MIDDLE CHILDHOOD
Behavior & Development

MIDDLE CHILDHOOD Behavior & Development

SECOND EDITION

Joyce Wolfgang Williams
Florida State University

Marjorie Stith
Kansas State University

Macmillan Publishing Co., Inc.
NEW YORK
Collier Macmillan Publishers
LONDON

Macmillan Publishing Co., Inc.
866 Third Avenue, New York, New York 10022

Collier Macmillan Canada, Ltd.

Library of Congress Cataloging in Publication Data
Williams, Joyce
    Middle childhood.
    Bibliography: p.
    Includes index.
    1. Child psychology. I. Stith, Marjorie, joint
author. II. Title.
BF721.W465   1980   155.4′24   79-10155
ISBN 0-02-427900-5

Printing: 2 3 4 5 6 7 8   Year: 0 1 2 3 4 5 6

Preface

This book grew out of our conviction that middle childhood is a fascinating area along the journey to maturity which has been detoured by many students in their study of the bewitching preschooler and the baffling adolescent. Middle childhood people are idea and action people who form a society well worth our attention.

Certain features of the book have been designed to foster learning and feeling. Objectives preceding each chapter should guide study and aid self-evaluation. THINK BACKs scattered throughout the text are designed to stimulate the readers to remember and think again about growing-up experiences and their meaning to them then and now. At the end of each chapter are three sections: "What's Next?" presents opportunities for further study through books, movies, and other media; "Catalysts for Discussion" is related to the content of the chapter; "Beyond the Classroom Experiences" offers suggestions for extending learning into the larger world through involvement with real children and provides means for establishing and examining relationships with them.

From time to time it has been necessary to refer to our subjects in the singular using the pronoun. For ease of reading, we have elected to use the masculine form in these instances. Our "he's" and "him's" refer to both girls and boys unless otherwise indicated.

Our indebtedness and deep appreciation in this venture are to many. Our students, families, friends, and colleagues have given inspiration and help in the gathering of information and ideas. Particular thanks go to Mrs. Nona Goodson for insisting that the work be undertaken and to Dr. Anne G. Buis for her support. Sincere gratitude is due Mrs. Isabella Torbert for superior workmanship in the preparation of the manuscript.

J. W. W.
M. S.

Two further words:

My gratitude I give my husband, mother, mother-in-law, Ann and Irma for child care performed during my necessary absences from the mother role; and to Leslie, Jr., Fred, Margaret-Alice, Joy, and Joel, my children, whose growth and development have inspired my efforts.

J. W. W.

Thanks, too, to Frank and Jenny and those in between who have provided me continuing glimpses of this delightful period of growing up.

M. S.

Contents

Prologue ix

1 Middle Childhood People 1

2 The Cultural Milieu 43

3 Focus on the Family 89

4 The Impact of School 137

5 Peer Influences and Activities 193

6 Physical Growth and Activities 231

7 Personality and Emotions 305

8 How Children Think 363

9 Moral and Religious Development 411

10 The Child in the Marketplace 447

11 Guidance 473

12 Children's Concepts 517

Epilogue 559

Bibliography 561

Index 595

Prologue

Smith (1957) has delightfully characterized middle childhood, recounting myriad adventures he shared with peers in his neighborhood. He fondly reports that after daring escapades, such as stealing materials from an unfinished house,

> We went home and when somebody said, "Where were you?" we said, "Out," and when somebody said, "What were you doing until this hour of night?" we said, as always, "Nothing."
>
> But about this doing nothing: we swung on swings. We went for walks. We lay on our backs in backyards and chewed grass . . . [we] read . . . and when we were done (my best friend) walked me home to my house, and when we got there I walked him back to his house, and then he——.
>
> We watched things: we watched people build houses, we watched men fix cars, we watched each other patch bicycle tires with rubber bands . . . our fathers playing cards, our mothers making jam, our sisters skipping rope, curling their hair. . . . We strung beads on strings . . . we tied each other up with string, and belts and clothesline. We sat in boxes; we sat under porches; we sat on roofs; we sat on limbs of trees. We stood on boards over excavations . . . on top of piles of leaves . . . under rain dripping from the eaves . . . up to our ears in snow. We looked at things like knives . . . and grasshoppers and clouds and dogs and people. We skipped and hopped and jumped. Not going anywhere——just skipping and hopping and jumping. . . . We sang and whistled and hummed and screamed.
>
> What I mean, Jack, we did a lot of nothing (pp. 93 and 97).

Chapter 1

Middle Childhood People

This chapter is designed to help you:

- recognize the commonalities and differences among individual middle childhood people
- see the current status of children in an historical context
- define child development as a discipline and delineate its major emphases.
- understand major problems in child study.
- identify main ways to study children, pointing up advantages and disadvantages.
- consider keys to meaningful observation.
- explain and use certain basic research terminology.
- review principles of development.
- identify the developmental tasks of middle childhood.
- appreciate the rights of children and understand the concept of advocacy

Who Are They?

Middle childhood people in the United States are the forty million between ages 5 and 12 who live in a host of settings with a variety of adult mentors and attend one or more of many forms of educational institutions. They engage in a multitude of recreational pursuits, are exposed to billions of facts, ideas, roles and images, and are disciplined in varying degrees by the significant others in their young lives. In spite of all the variation in their lifestyles and their stages of personal development they have much in common. There are certain givens characteristic of the majority of their age group: rights, roles, rules, games, jokes, errors, fads, wishes, changes, questions, attitudes, and concepts.

> Oh to be a child again—
> To be so pure and free,
> To search for four leaf clovers
> In fields of only three!
>
> *Author unknown*

Vignettes

Jane has recently moved to a new Midwest neighborhood and rides the bus to school. She has had trouble making friends among the other 11-year-olds in her class and doesn't have any neighborhood friends yet. She and her mother are very close, and she likes helping with the shopping and meals. Jane is an only child, and her father died several years ago. Her mother is a nurse who works the night shift. Jane sleeps alone in their duplex apartment. Jane loves to read and write poetry. She has a record collection which was her father's. She wants to attend college and become an English teacher.

David is 8 and belongs to one of the few Jewish families in his suburban New England neighborhood. He has learned much about his heritage and attends Hebrew school regularly. He looks forward to visits from his grandmother and to the good eggbread, bagels, lox, gefilte and blintzes she brings. David's father teaches music, and his mother manages a yogurt shop in a nearby shopping mall. He has an older brother in high school and a 5-year-old sister. He and his neighborhood friends like games of war and bike-riding.

Marie is 9 and has a twin brother Manuel. When they were babies they immigrated to a small town near the Mexican border, where they now live. At school they speak English, but at home they still speak Spanish because that is the only language their mother speaks. They attend a parochial school and wear uniforms each day. Marie and her girl friends like to play hopscotch and jump rope in the fenced playground near her home. Her father is a farm worker, and her mother works in a child care center. They all attend Mass on Sunday mornings and like to watch TV in the evenings after supper.

Fred is 7 and lives on a small farm in the south. He has a 12-year-old brother and two sisters ages 5 and 2. They tend a garden and have a few animals, but both their parents work in the city. Fred likes to camp-out in the field, to ride his neighbor's horse, and to work on Cub Scout badges in

Despite the variations in their lives, middle childhood people are more alike than different. *(Photo by Rindy Olsen.)*

his spare time. He attends a private school with his sister. His brother attends public school, and a lady comes to the home to care for the baby. His family enjoys annual vacations and frequently visits the grandmothers who live in other towns.

Ten-year-old Phil lives in a small apartment in Chinatown with three older sisters, a younger brother, and his parents. A cousin and his parents who recently immigrated from Hong Kong are also sharing the dwelling while looking for work. Phil attends public school, and on certain days goes to study the philosophy of Confucius and his native tongue at the Chinese language school. He enjoys the ancient stories and looks forward to the annual New Years parade and festivities. Phil likes to go with his father to visit his grandfather who still operates a tea shop in another part of the city. He likes the smell of herbs, grasses and teas in the little store, and his grandfather helps him with his problems.

Alice is 12. She and her brother Troy, age 10, live with their father in a two-story home. Their mother lives in an apartment several miles away, and they visit her each Wednesday and every other weekend. Their parents have been divorced two years, and Alice and Troy have learned to enjoy them separately. Mother has returned to school to complete a college degree, and Father is a university professor. Both children attend an experimental school at the university, and occasionally the whole family will attend a school function together. Alice is interested in drama and music. Troy has his own small garden plot and a science laboratory which he enjoys.

Tommy is 6, and he lives with his mother. His parents are divorced and he hears from his father only at Christmas. His mother works in a bank, and they live in a mobile home park where there are many, many children. After school Tommy stays at a child-care center until his mother picks him up after work. Tommy is very active, swims well and plays on a tee-ball team at the playground. He has a learning problem related to reading, and his mother works with him a lot in the evenings.

Sandra is 8 and lives in a ghetto in a large northern city with her grandmother who works in a store. Sandra's parents were killed in an accident when she was 5. She has two little sisters whom she dresses each morning and takes to daycare on her way to school. Sandra loves school and likes to learn. She goes to the library every day to check out books. She plays on the sidewalk near her apartment until Grandmother comes home. She helps with the housework and takes care of her sisters every evening.

Paul is 11. He lives with his father and a lady friend in a make-shift shelter on the edge of a large town. Ever since he can remember they have been on the move. He never knew his mother, but this is the fourth "friend" who has lived with his dad. His father cuts wood for a living. Paul attends a free school where he may study when and what he wishes. After school he is free and on his own until his father comes home late at night. Paul has tried grass, liquor, box-car living and other adult pastimes.

He is a rough-and-tumble boy who looks forward to becoming 16 so he can get out on his own.

Dora is 5 years old and mentally handicapped. She attends a special kindergarten to help develop her potential to its maximum. Her teenage brother drives her to and from school in the family car. Her father is a physician, and her mother is a government employee. Sometimes on the weekend, Dora stays at the respite care facility while her parents are out of town. She also goes with them to the beach, shopping, to the movies, and to visit their relatives. Dora is very affectionate and likes her cat, Tabby. She also likes TV and enjoys being outside when the weather is nice.

Red Eagle is a 6-year-old Indian boy living on a reservation. He has three brothers older than he and no sisters. His father farms, and his mother stays home. He rides the school bus each day, getting up before the sun rises and arriving home almost as it sets. He likes to learn by helping his father but doesn't enjoy school very much. He is embarrassed when the teacher asks him to read for the class. He likes to attend tribal meetings with his family and is learning some of the traditional dances of his people. He can also ride a horse, and looks forward to having one of his own.

Think Back

To your own childhood:
What is your earliest memory?
What happy things do you remember?
What sadness do you recall?
What sort of "nothing" things did you do?

What of Childhood?

As historians have recently discovered, the idea of childhood is a European invention of the last 400 years, and recognition of childhood as a distinct segment of life is a relatively new concept. The word *child* expressed kinship but did not denote age, and until the seventeenth century the word *boy* was used to refer to any dependent male up through age 50 (Plumb, 1976). In preindustrial and preurban societies children were given no special place nor consideration beyond infancy—they were viewed merely as miniature adults. This did not mean children were not loved; they were just thought to be able to function without special notice or care, more or less as equals to adults. Childhood in many cultures today is not delineated with special roles for children. Yet in the American culture there are definite periods when children are obedient and adults are dominant, children play and adults work, the child is supposed to be sexless while adults are expected to be sexually active. (Skolnick, 1976)

We know little about the ancient world's attitude toward children. Records of the training and education of Spartan youth in Greece and reports of the reverence of children for parents in early China are shreds of data which have endured. Because so many infants died in earlier civilizations, attitudes toward the young were casual. Life was too hard to bother too much with a child who would probably die anyway. The precision of age is a modern phenomenon. Formerly there were infants and noninitiate boys and girls, and there were adults. Near the end of the sixteenth century there dawned a new attitude toward the young. They were no longer seen as anonymous, as evidenced by the carvings of dead children which began to appear on parents' tombs.

A diary kept by the physician of Louis XIII reveals how very involved children were in adult activity. At 5 he enjoyed viewing a farce on adultery; prior to age 7 he was encouraged to be sexually explorative with his sister; at 7 he began learning to ride and shoot and started gambling. During the 1500's Jesuit priests advanced the idea that children were innocent and therefore should be protected from such adult involvements as sex: boys were no longer bedded together, separation of sexes began to develop, and "the child became an object of respect, a special creature with a different nature and different needs, which required separation and protection from the adult world" (Plumb, p. 209). But interest in their growth and development was from a philosophical rather than practical viewpoint (Kagan, 1972).

By 1700 there was distinct child literature, purged of adult sophistication and especially written for the young mind. The childhood period was becoming a world of its own. To distinguish it from adult clothing, the school dress for children in some European schools included two ribbons on each shoulder. Although the poor were unable to apply the new concept because of life conditions, the affluent began to view childhood in its new state. Boys were now allowed to wear long trousers whereas adults did not. And by the end of the eighteenth century, children began to be grouped by age in school. Prior to that time the method varied with life circumstances from tutoring in monasteries to learning on the street as a vagabond. A young boy might be bound to an older one and serve as his beggar, or his co-laborer, and occasionally they would attend lectures or classes together. (Plumb, 1976)

During the second half of the eighteenth century and into the nineteenth, there was a rise in the systematic study of children, indicative of increasing interest in them. This was not a scientific movement but centered primarily on moral development and child-rearing problems. The concept of individual differences was largely ignored, as was the question of heredity versus environment. The general belief at that period was that children were born in sin and therefore depraved, a notion which influenced the general treatment of the young. (Kagan, 1972)

In the early nineteenth century leisure activity for children and youth became more differentiated. Food was plainer: more milk and suet puddings were served. Children's clothes were drabber than adults' with gray, blue and black predominant. It was during this period that the role of the family in the child's development was recognized. Prior to this time infanticide was a major means of population control in Europe and in other societies which lacked other means of controlling birth.

Also in the early nineteenth century children were taught the three Rs as early as ages 2 or 3, and 9- and 10-year-olds attended college. Children could enter craft occupations or become apprenticed to professional men at early ages. In time the mixing of children of various ages for educational purposes began to be considered unhealthy, and precocious children virtually disappeared from the scene. With industrialization, children entered the mines and factories, but in these settings their presence was more abhorrent than in the crafts and in the professions. Hence, the child labor laws and the essential definition of childhood as a "time out" from the world of adult responsibility were instituted (Skolnick, 1976).

Social legislation eventually excluded children from public houses and from gambling and the purchase of tobacco, and by World War I there were three distinct ages: infancy, through age 4 or 5; childhood, to late puberty or early manhood; and adulthood.

With the rise of the scientific method, the possibility of rearing perfect children seemed feasible. At the core of this wish lay the desire for a no-nonsense child who would grow up quickly without quirks. (LeShan, 1973). But parents and teachers discovered that just as a gardener cannot make a flower grow by pasting on petals and leaves, children could not be *made* to grow. They could only be allowed to develop the self within them. A more recent need has been to replace the perfect image of children with spontaneity, self-realization, individual fulfillment, fruitful mistakes and failures. Current writers are calling for children to be allowed to feel that being young is good, that they *are a* person and not merely becoming one.

Children need an affirmation from adults that childhood is significant. Rousseau put it aptly: "Hold childhood in reverence and do not be in any hurry to judge it for good or ill. Give nature time to work before you take over her tasks, lest you interfere with her method . . . Nature wants children to be children before they are men. If we deliberately depart from this order, we shall get premature fruits which are neither ripe nor well flavored and which soon decay. We shall have youthful sages and grown-up children. Childhood has ways of seeing, thinking and feeling peculiar to itself, nothing can be more foolish than to substitute our ways for them."

Today, childhood in comparison with adulthood, is characterized as a period of being smaller in size, emotionally unstable, intellectually irrational, socially egocentric, dependent, and amoral in judgments. With development and growth, these characteristics are recognized as moving toward physical and emotional maturity, the ability to apply logic in decision-making, sociocentricity, independence in many areas of functioning, and moral judgments. As adults in a child's life recognize the changes typical in this period, they are better able to facilitate and ensure the changes. (Grotberg, 1976)

Caldwell (1976) has summarized recurrent themes concerning attitudes toward children and their development represented in the great works of art during the past five centuries:

- Childhood is a unique period, and children need to be accepted for what they are rather than as miniature adults.
- There is value in bringing adults back into the lives of children and children back into the lives of adults; the adult-child relationship is a reciprocally pleasureable one.
- The family is important; fathering is important.
- Skill training is also important, and there is need to orient children to the world of work.
- Many of children's activities are characterized by optimism, hope and joy; there is societal value in encouraging the expression of these feelings through art, music and dancing.
- Children's deep involvement in play develops physical skills, teaches them competition and sharing and allows them to practice roles for later living.

In a recent address at the annual meeting of the American Orthopsychiatric Associaiton, Urie Bronfenbrenner, a foremost authority in the acculturation of children, stated "the system for making human beings human in this society is breaking down." He predicted "impairment rather than improvement in the competence and character of the next generation of Americans." (Moore, 1975, p. 32). He cited factors responsible for this condition as over-emphasis on individualism, decline in committment to community, and the disintegration of the family at all income, race and educational levels. He pointed out the rise in social and emotional stress among children, including crime rates and child suicide as young as age 10. He called for committment to support for good child-care, concluding "A person cannot be committed to a child unless other people are committed to that person's committment to children . . . That's what these societies that are doing well and doing it cheaply have accomplished."

Child Development: What Does It Mean?

Child development is a discipline or body of knowledge dealing with patterns of growth and development; description, origins, and meanings of behavior; and the linkages among these broad areas. Child development, which focuses on infants, children, and adolescents, is one facet of the more encompassing area of human development in which the subjects range in age from conception through old age. Psychologists, sociologists, biologists, physicians, anthropologists, and home economists are all working in this area, using different viewpoints and guided by varying goals. Some of these professionals are more concerned with discovering basic information, others with building and testing theoretical frameworks, and others with applying principles to family life education and to community development.

Child development is a discipline which applies knowledge from both natural and social sciences to the child as an individual in the many roles and settings in which he functions in society. It is concerned with the normal and the abnormal child and encompasses the study of the growth, behavior, and development of the mental, physical, social, and emotional aspects from conception through adolescence.

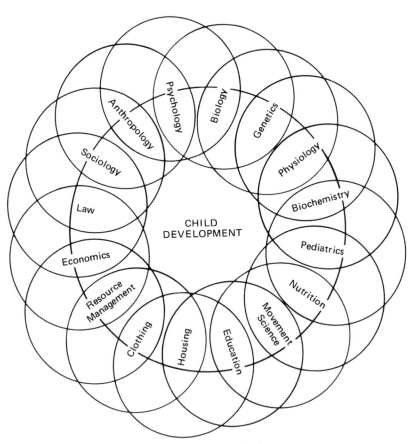

Figure 1-1. The interdisciplinary nature of child development.

As a field of study, child development emerged near the end of the last century under the name of child study. It has expanded and is now organized as a distinct entity concerned with conducting and providing facilities for research; providing education for students and professional personnel; and providing services for special groups in the community. Some child development centers are independent and privately operated; others are affiliated with colleges and universities as part of the home economics, education, psychology, or medicine curriculum.

The emphasis in early child study was largely on a descriptive account of individual children, followed by concern for physical growth and longitudinal studies involving large samples which resulted in the height-weight tables still seen on penny scales. There was little attention to cognitive development, but later the IQ concept was extolled and standardized testing spawned. Near mid century the mothering issue became paramount and more psychological aspects of development came under scrutiny. In each period there was a tendency to ride the current bandwagon while wearing blinders to findings of previous eras or concurrent research (Behrens and Maynard; and Murphy, 1972). Today concern is more focused on the total childhood experience, including research on family interaction and personality development, self-concept, life-styles, and the child's ecological unit.

It is in terms of the latter emphasis that this volume addresses itself to the growth and development of the child from 5 to 12 years of age—of the middle childhood years. A child entering this period of life is faced with new experiences and expectations. He has lost his appeal as a baby and must begin to shape and refine certain personality characteristics which will endear him to his peers and his elders as his world expands. He is not yet old enough to wield complete power over his environment, yet this yearning is growing within him. During the middle childhood years he will grow closer to friends and farther from family and home. He will meet new challenges as his body changes, his circle of acquaintances enlarges, and his cultural environment expands to include neighborhood, school, church, community organizations, and heterogeneous value systems.

Your question may be: Why this focus on the middle childhood years? A basic reason is that in much of our study this period is lost in the cracks! We understand the importance of beginnings, so infants and preschoolers have become the subjects of much discussion and research. It is easy to recognize the problems of adolescents, so they claim a major share of study. The middle childhood years, however, have remained a kind of no-man's land. Yet it is at this time when many aspects of development essential to a successful adult life occur. Body size increases, and proportions and contours continue to change. The ability to establish and maintain meaningful peer relations is acquired, and a positive self-concept is formed. The ability to reason emerges, and concept development is phenomenal. All this makes it necessary to examine and understand what takes place within a person during the "in-between" years—from ages 5 to 12.

A second purpose is personal: to know yourself better. Throughout this book there are "think backs" which will encourage you to recall experiences and problems of your own middle childhood years. These are the remembered years. Incidents can be retrieved and examined and analyzed. There is benefit in looking at a situation or a behavior, asking what caused it or how it could (or did) affect subsequent events, and to think through the feelings involved. No behavior can be fully understood outside an exploration of how the actor sees the behavior and how the behavior is perceived by others. This thinking back may help you to understand why you are who you are and ways you can continue to grow and change.

A third reason for such study is to be able to deal more effectively with the school-age child, since about 23 percent of the U.S. population is between ages 5 and 14. (See Figure 1.2) Through acquisition of knowledge and firsthand experience with children, attitudes may be formed or modified which will allow for more empathy with all children: young siblings or other relatives, one's own children or those in the neighborhood, children one deals with professionally as a teacher, counselor, nurse, community leader, business man, or in countless other roles. There is a body of knowledge about how children develop. What can we expect of 7-year-olds?

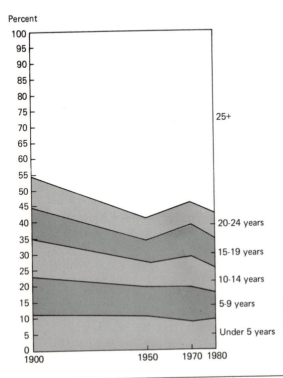

Figure 1-2. Detailed age distribution of population under 25 years: U.S. 1900–1980. (From *Profiles of Children*. Washington, D.C.: U.S. Government Printing Office, 1970, p. 14.)

How do children think? What makes them laugh? How do their interpersonal relationships develop? That's what this book is all about.

A final reason for concentrating in this area is to give you an opportunity to apply the underlying principles of behavior and development in real-life situations with middle childhood people. At the end of each chapter there are suggestions concerning interaction with children, as well as guidelines for analyzing what you see and experience in the light of what you are reading. It is impossible to learn to swim by merely memorizing certain rules or techniques or theory about water buoyancy and body movements. While knowledge of principles is important, it is not enough. You must try it . . . look at what happened . . . then try again. Certainly we must understand basic principles in knowing children, but there is more. To know children we must be with them. They cannot be placed under a microscope or examined variable by variable. We must take time to sit with them, listen to them, call them friend.

Problems of the Researcher

Certain problems are inherent in the study of an organism so complex as the child. If you are aware of these, you can exercise care in your own study attempts. You will be a better consumer of the written word: more alert to writings that generalize too far or incite undue alarm without sufficient evidence.

A major concern in child development research is the protection of the child. Care is necessary lest the subject of study become the victim. In animal study it is possible to control certain variables carefully while manipulating and examining others. Researchers with children do not have this option. In the controversy over the relative influence of heredity and environments on behavior and development, it has been difficult to study the effect of one variable while holding the other constant. Whereas some such manipulation might produce striking results, care must be taken that no damage ever comes to the children involved. Fear of such harm often makes parents reluctant or totally opposed to having their children participate in any type of research.

Another problem in research is reliance on recall as a technique for data collection. Since knowledge of the past often can be helpful in understanding the present, children and their parents and teachers are frequently asked to report from memory concerning particular events or circumstances. These persons may consciously or unconsciously tend to put themselves in a favorable light in such reporting. Even when there is complete integrity, memory is tricky. Time can cause descriptions to deteriorate, intensify, or otherwise become distorted. Certain unpleasantness is forgotten or an embarrassing or frightening event may blot out all memory of joy and contentment. Subjects tell only what they are able to recall and are willing to reveal.

Researcher bias is a third major concern. Researchers may through conscious or unconscious prejudice or incorrect interpretation of data draw conclusions that are false. It is extremely difficult to design an error-free study, particularly when the subjects are human. Even in the best conceived study, there is a temptation to place exaggerated practical significance on findings that are statistically significant. Generalizing from findings about groups to assumptions about individual persons is a temptation for researchers and readers alike. Herzog (1963) has termed this the "cookie cutter" approach. Prediction of individual behavior from evidence gathered on groups is risky because most measures of groups are expressed in averages or proportions, and the range of performance or characteristics varies from group to group. Group findings are better used in development of general policies or programs than in working with specific individuals from the group or from a totally different group.

The need for the student of children to read critically cannot be emphasized too strongly. In an age when one can find almost any "fact" in print, the discerning reader must be cautious concerning the source of the information, the representativeness of the sample on which conclusions are based, and the generalizability of the information presented to other children and settings. Relevance to reality, controlled variables, credibility of the reporter and the researcher are all vital concerns. A knowledge and understanding of basic principles of child development and a questioning mind can help guard against half-truths and falsehoods, which if believed and implemented into the guidance of children could bring irreparable damage to them.

Other obstacles to studying school-age children include hesitance on the part of school administrators and teachers to allow interruption of routine for such study, and feelings on the part of parents that time spent on research should be spent in teaching. There is also the fear that through such involvement children will gain ideas that would be contrary to parental teaching. There is a certain degree of reluctance on the part of the

---

Think Back

To a time you were a subject in a study:
How you were selected.
What you were asked to do.
What you thought of all this.
Who told you about it.

---

children too, particularly if they feel their privacy is being invaded, or that they are being treated as guinea pigs, or that their time is being wasted by research endeavors.

Ways of Studying Children

Approach: Longitudinal—Cross-sectional

The time span in which research is conducted affords one type of classification: cross-sectional and longitudinal. Regardless of the method employed, if data are collected from the same subjects over a period of time, usually years, the study is termed longitudinal. If the data are taken at a single point in time, the term "cross-sectional" may be used. Both types are concerned with studying changing patterns, but the approach is quite different for each.

In establishing height-weight tables using the longitudinal approach children could be weighed and measured each year from birth to age 12. Data collected yearly would be compiled to show progression with age. A cross-sectional study to establish a similar norm could be done in a few weeks or months by weighing or measuring a large group of children ranging in age from birth to age 12 and noting averages for each age. There are advantages to both techniques: Longitudinal data reveal individual and sometimes dramatic changes and differential patterns of growth. Cross-sectional data are less expensive to obtain in terms of time and money and yield information easily summarized into norms.

Projective Technique

A method by which researchers have attempted to evoke response data with a minimum of subject awareness is the projective technique. Projective techniques are aimed at revealing an individual's interests and wishes as he performs in a specific setting; and they may offer information he might not readily reveal in a questionnaire or interview situation (Henry, 1960).

Various researchers have classified these techniques in different ways. Among the classifications is one by Lindzey (1960) which includes the associative, construction, completion, ordering, and expressive types. Using the associative method one would note the first thought, image, or word that occurs to the subject upon presentation of a picture, word, sound, or other stimulus. The Rorschach Test (Rorschach, 1923) is a common example of this type. The Cloud Pictures of Struve and Stern (Struve, 1932; Stern, 1938) and the Word Association Test (Rapaport, Gill, and Schafer, 1946) are also examples of the associative form.

Construction techniques are those that call upon the subject to produce a creation, such as a story, from a picture stimulus. This involves the organizing of ideas as well as associative abilities. The Thematic Apperception Test (TAT) (Morgan and Murray, 1935) is among the most well-known of the construction type. Shneidman's Make-A-Picture Story (Shneidman, 1949) and the Children's Apperception Test (Bellak, 1954) are modified versions of the TAT. One 6-year-old, responding to the CAT picture showing a monkey and a tiger, told the following story: "One day all the animals decided to vote to see who would be king of the forest. The elephant got 64 votes. The lion got 97 votes. The monkey got 32 votes. That's how many monkeys voted!"

Completion techniques involve the presentation of an incomplete situation which the subject is to finish, such as the Sacks Sentence Completion Test (Sacks and Levy, 1950). Engle's adaptation of the Test of Insight into Human Motives is also an example of a completion technique (Engle, 1958).

Items from the Sacks (Sacks and Levy, 1950, pp. 377–378) instrument follow:

The people I like best . . .
My mother and I . . .
If my father would only . . .
My family treats me like . . .
Someday I . . .
When I am older . . .

In ordering techniques, the subject ranks or orders a series of pictures according to criteria laid down by the investigator, such as most liked or least liked. The Szondi (Fancher and Weinstein, 1958) is the best known of this classification. The Picture Arrangement Test (Tomkins and Miner, 1957) provides both ordering and construction features as it requires subjects to place into logical sequence pictures from an episode.

Expressive techniques include role playing or free-form drawings or paintings, in which not only the final product but the manner in which the subject goes about the task is of concern to the investigator. In the Machover Draw-A-Person Test, thickness of lines, location of drawing on the paper, size of the drawing, and symmetry are guides to interpretation (Machover, 1951). The Draw-A-Man samples in Figure 1-3 illustrate this technique. The head and facial features are considered expressive of social needs and a reflection of intellectual emotions. The interpretation of finger painting using the Napoli (1951) criteria would consider the color(s) used; the motions employed—smearing, scrubbing, patting, etc.—and verbalizations made during its creation.

The projective technique is primarily the tool of the clinical psychologist, and its use requires intensive training. The primary disadvantage of this method is the possibility of faulty interpretation of responses.

Figure 1-3. Three Draw-A-Man samples by the same child over a period of 10 months. (From *Child and Adolescent Psychology*, G. R. Medinnus and R. C. Johnson, p. 515. Copyright © 1969 by John Wiley & Sons, Inc. Used by permission of John Wiley & Sons, Inc.)

Questionnaire

A second way to collect information about children is by means of the questionnaire. It is limited, however, in its usefulness because children may find it difficult to understand the intent of the questions or be unable to read and write sufficiently well. The questionnaire is composed of a series of written questions. They may be open-ended and allow the respondent to state his answer in his own words: Tell the three things you most like to do on Saturday, or What do you like to do on Saturday? The child may be asked to select from a list of possible answers the one that most nearly describes his feelings or knowledge: Place an X by the activity listed which you would most like to do on Saturday:

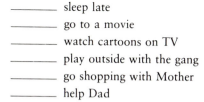

_____ sleep late
_____ go to a movie
_____ watch cartoons on TV
_____ play outside with the gang
_____ go shopping with Mother
_____ help Dad

Some investigators (Yarrow, M. R., 1960) believe that the anonymity provided by the questionnaire makes it especially valuable in ascertaining children's attitudes and values. The child may feel he is revealing his identity through his handwriting with the use of the open-ended question, however. The emotional reaction caused by the questionnaire items may be tested by using them in interviews prior to administering them in written form.

There are hazards in studying children via this method. The child may misinterpret an item or fail to complete the questionnaire. He may consistently mark the first or last alternative answer to each question, with no thought entering the decision, which is called position set. There is even the possibility that the subject is unwilling to respond seriously to the questions posed.

Interview

The interview may employ similar questions, but they are posed verbally, and responses are noted by the interviewer. An interview may be completely unstructured, during which the interviewer and subject informally discuss a topic or several topics, and notes or a tape recording are made of the conversation for later analysis. The interview may be semistructured, the interviewer following a schedule of questions but also conversing with the child in an informal manner. Some interviews are formally structured, and there can then be no interaction with the child: questions on the schedule are read, and answers are noted without comment. The structured interview might be difficult to use with a child since he would not understand why the interviewer could not talk to him or answer his questions.

Use of the interview technique with children under school-age is not particularly effective because of language deficiencies. However, with the great strides in language facility typical of the middle years, it is more useful during this stage of development. One drawback lies in the intensified resistance to revealing feelings, particularly to adults, common after age 8 or 9. To reduce such obstacles, investigators may play a game with the child prior to the interview or provide for him materials to handle or build with during the interview. Boys of the latter middle years may be reluctant to relate to a female interviewer because of the peer code of female disdain, but there are no systematic research findings in this regard.

Reducing anxiety and reluctance in conjunction with an interview may be achieved by planning some time for the child subject to become familiar with the environment and the interviewer. One researcher interviewing a fifth grade boy noticed unusual anxiety on his part upon entering the room in which the study was being conducted. During their get-acquainted discussion, he revealed that he thought she was going to kidnap him! An explicit verbal explanation of the purpose of the interview is important to the child of the middle years. A simple statement is sufficient, such as "I am trying to find out what girls and boys in Leon County know about money." Use of the funnel sequence for questioning, beginning with more general and less value-laden questions may facilitate relaxation and cooperation by the child.

Questions may be presented in a straightforward manner, such as "Do you prefer to be with your mother or your father?" Or they may be partially concealed in fantasy: "If you were shipwrecked on a desert island, would you rather have your mother or your father with you?" To disguise the intent of the question even further, one might ask the child to suggest which parent a boy in trouble would probably like to help him.

Questions for an interview should be formulated to avoid misunderstanding, variations in interpretation from child to child, and leading the child to any given response. If the child is being asked to provide responses he might find threatening and therefore would be reluctant to answer honestly, the following techniques (Yarrow, L. J., 1960) would be beneficial:

1. Suggest in the question that other children might feel similarly:
   "All children sometimes get mad at their brothers and sisters. What do you do when you get mad at yours?"
2. Present alternatives:
   "If you break something accidentally, do you try to fix it so that no one will ever know, or do you tell someone what happened and ask for their help?"
3. Avoid placing a child in a position where he has to deny some particular behavior by wording the question to assume he has in fact engaged in it:
   "When you don't like a meal your mother has served, what do you do about it?"
4. Give the child an opportunity to express a positive response before asking him to state negative opinions:
   "What do you like best about school? What things about school do you think need to be changed?"
5. Assure the child his responses will be kept confidential, thereby alleviating some of his fears at expressing his real opinions and feelings:
   "I am not going to put your name on this piece of paper, so you can say anything you want to."
6. Let the child know that what he thinks will not be graded nor criticized:
   "There are no right or wrong answers to the questions I will ask you. I am just interested in knowing what you think or feel about things."

One way to allay anxiety while drawing information about themselves from children is to use the group interview or conversation. Parkhurst has made extensive use of this method by which she brought together children of varying ages to talk about such topics as sportsmanship, anger, and conscience. The following excerpt from a fifteen-minute segment of conversation about conscience with Miss Parkhurst and a group of children ranging from age 8 to 12, recorded in her *Exploring the Child's World*, illustrates this technique (Parkhurst, 1951, pp. 155–157). She had just asked the children if they would like to give away their conscience. Stuart had decided that he would, but then anxiety got the better of him and he backtracked.

> STUART: "Well, I'd not like to give it away . . . because then, when I grow up, I might grow to be very bad. But I think I have another name for conscience."
>
> MISS P: "What is it?"
>
> STUART: "You can call it your subconscious mind."
>
> MISS P: "What's that—your subconscious mind?"
>
> STUART: "Your regular mind you just use every day, but your subconscious mind comes up for very important matters, and it's like ads and it makes you think more; like it tells you to count to ten before doing anything—"
>
> MISS P: "Just a minute, Stuart. What's the difference between your regular mind and your subconscious mind?"
>
> STUART: "Your regular mind is just your everyday mind, and your subconscious mind—"
>
> MISS P: (humorously) "Is your Sunday mind?"
>
> STUART: "Your subconscious mind is deep down inside of you, and I think that it sometimes comes out, and tells you things to do."
>
> MISS P: "How do you know that, Stuart?"
>
> STUART: "Well . . ."
>
> LOIS: "Your subconscious mind takes over when your regular mind isn't working."
>
> MISS P: "Convenient, isn't it?"
>
> DAVID: "Well, it's good to have!"
>
> TRUDY (8): "I disagree with Stuart between the subconscious and the conscience."
>
> MISS P: "The conscious mind?"
>
> TRUDY: "Yes. If he means an *everyday* mind, does he mean it is a Monday-Tuesday-Wednesday-Thursday-Friday-Saturday and Sunday? Or, is it the subconscious that has Saturday and Sunday?"
>
> MISS P: "What's the difference?"
>
> TRUDY: "I don't think there's very much difference, only it looks like there's two consciences, that when one goes to sleep the other wakes up, like a day nurse and a night nurse."

The length of an interview with a child should be in terms of his attention span. If he becomes fatigued, uninterested, or bored because of a prolonged session, his answers will tend to be less valid. To limit the length of the session, pose questions related to only one or two concepts. A second interview might be better than one very lengthy one.

Since in the interview method it is usually possible to explain any questions the child does not understand, as well as to avoid any lack of response due to reading difficulty, it is probably superior to the questionnaire for use with the 5–12 child. However, as in the questionnaire, the subject may mask his true feelings or respond as he thinks the interviewer wishes him to. The recording of his comments, if done manually, may also distract or otherwise annoy a child.

Experimental Laboratory

The experimental method is a major one used in collection of data about children. It is most commonly applied to study a suspected causative relationship between a phenomenon (dependent variable) and one or more other factors (independent variables). A situation is constructed in which the dependent variable is observed while the independent one(s) is introduced and varied in a systematic manner. All other variables are controlled to prevent their influencing the observed behavior. Changes in the dependent variable are noted and stated as a function of the preceding changes in the independent variable(s). The essential aspect in this method is control of variables, and measurement of changes are best done objectively or mechanically. Use of a laboratory with the experimental method facilitates control of certain conditions, hence the term laboratory method to mean experimental method (Bijou and Baer, 1960).

The laboratory method was employed in one study (Berenda, 1950) designed to measure the effects of group pressure on school-age children's decisions. The task was to judge the length of a series of lines. Each subject was asked to make a judgment about each line alone in the laboratory. He was then asked to make his judgments amid a group of peers who had been instructed to answer incorrectly seven of the twelve items. The variation in each subject's decisions was a measure of the influence of peer pressure on his answers.

One problem in using the experimental or laboratory method with children of middle childhood is that of space. Mobile laboratories have been used in this connection with some success. Another is timing. The effect of intersession events is a variable that is difficult to control, such as parental admonitions to "Do your best," or "Be a good boy." Discussion among the participants can also affect results. To reduce these effects adults involved with children participating in this type of study may be asked to refrain from discussion or commenting about their participation, and children may be requested not to discuss the experiment with others. Most experiments with the child between the ages of 6 and 13 are concerned with discrimination problems, such as the relative value of money. Serial learning, motivation, and problem solving have also been studied using this method. Undergraduate students of child development would not typically design and conduct studies of this type.

Observation

A major method of data collection in the study of children is direct observation. This method can allow one to note both similarities and differences among children, making it possible to see individual uniqueness along with certain principles which apply to the behavior and development of all. Through observation one may be able to cite needs for special attention as well as the relative effectiveness of specific or general treatment of the subjects. Through observation the student of child development may develop the empathy necessary to appreciate the pressures, pleasures, and problems of the children he is studying.

Observation has to do with careful looking, with awareness of action, feelings, and the surrounding environment. It demands close attention. As an observer, you may be a part of the situation or apart from it looking on. You may observe a group of children on a playground or in a classroom or at a hobby show. From a distance you may watch a couple of children playing jacks or a child trying to jump rope or climb a tree. As a participant-observer in a Brownie troop or a Sunday school class, you may look at children and later record their behavior. You may set up a standing appointment with a child so that you will have frequent opportunities to talk with him about the interests and concerns of children. You may plan various activities with him in order to note his reactions: a ball game, a cooky-making project, a hike, a game of cards. One disadvantage in being a participant-observer—which is really field observation—is that behavior is usually not recorded on the spot, but by recall. The sooner this can be done, the more accurate it will be. This disadvantage, however, is offset by the possibility of closeness to a child in a variety of situations. As he comes to trust you, he may allow you to enter more completely into the world of childhood.

In whatever way you choose to study children, observation plays a part. Direct observation, as a tool, depends on looking carefully at behavior and accurately recording it in some way: a running account; checking of pre-coded categories; using video equipment.

Observational aims might be ecological, normative, systematic, or idiographic (Wright, 1960). Ecological aims concern determining variation in behaviors in a number of environments: home, school, camp, playing field. The attempt in ecological studies, which are not very common, is to link behavior to certain natural settings. *Growing Up in River City* is an example of this type of study (Havighurst et al., 1962).

Normative studies are more numerous, their purpose being to determine central behavior tendencies and to establish norms for children of a particular age, sex, or other criterion. Studies of this type have resulted in height-weight tables (Bayley, 1956) and Gesell's Developmental Schedules (Gesell and Amatruda, 1951).

Systematic aims are evident in research designed to determine relationships between two or more universal behavioral variables, such as aggression and popularity or achievement and self-concept. Results are often in the form of generalizations without limiting references to specified environments or classes of children. Two examples of systematic studies which yielded contradicting generalizations because of failure to define terms carefully were those on social class and child rearing (Davis and Havighurst, 1947; Maccoby, Gibbs et al., 1954).

An idiographic study involves in-depth research on a specific child, noting various types of behavior in a single subject. The infant diaries so common in the early days of child development were idiographic in nature. Clinicians today often conduct idiographic studies on their subjects. Piaget used a modification of this approach in his early studies of cognitive development.

Techniques used in direct observation include time and event sampling as well as diary or subject description. In time sampling, a record is made of all behavior that occurs in a specified time period, based on predetermined categories. If we were interested in knowing how children use time during a study period, we would enumerate all possible behaviors and score each child at 30-second intervals during five-minute periods on a number of days. In event sampling, particular events or behaviors are recorded as they occur during a definite time period. For example, we might want to know how many times a child contacts another child per hour or how often in a given period he exhibits a tic.

Observation Tips

During the course of your study you will likely be observing children in the laboratory or in the field, as a participant-observer, or as an onlooker. In order to make the most of this, it is necessary to learn how to observe. A key to good observation, whether the subject is the contents of a test tube, the solar system, a primitive society, or children in their middle years, is the educated eye. The eye must rise above observer bias, feelings of sympathy or disdain, and superficial impressions to see reality as it exists. Otherwise, data collected through direct observation will be unreliable and misleading. Reality for each of us is a bit different, but an effort must be made to accurately record the situation and what happened, then attempt to explain or interpret what was seen and felt. Everyone has varying degrees of success in this task. The important point is to know when you are reporting and when you are interpreting!

The beginning observer is usually tempted to draw conclusions too quickly or to generalize beyond the data. In explaining what you saw, it is well to remember that while all behavior is caused, there are usually a number of interplaying reasons, rather than a single one. It is too easy and quite likely inaccurate to conclude that a child is boisterous or destructive because his mother works or because his father travels a lot of the time. Such factors are certainly part of the situation but certainly not the total picture.

Another difficulty the novice observer faces is expecting the child to always be clever or entertaining. Perhaps this is the result of examples cited in books on child development which seem to indicate that every

A vital part of observation is an educated eye. *(Photo by Rick Coleman.)*

time a child opens his mouth a bit of humor comes forth! This is not true. We must be aware of and attentive to the actions and moods of children, their body language as well as their vocalizing. We must attend to their quietness, their inabilities, their questions. Some children are quite verbal; others scarcely talk at all. This, too, is behavior that can increase understanding of the child.

If learning is to take place based on information gathered, the observer must cultivate objectivity and eliminate observer bias. The effect of observer bias may be a greater problem when the student is well acquainted with the subjects or when he has feelings of pressure or hostility during the observation. To be aware of these possibilities permit yourself to make allowance for such errors or to apply a sort of correction factor. Observer objectivity is fostered by a good attitude and an open mind.

The influence of the observer on the child is another factor to be considered: behavior may change if the subject is aware that he is under scrutiny. In order to minimize observer influence a one-way screen or mirror may be employed, shielding the observer from the observed. A less sophisticated form using the same principle may be found in wearing sunglasses, particularly the Polaroid type; thus the child cannot easily detect the eye motions of the observer. Children in the middle years are beginning to notice the dress and grooming of those older than they; they are fascinated by the unusual and the extreme. The presence of such stimuli can influence normal behavior. Unobtrusive note-taking reduces observer influence, and a concealed tape recorder may be used to eliminate the need for extensive writing.

Perhaps the most effective means of reducing observer influence results when the observer (or observers in general) becomes a familiar sight to those under study. When you become a part of the scene, your presence is unnoticed, and behavior will tend to be as though it were not being studied. This happens when regular and frequent involvement with the subjects is possible, even when you are a participant-observer.

Another key to successful learning through direct observation lies in deciding what to observe. Perhaps the goal will be answering specific questions: Is sex cleavage present? What fine motor skills are exhibited? How interested are the children in books and art materials?

On the other hand, the purpose of the observation might be to make a running account of occurrences:

The class noisily entered the cafeteria for lunch. Several girls teased the boys while waiting in line for trays; however the girls sat at one table and the boys at another. There was much talk about comic books and TV. Almost all the children had seen the Charlie Brown special last night.

Attention may be focused on one or two individuals:

Jerry doesn't seem to like girls. He always chooses to sit and work with boys. Today at the party when he got to the club house and saw Beth and Amy inside he refused to enter. When he discovered that because of rain we'd have to eat inside he agreed to come in—in his sock feet. He said he'd have to leave his shoes outside this girl place. I suppose he felt he would not be contaminated if he had "safe shoes" to put on after his sally into the Girl Scout Club House!

At other times attention may be focused on the total group:

The children arrived in the clearing with their sack lunches. It had been a fairly long walk, but they were full of energy. One group near the edge let out what sounded like a united scream and then retreated to the center of the area, still screaming. When I investigated I discovered they had seen a snake. Their antics alerted the rest of the group who seemed to break into companies of twenty-five or so, each taking turns rushing to the spot and then retreating, screaming all the while. Apparently there is a bit of fascination in things which are safely frightening—such as a small green snake that was probably shivering in his skin.

There may be a comparison with norms for the age:

The Steinlen children seem to be developing normally, exhibiting many of the characteristics typical of their ages. At 6, Fran has lost two teeth. She likes to help around the home, is learning to read and write, and is fascinated by her

---

new abilities. At 11, Don is interested in models, sports and reading. He talks about his friends and his Webelo leader with every breath but doesn't enjoy doing family things very much. He eats a lot.

Or concern may be centered on a specific aspect of development:

Judging from her unwillingness to try new things and to become involved with peers, Windy's self-concept is fairly low. She seems convinced that no one likes her and that she can't really do anything well. When asked to read a part in front of the class, she broke into tears and ran out of the room. At recess she is usually alone reading a book.

Depending on the focus of the experience students will prepare for observing in varying degrees, make notes differently, and present the report in a number of forms. But in all cases, writing the final report should follow the experience as closely as possible for the notes to be maximally meaningful as they are transcribed and interpreted. Whatever the form, basic information relative to the observation should be given: the date and inclusive times; the location and situation under which the observation was made; the age and sex of the subject. Include in your report what happened, possible reasons, and how you felt about it. In this way you can begin to understand children and yourself.

The Language of Research

While studying child development, you will encounter reports of research collected by a wide variety of methods and techniques. Regardless of the approach or the goals to be reached, there is a basic language of research which the reader must understand. Following is a brief clarification of some of the more common components of this language.

Subjects (sometimes abbreviated *Ss* in research writings) are the individuals about which information is desired—usually persons, sometimes rats, guinea pigs, mice, or dogs. The subjects compose what is termed the *sample,* which denotes the subjects as a group, or whole. For example, "The subjects were male Caucasians between 6 and 8 years of age, inclusive; the sample was 100." The sample size may also be denoted by the letter N. For instance, $N = 100$.

The *population* refers to the larger group in society which is being represented by the sample. Since it is impractical to gather certain facts about every child in a county, state, or nation, there are procedures for selecting a portion of the total population which allow findings from a smaller group to be applied to the total group from which the sample was chosen. If one were attempting to study the effects of television on third-graders in a certain school system, all third-graders in the system would be the population; the group chosen to participate in the study would comprise the sample; the individual participants would be the subjects.

In securing samples that are representative of the population from which they are chosen, great care must be taken. The ideal situation exists when every person in the population has an equal chance of being selected and when the selection of any one person does not affect the chance of any other person's being included in the sample. When such a situation exists, it is termed *random sampling*. Random sampling may be achieved by putting everyone's name in a hat and drawing the desired number of names, being sure to shake the hat well between each drawing. It may also be done by the use of tables of random numbers, when each name has been given a number.

Sometimes drawing a random sample is not feasible, especially if the population is a very large one. Imagine assigning numbers to or writing on paper slips the names of 30,000 children in order to draw a sample of 100! There are some alternative methods that yield samples that are also considered representative, although these approaches do not make it possible for everyone to have an equal chance of being selected. One of these is *systematic sampling*. In this method subjects may be chosen from a listing of names or numbers, every 10th person, for example, being selected. To draw 100 subjects from the above-mentioned 30,000 population, one would choose every 300th name.

Stratified sampling is another method by which representative groups may be selected. In this procedure a certain number or proportion of subjects is selected from several strata or categories of the population. In the school system of 30,000 children, sampling might be done by the grade level, socioeconomic class, or sex. In some cases each group would be proportionally represented; in other instances every group would be equally represented in the total sample.

Purposive sampling is a common method. In this approach the researcher includes as subjects whoever he can get to participate. With this method representativeness is sacrificed; however, much of the information currently available would have remained a mystery if the studies had been deferred until a representative sample were available.

Instrument is the term applied to the vehicle by which data are collected: a paper-and-pencil test, a series of pictures, an interview schedule, or an observation guide. A *standardized instrument* is one that has been used with hundreds of subjects and for which performance norms have been established. It has been found to be valid (testing what it purports to test) and reliable (consistent in yielding comparable results in repeated testings). Use of a standardized instrument permits one to compare individual performance with norms that may be national in scope, and makes one reasonably sure that the results obtained are a true representation of the subject's behavior, ability, knowledge, attitudes, and whatever is under test.

The *Hawthorne effect* refers to the influence of the researcher's presence or personality on the subjects' performance, whereas the *placebo effect* is the tendency for investigators to report positive findings relative to their more cherished theories.

Data is a Latin word that means "information," and the information gleaned in studies is referred to as *data*. Data are often expressed in relation to certain *variables,* or factors, being investigated in the research. Variables are of two main types, dependent and independent. *Independent variables* in a study are those that are varied so that the effect of such variation on particular behavior responses of the individual can be studied. These responses under investigation are called *dependent variables.* If one were interested in noting the play preferences of boys and girls at age 5, sex would be the independent variable. Play preferences would be the dependent variable. Results would be expressed in terms of the independent variable of sex: play preferences of boys and play preferences of girls.

Data are often expressed in what is termed measures of *central tendency,* which describe group trends but not individual variations. Three such measures are the *mean,* the *median,* and the *mode.* The mean is the average, determined by adding the numerical value earned by each subject and dividing the sum by the number of subjects. The mean height of fourth-graders might be 48″, but perhaps none of the fourth-graders in any given classroom would measure exactly that height. The median is the middle score or value in a set of results. If, in determining the allowances given elementary children in a certain town, one listed them from the least to the most, the median allowance would be that one which fell exactly in the middle of the listing. In even-numbered listings it would be the average of the two middle values. The mode is the most-often-occuring value in a set of scores. In IQ scores, if six children scored 98, but no other score was received by more than two children, 98 would be the mode. In making measures of central tendency more meaningful, the range is often reported also. The *range* is a notation of the lowest and highest scores in a particular collection of data. The *distribution* is a reporting of exactly how every subject did scorewise, either in chart or graph form. Perhaps the most common distribution is the bell-shaped curve. But distributions may fall into any shape, depending on the performance of the subjects. Given a distribution, one could determine the median, mode, mean, and range.

Persons engaged in research are usually concerned with finding *associations, relationships,* or *correlations* between certain variables. These three terms all denote degrees of relatedness between specific factors—as age, sex, weight—and certain behaviors or qualities—as aggression, security, IQ. Even strong associations, relationships, or correlations do not show "cause and effect," for it is not possible to say which caused the other. It is only possible to say there is an interdependence.

Relationships, associations, and correlations are often reported as positive, negative (or inverse), linear, and curvilinear. These adjectives tell in which direction the relationship moves. For example, a *positive correlation* between height and popularity would suggest as one grows taller, he also grows more popular; as one increases, so does the other. A *negative or inverse association* between weight and popularity would mean that as one increased, the other decreased; hence obese people might be less popular than slim-trim ones. A *linear relationship* would indicate that when the data were plotted on a graph, a straight or near-straight line would result. (See Figure 1-4.) On the other hand, a *curvilinear relationship* would be plotted as follows, indicating an increase and then a decrease in one variable. (See Figure 1-5.)

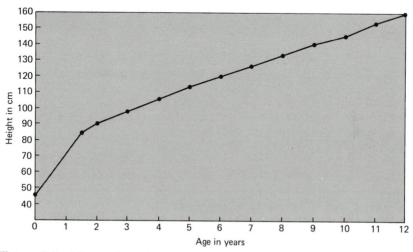

Figure 1-4. A linear relationship: age and height. (Based on data collected by N. Bayley, reported in *Child Development,* 27:47–54, 1956.)

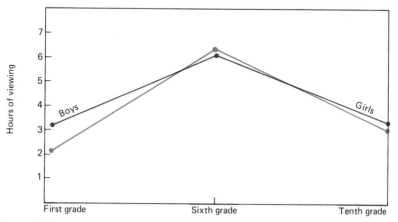

Figure 1-5. A curvilinear relationship: grade and average Sunday TV viewing time. (Based on data from *Television and Day-to-Day Life: Patterns of Use.* U.S. National Institute of Mental Health, Vol. 4, 1972, p. 141.)

When examining data from a sample of the population, there always remains the question whether or not the sample truly represented the total group. The science of *statistics* is given to this determination. By use of certain mathematical computations, called *sampling statistics,* one discovers to what extent the facts deduced from the data are actually true of the population, or true only of the sample. Theoretically, if a sample is chosen in a random manner, the findings should be applicable to the whole population. If the findings are reported as *statistically significant,* one can usually generalize from the sample to the population. This is true even when the summary statistic does not apply to the individual subjects. The degree of statistical significance is an indication of the extent to which the effect of chance has influenced findings. A finding *statistically significant at the .05 level* means that should you run the reported study on 100 different samples drawn at random from the same population, the results would be approximately the same for 95 of these samples; only 5 of the samples would yield information not applicable to the total population. Some findings are reported significant at other levels, as .01, .001, .10. Each denotes the degree to which the effect of chance has been ruled out in applying the findings from the sample to the population from which it was drawn (Sax, 1968; Weinberg and Schumaker, 1962).

Principles of Development

From research and observation certain principles that underlie development and behavior have been articulated. Once understanding of these is mastered, one should be able to deal more effectively with preschoolers, children of the middle years, adolescents, adults, and senior citizens. Through knowledge of the principles of development it is possible to set more realistic expectations for others, to note signs of deviant behavior, and to find comfort in the fact that annoying behavior is typical of the stage and will eventually disappear. Growth is usually interpreted as quantitative change—increase in height, weight, vocabulary, sense of humor, imagination; development connotes qualitative change—progression toward maturity, the integration of structures and functions.

Although young children are not inherently aware of growth and development, they soon learn that age is the ladder by which a child hopes to attain his dream, and they yearn to be bigger, older, and more astute at performing various status-gaining feats. By school age, the child notices when his clothes are too tight; he likes to show off new knowledge to parents and siblings; he enjoys demonstrating his independence. At this age boys may have adopted the idea that they are expected to employ aggressive behavior more than girls and exhibit tenderness less. To the child, growth and development are the keys that unlock all the forbidden doors in life; they are the magic gift of adults that bring power and social acceptance.

Think Back

To your childhood:
Whether you felt small or big, competent or not.
If you longed to be grown up.
If you thought you were growing about like other people were.

In studying growth and development, it is convenient to speak of periods, such as infancy, early childhood, middle childhood, and early and late adolescence. Each period has its characteristic traits and related potential problems. Certain factors seem to affect growth and development in all of these periods: sex, intelligence, race, glandular functioning, nutrition, health, ordinal position in the family, incentive, heredity, and parental attitude. Deviant development and growth are usually related to one or more of these factors (Hurlock, 1964).

The following principles of development summarize findings on the subject:

1. Development is similar for all, following genetic sequences yet influenced by environment; each child is unique.
2. Development is continuous, occurring in stages; children normally pass through each stage, often at different rates. Each stage has characteristic traits.
3. There is correlation among the rates and phases of the various structures and functions, the maturity of one facet affecting others, resulting in uneven growth tempo.
4. The rate of development is usually highest at the onset, closely associated with the principle of indigenous motivation which may cause a child's use of emerging developmental abilities to appear exaggerated and intense.
5. Behavior results from the interaction of a child's inner drives or needs, society's expectations of children his age, and his stage of growth and development.

Although each person is distinctly different from every other person, from his fingerprints to his voice print, from his personality to the shape of his ears and internal organs, the overall pattern of development is similar for all. Prenatal development has been studied in such great depth that the appearance of the finest details have been calculated to the day when they will occur. During middle childhood we can expect that primary teeth will be shed, that vocabulary will expand, that peer relations will go through certain phases, and that the basic emotions will find new modes of expression. The degree to which the various types of development progress will

---

be determined by certain genetic factors as well as the environment in which the child lives. As genetics determine one's eye color, environment determines what is available for the eye to see. Whereas the basic body type and efficiency of functioning are more genetic in origin, the environmental nutrition and care will determine the extent to which the body grows and the skills it acquires. The inherent brain capacity is set prior to birth. The stimulation it receives depends on the environment. Temperament, as well as height, skin and hair coloring, and growth timing are in part determined by constitutional components. Inheritance determines the limits of growth and development. One's environment either helps him achieve his genetic limit or prevents such attainment; but environment cannot cause one to surpass genetic potential.

The inter-relatedness of genetic and environmental factors on development is attested to by the following statement by Caspari (1967), p. 130:

> in many organisms the development of behavior patterns is strongly and irreversibly influenced by previous stimuli and by previously acquired behavior patterns . . . On the other hand, there exist many behavior patterns, particularly among higher animals and man, which are not only modified by learning but are also dependent on learning for their normal development. If the organism does not have the opportunity to learn, the behavior patterns either will not develop at all or will develop in an abnormal way. In these cases, the ability to learn particular behavior patterns, the necessity to learn them, the time when they can and must be learned seem to be themselves under genetic control.

While it remains true that environment determines the limits to which genetically-endowed potential may develop, even like environments may yield vast differences in development because of the genetic composition of given individuals operating in the environment. Therefore, the two factors remain interlocked in their influence on behavior and development. (Hirsch, 1967)

Growth and development never cease. The body manufactures millions of new cells daily. Each stimulus makes it imprint on the personality and the mind. Each moment the organism ages—called "growing up" among children. And some changes may be observed in specific stages—as that of hero worship, puberty, morality of contraint, concrete operations. Each child normally passes through each stage, but perhaps at a rate different from that of his older brother, his best friend, or even his twin sister. For example, in play, children usually progress through the solitary, onlooker, parallel, associative, and cooperative play stages. Play interests move from free, spontaneous endeavors to imaginative and constructive adventures, to collecting, sports, and reading. In peer relations children grow more peer-oriented with age—at first showing no preference for either sex, then a growing dislike for the opposite sex, finally an increasing preference for the opposite sex. Physically, the body exhibits certain stages of growth, as the formation, eruption, and shedding of teeth; the appearance of secondary and primary sex characteristics are common for the various stages.

Various structures and systems in the body have individual developmental rates and phases, yet there is a correlation among them. The progress in one area of development may affect the growth of another. For example, the brain grows at the most rapid rate, reaching its full size around age 12. Body weight and motor performance exhibit the slowest growth, reaching maximum effectiveness in the mid-twenties. Imagination grows in spurts between ages 2 and 6, and 12–16, declining at ages 10 and 20. These varied growth rates, along with those of intelligence and genital organs, are illustrated in Figure 1-6. As the child is experiencing growth in one aspect of development, he may demonstrate a lag in another aspect. It is common for young children who are learning to talk to reach a plateau in walking or vice versa. School-age children concerned with cognitive development may not show much progress in emotional or social realms. Those preoccupied with motor skills or social relationships may fall behind in intellectual progress. The child whose body has grown beyond his peers in maturity may find it difficult to relate socially to those in his own age group, whereas he who is mentally retarded may experience the same problem.

Development is usually more pronounced at its onset, often creating startling changes in appearance, ability, or behavior. With time its rate diminishes, and the new skill, attitude, or knowledge becomes more infused into the total person, causing the resultant change to be less exagger-

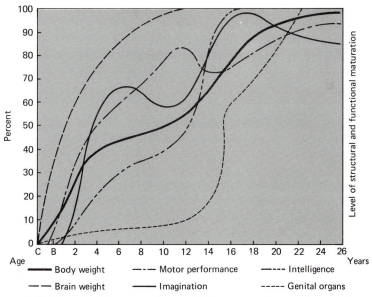

Figure 1-6. Hypothetical curves of growth for various factors of personality. (From *Human Development: A Science of Growth* by J. Pikunas, p. 39. Copyright © 1961, McGraw-Hill Book Company. Used with permission of McGraw-Hill Book Company.)

ated and intense. When children are first aware of an emerging ability or feature, they tend to emphasize it through actions or thoughts. This has been termed indigenous motivation—impetus from within the organism. An example is found in the child who sings the same song over and over, who prefers to eat only shrimp after discovering its flavor, who practices handball to the point of fatigue after finding what fun it is, who cannot be torn away from books after his reading skill has developed sufficiently.

One's behavior is inherently a function of his stage of growth and development, for with new talents and feelings, actions and thoughts are modified. Behavior is not wholly rooted in development. It is also shaped by the social setting, the significant others, the cultural norms, and the child's values and desires.

Developmental Tasks

Robert Havighurst (1952) is credited with formulating the theory of developmental tasks which links behavior with an inner push and outer pull. At each stage of development, certain tasks must be accomplished. These tasks are prescribed by the level of physical development, cultural demands or expectations of society, and aspirations or motivations within the individual. Developmental tasks do not form a curriculum for training children. Rather, this concept is the articulation of the learning and behavior that take place in the growing-up process in our society if the child is to function in a manner acceptable to himself and others.

Physical development of a child is the first determiner of things he learns to do. As the child's body matures, he is capable of different kinds of behavior. Even with practice, a child cannot learn to walk until his skeletal and muscular structures have grown enough to support and hold him in an upright position. Children cannot learn to play a game such as jacks or marbles until the fine muscle coordination has developed to a sufficient state to make such activity possible. This does not mean that all children are equally skillful in all activities. Skill depends not only on physical development, but also on incentive, opportunity for practice, attitudes of adults, and such things as body size and structure.

Our culture sets certain goals for good socialization. Americans value independence, sociability, and verbalization. Other societies may not value these same things, and therefore socialization processes in those societies do not push a child in these directions. Certain customs Americans take for granted—those dealing with food intake, toilet training, and the use of particular kinds of clothing. These customs are neither right nor wrong in the great scheme of things. Mealtime rituals vary from one culture to another. Nor are mealtime rituals the same in middle-class America as those in the ghetto.

Adults place emphasis on regulation of elimination functions and great restrictions on the child with the kind of clothing they require him to wear. In other cultures, regulation of elimination is fairly free and easy—and still children learn the ways of adults in their group. In some cultures, children wear little or no clothing, which may make the growing-up process easier.

As child-rearing practices vary from one country to another, so do they vary from group to group within our own country. What is considered unacceptable by one group may be quite highly prized by another. This is particularly true in the channeling of aggression. The middle class values verbal ways of settling differences, while the lower class values physical prowess.

One can also see this concept in language development. Middle-class children are taught that certain words are naughty; other words are acceptable. In lower-class communities "naughty" words might be quite acceptable. It is too bad if one's whole evaluation of a child and his worth hinges on whether the child uses a word labeled "bad" or whether the child confines his expressive language to words no worse than those labeled "slang." Even in middle-class America, the range of acceptable words has broadened quite a bit. Mouth-washed-out-with-soap words of a generation ago bring today at most a mild reproof.

In addition to the biological and cultural bases of developmental tasks, there is also a psychological basis: the aspiration or motivation within the child. Children try certain things in order to feel good about themselves, and in order to be accepted by others. Children might never learn to talk if there were no need to use verbal means of communication. Children modify their behavior in certain ways in order to be classified as regular fellows.

Havighurst has identified three great pushes that affect a child's development:

- The social push, thrusting the child out of the home into the peer group.
- The physical thrust into the world of games and work requiring neuromuscular skills.
- The intellectual push into the world of adult concepts, logic, symbolism, and communication and psychological environment and structure.

Adapted from *Developmental Tasks and Education* (Havighurst, 1952), the tasks of middle childhood are as follows:

1. *Learning physical skills necessary for ordinary games*—such as throwing, kicking, tumbling, swimming, and handling simple tools

    This is a period of general growth of muscle and bone, of increased muscular coordination. The peer group rewards a child for success and punishes him by indifference or disdain for failure in this task. Boys are expected to perfect these skills better than girls. Most children learn the necessary skills from the peer group. The school and community may need to help arrange play groups for awkward children to learn such skills without fear of punishment from age-mates.

2. *Building wholesome attitudes toward oneself as a growing organism*—such as habits of cleanliness, safety; realistic attitude toward self-adequacy and normality; wholesome attitude toward sex

   Physical growth such as dentition, postural habits, and muscular development is occurring. Healthy habits of diet, sleep, and exercise are not immediately rewarded but need to be stressed. Sexual curiosity and experimentation are present. Children are judged by physical appearance by both peers and adults. Success in this task is fostered by teaching routine health habit formation, correct information about sex, and encouraging physical neatness and orderliness. Community agencies may aid in general or in individual cases.

3. *Learning to get along with age-mates*—the give and take of social life among peers, to make friends and get along with everyone, to develop a social personality

   The child's circle of acquaintances broadens as he enters school, and he begins to compete with a larger group for the attention and approval of a mother-figure in the person of his teacher or another adult leader. He spends an increasing amount of time away from his family and must learn to derive more and more satisfaction from those outside his home. He learns how to follow rules in a group game, and how to treat friends. The school offers the major opportunity for accomplishment of this task.

4. *Learning an appropriate masculine or feminine social role*—to act the role which society expects of him

   In middle childhood the anatomical differences in boys and girls do not require a different sex role, but our culture expects them to be different in their expression of emotion, choice of play materials, and behavior in social situations. Reinforcement of these expectations comes in early identification with the parent of the same sex. The school usually fulfills the role of assisting the children who are having sex-role difficulty, while giving general reinforcement and encouragement to those who have already made satisfactory progress in this task achievement.

5. *Developing fundamental skills in reading, writing, and calculating*—

   The nervous system becomes mature enough to permit learning such abstractions during the middle years. The hand and eye muscles develop to a degree allowing manipulation of writing instruments and reading of the printed page. The technological and industrial strides in America have demanded accomplishment of this task. Reading speed, ability to spell and write, and arithmetic skills improve throughout middle childhood. Reading comprehension continues to improve indefinitely if learning continues. The other skills can also improve with special training and constant use. The school has the major responsibility for helping children achieve this task.

6. *Developing concepts necessary for everyday living*—acquiring a store of concepts sufficient for thinking effectively about ordinary occupational, civic and social matters

   By school entrance a child has a store of several hundred concepts—as roundness, sweetness, love, animal, food, anger. In the middle years the number of concepts swells to several thousand through experience and in reference to his early basic concepts. A child who has a correct concept of a camel, through pictures or actually seeing such an animal, can form a fairly accurate concept of a Ilama by seeing pictures of it and being told "it is a South American animal something like a camel."

7. *Developing conscience, morality, and a scale of values*—developing inner moral control, respect for moral values and the beginning of a rational scale of values

At birth the child values food and warmth. He gradually distinguishes good from bad. Through reward and punishment of parents he develops within himself the warning voice of conscience. Respect for rules of behavior is first learned in the home. The society expects children to "behave" correctly, and home and school jointly teach and refine social behavior through example, stories, punishments and rewards, and experience with peers.

8. *Achieving personal independence*—able to make plans and follow them and to act independently of parents and other adults to a degree

The young child is both physically and emotionally dependent on adults, and he views them as all-knowing and all-powerful. With success in his peer group and an ever-growing store of knowledge, he realizes adults are not infallible. He begins to free himself of parents and relate more to age-mates in choices related to recreation, choice of friends; and he becomes able to stay away from home for longer periods of time. He takes more responsibility for his safety and use of time. The school and the peer group provide laboratories for working through this task. Youth organizations likewise contribute to its achievement.

9. *Developing attitudes toward social groups and institutions*—defining and refining feelings about religion; social, political, and economic groups

The basic social attitudes are acquired by imitation of people with prestige, by collection and combination of experiences, by a single deeply emotional experience. From parents, teachers, peers, and through the mass media, the child during middle childhood gathers feelings and attitudes that are likely to remain with him throughout life. Every society inculcates its important and significant social attitudes during these years. The school in America fosters such basic democratic attitudes as religious and racial tolerance, respect for freedom of speech and other civil rights, political democracy, and international cooperation.

Children's Rights

No one is against children, but who is for them? As children's unique place in society has become recognized, specific actions have been taken relative to their protection and welfare. The Children's Charter is a classic document of 1930 enumerating their rights to spiritual and moral training. It calls for the guarding of personality; full preparation for birth; health protection, promotion and instruction; wholesome dwelling place and enriching home environment; safe school; community planning; education for citizenship, homemaking and parenthood; protection against accidents;

treatment of handicaps; fair treatment when in conflict; stable income and adequate standard of living; stimulation in youth organization.

Forty years later delegates to the seventh decade White House Conference on Children voiced some urgent concerns directed toward improving the lives of America's children. They called for a reordering of the national priorities to guarantee a basic family income adequate for children's needs; development of programs to eliminate racism which cripples children; comprehensive family-oriented child development programs including health services, day-care and early childhood education; a federally financed national child health care program; a child advocacy agency; massive funding for development of alternative optional forms of public education. The health, education and welfare and the bilingual-bicultural growth of all children was a major thrust of their deliberations, coupled with a call for a change in the national way of life that would bring people back into the lives of children (Report to the President, 1971).

Since the 1970 White House Conference on Children a new theme of children's welfare has related to their legal status, especially to the concept of their needs being rights. Two current approaches in the movement are to extend adult rights to children and to seek legally enforceable recognition of children's interests and needs. Whereas the thrust has sought to persuade adult society to treat children better, it has not changed the position of children in the society nor made them capable of securing better treatment for themselves (Rodham, 1976).

Although adult citizens have certain legal rights granted by the Constitution, children have far fewer ones. The very attributes which distinguish them from adults are the basis for withholding adult rights from them: age, degree of maturity, and circumstances. With respect to civil competence and liability, they are "non-persons" in the eyes of the law. (Rosenheim, 1976). Children's rights as legatees under wills, intestate successors or victims of crime have been long respected although they can only be exercised vicariously through adult representatives. However, they cannot be farmed out to nonrelated, unregulated caretakers and are immune from being sued or sold. Older children have more rights than middle childhood ones who cannot drive motor vehicles, drop out of school, vote, or work.

Glasser (1975) contends that children have but few legal rights, and even those are hard to enforce because there are few limits on the power of adults. He points out that when the biological family breaks down, children can be assigned to foster or adoptive parents or institutions and are then at the mercy of the state. He questions: Who really represents the child in court? Do children have the right to a permanent home?

Supreme Court decisions that have extended children's legal rights include: the Brown Case abolishing segregation in public schools, the Gault Case identifying their in-court rights, and the Yoder Case in which their rights to decline high school education on religious grounds were upheld. Children have also been granted by the high court the right to refuse to salute the flag when against their religious beliefs and to don a black arm band in protesting the Vietnam War. Their rights to protection from parental mistreatment have been traditionally based on the "best interest" theory, which has not always been provable. Continued reliance on this standard is under serious scrutiny by proponents of child advocacy.

Children are almost powerless to represent their own interests or to organize into politically powerful groups, and most adults allied with their cause have been relatively uninfluential in the political system. Except for the institutionalized, no other group in society is so dependent upon the choices of others. Children's rights cannot be clarified and secured until some specific institution or agency has recognized them and assumed the responsibility for enforcing the rights. This process will necessitate generating new lines of legal theory and involve both the legislative and judicial branches of government (Rodham, 1976).

Child Power is a relatively new term being used in attempts to gain for youngsters protection from the "state" under the Bill of Rights. The Children's Defense Fund is a part of the Washington Research Project begun in 1971 by citizens interested in improving and monitoring conditions under which children live in the nation. This group has assumed a role as children's advocate seeking: education for children formerly excluded from school (handicapped, non-English speaking, pregnant); privacy of social agency records; protection from medical experimentation or harmful research techniques; adequate health care; fair and humane services. The organization collects data and issues reports on selected conditions of youth, publishes reports, manuals and handbooks for parents, sponsors local task forces and speaks out in the press to increase public awareness of its findings (Cottle and Edelman, 1975).

The idea has been advanced that children be granted legal rights against their parents, for example, the right to divorce them. Such concepts have serious ranifications for parent-child relations as well as for services to families.

What's Next?

Centuries of Childhood. Ariès, P. N.Y.: Knopf, 1962.

Escape from Childhood. Holt, J. N.Y.: Ballantine, 1974.

Beyond the Best Interests of the Child. Goldstein, J. N.Y.: Free Press, 1973.

Harvard Educational Review, Vol. 43:4 and 44:1.

Exploring the Child's World. Parkhurst, H. N.Y.: Appleton-Century-Crofts, 1951.

Film: *Children Who Draw* (on observation) Macmillan Films, 34 McQuesten Pkwy., S., Mt. Vernon, N.Y. 10550 (44 min/color).

Filmstrip: *The Rights of Children* (7SV 945) Childcraft Education Corp, 23 Kilmer Rd., Edison, N.J. 08817.

Catalysts for Discussion

I.

Test your knowledge of the principles of growth and development by indicating which of the following statements are true and which are false.

1. Growth refers to quantitative changes, such as increase in size; whereas development refers to qualitative changes—progression toward maturity, and the integration of many structures and functions.
2. Types of change occurring in growth and development are size, proportion, disappearance of old features, and appearance of new features.
3. Development proceeds from general to specific, occurring in stages.
4. Development proceeds at different rates in different parts of the body, yet is continuous.
5. Developmental phases are correlated, the maturity of one facet affecting others.
6. The developmental laws are cephalocaudal (head downward) and proximodistal (trunk outward).
7. Growth and behavior follow genetic sequences.
8. Unfolding abilities are spontaneously expressed.
9. Behavior is largely controlled by human needs.
10. Behavior is a function of developmental status.
11. A useful yardstick by which to measure development is the concept of developmental tasks.
12. Forthcoming growth and behavior are predictable.
13. Deviant development may be caused by poor health, hormonal change, chemical imbalances, emotional deprivation, or other factors.
14. Young children are not particularly aware of growth unless someone mentions it to them.
15. Lack of knowledge concerning developmental stages in children can cause unrealistic expectations on the part of parents and other adults in a child's life.
16. Development follows a pattern, progressive and orderly.
17. Normally the child passes through each stage of development.
18. Each stage has characteristic traits.
19. Development is caused by maturation and learning, the environment influencing it as well as heredity.
20. The rate of growth and terminal status are different for each child, yet children are more alike than they are different.
21. Whenever a new developmental ability emerges, the child tends to use it, often causing his behavior to be exaggerated and intense.
22. The tempo of growth is uneven.
23. Growth rates and patterns can be modified.
24. There is a positive relationship between the various areas of development.
25. Many of children's activities at given stages are a result of the period of development.

You should have found all the above statements true, and the listing a summary of the principles.

Beyond the Classroom Experiences

1. To see a demonstration of the inherent problems in research, ask a friend to join you in observing children in a given situation. Each of you write a report of the experience in a prescribed form. Then compare for similarities and differences in what was observed and recorded.

2. Locate the following research tools in your library, noting their call number and general content:

   Child Development Abstracts.
   Psychological Abstracts.
   Sociological Abstracts.
   Dissertation Abstracts.
   Education Index.
   Child Development—published by the Society for Research in Child Development.
   Today's Child—published by Edwards Publications, Inc.
   Childhood Education—published by the Association for Childhood Education International.
   Young Children—published by the National Association for the Education of Young Children.
   Child Welfare—published by Child Welfare League of America.
   Journal of Home Economics—published by the American Home Economics Association.
   Research Journal of Home Economics—published by the American Home Economics Association.
   Children Today—published by the U.S. Dept. of Health, Education, and Welfare & Office of Child Development.
   Journal of Marriage and the Family—published by the National Council on Family Relations.
   Child and Family—published by the National Commission on Human Life, Reproduction & Rhythm.
   The Family Coordinator—published by the National Council on Family Relations.
   Monographs of the Society for Research in Child Development.
   Child development general texts.
   Other publications related to the field of child study.

3. Read a novel or biography about children. Some novels to consider:

   To Kill a Mockingbird, H. Lee. Philadelphia: Lippincott, 1960.
   Death in the Family, J. Agee. New York: Avon Books, 1959.
   The Learning Tree, G. Parks. Greenwich, Conn.: Fawcett, 1963.
   Manchild in the Promised Land, C. Brown. New York: Signet Books, 1965.
   Coming of Age in Mississippi, A. Moody. New York: Dell, 1970.
   Dibs: In Search of Self, V. Axline. Boston: Houghton Mifflin, 1964.
   To Brooklyn with Love, G. Green. New York: Trident Press, 1967.

   As you read, note passages or incidents which give you insight into the child's behavior or which help you to know him better. Give particular attention to the following:

   What was he like physically? Did this affect him in any way?

What was his neighborhood like: physical aspects, people, activities, socio-economic level?

What was his family like: parents, siblings? Values? How did he relate to them? What sort of guidance or discipline was used?

Who were his friends and how did they influence him?

What school did he attend and what was his response? Teachers? Curriculum?

What caused him to be angry, sad, fearful, hurt, affectionate? How did he express these feelings? What seemed to be funny to him?

Describe his moral and religious development.

What pressures did the child face?

State his ideas on:

Sex and his own sex role
Religion
Prejudice, fairness
Work
Goodness or morality
Death

4. Throughout the book suggestions are made concerning observation and activities with children. To make the most of these suggestions locate a child or a specific group of children with whom you can have ongoing frequent contact.

5. An Outline for Participant-Observer Data Collection

State setting
Include notes taken during experience
Try to account for the development and behavior noted
Relate observation to information presented in class

6. Chapter 16 and 17 in Peterson's (1974) *A Child Grows Up* demonstrates a diary approach with annotated text. This method of study may prove helpful in developing observational and analytical skills.

7. Discuss children's rights with various age groups, including children, parents, others in the community. Look for news articles where children's rights are an issue. Study and support legislation which seeks to provide for recognition of children's rights.

Chapter 2

The Cultural Milieu

This chapter is designed to help you:

- account for the great variety among the nation's children.
- suggest ways in which all children are alike and draw implications for living with them.
- consider the pluralistic values of the American society and their effects on children's development
- understand how the basic life themes of socio-economic class influence children's lives
- consider the major values of the American society and indicate reasons why poverty children may fail to exhibit evidences of their espousal.
- understand how the basic life themes of the lower class influence children's lives.
- discuss the special challenges faced by a child with minority group status.
- explain how children are acculturated.
- see the role of mass media in the lives of children—its contributions and disadvantages.

A Child's Legacy

The child of the middle years has two legacies that will continue to shape his life: the gift of heredity determined at the instant of fertilization, before society or even his parents knew of his existence; the endowment of environment, also bestowed at his conception and greatly enlarged at his birth when he enters a given society, culture, and family. Through the years those who would understand the complexity of human nature have tried to quantify and even to control these two factors, attempts that have resulted in the ongoing nature-nurture controversy.

Those who accept heredity as the superior influence have held that germ plasm is transmitted from generation to generation, thereby determining all life, including personality characteristics. Hitler's racism and desire to produce a superior people was an outgrowth of this viewpoint. Genetic counseling, which advises couples of the probability of the appearance of particular traits in their offspring based on their own traits, is perhaps a less radical manifestation. On the other hand, the environmentalistic-oriented scientists hypothesize that some factors can affect the germ plasm; that cell connections may be environmentally altered. In addition, the intrauterine environment may have a lasting affect on one's development; not only with respect to the proper development of body parts but even to emotionality, and utilization of inborn potential. Such social programs as Head Start and Follow Through are based on this theory.

Any environment less than maximally stimulating will inhibit one's achievement of full potential. Regardless of the superior environment stimulation, however, one cannot exceed the genetically-set limits of achievement. Efforts to refine such broad generalizations continue, but they are hampered by the fact that to control the variable of inheritance while varying that of environment is almost impossible, and vice versa.

It is known that certain physical characteristics are genetically transmitted, including coloring, general body build, and sex. It is strongly suspected that intellectual potential may be genetic in origin. There is support for the idea that even temperament may have genetic roots in terms of the individual's biochemistry. Even in this day of advanced technology, most children and parents are relatively powerless to alter these basics in their lives. They are not powerless, however, when it comes to the use and manipulation of the environment into which they are born. It is to this second legacy that closer attention will be given in this section. Hess (1970, p. 457) emphasizes its magnitude in these words:

> The social and physical circumstances in which man lives are primarily of his own making. He is responsible for magnificent cities and monstrous slums, massive projects of water control and widespread water pollution, powerful automobiles and chronic air pollution, mass media of communication and individual isolation. Within a major urban area are to be found extremes of personal trauma and personal comfort, deprivation and affluence, social cohesion and anomie. Man must adapt individually to the surroundings he has created collectively. It shapes his behavior and the behavior of his young. The study of socialization is the study of the effects of man-made environments upon man.

Hunt (1969) giving further emphasis to the importance of environment, particularly in the area of intellectual functioning, outlined several propositions regarding development he believed are no longer tenable. The first, that *rate of development is predetermined* (the idea of a constant IQ is illustrative of this stand) was tied to the notion that maturation and learning are two distinct and separate processes with maturation predetermined by heredity and learning controlled by the circumstances and environment encountered by the individual. The classical work of Skeels and Dye (1939) dealing with the positive effects of stimulation on the functioning of retarded children, as well as others, has made the idea of predetermined rate of development untenable and has underscored the role of environment and experience in total development.

The second assumption, that *maturation is independent of circumstances* is no longer credible even in the light of animal experiments in which varied rearing environments produced quite different behavior. In addition there is the classical orphanage study (Dennis and Sayegh, 1965) in which almost two-thirds of the children in their second year were not sitting alone and four-fifths of those in their fourth year were still not walking. In light of the norms for sitting alone (8.3 mo.) and walking (12.5–13.8 mo.) for family reared children, the role of circumstances and experience, even in motor development, becomes apparent.

Further credence is given this concept by the results of treatment instigated when 13 of the babies ranging in age from 7.2 months to 18.7 months were given an hour of additional experiences each day for 15 days. A significant gain was noted in developmental age for the experimental children in comparison to 8 matched controls who received no additional experience during that time.

The third fallacy, that *longitudinal prediction is possible,* based on IQ scores alone, has led to unfortunate educational practices; a bit like a self-fulfilling prophecy. In order to predict what a child will be like as an adult, one must specify the circumstances under which development will take place. Hunt pointed out that longitudinal prediction improves with age, but this can be accounted for by the tendency of individuals to remain within relatively stable social, economic and educational circumstances.

The idea of "readiness" is tied to this assumption. It is true that children are ready for certain experiences and not ready for others; but Hunt believed that considerations of "readiness" as a matter of predetermined maturation, distinct from learning or past experience, is basically wrong and potentially damaging. He is concerned with "the problem of the match"; that is, if a set of circumstances is to induce psychological development in the child, there must be "an appropriate relationship to the information and skills already accumulated by the child."

In rebuttal to Jensen's (1969) assertion that there is an innate difference in the intelligence of black children and white children, a group of behavioral scientists pointed out that, whereas differences in IQ scores exist, there is little evidence to indicate such differences are innate. Rather, "the evidence points overwhelmingly to the fact that when one compares blacks and whites of comparable cultural and educational background, differences in intelligence test scores diminish markedly; the more comparable the backgrounds, the less the difference." The thesis of the group is that social inequalities deprive certain groups of people—blacks in particular—of social, economic and educational advantages available to a large majority of the whites; existing social structures prevent black and white people even of the same social class from leading comparable lives. Therefore, they conclude: "no scientific discussion of racial differences can exclude an examination of political, historic, economic and psychological factors which are inextricably related to racial differences."

The place of one's birth and growing-up years is a vital determinant of the person one becomes. Since in this book we are primarily concerned with the child who is born and lives in the United States of America, in our consideration of the effects of environment we will speak in terms of the current American society.

Jerome Kagan (1974) pointed out that an environment can be classed as neither good nor bad except in relation to a specific species. Therefore, to evaluate the effect of environment on a child, we must also consider the demands the community makes upon the adolescent and young adult. A child must feel valued by significant adults in the community, his parents and a few others. To do this he must meet the goals set by the cultural expectation of his environment.

The cultivating of particular talents is important for development of a sense of worth since our society makes personal competence "synonymous with virtue" (p. 89). The value of a particular competence changes from one culture to another; in the United States academic success is of great importance. We value a sense of autonomy, the ability and desire to make decisions regarding one's own conduct, and independence. Children are socialized to make decisions which are in their own best interests and to decide conflicts themselves. Our permissive attitude toward sexuality grows out of our cultural requirement that young adults be heterosexually successful. There is much to celebrate in this listing, but also much is lacking: "insufficient emphasis on intimacy and too much on self-interest; insufficient emphasis on cooperation and too much on competitiveness; insufficient emphasis on altruism and too much on narcissism. . . . These values derive, in part from the form of our economy, our densely crowded, impersonal cities, and the fact that our educational institutions function as twelve-to-sixteen year selection sites for tomorrow's doctors, teachers, lawyers, administrators, scientists and business executives (Kagan, 1974, p. 90)." He continued by suggesting that in order to accomplish this ego idea there are appropriate accomplishments at each developmental level. During the school-age and preadolescent years, the child must successfully master basic school requirements (reading, writing, mathematics); be successful in peer-valued talents, and have access to desirable models for identification. The ease with which such tasks can be completed depends in part on the cultural milieu in which the child develops.

It is against this background tapestry that the American child must play his part on the world's stage. A closer examination of the American scene reveals that within the whole there exist divergent and unique cultures, or subcultures in which children live and grow up. Consider the variety of values, customs, beliefs, and traits one could find in America: the American Indian child of the Southwest, the black child in a northern ghetto, the child from Appalachia, the midwestern farmboy, the daughter of a wealthy family on the New England coast. There is no "typical" American child. Our classic picture of the freckle-faced, tousled-haired, Anglo-in-origin boy, riding his shiny red bike down a suburban street, closely followed by a cocker spaniel pup most assuredly does not adequately represent America's child of the middle years.

What in this society causes children to be different? How do these differences affect total development? What are the implications of such differences for adults involved with children in the middle years? Must the differences be minimized, ignored, annihilated; or can they be emphasized, understood, and used? What is it about American children that is the same? What are the implications of this sameness?

When we think of subgroups within the American culture, immediately many think of race and social class. Others will also think of nationality and religious affiliation. In addition there is rural-urban residence, age, sex, geographical location. All these factors tend to create distinct differences among Americans. Children prior to school age are measurably cognizant only of differences in external appearances, either in color or gross physical deviation or handicaps. They do not usually detect differences in social class, religion, or nationality per se. For many children, entering school is the first opportunity they have had to interact with children unlike themselves. Each, however, is certainly a product of the subculture into which he was born. Each brings to the new situation a set of "rules" for dealing with those he discovers different from himself.

It is difficult to totally reconcile the celebration of individuality and certain principles which undergird maximal growth and development while the good of the whole society is the sought goal. Yet the authors believe that those who choose to deal with children and their families must wrestle with this challenge. Our philosophy is centered in the idea of the individual worth of each person, not because of his productivity or even his behavior, but because of his humanness, his very being.

There are reasons for each person's behavior, many times not based on choice but on circumstance, for behavior emanates from needs that may or may not be consciously recognized. It is therefore necessary that we see the necessity for *choice-making* by all, including children. Ours is the role of avowing individual worth by making available alternatives from which they may select instead of adopting the position that we can make the best choices for others. Not only in the ghetto, but also in middle-class America too many people live and develop as they do, not because they find it satisfying, but because they have no other choice—because of their heritage, their environment, their ignorance, or psychological fetters that prohibit examination of other alternatives.

At the risk of being accused of dealing in semantic games, the concept of life-styles versus life conditions must be explored. There are many life-styles which enhance the development of children or individuals and group members. Examination, understanding, and appreciation of the varied value systems or family organizations must be our goal. However, there are certain conditions in the society which offer no choices and fail to enhance growth and development. These range from poor housing and inadequate garbage removal to lack of job opportunities and treatment by others which produces feelings of inferiority. Such conditions would not be alleviated even if "life-styles" were altered. Accepting life-styles while changing living conditions may well be the answer.

Another consideration lies in the *validity* of the choices people make. Not only must choice be available, but these choices must be acceptable, even when they are not the same as those we would have made. Honest acceptance and understanding of a multiplicity of life-styles, from breakfast foods to marriage and family management, is our responsibility. We can help in the education of others by expanding opportunities to explore various models. But ultimately we must respect their choice without condemnation.

When viewed with regard to the rights of others, even the principle of respecting choices becomes confounded. An adage in our culture suggests: my freedom to swing my arm ends where your nose begins. Yet even this rule of thumb is not clear-cut, as demonstrated in the consumption of alcoholic beverages. There exists a continuum which ranges from the view that such a practice is morally wrong and should be legally prohibited to the view that it is a vital part of the life-style. Where along this spectrum do rights of others supersede the individual's right to choose? A social drink may be offensive to many; driving while drinking potentially endangers others; a fender-bender accident due to driving while drinking elevates the cost of car insurance for everyone; a serious accident caused by a drinking driver could destroy others' property, even take the life of an innocent by-stander. The same dilemma exists with respect to pollution, population control, drug use, and a host of other social issues. The rights of the individual versus the good of the group is a continuing concern. Part of the solution is to see that the solution is not easy.

A third need is to *help children be flexible,* which is in itself a value, in order that they may be prepared to deal with new conditions and changing situations. They will be called on to make choices their parents never had to make, and we cannot give them the specific answers they will need in the year 2000. As they develop mechanisms for evaluation and choice-making, as they have opportunities to examine alternatives, weigh consequences and make choices, they will prepare for those future decisions. Although not simple, it is a necessary and exciting challenge. Roots of flexibility are nourished throughout the middle childhood years.

Continuing consideration for the humanity of each other and continuing education which begins early and continues throughout the life span may prove part of the solution. Individuals need to become aware of themselves and others as growing, worthwhile persons. Education for parenting, for example, although almost completely lacking, must begin when it counts, when children are forming concepts of themselves and internalizing value systems. Education that allows a child to explore alternatives, develop a positive self-image, and understand and reach out to others will allow youngsters to grow into persons who can foster this kind of development in their own children.

Social Class as a Determinant of Behavior

Race has been considered a significant variable causing differences in various aspects of personality and performance. When differences among races are examined in a situation where social class or socioeconomic status is carefully controlled, the effect of race is minimized (Chilman, 1966). This indicates that in our society, one's social standing or location in the economic structure is a more powerful force than the color of his skin. This should be encouraging, for although one does not have the option, nor the desire, to change his skin color in order to fare better, everyone has the theoretical prerogative to change his social class or subculture.

Consideration will be given to the child of minority group status, whether due to race, religion, or nationality. Primarily, however, attention will be given to the effect of social class on children, particularly during the middle years.

Since the majority of Americans are so-called middle class, and since the vast majority of students of child development come from this segment of our population, they are likely to have preconceived ideas about both the upper and lower classes, many of which may not be based on facts. There are factors related to socioeconomic status that demand attention: reported child abuse is more common among the poor than in middle class families (Gil, 1970); socioeconomic status of the family has emerged as the most powerful predictor of school success in studies conducted at both state and national levels (Coleman, 1966; Jencks, 1972); other conditions accompany poverty which may prove detrimental to the full development of children: poor housing, lack of parental education; lack of medical care.

The general tendency is to emphasize the differences between the classes; benefit can also come from noting similarities. Likewise, while describing people who are "deprived," "underprivileged," "disadvantaged," one may overlook areas in which they are advantaged. Every class and subculture has positive aspects. To know these and to help children appreciate and capitalize on them would contribute much to understanding, cooperation, and growth.

Upper Class

The child of America's upper class has probably been studied less than any other, partly because his plight did not seem perilous to the society, also because he is not as accessible for research as those from the middle and lower classes. He is more likely to attend private schools or receive private tutoring in his own home. He may study abroad and learn a great deal about the world through travel. He is surrounded by the great artworks of all time. It is assumed that he will gain education of the highest caliber, not to prepare him for the work-a-day world, but because it is part of the family tradition. He is not necessarily more intelligent owing to his family's affluence; he may be quite average in abilities; however, superior opportunitites may help him to develop his potential more fully than his other-class counterparts. His home life is likely to be less family-centered, often because of parental activities outside the home. He may be reared primarily by a governess, and although given all the material things a child could imagine, he may lack and long for the attention and companionship of his parents and other relatives.

The child from the upper-class home is usually spared the competition of making a name for himself, for he inherits this status. But he is often faced with adjusting to living away from his home and family while attending prep school, where he may find some pressure to become accepted by the Ivy League colleges. However, his misdoings are likely to become headlines.

Children whose families are considered upper-upper class differ from those whose families are thought of as lower-upper, or newly rich. The upper-upper-class family holds values that are not related to money: brains, creativity, beauty, breeding, loyalty, and stability. The child in this family respects family and lineage but develops disdain for such status symbols as conspicuous consumption. He believes money is important and enjoys the privileges and material items it can furnish without learning much about its value. He has been characterized as being more concerned with the past and the present than the future, more selflessly interested in his fellow man; and more strictly disciplined. These children follow educational patterns set by their parents and are relatively free to pursue any occupation they wish, from philanthropy to farming, since working is not a necessity but for diversion. Although the parents of the upper-upper class try hard not to spoil children, this is difficult because of their social position and the limelight surrounding it.

Children of the near rich may be somewhat different. They are not readily accepted by the upper-upper class because of their conspicuous consumption and the fact that their ancestors attended the wrong schools, married the wrong persons, and are buried in the wrong cemeteries. They are more likely to be spoiled and alienated from their parents because of the advantages they have enjoyed and the opportunities they have had to acculturate more upper-upper-class values (Bell, 1963; LeMasters, 1977; and Kirsten, 1968).

Whereas the middle class is characterized as valuing industry and thrift, the rich in America may be aptly described as valuing status, name, and tradition. The newly rich are concerned with glamour and material possessions.

Wixen (1973) has called the rich disadvantaged, claiming that "in many respects the children of the poor have more in common with them [children of the rich] than either has with the vast middle class between them." He cited a unique identity problem which results from impoverished role images and lack of sequential role progression, terming the condition *dysgradia*. The child with dysgradia suffers feelings of emptiness and unhappiness and may revert to fantasy or even prolonged sleep as a defense. Parents may contribute to dysgradia by the fact that they seldom demonstrate for the child advancement either in a career or even human relationships: they simply *are* successful in the former and often failures in the latter. Children living in large, isolated homes of the rich are even deprived of peer exposure, which for children in other classes provides a great deal of role information. Surrounded by servants, they may be prevented from learning how to assume responsibility for themselves. Parents' relations with their children in this group may be minimal due to their social involvements and the fact that hired personnel perform many nurturing functions.

Whereas newly-rich parents offer relatively unattainable images for their children, many in the upper-class have only sketchy ideas of their parents' occupations. One illustration from Wixen (1973, p. 40) will illustrate:

What does your dad do?
Oh he sails and plays golf. Sometimes he and mom go to France to live for a while.
I mean, how does he get the money to do those things?
I think that comes from the bank.
What do you want to be when you grow up?
I want to go to France.

Rich parents may experience guilt from not spending time with their children and make the children scapegoats, focusing on their shortcomings. Parents of the newly rich exemplify instant success and pleasure, and their children are particularly vulnerable to drugs and other growing-up problems.

Coles (1977) interviewed 85 children over a number of years: children of wealthy bankers, mine owners, ranchers, plantation owners. They resided in New Orleans, in Atlanta, Appalachia, Florida, Mississippi, or Boston. These children were broadly informed about the world and poverty and asked a great many questions.

One boy, who planned to attend Princeton, wondered why policemen, badly needed to contain "the mobs," were not trained in this college. Another could not understand why the mine owner would not let his daughter visit the mines. Another asked why, with so many rooms in the house, the family didn't let the poor people live in them. These children, between five and fourteen years of age, tended to be more liberal than their parents, more sensitive, curious about working people.

Coles went on to say that one cannot talk about *the* affluent any more than one can talk about *the* poor. Neither group has clear-cut, consistent psychological or cultural characteristics. There are, however, some resemblances based on "class, occupation, religion, common experiences, expectations, ideas conveyed to children" (p. 362). This intangible something which well-off Americans transmit to their children, Coles called *"entitlement"*: an emotional expression of those "familiar class-bound prerogatives, money and power," that has both psychological and social dimensions. He sensed on the part of parents and children, a feeling of confidence as far as material possessions and their place in the social scene, but along with this was a desire for something else for the children: responsible attitudes, and attempts to live up to their ideals, along with a sense of competence and self esteem. Without this there is a danger that the children of the well-to-do will turn away from life, forsake people, and become passionately involved with objects instead.

Middle Class

Middle class children are more often written about and studied, but to characterize in a truly typical way is almost impossible. The middle-class range is very broad, including such professionals as physicians, attorneys, and professors; those concerned with the distribution of such goods as real estate and cosmetics; those delivering such services as family life education and television repair.

Coles and Erickson (1971), in a photographic story, present some of the variety of the middle class: "families headed by men who are policemen, firemen, factory workers, bank-tellers or lower-level bank officers, school teachers, telephone repairmen, construction workers, clerks and typists, and small farmers and small store keepers and on and on." Suffice it to say that in the middle class, values include education, conspicuous consumption, social striving; such traits as honesty, moderation, cleanliness, thrift, and delayed gratification are endorsed but not always stringently adhered to. Most teachers in public schools are from this broad group of the population, and many of the procedures and standards in schools are said to be based on middle-class values (McCandless, 1967). Hence, children who have been reared to compete, achieve, and conform are more likely to succeed in school. These successful ones are most likely to have participated in Little League, the Scouts, Sunday school, and have had a fair amount of interaction with family in the home.

A profile of the American middle class family (U.S. News and World Report, 1977) reveals the following information:

- incomes range from $12,000 to $30,000 per year; average of $20,000
- 53 percent of all families are middle class
- 92 percent are white; as compared with 89 percent of total families
- median age of head of family is 43 years as compared to 45 years for all families in the United States
- average size is 3.7 persons as compared to the national average of 3.4 persons
- better than average education: of all families headed by a college graduate, two-thirds are middle class
- residence: 73 percent live in larger cities or suburbs; 24 percent live in small cities or towns; 3 percent live in rural areas.

Incomes are up, and so are taxes and costs of what the middle-class see as necessities of life: medical care; home ownership; college tuition; transportation; utilities. Even with a second income (both parents in the labor force) they may not be able to keep abreast of the cost of living increases plus higher-bracket federal tax rates. Meanwhile these middle-income families see others get getting benefits for which they cannot qualify, both tax breaks and subsidies for low income families and special exemptions enjoyed by high-income families.

Among the middle class there is a great deal of mobility, and many children do not spend all their lives among relatives in their native community. About 6 million children between ages 5 and 13 changed place of residence in 1970–71 (U.S. Bureau of the Census, 1972). It is more difficult for this child to put down roots and develop a sense of harmony between himself and his world. On the credit side, mobility allows the child to become acquainted with a larger world, with many people, and with varying customs. Children who have lived in Germany, Hawaii, or Japan are different from children who have lived only in one house or even in one town. These here-there-everywhere children can give a great deal to any group, but will perhaps need help in being a part of the group and in developing an "at home" feeling.

Consideration of the middle class warrants particular attention to the black middle class. In 1970, a fourth of the gainfully employed blacks in the United States were working in white-collar occupations. In the past three decades both the occupational structure and income of the black wage-earner have improved, contributing to a definable middle segment within the race. Typical white collar positions include: sales and clerical, teaching, social work, and government jobs. Kronus (1971, p. 8) characterized the position of the middle class black as follows: "The middle status black person, according to white standards, ranks above most other blacks, enjoying high prestige in the black community. However, when he judges his status in relation to whites, he finds himself somewhat lower in rank."

Lower Class

There are great numbers of children who are products of lower-class homes; a designation which refers not to their inherent worth as individuals nor to their moral character, but rather to their power and prestige within society. Within the last decade, the number of Americans living below the poverty line—$5,038 for a non-farm family of four in 1974—has been estimated at one-fifth of the total population. From 1973 to 1974 there was an 8 percent increase in children under 18 living below the poverty level: from 9.5 million in 1973 (14.2 percent of all children) to 10.2 million (15.5 percent of all children) in 1974 (Status of Children, 1974). By 1975, this figure had risen to 10.9 million (17 percent of all children). Children from female-headed households and black families were over-represented in these numbers. (See Figures 2-1 and 2-2.) In addition, Keniston (1977) suggests that one-third of all American children are born into families with such great financial stress that they will suffer basic deprivation. Nearly 8 million children are recipients of Aid to Families with Dependent Children (AFDC) in any single month. Nine million others live in low income families and are intermittent beneficiaries. Twenty-five million children participate in federally subsidized lunch programs with ten million of these receiving lunch totally or almost totally free. Then there are the children who live in families far above the poverty line,

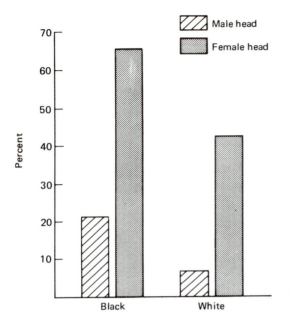

Figure 2-1. Percent of children under 18 years old in poverty families: 1974.

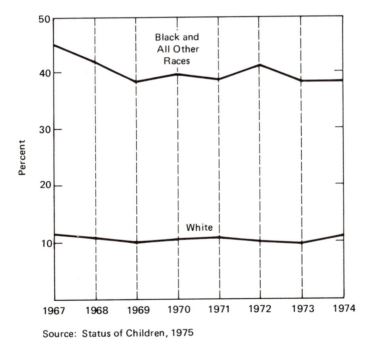

Source: Status of Children, 1975

Figure 2-2. Percent of children under 18 years old in poverty families: 1967 to 1974.

CHAPTER 2 / THE CULTURAL MILIEU

but also far below the median income level who are in difficult circumstances. (See Table 2-1 and compare with Table 2-2.) Sixty percent of the white children living in female headed households, and 75 percent of the children under six living in other households are in families with income which is 50 percent of the median income. Six out of ten of all black children, and five out of six black children in female-headed households live at this level. Median income for black families was 61 percent of that of white families in 1969, and by 1974 this percentage had decreased to 58 percent of the median income for white families.

Those who continue to think that persons in this segment of the population are happy-go-lucky without a care in the world have failed miserably to see the true facts. Psychosis, divorce, physical disease, alcoholism, illegitimate children, unemployment, slum housing, inadequate education are all serious problems that plague the lower-class family and that seriously affect the lives of its children. Not only do children in such families inherit

Slum housing is one factor which plagues lower-class families and can seriously affect the lives of children. *(Photo by Rick Coleman.)*

SOCIAL CLASS AS A DETERMINANT OF BEHAVIOR

Table 2-1 Intermediate Budget for Family of Four at Approximately the Median Income

Category	Annual Cost	Interpretation
Food	$ 3,548	$68 per week or 81¢ per meal per person
Housing	$ 3,236	$270 per month for rent or mortgage, utilities, home furnishings, and maintenance
Transportation	$ 1,171	$98 per month for car payments, gas, oil and repairs or 80¢ per day per person for public transportation
Clothing	$ 1,095	$23 per month per person for shoes, clothing, cleaning, laundry, and repairs
Personal care	$ 310	$1.49 per week per person for haircuts, soap, shampoo, toothpaste, etc.
Medical care	$ 742	$62 per month for health insurance, prescriptions, dental care, and uninsured portions of medical costs
Family consumption	$ 786	$3.78 per week per person for all leisure activities: vacations, entertainment, books, newspapers, etc.
Other costs	$ 661	$55 per month for gifts, contributions, life insurance, business-related and miscellaneous expenses
Compulsory social security and disability insurance	$ 780	5.4 percent of total income
Personal income tax	$ 2,010	14.0 percent of total income
	$14,339	

From *All Our Children: The American Family Under Pressure* by Kenneth Keniston and the Carnegie Council on Children, copyright © 1977 by Carnegie Corporation of New York. Reprinted by permission of Harcourt Brace Jovanovich, Inc.

these realities of life; they also inherit stereotype labels such as undependable, lazy, dirty, good-for-nothing, morally decadent, stupid (Chilman, 1966).

Great numbers of poor families live in the inner city. Stith (1969, p. 1) has captured their plight in these words:

Who are the people of the inner city? They are black and white, Indian, Spanish Americans, Gypsies; clean and filthy; ragged and neatly dressed; responsible

Table 2-2 **"Optimistic" Budget for Family of Four at Approximately Half the Median Income (150% of the current official poverty line)**

Category	Annual Cost	Interpretation
Food	$2,485	$48 per week or $11.95 per person for a week's food (30 percent lower than intermediate budget)
Housing	$1,239	$103 per month for rent, utilities, and furnishings
Transportation	$ 455	$38 per month or 31¢ per day per person
Clothing	$ 660	$14 per month per person
Personal care	$ 186	89¢ per week per person
Medical care	$ 737	$61 per month for all doctor visits, prescriptions, and health insurance
Family consumption	$ 294	$1.41 per week per person
Other costs	$ 327	$27 per month (50 percent lower than intermediate budget)
Compulsory social security and disability insurance	$ 472	6.4 percent of total income
Personal income tax	$ 520	7.1 percent of total income
	$7,375	

From *All Our Children: The American Family Under Pressure* by Kenneth Keniston and the Carnegie Council on Children, copyright © 1977 by Carnegie Corporation of New York. Reprinted by permission of Harcourt Brace Jovanovich, Inc.

and irresponsible; caring, unconcerned; at work, unemployed, desperately seeking a job with enough pay to make a go of things; men, women, youth, babies, women old before their time, disabled men, aged; immigrants from Alabama and Appalachia, natives whose parents were also poor. Among them are the sick, bewildered, frightened, lonely, frustrated, preyed upon, exploited. They are ill housed, inadequately fed, poorly clothed. They are illiterate, uneducated, and for the most part powerless. They seem not to understand nor to be able to fulfill the adult role in parenthood or in community life. They are faced with multitudinous problems: dollars and cents problems; relationship problems; situations that rob them of pride and dignity.

Children from lower-class homes or from racial or ethnic minorities are often called culturally deprived. One who is astute in perception will realize that these children are not culturally deprived until they leave their home and neighborhood environment. With this insight, one will further recognize that all persons are culturally deprived when out of familiar surroundings and circles. Consider the middle-class child who attends a private school for upper-class children; the English-speaking child who participates in a summer seminar in Mexico; the Catholic child who goes with a friend to a Baptist testimony meeting. In this sense, then, everyone is culturally deprived because there are situations for which our socialization process has not prepared us. This is the manner in which the poor child is culturally deprived. He functions adequately while he is in his home culture; he does not know how to act in settings that are so vastly different— as the typical classroom, club meeting, or other middle-class-oriented activity.

Think Back

To a time when you were culturally deprived (in a strange environment):
How you felt.
What you did to compensate for your deprivation.
How others acted toward you.
What someone did to make you feel better.
How you felt when you got out of the situation.

In another way it is impossible for a person to be "culturally deprived," for each child understands and acts from a frame of reference which comes from his own cultural subgroup. The poverty child has a vast store of knowledge and a broad array of skills, quite different from those of the middle-class child, yet useful to him in his life. Some poverty children know how to play craps, can point out a pimp, know what a pusher is, and can take you to a fence—human variety. At times their knowledge, not their lack of it, causes them to be mistaken. In a survey concerning economic concepts a poverty child was asked to tell the meaning of labor. Because she looked so puzzled and disturbed, the researcher attempted to put her at ease by continuing, "What would your father mean if he said 'I labored all day'?" The child sort of gasped as she asked, "Men can't have babies, can they?"

To be poor is not synonymous with being strong. However, in an attempt to understand the social ills of our time, we sometimes overlook positive inputs which may come to the poverty child from his family and community. In dealing with such strengths it is well to remember that there is no typical poverty home; wide variations exist in the inner city as well as in suburbia.

What, then, in the face of myriad handicaps, are the strengths of the poor? Even though both parents are more likely to be employed outside the home, they are proud of their children and want the best for them. They may be poor sources of information, but they demonstrate affection openly and have close family ties. They allow the child the freedom to roam, which some call neglect, but which gives him greater opportunity to learn more about his daily world than the normal middle-class child. Riessman (1965) has pointed out several advantages of the lower-class life-style: a mutually-aiding extended family; the reduced strain connected with competitiveness; the freedom from self-blame and protection; and the enjoyment of music, games, sports and cards.

Lewis (1972), after discussing characteristics of the culture of poverty, in which he believed only about 20 percent of the poor are enmeshed, presented several positive aspects of this generally negative condition: present-time orientation allows for spontaneity and adventure, enjoyment of the sensual, indulgence of impulses, all of which are blunted in the middle-class, future-oriented man; frequent use of violence is an outlet for hostility which may mean less suffering due to repression of such feelings; low aspirations reduce frustration; legitimization of short-term hedonism makes possible spontaneity and enjoyment. Lewis believes, however, that whatever effectively organizes the family and gives hope and a sense of identification with the larger group destroys the pathological core of this culture and allows new movement. He cites the Civil Rights movement as an example.

The pragmatic, fatalistic, physically aggressive, impulsive, distrustful, and despairing view of life often found among the poor is a mental health value-stretch needed for survival in their world of exploitation, with its attendant ills (Chilman, 1966). It is their way of coping with the realities; it is not necessarily the way they would behave or think if things were better for them. But these characteristics are obstacles to their realizing the better life, causing the so-called poverty cycle: "nice" people don't want their children associating with poor children because of their background and characteristics, intensifying the very behaviors and attitudes among the poor which make them objects of avoidance, discrimination, and suspicion.

The adult involved with children during their middle childhood years should know that the poor desire the same basic things in this life as do the middle class: advanced education, better jobs, better housing and neighborhoods, security, stable marriages, and good health. The problem lies in finding ways to achieve these ends for their children, often because of ignorance or inequity of opportunity. The poor are burdened with an inheritance of such feelings as powerlessness, hopelessness, fatalism, and anomie. Their life-styles are built on an orientation to the present and authoritarianism in dealing with children. They see education as a hope for a better tomorrow; they sacrifice to see that their children have the clothes and other necessities to attend school; and they put considerable pressure on their children to learn. Because parents are often poor helpers in the learning process, the poor are more apt to experience frustration and lose faith in the educational system than are their middle- and upper-class counterparts (Irelan, 1967).

Because of lack of language skills, children from the lower classes may appear more aggressive and less cooperative during the middle years. Unable to express their emotions in the ways socially acceptable to the middle class, they may resort to physical violence and language that is not acceptable to middle-class students. They are not astute at such subtle forms of aggression as gossip or sarcasm. They may appear to lack the basic commitment to cleanliness, thrift, honesty, and self-discipline. Manifestations of these values has not yet proven feasible nor practical in their situation in life. How can one be clean where there is no bathtub, and water must be carried several blocks; when soap is expensive and when hunger demands that food be the first priority on the shopping list? How can one learn to be thrifty when there is no money to be thrifty with? If thrift means saving, it is impractical, for the child of the poor has had to learn to grab before someone else does and that there is not even enough for today—let alone tomorrow. The lower-class child and his family may endorse the value of honesty as heartily as do those from other social groups. But he may be more tempted to betray this value because of his have-not status. And his betrayal is more often noted because it involves stealing bread instead of writing personal letters on company stationery or "taking" towels from a hotel suite. Self-discipline is difficult for the poverty child because he has not seen much reward for such behavior. He has seen that alcohol, drugs, and sex are used as escapes from reality in his world (McCandless, 1967). By school age he may have learned that these techniques are more relevant to his survival than keeping the stiff upper lip; grinning and bearing it; keeping the shoulder to the wheel, the ear to the ground, and the nose to the grindstone.

Although education has traditionally been available to the middle- and upper-class American child, this has not been true for the lower-class child. School attendance laws have not always been actively enforced for this group: funds were short, buildings were already crowded, these children were thought to be dumb, and they were obviously dirty. Consequently, theirs is a heritage of untold misinformation and superstition. Many of their parents have less than a sixth grade education; some cannot read or write. Because of ignorance and lack of opportunities to eradicate it, the poor are in the lowest segment of our society; in the next generation the story may change. The child-rearing practices, the language deficit, the health status, and the purchasing practices of the lower class contribute substantially to this burden. A brief presentation of facts relative to these factors seems warranted.

With larger-than-average families and often only one parent in the home, guidance of children among the poor tends to be more impulsive, harsh, inconsistent, physical, and punitive than are thought conducive to emotional health in children. Parents experience feelings of impotence in handling their children, and they themselves suffer from low self-esteem and a sense of defeat. Their relative distrust of new experiences, high rate of marital conflict and breakdown, and orientation toward fatalism reduce their effectiveness in guidance. These parents alternate in their encouragement and restriction of aggression and do not help the child to think and plan in terms of long-range commitments and successes; instead, the main object is to keep out of trouble. There is little support for and acceptance of the child as an individual; reasons for his misbehaviors are not usually sought (Chilman, 1966; Lewis, 1972).

In poverty homes there is apt to be little verbal communication among children and adults, and that which does occur tends to be abrupt, brief, and blunt. Interactive, conceptual, flexible communications are lacking in these homes. Not only does the language deficit cause the poor child to appear more aggressive; it penalizes him in educational testing situations and places him at a learning disadvantage upon school entrance. Workers in Head Start have reported children at age 5 or 6 did not know the names of the colors or what a block was.

As children reach the question-asking age prior to school entrance, communication takes on for them great importance. It is their main method of gathering information about their world. Language helps to define social roles and identification. It is a mode for mediating feelings and their expression, and of differentiating words and their referents (Landreth, 1967). When these purposes are not served by speech and listening, the child is more apt to suffer through retardation in achievement and grade placement, dropping out of school, and being unable to handle social situations.

The poor behave quite differently from other population segments with respect to health care (Irelan, 1967). They have a higher prevalence of many diseases, including schizophrenia. They have less accurate health information, delay treatment longer, and even define illness differently. There are poverty children who reach 18 and have never seen a dentist. To the poor, illness is not synonymous with physical discomfort as it is to those in higher economic strata; only when one is unable to fulfill his daily responsibilities is he considered sick. Mothers are less concerned with detecting children's illnesses or taking precautions against them. Treatment is sought at a relatively late stage. Low protein diets—the plight of the poor—make normal growth impossible. Even with the existing public health programs, self-medication is prevalent; friends and neighbors give advice; druggists or healers other than medical doctors are often consulted. The themes of fatalism and powerlessness are seen with respect to ill health: "If you're going to get sick, you're going to get sick; and there's no use worrying about it."

The low income of the poor is compounded by their consumer practices. Whereas research indicates this group spends most of their income on basic needs, purchase of such durable goods as cars, TV sets, and large household appliances make sizable inroads on their incomes. Most do not use a great deal of deliberation or shop widely to get the best buys. Instead they tend to depend on merchants or relatives for judgments as to what to buy. Few have savings of any size, and most do not have life insurance; only about half are covered by medical insurance. Not many carry out home production activities to supplement their cash purchases. Many probably do not make full use of the programs established to provide goods and services at free or reduced rates. The lack of education seems to be the most important factor in their ineffectiveness in the marketplace, coupled with the desire to be like others in their consumption. The preference for buying from peddlers and other neighborhood merchants may be due to inability to travel to other shopping areas or lack of availability of credit. The lure of installment buying, and the inflexibility of their income are two other economic pitfalls that often trap the poor (Irelan, 1967; Lewis, 1972).

In a survey (Rytina, et al., 1970) of 354 families representing the poor, the rich and middle income groups in a small Michigan town, stereotypes concerning the poor were highlighted. Three questions were asked: (1) Would you say that poor people work just as hard as rich people, or do you think poor people generally don't work as hard? (2) Do you believe poor people are on relief because of their personal characteristics? (3) Do you think poor people want to get ahead just as much as everyone else or do you think that basically poor people don't care too much about getting ahead? In each group black and white respondents were separated. Results are presented in Table 2-3.

Table 2-3 Opinions at Various Income Levels of Characteristics of the Poor (Percentage of Total)

	Poor		Middle Income		Rich	Total
Question	Black	White	Black	White	White	All
#1 No	3	13	4	30	39	25
#2 Yes	28	46	45	59	78	57
#3 No	0	19	6	29	46	23

The results indicate that a traditional view is that wealth is earned and deserved, the result of hard work, ability, motivation and other favorable personal attributes. People seem to believe that poverty also is earned and deserved, the result of not-so favorable personality traits: laziness, stupidity, lack of motivation.

Hess (1970) has summarized the plight of the poor, adapted here from *Carmichael's Manual of Child Psychology:*

General circumstances or conditions of lower-working-class life in metropolitan society:

1. Economic poverty.
2. Narrow range of power derived from status prestige or affiliation with an institution or organization.
3. Vulnerability to disaster.
4. Restricted range of alternative actions.
5. Awareness of lack of prestige and status in society.
6. Relatively small overlap in experience with those of the majority.

Consequences or effects of the circumstances of poverty on children:

1. Relationships tend to be structured in terms of power.
2. Feelings of low esteem, a sense of inefficacy, and passivity are present.
3. Life-styles of the poor seem to show a preference for the familiar and a simplification of the experience world: rejection of intellectuality and restriction of language and linguistic modes of communication.
4. There is reliance upon nonwork-related friendships and kinship contacts for social support and resources.
5. There is a low level of skill and experience in obtaining and evaluating information about events and resources that affect or might affect life.

Mediating processes which link social structure and behavior:

1. Functional tie between economic activities and child-rearing practices of adults either directly or through the salience of values rewarded on the job and therefore in the home.
2. Awareness in a person about his relative position in the hierarchy and the degree of prestige and opportunity that persons with his characteristics and who live in his community can command in the larger society.
3. Deprivation of essential experience, especially in early childhood, a central element in creating differences in performance between social status groups.
4. Transmission of social class differences through traditional cultural and religious values leading to different types of child-rearing practices.
5. Socialization of child into communication modes and thought strategies which become response patterns in specific interaction with salient parental figures, especially the mother: linguistic modes, regulatory strategies, cognitive styles, self-esteem.

Poor children in America may have more than poor children in many other nations of the world. However, cost of living is high and in the United States it "takes money" to earn money or save money. Moreover, Kensiton (1977, p. 26) reminds us that "the psychological pain—and the ethical shame—of American poverty are made greater by the fact that this country possesses the wealth and the energy to raise all children to a minimally decent standard of living."

Minority Groups—Who Are They?

Often children must not only live with the stigma of being poor but also contend with the fact that they are a member of a minority group in our total society.

> INCIDENT: BALTIMORE
> Once riding in old Baltimore,
>   Heart-filled, head-filled with glee,
> I saw a Baltimorean
>   Keep looking straight at me.
>
> Now I was eight and very small,
>   And he was no whit bigger,
> And so I smiled, but he poked out
>   His tongue, and called me, "Nigger."
>
> I saw the whole of Baltimore
>   From May until December;
> Of all the things that happened there
>   That's all that I remember.
>   *Countee Cullen, 1941, p. 138*

Minority group status, whether owing to skin color, religious beliefs, or nationality, imposes on children additional encumbrances with which to deal. Fourteen percent of all American families with children are black. Sixty-six percent of these families who live in poverty areas live below the poverty level. Children in black families are four times more likely to be poor than children in white families.

Williams *et al.* (1975) examined responses of children in the first to fourth grades to Euro-American (light skinned) and Afro-American (dark skinned) pictured figures. The children assigned one figure or the other to each of 24 evaluative adjectives. Among the light-skinned children, pro-Euro/anti-Afro bias reached a peak in the second grade and then declined. Among Afro-American children, there was, to only a slightly lesser extent, the same pro-Euro/anti-Afro bias with no discernible age trends. The authors pointed out that the problem of adequate self-concept development, which includes valuing themselves as they are, may be concentrated in the early school years rather than at the preschool level. At the preschool level the child may be able to identify himself as belonging to a minority group, but still may be caught in the trap of evaluating dark-skinned persons less positively than light-skinned persons.

In extreme cases, some American children must learn to speak and think in two completely different languages—for instance, the American Indian, the Cuban refugee, the Chicano. One language is necessary for communication at home and another for school and play with children from the majority groups. There is considerable additional stress upon a child in such circumstances (Rogers, 1969). Among children from 4 to 17 years of age, one in seven, 15 percent, come from ethnic origins corresponding to one of the ten languages covered in the survey of languages conducted by the National Center for Educational Statistics (Hill and Waggoner, 1977). One-half are from selected Spanish heritage (Mexican-American, Puerto Rican, Cuban, Central or South American); one-fourth from German heritage; approximately 14 percent from Italian heritage; the rest from European and Oriental heritages. Thirteen percent of all children, a total of 7.7 million children, between 4 and 18 years of age live in households in which a language other than English is the usual or second language. Two and a quarter million children live in households where non-English is the usual language, and in 75 percent of these instances the usual language is Spanish. These children do not participate in the educational system to the same extent as other children (Hill and Waggoner, 1977) in several ways: fewer attend school; more fall behind grade level; and fewer complete high school; from English dominant households, 85 percent complete high school; from non-English dominant households, 53 percent complete high school (See Tables 2-4 and 2-5.)

Minority groups in America today, unlike those of past generations, are looking on the positive side. They are saying, "We're proud to be black, or

Table 2-4 Percentage of Children Enrolled in School from English Dominant and Non-English Dominant Households

Age	English Dominant Households	Non-English Dominant Households
4–5	39	30
6–13	99	97
14–18	91	82
Total	91	82

Table 2-5 Percentage of Children at Expected Grade Level from English Dominant and Non-English Dominant Households

Grade	English Dominant Households	Non-English Dominant Households
1–4	91	85
5–8 *	88	77
9–12 **	86	65
1–12 **	88	77

* significant at .01 level; ** significant at .05 level

Dress and hair styling are often distinctive ways of identifying with one's cultural heritage. *(Photo by Lin Mitchell.)*

Indian, or Jewish, or whatever. We've a rich heritage of which to be proud. We don't want to lose our identity in the mass of the majority." This is a healthy approach. But families from these groups still face obstacles in the area of social mobility, equal housing and employment opportunities, legislative representation, extension of their cultural inheritances, and identity. It is from minority groups, often national in nature, that mass media, in all too many plots, have drawn the villian. Only in the past few years have public school texts, newspapers and comics, television shows and advertisements begun to portray members of minority groups as typical Americans.

The minority group child is often reared in a pattern unlike those of his peers who constitute the majority group. Mirandi (1977) pointed to some of the characteristics of the Chicano family that may lead to a different value focus than that found in Anglo families: male dominance; rigid sex-age grading so that the older order the younger, and men order the women; clearly established patterns of help and mutual aid among family members; strong familialistic orientation whereby individual need is subordinated to collective need. In the "child's" eye view the central feature is the home, and the people at home (Goodman and Beman, 1971).

Goodman and Beman (1971) surveyed children between 7 and 13 years of age in a Houston barrio about important people in their lives. In answer to the question: Who do you love? barrio children named no one except relations, whereas black and Anglo children included non-family members in their lists. Grandparents are important as affectionate, not authority, figures. Fathers are seen as warm and affectionate when the children are young, more distant as children grow older. Fathers are the perceived authority figures. Girls are closer to their mothers and more restricted in their contact with their fathers than are boys, but few children of either sex feel free enough to report asking questions of their fathers.

All these differences that set the child apart from the majority group require adjustments at school, in organizations, at play. He must make a choice: will he conform to the mores of his peers or display the values and customs of his own heritage or try to work out a suitable compromise? His status in the fluid society may be constantly changing, requiring even more flexibility in terms of identity and proper ways of behaving and relating. And it is *he* who is usually doing the changing—seldom his peers from the majority group.

Geographic Locale

The geographic locale in which one is reared and lives may be another societal factor that merits mention. Life for the child from rural America and that for the inner-city child may be as different as day and night. One is free to roam and explore the wonders of nature, to breathe the smell of new-mown hay and help with the birth of a baby calf, to go hunting and fishing or help can or freeze home-grown beans and corn. To the other the world may be a concrete jungle—smog to breathe, garbage to dodge, constant city sounds to ignore if he would concentrate on his homework, a frantic struggle to reach his school via bus, subway, or elevated train. His living quarters may not only be crowded, ten stories up, and noisy—but also dirty, old, and soon to be demolished for a new office building. The child of suburbia has another life: the advantages of the city nearby; yet the advantages of semi-countryside in trees, running brooks, birds, and squirrels. He knows the joy of wide pavements for skating, the backyard barbecue, the neighborhood Scout Troop. Yet his is the struggle to sleep on Saturday morning when Mr. Jones decides to mow his lawn at 6:00 A.M.; and his father is commonly the one who spends considerable time each day merely getting to and from work. In Suburbia, neighborhood dogs are more often the cause of backyard quarrels, and the problem of getting someone to transport the school-age child to his various commitments may be compounded by Mother's involvement in the garden club, PTA, League of Women Voters, and innumerable other civic and social groups.

We are predominantly an urban nation. By 1971, 68 percent of all families lived in urban areas. The rate of the shift from rural to urban has slowed: during the 1960s the growth rate in metropolitan areas was 16.6 percent; from 1970–74, it was 3.8 percent. The growth rate during these two periods for non-metropolitan areas remained about the same: 6.8 percent during the 1960s and 5 percent from 1970–74. There is a disproportionate representation of minority groups among metropolitan families: 82 percent of all Spanish origin families; 90 percent of all Puerto Rican families; 75 percent of all Mexican-American families; and 77 percent of all Black families live in cities. (Snapper, 1975).

Since almost 6 million children age 5–13 moved in 1970–71 (Bureau of the Census, 1972), the possible impact of mobility on children of schoolage warrants mention. Today, however, more executives are refusing to relocate. Important among the objectives cited (New York Times, 1975) are the adverse effects on the family. One moving company reported that in 1973, 37 percent of 300 of the companies for which it moves families had encountered some refusal from employees to relocate. The figure was up to 57 percent in 1974. In 1972, there was not enough of a problem to take a poll! As with most issues, there are both adverse and beneficial aspects of a family move. The view of the parents toward moving is apt to be transmitted to the children, so hopefully they would be looking for positive emphases rather than negative ones. Bossard and Boll (1960) have cautioned against the break in the continuity of life, the adjustments accompanying change of schools, the challenges in social contacts and acceptance, the significance of family status or lack of it, and the cumulative aspect of repeated moves.

The results of a 1973 study (Barrett and Noble, 1973) suggested that anxiety about negative effects of moving on the emotional adjustment of children may be largely unfounded. For more than four-fifths of the children, parents reported the move had "no" effect or "good" effects. Only one-fourth of the children between 6 and 10 years of age reported any difficulty with the change in schools; 90 percent reported easily making new friends. Older children, between 10 and 14 years of age, reported only a little more difficulty: one-third had trouble with school and 68 percent reported ease in making new friendships. Parents again pointed to both negative and positive aspects of moving. Although there may be some difficulty in establishing roots if moves are frequent, the child becomes acquainted with a larger world, many people and varying cultures. It would be appropriate for families who face a move to focus on adaptive strategies rather than on ways to avoid stress. The child who succeeds in making friends with one person in his new neighborhood is likely to gain acceptance with a larger group, and he who makes a special effort at being

Children experience mixed feelings during a family move. *(Photo by Lin Mitchell.)*

friendly usually will find others becoming friendly toward him. To display enough aggressiveness to attract attention without antagonizing the group seems a key to social acceptance among children; however, few children may be able to display such a subtle balance.

Think Back

To the place(s) where you grew up:
If your family ever moved.
The floor plan of your house(s).
Where you played; the gang's favorite spot.
Where you bought bubblegum and other goodies.
The route you took to school.
The kids in the neighborhood.
The advantages of your locale.
Things you wished were different.
Problems you had because of where you lived.

A study by Lehr and Hendrickson (1968) revealed that in the adjustment of elementary school children there was no significant difference between: those with siblings in the school they entered and those with none; those who had moved a major distance and those who moved a minor one; boys and girls. Among their other findings was the fact that children moving for the first time had positive attitudes about entering a new school, but leaving friends was more difficult than for those who had moved before. They concluded that if the moving family is intact and there has been no previous trauma, a change in residence for an upper-middle-class family is not in itself a traumatic event.

Mass Media

Since the appearance of mass media on the human scene, persons have been concerned with their effect on the lives of their consumers. Rivers and Schramm (1969) cited the complaint of such a critic who wrote in 1592:

> A company of idle youths, loathing honest labor and despising lawful trades, betake themselves to a vagabond and vicious life, in every corner of Cities and market Towns of the Realme, singing and selling ballads and pamphlets full of ribaudrie, and all scurrilous vanity, to the prophanation of God's name, and withdrawing people from Christian exercises, especially at faires, markets, and such public meetings.

Children's books and stories, including fairy tales and nursery rhymes, have received their share of public critical comment. Movies and comic books have seen a time of censorship. Magazines and television programs have likewise been the subject of close scrutiny. The perennial concern is that through mass media children will receive information or develop attitudes that will be contrary to those they receive from other sociocultural influences, including the home, church, and school. The incidence of sex, violence, and group stereotyping has been a recent cause for their evaluation.

The mass media have probably provided what their consumers sought and bought. There seems to be within most people a fascination for the bizarre, the tragic, the heart-rending. Those who have consumed a rather steady diet of such offerings have endangered their own morals and emotional well-being. Likewise, parents who have allowed children similar diets have abdicated their role in guidance toward the uplifting and edifying. Fortunately, unlike the society characterized in Orwell's *1984,* consumption of mass media is still voluntary and open to individual discretion. Children whose lives are filled with good things seldom seek harmful ones. It is better to make them intelligent consumers of mass media offerings than to shield them from them.

Mass media indeed exert considerable influence on the intellectual, social, and emotional development of children; even physical development may be affected. They provide not only entertainment but behavior models, facts upon which concepts may be based or revised, situations which call forth the basic emotions, opportunities for language experience, and escape from reality. They basically appeal to the curiosity and imagination of the child of the middle years—thirsty for knowledge, ideals, and adventure. They provide opportunities for the pursuit of his many interests, be they space exploration, animal care, stamp collection, or just learning about one's own sex role. While they may offer answers to questions or solutions to problems, they may also set in motion other questioning and even be the beginning of certain types of problems.

For communication to be successful, it must clear four hurdles (Rivers and Schramm, 1969): attracting attention, being accepted, being interpreted, and being stored for use. Failure in any of these aspects results in ineffectiveness. Therefore, persons guiding children's consumption may wish to intervene in the process at points that would make the impact of the media incomplete. Parents may wish to keep their children unaware of certain offerings by the media. Others look and listen with their children to guide in acceptance and interpretation of what is being seen, heard, or read. Others provide alternative information that interrupts storage.

For some parents and teachers, the problem is one of guiding children toward a balanced diet of mass media; for others the crises arise in connection with balancing mass media consumption with other areas of living, including family pursuits, active exercise, and social interactions with peers. Although mass media experiences can be very beneficial, they can never replace "real life" experiences with others and the world in which the child can be an active participant rather than a passive observer.

Reading

Perhaps those concerned with guiding children are less worried with respect to reading than they are with viewing movies or television. Yet even in the realm of the written word there lie questions concerning appropriateness of consumption.

Reading is usually considered a good thing for children to do. It fosters hand-eye coordination, intellectual enrichment, and stimulation of the imagination. It can be a relatively inexpensive form of entertainment. It is usually quiet and can be enjoyed alone or in groups. It is fostered by adults who read for their own pleasure and growth, who read to children, and who encourage children to read to them. Even this activity, however, can be used as an escape for children who have not mastered necessary physical or social skills that enable them to be at ease with their peers.

Reading tastes of children seem related to sex and age: boys typically interested more in the how and why of things; girls interested more often in the how and why of people. By the upper elementary grades, boys usually demand action and aggression in their books, while girls are intrigued by stories of home life, romance, and other social situations.

Books. In helping children select books they will enjoy, their interests and their abilities need to be considered. Quick indicators used by children to assess the relative reading ease in books include: thickness of the book, incidence of pictures, size of the type, and length of sentences and paragraphs. One 10-year-old confided that her test for choosing a book was whether or not there was conversation on the first page.

Fry (1968) has devised a more exact method of determining the grade level for which books are suited: the Readability Graph. A score is derived based on sentence length and syllable count by which the grade level of the material is estimated. (See Figure 2-6.) Fry's answer to a question concerning the accuracy of the score is a nontechnical one: "Probably within a grade level."

Suggested References for Children's Reading. A number of books have been written especially for the adult who is interested in guiding children in their use of this mass medium:

The Arbuthnot Anthology of Children's Literature. compiled by May H. Arbuthnot and Dorothy M. Broderick. (4th Ed.). Glenview, Ill.: Scott, Foresman, 1976.
> *A collection of poetry, folklore, fantasy, short stories, biographies and other non-fiction. Includes a history and discussion of children's literature with suggestions for using this literature with children.*

Children's Books Too Good to Miss, M. H. Arbuthnot. Cleveland: Western Reserve University, 1971.
> *An annotated listing of some 300 books that are considered to be good literature; to make a significant contribution to the child's wisdom, merriment,*

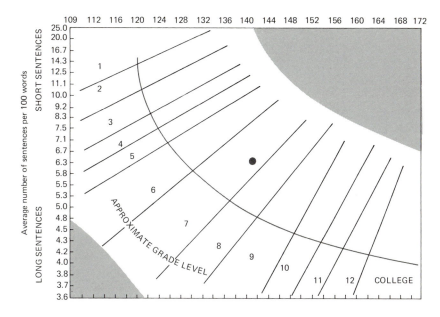

Average number of syllables per 100 words

DIRECTIONS: Randomly select 3 one-hundred word passages from a book or an article.
Plot average number of syllables and average number of sentences per 100 words
on graph to determine the grade level of the material. Choose more
passages per book if great variability is observed and conclude that the book
has uneven readability. Few books will fall in gray area but when they do grade
level scores are invalid.

EXAMPLE:

	Syllables	Sentences
1st Hundred Words	124	6.6
2nd Hundred Words	141	5.5
3rd Hundred Words	158	6.8
AVERAGE	141	6.3

READABILITY 7th GRADE (see dot plotted on graph)

Figure 2-6. Graph for estimating readability, by Edward Fry, Rutgers University Reading
Center, New Jersey. (From "A Readability Formula That Saves Time," *Journal of Reading,*
11:514–516, April 1968. Reprinted with permission of Edward Fry and the International
Reading Association.)

or appreciation of beauty; and to have child appeal. Categorized by age
groups: under 6; 6–8; 9–11; 12–14.

Children's Reading in the Home, M. H. Arbuthnot. Glenview, Ill.: Scott,
Foresman, 1969.

A discussion of good home environment for reading and ways to promote
lasting interest in books. An annotated listing of over 600 books grouped by

general age level with information concerning developmental characteristics that influence reading interests and choices.

A Parent's Guide to Children's Reading, (4th Ed.) N. Larrick. Garden City, N.Y.: Doubleday, 1975.

A handbook which answers questions parents ask about their children's reading, with suggested reading guidance methods and annotated bibliography.

Basic Book Collection for Elementary Grades, American Library Association, 50 E. Huron St., Chicago, Ill. 60611, 1960.

A listing of over 1,000 essential books for an elementary school library, including special lists of picture books, easy books, magazines, and references.

I Read, You Read, We Read, American Library Association, Chicago, Ill. 60611, 1971.

A collection of briefly annotated books, poems, stories, films and recordings particularly appropriate for disadvantaged children. Arranged by age group: 5–8, 9–11, 12–14.

Motivation to read generally moves from entertainment to location of information, and children encouraged toward this end will find books enhancing their hobbies, schoolwork, and citizenship. Reading is not a natural inclination but a habit that must be developed.

Magazines and Newspapers. But reading is not confined to books from the library. By middle childhood other forms of the written word become a part of the reading horizon. Magazines such as *Children's Digest, Ranger Rick, Highlights,* and *Child Life* usually have great appeal for the 5- to 10-year-old. Even some general or news periodicals intended for adults may be occasionally read in part. Only 29 percent of a group of sixth-graders had not read a magazine within a month; one-fifth had read five or more. Twenty-four percent of the first-graders surveyed received magazines of their own (Ward, Reale, and Levinson, 1972).

Some newspapers regularly include syndicated supplements designed particularly for children. These foster awareness of date, weather, and number; encourage visual discrimination of objects and knowledge about such popular items as animals. Other newspapers feature weekly local supplements which include articles and pictures of children's activities in the community. Often children enjoy the puzzles, quizzes, and advice columns in the newspaper, and some papers have letter columns especially for children. A few even employ child journalists to respond to queries by their peers. All these features help school-age children to develop a daily reading habit early in life.

The Comics. Comic books and strips are popular. Among first-graders more than 80 percent reported enjoying comics. Even though a third of the

Mass media exert considerable influence on children: intellectual, social, emotional, and even physical development may be affected. *(Photo by Rick Coleman.)*

sixth-graders had not read a comic in a month, another third had read five or more (Ward et al., 1972).

Comics are relatively inexpensive, usually easy reading, and highly illustrated and colored. The print is large, and the stories are short and exciting. They become social items through trading and sharing. It is not uncommon for boys to sit around in a group reading comics for considerable periods of time. Comic interests progress from animal stories such as Yogi Bear to invincible heroes such as Batman, and then to educational or classic comics. As other reading materials become available to the child, his interest in comics is likely to decline. By the end of middle childhood the incidence of comic reading has diminished greatly, except, of course, for the daily strips in the newspaper!

Research should generally reassure those concerned about the impact of comics on children (Klapper, 1960; Witty, 1941): there is no distinguishing characteristic between readers and nonreaders of comics; the comic reader exhibiting neurotic or delinquent symptoms most likely exhibited these tendencies prior to the time he began reading them.

Listening

The spoken word is increasing in its appeal to children, evidenced through their consumption of records, tapes, and cassettes. For the younger child who cannot yet read to himself very well, the recorded story is a joy both for him and for his parents. Many records are planned in conjunction with the storybook so that the child can follow the pictures and words as he listens. Later the primary consumption of recordings is in the musical realm. Whereas radio was once a major mass medium, its influence has declined greatly with the advent of television. In one study (Himmelweit et al., 1958) children were found to shun radio after being introduced to television, even if television were denied them. Radio is probably the most casually attended of the mass media for the child in middle childhood. Its major contribution today seems to be background entertainment for other

Children spend considerable time and money on media experiences. (*Photo by Lin Mitchell.*)

activities such as reading, washing dishes, or talking. Those whose interest in organized sports has developed sufficiently also rely on radio for the broadcasts not carried on TV. Ward et al. (1972) reported that one-fourth of first-graders in their study said they owned a radio; 80 percent of the sixth-graders did. Among first-graders 46 percent had listened to the radio "yesterday." Half the sixth-graders owned record players. Half the first-graders had played records within the week. Boys more often than girls had tape and cassette players.

Watching

Television and the Movies. The impact of television in the home and classroom has also contributed to the decline in popularity of another mass medium: the movie. Whereas the Saturday matinee was a ritual for the elementary school-age child of yesteryear, this is no longer true. In some communities the incidence of child-oriented movies is approaching zero, with the rise in the number of sex- and crime-oriented pictures billed. Children today probably see more movies in the classroom or over television at home than they view in the theater. Their movie interests are similar by age and sex to their reading interests. What the child receives from a movie will depend mainly on the type of child he is: what he thinks of himself, what he thinks others think of him, his concept of his rights and responsibilities. Whereas the young child remembers little of what he views on the movie screen, older children retain up to 70 percent of what adults remember, and these memories last up to three or four months. If the movie is exciting, it will cause the child to remember more than if it is dull or presents information or situations with which he is readily familiar. If the child identifies with a character in the movie, the effect of the movie is likely to be greater than if he does not. Children tend to identify with characters who are similar to them in age, sex, and race and whose actions are most relevant to their needs (Hurlock, 1964).

Movies provide pleasure, excitement beyond that afforded by everyday life, and ideas to use in play. They also suggest behavior modes and may influence attitudes toward certain types of people.

Many of the generalizations made about movies may also be applied to the medium which today enjoys by far the greatest popularity of all: television. Television sets are today in more than 98 percent of the nation's homes; over half have color (Ward et al., 1972). In many homes they play the major portion of every waking hour, potentially exposing children to a steady diet of news, drama, advertising, and other emotion-packed programming. Recent data indicate that the average viewing time of first grade children is about 3½ hours weekdays and between 2¼ and 3¼ on Sunday. By the sixth grade, these amounts have increased to 4 hours weekdays and 6½ on Sunday (U.S. National Institute of Mental Health, 1972).

More than 80 percent of a sixth grade group reported they do other things while watching TV: eat, draw, study, read, talk (Ward et al., 1972).

Ferguson (1975) administered questionnaires to 282 fourth- and sixth-graders to study the relationship of attitudes toward TV commercials and cognitive level, socioeconomic level, and TV exposure. She found the average hours viewed per week was 34.2 with the older group viewing a couple more than the younger. Television exposure was greatest among the middle class children, but only an hour more than the lower class. Saturday morning programs have audiences up to 97 percent, while weekday evening viewing is also high between 6:30 pm and 10:pm. In 1971, about 96 percent of all Americans, 180 million people, had access to a television set. This means that more families have televisions sets than have bathtubs, telephones, toasters, vacuum cleaners, or a daily newspaper (Lesser, 1974). By the time children complete high school they will have spent an average of 15,000 hours watching television, which means more time devoted to television than to any other activity except sleep. Whether or not television poses problems for the adults in guiding school-age children will depend on the amount of TV the children are viewing and what other activities are being neglected because of TV viewing.

What are the possible deleterious effects of too much television? They may be classified, as is development, into four categories.

In the physical realm, there is always the possibility that due to passive involvement with TV children will neglect other forms of recreation which naturally provide physical exercise. For some, normal routines such as eating and sleeping may be affected. Consumption of calorie-laden snacks in front of the TV set can reduce the appetite for more nutritionally adequate mealtime foods. Too much of this can cause obesity and other manifestations of malnutrition. Eyestrain may be caused if the children sit within 6 feet of the screen and if there is not a dim light to reduce the glare.

Emotionally, one's sensitivity may be dulled through a constant diet of crime, violence, and terror. Whereas it was once thought that TV served to drain emotions, evidence seems to indicate that it actually intensifies aggression. A content analysis (Gerbner, 1972; Gerbner and Gross, 1973) of a one-week sample of dramatic fiction on the networks during 1967 to 1972, revealed the great extent of violence in television fiction. There was at least one incident of violence in 80 percent of the plays sampled; during the six-year sample the frequencies of five per play or eight per hour remained constant. Children's cartoons had the greatest number of violent acts, although the 1969 figure of 30 incidents per hour was reduced to 17 per hour by 1972. Television violence is rewarded about as often as it is punished and even the "good guys" act in violent ways; so, there is little basis for the argument that negative consequences may inhibit violent action. The painful aspects of violence are deleted from television because network codes prevent showing some of the more bloody details. No research has been done on the amount or effect of verbal abuse or hostility, aggressive humor, or control over other people by use of threat (Stein and Friedrich, 1975).

The research of Bandura (1963a, 1963b), as well as others, supports the idea that aggressive behavior increases after a child views a film with aggressive models. According to Bandura (1969a) this behavior is due to learning new aggressive acts and also to the removal of inhibitions against performing acts already in the individual's repertoire. Unless environmental conditions or fear of punishment inhibit it, aggressive behavior increases. Laboratory situations are quite different from television in natural context, so generalizations may be questionable. What a child brings to television viewing—past experiences, self concept, conceptual development—determine in part the content for the child. Nevertheless, aggressive models probably lead more surely to imitation and removal of inhibitions than to a draining off of aggressive impulses, which is another viewpoint concerning the effect of television violence.

During middle childhood, children are less affected by television violence than during early childhood because they have more behavior and cognitive controls, more ability to distinguish fact and fancy, and are more tuned to adult values and prohibition about aggression (Stein and Friedrich, 1975). Research seems to indicate that increased aggression followed television violence in situations that were permissive in at least one of the following ways: aggression directed at peer rather than adult; no adult or an unrecognized adult was in the room; child was in a familiar classroom with a large number of children with little supervision. Where aggression either did not increase or decreased following the viewing of the filmed material, the situations were anxiety-producing: familiar adult was the target, rather than a child; children were in unfamiliar classroom. While "anxiety reaction to violence apparently becomes habituated over time, the aggression-arousing effects of violent television do not decline with repeated exposure. If anything, they accumulate" (Stein and Friedrich, 1975).

Many factors affect increase or decrease of aggressive behavior incident to watching television violence: the higher the habitual level of aggression, the greater the increase of such behavior; a high anger or frustration level may cause the person to be particularly attentive to filmed violence and prone to imitate it; imitative behavior is a little more likely if the model is rewarded than if the model is punished. In some cases showing the pay-off involved in the violence may increase aggressive behavior; cartoons arouse as much aggression as real people films. The most effective action parents can take to combat the effects of television violence is to limit viewing time, especially in the early years of development. Violence may have less effect on children's behavior if parents communicate their disapproval of aggression. Stein and Friedrich (1975) label this measure as limited! They point out that the more effective course of action is on the part of producers of programs: reduce the amount of violence presented.

Even in preschool years parents put few restrictions on television viewing (Friedrich and Stein, 1973). When parents attempt some control, it has greater effect at younger ages than when the child reaches preadolescence. Parents probably have an influence on viewing behavior by serving as models. Children's patterns of viewing violent and non-violent programs is related to the parents' viewing choices (Chaffee and McLeod, 1972). This correlation may be due to convenience as well as modeling, especially among older children. However, the pattern exists even in homes where there are two television sets and declines somewhat during adolescence, when children might be expected to be watching at the same hours as parents do.

Abel's (1976) work suggests that patterns of interpersonal communication influence children's choices in television viewing. In families where children are taught to avoid disturbance in parent-child relations (emphasis on child-parent relations) more than in families where children are exposed to contrasting views and are free to express ideas fully (emphasis on child-idea relations), children's viewing choices are influenced by what they perceive to be what their parents want them to watch. However, children from families who emphasize child-idea relations are more likely to know what sorts of programs their parents would choose to watch than are children from other families.

Prosocial behavior has been examined in relation to preschool children more than any other group. Research shows that children have demonstrated increased cooperation, sharing, understanding of other's feelings, and verbalization of own feeling, self regulation and imaginative play as a result of watching television programming such as Mister Rogers' Neighborhood. Such programs for older children are more recent in origin but may be effective in getting across the same kinds of messages. A big question, of course, is who decides what is prosocial in our pluralistic society. Stein and Friedrich (1975) suggest two elements which may establish a common ground: (1) affirmation of the unique worth of the individual, both in the televised segment and in the audience; (2) identification of values incorporated into the programming by the television producers in order to give the public choices about what they would watch or "buy" into.

Think Back

To your favorite TV program as a child:
Why you liked it.
Who watched it with you.
How it influenced you.

In some homes television has severely reduced social interaction among family members while in others it has fostered new family interests. In cases where it has reduced the child's involvement in other recreational activities, it may have reduced the social development normally experienced in games, sports, and other play endeavors. When used by parents as a pacifier of children, displacing discipline, the unfavorable effects are obvious.

Intellectually, television is an important source of information, language, and attitudes. It may spark reading or experimenting. It brings the whole world into the home of the viewer, helping keep him up to date on local and global happenings. It advises him of the latest products on the market. The child may believe that all that he sees on TV is truth personified, causing him to be gullible to advertising. Viewing presentations containing material inappropriate for his age and level of development may interfere with the development of some of his concepts, resulting in faulty or confused ideas and knowledge (Lesser, 1974). However, it appears there are limits inherent in the medium which makes it less effective than direct instruction: a teacher is needed for added rehearsal and to assure close attention to curriculum materials for best learning.

The data in one study (Himmelweit et al., 1958) indicated that stereotyping of certain ethnic groups is intensified through television viewing. Yet it made little change in attitudes toward marriage and family living. Mendelson and Young (1972) reported that standard English was spoken by good characters while one half of the bad characters had a foreign accent. Predominance of males is another bias: in prime-time between 70 and 75 percent of leading characters are male (Gerbner, 1972) and this is even more prevalent in children's programming, especially cartoons. The male roles are more powerful, more interesting, and more varied than female roles. Stein and Friedrich (1975) conclude their overview with this statement:

> The social knowledge available on television represents a composite of dominant American values with little recognition of the diversity in our society. Middle class white American male adults are portrayed as the most powerful and important members of society. Women, foreigners and lower-class men have a restricted set of options and little power. Most minority groups and people who are not adult, young, and beautiful are ignored almost completely. The one notable change in this picture has been an increased representation of black Americans in prestigious, relatively powerful positions. The images and stereotypes portrayed on television appear to be important sources of children's learning, particularly about activities and groups with which they have little contact. . . . Children should be made aware of a variety of possibilities for interpersonal relations, social roles, accepted activities, and group attitudes (p. 245).

The impact of educational television is yet to be fully determined. But as the child views the picture tube as a form of recreation and relaxation, his respect for it as a formal teaching medium may be threatened.

Although at this point in time one cannot conclude whether television is primarily bad or good, there is almost unanimous agreement on the fact that the well-adjusted child is less likely to be adversely affected than the poorly adjusted one, and the healthy child less than the unhealthy. Moreover, the maximal effect of TV will be felt when programs link with the child's immediate needs and interests and when the viewer is not already supplied with a set of values against which to assess those views presented via the tube (Hurlock, 1972).

Television watching may be an index of family tension in two general ways (Rosenblatt and Cunningham 1976): (1) television set operation could produce frustration and consequent tension with problems arising from noise, distraction, discrepant program preference; increased difficulty in carrying out alternative activities; (2) television set may serve as a coping mechanism, as a means of escape from a preexistent problem by making it possible to avoid tense interaction and expressions of anger and aggression.

Television will not be the last mass medium to exert influence on children and adults alike. Already scientists are experimenting with electronic devices that will permit the receiver to specifically order certain information or entertainment on his screen, including the comic strips missed while on vacation, a computer partner with whom to play chess, a tutorial program on the economics of the gold market, a quick rundown on the progress on some minor bill before the Congress, headlines written only microseconds ago, a biographical sketch of some person in the news you want to know better. Parents of tomorrow can then worry about the evils of machine-duplicated and machine-interposed communication, just as those of yesterday bemoaned the ballad and the pamphlet (Rivers and Schramm, 1969).

Children Learn What They Live

Children learn about and internalize the culture in which they are reared through observation, trial and error, and formal instruction. Their sources include parents and other adults, siblings and peers, the mass media, and community institutions. The process by which they "tune in" on what is right to do when, why things are as they are, where the limits are, and what the results of action will be is called acculturation.

Acculturation begins as soon as a child begins to perceive the world around him. With proper stimulation and experience, by school age, the child has acquired a functional use of the spoken language and has formed workable yet not totally refined concepts of even such abstractions as love, success, and fun. Most of this process has occurred in unplanned situations, through answers to his wondering questions of What? Why? Why not? Who? When? Where? and How? A great deal he has learned through the actions of his parents and other family members, through their planned or unplanned examples. Much has been acquired from stories told or read to him, programs on television, and adventures into the neighborhood with older children or adults. If he has older siblings, he has soaked up like a sponge from them; or he may do likewise from peers in the neighborhood or at church school.

By school age, the child is feeling pretty confident about his ability to handle his life and to deal with various situations he confronts. Little does he realize that his world is still confined, nor can he imagine the magnitude of that which will be opened to him as he, for the first time, passes through the portals of the larger society embodied for children in the kindergarten or elementary school. But if he has mastered functioning in his littlest world, the family, he may be well on his way to success in the larger one into which he will move.

What's Next?

1. *Beyond Freedom and Dignity*, B. F. Skinner. New York: Knopf, 1972.
2. *Child Development Through Literature*, Landau et al. Englewood Cliffs, N.J.: Prentice-Hall, 1972: "Nancy," by E. Enright, pp. 492–504; "And Now Miguel," by J. Krumgold, pp. 508–511.
3. *The Inner City Mother Goose*, E. Merriam. New York: Simon and Schuster, 1969.
4. *The Me Nobody Knows*, S. M. Joseph. New York: Avon, 1969: "Rejoice," p. 119.
5. "Like It Is in the Alley," R. Coles. *Daedalus*, **97** (Fall 1968), 1315–1320. Also in *Readings in Child Development and Personality*, 2nd ed., P. H. Mussen, J. J. Conger, and J. Kagan. New York: Harper & Row, 1970.
6. "How to Tame the TV Monster: A Pediatrician's Advice," T. B. Brazelton. *Redbook*, **138** (April 1972), 47, 49, 51.
7. "TV Violence and Child Aggression: Snow on the Screen," R. M. Liebert and J. M. Neale. *Psychology Today*, 5:11 (April 1972), 38–40.
8. "Legal Policies Affecting Children: A Lawyer's Request for Aid," Wald, Michael S. *Child Development*, 1976, **47**, 1–5.
9. "Let's Bring Back Heroes," Bennett, William J. *Newsweek*, August 15, 1977, 3.
10. Film: *Tommy Knight—Portrait of a Disadvantaged Child*. New York: McGraw-Hill, 1221 Avenue of the Americas, New York, N.Y. 10019. (16 min, b/w.)
11. Film: *My Childhood, Parts I and II*. Metromedia Productions Corp., 485 Lexington Ave., New York, N.Y. 10017. (51 min, b/w.)
12. Film: *Pizza Pizza Daddy-O*. University of California, Extension Media Center, Berkeley, California, 94720. (18 min., b/w)

13. Film: *Children in the City.* Paramount-Oxford Films, 5451 Marathon St., Los Angeles 90035. (8 min/color)

14. The following films may be obtained from Campus Film Distributors Corp., 2 Overhill Road, Scarsdale, New York 10583. The four films form a series on "Play and Cultural Continuity."

      Part I   *Appalachian Children*—25 min.
      Part II   *Southern Black Children*—27 min.
      Part III   *Mexican American Children*—27 min.
      Part IV   *Montana Indian Children*—27 min.

Catalysts for Discussion

I. "Persistent poverty over generations creates a culture of survival. Goals are short range, restricted. The outsider and the outside are suspect. One stays inside and gets what one can. Beating the system takes the place of using the system.

"Such a culture of poverty gets to the young early—how they learn to set goals, mobilize means, delay or fail to delay gratification. Very early too they learn in-group talk and thinking and just as their language use reflects less long-range goal analysis, it also tends toward a parochialism that makes it increasingly difficult to move or work outside the poverty neighborhood and the group. Make no mistake about it: it is a rich culture, intensely personalized and full of immediate rather than remote concerns. The issue is certainly not cultural deprivation, to be handled, like avitaminosis with a massive dose of compensatory enrichment" (Bruner, 1970).

II. "Drawing a Hand"—an editorial in the Baltimore *Sun* (1960).

"As Mrs. Klein told her first-graders to draw a picture of something for which they were thankful, she thought how little these children, the mixed offerings of a deteriorating neighborhood, actually had to be thankful for. She knew that most of the class would draw pictures of turkeys or of bountifully laden Thanksgiving tables. That was what they believed was expected of them.

"What took Mrs. Klein aback was Douglas' picture. Douglas she looked upon as her true child of misery, so scrubby and forlorn, and so likely to be found close in her shadow as they went outside for recess. Douglas' drawing was simply this:

"A hand, obviously, but whose hand? The class was captivated by the abstract image. 'I think it must be the hand of God that brings us food,' said one. 'A farmer,' said another, 'because they grow the turkeys.' 'It looks more like a policeman, and they protect us,' 'I think,' said Lavinia, who was always so serious and final, 'that it is supposed to be all the hands that help us, but Douglas could only draw one of them.'

"Mrs. Klein had almost forgotten Douglas in her pleasure at finding the class so responsive. When she had the others at work on their numbering, she bent over his desk and asked whose hand it was. Douglas mumbled, "It's yours, Teacher.'

"Then Mrs. Klein recalled that she had taken Douglas by the hand from time to time—she often did that with the children. But that it should have meant so much to Douglas. . . . Perhaps, she reflected, this was her Thanksgiving, and everybody's Thanksgiving. Not the material things given to us, but the chance in whatever small way to give something to others."

III. From "A Portrait of the Underprivileged" (Riessman, 1962).

"The deprived individual often feels alienated, left out, frustrated in what he can do. He holds the world, rather than himself, responsible for his misfortunes. Therefore, he is less likely to suffer from self-blame and is more direct in his expressions of aggression. He desires a better standard of living, but not necessarily the middle-class style. His beliefs about morality, punishment, custom, diet, traditional education, the role of women, and intellectuals are traditional in origin and manner. They are not open to reason nor are they flexible.

"He is generally not interested in politics but readily willing to believe in the corruptness of leaders. He fails to vote much of the time and generally belongs to few organizations. He places much value in his family and his personal comforts. He likes excitement, to get away from the humdrum of daily life: news, gossip, new gadgets, and sports are attractive to him. His desire to have new television sets and cars is part of this love for excitement.

"One of his most serious handicaps is his anti-intellectualism, seen in his antagonism to the school, his belief that life is a better teacher than are books, that theory is impractical. He seems to learn better when ideas can be manipulated with the hands and body; even in religion it is the hand-clapping and singing which appeals to him more than the dignified sermon. His respect for the physical prowess of prize fighters and baseball players demonstrates his physical orientation. Strength and endurance are his principal economic assets, representing one possible line of achievement he may pursue—hence his love for sports.

"His emphasis on masculinity is another manifestation of his physical orientation. Authority enforced through physical force is learned in the home where the father or even the mother use this means of keeping respect and order. Reading and attending school is often imaged as a prissy place dominated by women and female values."

Beyond the Classroom Experiences

1. Volunteer to become involved with children from subcultures different from your own—tutoring, recreation, friendship activities.
2. Begin a picture collection of the faces and activities of children in middle childhood, representing a variety of cultural backgrounds.

3. Read the biography of persons reared in socioeconomic classes different from your own. Compare their life-style and its effect on their development with that of yourself.

4. Interview a family with children that is just preparing to change residences or that has recently done so, noting feelings, problems, advantages they see.

5. Attend a movie with a child. Note his actions during the emotion-packed scenes. Use a questionnaire to assess his recall of main and extraneous facts from it the following day, week, and month.

6. Play a series of current records or tapes for children to test their knowledge of popular music. Determine their use of radio, records, and tapes to see if there is any connection with knowledge and listening time.

7. Ask children to interpret comic strips, including previous action in continued stories, to measure their perception, humor index, and recall.

8. Survey children with respect to the children's and adult magazines and newspapers received and read by them at home.

9. Take a child to the library. Note criteria on which he selects books to read. Use the Readability Graph to measure reading level of their content. Read one or more of his selections and later discuss the content with the child. Note his learning, recall, and feelings.

10. Survey children or parents to learn how TV viewing is controlled in homes, the attendant problems and possible solutions.

Chapter 3

Focus on the Family

This chapter is designed to help you:

- realize the many family forms that affect the lives of children.
- discover factors in families that infiuence child development and behavior.
- understand how school-age children view their homes and families and why.
- examine ways in which changing roles of men and women affect children.
- note the ramiflcations of ordinal position on personality and behavior.
- know ways to minimize sibling rivalry.
- consider possible effects of divorce on children.

Consideration of the child's family is as basic to understanding his development as is that of his society in general. This littlest world has provided his first encounter with the challenges of identity, acceptance, relationships, and achievement. The family can either prepare him for success in his ever-expanding world, or it may handicap him—perhaps irreparably.

The primary tasks of families are to develop their capacities to socialize children, to enhance the competence of their members to cope with the demands of other organizations in which they must function, to utilize resources of the community, and to provide the satisfactions and a mental health environment intrinsic to the well-being of people (White House Conference on Children, 1971).

The modern definition of the family is a changing one. In a bicentennial review of the family, Sudea (1976) makes the following statement: The American family is still an accepted pattern of living together. Its structure is varied but simple. It usually includes an adult pair living together in sexual relationship affirmed and accepted by civil, religious and family authority, with their children, and may include the parents and other relatives of both partners. However, none of these elements is essential, and it may still be a family. The form is quite varied and in recent years has become more so. Unmarried cohabitation, communal arrangements, single parent families and various other forms are tolerated if not wholly approved.

A Family Is a Family Is a Family . . .

A family might be differentiated from a dormitory or apartment house group by including in the definition the idea of supporting network of relationships: affectional, comradeship, economic, sexual. The most prevalent types of family forms and variations, modified from the report of the White House Conference on Children (1971) and Talbot (1976), include:

Nuclear Family. Husband, wife, and offspring living together in a common household; natural or adopted children. *Traditional:* husband the breadwinner, wife the home manager and child rearer. *Modern or evolving:* father contributing as a wage-earner, policy-maker and part-time partner in child caretaking; mother also works and has some help with management of home and children. *Androgynous household:* sharing parental and other household and work responsibilities by husband and wife; merging of heretofore exclusively masculine and feminine roles.

Single-Parent Family. Either man or woman (more often woman) and one or more children; children may be born to or adopted by parent. May result from death of spouse, divorce, separation, abandonment, or non-marriage.

Three-Generation Family. Three generations in a single household, in the home of either the aged parent or the grown child; parent, grown child, and grandchildren; aged couple, their grown child, and his offspring; married couple with their children and the aged parent.

Middle-Aged or Old-Aged Couple. Husband and wife; children, if any, are launched into school, career, marriage; husband only may be employed; both may be employed; neither may work (retirement stage).

Adoptive Parent: Foster Parent Family. Adoptive family may be a close equivalent of natural parenthood provided the parents are "well endowed for the job and well matched to their prospective charge" (Talbot, 1976, p. 23). In foster parenting, one or more children are placed with parents assigned by court or agency action.

Reconstituted Family. Family is formed through re-marriage and may include children from the previous unions of one or both partners and may subsequently include children born to the new partnership.

Kin Network. Nuclear household or unmarried members living in close geographical proximity and operating within a reciprocal system of exchange of goods and services.

Institutional Family. Children absent from natural or adoptive parents, care being provided by orphanges, residential school, or correctional institutions.

Communal, Collective, Cooperative Living. There is great variation in the setting up of these arrangements, varying from tight sets of rules governing how people will relate to each other and how the household will be managed, to quite flexible policies which are changed as the need arises through some type of democratic decision making process. *Collective marriage:* made up of from three to eight or ten people where all adults are married to each other and all are parents to the children. *Communal family:* households of more than one monogamous couple with children sharing common facilities, resources and experiences; socialization of children is a group activity. *Homosexual couple and child:* A male or female couple with a child who is formally or informally adopted.

A recent news article (Angove, 1972) featured an interview with a husky, bearded junior college graduate who listed his occupation as housewife. Upon completion of school Paul and Vicki both went job hunting, having agreed that whoever could earn the most money for the least hours of work would become employed; the other would be in charge of their modest apartment. Vicki is self-employed as a legal transcriber working 4–5 hours each day while Paul minds the stew, vacuums, and manages the home. After his chores are completed, he writes on his book while Vicki does glass ceramics. Both find the arrangement a lot of fun but see a role reversal may come in a couple of years when they have children. Paul indicates his fascination with this emerging family form in these words: "We might go on for the rest of our lives, switching back and forth every few years."

Think Back

To your family composition and routine when you were growing up:
Who slept where?
Who did what duties around the house?
Who was boss?
Who got up first?
What time was bedtime?
What did you do right after school each day?
What pets did you have?
Who lived in your house?
What did you like best about each family member?
What was your favorite activity with each parent?
What did the family do together?

Children are likely to move from one family form to another with increasing age: children in a nuclear family may experience the single-parent

Grandparents become parents of their grandchildren in some families. (*Photo by Lin Mitchell.*)

form and then a reconstituted nuclear form if death or divorce occurs and re-marriage follows. If the mother enters the labor force, they face new experiences and activities. If aging grandparents join the family, they move into a three-generation form. Variation in family form presents differing issues and problems for all family members, and both relationship and socialization aspects of the child's development will be in part influenced by the form of his family.

The family is undergoing change in composition as well as structure: postponement of marriage; child bearing completed earlier; fewer children; more women in the work force; fewer adults in the family. All these changes have effects in the lives and growth of children.

Women and Work

Average age at marriage for women born in the 50's and married in the 70's was 21.2 as compared to 20 years for women born in the 30's and married in the 50's. The seventies bride had her first child after 1.5 years of marriage and completed child bearing 8.4 years later. This contrasts with the fifties bride who had her first child after 1.4 years of marriage and completed child bearing 11.2 years later (Glick, 1977). This means a longer period of marriage after children are away from home which may precipitate different child-rearing practices growing out of new priorities in self-development and in the marriage relationship.

Later marriage may mean more education and work experience for women which in turn becomes part of the explanation for the great number of married women who enter or remain in the labor force. Increasingly, the presence of children makes no difference in this choice. The number of women who had both husband and children under six and were working, or looking for work, increased threefold between 1950 and 1975. Twenty-five years ago one-quarter of all married women worked outside the home; in 1970 one-half were doing so. This included 40 percent of all mothers, who had 26 million children, of whom six million were less than six years old. Over a million children were "latch-key" children—left at home alone while parents work.

By 1975, 52 percent of all married women with children between six and seventeen years of age were working; 37 percent of the married women with children under six were working (Figure 1, Toward a National Policy). Since the 1950's, mothers of school age children have been more likely to work than married women without children. The most rapid increase, however, has been among married women with young children: in 1974 one-third of all women with children under six were working, as were three of ten women with infants. Whether the mothers had infants or teenagers, two-thirds of those who worked were employed full-time.

By 1975 in only 34 of every 100 husband/wife families was the husband the sole breadwinner, as compared to 56 such families in 1950 (Carnegie Report, 1977, p. 4). Now the *typical* school age child has a mother who works outside the home.

Even larger percentages of single mothers work: 62 percent of all single mothers with children of school age: 54 percent with children under six; and 45 percent with children under three. Eighty percent of these mothers are working full-time.

Reasons for this increase are varied, but one cause is economic. A greater proportion (51 percent) of mothers whose husbands' incomes are $5,000 or less is in the labor force. However, even among these women there is an over-representation of women who have finished high school, an under-representation of high school dropouts and of younger mothers under age 25. But income is not the whole answer, for the most rapid increase over time has been among mothers married to husbands whose incomes were in the middle and high levels.

At least theoretically, as a result of this trend, more fathers are assuming home-related tasks. Probably children, too, in families with gainfully employed mothers are assuming more home-related duties. Herein lie implications for development, not only of sex-role identity but of specific skills and attitudes toward work of various types. The effect of the mothers' being employed outside the home has received much attention, particularly related to the rise in juvenile delinquency in our nation. Research seems to indicate it is not the fact that a mother is outside the home for employment but the provisions she makes for child supervision in her absence as well as how she spends her available time with her children that makes the difference. If in her absence the children receive supervision consistent with that she would give were she at home, they do not tend to suffer from her employment. Likewise, if in her time with them she engages in activities that are meaningful to them and to her, the mere quantity of time spent is subordinated, and the quality becomes of major importance. The mother's view of her employment and her relative satisfaction with her multirole life will also help determine the effect of such employment on the life of all family members. When mothers feel they have chosen to work, they tend to be more pleased and therefore more able to carry on home-related tasks.

From another viewpoint, Yorburg (1974) makes an interesting interpretation of the data from a study of successful working women. Earlier studies emphasized negative aspects of the relationship between these women and their mothers: lack of a close relationship traced to maternal hostility or rejection, strong identification with fathers, and "masculine" interests. More recent studies of women in male dominated professions place emphasis on the lack of over-protection in the mother-daughter relationship. These successful daughters are seen as identifying with their mothers, especially with mothers who work or have a career. Yorburg's view is that working mothers do not have the time or energy or need to over-protect or over-invest in their children. In summary he says: "Children identify strongly with models who are perceived as warm and nurturing. They identify with people who are viewed as having desired traits or resources—power, love, or competence in areas that the child feels are important. With rising status and changing roles of women, aspiring daughters are more likely to identify with their mothers as well as their fathers. And if their mothers have personality traits such as self-reliance and assertiveness, that are usually sex-typed for the opposite sex, daughters, too, will acquire these traits (p. 163)."

Working mothers in the one- or two-parent family, when there are no proper arrangements for childcare usually means, according to Bronfenbrenner (1977), "Nobody home." This empty time children fill up with something: television and peers. This peer-group culture, Bronfenbrenner suggests, may be an "ugly culture—a culture of destroy, of break, of act out. The essence of it is anomie, a social and emotional disintegration, inside and outside." He states that children, at home or away from home, need quality care and in addition need to spend a substantial amount of time with somebody who cares for them, cherishes them, and thinks they are important.

Society can help to arrange for these conditions in a number of ways: community-supported childcare systems which meet needs of families with school age children as well as younger children; parent education, giving priority and recognition to the work and skill involved in helping children grow; work situations which give status and economic stability to part-time employment for both men and women; emphasis on the community of the neighborhood; and involvement of children in worthwhile tasks or projects.

In a study involving 223 ten-year-old girls and boys representing both middle-class and working-class families and with either full-time employed or unemployed mothers, Gold and Andres (1978) found a number of relationships between maternal employment and the child's development. Children with employed mothers, who expressed satisfaction in their roles, had the most egalitarian sex-role concepts. There was some relationship between adjustment of children and employment of mothers: working-class boys with employed mothers having more adjustment problems. The longer the mother had been employed the greater this correlation. However, this may be more closely linked with the father-child relationship. Because these fathers seemed to be more critical of their sons, they may not have been perceived as appropriate role models. Boys with working mothers also did less with mathematics and language achievement tests than other middle class boys. Husbands and wives in families where the mother was employed were in greater agreement in their reports of behavior in the home and attitudes which depicted fear than were non-employed mothers and their husbands. It appears that the effect of maternal employment on the development of children is mediated by a number of factors and varies with the particular child behavior being examined.

Fewer Children—Fewer Adults

Families are smaller: fewer children; fewer adults other than parents in the home; and fewer parents, or more single parent families. In 1975 the number of births per 1,000 population was only 76 percent as high as ten years earlier in 1965 and only 49 percent as high as the rate in 1910. Women born in the 50's and having children in the 70's will give birth to only about 2.5 children per mother, which is about one child less than 20 years earlier (Glick, 1977). A decrease from a four-child family in the early part of the century to a two-child family today is a big one.

Another erosion in family size stems from the fewer number of adults other than parents in the home. The average household size in 1974 was

Today's American families have fewer children than in previous generations. *(Photo by Rick Coleman.)*

2.97, a record low (Snapper, 1975). In 1948, 9 percent of all families with children under six lived in a household with a relative who was family head. By 1974 this had dropped to 4 percent. In families with children from six to seventeen years, comparable figures were 5 percent in 1948 and 2 percent in 1974. (See Figure 3-1.) Unfortunately, there is no record of households where husband or wife is head and where relatives are also part of the family. However, we do know there has been a decrease in the number of families with children under 18 who are living in three-genera-tion households. In 1959, 13 percent of all black families with children were in three-generation households; by 1974 only 8 percent could be so classified. Among white families, the figure was 4 percent in 1959 and 3 percent in 1974.

In 1974, 85 percent of all families were husband-wife families (Table 3-1); however there has been more than a 25 percent increase in one-parent families during the last decade, with an 18 percent increase from 1970 to 1973. In 1974 one of six children under 18 years of age was living in a single-parent family. The most rapid increase is occurring in families with children under six (Figure 3-2).

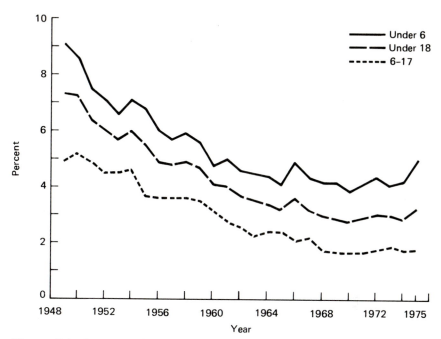

Figure 3-1. Percentage of families living with a relative as family head as a percentage of all families with children under 18, under 6, and 6 through 17 years of age, 1948–1975. (From *Toward a National Policy for Children*, p. 17.)

Table 3-1 Distribution of Primary Families by Sex of Head and Presence of Children, 1974 (Numbers in Thousands).

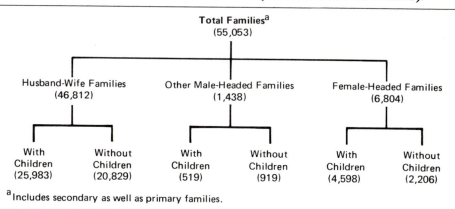

a Includes secondary as well as primary families.

Source: "Household and Family Characteristics: March 1974," Table 1, Series P-20, No. 276, *Current Population Reports, Population Characteristics*, Washington, D.C.: U.S. Bureau of the Census.

About 90 percent of all children with only one parent are living in independent families in which the single mother or father is family head. The great majority are headed by a woman, many of them quite young. In 1974, 12.4 percent of all families were headed by females; 34 percent of all black families and 10 percent of all white families. Only 2.6 percent of all single-parent families were headed by males. In 1974, one of every four parents under 25 years of age heading a household was without a spouse (Figure 3-3). In single-parent families, the head was less educated (Figure 3-4). Both of these conditions mean less income (Figure 3-5).

In the five years between 1970 and 1975 there was a 45 percent increase in the proportion of children living with mothers only. By 1975, one of five children was living with one parent only or with neither parent. Four of ten children born in the 70's will spend part of life in a one-parent family, usually with the mother as head (Carnegie Report, 1977).

Two things are happening: an increase in divorce and an increase of

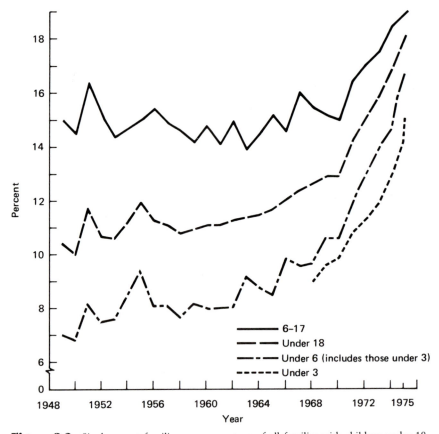

Figure 3-2. Single-parent families as a percentage of all families with children under 18, under 6. 6 through 17, and under 3 years of age, 1948–1975. (From *Toward a National Policy for Children,* p. 18.)

CHAPTER 3 / FOCUS ON THE FAMILY

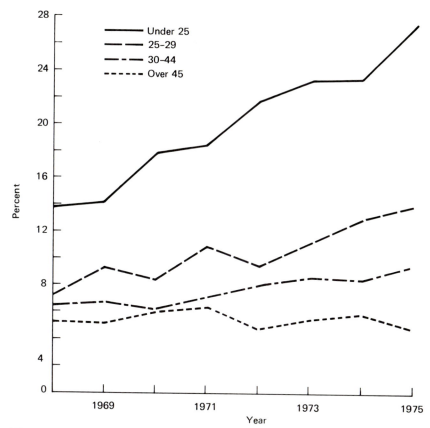

Figure 3-3. Percentage of single-parent family heads with children under 6 by age of family head, 1968–1975. (From *Toward a National Policy for Children*, p. 22.)

births to non-married women. In 1971, 11 percent of all births were to never-married women as compared to only 3 percent in 1950. A million of these never-married mothers are setting up households each year (Carnegie Report, 1977; Glick, 1977). There has been an eightfold increase of single couples of opposite sex living together, which represents about one percent of all couples and certainly is a new family form to be reckoned with. This arrangement may be the forerunner of marriage or of additional one-parent households when children are born (Carnegie Report, 1977).

Almost 16 million of the more than 48 million married women in America have celebrated their twenty-fifth wedding anniversaries and one and a quarter million have celebrated their golden anniversaries (Talbot, 1976). However, within the last century (1875–1975) there has been a six-teenfold increase in the divorce rate in the United States which is the highest for any nation reporting statistics to the United Nations. By 1971 a million children under 18 were involved in divorce, a number which tri-pled between 1953 and 1971 and a 700 percent increase since the turn of

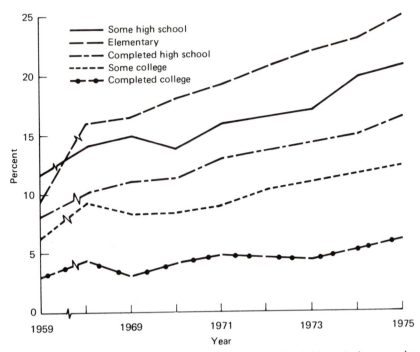

Figure 3-4. Percentage of families with children under 18, headed by a single spouse, by education of head, 1959–1975. (From *Toward a National Policy for Children*, p. 25.)

the century. In 1970 there were 35 divorced men for every 1,000 living with their wives; and 60 divorced women for every 1,000 living with their husbands. This compares to 28 per 1,000 men and 42 per 1,000 women in 1960. One in every five divorces is characterized by the presence of children.

Glick (1977) reminds us that smaller families mean children will spend more time interacting with parents. Parents' views vary more greatly from views of the children than would the views of childrens' siblings. The role of the parents in relation to each other is quite different because of fewer demands of the smaller number of children. The ability to limit and time births of children may have a positive effect on the health of the mother, and fewer children will allow the early ending of the child bearing period which has an effect on parental roles and family interaction. Bronfenbrenner's concern is that smaller families, particularly with fewer adults, dilutes family interaction and really cuts children off from interaction with adults and the world of work, leaving the void to be filled by same-age peers (Bronfenbrenner, 1974).

Continuing Influence

Regardless of the family makeup, the child will be influenced by that unit. By school age the family will have made basic impressions which he can-

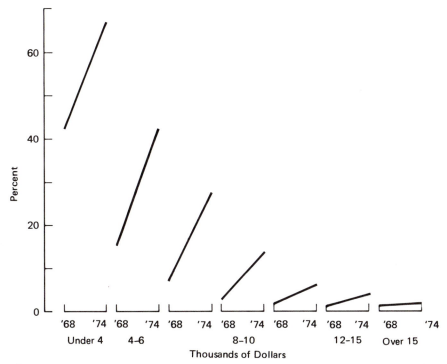

Figure 3-5. Female-headed families as a percentage of all family heads under 65 with children under 18 by income in previous year, 1968–1974. (From *Toward a National Policy for Children*, p. 23.)

not deny nor erase. His family will be ever with him, though not physically, at least psychologically. In the area of physical development, he carries his family's influence in his body build, attractiveness, general state of health, motor skills, and perhaps even food likes and dislikes and hygiene practices. Mentally, the family heritage may be expressed in his intellectual potential and curiosity, concept formation and refinement, language style and vocabulary, problem-solving and decision-making techniques.

Familial characteristics and influences will be revealed in his social skills, attitudes and relationships, recreational preferences, choices of friends, goals and aspirations. Emotionally, his general state of happiness and contentment; his expressions of such specific emotions as fear, anger, and love; his reactions to stress and success; his threshold of frustration will all have roots in the family. Whether he was a planned-for and wanted child, the age of his parents and siblings, his place in the family, family size—all have impact on his development. The neighborhood in which the family resided, the way the family worked and lived together, the values they espoused, the opportunities they provided—all were important in shaping the child of the middle years into the person he is.

Adults living and working with children can do so more effectively when they understand the vital mark of the family on these "middle people." At times, we marvel at a child's capabilities and characteristics when we realize the type of family life he has had. We may say he has "made it" in spite of and not because of his family. There is need to accept all children, regardless of their family type or status. By seeing how various family aspects influence development, such acceptance should be facilitated.

The impact of the nonfamily environment in the child's socialization has been inadequately researched (Hess, 1970). Such external aspects of physical and social environments as general condition, beauty, space, comfort, and resources in the home and community vary more between social classes than do the expressed values of parents.

Testing the assumed intrafamilial transmission of values, attitudes, and behavior, a number of studies (Hess, 1970; Jennings and Niemi, 1968; Sewell, 1961; Gildea et al., 1961) have revealed relatively low correlations between parents' attitudes and behavior and their children's behavior patterns. This suggests that values may arise from environmental conditions outside the family. If, in fact, parental influence on children is a function of the relative effectiveness of parental versus nonfamily modes, reinforcement schedules, authority figures, and mass media, the influence of such nonfamily factors on behavior may increase when a parent fails to exercise his options of socialization and control. Perhaps the socialization of working-class children is different not due to their parents' attitudes and values as much as it is due to an increase in nonfamily influence because of less powerful parental influence.

How Children View Their Family

Upon entering the school years, the child probably views his family idealistically. He is likely to have great pride in it, solely because it represents the best life he has known. For someone to criticize his mother or his family often hurts more than for someone to find fault with him. As he leaves the family, to spend time with other families in the neighborhood and in the larger community, he is likely to begin making comparisons and seeing things about his family he may not like. On the other hand, comparison of his family with others may reinforce his pride: "Mom, do you know the Conovers never had a vacation together? I told Anita we go somewhere every summer. Maybe she could go with us next year!"

With age, the child of the middle years loses his overt family loyalty. He will admit less and less that his family is important. If the truth were known, however, he is still glad his family is there to support, console, inspire, restrict. He is glad he has a home and family at mealtime and when he is tired and downtrodden. He likes to know there is always a group who will rally to his side when the rest of the world seems against him. Even in adulthood, desires for family support continue as evidenced by such continuing American traditions as getting home for the holidays.

Middle-class fifth-graders in a large southern city were questioned concerning their concepts of familism (McInnis, 1972). Some of their responses follow:

QUESTION: *What do you think are the most important things parents can do for their children or teach their children?*

"They can care for them and love them. They can teach their children good manners and to be polite to other people."

"Love them, send them to school, don't be cruel to them. If they are a boy their father should teach them baseball and things. If they are girls their mother should teach them to be lady-like and things."

QUESTION: *What is good about having brothers and sisters?*

"So if there is no one to play with you can play with your brother or sister."

"To play with them, to go swimming with them, to fight with them."

QUESTION: *What are some things you think a father should do in the family?*

"Earn money for the family. Keep the outside of the house nice by doing things or painting it."

"Wear the pants in the house (be the boss), decide the problems, do the bills, take care of the house outside."

QUESTION: *What are some things you think a mother should do in the family?*

"A mother should clean the dishes, mop the floor, clean the house and cook dinner."

"Cook the food, clean the house, make sure the kids get up in time for school, help the father with the money."

QUESTION: *How would you describe the ideal family?*

"A family that has two loving parents and at least two children to love each other and play together. The father would not have to go on long business trips and the mother and father had plenty of time to spend with their children."

"An ideal family to me would be a family of 5 or 6, have two cars, a two story house, a horse, and love for each other."

QUESTION: *Why do you think most people live in a family instead of living in other ways? List as many reasons for this as you can.*

"I believe people would rather live together than to be away from their family. They would probably want to use the same bill for all of their groceries."

"For company, love, helpfulness, someone to share your fears with, kindness, someone to help you with your problems."

The fifth-graders most often listed as the biggest problem in family life today: arguing, money, and divorces. They felt much of the problem was the children's fault. Older students were prone to blame parents and cite common problems: lack of communication, lack of family togetherness, and no love. Asked to comment on maternal employment, the 11-year-olds noted the extra money as a positive, but the burden it places on children as a negative aspect. When they pointed out the most important things parents can do to help children, 11-year-olds listed: send them to school, and help them with their homework. No 11-year-olds mentioned the need to help children love life and be happy.

Children quite early in life understand the kind of behavior adults value and what they frown upon. Children equate good behavior with obedience. They are aware earlier of adult disapproval of aggressive behavior than adult concern over withdrawn behavior. Children perceive fathers as more punitive than mothers. As children grow older, they tend to see the same-sex parent to a greater extent as the punisher.

In conversations with groups of third, fifth, and sixth grade boys and girls, the following ideas were brought out as the children discussed their opinions of adults.

> CHILD: Well, sometimes they treat you like a baby. Well, let me think of an example . . . when you fall down and skin your knee, they nurse you and everything.
>
> INTERVIEWER: Isn't that pretty nice?
>
> CHILD: Yes, but there are your friends watching you and you feel like a baby.
>
> CHILD: And it hurts. So they take that lotion stuff they put on it, and let's say it is just scraped up real badly and it's bleeding and then they put all this lotion junk on it. When they are moving this cotton ball around, it just stings. You want to yell out loud, but your company is there and you just get all red in the face.
>
> INTERVIEWER: So sometimes adults embarrass you. You don't like this.
>
> CHILD: And they don't know they embarrass you.
>
> CHILD: They always get mad at you when you embarrass them or you get your allowance taken away or you have to go to your room.

Being fair is important to children. Adults should keep this cardinal principle in mind.

> CHILD: When you play a game like "bombardment" and somebody gets hurt and you know it is really their own fault—they were showing off or something—then everybody gets the blame. . . . I just don't like that.
>
> CHILD: And each person in the family have the right amount of what they are doing. Like you not have all the jobs.

A sixth-grader cited an example of this common difficulty: lack of opportunity to give reasons for actions not approved by adults:

> CHILD: Sometimes parents just won't believe that something you did, you really didn't do on purpose.
>
> INTERVIEWER: Have you had this happen to you?
>
> CHILD: We went to Kansas City one Thanksgiving. I had braces and I was supposed to wear a head strap at night and my dad was hurrying me up with my packing because we were ready to leave except for me. And I forgot it and my mom was mad at me! "I know you were doing it just to get back at me! I made you wear it." I didn't mean to leave it. I thought about packing it. I was going to, but I just forgot it.

Children display a great deal of insight into parental behavior. Perhaps they spend as much time getting the measure of parents as parents spend taking the measures of children!

INTERVIEWER: Do you think for the most part adults are nice?

CHILD: Well, it depends on the mood they are in. When I want somebody to spend the night or something and my little sister breaks a dish or does something like that, then Mom is in a bad mood and I can't do what I want to do.

In one group, conversation turned to lying and stealing. The children agreed that most boys and girls are involved to some degree in this activity.

INTERVIEWER: Do you think parents like this?

CHILD: No, because they think they try so hard to bring you up right and then when you do something wrong it just makes them feel bad.

INTERVIEWER: Do you think this must be a disappointment to parents?

CHILD: Yes, they think they goofed.

And in another group this conversation took place:

CHILD: I wouldn't want to be an adult. Because when you are a kid you know you still have a long life ahead of you, but when you are an adult you really don't have that much time.

CHILD: You have too much to do, like paying bills and worrying about having enough money to pay them.

CHILD: And when you are a kid you can do a lot more things than the adults— like going outside and playing football and roughing around. But when you are an adult you have jobs, like a doctor. And a housewife has a lot of jobs, too—to clean up the house and do the dishes.

Perhaps children are more perceptive than they are perceived to be. They may have greater empathy for the parental role as well as greater facility for discerning the games adults play with children than we credit them with. This underscores the need for talking with children and listening to them. It is important to understand the view of the world from their vantage point and to take time to help them see reasons for parental behaviors.

Parenting and Family Relationships

To be the parents of school-age children is not an easy task. Everyone from the juvenile judge to the man in the barbershop finds fault with parents. As children become more and more the center of attention in the nation, standards for parents rise and parental self-images fall. With the rising divorce rates, increasing numbers of American parents are having to function alone in child care and guidance. As the number of mothers in the labor force swells, their roles as parents are altered, making the demands on them greater. Parental knowledge and authority are more challenged today than in yesteryear because of the mass media and rising educational level of children. Preparation for the parenting role is grossly inadequate. Parenthood is so surrounded by myth and folklore that parents are not aware of what parenthood means or demands until it has occurred. Consider the following myths by LeMasters (1977):

- Rearing children is fun.
- Children are sweet and cute.
- Children will turn out well if they have "good" parents.
- Today's parents are not as good as those of yesterday.
- Sex education myth: children won't get into trouble if they have been told the facts of life.
- There are no bad children-only bad parents.
- The one-parent family is pathological.
- Love is enough to sustain good parental performance.
- Childless married couples are frustrated and unhappy.
- Children improve a marriage.

Such beliefs on the part of either parents or society can only be frustrating when things do not work out so in real life, or when unreal expectations are placed upon people in the couple role or in the parent role.

Another myth that parents must contend with is that parenthood receives top priority in the nation. In reality, business and industry, schools and churches all place pressures on families that seem to pull them apart and place the role of parents far from first-place position. Talbot (1976), in illustrating the low-status accorded to childrearing in the economy, writes:

Child care workers are not even listed as a category in the U.S. Department of Labor's Table of Employment by Occupations. Mothers' helpers and housekeepers stand at the bottom of the list of earnings by occupation. They receive less pay on the average than lumbermen, teamsters, fishermen and garbage collectors. When a mother who is left alone to rear her children turns to Public Welfare for supportive aid, the allotment she receives is at the poverty level. Regardless of how many children a mother is responsible for or how busy they keep her, she is not considered to be "working" in a way that contributes to the Gross National Product unless she is gainfully employed outside her home (p. 29).

In the same vein, from the 1970 White House Conference on Children comes the following report:

In today's world parents find themselves at the mercy of a society which imposes pressures and priorities that allow neither time nor place for meaningful activities and relations between children and adults, which downgrade the role of parents and the functions of parenthood, and which prevent the parent from doing things he wants to do as a guide, friend, and companion to his children . . .

The frustrations are greatest for the family of poverty where the capacity for human response is crippled by hunger, cold, filth, sickness, and despair. For families who can get along, the rats are gone, but the rat race remains. The demands of a job or often two jobs, that claim mealtimes, evenings and weekends as well as days; the trips and moves necessary to get ahead or simply hold one's own; the ever increasing time spent in commuting, parties, evenings out, social and community obligations—all the things one has to do to meet so-called primary responsibilities—produce a situation in which a child often spends more time with a passive babysitter than a participating parent (White House Conference on Children, 1970; Report to the President, 241–243).

Notwithstanding the difficulty involved and the lack of training for parenthood, parents and family and parent-child interaction have high impact on children and their total development. Less and less we look at a particular action of a parent as producing a particular result. The parent-child system is a complex and intricate interaction pattern rather than one in which particular child behavior results from particular parental behavior.

During the early years of middle childhood, children seem to be inter-

Parent-child interaction has a high impact on the total development of children. (*Photo by Lin Mitchell.*)

ested in pleasing adults: first parents, and then teachers. However, with physical growth, increasing skills, and more contact with other children, pleasing adults becomes less pressing. Fitting in with and winning the approval of other children assume greater and greater importance. While adults are necessary, children have achieved enough trust, autonomy, and initiative that they want to become involved in a private world of their own where adults are usually not welcome. Withdrawal into the society of children occurs at a time children are least attractive to adults. Children rebel against cuddling, are more restless, usually are dirty, snaggle-toothed, and speak a language adults find too difficult to understand.

At home, vocalization assumes new patterns—children talk back and accuse parents of unfairness. Chores are forgotten; they fail to show up in time for dinner; embark enthusiastically on projects, only to have to be prodded to finish them. Some children disdain taking baths and keeping their rooms clean. One youngster declared: "After all, I have to live in it. And when it gets so messed up that I can't find my things, I'll clean it up." Children are not interested in the social amenities: greeting their mother's friends or explaining some project on which they are working. During elementary school years, children spend about six to seven hours a day away from home. This is in contrast to one hour a day during the preschool years and eight hours a day during adolescence.

All of this—but at the same time, a keen awareness of feelings and relationships within the family is present. Family values are internalized. Parents might be surprised to hear their sixth-graders handing out parental admonitions to their friends. "Nope, Saturday is our work day. I can't help it if you can talk your mother out of things. My mom means what she says." Large responsibilities can be accepted by children in emergencies and carried out very well. Parents are often amazed by their children's well-thought-out plans of action in certain situations.

This on-and-off behavior of children is the result of rejection of adult standards. In the fourth, fifth, and sixth grades, problem behavior reaches a peak: teasing, discourtesy, scuffling, rebelliousness, carelessness, untidiness, and disobedience. These children are frequently irritable, easily offended, and often discouraged. Physical aspects of problem behavior include facial tics, restlessness, nail-biting, and scratching.

There seems to be a change in the child's relationship to authority. Each child is dropping identification with adult society in order to establish strong bonds of identity with a group of his peers. There are several reasons for this rejection (Blair and Burton, 1951) of previously accepted standards.

- Physical changes bring the child to a new awareness of himself. John, particularly, feels he must assert his masculinity in a largely feminine world. Growth brings the need to say: "I am me." This new identity must be experimented with. The child has inadequate techniques for handling these new experiences and new feelings.

- Increased expectations of adults and more structuring of activities by adults create tension and anxiety. Adults become aware of the child in a new way and so demand more of him.
- Children arrive at a stage when they care only for their age mates.

These are push-pull children. While they are pushing away from the family, they still need the pull of the family to give security and allow them to try out new ways of acting and relating. Sometimes behavior of children leads parents to be somewhat rejecting of them. Parents cannot allow this to happen. Children need their families as much or more during the middle childhood years than any other time. In spite of the changes in family patterns and styles and the child's growing interest in people and things outside the family, the family is still the most significant influence in the life of the child.

So, what is it about the family that makes a difference to the children of school age? The overall climate of the home seems to be the major factor in the total development of its children, at any age (Sears, Maccoby, and Levin, 1957). During the preschool years, it is not isolated routines, such as toilet-training, bottle or breast-feeding, which make a child develop "properly" or not. Likewise, during the middle years, it is not whether a child has home chores, shares a room, has a specific bedtime, or is an only child which solely determines his development. It is the total atmosphere and attitude of the family which becomes the major force in shaping behavior and guiding development.

Basic in family adjustment and success is the relationship of the parents to each other. Children keenly sense how parents get along and are not often fooled when things are not as they should be. Children draw their first impressions of the adult world, including marriage, from their parents. They unconsciously absorb attitudes and ways of behaving from parental models. They learn through observation far more than they may ever be formally taught in the area of relationships.

Therefore, an important task of parenthood is to foster the deepening of a good husband-wife relationship. Mature parents who do not need to depend on children to meet their own emotional needs are in a better position to listen to the growth-beat of their children. A good husband-wife relationship also sets a standard for femininity and masculinity which children can follow.

Another important consideration is the recognition of the individuality of children during their growing up years. Democracy is important; individuality must be guarded. A group of children in an interview with Parkhurst (1951) listed rights which they believe important to children which may still be instructive for us:

- To be an integral part of the family.
- To be heard at times and about subjects they consider important.
- To have opinions properly evaluated.

- To explain.
- To receive objective, fair, and patient treatment.
- To ask questions.
- To be given reasons.
- To have a secret.

Parental attitudes about who children are and toward responsibility in regard to methods of guidance are key factors in the development of the climate of warmth and acceptance in which children seem to thrive. It is more helpful to examine patterns or configurations of interaction than simply to look at parent behaviors in isolated situations.

Baumrind (1971) identified groups of parents with varying patterns of interaction and examined associated characteristics of children. The main patterns were authoritarian (arbitrary control, no consideration of child's point of view); authoritative (firm control in a rational manner; encouragement of verbal give-and-take with child); permissive, rejecting-neglecting. Boys of authoritative parents were more friendly, cooperative and achievement-oriented than boys in other parent groups. Girls of authoritative parents were likely to be more dominant, achievement-oriented and independent than other girls. Masters (1975) pointed out the importance of attending to the fact that this research related a pattern of parental behaviors or characteristics with a pattern of child outcomes. If high authority were not accompanied by ability to communicate openly and to solicit the child's opinions, he wondered if it would be associated with independence in the child. Even though the subjects in this research were preschool children, the conclusion can be drawn that patterns of interaction are important.

Parental attitude not only toward children in general, but also toward their individual children is paramount in determining family impact on children of the middle years. Each child perceives himself as either being accepted or rejected by each of his parents. And he likewise has his own ideas whether or not each of his siblings is accepted or rejected. Quite naturally, if he feels rejected or less accepted than another child in his family, his attitudes and behavior will be different than if he perceives himself equally or even more accepted than his siblings.

Rejected children are likely to exhibit emotional unstability, restlessness, overactivity, troublemaking tendencies, resentment toward authority, quarrelsomeness, and an inclination to steal. Children perceived as accepted by parents are more likely to be cooperative, friendly, honest, straightforward, emotionally stable, deliberate, enthusiastic, and cheerful. The behavior of children who feel rejected is apt to make them even more rejected by those with whom they live, thereby intensifying the signs which caused their original feelings.

Family management and role assignment likewise enter the picture for the developing child. In our changing society it is increasingly difficult for children to distinguish sex-linked roles. It is sometimes difficult for them to distinguish sex itself, as a result of the changing modes of fashion and grooming.

A further word concerning the impact of social class and family life is appropriate in this context. From class to class, there tends to be variance in the roles played by each parent and in the goals the parents hold for the achievement of their children. Upper-class parents traditionally abdicate many of their roles to hired family employees: discipline, physical care of children, intellectual stimulation. They enjoy living with their children at times when there is apt to be little stress, such as in recreational or cultural activities. They are hopeful that their offspring will be genteel, cultured, compassionate, happy.

The middle-class parent is concerned with imparting to children self-reliance, independence, and initiative, qualities that will help him "get ahead" in life. Parental roles for this large population segment are more fluid and interchangeable. The husband-wife relationship is ideally one of mutual support, joint planning, and sharing, and their guidance of children more apt to be developmental or democratic.

The lower-class home is more often authoritarian in nature, and the husband and wife roles are distinctly defined and traditional in nature. There is a degree of emotional distance in this relationship which perhaps causes the mother-child bond to be stronger. The mother-child relationship in the lower class often resembles one between peers. Obedience and politeness are qualities which these parents seek to teach their children. They probably value "getting by" more than "getting ahead" (Irelan, 1967).

In a summary of research in parent-child relationships, Martin (1975) pointed out that almost any type of behavior can be interpreted in terms of the influence of the child on the parent or the influence of the parent on the child, and most of the time there is some degree of mutual influence. Whenever we look at parent-child relations, then, we must consider the interactive framework rather than simply the effect on children of certain parent actions.

Martin also deals with the importance of situational variables as affecting the interaction pattern of parents and children: who is present at time of interaction; the condition of the child's health and energy level; other stresses in the life of the parent; and what happened immediately preceding the behavior in question. The following selected conclusions are drawn from a review of research on parent-child relations (Martin, 1975):

1. Parental restrictiveness combined with hostility is related to adult-directed dependency; parental permissiveness or laxity combined with low warmth (parental hostility) is related to peer-directed dependency.
2. Internalized reactions to transgression in middle class children are correlated with maternal warmth, with disciplinary practices characterized by clear statements of expectations and consequences of deviation, and by the use of the "affective relationship"; that is, making the child feel badly by

describing how badly he is making others feel. A model for self-control increases the likelihood of self-control on the part of the child.

3. Girls are socialized (take on the prohibitions, proscriptions, and associated values and beliefs of the culture) more readily than boys and there is some indication that girls may be more subject to oversocialization than boys.

4. Independent behavior is associated with a parent-child interaction pattern in which age-appropriate behavior is demanded; rules are firmly and consistently enforced; affection and approval are given to the child, who is encouraged and listened to.

5. Achievement behavior in children is directly related to demands for such behavior and parental reinforcement of such behavior.

6. In girls, high achievement may be associated with relatively low level of parental acceptance.

7. Parental permissiveness or laxity is generally related to aggression in adolescents and six- to twelve-year-olds.

8. Parental punitiveness and non-acceptance are positively related to childhood aggression at all ages.

9. Configurations in which permissiveness and punitiveness are combined, either between the parents or within the same parent, are likely to be associated with aggression.

10. Aggressive children are likely to have parents who are models of aggressive behavior either in the form of antisocial acts or in inter-parent conflict or both.

11. At older age levels the variable of parental warmth (or acceptance) is of importance. Non-acceptance seems to be associated with both withdrawn neurotic behavior and with psychosomatic disorders in children.

Think Back

To your childhood:
Whether or not your mother worked.
How you felt about her role.
Whether your father shared the tasks at home.
What you thought about other families in which there were divorces; working mothers; adopted children; step parents.

The One-Parent Family

Martin's review (1975) of parent-child relations dealt exclusively with research among intact families; while in modern America the one-parent family is becoming more and more a reality, and the effects of this family pattern on children in the middle years are worthy of consideration. Certainly the circumstance that caused the loss of one parent would be an important factor, whether it was illegitimacy, death, imprisonment, desertion, military service, adoption, or divorce. Whatever the cause, the way

Single parents often feel job demands rob them of adequate time with children. *(Photo by Lin Mitchell.)*

the child perceives the cause and is helped to adjust to the family situation is the key to how the one-parent family will affect development.

Single parent families mean father-absent families in the great majority of cases, which is a syndrome rather than a single easily-defined variable in the life of a child. Biller (1977), in a brief summary of some of his research, reminds us that "many factors must be considered in the father-absent situation: type (constant, intermittent, temporary), length, cause, the child's age and sex, his constitutional characteristics and developmental status, the mother's reaction to husband-absence, the quality of mother-child interaction, the family's socioeconomic status and the availability of surrogate models." Many adverse generalizations can be made about the approximately seven million children in the United States growing up in fatherless homes. On the basis of a review of almost 400 studies (Herzog and Sudia, 1968) there is no clear-cut research evidence indicating correlation between the incidence of adverse traits or behavior and the absence of fathers, per se. Herzog and Sudia have drawn three conclusions: (1) Existing data do not permit a decisive answer to questions about the effect of fatherlessness on children. (2) To increase knowledge about the effects on children of growing up in fatherless homes, we must look at the family in a different way: Is this a new family form? What is the role of the mother in such a home? What other male role models are available? (3) Father absence (just as working mothers) is not a single variable which is the determining factor in whatever results are found; rather it is a cluster of interacting factors which "on this one hand, mediate the effect of that variable and, on the other hand, provide clues to methods of diminishing some adverse elements in its effects." In fact, the child whose father is not in the home may be less paternally deprived than selected father-present children, because the child whose father is absent may seek out some type of father surrogate, whereas the latter may develop negative images of males (Biller, 1968a, 1974). This is especially true for father-absent children who have competent mothers. On the other hand, children who have domineering mothers and ineffectual fathers are more likely to develop personality defects. Children with too-busy fathers may also suffer paternal deprivation. There seems to be poor personal adjustment among children whose fathers are home a great deal but are not very nurturant and among children whose fathers are seldom home but highly nurturant. Particularly in the cognitive domain, children thrive best with available nurturant fathers (Biller, 1974a; Reuter and Biller, 1973).

Fathering and mothering are different, each unique and qualitatively different (Lamb, 1977), and both girls and boys seem to profit from contact with both parents, who meet different growth needs. Pederson (1976) suggests the father exerts both direct effects and effects mediated by the mother. The father's interaction is different from that of the mother: more rough housing; active arousing play; more limited contact than the mother which enhances novelty value; interaction more tied to play than to meeting physical needs; therefore it forms one of the bridges to the larger environment particularly for the infant. In addition, support of the husband to the wife seems to add to her effectiveness in mothering.

Pederson (1976) points out that children growing up in a single parent household headed by the mother may be affected by any of a number of factors: the changed family structure with consequent differences in maternal role behavior; "the child's diminished or changed quality of interaction with a male adult; proportionately greater interaction with the mother; the presence of surrogate caregivers associated with the mother's employment; a qualitatively different maternal behavior, vis-a-vis the child, because of the emotional meaning of the father's absence to her."

Bigner (1977) examined attitudes toward fathering and father-child interaction patterns of middle class fathers and their young children. As attitude scores indicated a more developmental approach, there was an increase in activity with the child. Older fathers spent more time with children; however, as the child's age increased, there was less interaction between father and child. Perhaps the father felt that as the child grows older, help was less needed than at younger ages. Fathers with two or three children had higher attitude scores (more developmental) but reported less interaction than fathers with only one child. This finding suggests that as the father gains experience he becomes less rigid and has more accurate expectations about the child; and may also point up the possibility that children modify parents' behavior.

The role of the American father has become less and less clearly defined in the past decades (Brazelton, 1970). The depression eroded his capacity as a breadwinner, closely followed by entry of women into the work force during World War II. Whereas fathers of yesteryear patriarchially dominated their household, controlling children and womenfolk with a glance, today fathers feel unsure, insecure, inadequate, and even guilty about their contribution to the family. They are often torn between an interest in their children and a desire to succeed in their job. One corporation executive explained why a very able young man in the company had not risen to high-paying rank in these words: "He chooses to spend his free time on the floor with his children." Because it seems that regardless of what they do someone in society criticizes it, fathers tend to substitute more satisfying activities for those of fathering. Spending the weekend playing golf or at the office seems better than facing the challenges of teasing, wiggling, arguing children. And eventually the family must learn to function in his absence.

This role-definition dilemma faced by today's mothers and fathers presents the question: Are roles to be equal or is devotion to the family to be equal? Ideally, a clearly defined parent role might aid fathers in their own identity as well as male youngsters looking for a model to emulate. The difficulty lies in the fact that we are somewhat fettered with a male stereotype which defines many parenting activities as more feminine than masculine.

Divorce and Reconstituted Families

In 1974 more than a million children were involved in the divorce of their parents (Figure 3-6). There has been an increase of 135 percent in the number of divorces from 1962 to 1974, or 2.2 per 1,000 population in 1962 to 4.6 per 1,000 population in 1974.

Divorce must be understood as a process rather than an event if we are to see the implication of this action, particularly in the lives of children. Green (1977) suggests that adults go through a process or series of adjustments, all of which have impact upon the children involved. How the children fare depends to some extent on how parents move through these stages. The steps he outlines begin before the divorce and continue after it has become final: disillusionment with the relationship; erosion; disengagement at which time there is probably no desire for reconciliation; physical separation; mourning period; second adolescence during which time the parent attempts to find a new place for himself to test out the world; hard work at resolution of the conflict and at adopting a new style of life. Landis (1960) has outlined some potential traumatic situations to be faced by the child of a divorce:

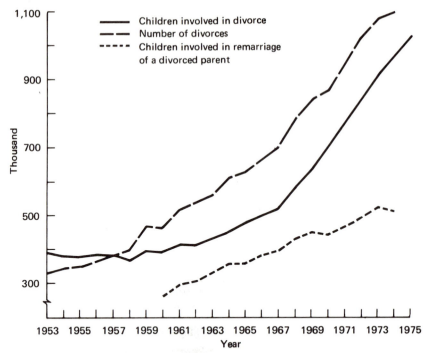

Figure 3-6. Number of divorces and estimated number of children involved in divorce and remarriage (in thousands), 1953–1975. (From *Toward a National Policy for Children*, p. 19.)

- The necessity to adjust to the knowledge that the divorce is imminent.
- The necessity to adjust to the fact of the divorce.
- The possibility that before or after the divorce the parents will make the child a weapon to fight each other.
- The necessity for redefining relationships with parents.
- The new status of being a child of divorce and the necessary adjustments with the peer group.
- The possibility of recognizing the implications of the parents' marriage failure (for their own marriageability, perhaps).
- The necessity to adjust further if the parents remarry.

In dealing with these traumas the child may see his mother enter the labor force, or move to a new neighborhood of more modest means. He may have to share parental love with step-siblings, and suffer guilt feelings if he perceives himself as having caused the divorce. He may be the victim of over-indulgence by well-meaning relatives and friends and use this as an unsound emotional crutch. He may find himself the center of conflict over visiting arrangements with the absent parent, and subjected to constant questioning about the ex-spouse during and following visits with each of them. Divorcing or divorced parents who are aware of these possible strains on their developing children can take appropriate steps to minimize them.

A long range study begun in 1970 (Kelly and Wallerstein, 1976; Wallerstein and Kelly, 1975; Wallerstein and Kelly, 1976) has centered upon the effect of divorce on children at various developmental stages. The researchers used a clinical method and dealt with children just after divorce and one year later. Quite different effects were found among younger school age children (7 to 8) as opposed to older school age children (9 to 10).

Among the younger children the most striking response to divorce of the parents was a pervasive sadness. This was the case even when there was no overt parental upset. These children seemed unable to mobilize any defenses against this stress. "While some parents planned ways to help their children cope with their distress many were too preoccupied with their own bitterness, humiliation, and plans for revenge to be supportively available" (Kelly and Wallerstein, 1976, p. 23). In addition, the younger children were frightened about the unstable family situation; they were worried that there was no safe place for them to take refuge. Some were afraid they were wanted by no one, or could themselves be "divorced" by the parent in whose custody they lived. Many of the children played out deprivation fantasies; wanted many fancy things; became increasingly selfish; displayed great hunger. These children, in contrast to preschool children, did not predominately see themselves as responsible for the divorce. Wishes for reconciliation, however, were widespread, open and enduring in these children. None of the children, contrary to some popular thought, was relieved or pleased about the divorce, even when it came after a period of conflict and unhappiness before the divorce.

In regard to the father, children had a deep sense of loss that seemed unrelated to the pre-divorce father-child relationship. Many of the children in addition to coping with their own loss, also bore the "brunt of their parents' bitterness and continuing rage toward each other as it was reenacted during the visits" (Kelly and Wallerstein, 1976).

Green (1977) suggested a number of games children and parents play during this period which can be quite hurtful to the children in their adjustment to the new situation: It's Okay—in which the parent tries to mask his feelings and put on a happy face for the sake of the child, who knows that things are wrong and needs to understand some of the changes going on; Messenger Game—in which the parents send messages to each other by the child, many times things they do not want to say to each other, and so the child gets the brunt of the anger really meant for the partner; I Spy—in which one or both parents tries to keep up with what the spouse is doing when the child comes back from a visit; Disneyland Daddy (or Mommy)—in which every visit is like two days of Christmas; You're Just Like, or Put Down—in which the parent reminds the child that all his "bad traits" come from his father or mother such as "You are stubborn just like your father," or "You are wearing make-up just like your mother—too much"; Friendly Divorce Myth—in which the parents fail to cut the spouse cords and keep only the parent cords between them which may cause continual fighting and discord which is what led to the divorce in the first place; I Wish—played by the child in which he toys with a reconciliation fantasy.

A number of boys in the Kelly-Wallerstein study requested their mother to remarry and expressed a need for a father to provide discipline and external controls. It was easier for children to express anger toward the mother, than toward the father, for causing the divorce. Even so, more anger was expressed in other ways: toward teachers, friends, siblings, or in preschool-like temper tantrums. But even more than anger, there seemed to be fear of antagonizing the all-powerful mother who drove the father away. Some children felt physically torn by conflicting loyalties. These young children, unlike older children, could not reject one parent totally and align solely with the other.

At the end of a year, the older children's responses had modified; they had a sad resigned attitude and realistically accepted the divorce as final, in contrast to younger children who continued to have fantasies of the father's return. There was, however, a strong loyalty to the father, a wish to see him more often, and a desire for the whole situation to be finalized.

> Mary, nine years old at follow-up said, "Divorce is better for my parents, but not for me . . . If my father could visit more often, I probably wouldn't mind so much." But Mary added, "He doesn't like to keep regular schedules." Asked what she might tell a child whose parents were getting a divorce, Mary said she couldn't say, "Don't worry, you'll be a lot happier," because that wouldn't be true.

Older school-age children, in contrast to younger children, were able to perceive the family disruption and the parental conflict with clarity and soberness (Wallerstein, 1976). During the counseling sessions with ten-year-olds, the authors encountered various coping devices: bravado, support seeking, conscious avoidance, denial, nervous movement, courage. These were labeled as age-appropriate ways of management of the "profound underlying feelings of loss and rejection, of helplessness and loneliness that pervaded these children" (p. 258). The children experienced great suffering as well as grief over the departure or loss of the parents. They were also fearful about what the future was for their diminished family. For some, their greater understanding of reality and the consequences of divorce added to their fears; for others, it made them more able to handle the impact of this event on their lives. There was also some evidence of being ashamed of their parents and their behavior and of the implied rejection of themselves by the departure of a parent, that caused them to perceive themselves as unloved. Some showed fear of being "next" among the people whom the parent would stop loving and would leave behind, or worried that something would happen to the one remaining parent, leaving the child totally alone.

The pain these children felt often galvanized them into organized activity which may have been linked to the attempt to overcome their sense of powerlessness and loneliness at being excluded from the action area, and to their sense of shame and rejection. Sometimes it was an attempt to undo the separation, resulting almost in harassment of the parent in order to force a reconciliation. Some of the children used this "pain energy" to master new and exciting activities. One child, whose father was in public relations, published a magazine with articles and drawings about the pending divorce and other events of interest which she sold in her school and in the community. In such ways the pain is transferred to the pleasure of achievement.

These children had feelings of intense anger, not expressed in younger children; anger directed at fathers, mothers, sometimes at both and expressed through increased temper tantrums, excessive demands and dictatorial attitudes. Most anger was directed at the parent who the child thought had initiated the divorce. The anger was present, even when the child could reconstruct scenes of conflict between the parents. In part, it is based on a moral stance that judges this action as "not good," while all the time the parents have been pushing the child to "be good." Children have a difficult time reconciling this precept with the practice, which in their eyes represents conflict. The child may thus see himself as unable to control his own conscience, and so petty stealing and lying may make their appearance.

Although few of these children felt themselves to be responsible for the divorce, in many cases they saw themselves as the one who should worry about and protect one or the other of the parents from loneliness and from the unknown future.

Blaine (1969) suggested that children, particularly those under ten, can tolerate more family discord than most adults realize; they are familiar with feelings of anger and frustration within themselves. Threat of separation, however, is quite a different problem. A deep fear that children have concerns being deserted or abandoned by a parent. Divorce makes this fear a reality; and if one parent, why not both? Disruption of the family may be necessary for many reasons, but along with attention to the adults in the situation, it is necessary to plan support systems for the children involved.

The higher divorce rate brings into focus another increasing family form—the reconstituted family. There are approximately eight million such families in America involving seven million children living with a step-parent (Duberman, 1975). In one in every eight marriages the partners have been married before; one in every five marriages is a remarriage for at least one partner.

One of the difficulties faced by the reconstituted family is its categorization by society and by itself as deviant. It exhibits greater stress, ambivalence and lack of cohesiveness than primary families.

In a study of 88 reconstituted families, Duberman (1975) looked at many facets of the relationship. All families perceived their greatest problems as "children" and "outside influences," except that middle class husbands named "money" as the greatest problem. In a study by Blood and Wolfe (1960) first-time married couples named "money" as the biggest area of disagreement; "children" second; and "in-laws" was rated third. Stepfathers were more likely to establish good relations with children than were stepmothers. Mothers spend more time with children which means more room for misunderstandings. Also, men find more social acceptance in the stepfather role than women, who still suffer from the Cinderella syndrome.

Younger stepmothers have better relationships with children than do older stepmothers. Age makes no difference for fathers, nor does education nor religious affiliation. Stepmothers had better relationships with younger children (under 13) than with older children (over 13). Again, there was no correlation for fathers in this area.

A new child in the reconstituted family strengthened the relationship with the parent and stepchild, which may have emanated from the feeling of security between the husband and wife. However, when there were two sets of children, the likelihood of a new child lessened. In families where there were better relationships between the husband and wife, there were also better parent-child relationships and better relationships between stepsiblings, as illustrated by the following percentages:

Table 3-2

	Poor to Good Parent-Child Relationships	Excellent Parent-Child Relationships
Poor to Good Husband/Wife Relationships	84%	39%
Excellent Husband/Wife Relationships	16%	61%

Forty-five of Duberman's (1975) families had two sets of children. The lower the social class, the better the relationship between siblings, which may be related to the fact that there are often more non-nuclear family members in lower class families than in middle class families. If the siblings were living together there were likely to be better relationships than if they were living apart. The relationship between the parents and child did not seem to be influenced by the kin group, but if outsiders were accepting, the stepparents were likely to attain "excellent" relations with their step-children.

Family Planning

Between 1971 and 1973 the U.S. government was authorized to spend $382 million in activities through the Office of Population Affairs. This reflects to some degree the current concern in our nation that children be planned and wanted by their parents. Welfare and other family-oriented agencies have long emphasized the importance of the individual in this area.

Although the lifelong effects of being unwanted have not been thoroughly investigated, longitudinal research in Sweden (Forssman and Thuwe, 1966) has strongly suggested that unwanted children are worse off in every respect. The study involved 120 children born to mothers whose requests for legal abortions had been denied and 120 presumably wanted children born at the same time in the same hospital or township. Data collected on the sample until the age of 21 indicated that 60 percent of the unwanted, compared to 28 of the other group, were reared either in children's homes, foster or divorced homes, or were born out of wedlock and never legitimized. Twenty-eight percent of the unwanted group received psychiatric care compared to 15 percent in the control group. More had delinquency records, 18 compared with 8 percent. More were declared unfit for military service, 15 to 7 percent. Fewer of the unwanted children attended college, 14 percent as compared to 33 percent.

Children arrive with the same needs whether they were planned or unplanned, and whether they are wanted or not has potential bearing on their development from the moment of conception. We know that maternal emotions during pregnancy affect the emotionality of the offspring, which could influence their entire life. The parental feelings of acceptance or rejection influence the development of trust in the first few days and weeks of life as well as child-rearing practices and the overall personal-social and intellectual functioning of children. The ultimate size of a family has bearing on its economic situation, life-style, and the ways in which the basic needs of each family member are met.

There were an estimated 4.7 million unwanted births in the United States between 1960 and 1965. This represents almost 20 percent of all births. In families with a large number of children, 44 percent of all fifth-born children and half of all children born in the sixth or higher positions were reportedly unwanted by one or both parents.

Several of the commonly held assumptions concerning poor people and children lack empirical support. Invalid are such ideas as all poor people

(1) want many children because child rearing makes them happy, (2) have nothing better to do than bear children, and (3) have children to uphold the masculine virility of the husband. Poor women want the same number of children as other American women: three or less. However, they become trapped by poverty. Among the poor, 42 percent of all births between 1960 and 1965 were not wanted. Among the black poor and near-poor, over half of all births were reported as unwanted (Westoff and Westoff, 1971).

Advancements in contraceptive methods could have a marked effect on this problem. The average American woman using no contraception of any type could expect to bear an average of 9 or 10 children during her reproductive lifetime. The current average is slightly over 3. In the 1965 Fertility Study three out of four women who intended to have no more children had failed to control either one or both aspects of family planning, namely the number of children desired or the desired spacing of those offspring. Only 26 percent reportedly were completely successful in determining the number and time when they would produce their children (Westoff and Westoff, 1971).

This evidence emphasizes the fact that family planning is practiced in varying degrees, depending on the religious belief, desire, knowledge, and other circumstantial factors such as health and income of the couple or woman. It is not our purpose to propose contraception, family size, nor population control for any family. Our intention is to point out that many children in our nation are illegitimate; others are battered or living in crowded conditions without adequate care and opportunity; and others within all socioeconomic levels are unwanted by parents who could or would not practice family planning.

Child Abuse

Connected with the issue of planned parenthood is the issue of child abuse, that is becoming a prominent concern in our society. Estimates of actual instances vary, but most agree that even the high estimates do not fully reveal the total problem. We must take into account not only severely battered children, but also sexually abused children, neglected (physically, morally, educationally) children, and emotionally neglected children. Gil (1970) places upper limits of physical abuse higher than others: 2,500,000 to 4,000,000 incidents in the 13,000 to 21,000 per million population.

Even more revealing of our lack of pro-child ideology than these estimates is our inability to reach closure on the issue of definition of abuse, particularly when we move beyond the "restricted phenomenon of 'physical abuse' to such operationally ambiguous concepts as 'emotional abuse' " (Garbarino, 1977). This researcher makes two telling points in his discussion. The first is that child abuse is one end of a continuum of treatment of children, rather than a qualitatively different interaction from all others. As many as 25 percent of American families are in danger of being "abuse prone" because of some combination of child rearing ignorance, unrealistic expectations concerning children's growth and behavior, and propensity toward violence.

Garbarino (1977) suggests three factors which facilitate effective adaptation to the parental role, lack of which may set up conditions leading to abuse prone families: (1) rehearsal of the role of parent or care-giver, (2) clarity about expectations, and (3) minimal life-style change. Abusing parents may have themselves been abused and in other ways may have lacked appropriate role models in parenting. There is very little opportunity for people to learn about children and parenting before they are in the midst of the no-turn-back job of raising children. Numbers of parents, particularly young ones, have little idea about how children develop or about the substantial changes in life-style they require: reordering priorities concerning gratification of one's own needs; valuing needs of child appropriately. Furthermore, we give very little support to parents in understanding the necessity of such changes, nor support in adjusting to such changes.

Garbarino's second point is that child abuse requires cultural conditions that support it. There must be cultural justification for the use of force against children, and America fulfills this condition. In a survey in 1970, 90 percent of the parents responding reported using physical force in rearing their children; in a 1965 survey, one quarter of the respondents reported spanking a child under six months of age and one half reported spanking a year-old-child; two thirds of the clergy and police surveyed in 1974 condoned spanking children. These figures need to be coupled with the idea of child abuse as a continuum and with the prevalence of "abuse-prone" families.

The second necessary condition is isolation from parental support systems, which may be brought about either because of gaps in the resources available or failure on the part of parents to use what is available. In light of the myth of the self-sufficient family, it is possible for parents to isolate themselves from the neighborhood and the larger community which is increasingly the case as stress within the family mounts. Furthermore, Bronfenbrenner (1977) reminds us that the United States is the only country in the world without a national program to provide child care for working parents, a minimum family income, and health care for families with young children. The merits of such a national policy is beyond the scope of this discussion, but the fact remains that parents need support systems to provide optimal environments for the growth of children.

Bronfenbrenner (1977) believes there is no such thing as individual or self-sufficiency, for people must support each other. This is certainly true of the children and parents within the family and the family within the community. The parent-child system is an interactional one; so is the family-community system.

Ordinal Position

No two children are born into the same family. The first child inherits a family-size of three; his first sibling helps constitute a family of four, etc. The ages of parents and siblings are different at the birth of each child. The number of other relatives is different. So no two children are born into the same family, and the position one holds in the family is a major determinant of development. Ordinal position or position within the sibling group has been a popular topic of investigation, and generalizations have been made characterizing the eldest, middle, youngest, and only child (Pepper, 1971; Ansbacher and Ansbacher, 1956; Toman, 1970; Boroson, 1971; Dinkmeyer and Dreikurs, 1963; DeFee and Himelstein, 1969). An acquaintance with these characteristics, discussed in the following paragraphs, should help one evaluate the effects of ordinal position on his own development and should assist him in recognizing the effect of ordinal position on the children with whom he lives and works.

First-borns are likely to be more like their parents than later-borns. Having become accustomed to a world of adults prior to a knowledge of the world of children, the eldest child typically has highly developed standards for himself and others. He finds rules and laws important, and he is more often the teacher's or parent's "pet." Primarily owing to his close association with parents and other adults prior to the arrival of siblings in the home, he tends to be more mature and serious than those in other ordinal positions. He has usually received more attention and help than later children merely because there were less demands on parental time during his early life. He may have also been given more responsibilities in the home and more opportunities for experience education. Often finding positive deeds a major attention source, he is usually more conscientious in his schoolwork and consequently performs better on achievement tests.

The first-born is apt to have high ambitions and organizational ability, assuming the role of leader or protector, as he finds that to help and protect others places him in a position of control, which he likes. Because he strives for perfection, he is often quite sensitive to criticism, more reactive to anxiety situations, and more prone to worry than are his siblings. He is sensitive to pain and failure. He may relish contemplation of past accomplishments far more than the anticipation of the future when he may fail. Having once been the center of attention in his family, the eldest child continues to yearn to be first—in competitive activities and in the opinion of others. He is aggressive yet conservative—torn by the desire to achieve, yet fearful that he will not succeed. He is likely to excel in such fields as education, religion, science, and literature—where seriousness, intellectual prowess, and high goals are vital. And first-borns are disproportionately represented in colleges, *Who's Who,* and the American astronaut program.

Unless the first-born perceives himself as being revered, he may suffer feelings of being unloved or neglected. Many of his characteristics are prone to contribute to his being less accepted by his peers, and as a result he may have fewer friends than those born into other ordinal positions. First-borns are the most likely to become problem children and to experience emotional maladjustment in adulthood.

Only children are a specialized type of first-borns in that they retain the "center of attention" status throughout their life in the family. They are generally characterized much the same as first-borns who have siblings. They typically compete with Father and are babied by Mother. Having no siblings with whom to form alliances against parents, onlies are likely to pit parent against parent to get their own way. They may become quite self-centered because of pampering, and feel insecure if parental anxiety over their welfare is extreme. They learn to depend on others and refuse to cooperate when they fail to get their own way. They are prone to perceive themselves as unfairly treated unless others give in to them. They may employ infantile behavior to reach goals and have a high tendency for neurotic disorders. They may worry about disappointing their parents if they are made to feel the parents' success lies in them. They may not relate well to peers because of lack of regular association with children.

Children ages 5–10 were studied to see if first-borns were indeed more fearful than latter-borns in a dental situation (DeFee and Himelstein, 1969). Dentists rated each child with regard to his cooperation, state of fright, amount of crying, and sensitivity to pain. Differences between only or first-born and latter-born children were significant at the .001 level on each of the criteria. The study supports the generalization that first-borns possess a greater amount of fear in anxiety-producing situations than do those of later-birth order.

The middle child is usually one who feels "sandwiched-in." He has never known his parents' undivided attention. Whereas in large families the middle child knows less strife and conflict, in small families he may benefit from more individual attention. He may feel unloved and abused, as he is not old enough to share the experiences of the older siblings but too old to compete with younger ones. The middle child is likely to erroneously perceive himself as being less intelligent than the first-born, and he may turn to nonacademic endeavors, such as sports or the arts, as his source of attention. He likes physical activity and is action-oriented. Although he often learns cooperation better than the first-born, a middle child is more likely to become a revolutionary. He is more practical than theoretical, and relates to such fields as social welfare, entertainment, and art. He is generally easygoing, cheerful, gentle, analytical, yet unconcerned.

The last-born child faces the risk of receiving help past the age at which he needs it, particularly if family members realize he is indeed the "caboose." In this case, he may settle into the "baby" role and expect others to serve him the rest of his life. If there is a considerable age span between him and his nearest sibling, he may take on the characteristics of an only child. Because of his "cuteness," and the fact that he is not given much responsibility, the youngest child may not develop a feeling of independence. He may feel inferior because everyone else in the family is older, stronger, and more experienced than he. He may, therefore, find his forte in being the weakest, most charming, or the "boss." The last-born may become discouraged and give up in despair, evading direct struggles with his siblings. On the other hand, he may become the most ambitious and excel all because of the many older examples he has to emulate. The proportion of last-borns among "problem children" is second only to first-borns.

In a brief review of effects of ordinal position as it relates to parent-child relationships and development of the child's personality, Martin (1975) points out several findings. First-born females are more likely than later-born females to seek an affiliative relationship with other people when stressed or anxious (Gerald and Rabbie, 1961; Schachter, 1959). First-borns tend toward adult-directed dependency and general conformance with social expectations of others (MacDonald, 1969) which is more true of first-born boys and first-born girls with younger brothers than of other ordinal positions and sex-of-sibling combinations. Mothers seem more involved with and responsive to and directing of first-borns than with later-borns (Koch, 1954; Lasko, 1954; Hilton, 1967) which may explain differences associated with ordinal position in terms of differential parental response. "The greater intrusive directiveness of mothers of only and first-born children may contribute to their children's dependency (and perhaps to conformity under stress) by depriving them of the opportunity to develop self-determined goals and practice self-initiated behavior" (Martin, 1975, p. 526).

Breland (1974) examined scores of 800,000 National Merit Scholarship participants and reported that first-borns and those of smaller families scored higher, even when socioeconomic variables were controlled. First of two children scored highest, twins lowest, and only children next to lowest. He concluded that lower achievement scores were related to twin status, larger families, later birth order, and closely spaced siblings. These findings are explained in part by the "isolation" hypothesis (Farber, 1970): children who grow up isolated from other children may have an advantage possibly because of more interaction with adults and avoidance of close relationships with siblings at low verbal levels. This does not explain findings for only children who should do better than all others. Breland suggests that first-borns played a sort of parent-surrogate or foreman role to younger children and mediated between parents and later-borns, which gave excellent opportunity for developing verbal skills.

Adams and Phillips (1972) suggest that differences in intellectual and academic functioning of first-borns as compared to later-borns disappear when motivation is held constant. First-borns more than later-borns receive early training in independence and responsibility from parents and

No particular size family nor years between children has been proven better than any other. *(Photo by Lin Mitchell.)*

more pressure to be responsible. The authors concluded that "not only do parents have higher aspirations for and expect more achievement for the first born children, but, as evidenced by their higher school motivation, first borns appear to be living up to this expectation."

Evidence suggests that later borns are more affected by older siblings than the other way round. Females are more affected by males than males by females. First borns show higher power tactics, with second and later borns showing consistent reactions, which include aggression against such power plays. In addition, first borns and only children are pushed for school grades, college graduation and to eminence by their need to achieve. In high-anxiety situations, first borns are more apt to seek the help of others, while later borns are more likely to handle their anxieties in isolation, either effectively or ineffectually. First borns in conditions of uncertainty are more likely to conform to the opinion of others. Sutton-Smith and Rosenberg (1970) suggest that these reactions may be closely linked to the mother-child interaction during infancy. The mother may have been more responsive to and "there" for the first-born and therefore reinforced the seeking help actions of the child. With later borns the mother is more relaxed and does not respond as anxiously to the child who then learns to handle more of his own frustrations.

The qualities typical of each ordinal position are minimized when the sexes of successive children tend to alternate. Spacing of six years or more allows children to develop more individually. Skillful parents who do not call attention to sibling differences and who afford each child equal opportunities to develop his talents and his individual personality will find their offspring less likely to fall into stereotypes. The greater the competition between the parents, the greater is subsequent competition among the children, particularly between the first and second children. Competition is reflected subtly by differences in attitudes, opinions, and interests.

Think Back

About your ordinal position:
Where you were.
What difference this made.
The advantages and disadvantages.
What position you wished you held.

Sibling Relationships

With the advent of the second child a phenomenon occurs which is worrisome to all family members: sibling rivalry. It has overtones of jealousy, competition, attention-getting, but it is a natural and unavoidable occurrence. With the increase in family size, the number of relationships multiplies, and the potential for disagreement, misunderstanding, taunting, and reacting grows. This quarrelsome behavior is often a source of concern for adults.

Children will not be able to analyze why they feel unhappy toward a brother or sister, but they usually will display their feelings for all to see. Some of this is normal and comes from the fact that one "lets down" at home. It seems more necessary to be on best behavior away from home than at home among those with whom one feels more at ease. Parents may not be able to determine the cause; but they should be able to handle the rivalry in a positive way in order for the family to develop mutual respect and unity while still allowing for individuality of its members.

In a study of sibling relationships (Sutton-Smith and Rosenberg, 1970), 95 fifth and sixth graders were asked: How do you get your sibling to do what you want him (her) to do? How does your sibling get you to do what he (she) wants you to do? The greatest agreement among the children was that the first born, whether male or female, is perceived both by the first-born and second-born, no matter the sex, as more bossy. Non-first borns, with the exception of boys who have older sisters, tend to use a "low-power" procedure of appealing to others outside the sibling dyad for help: crying, pouting, sulking, or threatening to tell tales or using prayer. The boy with an older sister is more apt to feel less powerlessness and use such techniques as breaking or taking things, bribery and blackmail. Boys are seen as more likely to beat up, hit, wrestle or chase a sibling to accomplish goals; girls are seen as more likely to scratch, pinch, or tattle. First-born girls are the only ones seen as explaining, asking or taking turns.

The majority did not want to change places with any sibling. In only one category was there more than one or two who expressed a desire to exchange: 8 of 23 later-born girls wanted to change places with older sisters. When asked who had most fun, males gave the edge to later borns and females thought first borns had a better position. It may be that first born children feel greater closeness to their parents and a need to carry out surrogate responsibilities. These responsibilities are more typical of female sex role requirements, so enhance the development of girls and place a stress on first-born boys.

Sibling rivalry should be accepted as normal, rooted in the desire to be the most loved. Individual attention and recognition of each child's attributes, talents, and accomplishments will help to minimize it. Encouraging children to vent their feelings of hostility in socially acceptable ways can help to drain off its manifestations.

Unemotional discussion of feelings and conflict areas in anticipation of such or after they have occurred can provide growth experiences for all. Doing things to help one another, promoting a spirit of "we-ness," reduces rivalry through understanding. Siblings perform some functions for one another which are unique, and these functions will be more easily facilitated when rivalry is minimized.

Siblings are teachers of the culture. They transmit attitudes of the family as well as factual information about the world. They provide a sense of security and pride. They serve as testing grounds for relationships and emotional behavior. They are a potential source of friends, interests, and joint endeavors. Older siblings can serve as role models, and younger ones often afford opportunity to practice an "older" role.

When children are close together, there is almost always competition for the attention and love of parents. A sibling who has just reached puberty is critical of the untidiness and boisterousness of younger children. There must be strict attention to what is fair. Even with care, there may be accusations of partiality in relation to certain actions of parents. Parents must deal with these feelings as adults and understand the anxieties of children in this regard.

Difficulties between siblings arise from many sources. When one child is "out of sorts," there is more quarreling. Siblings of the same sex have more arguments than those of opposite sex. Younger siblings want to go along with the older ones, and the older ones hate to have tagalongs.

Arguments arise over lack of respect for property rights. Children need a special spot of their very own, not to be molested by anyone. A particularly difficult situation arises when parents demand too much free baby-sitting for younger siblings. Some sort of equitable arrangement must be worked out. In addition, child society is a horizontal one. It is easier for age-mates to get along than to work out difficulties with older or younger people.

Discussing the advantage of having a twin, a fifth-grader said: "It would be nice to have someone you could really talk to and know they understand you. I have an older brother. If I talk to him about things, he thinks I am stupid." And another fifth-grader chimed in: "And your younger brother don't know what you're talking about." Nevertheless, when an outsider "attacks a family member," it is gratifying to see the ranks close—all for one and one for all.

Children need to learn to get along with people of different ages, and people within the family and outside the family. Parents and other adults are example setters in relationships. Children learn to settle their difficulties and to make concessions to the needs and weaknesses of other people, just as they learn a great many other things by watching what adults do, following their examples, and by internalizing their values. If parents are to help children get along, there must be no favoritism. "Fairness" does not always mean the same thing for every child, but it does mean that each child shall have the things he needs.

The Daily Special (Stirling, 1955) deals with this problem. In this play, two children work out their problems concerning use of the recreation room. One child has a boat to finish and the other is expecting an important, but unplanned for, out-of-town guest. Not the least important item in helping them reach a decision is the example of the father as he adjusts important plans in the light of a new situation.

Parents can see to it that each child is a contributing member of the household. It is important to children to recognize themselves as important and necessary parts of the family, responsible in part for its functioning. The child will be able to develop patterns of responsibility in this way.

But regardless of the form, the size and composition, the socioeconomic status, and the location of the family, the major tasks of parents and other adults guiding children through middle childhood cited by Duvall (1957) include being sensitive to and providing for children's growth needs; enjoying life through children's eyes; and letting the child go and grow. Those who are emotionally stable themselves will find these tasks much easier. Vicarious living through one's children places a heavy burden on a child. Overprotection and overconcern can stifle his natural growth and development. The child whose parents or teachers are not cognizant of his needs is seriously deprived.

He who grows up with opportunities to explore, to succeed, to love and be loved has a head start in the human race.

What's Next?

1. *Talking About Divorce: A Dialogue Between Parent and Child.* Earl A. Grollman. Boston: Beacon Press, 1975. A somewhat different version of this appeared in MS Magazine, 1976, October, 77–82, under the title: Talking About Divorce which was presented as a story for young children.
2. *What Is a Mother?* L. McGrath and J. Scobey. New York: Simon and Schuster, 1968.
3. "Family Roles Scale." In R. O. Blood, "A Situational Approach to the Study of Permissiveness in Child Rearing." *American Sociological Review,* **18** (1953), 84–87.
4. "An Indian's Soliloquy," B. W. Aginsky. *The American Journal of Sociology,* **46** (1940), 43–44.
5. *Growing Up in River City*, R. J. Havighurst et al. New York: Wiley, 1962: "Two Boys," pp. 16–19; "Community Conditions for the Development of Talent," pp. 25–27.
6. *Child Development Through Literature*, Landau et al. Englewood Cliffs, N.J.: Prentice-Hall, 1972: "Destroying Angel," by E. Cameron, pp. 321–327.
7. Film: *Jamie, The Story of a Sibling.* National Film Board of Canada, 680 Fifth Avenue, New York, N.Y. 10019. (29 min, b/w.)
8. Film: *The Summer We Moved to Elm Street.* National Film Board of Canada, 680 Fifth Avenue, New York, N.Y. 10019. (29 min, color.)
9. Film: *Mothers After Divorce.* Polymorph Films, 331 Newbury St., Boston, 02115. (20 min., color)
10. Film: *Stepparenting: New Families, Old Ties.* Polymorph Films, 331 Newbury Street; Boston, 02115 (25 min.; color)

Catalysts for Discussion

I. Children's Concepts of Family

According to Vicki, age 10, a mother is "a very special person. In the first place a mother 'gives up' nine months of her life in order to bring each of her children into the world. She feeds each child and keeps him warm even before he is born. After he is born she must protect him from harm and help him with all his problems until he can do these things for himself, which occurs when he gets married. But even then a mother's job is not done—she must help him with his children, since she has been through it all before and knows just what to do."

II. Test Your Ordinal Position Stereotype: Select the seven statements below which most closely describe you.

I always tried to please my parents.
I liked school when I was young.
I don't like to make decisions alone.

I tend to worry and get depressed rather easily.
I have high expectations of others.
I am more mature and serious than my peers.
Being corrected when I was young did not bother me much.
I like large parties and opportunities to meet new people.
I like to be told that I am loved.
I'm rather good in the creative arts.
I try to circumvent rules whenever possible.
I have a lot of friends.
I am poor in spelling, and my handwriting is difficult to read.

(If you checked a majority of the first six statements, you are indicating traits typically associated with first-born or only children; if you checked a majority of the last seven, you are indicating traits typically associated with latter-borns. If your ordinal position within your family is contrary to that indicated by your responses to the items, there are probably some very good explanations in terms of skilled parents, spacing of children, or sibling sex differences.)

III. ABC's: One Version.
   The basic idea for this piece is from Suzanne Volin LaBreque

A is   for After, as in after supper, after I read the paper, after your nap. Father is always going to play after.

B is   for Before, as in before you come to supper, before you get any dessert, before you go out to play. Mostly things you don't want to do but have to.

C is   for Can't, as in can't you stop that singing? Can't you turn down the radio? Can't you ever come in when you're called? Means you can and you darn well better.

D is   for Don't, as in don't let me catch you doing that again. Don't come in the house with those muddy shoes; don't expect me to do it for you again; don't talk to your mother like that; don't you ever hit him again; don't lie to me. Most sentences begin with don't.

E is   for Either, as in either you eat your spinach—or clean up your room—or get your homework done—or else. Or else is never quite defined but it sounds dark and foreboding. One is never quite sure.

F is   for Fair, as in fair is fair—there are rules, you know. Funny how nobody ever stops to think about what's not fair—like what jobs you have to do or where you get to go or having to go to bed at the same time as your little brother.

G is   for Get Moving! And that means move—but just not anywhere. It may mean wash up or take the trash out or run an errand. If you missed out on the first part—you're in trouble.

H is   for How, as in how in the world did you tear your shirt, or scratch your face, or forget your coat? One never really has the answers to such questions.

I is   for If, as in if you do that again you'll be sorry. Another one of those vague nameless threats—but, of course, sometimes you *are* sorry!

J is   for Just, as in just try that again if you dare. It is usually said with no explanation, but most of the time it means be careful where you dare to do it again.

K is   for Keep Out, as in keep out of the cooky jar; keep out of the living room; keep out of the kitchen when the floor is clean or while I'm cooking.

L is   for Leave, as in leave your brother alone—never mind that it is your brother who is doing the bothering and it's you whose being bothered. Sometimes you just can't explain or nobody will let you.

M is   for Messy, as in your room, or your pants after football practice on the way home from school, or the way you comb your hair. Sometimes it's just the way you are.

N is   for No. So many No's that it's simpler not to ask about anything. Just do it. Maybe nobody will ask about it.

O is   for Old, as in you are too old to act like that, or old enough to know better, or older than your little brother so you need to set an example. You are never old enough to do the things you want to do—just the things other people want you to do.

P is   for Put, as in put your things away, or put your jacket on even when it isn't cold, or put the dog out even when it *is* cold out, or put your jacks away because the baby might swallow them. Why can't things be out where you can see them and find them and think about them? They always have to be put on hooks or in boxes or up on shelves.

Q is   for Quiet! Seems everything is noisy some days: bouncing a ball against the garage door; talking on the telephone; tossing rocks across the roof; listening to records— especially the good ones. How come you can't decide what's noisy and what's quiet?

R is   for Ready, as in aren't you ready yet? You'll be late for school. You can't rush all the time, you have to stop and think and look and try things out. You just forget about what time it is.

S is   for Stop. You wish sometime somebody would say go instead of Stop. What are you supposed to do when you stop? To stop is to nothing and you can't just "nothing" for very long at a time—you need to "something."

T is   for Times and Told, as in how many times have I told you to empty the trash or clean your room or mow the yard or clear the table. You wonder what would happen if you had the answer to that one! It usually concerns things that are easy to forget.

U is   for Unless, as in unless I hear you practicing, or unless I see an improvement in your grades, then . . . and the sentence falls. It's not fair to be grounded for a week just because you hate to practice. It seems all out of proportion.

V is   for Vegetables, as in eat your vegetables if you want ice cream, or want to invite a friend over, or to go play or go to a birthday party.

X is   for Xcuse, as in that's no excuse for breaking his toy, for fighting, for being late, or lying, or cheating

Y is   for Young, as in you're too young to stay up for the late TV show, or to plan an overnight with your friend, or to be out after dark or to see a groovy movie. You wonder when you will not be too old or too young—what is the just right age— surely not right now.

Z is   for ZERO, as in your allowance will be zero this week because you disobeyed, or made a C, or didn't take out the garbage. ZERO is also what a child feels like when he lives with this alphabet.

Beyond the Classroom Experiences

1. Ask some of McInnis' questions to 5–12-year-olds. Compile their responses and compare with her data.
2. Interview two or three fathers of middle childhood people concerning their feelings about and ways of fulfilling the father role, what they do to strengthen the father-child relationship, and how their wives help them in this regard.
3. Conduct a group interview with children concerning their view of adults. Or ask several children to write a story or an essay on the subject.
4. List LeMasters' myths of parenthood and ask several parents to mark them true or false. Ask some of your college-age friends to do likewise. See if experience plays any role in this regard. Discuss the myths with parents to see how they have learned through experience.
5. Ask children with working mothers about this phenomenon. Have them note the advantages and disadvantages and state their feelings on the topic. If possible, also talk with their mothers about this practice. Note provisions made for childcare in the mother's absence as well as the kinds of things the mothers do with their children during their nonworking hours. Compare this latter listing with what nonworking mothers do with their children.
6. Attend a meeting of Parents Without Partners to see the kinds of concerns and problems faced in one-parent families.
7. Discuss with parents how they deal with sibling rivalry. Compile their suggestions.

Chapter 4

The Impact of School

This chapter is designed to help you:

- understand the importance of preparation for school.
- see the importance of strengthening home-school communication.
- understand how school is perceived by children.
- delineate the roles assumed by the school teacher of middle childhood people.
- examine briefly some of the approaches to the education of children ages 5 to 12.
- recognize the current school-related issues affecting children and their families.

A Parent's Soliloquy

I guess all along I've known that today would come, but why did it have to come so soon, and why did the world have to be in such a shape when it was time for my son to take his first step alone in it? Here he stands, dressed in his favorite new jeans and shirt, his hair all brushed, eyes sparkling with excitement, a brand-new plaid book satchel in hand and on his lips the words of wonder: "I'm ready for school, Mom!"

Only time will verify his assertion, for who ever knows when a child is ready to leave the security of home and family to face the larger scene. But he is confident—he pulls away from me—he's on his way to school.

Until now I have been his teacher, the maker of rules, the healer of hurts, the dietician, coach and helping hand for street-crossing. And he has been my willing student. Today the world takes over some of these duties from me. May it deal with him gently yet teach him thoroughly.

He still has much to learn: that the individual, though a free spirit, is subject to the welfare of the group; that the majority, though often in command, is not always right; that the best in life is not always bought with money; that one need not be famous to be great, nor rich to be happy. That to be tender or to laugh at oneself is not a sign of weakness but of strength. That success is elusive both in definition and attainment. May he somehow understand that learning never ends, that love never really loses, that long-range goals and the anticipation of their achievement are worth the waiting and the work.

I have tried to teach my son the necessity of rights and responsibilities. As he steps into the world may his respect for them grow, his understanding of them increase, and his commitment to them be unselfish and unwavering. I've tried to instill in him an attitude toward work that he will give it his best and finish what he begins. There will be times when the job becomes tiring, tedious or difficult, and he is tempted to give up or to accept compromising standards of workmanship.

I have tried to teach him the need for mutual respect in his relations with others, to live the golden rule and the silver rule, to forgive and admit when he has been wrong. As he moves away from me, he somehow has to learn that all men are not honest, nor beautiful, friendly nor intelligent. At the same time he must remember that all men are of worth because of what they are—not because of what they do. He will need help in looking for the best in each and in building caring-helping relationships, in revealing himself to others.

I have tried to help him see the need for a healthy body and ways to keep himself physically fit. As his horizons expand, I hope he will remember the necessity for rest and the need for exercise. That he will know a variety of bounties from Nature's garden, pasture, field and stream. That he will be strong in resisting temptations to harm himself in pleasure-seeking and physical abuse.

I have shared with my son my own sense of wonder and joy and peace as I try to understand the universe and the Supreme Being which in our family we call God. These beliefs will be challenged in a hundred ways in his lifetime, but perhaps he will remember that nothing is impossible and that there is room in life for both faith and logic.

Today the world becomes my son's teacher, allowing him to grow into the man he could never become under my tutelage alone. So he goes forth

The first day of school marks a new beginning and an expanding world. (Photo by Lin Mitchell.)

this morning to walk new paths, meet different people, to reach for himself as he can become.

"Goodbye, son. Have a good day at school."

Education: The State of the Art

America's free public school system, with attendant compulsory education laws, has been called one of America's greatest contributions to the world. The school has been looked to as the salvation of democracy, the solver of social and economic problems, the inspirer of greatness in our children. Yet in the past decade the growing criticism of this institution has been a boom in private schools, parent groups making more specific demands, legislative bodies placing the school under closer scrutiny, teachers striking in behalf of their students' welfare, students picketing, the emergence of an idea that educational vouchers be issued by the government to allow parents to "shop" for the best possible education for their children. Americans have experienced a new awakening to the potential the school holds for their children and are determined that that potential be realized to its

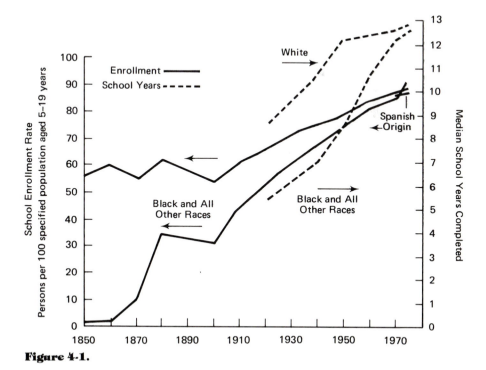

Figure 4-1.

fullest extent. Formal schooling is still recognized as one of the major ways children learn, and the age at which children begin group education is declining steadily. But such myths as that teachers know and children don't know and that the schoolroom is the only place to learn are being exploded daily.

Our nation is seeing a rise in experimental and innovative educational strategies. Teacher preparation today is encompassing more areas of study than in former years. More supportive personnel for teachers, from supervisers and consultants to aides who grade papers and supervise the lunch hour, are being made available to free the teacher for performance of the duties her position demands. Educators are recognizing the increasing need for individualized instruction and attention because of varying motivational levels and abilities of students. They are admitting that to teach only toward the average and to do so in an authoritarian, sterile way may not produce maximal results in terms of student growth and achievement.

School: A Whole New World

One first-grader revealed his exuberance on entering his classroom the first day when he exclaimed, "Oh, boy! A whole new world to mess up!" But the first few days may bring some feelings of doubt and wonder too. There is always someone who cries for his mother; and there are probably hosts of others who would like to. For it occurs to the child upon entering school that he may forever be cut off from his family, that he may never see Mother and Daddy again, that they may forget to pick him up after school. There are many strange new people and new rules. The bathroom facilities may even be strange, and probably the lunch line is a new routine for many. There is a new "boss," the teacher, and she may employ totally different techniques for guiding children than the parents have used. There is usually a rest time that can be disconcerting if one is not used to lying down in the middle of the day. There is the need to sit in one's seat and raise a hand to gain recognition in many classrooms. There are things one must remember to do, and not to do; eventually the teacher will expect the child to be able to concentrate on a particular task, which may be a new experience. School is certainly not just a new world to mess up—but a world in which to learn and function.

Mitch, a second-grader, came home from school with this observation: "There are about two million things I don't know, and I've got to learn them all in the second grade." He was elated with the prospect of the great adventure ahead. It is too bad that for some children there is never this exhilaration in relation to school activities, or that it is stifled. Too often, sixth-graders have developed a ho-hum attitude about the whole process.

In his recent book, Bloom proposes it is possible for 95 percent of students to learn all the school has to teach them, at about equal level of mastery. He contends 1–3 percent cannot master the material, and 1–2 percent have superior learning abilities. He believes school learning success is highly alterable under appropriate learning conditions, and that past experiences, motivation to learn, and cues about what to learn, participation opportunities, and reinforcement and feedback are the necessary qualities for instruction. Bloom contends better learners are less influenced by the method used to teach them whereas poor learners are highly susceptible to the specific approach. He sees children entering school fairly equal in their feelings and attitudes about the process, the subjects to be studied, and about themselves in relation to school (Harvey and Horton, 1977).

Preparation for school entrance is a process which begins very early in life. Children's attitudes toward learning and even formal education are learned in subtle comments, observations, experiences they encounter in their family. The mass media also have some impact on their concepts of education. Older siblings and children in their neighborhood teach them about school. Likewise, certain knowledge and abilities necessary for successful school entrance are gained primarily through the family's efforts.

White (1975) summarized vast data relative to the role of family in education in these words: "the informal education that families provide for their children makes more of an impact on a child's total educational development than the formal educational system. If a family does its job well, the professional can then provide effective training. If not, there may be little the professional can do to save the child from mediocrity. This grim assessment is a direct conclusion from the findings of thousands of programs in remedial education, such as Head Start and Follow Through programs." (p. 4) He emphasizes the great importance of experiences and environment during the *very first year of life* with regard to learning success throughout life. He points out that too many families ignore infants most of their first year, missing the vital opportunity to impact on their potential in positive, meaningful ways through stimulation, psycho-motor involvement and association with adults.

The home contributes to school success by fostering a continuing, concentrated, intimate relationship between the child and the parent(s). By nurturing the verbal dimension of his development through reading, talking and encouraging the child in self expression, school readiness and success are facilitated. When the home activities are congruent with school demands, there is effective carry-over: a time and a place to study, help with work when necessary, support for academic efforts, and interest in school-related activities. The cultural level of the home also contributes to school success: when children are encouraged to read and discuss and are able to attend cultural activities, school work is more meaningful and successful (Kifer, 1977).

A statewide study in New York of factors affecting school performance at all grade levels revealed that 58 percent of the variation in student achievement could be predicted by three factors: broken homes, over-crowded housing and the educational level of the head of the household (Report of N.Y. State Commission).

White and his associates (1973) conducted research with 1,100 pre-schoolers to determine the characteristics of a competent six-year-old. They found twelve competencies which distinguished the least talented children from the most talented ones, and concluded these qualities would help children achieve success in school. All can be learned at home.

Some of the qualities were social in nature. These included using adults as resources and gaining their attention in acceptable ways. The talented children typically moved toward or touched an adult or showed something to them to gain their attention. They used adults as resources in meeting their own needs by gesturing or making requests. The competent children were able to show both affection and hostility to adults and peers. They used friendly comments, statements of dislike, hugging and physical resis-tance with both groups. They were able to compete with peers, to play the leader or follower role as the situation demanded. They showed pride in their personal accomplishments and possessions. They freely expressed their desire to grow up through their comments or adult role-playing.

The other group of qualities were non-social competencies. The talented children showed extensive language, vocabulary and grammar mastery. They demonstrated intellectual competence in their ability to sense disso-nance and to note discrepancies. They were able to plan and carryout multi-step activities; and they were able to do two things at one time, such as working and talking. These qualities may constitute some standard by which to judge the readiness of children for school entrance. All can be ob-served in the everyday repertoire of children.

Among the skills which facilitate school success and happiness are the ability to share, take turns and help others. Whereas the preschool child is not cognitively ready to thoroughly master these tasks, he can learn through habit to consider the rights and feelings of others. A basic respect for persons in authority is another requisite for good adjustment to the school setting. Ability to follow directions and obey rules reduces the need for correction by the new adults the child encounters. Confidence in him-self and his ability to function apart from his parents facilitates the child's school performance. Familiarity with the materials with which he will work, such as books, crayons, and games makes the transition easier. Ex-perience concentrating on small activities for extended periods and com-pleting a task are other boons to success in school work. Exposure to rou-tine, time structuring and sequencing provides an advantage in formal learning.

Most children anticipate school entrance. Those fortunate enough to at-tend schools which are child-centered and sensitive to their needs and abil-ities and whose families support and encourage their learning efforts, may maintain a fair degree of excitement throughout their formal educative process.

Varied Approaches

Children aged 5–12 are experiencing varying degrees of achievement and personal fulfillment through a host of innovative educational adventures. Some representative ones and a brief description of them follows: (Smith, et al, 1972)

Grass Roots, Independent, Parent-initiated, and Alternative Schools. Schools operate outside the regular public school framework. Some are sponsored by the school systems to meet parent demands; most are community or parent-sponsored. Attendance, curriculum, staffing, materials and equipment provisions, goals and clientele often vary considerably from the public school classroom.

Educational Parks. Expensive campuses house a number of school populations from ghetto and middle class neighborhoods and feature superior services and facilities. Students are selected by computer from applicants.

Schools today employ a host of innovations in an attempt to make learning more effective. (Photo by Rick Coleman.)

Middle Schools. Designed to serve children in grades 5 or 6 through 8, these schools typically feature team-teaching, some divergence from the traditional elementary approaches to education (such as changing classes), social activities geared to the prepubescent and pubescent age child.

Open Classrooms. This system employs a more sympathetic approach with a more informal atmosphere for learning.

Non-graded Schools. This program is designed to eliminate problems of non-promotion by fostering the continual progression of each child without set levels or grade levels. Children are grouped homogeneously according to their instructional level in each particular subject matter area. There is more individuality of learning possible and the "no failure" feeling is encouraged.

Extended School Year. This system includes the operation of the school on a 210-day-school-year for better plant utilization and/or completion of 12 years of education in 11 years. In some districts children rotate vacation periods for maximal use of the facility. In others they attend more total days to achieve early graduation.

Modular Scheduling. The advantage of modular scheduling is that it allows for flexibility in time-use within the school day to provide longer periods for projects or laboratory classes and shorter periods for other activities. It may allow children to experience more electives or more in-depth study or individual tutoring or club activities.

Behavioral Objectives. The practice of establishing evaluative criteria according to what a child will be able to do, under given conditions and to a specific extent is the basis of this system. Ideally, these objectives allow children to know better what the educational expectations of him are, hence, fulfill them more fully.

Alternative Grading—Non-traditional Reporting of Student Performance. Written profiles, notation of progress in conjunction with needs for improvement, and/or parent-teacher conferences are used. In some instances, grading is based on achievement of specific objectives rather than on comparison with peers.

Computer Assisted Instruction (CAI). Machines are used for student retrieval of information on tapes or in computer banks. An NEA survey revealed that only one percent of teachers used this approach. It is impersonal and quite expensive.

The Inquiry Method. An inductive approach to education, in which the student discovers facts as opposed to being told them per se is the basis of this method.

Accountability-Responsibility. Documentation of student accomplishment relative to time, funds expended, and personnel involved is employed.

Individually Prescribed Instruction—(IPI). Units designed for individual students to allow self-pacing, initiation and direction, self motivation and evaluation are used. They are designed to help solve the problem of individual differences in a given group.

CHARACTERISTICS OF MIDDLE SCHOOL STUDENTS AGES 11-13 (FENWICK, 1977)

- Crucial time for synthesizing values and attitudes of self
- Fundamental questions about personal and social issues are being answered
- Turbulent, shifting and often conflicting emotions = need forum for discussion of fears
- Moody, lack of self-confidence-Who Am I? = curriculum to reaffirm personal worth
- Conformity to peers and intolerance of others = multicultural education
- Unpredictable reaction to adult affection = variety of adults available
- Rapid physical growth and skewed responses = differentiated assignments and independent study
- Testing of home values = values clarification opportunities
- Ability to grasp moral and ethical concepts and social responsibility awareness
- Clear sex role and heterosexual interests = guidance in sex role contradictions
- Transition from childhood to adolescence = empathetic instructional techniques

The Roles of a Teacher

In addition to home preparation for school, there are other factors that influence the child's performance and happiness there. A primary one is the teacher's attitudes and actions day by day. Unfortunately, all persons entering the educational field have not been well prepared, personally suited to teaching, nor happy in their occupation. And regardless of the physical facilities of the school, the type of teaching materials available, the class size and schedule, the teacher is the main component in a child's educational experience. If the teacher is not well adjusted and does not have the welfare of each child in the class in mind as plans are made and executed, learning and growth will not be maximized. It is the teacher, more than the physician, the attorney, the journalist, or the superstar, who has the best opportunity to inspire and prepare the leaders of tomorrow for the nation and the world.

What, then, are the primary functions the teacher is expected to fulfill in enhancing the growth of the children? She becomes the substitute mother for younger children and a behavior model for those of all ages. She deals with values and attitudes. She is charged with fostering all aspects of growth and development and is expected to understand children's motivation. Through her teaching, children should learn not only how to read but how to reason; not only what people in faraway lands eat but how to select foods in the school cafeteria; not only how to play ball but how to win and how to lose—good sportsmanship. The teacher is expected to call forth through her skill and ingenuity the inner-motivation of her students and to evaluate the effects of this motivation in terms of performance and learning. Likewise, she can help children to see the need for evaluation and foster in them the ability and desire for self-assessment which will facilitate their progress in school, and in all of life. This latter function is sometimes hampered by rigid grading scales imposed by the system on the teaching-learning process. The teacher is responsible for planning meaningful learning experiences for students.

Although often unprepared for the task, teachers are expected to help children with their personal problems—whatever they are. Although they are not therapists they can, through referral, cooperation, and encouragement, aid in the efforts of such specialists as the school psychologist, the speech therapist, the school nurse, and the guidance counselor who are helping to remedy specific difficulties that interfere with a child's normal adjustment and success in the educational setting. It is the role of the teacher to minister to certain special needs of the new child, the transient child, the handicapped child, the behavior problem, the child of poverty, the gifted, the slow-learner (Rogers, 1969).

The new child may long for security within the strange peer group. The teacher may be able to provide this as she gives him opportunities to join group work, to demonstrate some special ability, to assume a definite responsibility that will contribute to the class success.

The transient child may suffer insecurity from a number of moves and perhaps, in addition, the stigma of being poor if his family are migrant workers. He may exhibit feelings of indifference or hopelessness toward his schoolwork. The teacher can help him set goals which he can reasonably fulfill within the relatively short period he will be in her class. She can call on him to share with the class the experiences of having lived in many areas of the nation. She might also be able to reduce the shock of his transfer by corresponding with his previous teacher and contacting the school to which he will move.

By accepting the limitations of the handicapped child while still setting high expectations for him, the teacher may be able to minimize the apprehension of this student and that of other students toward him. To treat him as far as possible like all the others in class and encourage his participation to some degree in all activities may help alleviate his feeling of being different or special.

To understand the cause of the undesirable behavior on the part of habitual troublemakers in the group is the teacher's task. Background circumstances or experiences as well as physical and emotional composition are usually behind behavior problems in the classroom. Relating to these children in a meaningful way—through assignment of special responsibilities within the classroom, provision of work materials that are interesting to them, and helping them to feel successful and accepted in the group—usually contributes to the solution of such problems.

Knowlege of the life circumstances of the child of poverty can go a long way in making his school experience meaningful and successful. Coupled with physical impairments because of poor nutrition and health care, lack of intellectual skills because of language deficiency and parents who are poor information sources, and often a home in which there is continual noise and no place to study, the low-income child is not usually as motivated by competition and desire for good grades as are middle class children. The use of short-term tangible rewards which are valued by his peer group helps improve his school performance (Irelan, 1967). The teacher who transmits to the poverty child her belief in him, who provides opportunities for his experiences to be meaningful in class study, and who treats him as a child—not a poor child—may be able to build his self-image sufficiently to motivate him to do his best.

Another function that many teachers assume is helping parents understand children better. Often a child's malajustment stems from problems at home because of lack of parent understanding. Teachers possess knowledge of growth and development which could aid parents, and most parents are eager to learn. Although education for the parenting role is not formalized in many communities, there is an ongoing concern for this type of help in the nation. It occurs in such informal situations as the parent-teacher conference, the PTA program meeting, and the parent study group at the community center. And teachers are called upon to conduct them all from time to time.

There is a growing emphasis on interaction between the teacher and parent. This is an opportunity for parent education and also for teacher education. A conference with a parent is a two-way street, in which the teacher both shares what she knows about the child and gains new insight into the child's behavior and motivation from the parent. So you're going to confer with a parent. Shall the meeting be a confrontation or one of mutual exchange?

Many parents feel apprehensive about discussing their child with a professional, even prior to an invitation to do so. They desire any suggestions to be gained thereby, but fear even helpful comments will reflect on their parenting abilities. The way the invitation comes, and the wording, can help set the tone for the meeting. If it is a written communication brought home by the child or a personal phone call, parents will be looking for clues that indicate the kind of trouble their child is in. If they can be helped to see that other parents are also being invited to confer, it should help. If they can have some choice of times and be given a brief idea of the purpose of the meeting, their fears may be somewhat allayed. When the invitation is extended to both parents or guardians, it may encourage them to attend together and help them feel more united. For example:

Dear Mr. and Mrs. Montgomery,

Each year many parents express interest in an informal conference to discuss how their children are doing in school. I am now planning these opportunities and hope you will select and indicate on the tear-off below the date and hour when we might have a chance to review some of Kevin's work in the fourth grade. We could get together either here at school or in your home, depending upon your wishes. Please let me hear from you soon.

Cordially,

In some schools the child being discussed is invited to participate in the conference. This prevents anxiety on his part that the teacher and parents are ganging up on him.

If the parents choose to come to school, it is well that they are not kept waiting while other parents are conferring within ear range. One mother, asked to sit outside a small office where another mother was conferring, told of her fear that the next parent would overhear test results and behavioral problem analysis just as she was hearing the two-way conversation inside. In planning the physical facilities for a parent conference, it would help put the parents more at ease if the teacher is seated next to them at a table rather than across a desk. It is helpful if there can also be available concrete examples of items to be discussed, such as test papers, artwork, or other work samples. It is well to allow work samples to be taken home to share with an absent parent.

The opening words of the conference should be friendly and positive. The teacher should have planned the main points she wishes to discuss. Those who have done insufficient planning for such a conference often blurt out criticisms and never get around to pointing out the many fine qualities of the child.

The goal of the conference should be an honest, helpful exchange of information and ideas. It should not be to convince the parent his child is brilliant, doomed, perfect, or impossible. The total welfare of the child as well as the pride of parents should be kept in mind.

Putting the parent on the defensive is to be avoided. The teacher in a church-related school relied on the child's account of Daddy's drinking and confronted the father in these words: "I understand you have an alcohol problem."

Time for the parents to bring up questions or items for discussion is vital. Teachers should encourage the parents to help explain the causes of behavior or learning problems encountered by the child so that together they may plan ways to help him. Often parents will want to know what they can do at home to correlate with the school's attempts to foster the child's growth. One teacher suggested that an elementary child who found losing difficult to bear be given more opportunities at home to play board games in order to practice, among his family, being a good loser. Another recommended the child be encouraged to eat breakfast each day in order to increase his attention and energy in the classroom.

A parent suggested that the teacher join her in helping the child to see acceptable ways of expressing displeasure and anger. Another discussed a kidney operation that made it necessary for her child to be frequently allowed to use the restroom.

Extreme care should be taken in sharing and interpreting test results or other evaluative measure with parents. One teacher told a parent that his child was lacking in moral development, substantiating this "fact" by reporting the child used the playground shovel as a gun and threw sand, both of which were against the school rules. Another teacher interpreted a child's desire to look out the window as a sign he was not using his free time well. Many times parents are unduly upset when their child's IQ score is not as high as their own or as that of their neighbor's child. IQ score should preferably not be shared at all. If grades are used, the teacher should be able to explain the system in effect, assuring the parent that any system is imperfect and that factors other than basic worth and ability may be causing the child to perform below average. It would also be helpful to impress on parents that being average and being a follower rather than a leader are quite all right.

The conference should also end on a postive note, perhaps with the mention of a future conference to discuss the success of any plans jointly made by the parents and teacher. A follow-up note thanking the parents for their interest is another way to encourage future cooperation.

Teachers should be mindful of their appearance on days of parent conference. Obviously they should be neatly groomed but they should refrain from overdressing, since dress is one factor that can easily put a parent ill at ease. If visiting in the child's home, the teacher should accept any hospitality offered, such as refreshments, because many families feel refusal of such courtesies symbolizes a superior attitude.

TELL THE PRINCIPAL TO SPEAK ENGLISH

Dear Ann Landers: You are supposed to be a smart cookie. Can you figure this out? I bet my wife ten dollars you'd flunk just as we did.

The parent of a Houston high school pupil received a message from the school principal concerning a special meeting on a proposed new education program.

The message read: "Our school's cross-graded, multi-ethnic, individualized learning program is designed to enhance the concept of an openended learning program with emphasis on a continuum of multiethnic, academically enriched learning, using the identified intellectually gifted child as the agent or director of his own learning. Major emphasis is on cross-graded, multi-ethnic learning with the main objective being to learn respect for the uniqueness of a person." The parent responded: "Dear Principal: I have a college degree, speak two foreign languages and know four Indian dialects. I've attended a number of county fairs and three goat ropings but I haven't the faintest idea as to what the hell you are talking about." It was signed: "Two Dummies in Fort Worth."

Dear Friends: I don't think you are dummies. That principal needs to learn how to express himself in simple terms.

What he means is: "We are planning a program for students of all races which we hope will encourage the brighter ones to move ahead at their own speed. Grading will be geared to the learning level of the student. In this way we hope to teach and grade each student according to his ability to learn." P.S. Pay your wife the ten dollars. Or better yet, send it to your local Heart Association.

The behavior of childen in school is thought to be highly dependent on the behavior of their teachers. Those who use force are more likely to elicit greater student resistance, whereas those who employ democratic techniques tend to foster cooperation, initiative, and interest in their students. Most children do best when their teachers are well prepared, know their subject matter, use democratic methods, are interested in their students, and are not overly concerned with their own problems. In contrast, children cannot experience optimal growth when their teachers are rigidly authoritarian, hostile, or unresponsive to student needs, indecisive, poorly prepared, or too preoccupied with their own problems (Mussen, Conger, and Kagan, 1969).

Teacher attitude, behavior mode, stance, and performance flavor, all affect the children they teach (Goldberg, 1966). Their classroom control, approach to dissemination of content, and the interpersonal climate they create and maintain are important factors in learning. Studies of teacher characteristics and processes show variation in pupil achievement in class is related to teacher performance. A particular teacher affects different pupils differently. One study considered the relationship of teacher personality to achievements of four distinct types of learning. Teachers were identified as either turbulent (a concern for ideas, inconsistency, sloppy in routine), self-controlling (a concern for people), or fearful (anxious, insecure, disorganized and variable). Students were grouped as conformers, opposers, waverers, or strivers. It was found that conformers and strivers' achievement was unaffected by teacher style. They did well regardless. However, the opposers and waverers performed best with the self-controlling teacher. The fearful teachers were the least effective of all. The turbulent ones succeeded best teaching math and science to all the learning groups.

First-graders randomly selected from classrooms of ten impulsive and ten reflective teachers were tested in the fall and spring for the tendency to be impulsive or reflective (Yando and Kagan, 1968). Children's score changes were related to the tempo of the teacher: those taught by experienced reflective teachers showed the greatest increase in response time during the year. This effect was more marked for boys than girls. It is possible that the increase in response time was mediated both by modeling effects and direct reinforcement. As a practical application, it was suggested that the teacher tempo be tailored to the child's tempo; for example, placing extremely impulsive boys with teachers who are temperamentally reflective to promote the adoption of a more reflective disposition and perhaps facilitate reading progress.

When asked to tell why they dislike school, children are likely to mention the teacher. As children grow older there seems to be increasing dissatisfaction with teachers, either related to their personality or teaching ability. This is due in part to peer pressure to be *for* children and *against* adults!

At the elementary school level children tend to judge teachers more on the basis of personality, mentioning qualities such as sympathetic and cheerful, neat, fair, enthusiastic, understanding, and willing to join in play activities as desirable traits. The relationship between teacher characteristics and student academic and social progress has been investigated. In one study (Heil and Washburne, 1961) it was found that children made the geatest academic progress under the self-controlled teacher who is methodical, feels secure when things run smoothly, is not interested in putting herself in the limelight, is sensitive to the reactions of others, and executes others' ideas effectively. Growth in students' "friendliness" also was significantly greater under this type of teacher. The least academic growth was measured in students taught by fearful teachers who tend to be helpless, dependent, and defensive, afraid of doing the wrong thing and prone to stick by the rules no matter whom it hurts. Neither does students' friendliness increase as much when taught by the fearful or turbulent teacher. This teacher was characterized as not identifying closely with others; having little interest in orderliness; mainly interested in uninhibited and unconventional thinking, imagining, and conjecturing; not empathetic or warm; blunt, tense, and unpredictable. In the same vein, hostile and dominating teachers generally appear to affect pupil adjustment adversely. Examples of dominating behavior include the use of force, commands, threats, shame, blame, and rigid insistence on conformity.

Ideas expressed about what teachers should be like were collected by the Wichita City Teachers' Association (1967–68) and gathered for publication under the title *The Teacher and I*. Some of them follow:

- She should be "honest," really honest, pointing out mistakes and assuring herself that "I" can reach the goals set for me. She could help me by being consistent. She could help by allowing me to experiment with my own abilities.
- I would like to be free to think for myself. When I forget I wish my teacher would allow me to think about why I forgot. Learning about myself is important to me.
- I want to know that my teacher loves me, that my mistakes are acceptable, that she will correct my mistakes, but will still like me. If my teacher makes a mistake I still like her. If I'm always scared of making mistakes I may not want to try a lot of things.
- I would be encouraged to do better if I knew the teacher liked me. If she would just listen to me and not jump to conclusions before she finds out all the facts. If

I knew she trusted me and had faith in me I would probably be good and work harder. I want her to have faith in me until she has good reasons for losing her faith in me. I would like for her to give me encouragement when I do something well or when I need encouragement. I would like to be reprimanded and corrected when I need it—in short, I would work much harder if I knew that someone was really interested in me.

Over 1,000 children attending schools designated by administrators as "liked by kids" were interviewed to see why. Fifty-three percent said it was because of the teachers! "They are nice . . . not mean . . . concerned . . . smart . . . happy . . . good and fun to be with." Other people who seem to make school enjoyable were mentioned: "The principal comes into our room often" "Secretaries, lunchroom personnel and custodians are nice."

Curriculum aspects mentioned by the respondents are represented in these comments: "You learn in a fun way- there is not pressure." "You don't have to be quiet all the time"; "I can work at my own speed." "There are lots of choices and freedom" "The work is just right for us."

The uniqueness of the school was another important dimension in its likeableness: Fairness, Unity, and school spirit were often mentioned. Children said "hardly anyone gets in a fight." "I can find a quiet place when I want it." "It's like a big family." "You can leave the lunchroom anytime."

Finally, there were things about the school which contributed to self enhancement and personal worth. "Sometime each day this school tries to make each child feel 10 feet tall." "You don't have to be popular to make it." "You don't have to do everything that everyone else has to do." (Hicks and Buhler, 1977).

Current Issues in Education

There are many problems to solve and decisions to make if the school is to move children toward their maximum potential with optimum effectiveness. The development of children is affected by the attitudes, positions and actions of their families, teachers, administrators, legislators and community leaders with respect to these issues.

Financing

Since 1971 educational spending has surpassed defense spending in the U.S.; in 1975, it was $120 billion. That year there were 33,199,000 American children between ages 5 and 13. The average expenditure per pupil by states was $1,112, with a range from $983 to $2,241. With approximately 10 percent of the children attending private schools, a rise in the Southeast since 1968 and a decline in the Northeast (HEW, 1976), it would seem that public education's financial picture should have improved. But costs of educational facilities, materials and services continue to rise. The host of teacher unions picketing schools for more lucrative contracts, the school districts closing their doors mid-year due to budget depletions, and the failing school bond issues and elections to raise the millage attest that the mere monetary sustenance of public education is in serious jeopardy.

There has been a call for more accountability in education, for a reduction of administrators, supervisers, and of such subjects as music, physical education, and art. Increasing numbers of parents and other adults have formed volunteer groups to assist with clerical and teaching duties to curb educational costs. Children have been used in TV appeals to the public to support funding efforts. In the future the federal government is expected to promote study and action by states relative to school finance and provide direct financial support through categorical aid and revenue sharing. Orlich and Ratcliff (1977) contend that attempts to run public education like big business will reduce the very humanizing element which is distinctive of American educational theory. They believe that accountability does not take into consideration the process of change, the complexity of educational roles, and the student's freedom to learn.

Violence and Vandalism

Violence in schools has become such a concern that many state legislatures have passed legislation related to school crime, and a special congressional committee was instituted to investigate the problem. Physical assault and vandalism have increased dramatically in recent years, among children of all ages. Attendant problems of weapons, drugs, and rampant absenteeism because of fear of attack compound the issue for school personnel, parents and students. A 1975 report by the National Education Association cited a 58 percent rise in assault, a 62 percent increase in sex offenses, an 81 percent escalation in drug related crimes, and a 117 percent jump in robbery over a four year period in American schools. The congressional committee reported "Schools voicing a concern over the escalating rates of violence can be found in any city, suburb, or town regardless of geographical location or per capita income." (p.8) Teachers and students alike are the victims. Some campuses have instituted full-time police protection. Many systems have initiated night guards, and installed protective devices and alarms (Challenge for the Third Century, 1977). One mother reported requiring her daughters to wear pants to school for personal protection from sexual overtures.

Parent Involvement

Parent involvement has risen in recent years. More are employed part-time as aids under federal projects. Some districts have organized volunteer ser-

Vandalism by two youngsters to elementary school amounted to thousands of dollars.

vice groups, composed primarily of teachers. Leaders in parent-teacher organizations are speaking out on curriculum more and Halloween carnivals less. Citizens are making their voices heard at the ballot box by defeating bond issues, and through elected representatives. The result has been the curtailment of educational funds.

The 1976 national PTA President interpreted parents' increased involvement in the affairs of public schools as a plus for education and reports that some parents serve as a third party in bargaining and in formulating bargaining demands, work as organizers of boycotts and suits against striking teachers in order to keep schools open, and help set educational goals and determine priorities and objectives in individual schools and classrooms. The PTA President does not believe American parents are trying to usurp the professional duties of teachers and administrators (Kimmel, 1976).

Parental Confidence and Expectations

In its third annual report to Congress, HEW reported a marked decline in parental confidence in school administrators. Half of the public contacted reported they feel that too little money is being spent to improve education and that lack of discipline is the foremost problem in today's American public schools (1976). The majority of respondents equated the recent declines in standardized test scores with a general decline in educational quality. There was increased demand for accountability concerning the precise results of education. Other primary problems cited were lack of adequate financial support, few quality teachers, the use of drugs, large school size, and the integration/segregation issue. Over three fourths voiced objections to busing across district lines.

Gallup (1976) found similar trends in his eighth annual poll. Some fifteen hundred adults in a modified probability sample indicated lack of discipline was the major problem in public schools. The second ranked problem was integration/segregation/busing. Lack of proper financial support and poor curriculum were other major concerns. The latter concern rose from seventh to fourth place in one year of his reporting.

During the in-home interviews held, a trend was noted toward more traditional values in the responses given, and parents with children in private and parochial schools gave lower ratings to the public school than those whose children were involved in public education. Fifty-one percent called for more focus on the basic skills to improve local education, and 67 percent favored schools assuming more responsibility for moral education. Other needs noted included stricter discipline, improved parent-school relationships, and meeting the needs of individual students. Over half believed schools should have career education, and 90 percent said they would like to serve on school committees.

Asked to indicate the prime qualities important in children's development, the group ranked learning to think for oneself, getting along with others and willingness to accept responsibility highest. They characterized the ideal teacher as one with the ability to communicate, to relate and understand, to discipline firmly and fairly, to inspire and motivate her students and who could serve as a model for children.

Demands for Privacy

Congress has amended the General Education Provisions Act by the adoption of the so-called "Buckley Amendment," adding a new "Family Educational Rights and Privacy Act of 1974," effective November 20, 1974. The enactment of this amendment was presumably fostered by the general feeling that parents are being denied information about their children. The Act reads in part, "any and all records, files, and data directly related to their children, including all material that is incorporated into each student's cumulative record folder, and intended for school use or to be available to parties outside the school or school system, and specifically including, but not necessarily limited to, identifying data, academic work completed, level of achievement (grades, standardized achievement test scores), attendance data, scores on standardized intelligence, aptitude, and psychological tests, interest inventory results, health data, family background information, teacher or counselor ratings and observations, and verified reports of serious or recurrent behavior patterns" (Fellows, 1977).

Alternative Education

During the late fifties and the sixties, alternative schools were begun by parents and professionals who felt that the traditional public and private institutions were not contributing to their children's full development. Although the movement has not disappeared, the errors it caused have made current parents think twice before patronizing its offerings. Wolynski (1976) recounts her experiences in the "school without pain" she attended in Greenwich Village. Now a graduate of NYU, she describes her 9 years of school as "a misspent youth." Since the curriculum was devoted to cultivation of innate creativity, children abandoned any study which they disliked. Children were taught to hate intellectuality and reading was not introduced until grade three so it would not discourage creative spontaneity. Interpersonal relationships were a focus of attention, but as the children entered traditional high schools, they became the culturally disadvantaged and the underachievers. Most endured severe education hardships in their quest for higher education, and a number have been in mental institutions.

A plethora of writers are continuing to criticize the traditional educational approaches. Holt (1976) and Silberman (1970) have been among the more caustic in their comments: Holt has called education which is compulsory and competitive "perhaps the most authoritarian and dangerous of all the social inventions of mankind." (p.4) He claims that in 1970 funding for education, only one-third of one percent was related to changing the educational approach. He proposed the true educative process should involve doing interesting things in order to help the student to become more informed, competent and wise. He charges that the current typical approaches kill curiosity, energy, resourcefulness and confidence. He calls for more choice, freedom, action, talk, cooperation, movement, excitement, energy and joy. He demands that the comparisons, testing, gold-starring, grading, coercion, pecking-ordering, humiliation, threat, punishment and fear which are reportedly wide-spread in the public and private school systems be eliminated.

Among the myths Holt sees spawned in American schools are the following:

- Compulsory attendance laws are to make sure children learn all the important things the schools teach.
- Everything important must be learned in school.
- Learning and doing are different kinds of acts.
- The best way to teach a difficult act is to break it into as many separate skills as possible and teach them one by one.
- The school system wants all children to be winners.
- There has to be an "outcome" from every educational endeavor or activity.
- Success and happiness can only come out of sacrifice, pain and struggle.
- Everything important about children can be tested and measured; the rest is not important.
- Good grades signify a good education.

Silberman charged American schools for mutilation of spontaneity and sense of self, for the petty rules, intellectually sterile and esthetically barren environments, the lack of civility and unconscious contempt for students, the grim and joyless classrooms. He claims school record-keeping is full of

The "play" yard in this grassroots school reflects provisions for free experimentation in learning. (Photo by Lin Mitchell.)

Inside free school space in many cases is utilized for materials rather than desks. (Photo by Lin Mitchell.)

gossipy, malicious pseudopsychological observations and diagnoses, and that labels of "stupid" and "pre-delinquent" are assigned to students there. Some districts are said to maintain separate sets of reports: one for parents to view under the federal law granting them permission to see such records; another for others, including future employers. He points out that schools teach not only the official curriculum but also ideas and attitudes expressed or implied in materials, consciously taught by teachers and even unconsciously taught by teachers.

Gross (1977) advocates a reform in education that will allow the elementary school to provide: recreational facilities for infants through the middle years, early and late afternoon care, tutoring and homework help, a craft center, support and discussion groups for parents, a center for psychiatric services, provision for breakfast, lunch and nutritional snacks, a swap center for outgrown clothing, and facilities for summer activities. She calls for less testing and more time to listen, for less written reports and more family visits, for schools to broaden their traditional areas of service and become extended family centers for total family development.

Elkind (1977) discusses the need to provide a curriculum balanced between individuality and realization of full potential and human sociability that allows one to relate to others and subordinate certain personal inclinations for the benefit of others. He believes the needs and abilities of the child are the vital considerations and that there is no single answer. The affective curricula, such as value clarification, moral discussions, and class meetings have typically expected children in elementary grades to think of painful subjects at the wrong time, reflect and rank feelings they may be incapable of analyzing. Elkind sees this approach as a worthy one, only, when it is geared to the children's emotional and cognitive level.

The current decline in learning as evidenced by drops in SAT scores may be but a result of Sputnik-spawned educational strategies which were too difficult and pressurizing. Recent data from the National Assessment of Academic Achievement show reading scores of nine-year-olds have risen between 1973 and 1977, perhaps due to more concrete, child-centered curricula. Lower grade children in 1976 were reading better than in 1970, continuing a trend which began in 1931. In general, their scoring was high on basic skills tests, probably the result of federally-funded reading programs. Basic word recognition was high (Farr, 1977). The open-education approach featuring a heavily experience-based curriculum and children responsible for their own learning has shown evidences of aimlessness and innovation for its own sake.

Lehane (1977) has conceived an education curriculum based on the psychological and social development of children that proposes the priority on learning experience type proceed from incidental in kindergarten-primary grades, to informal in the intermediate grades, to interpersonal in the middle or junior high school, and finally to formal at the high school level. His scheme is outlined below to show the relative priorities of the four types of experiences over the K-12 period:

	K-primary	Intermediate	Middle/Jr. High	Senior High
incidental	1	4	3	2
informal	2	1	4	3
interpersonal	3	2	1	4
formal	4	3	2	1

A developmentally-based approach, incidental experiences are life-centered; informal ones include exploration through learning centers and labs; interpersonal approaches offer discussion, teams and projects; and formal methods include lectures, recitations and specific learning objectives.

Back to Basics Movement

But parents and legislators are calling for more accountability, and over a third of the state legislatures have mandated basic skill assessment of students at certain levels of schooling. One of the major thrusts in the past few years has been the cry for "back to basics" education. The Council for Basic Education, a 5,000 member, Washington-based force, is the most articulate group which sponsors publications and assistance to parent groups. Although national in scope, this movement is regional or local in specific objectives concerning both content and process.

While critical thinking, intercultural understanding, artistic perception and scientific skepticism *are* basic, the "back to basic" advocates generally refer to teaching the 3 R's, phonics, patriotism and Puritanism in a no-nonsense setting with the teacher in a dominant role. The methods they call for are drill, recitation, frequent testing, daily homework, and traditional letter grade reporting. They believe strict discipline, including corporal punishment and defined dress standards, should be returned to the schoolroom; and they don't favor social promotion, "frills" such as sex education, driver education, and electives including drama, art, and music. Also they call for reduction in the social services provided by the school (Brodinsky, 1977).

Fundamental schools is another term in "back to basics" movement. The term implies stress on excellence through doing your best, citizenship, respect and personal responsibility, appreciation of the traditional values and ethics through heritage education, and reasoning and spelling (Wellington, 1977).

These movements are reportedly the result of increased parental involvement in schools, the criticism of employers that today's graduates lack such basic skills as reading, and the feeling of minority groups that they have been short-changed. Four-fifths of the nation's school boards favor increased emphasis on the 3 R's. Some state legislatures have passed statutes disallowing social promotion and requiring proficiency testing at specified grade levels (Brodinsky, 1977). A 1975 Gallup poll indicated 60 percent of American parents would send children to alternative schools to receive more discipline and the 3 R's.

Student Evaluation

A trend toward more exactness in reporting the progress of students has been noted with the advent of teaching machines, programmed learning, and computed-managed learning. The delineation of behavioral objectives that state precisely what the child should be able to do, under what conditions and to what extent, has facilitated evaluation beyond a mere comparison with other learners on a percentage scale.

Criterion-based reporting involves a listing of objectives with which the students, and sometimes parents, agree to work. The reports to parents at given intervals indicate M for mastery or A for achievement of the specific objective. P can denote progress but not full mastery. R may denote review or reinforcement. L indicates a loss of proficiency whereas N or Y merely

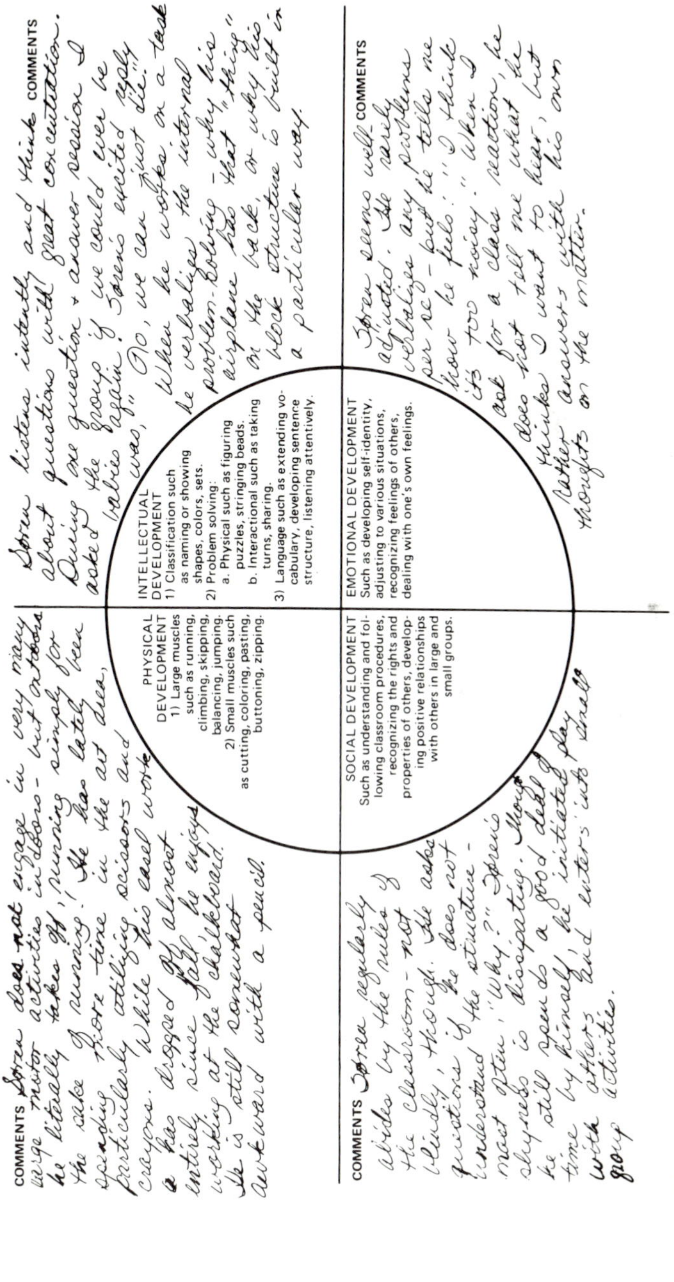

COMMENTS Soren listens intently and thinks COMMENTS about new question & answer session. During one question + answer session I asked the group if we could ever be inside again. Soren said, "Why was," "No, we can just die." When he works on a task he verbalizes the internal problem-solving – why his airplane flies that "thing" or the lack or why the block structure is built in a particular way.

INTELLECTUAL DEVELOPMENT
1) Classification such as naming or showing shapes, colors, sets.
2) Problem solving:
   a. Physical such as figuring puzzles, stringing beads.
   b. Interactional such as taking turns, sharing.
3) Language such as extending vocabulary, developing sentence structure, listening attentively.

PHYSICAL DEVELOPMENT
1) Large muscles such as running, climbing, skipping, balancing, jumping.
2) Small muscles such as cutting, coloring, pasting, buttoning, zipping.

EMOTIONAL DEVELOPMENT
Such as developing self-identity, adjusting to various situations, recognizing feelings of others, dealing with one's own feelings.

SOCIAL DEVELOPMENT
Such as understanding and following classroom procedures, recognizing the rights and properties of others, developing positive relationships with others in large and small groups.

COMMENTS Soren does not engage in very many large motor activities indoors - but outdoors he literally takes off, running simply for the sake of running. He has lately been spending more time in the art area, particularly utilizing scissors and crayons. While the easel work a bit dragged by almost entirely since fall, he enjoys working at the chalkboard. He is still somewhat awkward with a pencil.

COMMENTS Soren regularly abides by the rules of the classroom - not blindly though. He asks questions if he does not understand the structure - most often "why?" Soren always is disagreeing. Though he still needs a good deal of play time by himself, he initiated play with others and enters into small group activities.

Soren seems well COMMENTS adjusted. He easily verbalizes any problems per se - but he tells me how he feels. "When it's too steamy reaction, he act for a direct reaction, he does not tell me what he thinks. I want to hear, but rather answers with his own thoughts on the matter.

Figure 4-2. An elementary grade report form.

means the objective was not under consideration that grading period or is yet to be taught (McClendon, 1976).

The advantages of this approach are: avoidance of intra-group competition, a focus on strengths and weaknesses, and a specific indication of what a child is able to do in the subject matter area. Some examples from the communications skills section:

- identifies parts of speech
- speaks clearly
- reads for details
- organizes related ideas for oral presentation

A summary of alternatives to group standardized testing included approaches which may be fairer and more indicative of student progress. It includes oral presentations, contracts, self-evaluation measures, peer evaluations, parent-teacher conferences, criterion-referenced tests, individual diagnostic tests, teacher made tests, and school letter grades.

Bolstad and Johnson (1977) report teachers are able to accurately discriminate between students on the basis of classroom behavior. Ten teachers of third and fourth grade combination classes were each asked to select a boy and a girl they considered "best behaved," "average in behavior," and "least well-behaved" in classroom conduct. Socioeconomic status and reading achievement scores were noted for each child named.

Trained observers conducted 200 minutes of time sampling related to the students' ability to work independently, in a group, interacting with peers, and willingness to volunteer as well as non-attention, noisiness, and physically negative behaviors. Boys obtained significantly lower ratings of appropriate behavior than girls. Teachers' ratings were convergent with the assessment by observers, and the most strongly related categories were attention to task and peer interaction. The researchers questioned if SES and achievement scores may have influenced teacher ratings since these two factors also obtained a degree of convergence with teacher ratings.

Retention

The Dropout Prevention Program is a federally supported effort to help keep elementary and secondary children in school through the use of innovative methods, materials, systems and programs. In 1974 there were nine demonstration projects conducted, and dropout rates increased. Projects with reading and math components reported average gains of 1.5 to 2.0 yrs. in student achievement (Snapper, 1976).

Most elementary school children in 1972 enrolled in their modal grade. A larger percentage of black as opposed to white children are enrolled both below and above modal grade.

In 1971 over a million elementary school students failed in school. Although it is thought by some to provide a year to grow, learn to conform, increase personal motivation, enrich learning repertoire, or raise the learning rate of non-promoted children, there is overwhelming research evidence showing retention is damaging to children who experience it. According to Bocks (1977), children who do not advance with their classmates are punished by parents, taunted by siblings, ostracized by peers and viewed with skepticism by teachers. They are characterized by their peers as more grouchy, rude, and selfish, and their placement in sociometric measures declines over the year in which they are retained.

A 1970 study by Godfrey indicated, just as did work in the 1930's and 1940's, that retained sixth and seventh grade students did not catch-up. Their self-concept scores declined. Dobbs and Neville (1967) matched retained first and second graders with promoted ones. The reading and arithmetic achievement gain of the promoted group was significantly higher than the non-promoted at the end of a two-year period.

Finlayson (1977) suggests that the maturation of children during middle childhood may contribute more to lowered self-concepts than nonpromotion, because of their increasing realistic self-view in terms of ability. He cites data from a two-year study with first graders using the FACES Scale to assess self-concept. The promoted, borderline and non-promoted groups all showed increases in self-concept scores between May and October of their first year. The retained showed a continued increase during the second year while the other groups declined. The promoted group declined the most.

Research indicates non-promotion does not ensure greater mastery of elementary subject matter, but holds many social-psychological consequences. Threat of non-promotion does not generally motivate children, and they tend to grow best in the same class with their age-mates.

Minority Education

Even though introduction of white life styles has created conflict and changes in the life of Indian children living on reservations, the basic cultural and value systems continue to operate in a subtle way. Traditions, rituals and ceremonies continue on special occasions. The modes and codes of learning they experience affect their performance in public schools outside their community. Indian children are accustomed to learning through family and community activities in an informal, unpressured atmosphere. They learn a great deal through observation of adult models and by asking questions. They are given some supervised participation in acquiring a new skill and then left alone to try it first, in private, without adult pressure. This builds the concept of self-initiation and self-evaluation. Learning through public mistakes is not a valued way of learning for the Indian. Children use little speech to explain what they have learned because much can be demonstrated through their actions. Indian children accompany their parents and other adults to community functions where

Learning to do bead work at school reinforces the Indian child's cultural heritage.

they see leadership based on community consent; no required participation or prescribed degree of participation is enforced. They observe that all are free to speak but no one is designated, and there is no limit on the time they speak. They realize that attendance is by choice, and see withdrawal of support evidenced by leaving the function.

The Indian culture does not value individual competition or persons standing out in a crowd. Therefore, personal competition is not always an effective motivator in learning, and Indian children are often characterized as "shy." The Indian culture does value freedom to roam in nature, and the classroom is thought by many to be confining. Indian children learn to classify and categorize horses and cows early in life, but often geodesic domes and obtuse triangles seem useless concepts in their everyday life.

Brewer (1977) offers some guidelines for the public education of Indian children: Treat them with dignity and respect. Do not equate "lighting up" as a sign of learning; lowered eyelids may signal the same phenomenon. Place value on careful, accurate performance and not on merely speedy response. Find gentle ways of recognizing a child's worth without public display. Capitalize on the observation of adult models and quiet exploration through manipulation and sensory discovery.

Multi-cultural education is a new thrust designed to help children recognize and prize diversity, develop increased understanding of other cultural patterns, acquire a respect for other cultural groups and promote interaction among groups. In an attempt to make public education more relevant to its Indian students, tribal communities from 12 reservations in the Pacific Northwest have developed 130 pieces of language arts material incorporating legends, stories and activity units reflective of their culture for use in primary education. Each tribe holds the copyright for the items its representatives developed, and both Indian and non-Indian children using the authentic new materials show approval and a keener interest in their study (Coburn, 1977).

Busing

Busing has been a part of American public education since 1919. When during the later 1900's rural children were transported to larger, consolidated schools, parental objection was high. Porter (1977) contends that parental reaction to busing that attempts to achieve racial integration is actually a protest against the development of a multiracial society. Busing is to "get the child safely to a better education than he otherwise might have," said James E. Allen, former U.S. Commissioner of Education (Phi Delta Kappan, May 1972, p. 545).

The past decade has seen parental furor over busing to achieve racial balance similar to the reactions of parents when rural children were bused for regional consolidation earlier in the century. In the heavily segregated South the movement has gone more smoothly than in the large northern cities such as Boston. In 1975 an HEW survey indicated that in the Northeast, Midwest and the Border States 60 percent of the black students were still attending "intensely segregated" schools whereas only 20 percent in the south were so assigned. There is a growing agreement in academic circles over what busing has actually achieved for black students. There are no longitudinal studies, little research and no real comparisons on which to base conclusions (The Times Educational Supplement, 1976).

The U.S. Commission on Civil Rights Report on Public School Desegregation cites: desegregation has produced more positive attitudes toward schools and little change in educational quality. Fifty percent of U.S. students are bused, less than 7 percent for desegregation purposes (NEA Teacher Rights, 1977).

The data on the impact of busing to achieve school desegregation on the bi-racial urban future are inconclusive because there are so many variables at play in such a complex situation. At present it is impossible to demonstrate that school integration in itself causes substantial white flight. Other factors contributing to this phenomenon are rising inter-city crime, reduction in city services. More families of both black and white races are seeking suburbia today (Orfield, 1976).

Integrated schools tend to produce less positive academic self-images than nonintegrated ones which are less pressurizing and competitive in comparison (Coleman, 1966; Levine, 1968). Segregation insulates the disadvantaged during early years from acquiring negative attitudes toward the nondisadvantaged (Havighurst and Moorefield, 1967).

Just as no single educational reform has substantially affected students' academic achievement, school integration as a single factor has not either, according to a review of research by Armor (1972). Studies of the impact of integration in Boston, White Plains, Ann Arbor, and Riverside revealed no significant difference in grade equivalent gains among 3- to 6-graders bused and non-bused. Although children in some grades in New Haven and Hartford showed gains, the trend was non-consistent over all grades studied. Integration does not seem to have affected self-esteem in any consistent or significant way; however, it reportedly heightens racial identity and consciousness and because of increasing ideological solidarity and behavioral withdrawal among the races involved, inter-racial experiences decline over time.

Two hundred eighty-four students in grades 5 through 12 were interviewed at the end of one year of busing in Louisville and Jefferson County to assess their feelings about busing. The majority of blacks and whites reported they were doing as well or better than previously, and that the quality of education they were receiving was equal or better than before. They perceived an increase in friendly interracial contact. Fifty-two percent of the white and 90 percent of the black students said they believed the principle of integration was a good one, and there was little difference in the degree of support for the principle between bused and non-bused students.

Educating the Handicapped

At the beginning of the 1978–79 school year, the impact of Public Law 94-142 was felt in many school systems as some 7 million handicapped children gained the right to "free, appropriate public education." Among the children so classified are those who are mentally retarded, hard of hearing, deaf, speech impaired, visually handicapped, seriously emotionally disturbed, orthopedically impaired, other health impaired, those with specific learning disabilities. The law provides that no child can be denied educational opportunity, no matter how severe his handicap. Public systems unable to service these children must make arrangements for their education in private institutions with no cost to the parents. The law further requires that the education of these children be "to the maximum extent appropriate with children who are not handicapped."

Some problems arising in implementation of the new law include

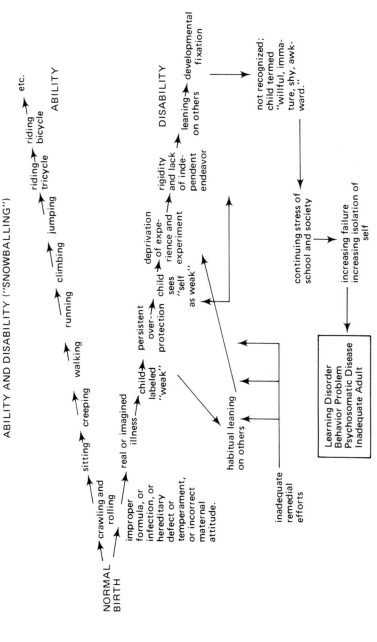

Figure 4-8. Wunderlich *Kids, Brains and Learning*, 1970. [Reprinted from *Physical Therapy* (Vol. 47; 700–708, August 1967) with permission of the American Physical Therapy Association.]

classroom teachers who are not trained to teach the handicapped and the loss of special state funds when handicapped children are no longer receiving separate special education. It is believed that with time handicapped children will benefit from improved self-concepts due to their equal treatment, and that their non-handicapped peers will become more accepting of various disabilities.

Learning Disabilities

Although a number of terms have been used to describe children with learning problems or disabilities, Wunderlich (1970) notes that *brain dysorganized* is the broadest and perhaps most descriptive. It implies a damaged or reversed portion, an irregularity in the transmitting network or faulty power input to the brain. He reports that 15 to 20 percent of the school population may be categorized as slow learners and ten percent as having learning disabilities. The causes of non-optimum brain development include malnutrition, accidents and poisoning, disease, heredity, oxygen lack at birth and lack of stimulation.

Children with learning problems may also have behavior deviations, psychosomatic conditions, excessive energy expenditure or inadequate effort in their work. Their poor performance is usually caused by an imbalance in the child's capacities to deal with stress and the amount of stress he is put under: "the strain of trying to keep up."

Children who experience difficulty learning such skills as reading, writing, and arithmetic are usually interested in music, and may excel in drumming, swimming, skiing and bike riding. They typically experience developmental fixation, remaining at a set primitive level of functioning. Better learning conditions such as structuring of tasks, breaking them into small parts or moving them closer to the fixation level of functioning contribute to progress for these children. Labeling them helps not at all.

Among the learning disorders of most concern to parents are reading disabilities. They tend to occur more in males and may be caused by a lack of general learning ability, improper instruction, brain injury, or visual or auditory imperception. Auditory imperception is among the most common causes. Such non-organic factors as poor motivation because of a depressed environment or emotional reaction in retaliation against family members can also impede reading progress. Specific development dyslexia is another cause. This condition is often the result of an hereditary brain dysfunction characterized by poor right-left orientation that becomes evident in math and reading, and in problems constructing geometric shapes or matching printed words with heard sounds. The problem is believed to stem from maturation lag in the parietal lobe of the brain. The condition may be relatively unnoticed but can be magnified by a severe case of measles, dehydration, detached mothering or excessively restricting environment. The use of large print, working at arm's length rather than close to the body, and large spacing between letters and numbers contribute to inprovement of reading skills in these children.

Children with reading difficulties are more often male, blonde, allergic. They often also suffer from "mishearing," an auditory problem related to chronic congestion of the Eustachian tube. They typically have a higher percentage of family problems than other children; have a frail, pale look; wiggle a lot during seat work, demonstrate laborious working patterns, and have poor posture when at their desk.

Specific language disability children are those who cannot seem to master reading, writing and spelling. Ten percent of those with normal intelligence experience this problem, even though they are typically good in science and math. Theirs is often an hereditary tendency involving right-

Table 4-1 Vulnerability Factors

Biologic	Environmental
Organic	1. Maternal deprivation
1. Abnormal gestation or labor	a. Absent mothering
2. Prematurity	b. Poor quality mothering
3. Crippling disorders, birth defects, prolonged illness, accidents, etc.	2. Absent playmates
4. Brain dysfunction	3. Constrictions and restrictions of opportunities
a. Cerebral palsy	a. Tactile opportunities (heavily clothed infant)
b. Convulsive disorders	b. Range of exploration (e.g., playpen)
c. Minimal brain dysfunction	c. Movement experiences (hypokinetic disease)
d. Occult	d. Visual or auditory deprivation
5. Visual and auditory disorders	4. Failure to provide in critical periods (lack of imprinting)
6. Allergic rhinitis and sinusitis	5. Chronic fixed parental attitudes
7. Malnutrition	6. Absence of structure
Genetic	a. Overpermissiveness
1. Intellectual inferiority	b. Indulgent overprotection
2. Mixed dominance (some cases)	7. Absence of choice
3. Incomplete dominance (some cases)	a. Overstructuring
4. Left handedness (some cases)	b. Dominating overprotection
5. Specific dyslexia	8. Crowding
6. Temperamental individuality	
7. Hereditary metabolic disease	
8. Hereditary slow maturer (late bloomer)	

Wunderlich *Kids, Brains and Learning,* 1970.

left confusion, ambidexterity, clumsiness, perceptual abnormalities and weak language skills. They benefit from special learning environments which require daily performance acts involving words. When they are able to type, trace over, cut out or write words in sand, they "experience" the words just as they might trucks or blocks, and learn to feel comfortable with them. Gradual increments of involvement and respect for the child's innovations with the words are other important aspects of helping these learners succeed.

Abraham (1964) has noted some characteristics most frequently cited among slow learners:

1. Short attention and interest span.
2. Limited imagination and limited creative thinking.
3. Slow reaction time.
4. Apathy, difference, dependence, placidity—but frequent presence of excitability, sensitivity.
5. Academic retardation, especially in reading; achievement age laging behind chronological age.
6. Absence or easy loss of self-confidence.
7. Gullibility, instability, shyness, submissiveness.
8. Low power of retention and memory.
9. Inability to do abstract thinking, to handle symbols, to evaluate results, to foresee consequences of acts.
10. Failure to transfer ideas, to extend beyond local point of view in time or place, to retain interest if results are deferred or intangible.
11. Limited powers of self-direction, of adapting to change in situations and people.
12. Low levels of initiative, vocabulary, standards of workmanship, persistence, concentration, reasoning, defining, discriminating, analyzing.
13. Ease of confusion; fears, anxieties.
14. Laziness—but perhaps due to ill health or emotional maladjustment rather than as a constitutional factor.
15. Action based on impulse; insistence on quick results; inclination toward jumping to conclusions.
16. Less well-developed physically—height, weight, proportion, general health, unexplained fatigue.

He stresses the fact that identification of slow-learning children should begin early, that no single index or device is alone sufficient, and the identification process should continue over a relatively long period of time.

This group are generally identified by scores between 75 and 90 on a verbal intelligence test. Among the general school population, 15 to 17 or 18 percent may be so classified. Children who are considered slow learners are behind the average both in rate and level of typical intellectual growth. They are not as discriminating, nor as able to judge or abstract, develop initiative, direct their own activities, or detect and correct their errors as are normal children of equal age; and since their rate of intellectual growth is slower than the average or the gifted, they tend to grow farther behind with progressing age. Their inability to keep up with their peers affects their social and emotional adjustment. Whereas their emotional and social needs are the same as those of all children, they have more difficulty in making satisfactory adjustments to these needs because of intellectual limitations. Deviate, antisocial, unacceptable behavior in school is not rare. Therefore, they are apt to provide one of the most challenging, continuing problems of the classroom teacher. Such behavior is not, however, an intrinsic part of the psychological makeup of these children; instead it is due to the continual frustration they experience because of failures in areas where success is valued by them and their society.

Physically, slow learners are slightly below average in build, size, and motor ability. Yet they cannot be identified by their appearance. Their physical and motor abilities may be sufficient for them to excel in those athletic activities that do not emphasize mental or intellectual skills to an extremely high degree, thereby affording them a measure of status and sense of accomplishment (Johnson, 1963).

Helping the slow learner achieve a sense of dignity and value through programs suited to his abilities and then valuing his achievements are important goals of adults involved with his growth and development. Some special goals in working with a child of this type are exercising great patience; using methods and materials geared to his level of understanding and ability and helping him make the most of it; and keeping his motivation high through approval of his accomplishments (Hawkes and Pease, 1962).

Dyslexia means word blindness and implies something wrong with one's reading. It is a name given to a disturbed function of the symbolic and perceptual abilities, which is estimated to affect 3 to 5 percent of the U.S. school population. It is often discovered upon school entrance because of its relation to reading problems. The ratio of boys to girls with this problem is about 4 to 1, and there is evidence that heredity may be a factor in its incidence (Wagner, 1971).

Other factors that have been postulated are language and race, bilingualism in the home, teaching reading too early or too late, and brain damage. In addition to reading impairment, dyslexia may also affect arithmetic skills and spelling (Keeney and Keeney, 1968). Some characteristic signs of the disorder, when present in a cluster, are poor ability to associate sounds with letters, the reversal of letters and numbers, mirror writing, difficulty discriminating between the letters *d* and *b* or *d* and *p*.

The dyslexic child may also find it difficult to work puzzles, hold a pencil correctly, or walk a chalkline. Behavior typical of the disorder includes clumsiness, overactivity, destructiveness, nervous mannerisms, lack of concentration, and short attention span. One can readily see how dyslexia would hinder a child's normal progress in school. Wagner (1971) advocates a regular 15-minute tutoring session each day in the home, conducted by a parent, friend, older sibling, or some other person who has the temperament and ability to help the child learn to concentrate and to feel success in small tasks. Consistency and lack of confusion are keys to helping the child with this problem. Early help is vital, and school systems are beginning to organize special classes for those with dyslexia. Two national organizations devoted to further the cause of these children are (1) the Association for Children with Learning Disabilities, 2200 Brownville Road, Pittsburgh, Pa. 15210, and (2) the Orton Society, Inc., Box 153, Pomfret, Conn. 06258. Both publish materials and offer individual memberships (Wagner, 1971).

Learning disabilities are universal and experienced by everyone. They vary accordingly to intensity and specificity. Some are severe enough to divert, stunt, or inhibit children from reaching their full potential in life.

What happens between the *brain-damaged* child and his parents is of major importance. Probably no parent is psychologically ready for this challenge. Their attitudes and actions, as well as the feelings and work of professionals who may be privileged to minister to this child, shape his ultimate destiny.

B. K. Smith (1968) has painted the picture beautifully:

> We know of the child with learning disabilities. We feel his vague hunger for a food he has never tasted and we recognize his sense of self-blame that he has not eaten.
>
> His days are days of shadows, and he knows no sun. The fog lifts from time to time, showing him a bit of the world or a piece of life, tantalizing as a veiled woman who reveals only a portion of her mystery.
>
> He walks through a forest of huge and rough-barked trees. There is an occasional path which he can follow, but it often ends without taking him to the clearing. There is no guide, and he stumbles.
>
> He is like the small boy who was lifted from the ground by a tornado. As he whirled within the cylinder of the storm, he saw birds and bits of wood, leaves from trees, and debris twirling with him in a frenzied cycle which held him in its power.
>
> It matters not what we call him. A child with learning disabilities. Or one with minimal brain dysfunction. A perceptually handicapped child. Or a brain-damaged one. Kim or Alice. Polly. Frank. Ted. Joel or Timmy. What we call him is but a tag. What we see and feel about him prompts action.
>
> He is a child who knows he is different. He is a child who "cannot" while other children "can." He may live in a kaleidoscopic world of twirling lights and pieces. He knows a pain too deep for crying. He is like a kite without a string. His world comes in pieces, like a gigantic puzzle he cannot solve. It tilts; it fragments; it turns completely upside-down.
>
> Steady hands are needed. Many hands lifting, turning, working together to bring life into focus and to right for him his world of upside-down.

The Gifted

A gifted child is one who performs much better than his age group in a way which gives promise to future high level achievement or contribution. Gifted children comprise a relatively small group in the school population, and sometimes there are no provisions made to foster their fulfillment of potential beyond the normal classroom activity. Some school systems group them for special activities and opportunities on a periodic basis. Individual teachers may also provide supplementary challenges and stimulation for such pupils in their class. A gifted child may be talented in many areas or in only a few. He may even be handicapped in some area of endeavor. He may come from any level of society, any race or section of the country. Bloom (1977) estimates that about 1 to 2 percent of students have superior learning abilities.

Comparative studies indicate gifted children are likely to be stronger, larger, healthier and have more interests than their peers. They tend to be more sociable, happy and alert. They usually learn more and absorb more quickly than other children, and are able to concentrate, discriminate, solve problems, create and endure at a task better than most. Gifted children tend to turn out better than the average adult, maintain their mental powers and their good health. Even their marital success tends to be above average (Terman, 1925, 1959).

There is no simple way to determine whether or not a child is gifted. Through observation, developmental records, performance and testing he may be identified. Parents may not be able to recognize giftedness because they are necessarily biased or because they have no norms for comparison. Some are amazed to learn of their child's giftedness! Prior to age 3 or 4 testing does not yield dependable results. But some early signs of superior intellectual development may include language abilities, recall of detail, long attention span, deep questioning, self-taught reading, a knack for color and design, ability to carry a tune quite well, and understanding and management of human relations situations.

As a whole the gifted child is just as socially adjusted as the average child. But his relations with other children will depend on his social attitudes and behavior, his verbal facility, and the attitudes others have toward gifted people. If he is unpopular, it could be due to jealousy or fear on the part of children who feel inferior to him. Or it could be that the gifted child is dissatisfied with the standards or abilities of other children to discuss and learn. Such feelings are intensified if the gifted child is singled out as being special. The teacher can contribute most to the development of the gifted child by treating him as an integral part of the total class, and in addition providing a wealth of opportunities for him to go beyond the average student in his thirst for learning, through reading, special projects, and other enriching activities related to the class work.

Whereas parents and teachers may feel very proud of a gifted child, the temptation is to push him too quickly toward advanced work and accomplishments. He, like all children, needs to experience the normal joys of childhood. He needs association with other children, approval for a job well-done, and opportunities to develop his interests without being placed in the limelight. He will benefit from regular duties around the home and freedom from overscheduling of his time. His accomplishments should not be emphasized to the detriment of the other children in his family and in his classroom.

Think Back

To elementary school days:
How you got to and from school.
What you did before school; at recess; after lunch.
What happened to children who were late.
How the routine changed when it was rainy or very cold.
How often report cards went home and who signed them.
How you felt about grades.
Some things you remember learning.
How you felt about leaving elementary school.

Myths of Education

One interesting way to view the teaching-learning process is to cite so-called myths of education under which many systems still operate. Adapted from *Report to the President* (White House Conference on Children, 1971), some of these myths are as follows:

MYTH 1: *All children come to school to learn.*
Children come to school for many reasons; some because they must. But some do not even know what learning is—certainly not the learning the teacher has cited in her behavioral objectives. They may bring with them not only a poor concept of learning but grossly inadequate tools with which to work: weak eyes, undernourished bodies, exhaustion, emotional problems, undetected illness, unstimulating environments. One of the teacher's foremost roles is to develop children's attitudes toward learning, to foster their interest in it, and to help them acquire the basic skills needed to learn.

MYTH 2: *All parents can help teach.*

While parents do transmit facts and attitudes in the home, parents from the lower socioeconomic group are often poor information sources for their children, and sometimes they consider the duty of teaching belongs solely to the school. In many homes there is not the proper atmosphere for home study. In some homes there are so many responsibilities given children that they have inadequate time to study. Even the teacher who asks students to bring a picture from a magazine or an empty milk carton from home may be assuming too much—as well as placing the child in a potentially embarrassing situation in the eyes of his peers. Repeated experiences such as these can become a cause for a child to wish to leave school. One mother who is a teacher herself told of taking a half-gallon paper milk carton to her son's class in response to the teacher's request. She was met with scornful eyes and these words from the teacher: "Oh, that's not what we need! Don't you buy your milk in those gallon plastic bottles?"

MYTH 3: *Teachers know and children don't.*

Perhaps the old adage "Children should be seen and not heard" has perpetuated practices from a philosophy long-ago abandoned by developmentalists but still preserved in authoritarian school models. It is one of the most destructive educational assumptions, and runs counter to both the idea of encouraging children to think for themselves and to learning theories which suggest that with increasing age, children depend more on peers than adults for information. With the growth of media, the mobility of families, and the mushrooming of knowledge, children are increasingly more informed than they were in previous generations. It should be possible to involve the student in both the teaching and learning roles. An example of this idea is embodied in cross-age teaching, where students work with younger children. This method not only allows the teacher to give attention to special needs and extend her creative contributions; it also reinforces the learning of the student-teacher, aids the socialization of the younger learner, and improves the self-image of all involved. By recognizing that children often have had experiences and gained knowledge that the teacher herself has not experienced, cross-cultural understanding can be fostered, self-confidence is enhanced, and a more cooperative spirit can pervade the classroom.

MYTH 4: *All children in a family will perform similarly.*

Preconceived expectations of children, based on the performance of an older sibling, on information in cumulative folders, or on hearsay from the teacher's lounge or the neighborhood grapevine are potential sources of doom for some children. Children sense and act in terms of leader expectations more than many like to admit. Whereas expectations that are too high can be damaging, those set too low can also be debilitating. Unrealistic demands can stifle initiative, create hostility, and even cause emotional disorganization in children and adults. The wise teacher uses background information only as one of many indicators of a child's potential; she adds to it other facts as she begins to help the child set goals and plan and evaluate progress. She never compares the child with others in his family whom she has taught!

MYTH 5: *All teachers love children.*

The attitude of the teacher toward children can be of prime importance, just as the parental attitudes affect the climate and success of the home. There are teachers who actually dislike children; among this number may be some who became teachers simply because there seemed nothing else to become. Children are astute in their perception of a teacher's real feelings for them, and it has been suggested that a child's feeling that his teacher dislikes him might be grounds for his transfer to another classroom—for he is very often quite right in his feeling!

MYTH 6: *Age is the best determinant for school placement.*

Traditionally schools have grouped children according to chronological age. Whereas this is still a widespread practice, grouping according to other factors is also proving successful. Grouping by developmental level allows more opportunity for children to achieve mastery. With vertical movement according to needs and learning patterns, children who are accomplished in math or science work with others of similar abilities but perhaps of different ages. Those who are experiencing difficulty in reading or in music work with others who are at their same level of progression. The ungraded school facilitates vertical movement.

Friendship grouping can expedite task accomplishment in some cases (Klausmeier, 1966). Interest grouping is effective if performance on the same level is not critical, such as may be true in a skating or stamp club. Ad hoc grouping allows short-term activities to be conducted within a group but does not bind the group members for an extended period. Differential-ability grouping is useful when the representation of different abilities is desired within a group. A variety of different groupings within a given day or unit allows children to be leaders, followers, teachers, learners, the best, less than the best—and it promotes acceptance of everyone, not just the other "blue bird readers."

MYTH 7: *Competition in school is good for everyone.*

Whereas the free enterprise system on which our nation operates is based on competition, this is not a major tenet of the American philosophy of child rearing. Although competition may be related to the urge for survival, the intensification of this trait seems largely dependent on the society's attitude toward it. Competition is unavoidable. And the school setting has lent itself to this value because of its emphasis on speed and accuracy of performance. However, if competition is the crutch on which interest in learning is contingent—that is, if the only reason children want to learn is to make a good grade—something is wrong in the system. Imagine a school in which students whose averages are high receive the special privilege of a study hall painted pink while those with averages below 85 percent must study in a gray room (Lobsenz, 1962)!

The importance of getting ahead was found to be the hidden curriculum among first-graders studied by Kessen in 1974 (Radloff, 1976). The spirit of promotionalism and outshining the competition ran high; the obsession to finish the blue set in reading and get on to the orange and then to the purple over-shadowed the desire to learn about the topics seemingly covered in the reading. The children seemed to solve problems more on such teacher cues as nods and smiles than by focusing on the facts at hand. They seemed more motivated to get to another task than in pleasing the teacher or understanding the material. There was a high level of anxiety in the class, particularly with respect to evaluation. They were more interested in knowing how they were doing in comparison with others than how they were personally progressing. Their sense of accomplishment was generally high. But they enjoyed art and music most because they were harder to grade. Those children who were unable to get on the fast track to success suffered most from the system: they had lower status in the group, perceived themselves as less valuable and seemed to live up to their peers' expectations. Kessen concluded that "Schools only sharpen those values which society and parents revere, and we'll have to change our society before we change our schools."

It is not a pretty picture: middle class parents demand more homework, stricter grading, advanced classes so their children will be able to compete in the academic marketplace. They want their child to be the smartest, most popular, most talented, best mannered, and a host of other superlatives. Most teachers were schooled on a competitive basis, and they were able to survive the system; some reason that if it worked for their generation, it will work for the current one. Many schools have decreed grading scales something like the following:

A = 98–100%
A– = 95–97
B+ = 91–94
B = 88–90
B– = 85–87
C+ = 81–84
C = 78–80
C– = 75–77
D = 65–74
F = below 65

This type of preset grading scale makes some faulty assumptions, namely that there has been perfect teaching; the stimulus was the same for every child; the evaluation device was perfect; the only variable is student learning. Whether teachers fail to recognize the fallacies of the approach or whether they simply do not know what course to take to remedy the situation, most ascribe to the system to some degree.

Children need to experience success and to feel worthwhile. Yet if they must depend on grades for the meeting of this need, some are bound to consider themselves failures or worthless. As they feel the pressures of competition, they may lose the love of learning for learning's sake—or they may begin to lose self-confidence and see their peers as threats and rivals for the teacher's praise. It is important that each child know he is worthy—whether he succeeds, fails, or chooses not to compete at all.

MYTH 8: *Failure is good for children.*

Since the graded plan of education began in Boston about the middle of the nineteenth century, the problem of promotion and retention has been a challenge to parents, teachers, and children. Each year thousands of children are retained, costing school systems millions of additional dollars and in some instances beginning a failure syndrome that will be lifelong (Snipes, 1965). Even in these modern times, when other complex problems are being solved through research, technology, and ingenuity, this problem in schools throughout the land continues. The education books term it nonpromotion; the teacher says it's retention or repeating; the embarrassed mother describes the action as "keeping Johnny back"; and Johnny calls it failure! This decision is meant to benefit his adjustment, achievement, and ability to learn. Many instances of children's school failure stem from home crises: alcoholism, rejection, separation, and deprivation. Once he has failed, the child finds it increasingly difficult to catch up on his own and is likely to become the object of embarrassing attention at home and at school. Some become clowns to gain acceptance; others hide or withdraw into their own little world. Still others bare their teeth and fight a losing battle. Very few children perceive failure as a stepping-stone to a successful and satisfying school career or life. Children who fail may feel like "a balloon with its skin off," which was one youngster's definition of the word "nothing."

Repeated failure has a definite undesirable effect on subsequent goalsetting and may be an indication that a child is acquiring poor attitudes about himself and the school. Children who fail and their parents have more negative attitudes toward school than those who are promoted. More than one writer has called child failure a failure of the school in classifying, stimulating, and motivating children, failure in selection of appropriate teaching techniques.

Think Back

To some of your elementary school teachers:
Their names.

Their favorite sayings.

How they punished misbehavior.

The presents you gave them on special occasions.

The nicknames you had for them.

What you liked best, least about them.

How to Hear Their Drumbeat

Perhaps Thoreau (1942) summed up the challenge to the school in his *Walden:* "If a man does not keep pace with his companions, perhaps it is because he hears a different drummer. Let him step to the music which he hears, however measured or far away." May educators tune in more acutely.

In a preliminary report of a project to find ways of helping a prepuberty boy work through conflicts with his family, school, and neighborhood, Murphy and Morgan (1963) discussed growth experiences provided for the youngster which were in keeping with his "inner drumbeat." When the project began, Peter had developed destructive tendencies, had no goals for himself, would not attempt to overcome difficulties in schoolwork, and had no interest in sports. He expected to get what he wanted without any effort on his part, and cheated and ignored the rules of his peer group and of authorities in his life. He did not like Boy Scouts, nor was he able to make good use of any of the neighborhood opportunities. He seemed totally uninterested in any achievement for its own sake or in any program based on achievement awards. Peter was underachieving in school. Although he wanted to be first or best in everything, he found it difficult to give his attention to learning a skill and would not put forth any effort.

A young adult was enlisted to work with Peter on a one-to-one basis. The first project he introduced was the making of a sling modeled after the one David used to kill Goliath. There was no lagging interest: Peter was fascinated and quickly understood the principle involved in its use. He practiced with the sling, using rocks of varying sizes, staying with it until his skill improved. Next the growth experience provider (GEP) began to stimulate Peter's mild interest in fishing by teaching him how to tie flies. This led to the construction of tools used to improve Peter's fishing skill, which eventually developed into a small business venture. Since there was no money for fishing equipment, the GEP helped Peter make rods from radio antennae bought for ten cents each at the local junkyard.

Then Peter discovered there were things to learn about fishing: best times and places for particular kinds of fish, correct methods of fishing, right kind of bait, and methods of bating the hook—all were important.

During this time the boy who didn't like to read was reading—books on fishing and fly-tying.

Peter's interest in fishing led to construction of an aquarium. He found inexpensive materials and continued his reading to find ways to complete the project. During this time, Peter was also having experiences in construction of a small park area. With the money he was paid for this work, Peter decided to buy materials and build his own boat, which required more study, planning, and ingenuity.

All of the things happening to Peter affected his schoolwork. His grades went up; his attitude improved; he went out for football; he was better behaved; and he became more popular with his peers. Someone had tapped his inner resources; helped him understand his own abilities; and provided success experiences which spilled over into every area of his life. Learning was exciting to this boy when the learning dealt with things that had relevance to him.

Another way individual drumbeats were heard in elementary grades was through a housewife aide program (Cowen, 1969) in which first-graders judged to have or likely to develop persistent problems were the target population. The program involved working with the mother of each child to collect in-depth information about his background and behavior, psychological evaluation, and close observation. It featured regular periods of attention by trained semivolunteer mothers who spent time playing, reading, talking, and doing art activities with the children. "Sue was a tiny, underdeveloped and immature first-grader. Her intellectual potential was average or above average, but she was entirely antagonistic to school and to schoolwork . . . she spent most of her time walking around the room, annoying the other youngsters. . . . She would often sneak out of the room and play in the halls. . . ." After several weeks of participation in the program she became less restless, left the classroom less often, paid attention for longer periods of time, and was even trying to learn to read. "Two years later Sue continued to make normal progress."

Other evidence to the worth of the program:

> Carl, who has never been able to function in a classroom situation, is miraculously learning to read. Dave, who didn't lift a pencil for three months, now asks permission to stay after school to finish his work. Tom had no regard for rules or the people who enforce them. Recently, he began to raise his hand instead of calling out, and he hasn't raced to be the first in line for months. . . . As for Gerald, he never looks up from his desk in the classroom and cannot speak above a mumble, but now he lifts his head and yells for joy when his aide comes to pick him up.

In a report on a camping program for troubled youngsters, Smith (1970, pp. 18–19) reported the following conversation between the counselors, Jeff and William, and a group of boys as they read together a letter from the Beavers, a contingent from the camp who was away on an extended trip. The letter was mailed from Bexar County, near San Antonio.

DAVID: Oh boy, at the Alamo. Have they been there?

WILLIAM: They've not only been there. They spent nearly a whole day. Now they're camping in a park outside of San Antonio before they move on to Fredricksburg.

ROBERT: Will we get to take a trip? Will we?

RONNIE (almost disdainfully): Of course we will. As soon as we decide on what we want to do.

JERRY: It takes a lot of planning. You gotta think of everything, man, before you go on one of them trips.

Smith continues:

Jeff listens to the letter, watches the absorbed faces of the boys and thinks of the particular kinds of experiences the letter represents. If such a letter as this were labeled "English," none of the boys would show interest. Yet Jeff knows that the Beavers sent out almost 200 letters to chambers of commerce, historical associations, factories, processing plants, and civil groups while they were planning this nine-week excursion. He recalls the history books they read, and the geographies, in order to decide where to go and what to see. He knows that the boys, traveling by camp bus, have to plan each meal (which they cook outdoors) to fit in with their daily allotment of 35 cents per meal per person. Before they began their trip, they had to outline their plans and write out their objectives. They keep a daily log of their trip, evaluating each day's experiences. While the boys exclaim excitedly about the Beavers and their adventure, Jeff smiles to himself, thinking of the varied clothing learning wears. In the setting of the camp and travel, the boys make decisions which have direct relation to the present, to reality, and to comfort, and they are willing and able to work toward these immediate goals where they cannot or could not in the more abstract school setting.

Dodge (1966) shared creative approaches to tutoring which are designed to capture the interest and foster the growth of children. An *imagination walk* can stretch the imagination, facilitate expression of feelings and aid verbalization skills. This allows the tutor and child to discuss the objects and persons observed, to consider together how it might feel to be a blade of grass, or to determine what sort of person a given stranger is. Making a *hiptionary* of slang words and their standard English synonyms is an approach which adds to, without replacing, a child's own language. Map-making to show one's route from home to school and the various services and places en route helps children develop awareness, and expansion of the map on a larger scale could lead to making travel plans and attendant decisions. Students dictating accounts from their lives which are then typed up and duplicated for exchange with each other can help reading and composing skills. These compositions are enjoyable because they are in their own language and on topics of personal interest to them.

One special education fourth grade teacher directed her class in making books on various topics, such as April Fool's Day, in which each student contributed a verbal story which she duplicated. After they were bound, the books were placed in the school library for other students in the school to use. The special education class was flattered when some of their volumes were missing from the shelves, concluding they must have been well-liked if other students took them home to keep!

How else can teachers hear students' drumbeats? One way is certainly a study of their records. This action yields information concerning health problems that have been detected previously and, hopefully, information concerning their correction or treatment. A teacher who knew of a child's diabetic condition would not insist that he eat the roll served on his lunch plate. She would be on the alert to his having an insulin reaction or going into a diabetic coma. Likewise she who knew of an epileptic student would know what to do in case of a seizure. She would place children with hearing difficulties near the front of the room. She would refrain from pressuring into public performance the child who is shy or who stutters.

The cumulative folder would also provide some insight into the past performance of a student and perhaps provide clues as to areas of learning deficiency or excellence. It would help the teacher know more about the family socioeconomic status, composition, neighborhood, religious orientation, and mobility. A teacher could ascertain many useful facts from this record but should not prejudge or predestine a child on the basis of these.

Home contacts, either by personal visits or parent-teacher conferences at school or via telephone, help a teacher see the child's home situation in better perspective and should put her in a better position to understand why he acts as he does at school. The teacher who makes such a home contact before the school year begins indicates to the parents and to the child that she is interested in him. It also allows the teacher to know her students by name from the first day of school—which can mean a lot. Other home contacts, made when the child is doing well, can reinforce feelings of trust and confidence. If the only parent-family interaction occurs when the child is in trouble, little positive communication occurs. If home contacts are made on the parent's home ground, they may be less threatening. But teachers must guard against appearing to be inspecting or snooping into the home and the lives of family members. Even the apparel worn by the teacher on a home visit is a factor in the success of the visit: it should be modest, though tasteful.

Perhaps the most successful means of understanding children is through personal interaction with them in a variety of situations. Elementary school teachers have countless contacts with individual children on any given day. The personal organization and management of relationships during these encounters are a key to successfulness in the teaching-learning process. For some children, the teacher is their prototype. Every movement and word communicates to these children, and they often emulate her as closely as possible. It is during the early school years that the child may quote his teacher to his parents on every occasion possible. Some parents feel threatened by this action, but it is a natural one and does not indicate loss of love and respect for the parents. It should, however, indicate to the teacher her extreme position of influence in children's lives and encourage her to be ever more worthy of emulation. Perhaps the traditional community expectations that teachers be spotless in character and blameless in action stem from this fact.

What's Next?

1. *Human Characteristics and School Learning,* Bloom, B. New York: McGraw-Hill, 1976.
2. *Crisis in the Classroom,* Silberman. New York: Random House, 1970.
3. *How Children Fail,* J. Holt. New York: Pitman, 1964.
4. *How Children Learn,* J. Holt. New York: Pitman, 1967.
5. *Instead of Education,* J. Holt. New York: Dutton, 1976.
6. *Teacher,* S. Ashton-Warner. New York: Simon and Schuster, 1963.
7. *The Authentic Teacher,* C. Moustakas. Cambridge, Mass.: Doyle, 1966.
8. *The Empty Spoon,* S. Decker. New York: Harper & Row, 1969.
9. *Freedom to Learn,* C. Rogers. Columbus, Ohio: Merrill, 1969.
10. *Free Schools,* J. Kozol. Boston: Houghton Mifflin, 1972.
11. *The Lives of Children,* G. Dennison. New York: Vintage, 1969.
12. *Closer Look,* P.O. Box 1492, Washington, D.C. 20013 for information about handicapped and learning problems.
13. *Child Development Through Literature,* Landau et al. Englewood Cliffs, N.J.: Prentice-Hall, 1972: "See How They Run," by M. Vroman, pp. 424–440.
14. Film: *A Desk for Billie,* National Education Ass'n., 1201 16th St., N.W., Washington, D.C. 20036. (57 min, b/w.)
15. Film: *Children as People* (on alternative schooling), Polymorph Films, 331 Newbury St., Boston, MA 02115. (28 min, b/w.)
16. Film: *Children Without.* Modern Talking Picture Service, 2323 New Hyde Park Rd., New Hyde Park, N.Y. 11040. (29 min, b/w.)
17. Film: *Summerhill* (*free school*) Nat'l Film Board of Canada, 1251 Ave. of the Americas, NY 10020 (28 min/color)

Catalysts for Discussion

I. Other "myths" of education identified by Learning Forum group "Confronting the Myths of Education" at the 1970 White House Conference on Children—Dwight Allen, Chairman.

1. Teachers are neuter.
2. Someone must win—someone must lose.
3. All learning occurs in the classroom.
4. Tests are infallible.

5. Learning is painful.
6. Punishment motivates—a flogging will cure.
7. Uniqueness is bad.
8. Democracy won't work with children.
9. Schools teach the truth.
10. There is no difference among people.
11. Teachers don't care.
12. Anyone can learn if he wishes.
13. Intelligence is fixed.
14. Grading is good.
15. I (the teacher or parent) can't change the system because "they" won't let me.

The above-mentioned myths would make good topics for independent research, debate, class discussion, or drama.

II. School Readiness
   To help parents answer the question, "Should I keep my child out of school for another year?" Jordan and Massey (1967) have devised a school readiness test which assesses number concepts, discrimination of form, color naming, symbol matching, speaking vocabulary, listening vocabulary, and general information. Items from the General Readiness Checklist follow:

Will your child be 5 years 3 months or older when he begins kindergarten?
Can strangers easily understand your child's speech?
Can your child:
Pay attention to a short story when it is read, and answer simple questions about it?
Draw and color, beyond a simple scribble?
Tie a knot?
Zip a zipper?
Walk backward a distance of 5 or 6 feet?
Stand on one foot for 5 to 10 seconds?
Alternate feet when walking down stairs?
Walk a straight line?
Fasten buttons that he can see?
Tell his left hand from his right?
Use a knife for spreading jam or butter?
Take care of his toilet needs by himself?
Set the table with the correct number of knives, forks and spoons?
Be away from you 2 or 3 hours without being upset?
Cross a residential street safely?
Print his first name?
See a straight pin on the floor while standing up?
Draw or copy a plus, a box, and a ball?

III. Letters from nine- and ten-year-olds to their student teacher:

   Dear Miss Olsen,
   I am your friend no matter how mean you get. I like you a lot. I am your friend even if you give an 85 page test.
                                                        Your friend (I hope)
                                                        Nora

Hi Miss Olsen, I'm Kirk McMann. I've always got candy. But I only eat it at P.E. I have sour apple and cherry. I'll give you two of each.

To Miss Olsen
I love you. You are the nices, sweetes, prettyes teacher I every met. With lots of love and Kisses. Janice M.

Miss Olsen,
You are the greatest! Even if you like Nora, Dinky and Patti the most in this school.
From Debbie and Judy

To the Olsen
I like you a super lot. I thank you for talking to me when I wanted you to. And teaching me math. And everything. If I've ever been mad at you, I'm not sorry because love means never having to say you're sorry.

Dear Miss Olsen,
I hope your feeling happy. I hope your feeling gay. I don't mean to make you feel sappy. But heres what I have to say: I'll send you a card on father's day not for you
but for your father.
Here's my address and phone number. If they say beauty shop or something like that just say may I speak to Michelle.

Sincerely yours,
Michelle

IV. "Curriculum Fable" (Shibler, in Moore, 1972)

Once upon a time, the animals decided they must do something heroic to meet the problems of a "new world," so they organized a school. They adopted an activity curriculum consisting of running, climbing, swimming, and flying and to make it easier to administer, all the animals took all the subjects.

The duck was excellent in his swimming, better in fact, than his instructor, and made passing grades in flying; but he was very poor in running. This was kept up until his web feet were badly worn and he was only average in swimming.

The rabbit started at the top of the class in running, but had a nervous breakdown because of so much make-up work in swimming.

The squirrel was excellent in climbing until he developed frustration in flying class where his teacher made him start from the ground up instead of from the tree-top down. He also developed charley horses from over exertion and then got a C in climbing and a D in running.

At the end of the year an abnormal eel who could swim exceedingly well and also run, climb, and fly a little had the highest average and was valedictorian.

The prairie dogs stayed out of school and fought the tax levy because the administration would not add digging and burrowing to the curriculum. They apprenticed their children to a badger and later joined ground hogs and gophers to start a successful private school.

V. A child's enjoyment of school (Barth, 1970) is related to—

1. The number of significant options available to him each day:
Choice of working alone or in groups
Investigation and exploration or reading and accepting a variety of learning methods and materials

---

2. Having a voice in determining the activity in which he will be engaged:
   Physical mobility
   Conscious commitment
   Teacher's respect of his choices
3. Being able to pose his own problems and decide the manner in which he will pursue their solution:
   Thought-provoking materials
   Freedom to apply imagination and energy
4. The extent he is permitted to collaborate with peers:
   Cross-fertilization of ideas
   Cooperative problem-solving
   Social learning
   Spiraling curiosity
5. The extent to which he is trusted by adults:
   Trust until untrustworthiness is shown
   Unsupervised work in and out of the classroom
   Use of expensive equipment alone and together
6. The extent it has a climate of consistent order:
   No destroying equipment
   No interference with the work of others
   Results of infraction is loss of privilege in which violation occurred
7. The extent to which comparisons between his performance and those of other children are minimized:
   Ad hoc rather than ability grouping
   Work samples rather than grades sent to parents
   Maintenance of extensive work folders for parental review
   Freedom of choice of activity on interest, not sex
   Considering mistakes helpful rather than wrong

VI. Some statements relative to grading in this century:

1913—Cornell Educational Laboratories (Finkelstein, 1913):
   We recommend that every institution of learning, at least every high school and college, adopt a five-division marking system, based upon a distribution which should, in the long run, not deviate appreciably from the following: Excellent, 3 per cent.; superior, 21 per cent.; medium, 45 per cent.; inferior, 19 per cent.; very poor, 12 per cent.

1939—(Cole, 1939)
   A pupil's mark is important to him because it summarized the extent to which he has succeeded in doing what he was supposed to do. Those who want to abolish all marks, so that pupils may work for the mere love of working, forget that a mark is objective evidence of the teacher's opinion and as such informs the pupil of his standing. Without marks an inefficient pupil will work happily and busily for months without ever knowing that he should improve. A student of any age has a right to know what those best equipped to judge think of his competency.

1969—(Simon, 1969)
   One of the ugliest words you hear in school is that conglomerate "Whadjaget"?

Simon believes the grading system to be "the most destructive, demeaning, and pointless thing in education," and lists its only visible contributions as permitting the assistant principal to decide who is on probation and who can take an honor section; or determining who will go to Vietnam, who drops out, and who stays on the football team! He also refers to the ways it detracts from learning: Who reads the chapters that won't be on the test? Who reads the novels or plays that are not assigned? And who signs up for courses about which they are curious but which might earn them a low grade? Finally, he states, "What our students get out of a course boils down to a single, crude letter of the alphabet."

VII. Poor Scholar's Soliloquy (Corey, 1944)

No I'm not very good in school. This is my second year in the seventh grade and I'm bigger and taller than the other kids. They like me all right, though, even if I don't say much in the schoolroom, because outside I can tell them how to do a lot of things. They tag me around and that sort of makes up for what goes on in school.

I don't know why the teachers don't like me. They never have very much. Seems like they don't think you know anything unless they can name the book it comes out of. I've got a lot of books in my own room at home—books like *Popular Science Mechanical Encyclopedia,* and the Sears' and Ward's catalogues, but I don't very often just sit down and read them through like they make us do in school. I use my books when I want to find something out, like whenever Mom buys anything secondhand I look it up in Sears' or Ward's first and tell her if she's getting stung or not. I can use the index in a hurry to find the things I want.

In school, though, we've got to learn whatever is in the book and I just can't memorize the stuff. Last year I stayed after school every night for two weeks trying to learn the names of the Presidents. Of course I knew some of them like Washington and Jefferson and Lincoln, but there must have been thirty altogether and I never did get them straight.

I'm not too sorry though because the kids who learned the Presidents had to turn right around and learn all the Vice Presidents. I am taking the seventh grade over but our teacher this year isn't so interested in the names of the Presidents. She has us trying to learn the names of all the great American inventors.

I guess I just can't remember names in history. Anyway, this year I've been trying to learn about trucks because my uncle owns three and he says I can drive one when I'm sixteen. I already know the horsepower and number of forward and backward speeds of twenty-six American trucks, some of them Diesels, and I can spot each make a long way off. It's funny how that Diesel works. I started to tell my teacher about it last Wednesday in science class when the pump we were using to make a vacuum in a bell jar got hot, but she said she didn't see what a Diesel engine had to do with our experiment on air pressure so I just kept still. The kids seemed interested though. I took four of them around to my uncle's garage after school and we saw the mechanic, Gus, tearing a big truck Diesel down. Boy, does he know his stuff!

I'm not very good in geography either. They call it economic geography this year. We've been studying the imports and exports of Chile all week but I couldn't tell you what they are. Maybe the reason is I had to miss school yesterday because my uncle took me and his big trailer truck down state about two hundred miles and we brought almost ten tons of stock to the Chicago market.

He had told me where we were going and I had to figure out the highways to take and also the mileage. He didn't do anything but drive and turn where I told him to. Was that fun! I sat with a map in my lap and told him to turn south or southeast or some other direction. We made seven stops and drove over five hundred miles round trip. I'm figuring now what his oil cost and also the wear and tear on the truck—he calls it depreciation—so we'll know how much we made.

I even write out all the bills and send letters to the farmers about what their pigs and beef cattle brought at the stockyards. I only made three mistakes in 17 letters last time, my aunt said—all commas. She's been through high school and reads them over. I wish I could write school themes that way. The last one I had to write was on, "What a Daffodil Thinks of Spring," and I just couldn't get going.

I don't do very well in school in arithmetic either. Seems I just can't keep my mind on the problems. We had one the other day like this:

If a 57 foot telephone pole falls across a cement highway so that $17^3/6$ feet extend from one side and $14^9/17$ feet from the other, how wide is the highway?

That seemed to me like an awfully silly way to get the width of a highway. I didn't even try to answer it because it didn't say whether the pole had fallen straight across or not.

Even in shop I don't get very good grades. All of us kids made a broom holder and a bookend this term and mine were sloppy. I just couldn't get interested. Mom doesn't use a broom anymore with her new vaccum cleaner and all our books are in a bookcase with glass doors in the parlor. Anyway, I wanted to make an end gate for my uncle's trailer but the shop teacher said that meant using metal and wood both and I'd have to learn how to work with wood first. I didn't see why but I kept still and made a tie rack at school and the tail gate after school at my uncle's garage. He said I saved him $10.

Civics is hard for me, too. I've been staying after school trying to learn the "Articles of Confederation" for almost a week because the teacher said we couldn't be good citizens unless we did. I really tried, because I want to be a good citizen. I did hate to stay after school, though, because a bunch of us boys from the south end of town have been cleaning up the old lot across from Taylor's Machine Shop to make a playground out of it for the little kids from the Methodist home. I made the jungle gym from old pipe and the guys made me Grand Mogul to keep the playground going. We raised enough money collecting scrap this month to build a wire fence clear around the lot.

Dad says I can quit school when I'm fifteen and I'm sort of anxious to because there are a lot of things I want to learn how to do and as my uncle says, I'm not getting any younger.

Beyond the Classroom Experiences

1. Visit schools operating under various philosophies, plans, and curricula. If possible, talk with children and parents about their learning and how they feel about it. Note the relative percentage of students vs. teacher-initiated activity; positive vs. negative reinforcements; "good" vs. "bad" behavior; noise and motion vs. quiet and passivity. Note if use is made of books or of less traditional media.

2. Talk with a preschooler about his concept of school, noting if he is excited or afraid, where he got his ideas, what he thinks school is for. Talk with first-graders about their first day at school: what surprised them and how they felt.

3. Survey children of varying ages concerning what is important in a teacher. See if age influences opinion.

4. Observe cross-age teaching to see what methods children use to transmit information to their younger peers. Look for evidences of involvement, excitement, productivity.

5. Discuss with principals, parents, and teachers grading scales used in local schools for children ages 5–12. Note the assumptions underlying these scales. Determine if developmental principles are taken into consideration.

6. Attend a PTA meeting. Note the business items discussed; program presented; interaction of parents and teachers. What was your reaction to content and tenor of meeting in the light of developmental needs of children?

7. Discuss with a child his report card to see how he interprets the information, how he feels about it, the relative importance it has for him, and why he received certain marks or comments.

8. Contact local school personnel concerning violence and vandalism prevalence and control.

9. Compare the back to basics curriculum with the curriculum being followed in local schools to see if there are appreciable differences, and if so, what.

10. Visit some alternative school settings and evaluate student interest, involvement, achievement and attitudes.

Chapter 5

Peer Influences and Activities

This chapter is designed to help you:

- become familiar with the social development of the child of the middle years.
- identify the contributions of the peer group to its members.
- account for the sex cleavage so typical of this age.
- cite some problems that would logically arise during school age due to social development.
- examine the bases for friendship among children.
- understand the use of the sociometric technique in assessing peer acceptance in a group.
- be familiar with the goals and contributions of youth organizations.
- know the desirable traits of adults leading youth groups.
- explore the pros and cons concerning the place of lessons, organized sports, and group affiliations for this age group.

The Child Society

Although the mind, body, and emotions continue to grow and develop at a steady, even pace during middle childhood, the social side of life moves ahead in a bounding fashion for the child whose world has suddenly expanded through school entrance and its accompanying activities and experiences. Certain factors that contribute to the sequence of social growth are organic in nature, whereas others are functions of the culture.

But this phase of development cannot be thought of as a straight road from childhood to adulthood; there occurs during the middle years a necessary detour on the road to maturity, via the peer group. At this time relationships with adults often digress, whereas those with age-mates flourish. And herein lie potential problems for parents and professionals dealing with children which require an understanding of the socialization during this stage of growing.

Consider the following occurrences at this period to gain a general feeling for the challenges inherent in middle childhood socialization patterns. Children seem to draw together and gain strength from each other as they pull away from adults in their desire for independence. This subculture, the society of children, has traditions, games, values, loyalties, and rules separate and apart from the adult society in which it exists. These are handed down from one generation of children to the next.

Part of the dilemma faced by adults is that times have changed since they were children, and many adults have forgotten how very strong and intense the membership in the child society was and is. They assume that all is open for them to see, when actually there may be conscious efforts by their children to exclude them from that special sphere (Rogers, 1969).

> . . . school-age children learn to keep their thoughts from adults. They stop thinking out loud, and, besides, practice deliberate guile and deception. To fortify their sometimes hostile, sometimes bland taciturnity toward adults, together with their peer-group solidarity, they form secret societies. Although a given club may last no more than days or weeks, it may be protected by mortal oaths

Establishment of satisfactory peer relationships is of crucial importance; failure to do so often continues into adulthood. (Photo by Rick Coleman.)

and covenants, binding for life and countersigned in blood (or perhaps red ink) (Stone and Church, 1968(a), p. 362).

When communication begins to lessen, parents should still keep the opportunities open. They can still judge children's progress toward maturity by noting the topic of their conversations and jokes, the plans they make, the words they use, and the methods by which they make decisions.

The Peer Group

One of the tasks of the middle childhood person is to make attachments to age mates—the formation and use of the peer group. This does not mean that home and family no longer are important to children. The family base and activities may be the key to beneficial peer interaction. The child is better able to use the peer group if he operates from a framework of strong self-esteem, self-worth and acceptance.

It is important to examine the impact of dependence on peers as this affects the activities and attitudes of children. Perhaps at this stage of development it would be better to approach this period with the idea of helping the child to keep one foot in the adult world while he reaches out for information and experience to the peer group. Recent research points in this direction.

Based on scores on the Dilemma Test (Bronfenbrenner *et al*, 1965) in which subjects responded to a series of conflict situations by choosing between peer norms and adult values, 432 sixth graders were classified as either peer-oriented or adult-oriented (Condry and Siman, 1974). The peer-oriented boys spent more time with friends than with family and had more friends "not in your classroom." There was the same trend among the girls in the sample, although the differences were not statistically significant. Peer-oriented boys and girls reported more friends who "live near you" than the adult-oriented children did.

Behavior of the children was examined through self report and teacher ratings. Peer-oriented subjects engaged in more socially undesirable (Category I) behavior such as playing hooky, smoking, doing something illegally; and in more affiliation-oriented activities (Category II) such as listening to records, talking about other kids, going to movies or parties. Adult-oriented children engaged in more socially desirable (Category III) behavior such as helping someone, making or building something, and talking about books. Adult-oriented subjects saw themselves as dependable and obedient, more conforming to adults and less conforming to peers. They endorsed socially desirable values: being on time, doing school lessons and work around the house and not using bad language.

Peer-oriented children, on the whole, had negative attitudes about themselves and did less well in school than adult-oriented children. Their social interaction was marked by a distance and a lack of concern: they reported saying and doing things to hurt other people but less often "feeling badly" about this than other children. They most often reported not being able to keep their minds on what they were supposed to be doing, not being able to think of right answers at school and expecting bad things to happen, and were seemingly less concerned or anxious about these things than other children. Less often than adult-oriented children, peer-oriented children reported feeling good or happy about any of their activities or associations. Even though they were much less willing to spend an afternoon with their parents than adult-oriented children, peer-oriented children were not more willing to spend an afternoon with their friends. Peer-oriented children reported themselves to be mean, disobedient, and less dependable more often than adult-oriented children.

Adult-oriented children, more than peer-oriented children, conformed to adult values and seemed to feel comfortable in this conformity. Girls "feel happy about the ways things are going" and that "the things I do turn out right." Boys "feel good about the things I've done" and "about the things that are going to happen." These adult-oriented children had significantly higher overall self-esteem scores than the peer-oriented children.

The parents of adult-oriented children were much more active and involved with them than the parents of peer-oriented children: they gave more support to both boys and girls, and more control to boys. Peer-oriented children were a little more punished, but not significantly so. Parents of adult-oriented children were nurturant, demanding, consistent, and gave companionship and discipline. Mothers of peer-oriented boys were seen as significantly higher on only one trait, nagging and scolding.

The authors concluded that the family environment of the peer-oriented children is inadequate, so they are pushed into dependence on the peer group. Dependence on a group may meet different needs: information dependence versus affect dependence (Jones and Gerard, 1967), the desire to obtain information versus the desire to obtain emotional support. The person who is dependent on the group for information may feel free to move in and out of the group, either when informational needs are not being met or when the group begins to engage in anti-social behavior. The person who depends on the group for emotional support, however, would be more likly to conform and to take part in anti-social activities. Children who do not receive support within the family may be forced to look for this support among their peers. This would explain the ambivalent feelings reported. They cannot "buy into" the values of the adult world because of lack of help, but cannot feel entirely comfortable with the values of the peer group.

The higher self-esteem of the adult-oriented children emphasizes this family-inadequcy conclusion, also. Coopersmith's (1968) research points to the importance of parental involvement: children with high self-esteem were more likely to have concerned, demanding, consistent, encouraging parents than were other children. The involvement of parents with the children seems to make the difference, allowing the children to remain dependent while safely exploring other bases of support and learning from their peers.

Peer Group Functions

This is not to say the child's peer group is not important. It remains an important consideration for it performs for the child many of the same functions it serves for the adult. It is, in one sense, preparing him for the very life he is shunning through his disassociation with adults during this period.

Companionship. One basic function that peers serve is that of companionship—people to be with, to think with, and to talk with. The peer group helps you avoid boredom and loneliness. It provides a source of activity in those unstructured hours between school dismissal and the home's demands. It brings to life the looked-forward-to vacation times and weekends. The peer group helps to construct and inhabit tree houses, to concoct and consume ice-tray popsicles, to create and stage neighborhood fairs and dramas, and so on. It provides contacts with whom to exchange old comics, cereal box treasures, jokes and riddles, and boastful tales of accomplishment and adventure.

It is a transmitter of child culture, of superstitions, of games and ideas.

Birthday parties are often the child's first social experience outside the family. (Photo by Lin Mitchell.)

Not many of us learned from a book or a physical education teacher how to play scissors-paper-rock, or to give an Indian wrist burn. Few adults teach children to avoid stepping on a crack in the sidewalk because to do so would break a mother's back. (Step on a crack/Break your mother's back.) The sing-songy chants so common among children of this age have not come from a music book; few adults would desire their perpetuation. And yet they continue as a part of Americana—and a delightful part, to say the least! Long live the child's peer culture.

Testing Ground for Behavior. Another basic function of the peer group is to form the testing ground for behavior and the yardstick for one's inheritance. A child may discover for the first time that the behavior patterns that bring him success at home do not work among his friends at school or in community clubs or recreation centers. The tear may be replaced by the fist and the sulk by the give-and-take technique. To get along in the larger groups, not bound by kinship ties or adult-imposed rules, may require of the child much refinement or alteration of his social style. This he must usually learn by trial and error. It may even require him to establish two or more codes of behavior—one to satisfy his peers, and one to please his family. Conflict at home may result if he abandons the old ways and acts among his family in ways that are accepted by his peers. Most parents hope they have by school age instilled into their children some basic values that will guide their relationships: honesty, fidelity, consideration, fairness, and cleanliness. To succeed in the peer group may require some alteration of these attitudes.

The peer group supports the child's bid for independence from adults, giving him courage to protest family decisions ranging from trivial to highly important considerations: bedtime hour, amount of allowance, dress code, patterns of communication, assignment of chores, and choice of social activities. The group seems to give impetus to the youngster's seeking greater freedom and responsibility. With peer group support, children will often perform acts they would never dare attempt alone.

Transmitting Knowledge. Passing on of knowledge is also a peer group function—not only about incidental things but about biology, physics, chemistry, psychology, art, music, and literature. Each child brings to the peer group a different store of facts, a slightly different area of intellectual interest and experience, and different sources of information. Pooled, the total is phenomenal. Just as this age places more faith in the TV advertisement than in Dad's statement of fact, so children in the middle years believe what their peers tell them about life. And although some misinformation is transmitted, a great deal of factual knowledge is given and gained in the group. Some of it is generated by the children's spirit of discovery and learned through misjudgment. The boys who jumped from a tree limb to test their flying ability will probably have concrete evidence that gravity is a force in nature. And the girls who tried to concoct a cake by intuition will have new respect for chemistry—though they may not call it such.

Teaching Rules and Logical Consequences. The peer group is a great teacher of rules and logical consequences. Usually there is a strong code, whether it is in a game of baseball or a case of spitball-throwing behind the teacher's back. Both competition and cooperation are learned with one's peers. The group process, the roles of leader and follower, decision-making, and problem-solving are given emphasis, although nothing may ever be identified as such. Group penalties may not always be just, and they may be based on meager evidence, but they are frequently imposed and are often quite stringent. Ignoring or ostracizing a group member is a common form of punishment for violation of the group code. Fortunately, the period of punishment is not extended in most cases.

Acceptance in the Group

The child's success in social development will be contingent on many factors: his early experiences with his family; his parents' attitudes toward

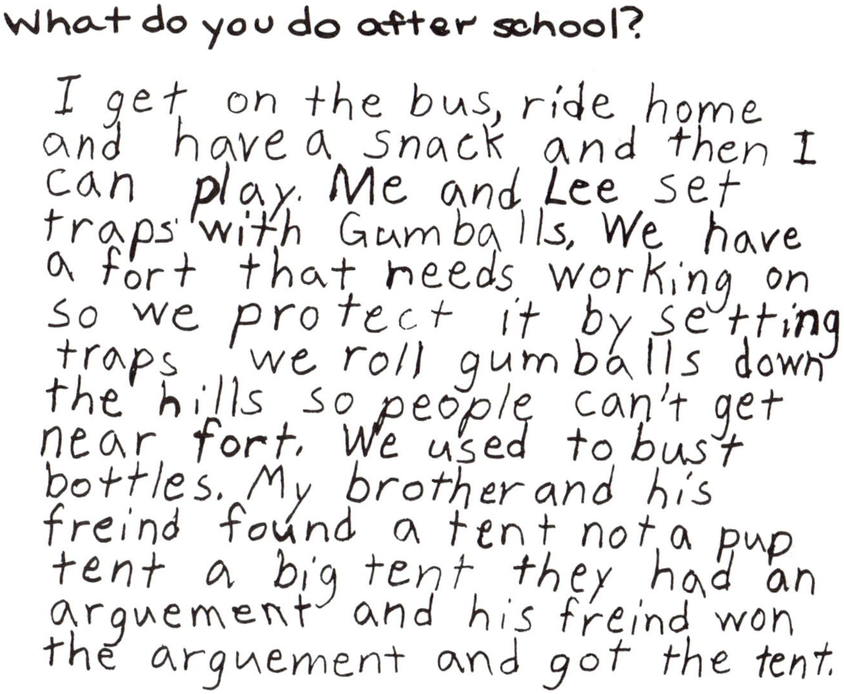

What do you do after school?

I get on the bus, ride home and have a snack and then I can play. Me and Lee set traps with Gumballs, We have a fort that needs working on so we protect it by setting traps we roll gumballs down the hills so people can't get near fort. We used to bust bottles. My brother and his freind found a tent not a pup tent a big tent they had an arguement and his freind won the arguement and got the tent.

Figure 5-1. Written by a nine-year-old boy.

him and their accompanying discipline style; his self-concept; the opportunities to interact with his peers and the family's reaction to these interactions; his ordinal position in the family; and his own individual traits. Acceptance by one's peers may pose a problem, particularly if the child has some physical or personality trait that may be feared or disliked.

A study (Richardson and Royce, 1968) of 10- to 12-year-old campers of Negro, Anglo, and Puerto Rican heritage measured the relative importance of physical disability and skin color to children selecting the "most liked" and "least liked" among their peers. Half the subjects were asked to rank-order six drawings showing children with handicaps. Both boys and girls selected the nonhandicapped child as best liked. Girls designated the obese child (cosmetic handicap) as least liked, whereas boys singled out a boy with an amputated left forearm (functional handicap).

The other children were divided into two groups. Half were shown a series of drawings in which the best- and least-liked children were black and the intermediate drawings were white. The other half viewed a series in which the best- and least-liked were white and the intermediate drawings were of black children. There were no significant changes in the ranking of the drawings. The conclusion drawn was that for these low-income children physical disability was a more powerful preference factor than skin color.

Establishment of satisfactory social relations during this age is paramount to success in subsequent stages of development, and failure to relate with peers during the school years often continues into adulthood. The skillful parent or professional working with children will watch for signs of failure in social development and help where possible to facilitate this important part of growing up.

Popularity is an area that causes problems for some children with respect to their social adjustment. Moderate self-concepts seem to contribute to popularity more than high or low ones (Reese, 1961). Friendliness and sociability foster acceptance by others while withdrawal and hostility reduce it (Smith, G. H., 1950). Above-average intelligence is a boon to social acceptance as are academic achievement and athletic skills (Gronlund, 1959). Pleasing appearance also helps one to be popular—at all ages, perhaps. Contributing to reduce popularity may be membership in a low-status group; possession of some disliked trait, as overtalking; lack of social experience; low desire to belong (Rogers, D., 1969).

Conformity is another aspect of social development with which children must deal. Conformity to the group rules and goals varies with both social class and subculture. Rural children tend to conform more than urban ones, and lower-class children more than upper-class ones (Iscoe et al., 1953). The child must struggle to conform to the proper degree so that he is not rejected by peers for being odd nor punished by others for his conformity.

While group pressure is strong, it is not always easy to follow the group, especially when the child has other ideas. In one study (Berenda, 1966) ninety children were asked to do a line matching test. Each child was brought into a situation in which eight other children had been instructed to give wrong answers in seven out of the twelve trials. More of the younger children than older children followed the wrong answer of the group. More children followed the majority group of answers when the length of the line was difficult to determine—when the material was more ambiguous. Although the children followed the group in many instances, it was not easy! A 7-year-old girl said she felt her "heartbeat go down" when the group gave answers she thought were incorrect. One boy tried to explain why some children followed the group even when it was wrong by saying that if one does too much disagreeing with people, they will think he is always disagreeable and get the wrong impression. Another boy explained that he knew the others were wrong, but that it was like a jury. There were nine children; and he was the only one against eight, and the majority wins. Anyway, he wondered how he could have proved he was right.

The conclusion was that although the children followed the group, they did not do this simply by blind faith in the majority or on instinct to imitate. They were affected by real factors in the situation. This points up, however, the strong pull of the group even when conformity is painful. Groups meet the child's need for companionship, support, and socialization. "There is a saying that God makes brothers, but man makes friends" (Mead and Heyman, 1965). Although families continue to be important, friendships take on added importance during middle childhood years.

Rejection among children is a fact of life, and usually during middle childhood expressions of rejection are not subtle but quite blatant. Membership in the wrong group, be it racial, ethnic, socioeconomic, or ability-based can cause ostracism. Lack of social experience because of home location, state of health, family patterns, or even shyness, can reduce popularity during these years.

Children who do not relate well to the group may be mavericks who really care very little for the group setting. They may be shy, merely unnoticed and neglected. Or they could greatly desire to belong to the group but be actively rebuffed. Extreme rejection may take the form of prejudice against or blanket disdain for children of a certain race, ethnic group, or religious group, or section of town (Rogers, D., 1969).

A study (Grottman, 1977) involving Head Start children throws light on different aspects of social isolation: low frequency of peer interaction and low levels of peer acceptance. In this research, sociometric assessments were used to measure acceptance and rejection by peers, and observational techniques were used to measure behavior when the child was alone, interacting with peers, or interacting with teachers. No relationship between frequency of peer interaction and peer acceptance was found, suggesting that these tap quite different dimensions of behavior. The children who had the lowest means on peer acceptance were those labeled as children who were tuned-out or off-tract when alone. These children were rated high on a set of shy, anxious and fearful behavior coded "hovering." These children were neither accepted nor rejected by their peers, but rather ignored by them. These children may need a very different support system and set of skills than the children who are actively rejected by peers or who have hostile interactions with peers.

Whatever the case, the helpful adult must discover the cause of the rejection but at the same time help the child learn the social rules of the society. It may be necessary to semistructure a situation in which the rejected child will have opportunity to demonstrate his abilities to his peers. Sometimes class lessons can be related to being a better friend, or some allied consideration. When significant adults show their respect for rejected children, peers may begin to take a second look.

Data indicate (Gronlund, 1959) that a number of children go through school with very few friends and sometimes without a friend at all: in one school system 6 percent of third to sixth graders were not selected by any classmate in a sociometric questionnaire; another 12 percent were selected by only one. Isolated children have fewer opportunities for social learning from their peers, an important developmental task of this stage of development. Isolated children, also, are more likely to drop out of school (Ullman, 1957), to become delinquent (Roff, Seels and Golden, 1972), and to have mental health problems (Cowen et al, 1973). Can children be taught skills that will make them more accepted and less rejected by other children?

Odin and Asher (1977) set up a situation in which a group of third and fourth grade isolates were coached in social skills. After four weeks of training, the coached group showed an increase on a play sociometric rating which was significantly greater than a similar group who had played games with peers to increase game skills, or a control group of isolates who, along with a group of their peers, had played individual games. The same increase was evident a year later (see Figure 5-2), when the mean sociometric play score of the coached children was only a bit below the classroom mean. The peer-pairing group made some gain; the control group, no gain. Four of eight of the coached children received scores above the classroom mean. For only one of seven in each of the other groups was this the case.

The instruction began with identification of social skills which were considered useful in making a game fun or enjoyable to play with another person: participation (getting started, paying attention); cooperation (taking turns, sharing materials); communication (talking with and listening to the other person); validation and support (giving attention or help, looking at the person, smiling, being friendly). The coach proposed the concepts, then asked the child to give specific examples of the concept from the game

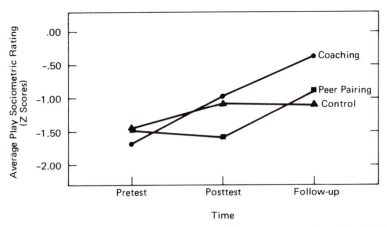

Figure 5-2. Average play sociometric ratings for groups across time. (From S. Oden and S. R. Asher, "Coaching Children in Social Skills for Friendship Making." *Child Development*, 1977, 48:2, 504.)

---

experience just finished. The coach repeated or rephrased the child's example and clarified or extended it as necessary. The child was asked also to give examples of opposite kinds of behavior, and to evaluate the two kinds of behavior: which would be likely to make the game more fun for both players. The child was instructed to try out the behaviors, and immediately after the next play session the coach had a de-briefing session with him: did you get a chance to try out any of the ideas we talked about last time? Later on the coach also asked if there had been any opportunities to try out the ideas in a classroom situation.

Whereas the coaching did make a difference in play sociometric scores, it did not generalize to work situations. There was, however, a slight increase in the number of friendship nominations for the children in the coached group. Intervention at earlier ages than nine and ten might lessen the child's coming to see himself as an isolate and therefore make social acceptance skills easier to learn.

Friendships

Children need other children. They must learn to create perceptions of children and adults. How is this done? How do children define friends? What is important to them? As the child becomes able to differentiate among other people, self-concept development is assisted and the individual is better able to anticipate his own and others' behavior, thus aiding social interaction.

In a study of children's perceptions of peers (Scarlett, Press and Crockett, 1971), 108 boys from first, third and fifth grades were asked to describe four persons: a boy he liked; one he disliked; a girl he liked; one he disliked. Each subject was also asked to re-tell a recorded story and specifically to describe the two boys in the story. Responses were assigned to one of four categories: *concrete-we constructs:* in which the subject described what he and the person did together (e.g., we play together); *egocentric-concrete constructs:* in which the subject described some behavior of the peer in a particular situation with the subject himself as object of the action (e.g., he hits me; he gives me things); *nonegocentric-concrete constructs:* in which the subject continued to describe concrete behavior, but did not include himself as object of such behavior (e.g., he plays baseball; he hits people all the time); *abstract constructs:* in which the subject referred to qualities that were not limited to a specific context (e.g., he is intelligent; he is kind).

First grade boys used more egocentric-concrete constructs. Nonegocentric constructs were the next most commonly used. The same was true for third graders; but in this group there was a greater proportion of nonegocentric constructs, both concrete and abstract, than among first graders. Among fifth graders, abstract constructs were most common, followed by nonegocentric concrete constructs. In relation to the fictional boys, the number and level of the constructs increased with the age of the subjects.

Experience with a person (more frequent interaction), independent of increasing age, should produce an increase in the contruct level used and fuller descriptions (Crockett, 1965). The boys produced significantly more responses to describe "liked boys than "disliked boys". No significant difference was found in the descriptions of "liked" and "disliked" girls. Another difference which appeared was the number of concepts used to describe boys and girls. At each grade level, boys were described more fully than girls. At the fifth grade, however, "disliked" girls were described more fully than "liked" girls. Supnick (1967) reported the opposite condition among high school males who described "liked girls" in more detail than "disliked girls". The younger boys had global undifferentiated concepts of girls: "All girls are the same, really"; "They all look alike and do the same stupid stuff."

Scarlett *et al.* (1971) concluded that with increasing age there were increasingly perceptive descriptions of people in differing roles. In addition, relationships between people affect the perception held and the resulting descriptions. It may be that changes in behavior parallel this shift from egocentric to nonegocentric and from concrete to abstract conceptualizations. Piaget (1966), according to Scarlett (1971), suggested that the rise in inferential thinking and the decrease in egocentricity comes about as a result of the interaction of increased cognitive ability and the growing desire of the individual to cooperate with others. However, Scarlett *et al.* (1971) reminds us that constraint should be used in drawing inferences about the actual interactions of the children based on their conceptualizations. The children who conceptualize at the lowest level may still be able to deal with their peers in a much more mature manner than indicated by their verbal construct. For example, one of the youngest boys who said, " I don't like John because he stole my milk once," may be quite able to behave as if he thought of John as dishonest and to protect himself accordingly. These data point to the conclusion that children with increasing age and cognitive skills find their peers more interesting and unique as evidenced by descriptive constructs employed.

Bigner (1974) employed the same methodology with a sample of siblings and reported slightly different results. His sample consisted of 240 sibling pairs at kindergarten, second, fourth, sixth and eighth grade levels. At each grade level there were 24 males and 24 females who were second-born in a two-child family with half the sample closely spaced to sibling (12 to 20 months) and half the sample distantly spaced from sibling (28 to 48 months). In each of these divisions, half of the children had an older brother and half had an older sister. The children were asked to describe their older sibling in terms of what the sibling did and what the subject liked and disliked about that brother or sister. The responses were coded in the same manner as used in the Scarlett (1971) study.

With increasing age there was the expected shift from the use of concrete and egocentric constructs in describing siblings to nonegocentric and abstract modes. The qualities which the children liked in older siblings were described, however, with concrete-we and egocentric responses and disliked qualities were described in nonegocentric-concrete and abstract responses; this was true across all ages. Female siblings were described in more detail by kindergarteners, second and fourth graders, while male siblings were described in more detail by sixth- and eighth-graders. With increasing age, lower level concepts were used more often to describe female siblings, higher level constructs to describe male siblings.

In Scarlett's data, the number of responses increased, and abstract and egocentric concrete constructs were the most used descriptors for liked males (close interaction); whereas nonegocentric-concrete constructs were more often used to describe disliked peers, neither of these concept levels reached statistical significance. We would expect, then, that closely-spaced siblings, who presumably have greater interaction than distantly spaced ones, would follow this general pattern. Bigner's data (1974) indicate that

Children have definite criteria on which they select friends. (Photo by Lin Mitchell.)

children who were closely spaced to their older sibling used a greater number of constructs with increasing age than children who were distantly spaced from older siblings. In closely spaced pairs, the subject used more egocentric concrete constructs, with nonegocentric responses coming next. In distantly spaced pairs, the subject used more nonegocentric-concrete constructs followed by egocentric-concrete constructs. This held true over the age span investigated in this study. Closely spaced children responded with dynamic and positive content about siblings. They talked about psychologically close "care-taking" activities. The distantly spaced siblings were psychologically distant and the activities of these older siblings could be described in more general terms.

In a study of friendship expectations (FE) of Canadian and Scottish children from 6 to 14 years of age, Bigelow (1977) analyzed essays describing best friends, coding them in reference to 25 FE dimensions which he had defined. Four of these appeared in fewer than 5 percent of the essays and were dropped from further consideration: mutual activities, similarity of personal characteristics, physical attractiveness and ritualistic social exchange. Of the remaining 21, eleven increased in importance with age: common activities; evaluation; propinquity; character admiration (same rank as propinquity); acceptance; loyalty; commitment; genuineness; common interests; and intimacy potential. The last FE was mentioned only by girls. Three dimensions, ego-reinforcement, reciprocity of liking, and having friend as a receiver, did not increase in importance with age. Bigelow suggested these affective values remain basically important throughout childhood and that only the cognitive values of friendship change over time. Egoreinforcement and reciprocal liking may transcend the age-related changes in the conceptual basis of friendship expectations.

The data support the idea of an invariant sequence in the development of friendship expectations. Three stages are defined. The first stage involves common activities and propinquity, or the more superficial aspects of friendship. The second stage places emphasis on norms and rules of friendship; the dimensions deal mainly with character admiration and are similar to moral values that are socially sanctioned. The third stage includes empathy, understanding and self-disclosure. Disposition attributes are important in this stage. This level is closely linked to the ideas expressed by Maslow (1954) and Rogers (1962): "unconditional positive regard" and "self actualization."

Important questions concerning the development of friendship patterns are raised by Bigelow.

1. To what extent are the friendship expectations of a person important in determining the likelihood of his being chosen as a friend?
2. Are friendship choices made according to characteristics of the general stage of development or in reference to specific friendship expectations?
3. Are there friendship expectations that a child may not be able to verbalize, but which are important to friendship choices? Is there a non-verbal tech-

nique for exploring friendship expectations of children; and would this give very different results and bring new understanding in this area?

4. What are the roles of social influence and developing cognitive skills in conceptualization of friendship expectations? How well does friendship expectation development parallel intellectual growth? This question grows out of the fact that less than half the 13- and 14-year-olds, who supposedly are at the period of mastering formal operational thought, were at Stage 3 of Friendship Expectations as proposed by Bigelow. These children may, of course, understand advanced friendship expectations, but for some reason may not be willing to express them: lack of verbal skills, shyness, or other inhibitions from the social framework in which they live.

Preschoolers usually have one or two friends. During the early school years, the number of close friends increases from four to six or eight. Some older children would rather do things with one or two best friends. Some children tend toward intensive friendships, a best friend or two, while others tend toward extensive friendships, the neighborhood group or "gang." These may change over time. In a one-to-one relationship there is more sharing of experiences and fantasies, more involvement with one another. In a group of three or more there is more activity probably centered around mutual interest or games (Waldrop and Halverson, 1975).

Waldrop and Halverson (1975) examined the peer-involvement practices of 62 seven-and-a-half-year-old children by coding a play diary which each mother kept for a week (the Week in Review) and through interviews with the mothers and with the children, gathered data on such things as: number of hours with peers, with one peer, with more than one peer; number of peers seen; number of times child initiated the getting together or determined the activity chosen; number of peers in neighborhood; proportion of friends of same sex and of those within one year of age of child.

The pattern of a peer-oriented seven-and-a-half-year-old girl was somewhat different from that of a seven-and-a-half-year-old boy. Play in groups of three or more was more characteristic of boys than of girls. "For boys, social ease, importance of peers and hours with peers were associated with measures of extension. For girls, social ease, importance of peers and hours with peers were associated with measures of intensiveness (Waldrop and Halverson, 1975, p. 25)." Intensiveness was defined in terms of frequent mention of a best friend by both mother and child; referral to the best friend daily in the Week in Review. Extension was defined in terms of frequent mention by both mother and child of group activity such as playing ball or being on the playground or outside with a group of children.

Girls saw more peers, had a higher percentage of time in which they initiated getting together with peers or choosing the play activity and were rated higher on importance of peers. Boys were higher than girls (but not significantly so) on the number of hours spent with more than one peer.

The differences in boys and girls in extensive vs. intensive peer relationships may be explained by different play interests. Boys more than girls chose games (Sutton-Smith, Rosenberg and Morgan, 1963) involving unrestrained movement, such as football and baseball, or pretended assaults, such as cops and robbers or cowboys. Girls, on the other hand, chose nurturing activities, such as dolls, dressing up, house, or restrained, precise movement such as hopscotch, jump rope, or jacks.

Boys are more active and noisy which leads them to extensive relations rather than intensive ones. They may be thrown into group situations more than girls because they may be told more often, because of the above characteristics, to "go out and play." The less noisy, less rowdy girls, who are less motorically active and more person-oriented would probably be permitted to play inside more often, where a relationship with one friend, rather than a group, is more apt to occur.

Children need to get along with people of the same age and those of different ages. The child who is popular is usually rated as cheerful, generous, friendly, cooperative, honest, and even-tempered. He is a good sport and has a sense of humor. Children are conscious of their appearance and rate attractiveness as important in popularity. The more contacts the child has with the group, the greater his chance to form friendships and to be accepted by the group. The child from a happy home is more likely to be popular than the child from a home where there is friction.

While such obvious physical characteristics as obesity and disability have been found reliably related to children's social acceptance, evidence (Kleck, Richardson, and Ronald, 1974) is now suggesting that less obvious physical traits are also important clues to interpersonal attraction. Nine- to fourteen-year-olds in a camp setting, asked to select "a friend" and the "better looking" boy from paired photographs representing unknown high- and low-socially accepted former campers, chose the high-acceptance child a significantly greater number of times. Again, the chosen child was regarded as the more attractive of the pair. Attractiveness judgments were reportedly based on facial cues 73 percent of the time. The most often mentioned influencers of attractiveness were the hair, eyes, teeth, and mouth. Responses referred to the unattractiveness of the unchosen one in the pair 73 percent of the time. Over half of the children mentioned such features as posture, head and body size and affect cues such as "looking sad." Approximately 20 percent also mentioned action clues: he looks like he would like to kill his mother.

Attractiveness or lack of it may continue to be important to children even after a significant period of interaction. It may be that attractive children are more at ease and therefore able to behave in ways which cause other children to accord them high acceptance.

Good friends are important to children, but so is an enemy. To have someone on the outside seems to give more "in-ness" to the inside! Belongingness and exclusion are two sides of the same coin. Something of this aspect of a secret club is portrayed in the following quotation (*New Yorker,* September 18, 1954):

The rules of a secret society of nine- and ten-year-old girls in a certain community on Long Island that shall here be nameless are as follows:

1. Do not tell a white lie unless necessary.
2. Do not hurt anyone in any way.
3. Do not hit anyone except Ronny.
4. Do not tell a black lie.
5. Do not use words worse than "brat."
6. Do not curse at all.
7. Do not make faces except at Ronny.
8. Do not be selfish.
9. Do not make a hog or a pig of yourself.
10. Do not tattle except on Ronny.
11. Do not steal except from Ronny.
12. Do not destroy other people's property, except Ronny's.
13. Do not be a sneak.
14. Do not be grumpy except to Ronny.
15. Do not answer back except to Ronny.

Think Back

To your closest friends when you were young:
Where they lived.
What about their family life was different from yours.
Some daring adventures you shared.
The secret meeting place or special code you used.
Some things you never told your parents about doing.

In including or excluding persons as friends, social interaction, facial recognition skills are important. Little is known about how this complex visual image information is processed, how it is encoded or the social factors that affect this processing. Feinman and Entwisle (1976) used color slides of black and white children to test the facial recognition ability of black and white children from seven to ten years of age in both segregated and non-segregated schools. Recognition ability increased with increasing age of the subjects. The rate of increase was not so great after grade three. Other research (Feinman and Entwisle, 1973) indicated that this ability continues to level off, and that adults are only slightly better than sixth graders.

Children from segregated schools had better overall scores than children from integrated schools. It is the scores from the second and third graders that produce this difference, with the segregated third graders doing as well as the integrated sixth graders. Girls are better than boys at every grade level. Female pictures are remembered better than male pictures by children at all ages and of both sexes. The difference score is greater for males than for females.

Both races recognize pictures of their own race better than pictures of the other race with blacks better at recognizing white faces than whites are at recognizing blacks. The difference in own-other scores was greater for children who attended segregated schools than for those who attended integrated schools. The difference was more pronounced for children living in segregated neighborhoods. Subsequent analysis suggested that integration of neighborhoods may have a greater effect on recognition scores than integration of schools.

In order to explain these data, the authors suggested that persons may pay closer attention to small cues differentiating persons above them in social class and that blacks have had more experience in looking at white faces than vice versa (i.e., television). The higher scores in segregated schools and the smaller own-other difference scores in integrated schools may be linked to the fact that segregated neighborhoods have an impact on children in limiting experience with black faces, and many of the children in integrated schools come from segregated neighborhoods. It seems that own-other difference scores are significant for all children except when the majority of people in the neighborhood are of the other race. One benefit of early integration which the authors pointed out is that there is improvement of recognition ability of opposite race persons. This ability evidently must be developed in the childhood years, with little improvement during adolescence and adulthood.

Sociometry

Aside from mere observation and conjecture as to the social structure in a group of children, one may wonder how to identify problems which children may have with the structure. An objective approach to such diagnosis lies in *sociometry,* a term derived from Latin meaning "social" or "companion measurement." The originator of sociometric tests was Jacob L. Moreno (1934), and through this method one may identify social relations in a group, organize the group in ways to aid social development, and evaluate the growth in group acceptance by the various members. It lends itself to use in the classroom, the club, the factory, and the community setting. It is a simple technique—quick to administer and requiring no expenditure of funds.

The technique involves posing a sociometric question to the subjects, collecting their answers, and arranging the data into a graphic form. The question should relate to working in close proximity—as in project or study groups. Or spending leisure time together—as with play or party companions. "Whom do you like best?" or "Who are your best friends?"

Conformity is a strong desire among peer-group members: eating out of lunchbox tops. (Photo by Lin Mitchell.)

are not considered appropriate queries. The question should also elicit positive, rather than negative, choices, since identifying those one would least like to be with could reinforce such a feeling.

Respondents are often asked to make three ranked choices. In order for all persons in the group to have a "fair" chance, the technique should be employed only after everyone has had opportunity to know everyone else, and all members of the group should be present. In addition, it is important to assure the group that the choices will be kept strictly confidential; but the data could be used in some later grouping activity, lest children become suspicious as to the need for gathering it. For example, if the question concerned their choices for project work, the teacher might well assign them to the approximate work groups their choices dictated. With children below the fourth grade, it is recommended that choices be made orally in private interviews with the teacher. In higher grades, they may be written on a prepared form or a blank sheet of paper. Use of sociometry at seven- or eight-week periods permits one to see changes within the group structure and allows the pupils to view the choices as realistic.

A sociogram can be used to arrange the data into a meaningful form. Using symbols to designate group members and drawing lines and arrows

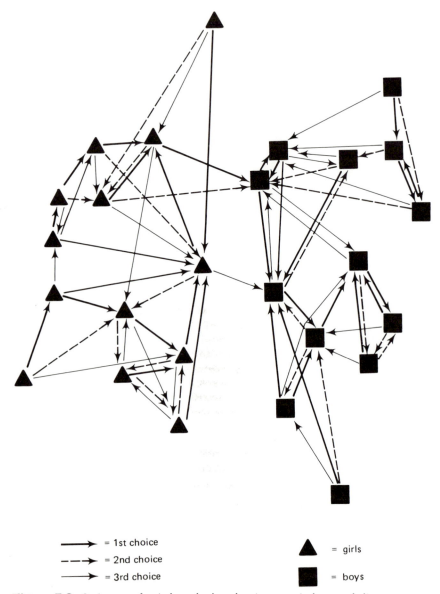

⟶ = 1st choice	▲ = girls
---→ = 2nd choice	
⟶ = 3rd choice	■ = boys

Figure 5-3. Sociogram of a sixth grade class showing stars, isolates, and cliques.

to indicate direction of choice, you can graphically represent the preferences expressed. (See Figure 5-3.) The target diagram utilizing four concentric circles and grouping the most-chosen persons in the center and the least-chosen in the outer circle may also be employed. In the upper elementary grades, when division of the sexes in occurring, the sociogram may be divided on this criterion for further inspection. Those students who receive a large number of choices are called *stars*; they are usually considered the group leaders or potentials leaders. Those who receive no choices are termed *isolates*. Subgroups within the group are called *cliques*, and *cleavage* is indicated when there is lack of sociometric choices among the cliques.

The sociogram may be made more meaningful when other data are also collected relative to the subjects. This may be based on the teacher's observation, anecdotal recording, or investigation of pupil permanent folders. Respondents may be asked to provide written reasons for their choices or to state these orally in private interviews with the teacher. When the teacher understands the reasons for the choices, she is in a better position to facilitate group cohesiveness and foster a sense of worth in each child (Gronlund, 1959).

A number of personal and social factors may affect sociometric results, among them intelligence, achievement, age, skill, physical appearance, interests, values, and personality characteristics. Too great a deviation from other group members on these personal traits seems to contribute to lower sociometric status on the part of the deviant. The community social structure, their family experiences, their residential proximity to other children, and social cleavages in the community have also been found to affect sociometric choices.

Various problems may be highlighted by the use of sociometry: the lack of mutual relationships; a decline in sociometric status; unrealistic social aspirations; extreme dependence on the peer group. In each case a study of the factors causing the social difficulty will suggest the type of remedial action necessary.

Think Back

To feelings of aloneness:
When your family life differed from that of your friends.
When you were ashamed of yourself; when you felt superior.
When there was no one to play with.
When you were not chosen.

One who uses sociometry to study socialization of children should bear in mind several facts: the sociogram represents desired associations, not actual ones; the group structure and desires are ever-changing, not static; the technique does not explain why but only shows which children are most or least chosen.

The "guess who" technique employed in Tyron's research (1939) also lends itself to a study of acceptance. It is possible to achieve a measure of peer acceptance by asking the group to respond to such questions as

"Who's the most fun to be with?" "Who gets mad easiest?" "Who studies the hardest?"—and then noting which characteristics are assigned to the various group members. Used in conjunction with a ranking of qualities the same group deems good or bad in their peers, these designations would be more meaningful.

Youth Organizations and Activities

Whereas most peer relationships are not in formalized settings during middle childhood, clubs and other organizations with youth memberships provide some structured opportunities for interpersonal interaction during this period. Children will form their own groups, such as the Dennis the Menace Club which met each week at a special place. With the coming of winter and the continual loss of membership cards, the club broke up. They may institute secret organizations, like the Pottawatomie Pack formed by boys; or the Batman Club, a group of girls who meet in Kay's backyard on the trampoline. One club had five members. They met every Saturday afternoon under a bridge at the edge of town. They counted cars and marked down every one that needed washing.

Children at this age also belong to nationally known as well as locally conceived organizations planned for them, becoming more active as their age increases. Schools sponsor subject-matter groups—such as the science or library club; those planned to promote recreation and aesthetics—such as the drama club or Junior Garden Clubs of America; some that foster physical efficiency—such as the skating club or intramural teams. Others may center around a vocational interest—such as Future Teachers of America. Still others have as their goal the teaching of civic, moral, and social responsibility—namely Camp Fire Girls, Boys and Girls Clubs of America, Scouts, Gray-Y, Tri-Y, and 4-H. (See Figure 5-4.)

These programs place major emphasis on personal involvement, improvement, and achievement. Yet they provide small and large group opportunities for their members. The structure of such organizations fosters healthy communication and active cooperation between the child and the adult leaders, facilitating such relationships in camping situations, at fairs, and in other settings that encourage informal banter and sharing of confidences and fears.

Youth activities sponsored by churches and synagogues offer many opportunities for growth and development. Perhaps the program reaching the largest number of children is Sunday school. In some areas children of certain faiths are given released time during the regular school day to receive religious instruction in their various houses of worship. Others attend special classes or activities prior to or following school on a daily or weekly

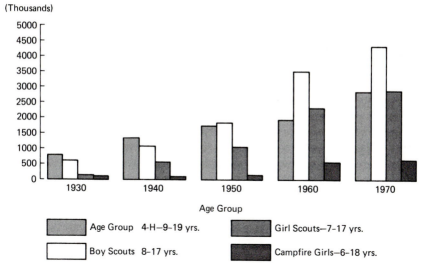

Figure 5-4. Membership in youth service organizations: U.S., 1930–1970. (From *Profiles of Children*. Washington, D.C.: U.S. Government Printing Office, 1970, p. 35.)

basis. Informal programs in many churches include choirs, sports, drama, camping, dancing, and other recreation.

Depending on the particular orientation of an organization, it can benefit members by offering opportunities for them to apply the knowledge acquired in school and elsewhere, promote a wholesome use of leisure time, foster socialization with peers, and develop leadership and skills in the democratic process. Whereas the members hold the offices and collectively make the decisions, there is available skillful adult guidance, which is lacking in the informal groupings children create themselves in backyards, secret clubhouses, and basements.

Group loyalty and identity are likewise enhanced by formal membership, with the attendant membership card, uniform, insignia, and official publications. Such traits as trustworthiness, clear thinking, cleanliness, and kindness become a group goal, and the spirit is catching. Although these organizations have not in the past catered to these needs among certain segments of the population, there is a current trend to make their services available to all children. These groups quite often consciously try to include the family in some of their activities, encouraging increased understanding between the member and his parents and siblings. When everyone else in the group brings his mother or brother to a function, it becomes the "in" thing to do, and with such group support, a child has the courage to also invite a member of his family. In such cases consideration should be given to the child whose family will not or cannot participate. Perhaps a plan for a "big brother" or "foster aunt" can be arranged.

In addition, the child comes in contact with attitudes and behaviors different from those within his family. He begins to accept other points of view; he becomes an individual in his own right. Adults place high value on group life and social acceptance in the present culture; so American children learn independence earlier than children in other cultures. American children, at an earlier age than Swiss children, for example, choose to accept the advice of another child on a project in preference to that of an adult. Swiss children have less confidence in their peers, believe longer in the omniscience of adult authorities, and are more afraid of their teachers than are American children of the same ages (Boehm, 1957).

What boys and girls expect from a group of this type is determined by their needs, their drives, and their hopes and fears. If the group's activities meet reasonably well the expectations of its members, it will be a useful tool of society to acculturate and educate the child. The adult leader in youth groups should be attuned to the needs and wishes of the membership while still guiding their efforts in worthwhile undertakings. The function of such a leader is not to give boys and girls "what they want" but to help them toward an intelligent grasp of what it is they ultimately desire. For example, their interest in a dramatic club might not necessarily mean they will be fond of memorizing lines; rather, it may indicate their wish to gain the prestige which accompanies performance or to have the feeling of being someone else for a time. Fedder (1965) has listed several functions of the effective adult leader of youth groups:

- Developing group morale.
- Furnishing resources for the group's use in planning and executing plans.
- Fostering initiative, curiosity, self-direction and sense of responsibility in members.
- Guiding resolution of disagreements within the group through open discussion of the issues involved.
- Representing verbally and by example constructive values in which members can believe.

Adult leaders of youth groups need the same characteristics as a successful parent or teacher, plus a few more. Where the parent or teacher possesses a legal or moral force, this leader must rely on his skill in maintaining members' interest in the activities of the group. One who senses and accepts their group need is valued, as well as someone who will talk seriously with them when they feel this need. Young people admire someone who has a wide range of knowledge, who can build and play skillfully with his hands, who is warm and genuine. Willingness is no longer the only legitimate criterion for such a leader if success is to be achieved.

Parents may equate their children's membership and participation in organized youth groups with social success or even family social standing. Some even consider their parental duty largely done when they enroll the child in a group and furnish transportation to its functions. Youth groups can aid the parent who wishes to help his child's social development if the decision to participate in them is basically the child's decision, and if care is taken not to overload his schedule with same. Children may desire to join every group of which they hear, only to find that doing so leaves insufficient time for play or family activities or even study. There then comes the case of being an inactive member, which does not help the child nor the group. This may result in overfatigue and its attendant grouchiness; poor school performance and guilt and pressure; conflict at home; and even a general disgust with all memberships.

Parents would do well to help the child consider all possible membership commitments and perhaps suggest a limit. At the end of each membership year, the child could be encouraged to evaluate the joy and growth provided by each membership and then decide whether to continue it or find a new affiliation, or reduce the total memberships. But children should be taught and helped to be active—contributing members of whatever group they select. This is the time they need to learn to accept responsibility, to work cooperatively toward a common goal, to be both a leader and a follower, and to support the spirit of the group. Short-term memberships as that provided by YMCA summer day camps may be a good first experience.

As the decision is being made concerning group membership, parents should also bear in mind the suitability of the group's activities to the stage of growth of their children. A prime example is the Little League sports program, so popular in most communities. Whereas this activity is quite suitable for children in the latter part of middle childhood, it is not appropriate for younger children, for several reasons. Children under age 10 are not sufficiently group-oriented to work as a team for a season. Their interests and skills are not developed to the point where they can feel continuing success on a team. Their bodies are still growing, and injury to bones and muscles at this age is likely to cause permanent damage. Emotionally they are not mature enough to withstand the intense pressure and competition of such leagues. Their self-concept has not developed to the point where striking out is taken in stride, and tears may result. Whereas the thought of wearing a uniform and owning one's own glove and cap may be initially appealing to the 6- or 8-year-old, the newness is likely to wear off long before the season is over. And parents are tempted to insist on continued participation because of the expenses they have incurred—sometimes creating a lifelong disdain for sports in the child.

Faced with the prospect of Little League participation prior to developmental readiness in the child, the wise parent will find some way to defer the temptation to gain status from the child's involvement. When a number of parents decide to discourage Little League teams for children who are not yet ready, it is easier on the children to say "no."

Short-term commitments providing group experiences are found in summer camps, ranging from two-week day camp sessions to spend-the-night sessions of several weeks' duration. Children just beginning middle childhood may view participation in such activities with apprehension or even dread. Helping them face this unknown may be accomplished by getting a copy of the daily routine for discussion, or by a visit to the camp area prior to the beginning of camp, or by finding a friend who has attended the camp before or who is planning to attend the same session as the fearful child. Day camps would provide a good preparation for longer overnight camping adventures. Through camping, children learn group spirit; the traditional camping songs they will sing throughout childhood; swimming, hiking, nature study, crafts; and perhaps outdoor cooking and other "pioneer" skills.

They also experience other things: care of their own possessions; homesickness; how it feels to have a spider run across your face at night; what happens when you drop your soap in the sand coming back from the bathhouse; how a "new" food tastes; the joy of receiving a letter from Mom and Dad; the pain of poison ivy; the fun of horseback riding or doing a belly buster off the diving board. The letter in Figure 5-5 was written by an 8-year-old during his first camping experience.

Lessons can claim numerous hours of a child's time and need to be balanced with other time demands and needs. (Photo by Lin Mitchell.)

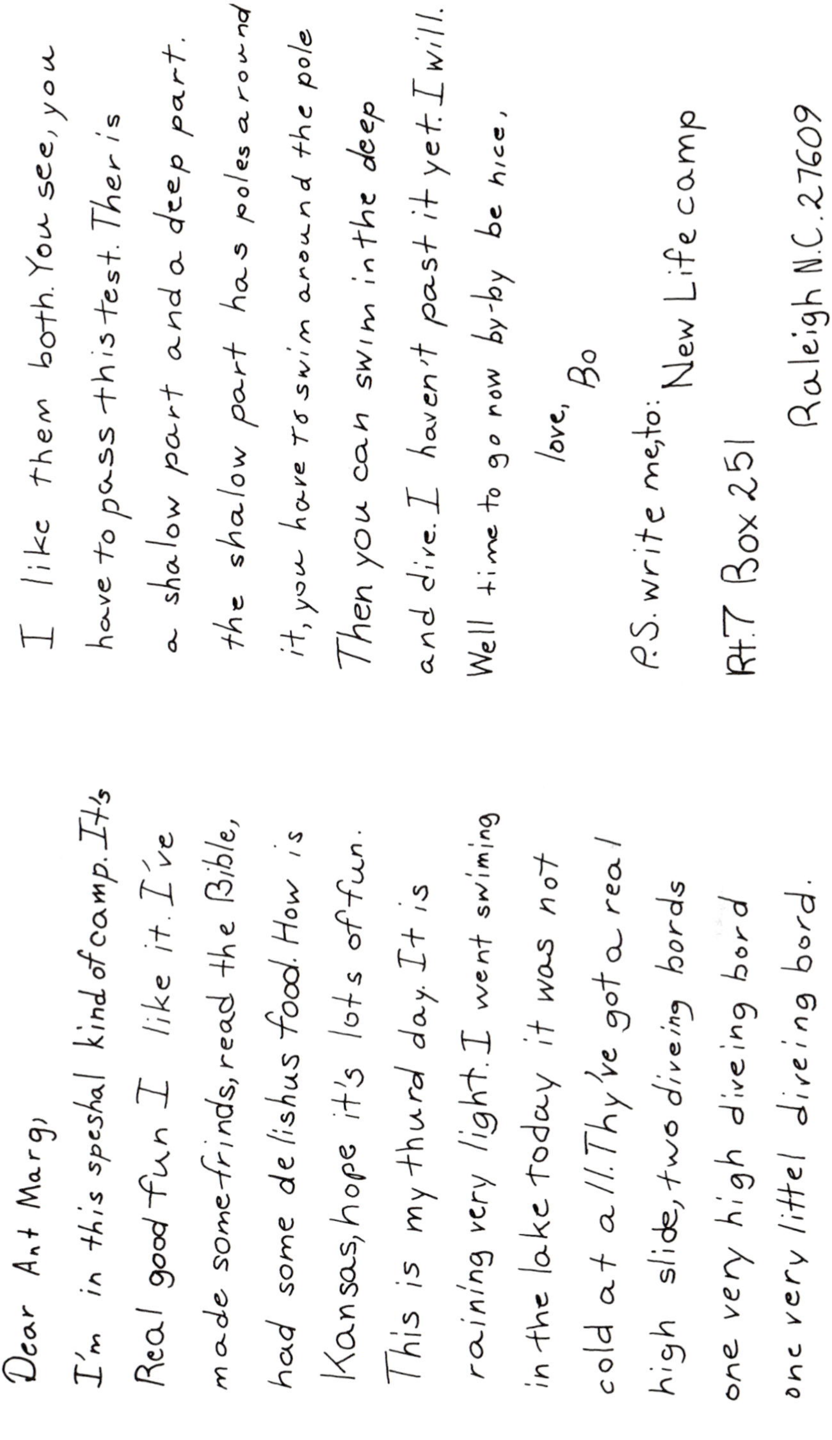

Dear Ant Marg,

I'm in this speshal kind of camp. It's Real good fun I like it. I've made some frinds, read the Bible, had some delishus food. How is Kansas, hope it's lots of fun. This is my thurd day. It is raining very light. I went swiming in the lake today it was not cold at all. Thy've got a real high slide, two diveing bords one very high diveing bord one very littel diveing bord.

I like them both. You see, you have to pass this test. Ther is a shalow part and a deep part. the shalow part has poles around it, you have to swim around the pole Then you can swim in the deep and dive. I haven't past it yet. I will. Well time to go now by-by be nice,

love,
Bo

P.S. write me, to: New Life camp
Rt. 7 Box 251
Raleigh N.C. 27609

Figure 5-5. A letter from camp.

Children acquire many skills without lessons, per se. (Photo by Lin Mitchell.)

Little Theatre is another group activity in many communities which may provide opportunities for children to develop social skills as well as dramatic abilities. Usually only one or two plays are cast annually which involve primarily children. Here again, if the child is developmentally ready and honestly desires to engage in these, he may benefit from the experience. Little Theatre is not the place to "make" a shy child blossom. It may, instead, increase the shame he feels at not being able to perform before others. If practices are long or too frequent, participation may be damaging to schoolwork or emotional stability. Sometimes the thought of costumes is the appealing factor to children. Parents need to help them see prior to their commitment to a production that participation will require learning, practice, and cooperation.

Lessons that children take are numerous: voice, dance, drama, art, swimming, tennis, karate, instrumental music, tumbling, ceramics, acrobatics, skiing, horseback riding, baton, needlecraft, diving, French. These experiences can contribute much to total development and to self-concept when carefully selected to suit the child's abilities and desires and when they are not burdensome on his personal schedule. As with memberships in organizations, children may tend to overextend themselves, the result being frustration and little leisure time. Lessons should be related to the stage of development of the child—something he enjoys, and not too demanding. Practice time as well as lesson time must be estimated in scheduling. Costs in time, energy, and money are considerations to be dealt with.

Think Back

To middle childhood activities:
Secret clubs you were part of.
Community and church-sponsored organizations you joined.
Lessons you took.
Camping: preparation, homesickness, daily routine.
Other youngsters participating.
Involvement of adults.

Sequence of Social Development

A general knowledge of the normal pattern of social development will help the adults in a child's life facilitate this aspect of his growing up. Parental reaction to the various stages can intensify or diminish such urges as tattling, moodiness, criticism. Adults who accept the painful aspects as natural, knowing that they will pass, can make life much more pleasant for all concerned. Those who fight the stages and their characteristic traits can find children's growing-up years a real nightmare. In general, socialization moves from individualized to group concerns, from adult to age mates, from family to peers, from egocentric to non-egocentric patterns. Whereas no chart can deal with all characteristics, and although no child can be neatly boxed into place in any chart, the following characteristics at various age levels might be helpful in understanding growth in this area.

Medinnus (Johnson and Medinnus, 1969) has characterized the socially *immature* children in early and late middle childhood as follows:

GRADES 1–3
- Does not play with peers in a controlled manner when not directly supervised.
- Wants to be "It" all the time; jealousy when playing; will not take turns.
- Will not share readily.
- Withdraws from the group.
- Inconsiderate—pushes, shoves.
- Lacks respect for others' property.
- Does not cooperate in group activities; does not assume his share of the responsibility.
- Interrupts; talks and bothers neighbors.
- Plays with children younger than himself.

5 Years	6 Years	7 Years	8 Years
General	General	General	General
friendly competent dependable likes praise, to dress up, feel independent project-minded interested in adult activities	excitable preoccupied with self dependable likes to help dawdles tends to go to extremes in behavior active	intensively preoccupied dissatisfied complaining competitive blaming sulks, mutters good listener alibis has musing moods minor strains of sadness	brassy expansive evaluative argumentative sensitive to criticism peer-oriented loud, continually talking independent worker
Relationship with Peers	Relationship with Peers	Relationship with Peers	Relationship with Peers
poor group member tattletale demanding hits and pushes needs adult supervision	poor group member but plays well with companion tattletale demanding has no group loyalty needs adult supervision plays with food	participates in group play that is loosely organized strong loyalty of short duration needs adult supervision not a good loser shows evidence of sex cleavage likes secrets with friends	engages in spontaneous grouping—is short lived highly critical of siblings muddles through, but play continues evidence that sexes are growing apart
Relationship with Adults	Relationship with Adults	Relationship with Adults	Relationship with Adults
companionable likes: to help parents, to run simple er-	companionable delightful demanding	nags challenges parents sensitive to other's	not consistently obedient demanding of mother challenges parents

rands, conversation with adults	hesitant wants approval	attitudes fond of teacher show-off	expects and asks for praise can admit wrongdoing to adults eavesdrops on adults
Physical-Motor Devl.	**Physical-Motor Devl.**	**Physical-Motor Devl.**	**Physical-Motor Devl.**
hops and skips cuts, pastes, draws handles: sled, tricycle well, tools geared to size, most dressing	1 or 2 permanent teeth ugly duckling stage losing knock-knees and protruding abdomen active has most basic motor skills practices and combines skills frustrated by lack of fine motor skills eye-hand coordination artistic likes to sing	permanent teeth appearing rapidly may show "tics" steady, smooth growth handles dressing completely well coordinated practices motor skills well established hand-eye coordination can whistle and throw with skill	10–11 permanent teeth losing baby body look writes with effort may swim well bicycles, roller skates interest in games requiring coordination and small muscle control
Interests-Intelligence	**Interests-Intelligence**	**Interests-Intelligence**	**Interests-Intelligence**
knows numbers up to 10 vague concept of time has questions that are purposeful more goal-directed than at 4 years enjoys being read to	advancing vocabulary knows numbers up to 30 knows common coins writes some numbers and letters backwards carries on long conversations imaginative play losing interest in toys interested in school subjects	knows basic number concepts fair concept of time beginning of sexual curiosity uses "bathroom" language periods of self-absorption	makes small change can tell day of month and year interest in past is skeptical likes: leisure-time reading collections dramatic play sense of humor

9 Years	10 Years	11 & 12 Years
General	General	General
independent	alert	critical of adults
widening interests	poised	rebels at routine
truthful	casual and relaxed	moody
honest	interesting	resents being told what to do
more self-dependent	congenial	strives for unreasonable indepen-
more self-motivated	clear on age-sex roles	dence
strong peer orientation	likes privacy	considerable individual differences
resents interruption		craves alone periods
bossy		strong urge to conform to group
competitive		mores
aware of grades		intense interest in teams
Relationship with Peers	Relationship with Peers	Relationship with Peers
joins in spontaneous groups of one sex	likes rules and teamwork is intense in friendship	interested in organized competitive games
may have friends outside of immediate neighborhood	highly selective in friendship strong indication of sex cleavage	membership in clubs is important enjoys participating in commmunity drives
shares reluctantly	affectionate with peers of same sex	Boys: admires boys who are skillful, bold, daring
expresses contempt for op- posite sex		Girls: interested in boys
begins secret codes and lan- guages		
interest in team sports		
impatient		
Relationship with Adults	Relationship with Adults	Relationship with Adults
needs reminders	loyal	hero worships adults not present
can accept blame but "who started it?"	hero worships	highly critical of adults
	affectionate with parents	refrains from communication with

Physical-Motor Devl.	Physical-Motor Devl.	Physical-Motor Devl.
makes increasingly accurate estimates of adults begins to pull away from parents more interested in friends respect for teacher more than love	finds mother all important has great pride in father enjoys creative companionship with parents	adults challenges adults' knowledge
slow, even growth cares for own needs variation in size perfecting motor skills uses tools increasingly well not graceful	14–16 permanent teeth Girl: may begin rapid increase in weight, on brink of pubescence interested in hazardous activities motor skills well in hand uses motor skills for group participation begins development of selective motor skills	Girl: rapid increase in weight; begins to show secondary sex characteristics Boy: ahead of girls in physical endurance good personal hygiene increases in muscle growth may prefer to be a spectator has strongly individualized motor-skill interests may show self-consciousness in learning new skills

Interests-Intelligence	Interests-Intelligence	Interests-Intelligence
clearly acquiring a conscience manners appearing at lunch perfecting tool-subject skills inventories possessions collects things relates events well art appreciation beginning	begins to use fractions can budget time uses thought and reasoning interested in other's ideas short interest span begins to show talents asserts leadership likes to read	critical of own art products increases ability for delayed gratification increases ability to use logic interests: earning money and jobs religion world about him develops tool-subjects to high level highly moral in evaluation

Adaptation of data from pp. 316–330 in *Behavior and Development from 5 to 12* by Glenn R. Hawkes and Damaris Pease. Copyright © 1962 by Glenn R. Hawkes and Damaris Pease. Reprinted by permission of Harper & Row, Publishers, Inc.

- Does not play or work well with others in his group.
- Picks fights; consistently employs pugilistic tactics rather than attempting to "talk it out."
- Uncooperative in planning games.
- Drops out of games when decisions are made against him (e.g., being called "out" in baseball).
- Wants his own way.
- Tattles; tendency to report every slight infraction of rules and wrong behavior which is of little actual importance; judgment of wrong behavior corresponds to the evaluation of a younger child.
- Rapid changes in friendship loyalties—i.e., a sudden turn against one's seemingly best friend.
- Extreme shyness with marked tendency to hang his head or cover the face when asked questions.
- Does not observe common courtesies:
  Walks in front of people.
  Interrupts when others are talking.
  Does not use "please" and "thank you."
- Lacks respect for others.
- Child feels that rules are made for everyone but him; consequently makes own rules and does not follow the rules of the group.

What's Next?

1. *Where Did You Go? Out. What Did You Do? Nothing,* R. P. Smith. New York: Norton, 1957.
2. *Child Development Through Literature,* Landau et al. Englewood Cliffs, N.J.,: Prentice-Hall, 1972: "Fight," by S. Crane, pp. 462–470; "Doctor Jack-O'-Lantern," by R. Yates, pp. 441–453; "The First Day of School," by W. Saroyan, pp. 457–461.
3. Film: *Six-, Seven- and Eight-Year-Olds—The Society of Children.* McGraw-Hill, 1221 Avenue of the Americas, New York, N.Y. 10019. (29 min, b/w.)
4. Film: *From Ten to Twelve.* National Film Board of Canada, 680 5th Avenue, New York, N.Y. 10019. (26 min, b/w.)
5. Film: *Peers in Middle Childhood,* Mental Health Film Board, 8 East 93rd St., N.Y. 10028 (23 min, color)

Catalysts for Discussion

I.

Children ages 7–11 were asked to tell what friendship was. Among their ideas were the following:

Someone who would listen to your problems and is just like another sister—girl, 11.
Someone who gives you something and can spend the night with you—boy, 10.
Someone who when he hits you lets you hit him back—boy, 8.
Somebody who can do things for you and can play with you—boy, 6.

II.
They select friends if they:

like the same things.
play by the rules.
let them have other friends, too.
are nice, fun and fair, pretty, smart.
help with your homework.
are good sports.
can keep a secret.

They don't like other boys and girls who:

lie.
are bossy.
are impolite.
push and crowd in line.

III.
Apply your knowledge concerning the sociometric technique and the factors which often influence sociometric choices in suggesting action in each of the following situations:

You are a third grade teacher. A sociogram has revealed that several children from poor homes are isolates. Why might this be true, and what might you do to help?

You are the parent of a very bright child who has been identified as an isolate in his fifth grade class. What might you do to help him become more accepted by his peers?

You are the parent of a child who is part of a very strong clique in their sixth grade class. What might have contributed to this situation? Is it desirable or undesirable? If undesirable, what could you do to help the teacher remedy the situation?

IV.
From the pages of a child's autograph book:

When you get old and think you're sweet
Take off your shoes and smell your feet.

*   *   *

down	and	you	if
and	you	love	you
up	will	I	love
read	see	that	me

*   *   *

Y.T.H.F.O.A.A.T.L.D.S.O.I.

*   *   *

Y	Y	U	R
Y	Y	U	B
I	C	U	R
Y	Y	4	Me

Yours till the ocean wears rubber pants.

*   *   *

Never make love by the garden gate.
Love is blind, but the neighbors ain't.

Beyond the Classroom Experiences

1. Observe a group of children in such free-forms as after-school play, camping, or weekend "doings." Look for examples of peer group functions.
2. Interview children about their formal and informal "clubs," and see if they will share with you their "rules," "purposes," and practices. If possible, attend one of these functions on their invitation. Look for ways this contributes to their development. Ask them to interpret the club's laws, motto, or creed.
3. Use a series of pictures to elicit children's responses to people with various handicaps, both functional and cosmetic. Look for differences in boys' and girls' attitudes. Compare your findings with those of Richardson and Royce.
4. Become involved in an organized activity for middle childhood people, such as a Sunday school class, a Scout troop, or recreational programs. Try to determine your assets and liabilities in this role. Look for growth in the children over a period of time. Note what approaches and activities seem best for the various ages. Check your progress in fulfilling the functions Fedder has delineated for an adult leader of youth groups. Look for sex cleavage, hero worship, group loyalty, and ways of dealing with difficulty.
5. Attend the casting, practice, and performance of Little Theatre productions involving children. Note their interest, problems, joys. Talk with them about how they learn their parts, how participation affects other aspects of life.
6. Become involved in a summer camping program for middle childhood people. Note the attitudes of beginning campers, their growth in time, the things that cause them difficulty and how they handle such. Note what portions of the camping experience seem particularly popular or painful, and try to determine the reasons for this. Look for examples of hero worship for camp leaders and the prevalence of sex cleavage.
7. Collect data relative to a child's use of time. Note the proportion claimed by school, free play, membership, lessons, sleep, and other activities. Discuss time use with children to assess their feelings.

Chapter 6

Physical
Growth
and Activities

This chapter is designed to help you:

- understand the physical changes that occur during ages 5–12.
- see implications of physical development on behavior.
- become acquainted with ways to assess physical well-being and possible problems.
- note the place of motor skills in the life of the school-age child.
- examine motor abilities developing at this age and provisions for motor development which should be provided.
- see the role of play in the total development of the child.
- understand the nutritional needs of middle childhood and factors regulating caloric needs.
- note the possible effects of illness and be acquainted with the common health problems at this stage.

If asked to judge a child's age, your first clue would be that provided by his physical appearance, for it is the most readily observable aspect of development. Although this is a helpful index, it can be misleading when considered alone. For example, a group of first-graders is shown on p. 234. Note their range in height and build. A child who looks one age quite often thinks or acts another age, and the latter may provide a more accurate basis for judgment. All types of development do not proceed at the same rate, and each child will grow at his own rate and in his own way. Each child has his own timing device, genetically set, which determines his individual rate of development. If it is important to analyze a child's growth (a comparison of his current status with his past growth pattern provides the most accurate picture) for it is in this manner that the uniqueness of the individual is taken into account. Nevertheless, physical growth is an important consideration; knowledge and appreciation of its intricacies are vital to the parent or professional involved in guiding children.

How the Body Changes

The genes control the ultimate possible body, as far as environment will allow. The peak of growth under the control of the genes occurs prenatally when in approximately nine months two cells multiply into billions. If this rate were to continue to age 20, adults would be 20 feet tall and weigh many times the weight of the earth. Fortunately, the rate of physical growth quickly decelerates between birth and ages 4 or 5, continuing to decline slowly until the pubescent spurt around age 10 to 12, when it increases. The endocrine system is responsible for this later growth, under

Children of the same age present a variety of body sizes. (Photo by Rick Coleman.)

the direction of the genes. The chemical agents in this system are the hormones, secretions which act both on the body at large and on each other, constituting a complex regulation mechanism. The pituitary gland is the predominant one in the endocrine system. Its action is triggered by impulses from the hypothalamus, located in the midsection of the brain believed to contain vital autonomic nervous centers. The anterior pituitary lobe controls all gland action involving growth, emitting trophic (nourishing) hormones which are transported by the bloodstream to stimulate the other glands in the system concerned with growth: the thyroid, adrenals, and gonads. These glands respond to the action of the pituitary by increasing their own hormones, the rising levels of which feed back signals to the pituitary or hypothalamus, reducing the trophic secretions.

The pituitary gland also secretes the growth hormone, somatotrophin, which acts directly on tissues to stimulate growth of bones and production of protein. Somatotrophin is only produced in response to certain body stimuli, such as rapid lowering in blood sugar, a rise in certain amino acids in the blood, physical exercise, and emotion. The action of the growth hormone is assisted by other hormones, especially that produced by the thyroid gland, which acts primarily on the brain, teeth, and bones. In the absence of this thyrotrophic hormone the growth hormone is partially inactive. The action of the thyroid gland is also thought to play a part in maintaining proper proportions during growth and in regulating the production of energy and metabolism of food.

Puberty is triggered by the action of the pituitary gland on the adrenals and ovaries in girls and the adrenals and testes in boys. In both sexes the adrenal hormones stimulate the growth of long bones, assisted by estrogens in girls. Boys experience more long-bone growth because of greater amounts of androgens for longer periods. Estrogens in girls and testosterones in boys bring about the maturation of the reproductive system and such secondary sex characteristics as breast development, beard, and pubic hair (Tanner and Taylor, 1969).

For growth to proceed in a normal, orderly pattern, the endocrine secretions must occur in the proper amounts at the proper times. Whether or not the amounts are optimum is determined not only by the pituitary but also by the thyroid and gonads. The growth tempo is largely due to small differences in the rate of hormone secretion, individual variations resulting probably from the setting of feedback mechanisms in the brain.

Sex, birth weight, body build, and rate of maturing offer the best information for predicting what a given child should accomplish under good conditions. All these except sex may be subject to environmental forces, even though they are genetically determined.

Physical growth during most of middle childhood may be characterized as steady but not spectacular. However, some pretty spectacular things do happen to the body during these years, such as the shedding and erupting of teeth, the changing of body proportion and profile, the acquisition of motor skills, and the weathering of common childhood diseases and accidents. Whereas all aspects of growth are integrated and similarly affected by heredity, state of health, nutrition, and exercise, the various parts of the body have individual growth rates.

Many structures in the body follow the normal height curve in growth (see Figure 6-1): the skeleton, muscles, liver, spleen, kidneys, and face. Others—the brain and skull, reproductive organs, tonsil lymphoid tissue, adenoids, intestines, and subcutaneous fat—do not. The head experiences rapid growth prenatally and during infancy. The brain, skull, eyes, and ears develop earlier than any other part of the body, demonstrating the cephalocaucal law: development proceeds from head to toe. The brain attains its maximum weight during middle childhood. Increasing shortsightedness at puberty is thought to be due to the growth of the eye, myopia increasing continually from birth to maturity. The sex organs show very little change from birth until the prepubescent growth spurt (Tanner, 1970). Each system and organ reaches maturity at its own time, resulting in asynchronous growth or split growth.

Those of earlier ages regarded children as little adults. The fallacy of this notion is supported in many ways, not the least being the fact that even body proportions of children are considerably different from those of adults. Perhaps the relationship of the head to the remainder of the body is

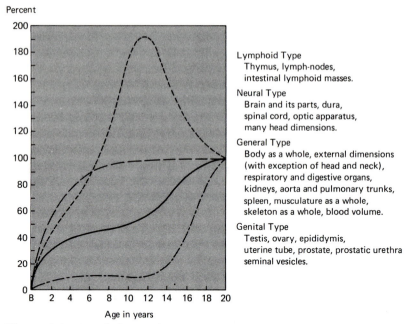

Percent

Lymphoid Type
Thymus, lymph-nodes,
intestinal lymphoid masses.

Neural Type
Brain and its parts, dura,
spinal cord, optic apparatus,
many head dimensions.

General Type
Body as a whole, external dimensions
(with exception of head and neck),
respiratory and digestive organs,
kidneys, aorta and pulmonary trunks,
spleen, musculature as a whole,
skeleton as a whole, blood volume.

Genital Type
Testis, ovary, epididymis,
uterine tube, prostate, prostatic urethra
seminal vesicles.

Age in years

Figure 6-1. A graph showing the major types of postnatal growth of the various parts and organs of the body. The several curves are drawn to a common scale by computing their values at successive ages in terms of their total postnatal increments (to 20 years). (From J. A. Harris et al., *The Measurement of Man.* University of Minnesota Press, Minneapolis, © 1930, U. of M.)

the most outstanding evidence in this connection: due to the early rapid growth of the brain, the child's head at age 5 has attained 91 percent of its mature size while the body height is less than 75 percent is adult size. The surface area of the child's head at age 5 accounts for 13 percent of his total body surface while that of an adult accounts for 8 percent.

Although the body contours of boys and girls differ little prior to puberty, between the ages of 4 and 8 there does occur a flattening of the forehead and a slenderizing of the arms and legs. During middle childhood the nose grows considerably, the shoulder line becomes squarer, the abdomen flattens, and the waistline is more clearly indicated. Throughout childhood there are no marked sex differences in body proportions, but with the onset of puberty the girls' hips widen; the boys' shoulders increase similarly. During this later period the hands and feet also grow rapidly, giving new proportions to the total appearance. Boys' cheekbones become more prominent, and hair lines begin to recede, forming a new facial pattern.

The school-age child has grown beyond the stocky look of the preschooler. School readiness may be partially determined from the body configuration: the characteristic body build of middle childhood, slender and lanky, is more often found among those children who are ready for school, while the topheavy look of early childhood is an indication the child probably is not sufficiently matured for this new undertaking. (See Figure 6-2.) Body maturity correlates with first grade achievement. It is reflected in superficial body features and also in the maturational level of the central nervous system which underlies such behaviors as readiness to submit to restraints and apply oneself to tasks. By age six the trunk is almost twice as long and twice as wide as it was at birth.

With rapid changes in proportion, there comes a temporary loss of control over the body. The resulting awkwardness and clumsiness as a child attempts to revise his skills can cause great consternation and actually constitute a social handicap. At this juncture the child may feel the loss of physical attractiveness if comment is made about the new appearance and behavior.

During middle childhood the body experiences change in both structure and function. Such obvious structural changes as increased height and weight are accompanied by internal growth of the heart, lungs, kidneys, and stomach, all of which contribute to the child's increasing abilities to function physically with greater precision.

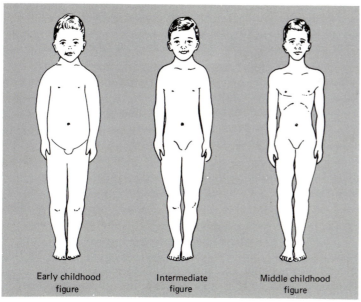

| Early childhood figure | Intermediate figure | Middle childhood figure |

Figure 6-2. Three types of body configuration seen in middle childhood. (Reprinted from M. D. Simon, "Body Configuration and School Readiness," *Child Development,* 30, 1959, Fig. 1, p. 496. Copyright © 1959, The Society for Research in Child Development, Inc. Used by permission of the author and the publisher.)

Weight

Girls weigh less than boys at birth but they are equal by age 8. They surpass boys in weight by age 9 or 10, remaining the heavier sex until around age 14½. Boys surpass the girls' weight again during adolescence and typically maintain this lead throughout life. Weight gain is constant from age 3 to puberty, averaging 2.0–2.7 kg per year (a kilogram equals 2.2 pounds). Weight gain in fatty tissue balances the drop in muscle and skeletal velocity in middle childhood. As childhood progresses, bone and muscle contribute increasing shares to the total body weight. Weight is an index to both physical and mental health in children. It is contingent on body build, diet, and psychological factors. Weight is easier to measure than is skeletal growth, but it is much less useful in assessing growth since it represents a conglomerate of different types of tissue, with varying growth rates. Failure to gain weight may signify nothing more than the relation of diet to exercise and metabolism. Failure to gain in height would call for immediate investigation (Tanner, 1970). (See Figures 6-3, 4, 5, 6.)

Height

Between the ages of 6 and 12 height increases 5 or 6 percent of total height each year, the rate of annual gain decreasing with age except during the pubescent growth spurt. Eichorn (1972) reports the average height of 5-7-year-olds has increased about .4 to .8 inches each decade for the last seven; for 10-14-year-olds, the increase is .8 to 1.2 inches per decade.

The height growth spurt for girls precedes menarche, and for boys it is closely timed with genital development. Prediction of the adult height of a child is somewhat contingent on the time the pubescent growth spurt occurred for him. The early maturer is generally shorter as an adult than his child height may have indicated. The later maturer is often taller as an adult than one would have expected. Since there is a close relationship between the age at which a child matures and the age his same-sexed parent matured, knowledge of the parent's growth history will increase the predictive accuracy (Garn et al., 1960) On the average, boys are taller than girls. Girls' height is often complete by age 16, whereas boys' height typically continues to 18 or older. (See Figures 6-3, 4, 5, 6.)

Skeletal maturity is a true common scale of development and is typically measured by X-ray of the hand. The amount of radiation from such an X-ray is equal to that which a child would receive from a week's vacation in the mountains; therefore, periodic assessments of this type offer little hazard to the child. (See Figure 6-7.) Skeletal growth is closely related to the onset of adolescence; the physiological processes controlling both seem linked. The maturity of the hand bones is used as a measure of school readiness in some areas. In some cultures readiness to attend school is assessed by a child's ability to touch his left ear with his right hand, the arm

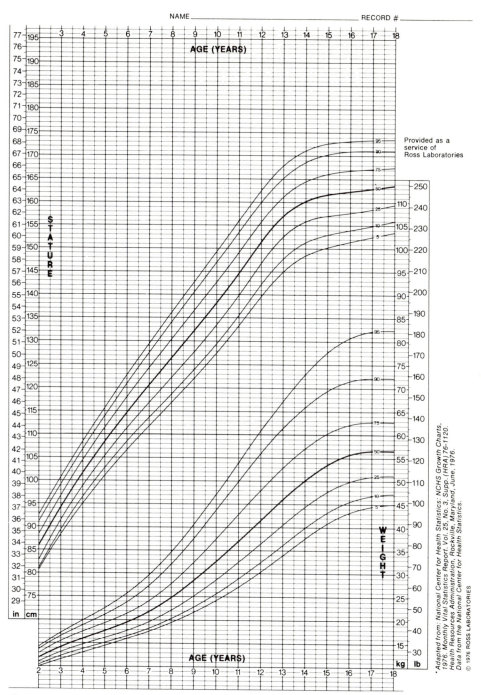

NAME_____ RECORD #_____

AGE (YEARS)

STATURE

WEIGHT

in cm   AGE (YEARS)   kg lb

Provided as a
service of
Ross Laboratories

*Adapted from: National Center for Health Statistics: NCHS Growth Charts, 1976. Monthly Vital Statistics Report. Vol. 25, No. 3, Supp. (HRA) 76-1120. Health Resources Administration, Rockville, Maryland, June, 1976. Data from the National Center for Health Statistics.

© 1976 ROSS LABORATORIES

Figure 6-3. Girls 2 to 18 years: physical growth NCHS percentiles.*

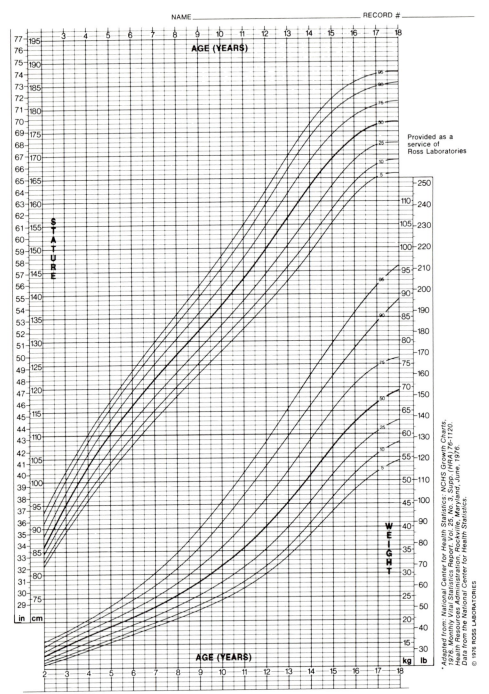

*Adapted from: National Center for Health Statistics: NCHS Growth Charts, 1976. Monthly Vital Statistics Report, Vol. 25, No. 3, Supp. (HRA) 76-1120. Health Resources Administration, Rockville, Maryland, June, 1976. Data from the National Center for Health Statistics.

Provided as a service of Ross Laboratories

Figure 6-4. Boys 2 to 18 years: physical growth NCHS percentiles.*

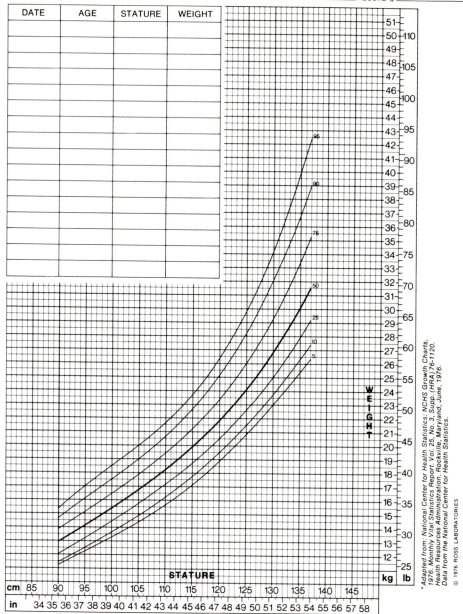

Figure 6-5. Girls: prepubescent physical growth NCHS percentiles.*

* Adapted from: National Center for Health Statistics: NCHS Growth Charts, 1976. Monthly Vital Statistics Report. Vol. 25, No. 3, Supp. (HRA) 76-1120. Health Resources Administration, Rockville, Maryland, June, 1976. Data from the National Center for Health Statistics.

© 1976 ROSS LABORATORIES

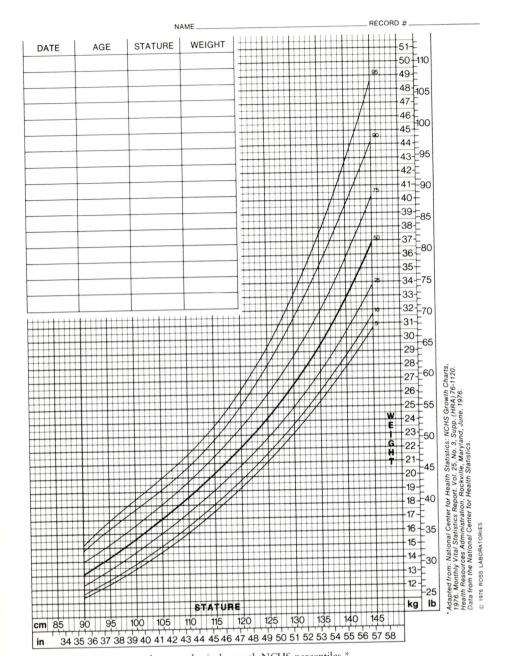

Figure 6-6. Boys: prepubescent physical growth NCHS percentiles.*

* Adapted from: National Center for Health Statistics: NCHS Growth Charts, 1976. Monthly Vital Statistics Report. Vol. 25, No. 3, Supp. (HRA) 76-1120. Health Resources Administration. Rockville, Maryland, June, 1976. Data from the National Center for Health Statistics.

© 1976 ROSS LABORATORIES

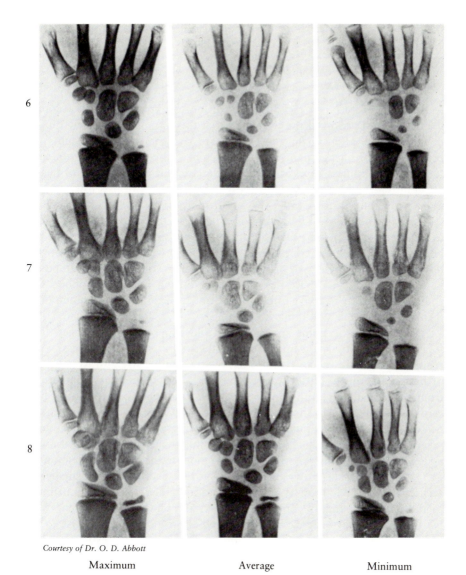

| Maximum | Average | Minimum |

Figure 6-7. Variations in carpal development of girls 6–7–8 years of age. (From *Robert's Nutrition Work with Children*, E. A. Martin, p. 100. Copyright © 1954, The University of Chicago Press. Used by permission.)

passing the top of the head. Both approaches utilize the skeletal development index.

There is consistency in acceleration or retardation of the skeleton and general body maturity. At all ages from 6 to 13, children who are advanced skeletally have erupted on the average more teeth than those who are skeletally retarded. Dentition may sometimes be used as a measure of skeletal development. Those with early adolescence erupt teeth earlier (Tanner, 1970).

Muscle Growth

At age 5 or 6 there is a rapid increase in muscle growth, which accounts for the major portion of the weight gain at this age. While no new muscle fibers develop after birth, those that are present grow in length and breadth and are accompanied by changes in composition, allowing their functional usefulness to expand. Both exercise and general state of health affect muscular development and status, illness or lack of use, lowering the muscle tone and causing fatigue to occur more easily.

The extreme physical flexibility of children in this growth period is due to muscle growth and the fact that ligaments are not yet firmly attached to bones. Their acrobatic contortions may be observed as they play on the floor, climb the jungle gym or trees, and perform tricks on the trampoline or monkey bars. Acrobatic lessons begun during middle childhood can channel the ability to move into an art form. If flexibility is not maintained through practice, it will diminish with age.

As the muscles become stronger the child experiences a stronger drive for muscular activity, wanting to be always on the go, restless when required to remain inactive, and often overtaxing his strength to the point of fatigue or injury. Little League elbow is a muscular injury that results from pitching that requires rotary movements of the forearm and a firm grip of the hand, as in throwing a curve ball. Whereas mild cases require no treatment, massage, immobilization, or surgery may be needed in more severe instances. Growth spurts can cause muscle aches, especially at night, as the developing muscles strive to accommodate the growing skeleton.

The heart muscle grows more slowly in these years and is smaller in relation to the body than at any other period of life. This fact contributes to the danger of highly competitive sports for school-age children. With maturity, the heartbeat slows down, and the blood pressure rises. The heart continues to increase in size until around age 20. Respiration rate slows to about 17–25 at this period.

The most common cause of heart disease in children is rheumatic fever, believed to be the result of a streptococcal infection. The potential damage to the heart is in the form of scarred valves or adhesion of the valve leaflets which affect the blood supply. Because of the greater work demanded of the muscle due to leaking or obstructed valves, the heart enlarges. Later it develops irregularities in rhythm. If the heart is permanently damaged, the disease may be fatal. Surgery is now able to remedy some of the damage and allow persons to live moderately active lives under medical care.

Bone Development

The bones also experience change at this period, both in size and composition, bone development continuing into the twenties. The maturity of skeletal development may be assessed through X-ray of the hand and wrist, and may predict the approximate age at which puberty will be reached. A child's bones have proportionately more water and protein-like materials and less minerals than do those of adults. The blood supply to these growing structures is greater, and the ligaments are less firmly attached, with larger spaces between the bones at the joints. These characteristics make a child more susceptible to bone infection carried by the bloodstream, less resistant to extreme pressures and muscle pull, and more flexible in movement than the adult (Breckenridge and Vincent, 1965).

Some factors related to proper bone development during middle childhood include posture, ballet dancing, and shoes. There is no perfect posture but a normal range of variation. Loose-jointed, gangling, sway-backed postures are not uncommon at this age. Bad posture can result from laziness, poor muscle development, and general debility. Any marked change in the posture of a child deserves a thorough medical checkup to determine the cause. At birth the baby's spine shows a continuous backward curve from pelvis to skull. With growth the spine develops subcurves in response to the demand of upright posture. The adult spine shows a forward curvature in the neck region, a backward curvature in the chest area, and a forward curvature in the lower back. Poor posture imposes added burdens on bones, ligaments, and joints. Upright posture is maintained by continuous muscular activity.

Ballet dancing has often been wrongly accused of damaging growing feet. When properly controlled it can be quite beneficial. It develops the intrinsic muscles of the feet and also the calf muscles. It improves the general tone and posture of the body. Structural changes of the foot can occur if the amount of dancing is excessive or if the child engages in toe dancing prior to age 13. Ballet dancing should be moderate in amount until around age 12 or 13.

Children's feet grow rapidly. A change in shoe size typically occurs every one or two months under age 6, every 2–3 months at ages 6–10 years, and every 3–4 months at ages 10–12 years. Usually one foot is larger than the other. Crowding the foot in ill-fitting shoes may result in permanent injury, poor posture, and foot-related problems in adulthood. Barefoot walking is the best possible treatment for growing feet and one great difficulty in fostering the developing foot is to persuade parents to allow their children's feet to develop unhampered by rigid shoes. A shoe does not help arches nor muscles develop. Activity and freedom of movement allow muscles, ligaments, and bones to grow normally. Walking barefooted on a lawn or rug, dancing, walking on tiptoes, and picking up marbles with the toes are among the healthy exercises for feet. Shoes should allow the feet to grow unhampered and to breathe normally to prevent fungus infections (Flatt, 1964).

Fatty Tissue

The amount of adipose, or fatty tissue, in the body during middle childhood is relatively unchanged unless there is a change in eating habits. Subcutaneous fat increases from the 7th prenatal month to about 9 months of age, then decreases until age 6 to 8. Girls have more fat, and it is placed differently, giving them softer contours. The onset of puberty marks an increase in fat. Girls' trunk fat increases steadily until adulthood. Boys' fat decreases during adolescence (Stolz and Stolz, 1951).

Evidence from animal studies suggests that the number of fat storage cells in the adipose tissue is determined early in life, perhaps by age 18 months in humans. Overfeeding during those early months could then cause problems of obesity later in life. The relationship of muscle to fatty tissue in the body can affect the types of activities in which children engage as well as the self-image and personality.

The Nervous System

The impact of early environment is also seen in the growth of the nervous system. The skeletal capacity to house the brain as well as the ultimate size of the brain is dependent on conditions and nutrition prenatally and prior to school entrance. The quantitative growth of the nervous system is relatively slow after age 4. Neural development by middle childhood primarily consists of the maturing of cells present at birth and approaches maturity by the time of school entrance. Myelination is usually completed between ages 6 and 8. By age 8 the brain is nearly its mature size, but the development of intracerebral association tracts and the building up of gray matter continue.

Epidermal Development

The epidermal development during middle childhood is evident in the skin's becoming less delicate, and darkening of the hair. Skin color is quite a "part" of the child's self-image as well as a factor in the assessment of others, becoming so around age 4. Skin irregularities can be cause for concern to the child of this age, among them freckles, warts, and moles. Freckles usually appear in susceptible youngsters around the age of 6 years. Redheads and blue-eyed blondes have a skin type sensitive to sunlight, and freckles are a result of exposure to light. Once they appear they are lifetime acquisitions. They do not become cancerous and are often considered attractive beauty spots. Warts are caused by viruses, not by holding frogs. They may disappear spontaneously or can be removed by chemicals, electrodesiccation, or excision.

Moles are skin lesions that develop early in life, usually not after age 30. They enlarge slowly and most become elevated. They are usually removed for cosmetic reasons but should be removed promptly if they become infected or are constantly irritated by clothing or activity. With age they tend to disappear. The average person in his twenties has 40 to 50 moles, but by age 60 the average is only 4. Moles that darken, increase in size, or appear after age 30 can be dangerous and should be removed. Malignant melanoma usually requires surgery (Bluefarb, 1964).

While some children find freckles a source of recognition in contests, others wish with all their might they could be rid of skin irregularities. In one family there was a legend that it was possible to transfer freckles from the face to another part of the body: On May 1, the person desiring to move his freckles was to arise without speaking to anyone, go outside and wet his hands with the dew of the grass, "wash" the freckles off his face and "transfer" them elsewhere. One son proudly displayed the freckles on his shoulders as a result of this ritual.

Children also believe that warts may be treated by various rituals, including tieing knots in a string and burying it under the back doorstep and saying "magic words." Children also employ this method to rid themselves of styes: Standing in a crossroad they say, "Stye, stye, leave my eye/Jump on the first one passing by."

The Digestive System

The maturing digestive system shows fewer upsets and retains food for longer periods of time. Therefore, meals do not have to be served as often nor as promptly as for preschoolers. Calorie needs in relation to stomach size are not as great as they were earlier or as they will be during the pubescent spurt. With this reduced need for calories, children need to be guided in selecting more body-building foods such as proteins, minerals, and vitamins and in minimizing "empty calories" furnished by sweets, soft drinks, starches, and excess fats. Bladder capacity will vary widely among children, boys having less than girls. Such factors as emotional state, temperature, humidity, and fluid ingestion will also influence the frequency of urination (Martin and Vincent, 1960).

Ears and Eyes

Hearing acuity is thought to increase between ages 3 and 13. Ear infections are less likely to occur than during preschool years. Because of the Eustachian tube's lengthening, narrowing, and becoming more slanted, it is more difficult for disease organisms to invade.

There is a discrepancy concerning the age at which 20/20 vision is normally achieved, but it is after age 7 that the eyeball reaches its full weight and several years later that full development is complete. Binocular vision is well developed for many children by age 6, but large print is recommended for children throughout the elementary school years (Breckenridge and Vincent, 1965).

The impact of corrective devices for the ear and eye can be negligible or traumatic for the child, depending on how others react to their acquisition. Children often make fun of hearing aides or eyeglasses. Their wearers may secretly omit their use to avoid being singled out or referred to by such an uncomplimentary term as "Four Eyes." The less visible hearing devices and stylish glasses made for children today can reduce the stigma. Depending on the needed correction, the personality, and the age of the child, contact lenses are also a way to make vision disabilities less conspicuous. Some children may use their defect as a source of special attention. Teachers should be aware of such impairments and make necessary allowances in seating and working arrangements. They may also help other children to be more accepting by including a study of the sense organs in health or science curriculum. Children who become fascinated by the operation of a hearing device, for example, may thereafter view it as a status symbol instead of a stigma.

Physically visible irregularities of the eyes and ears may also affect the self-concept of a child, including cross-eye or walleye and protruding ears. An eye that turns in or out during early childhood may lose its vision unless treated. No child will outgrow an eye condition of this type. Corrective lenses or surgery may be the recommended treatment. Corrective surgery to draw protruding ears close to the head is relatively simple and may do much to enhance body image.

The Reproductive System

The changes in the child's reproductive system during the last portion of middle childhood are likely to be dramatic since puberty typically begins for girls between ages 8 and 14 and for boys between 10 and 14½ (Tanner, 1970). Puberty is the time when the testes, prostate gland, seminal vesicles, ovaries, uterus and vagina suddenly enlarge. The age at which this takes place is basically determined by genetics, but malnutrition can delay its onset since the physical changes will not occur until the body has reached a certain size or maturity level. Maturation is occurring earlier today than it did a century ago: the average age for menarche in the U.S. in 1900 was 14.2; today it is 12.8. If physical growth is rapid, puberty comes earlier than if it is slow. The potential speed of the body to grow is also genetically controlled, but the achieved speed is a function of the environment.

In girls, development of breast buds is the first sign of puberty. Appearance of pubic hair may precede this development but typically accompanies it. The uterus and vagina mature simultaneously with breast growth. Between ages 10 and 16½ menarche or the first menstrual period usually occurs. This event marks the maturity of the uterus but not full reproductive ability. There is a 12 to 18 month period of sterility following menarche. The period of maximum growth usually begins prior to menarche, from age 9½ through age 14½, and continues afterwards. Girls grow about 6 cm. more following menarche. Girls also gain axillary hair and experience hip widening during this period of body changes.

In boys accelerated growth of the testes and scrotum signal the onset of puberty, a process which usually occurs between ages 10 and 13½ but may be delayed until age 14½ to 18. This enlargement is mainly due to the increase in Leydig cells which produce the male hormone testosterone. Appearance of pubic hair may accompany the changes but may come slightly later. About a year following the initial changes in the male genitalia, penis growth and height increase take place. The height spurt typically comes between ages 10½ and 16 and is complete sometime between ages 13 and 17½. Prostate gland and seminal vesicles enlarge, and approximately a year following the penis growth the first ejaculation occurs. This event usually occurs during sleep and is thus termed nocturnal emission. The nocturnal emission is the body's way of discharging accumulated sperm being produced in the testes. It is a normal bodily function and may occur irregularly, on several successive nights or months apart. In about 20 boys in 1,000 under age 14, one or both testes may fail to descend into the scrotum normally, producing a condition known as crystorchidism. Unless the condition responds to hormonal treatment, some degree of sterility may be present. About two years following the growth of pubic hair, axillary and facial hair change, darkening and becoming coarser. Body hair continues to change following puberty, following hereditary patterns in its distribution. Marked voice changes become evident as puberty progresses due to the action of testosterone on the larynx.

In both sexes genitalia and breast development acceleration is related to skeletal development. Boys have about two more years of pre-adolescent growth than girls. Their shoulders widen as girls hips widen due to the presence of cartilage cells specialized to multiply in response to the respective sex hormones. Variation in the closeness of pubertal events is thought to be due to the integration of hypothalamic and pituitary progresses since each controls different changes in the reproductive system. Deposition of fat causes the more rounded look of girls, while increase in musculature contributes to the angular appearance of boys. Precocious puberty at very early ages is either due to an isolated developmental defect or brain lesions. The youngest mother on record gave birth to a full-term healthy infant delivered by Caesarian section when she was 5 years 8 months of age. (Knepp, 1967)

Dentition

The dentition of the school-age child is one of the few readily observable aspects of his growth and development. This is another of the physical manifestations of prenatal environment, since both primary and deciduous teeth begin to form *in utero*. Around age 5 or 6 the deciduous or baby teeth begin to loosen and shed, the resulting spaces often being status symbols of a sort among the play group. Girls typically lose their teeth earlier than boys. To children this loss is usually an outward sign that they are "growing up." The fact that this heralds the so-called ugly-duckling stage, the "spacy look" and the "hissing speech" seems relatively unimportant to them. Great excitement will probably surround the loss of the first five or six incisors, but the process may become old hat by the time all twenty have been shed by age 12. Likewise, as the first permanent teeth emerge there will be an aura of delight which is altogether absent by the time the last molars, "wisdom teeth," appear, often via the surgeon's knife, at age 18 or 20. Combined with the fascination of gaining status through a tooth loss, the monetary rewards bestowed by the "good fairy" and the idea that each new tooth acquisition puts them farther and farther away from babyhood can tempt children to hasten nature's process of tooth shedding. This can have bad effects: Whereas natural shedding is closely followed by eruption of the permanent tooth, prematurely pulling a tooth increases the possibility that the jaw may shrink and the resulting space may be too small for the permanent tooth. Also, prolonged absence of teeth increases the chances that the lisping, which naturally occurs when several front teeth are missing, may become a permanent speech defect.

The condition of the permanent teeth during the years of middle childhood will have its roots in the condition of the deciduous teeth. Many parents do not realize that these baby teeth serve important functions in addition to allowing the child to eat. Teeth facilitate speech and accompanying speech patterns; absence of them impairs proper speech, as is often evident around age 6 or 7 when several central ones are absent. Teeth give shape to the face and serve as space-maintainers. Children whose deciduous teeth have not been properly cared for are more likely to experience malocclusion, or improper meshing of the upper and lower sets of teeth, with accompanying appearance, speaking, and eating problems.

The keystone to dentition is the first permanent molar, which usually erupts around age 6 and is subsequently commonly called the 6-year molar. (See Figure 6-8.) Many times parents who place little importance on proper care of baby teeth fail to realize that these 6-year molars are permanent; hence the decay may be so extensive that the tooth is lost, posing alignment problems which may well affect the total mouth thereafter. Improper alignment of the teeth can also be caused if the rate of jaw growth and eruption of teeth are incongruous or if through inheritance the child acquires a small jaw and large teeth. If the jaw develops rapidly

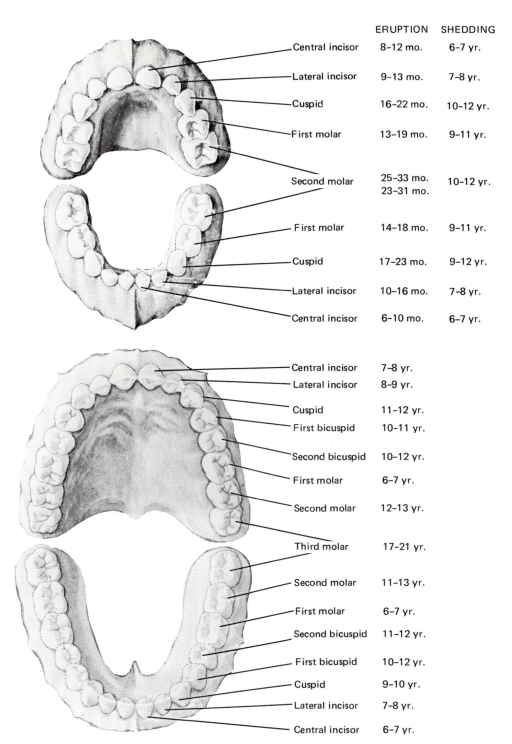

	ERUPTION	SHEDDING
Central incisor	8–12 mo.	6–7 yr.
Lateral incisor	9–13 mo.	7–8 yr.
Cuspid	16–22 mo.	10–12 yr.
First molar	13–19 mo.	9–11 yr.
Second molar	25–33 mo. 23–31 mo.	10–12 yr.
First molar	14–18 mo.	9–11 yr.
Cuspid	17–23 mo.	9–12 yr.
Lateral incisor	10–16 mo.	7–8 yr.
Central incisor	6–10 mo.	6–7 yr.
Central incisor	7–8 yr.	
Lateral incisor	8–9 yr.	
Cuspid	11–12 yr.	
First bicuspid	10–11 yr.	
Second bicuspid	10–12 yr.	
First molar	6–7 yr.	
Second molar	12–13 yr.	
Third molar	17–21 yr.	
Second molar	11–13 yr.	
First molar	6–7 yr.	
Second bicuspid	11–12 yr.	
First bicuspid	10–12 yr.	
Cuspid	9–10 yr.	
Lateral incisor	7–8 yr.	
Central incisor	6–7 yr.	

Figure 6-8. *Top:* Eruption and shedding of primary teeth. *Bottom:* Eruption of permanent teeth. (Adapted from *Your Child's Teeth,* published by the American Dental Association.)

while teeth erupt slowly, wide spaces may result between teeth. On the other hand, if the teeth erupt more quickly than the jaw matures, over-crowding is common. The achievement of proper alignment may involve orthodontic treatment during the school-age period. Whereas there is no set age for such manipulation to begin, regular dental examinations will allow the family dentist to determine the proper time to recommend such.

Irregularities requiring orthodontic treatment may result from heredi-tary crowding or spacing, early loss of primary teeth, dietary and growth disorders, and undesirable habits as prolonged thumb-sucking with pres-sure against the teeth. Unless corrected, improper alignment can interfere with speech and chewing and cause facial distortion which may lead to psychological problems. Orthodontists appeal to children's sense of physi-cal attractivenes and well-being in seeking the cooperation of the children to wear and care for their "braces" correctly.

Wearing dental appliances to correct the malalignment of the teeth has become almost a status symbol among the children of the middle class. Yet their use may still involve special notice from peers and adults. Most children adjust nicely to their bands and retaining appliances as they learn to eat, talk, and brush with them present.

Maintenance of effective dentition is based on proper dental care from the time baby teeth erupt throughout the life of the teeth, yet few children regularly see a dentist. By school entrance over half of America's children have three or more cavities. Materials for the Head Start Program recom-mend budgeting to cover repair of 6 caries for each 5-year-old (Worth, 1971). Between the ages of 6 and 15 the average child acquires one or two caries annually (Peckos, 1957). In addition to regular dental checkups, children of these ages benefit from nutritionally adequate diets, topical fluoride applications to strengthen tooth enamel, regular tooth-brushing immediately following ingestion of carbohydrate foods, and flossing at bedtime. Fluoridation of the public water supply or use of fluoride tablets aids dentition during the time teeth are forming but are of little value once the teeth have erupted. The latest weapon in the war against dental decay is a plastic tooth paint or sealant which can reduce cavities on the biting surfaces of teeth by 40 percent. The substance is brushed on the teeth semiannually.

Assessing Normalcy of Growth

Everyone has always known that children grow, but to quantify and evalu-ate growth is an illusive challenge. Even though physical growth lends it-self to more exact study than the other types of growth, it has posed a con-tinuing challenge to those who strive to achieve its accurate measurement and assessment. The growth studies conducted early in this century sought to establish norms based on average sizes at various ages, producing the familiar height-weight tables still seen on penny scales and found in the offices of pediatricians. Since they were summary measures based on thousands of subjects, most children do not exactly measure and weigh according to the charts. The main disadvantage, therefore, lies in determining how much variation from the norm is normal and healthy.

As skill improved in taking such anthropometric measurements as that of the head, chest, pelvic girdle, and shoulder width, scarcely a part of the child's body escaped investigation. Still, norms established in this way failed to take into account individual differences, and the averages determined excluded such important physical determinants as environmental factors and rate of growth. A more accurate picture based on norms may be achieved when curves or channels of growth are drawn on coordinate paper and an individual child's growth over a long period of time is plotted in relation to the norms. The child who is experiencing normal physical development will then tend to maintain the same relative position in respect to those of his age group (Stuart and Meredith, 1946).

The Fels Composite Sheet (Sontag and Reynolds, 1945) provides for complex plotting of individual deviation from group mean scores concerned with such aspects of growth as height, weight, skeletal development, and dentition. (See Figure 6-9.) Standard scores represent the difference between the normative value and actual value at a given age divided by the standard deviation for that age. This allows a view of growth progress of a given child in relation to that of the average growth for his age group. Because of the need to employ statistical measures with which the average parent or teacher is unfamiliar, the everyday usefulness of this method is limited.

The Wetzel Grid (Wetzel, 1943) was designed to chart height, weight, and physique type in relation to chronological age, taking into consideration developmental level and basal metabolism. Use of devices of this type facilitates location of gross growth malfunction. However, as in all evaluations, the cause of the deviations cannot thus be identified; comprehensive health histories and thorough physical examinations are necessary in making such determinations.

A method of study that has been employed by the earth sciences for over a century is now being utilized in growth studies, metabolic studies, orthopedics, and other biomedical research and clinical practice. It is called stereographic anthropometry (Herron, 1969), the scientific study of human body shape and size based on 3-dimensional images or models. (See Figure 6-10.) Through the use of a special camera and a technique known as stereophotogrammetry, photographs may be taken of the subject's body while he is standing in a frame which serves as ground zero. A slide projector throws grid marks on the body to help mark differences in its various body levels. A plotter machine traces the contour lines to pro-

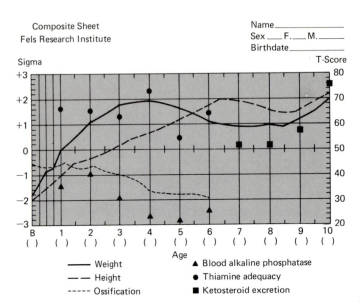

Figure 6-9. The Fels Composite Sheet showing growth of a girl from birth to 10 years. The abscissa is in units of chronological age. The left ordinate is expressed in units of 1 or more standard deviations (sigma) of expected values for a specific age on the abscissa; the right ordinate, in units of the T score in which 50 represents the expected mean. At birth the child was 2 sigmas below the mean for height and weight, but by 4 years was above the mean in weight and near the mean in height. From this record one can conclude that at birth she was small but well proportioned and at 4 was of stocky body build. Various other factors are indicated according to the key below the chart. (From Lester W. Sontag and Earl L. Reynolds, "The Fels Composite Sheet. I. A Practical Method for Analyzing Growth Progress," *The Journal of Pediatrics*, **26**:327–335, 1945. Reproduced by permission of L. W. Sontag and the publisher.)

duce a map of the body's hills and valleys. Relationships between the size of various body parts can thus be determined. The notable advantages of this method over conventional ones are that it is a noncontact procedure; the data are amenable to mathematical manipulation; measures can be made to predetermined limits of accuracy; and it is rapid. When the shortage of necessary equipment is overcome this approach will play an increasingly important role in the biomedical sciences and ultimately provide wide opportunities to realize a long overdue contribution to knowledge of bodily structures and function in health and disease.

Attempts have been made to classify body types and even to assign personality characteristics to each. Sheldon's somatotype classification involves the endomorph, mesomorph, and ectomorph groups (Sheldon, 1940). As a child the endomorph is plump and tends to put on weight as he grows older. He is characterized as having short arms and legs, a thick body, and large skeleton. He has a considerable amount of subcutaneous

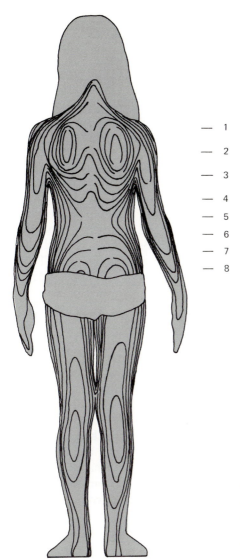

— 1
— 2
— 3
— 4
— 5
— 6
— 7
— 8

Figure 6-10. Illustration of stereographic anthropometry. (From R. E. Herron, "Stereophotogrammetry in Biology and Medicine," *Photographic Applications in Science, Technology and Medicine,* 5, no. 19, 1970, Fig. 15, p. 32. Used by permission of the author and the publisher.)

Scale 1/8.33
Units - cm

10 cm

fat. The mesomorph has much less fat than the endomorph, with muscle and bone predominating. Broad shoulders and heavily muscled arms and legs fit him to be the strong athlete. The ectomorph is linear, with a thin face, narrow chest and abdomen, spindly arms and legs. He has very little subcutaneous fat and seldom becomes obese. His muscles are neither strong nor large. Most people have some of each type in their somatotype. Although most somatotyping has been done on adults, there is some evidence that childhood growth is related to the adult somatotype achieved. At present, data are lacking with which to predict growth based on somatotype determined at birth.

In an attempt to relate body-build stereotyping to personality development, boys 5–6 years old, 14–15 years old and men 19–20 years of age were asked to judge photographs of boys representing Sheldon's three body types: endomorph, mesomorph, and ectomorph. They were to indicate which pictured boy best fit paired words such as healthy-sick, fights-doesn't fight, and brave-afraid. Later they judged the words as good or bad, and finally they selected the words in the listing which described themselves. At all age levels the chubby and average subjects viewed the endomorph unfavorably and the mesomorph favorably. They viewed the ectomorph more desireable than the endomorph but less so than the mesomorph. Subjects with unfavored physiques described their behavior as consistent with a more favored physique, whereas those with a favored physique identified with the characteristics of the favored mesomorph. These data suggest that a negative body concept is inculcated in chubby children while in average children a positive body concept is formed (Lerner and Korn, 1972).

Kurtz (1968) suggests that one views his body in at least three ways: the value, goodness or badness; the potency, strong or weak; the activity, active or passive. One's attitudes toward his body are closely related to his sex. In our society great awareness of bodily appearance is more acceptable in women than in men, and women are aware of their distinguishing characteristics in considerably greater detail than men. Men are not supposed to take such obvious and active interest in how they look. In general we view mesomorphs with more desirability than the other body types, assigning less desirable personality attributes to the extreme: the skinny are thought to be miserly and mean, the fat to be gluttonous, unattractive, and insensitive. Height is also related to how people feel about their bodies. Height, particularly in men, is related to dominance, self-confidence, and leadership. Shortness is seen by many as a liability. People do have total body impressions which can have important consequences in terms of self-concept, goal-setting, and even performance.

Bayley and Bayer (1946) have devised an androgyny classification based on the amount of masculinity present in females and the degree of femininity in males. They feel that the undifferentiated body build of early childhood suggests a neuter quality which at puberty may change toward the hyperfeminine or hypermasculine, or may remain intermediate (asexual). While the final androgyny score cannot be determined until maturity, these investigators have been able to roughly categorize children prior to puberty with respect to this index. The method involves the distribution of fat and muscle, women depositing more fat than men and men developing larger muscles. They believe the androgyny type is an innate trait, uniquely characteristic of each individual throughout life. In recent years the women contenders for the Olympics have been tested for their degree of masculinity and femininity through examination of a hair of their head, in a move to exclude from female competition women who are more masculine than feminine in genetic makeup.

It is obvious that the factor preventing exact measurement and assessment of physical growth is individual uniqueness, produced by a number of things: heredity, ethnic background, sex, family style and socioeconomic status, nutrition, exercise, state of health, emotional climate.

One readily observes similarities in the physical appearances of children and one or both of their parents. There are similarities in the growth pattern within a family. This does not mean that all the children will look alike or have the same terminal size, but the total growth patterns of the siblings are apt to be more alike than that of unrelated children. An attempt to relate body size of parents and their offspring has resulted in parent-specific age-size tables (see Table 6-1), compiled at the Fels Institute (Garn and Rohmann, 1966). The values are based on longitudinal analyses of the statural growth of over 500 children and are standards generally applicable to well-nourished American-born children of the middle socioeconomic class of northwestern European ancestry. The midparent value represents the average of paternal and maternal statures at age 30. To use the table, determine the mid-parent stature and present age of the child in question, and read out in the sex-appropriate column. Not only growth pattern but general body type is an inherited characteristic. Racial characteristics such as skin color, hair texture, body size, and specific physical features are genetically endowed. Sex is genetically determined, of course. Some diseases or physical weaknesses are inherited.

Environmental factors create physical differences, too. The socioeconomic status of the family and the family style impinge on physical development through diet and eating habits, exercise and rest, health care, emotional climate, and psychological pressures. Family values place varying emphases on physical appearances and abilities.

Hathaway (1957) compiled data from American cross-sectional studies which indicate children today are larger than were their parents, even though the range of heights and weights for all ages has been unaffected by time. There are still big children and adults and little ones. But all are a little bigger than were their counterparts in past generations. The growth trend is thought to be related to nutrition and control of disease, and children from the more privileged groups the world over gain more weight and gain it sooner than those from less privileged families.

Race and climate are two factors that are difficult to separate from socioeconomic status and nutrition in the total growth picture. Japanese children born and reared in California were taller and heavier than those born of similar parentage and reared in Japan (Greulich, 1957). The Cali-

Table 6-1 Parent-Specific Age-Size Tables for Boys and Girls of Three Selected Midparent Values

	Boys Parental Midpoint				Girls Parental Midpoint		
Age	163 cm	169 cm	175 cm	Age	163 cm	169 cm	175 cm
1–0	73.1	75.1	77.1	1–0	73.0	74.0	74.6
2–0	85.4	87.4	88.9	2–0	84.0	85.5	88.2
3–0	93.2	96.0	98.3	3–0	90.4	93.8	96.5
4–0	99.5	103.1	106.3	4–0	96.8	103.9	103.8
5–0	105.6	110.0	112.7	5–0	103.5	109.1	111.0
6–0	110.9	115.4	118.7	6–0	110.2	115.0	117.3
7–0	116.2	121.3	124.6	7–0	116.5	120.2	124.0
8–0	121.6	126.8	130.4	8–0	122.4	125.8	130.2
9–0	126.9	131.9	136.0	9–0	128.6	131.4	136.6
10–0	132.5	137.4	141.5	10–0	135.1	136.9	143.1
11–0	138.5	143.0	146.8	11–0	141.6	143.4	149.6
12–0	144.7	148.4	152.4	12–0	147.8	150.3	155.8
13–0	151.0	154.9	159.6	13–0	154.2	157.0	161.7
14–0	158.8	161.6	167.8	14–0	158.8	160.4	165.9
15–0	165.8	167.9	174.7	15–0	159.8	162.2	168.4
16–0	169.4	172.8	176.6	16–0	160.5	163.4	169.7
17–0	170.9	175.4	177.8	17–0	160.8	164.0	170.9
18–0	171.5	176.2	178.6	18–0	161.0	164.3	171.8

The values shown are based on fully longitudinal analyses of the statural growth of more than 500 children representing in excess of 12,000 observations in all. The midparent value, here the average of paternal and maternal statures, refers to parental size at age thirty. To use, determine the midparent stature and present age of the child in question, reading out in the sex-appropriate column. One inch equals 2.5 cm.

Source: Fels Parent-Specific Size Tables for Midparent Categories shown smoothed and arranged by James Eagen. From S. M. Garn and C. G. Rohmann, "Interaction of Nutrition and Genetics in the Timing of Growth and Development," *Pediatric Clinics of North America*, 13 (1966), 353–379. Reprinted by permission of Dr. Stanley M. Garn.

fornia-reared Japanese children were also more advanced in skeletal development. These differences are generally attributed to better food and living conditions, but climate could also be a contributing factor.

Children tend to be consistently advanced or retarded in maturity during their whole growth period after age 3. Yet there is no difference in height between early- and late-maturing boys when both have finished growing. Physically advanced children score slightly higher in most mental measures than the physically less mature. Postmenarcheal girls score higher than premenarcheal girls of the same age. Thus in age-linked examinations fast maturers have a significantly better chance. Children with many siblings are shorter in stature and score less on intelligence tests. Physique can affect self-concept and experience, thus affecting mental performance. Late developers may feel something is wrong with them and not try as hard. They may show more attention-getting behavior, be more restless, bossy, and talkative. They may be less popular and have higher anxiety. Early maturers, on the other hand, also have potential problems. They may be embarrassed by their new body and have a longer period of frustration with the sex drive (Tanner, 1970).

Physical individuality has considerable psychological efects on children during the 6–12 age period when it is important to be accepted by one's peers and to achieve such vital developmental tasks as the acquisition of motor and social skills. Being physically different from one's peers tends to elicit negative response and different treatment. Weight differences or physical handicaps are among the most common causes of such responses and differences. Feelings of inferiority, inadequacy, and rejection may be the result.

Food and Nutrition

"We are what we eat" is an old adage laden with truth. Some researchers (Drillien, 1957; Landreth, 1967) suggest that it takes two generations of proper nutrition to produce healthy children. By school age the child has tasted the majority of the foods eaten within his culture. He has established some basic attitudes about food and some eating habits that may stay with him for the remainder of his life. Still, there are certain nutritional requirements the body needs to maintain good health, and it is quite possible to be well fed but poorly nourished. The effects of malnutrition are manifest not only in specific diseases such as pellagra, scurvy, night blindness, and kwashiorkor (not common in the United States) but in such common conditions as obesity, lethargy, apathy, hyperactivity, tooth decay, anemia, skinny bodies, and poor posture.

There are a number of reasons why children are not well nourished: poor food habits, poor food and health practices, and physical defects and diseases. Poor food habits may stem from psychological problems often begun in infancy and early childhood because of parental anxiety and conflicts over food. Some basic guidelines for helping to avoid poor food habits: provide pleasant experiences with food; be sure the child has adequate exercise, rest, and sleep; serve attractive food to him; be sure the initial servings are small; allow the child some freedom of choice in his food and some freedom to eat it in his own way; relax to prevent intensification of feelings about food and mealtime. Physicians today urge parents not to create tension in youngsters by criticizing their diets of hamburgers and milk shakes, pointing out that these foods contain many needed nutrients essential for growth. Ignorance of the body's food needs is probably a prime cause of poor nutrition, coupled in some households with inadequate financial resources. Too little food, too much food, and poor selection of food are results of such ignorance and inadequacy.

Some typical food practices that can affect nutrition are hurried meals that produce pressure and strain, empty-calorie snacks, and fad diets. Snacks can be a desirable addition to the diet of a growing child if they are chosen to contribute more than energy. Fad diets may be dangerous when they deprive the users of nutrients required for good nutrition. Some of these call for omission of milk, meat, or eggs. Others call for special "health" foods which are sometimes purchased at the sacrifice of the basic foods needed by the whole family.

Such poor health practices as too little sleep, lack of outdoor play, and overexercise are cited as deterrents to good nutrition in children. Physical defects that may also contribute to this condition include: defective tonsils and adenoids that reduce appetite; poor teeth that make eating painful; heart conditions that render this muscle unable to pump sufficient blood to distribute nutrients to the body properly; and diabetes, tuberculosis, and cerebral palsy—all of which complicate the nutritional picture considerably (Martin, 1954).

For all people food serves three basic functions: growth and repair, energy, and regulation of body processes. To serve these functions, there are seven food components, present in varying amounts in the thousands of foods consumed daily. The following diagram shows the components in relation to the main functions they serve in the body (Wilson et al., 1965):

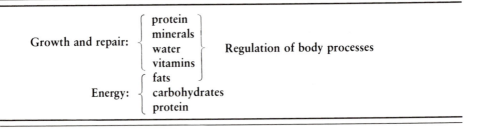

Growth and repair:
protein
minerals
water
vitamins

Regulation of body processes

Energy:
fats
carbohydrates
protein

Only three of these components carry caloric value (Fleck and Munves, 1966):

protein—4 calories per gram
carbohydrates—4 calories per gram
fats—9 calories per gram

Any of the three may be used by the body for energy or be stored as body fat if not expended. The other food components do not contribute to increases in body fat. One can readily see from these few facts that some foods will contribute more to problems of obesity than will others: fried foods will furnish more calories than boiled ones; starchy and sweet foods will generally have higher calorie value than those high in water and cellulose. Vitamin and mineral pills contain no calories but may improve the appetite and thus cause weight gain.

The caloric need of each individual is contingent on several factors, and each person must select his foods accordingly in order to maintain an optimum body size. One such factor is body size and state of growth. During the 6–12 period body size is not increasing at a very rapid rate, and the caloric need will not be as high as during the pubescent spurt when a great deal of growth is occurring. At all ages, persons with larger bodies need more calories to maintain their size than those with small bodies, if other factors are constant.

The efficiency of the body in processing foods is another variable. Some people's bodies utilize foods better and faster than others. These people may be able to eat a given diet and remain slender while other persons on the same diet will gain weight, since their bodies are not as efficient in processing foods.

The basal metabolism is another factor. This term represents the number of calories needed to maintain life in the body without exercise, i.e., digestive peristalsis, circulation of the blood, and production of body chemicals. The larger the body, the more calories needed to keep its basic processes functioning. Exercise is another important determinant of caloric needs, active persons requiring more than sedentary ones. Whereas body build is established by heredity, body size reflects environmental manipulation.

Obesity

A common misconception in terms of obesity is that fat children are healthy children. This is probably almost totally false. Fat children are either the product of body malfunction, as in the case of an underactive thyroid gland; or the victims of poor eating habits due to family patterns; or the sufferers of psychological problems.

The first step in helping the fat child is to determine the cause of his problems. A thorough medical examination and psychological testing may be most helpful in this determination. Even persons with underactive thyroid glands can control their weight through diet; most do not know this and use the body malfunction as an excuse to overeat.

Many obese children have fat parents, or mothers who derive much pleasure and satisfaction from preparing delicious things for the family to eat. Reeducation of parent and child concerning nutrition and food selection may be the key to solving the problem. An exercise program might be helpful if the overweight condition is being intensified by inactivity.

Obesity begins in childhood most of the time, and fat children typically become fat teen-agers and fat adults. For this reason children need to be helped to overcome whatever the obstacle as early as possible.

Once obesity is a fact of life, the child is often unable to develop socially because of ostracism or ridicule by his peers. To compensate for this failure, he may turn to food as a solace, thereby doubling his problem. He may become shy and withdrawn or a behavior problem as he lashes out at those who tease and reject him because of his size. Emotional maladjustment is a common accompaniment of obesity in children. Fat children also grow and mature faster, rendering them physically ready for experiences they may not be prepared to handle. Yet many parents are not aware of the dangers of this condition, and schools do little to help remedy it.

Winick (1975) summarized findings from a conference on child obesity sponsored by the Institute of Human Nutrition at Columbia University, College of Physicians and Surgeons which indicate a great deal is now known about the causes, characteristics, effects and treatments of this significant health hazard. An indication of the genetic factor in this phenomenon is seen in the fact that a child has only a 7 percent chance of obesity if neither parent is obese, while the child with an obese parent has a 40 percent chance and the probability rises to 80 percent if both parents are obese. Other constitutional factors contributing to obesity include brain lesions and metabolic syndromes.

A relatively new concept about obesity, postulated by Hirsch (1969) concerns the number of fat cells formed in the body in early life. He has found that while the non-obese person has approximately 300 billion adipose cells, the obese person has about twice that number. Either too many fat cells or fat cells that are too big can lead to obesity. Alteration of fat cell number can only be accomplished through dietary management early in life. A thirteen-year-old who already has the adult number of fat cells has little chance of escaping adult obesity. A youngster who has an excess number for his age but has not yet reached the adult quantity may be able to "grow out of obesity" by weight maintenance.

Garn (1975) has identified the parameters for determining obesity and leanness as at or above the 85th percentile for the triceps fat fold for age and sex and at or below the 15th percentile on the same measure, respectively. He contends this approach is more sound than the typical value of being 20 percent beyond the weight norm for one's age and sex.

There is some evidence that obesity is affected by socioeconomic status, poor children being leaner than affluent ones. Income held constant, ethnic differences also emerge: black infants are fatter than white ones, but as children the reverse is true. Puerto Ricans are fatter than blacks or whites at similar economic levels. Affluence seems to result in fat children's becoming thin adults, and it is conjectured that body configuration influences social mobility.

Factors causing infant obesity, which often becomes juvenile obesity, include excessive weight gain in pregnancy, brain damage, overzealous bottle feeding, early introduction of high-calorie solids, and family attitude toward weight gain. Peak periods in which obesity develops are: late infancy, at about age 6, and during adolescence. The literature suggests that fat children do not eat more than lean children and that adolescents reportedly eat when they are bored rather than hungry.

Obese children are physically different from their peers in more than body configuration. They are generally taller and their skeletal development is advanced. Yet they are far less active and exercise in nonrhythmical patterns. They experience earlier puberty and have higher levels of hemoglobin and certain vitamins. They also have higher fat-free weight. Since obesity and sedentary activity patterns are two of five factors which predispose coronary heart disease, their chances of heart disease may be greater. Some public health programs have developed routine screening for children with a parent who has experienced a coronary occlusion before age 50, and others do routine checks on serum cholesterol, blood pressure and endurance in even healthy children.

There are three major approaches to the obesity program: diet care from infancy, psychological support, and increased exercise. Hormones currently have little or no place in treatment: while thyroid hormone causes weight loss, it is in nitrogen and calcium stores with little loss of body fat. The cardiovascular and skeletal side-effects constitute a hazard in its use. There is presently no hormonal agent which can safely attack the problem.

Gradually changing behavior through modification schedules, shifting the responsibility from the therapist to the family and child seems to offer promise as a useful tool. Mayer (1975) reports a highly successful one-hour daily exercise program among school children resulted in weight reduction in 60 percent of the participants but notes that three years later the effects had been obliterated due to the sedentary nature of modern childhood.

Although not a problem of the dimension as that of the obese child, the too-thin child may need special help. Perhaps his body size is due to undernutrition, unappetizing meals, excess fatigue, and tension. Refusal to eat may be a weapon against a rejecting parent or a method of focusing attention on himself.

Food Selection

Contrary to popular belief, most people, most of all children, will not get an adequate diet through sheer intuition (Todhunter, 1969). It is for this reason that basic food guides have been created and that recommended daily allowances of specific nutrients have been determined.

Davis's study (1928) is often used to support the notion that children innately know what foods their bodies need and ingest appropriately. One who carefully reviews the research can see that this conclusion is not correct. Due to the age of the subjects there was no peer pressure. The effect of advertising was not present. The sample numbered but three, and the subjects had only healthful foods from which to choose: bone jelly and marrow, whole grain cereals, eggs, milk, muscle meats, glandular organs, and vegetables and fruits. All foods were fresh, and there were no sugars, butter, cream, or cheese available. Davis included at the end of her report a word of caution which has been ignored by those who have cited her research in support of the innate ability theory of child diet: "From the standpoint of nutrition, conclusions as to the success of the self-selected diet for these infants are not warranted from a continuance of it for periods of only six (two infants) and twelve (one infant) months."

The Recommended Dietary Allowances for certain nutrients were developed in the early 1940s and have been revised in the light of research periodically since that time. The most current ones are presented in Table 6-2. These may serve as a safe guide for planning children's diets under normal conditions. They are intended for use by people in good health; needs in disease or in a suboptimum nutritional state require special consideration.

A simpler guide to food selection is the Basic Four, pictured in Figure 6-11. It is very easy for children to learn this pattern and to self-check their daily intake. Children enrolled in Project Head Start have learned it and reportedly often query their parents concerning reasons proper foods have not been served in a given period. With careful selection, children in the 6-

School food service plays a vital role in the nutritional well-being of the majority of school-aged children. (Photo by Lin Mitchell.)

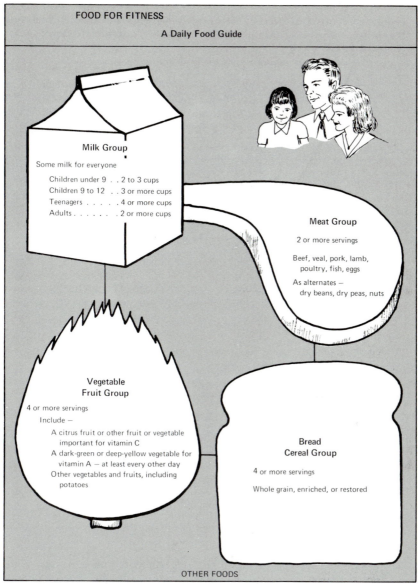

FOOD FOR FITNESS

A Daily Food Guide

Milk Group

Some milk for everyone

Children under 9 . . 2 to 3 cups
Children 9 to 12 . . 3 or more cups
Teenagers . . . . . 4 or more cups
Adults . . . . 2 or more cups

Meat Group

2 or more servings

Beef, veal, pork, lamb,
poultry, fish, eggs

As alternates —
dry beans, dry peas, nuts

**Vegetable
Fruit Group**

4 or more servings
Include —
A citrus fruit or other fruit or vegetable
important for vitamin C
A dark-green or deep-yellow vegetable for
vitamin A — at least every other day
Other vegetables and fruits, including
potatoes

**Bread
Cereal Group**

4 or more servings

Whole grain, enriched, or restored

OTHER FOODS

Figure 6-11. To round out meals and most energy needs, most everyone will use some foods not specified in the Four Food Groups. Such foods include breads, cereals, flours, sugars, butter, margarine, other fats. These often are ingredients in a recipe or added to other foods during preparation or at table. Try to include some vegetable oils among the fats used. (Modified from *Leaflet 424*, Institute of Home Economics, U.S.D.A., Washington, D.C.)

Table 6-2   Food and Nutrition Board, National Academy of Sciences–National Research Council Recommended Daily Dietary Allowances,[a] Revised 1974

Designed for the maintenance of good nutrition of practically all healthy people in the U.S.A.

	Age	Weight		Height		Energy	Protein	Vitamin A Activity		Vitamin D	Vitamin E Activity[e]
	(years)	(kg)	(lbs)	(cm)	(in)	(kcal)[b]	(g)	(RE)[c]	(IU)	(IU)	(IU)
Infants	0.0–0.5	6	14	60	24	kg × 117	kg × 2.2	420[d]	1,400	400	4
	0.5–1.0	9	20	71	28	kg × 108	kg × 2.0	400	2,000	400	5
Children	1–3	13	28	86	34	1,300	23	400	2,000	400	7
	4–6	20	44	110	44	1,800	30	500	2,500	400	9
	7–10	30	66	135	54	2,400	36	700	3,300	400	10
Males	11–14	44	97	158	63	2,800	44	1,000	5,000	400	12
	15–18	61	134	172	69	3,000	54	1,000	5,000	400	15
	19–22	67	147	172	69	3,000	54	1,000	5,000	400	15
	23–50	70	154	172	69	2,700	56	1,000	5,000		15
	51+	70	154	172	69	2,400	56	1,000	5,000		15
Females	11–14	44	97	155	62	2,400	44	800	4,000	400	12
	15–18	54	119	162	65	2,100	48	800	4,000	400	12
	19–22	58	128	162	65	2,100	46	800	4,000	400	12
	23–50	58	128	162	65	2,000	46	800	4,000		12
	51+	58	128	162	65	1,800	46	800	4,000		12
Pregnant						+300	+30	1,000	5,000	400	15
Lactating						+500	+20	1,200	6,000	400	15

[a] The allowances are intended to provide for individual variations among most normal persons as they live in the United States under usual environmental stresses. Diets should be based on a variety of common foods in order to provide other nutrients for which human requirements have been less well defined. See text for more detailed discussion of allowances and of nutrients not tabulated. See Table I (p. 6) for weights and heights by individual year of age.

[b] Kilojoules (kJ) = 4.2 × kcal.

[c] Retinol equivalents.

[d] Assumed to be all as retinol in milk during the first six months of life. All subsequent intakes are assumed to be half as retinol and half as β-carotene when calculated from international units. As retinol equivalents, three fourths are as retinol and one fourth as β-carotene.

12 age group will be able to fulfill the requirements and consume some "fun" foods such as candy or soft drinks without exceeding the 2000–2500 caloric intake which this age usually demands.

School Food Service. Grants-in-aid of federal resources are provided to non-profit schools in U.S. states and territories to provide low-cost food service to children of high school age and under through cash subsidies and distribution of agricultural commodities under the provisions of the National School Lunch Act, Public Law 87-823, passed in 1946 and amended periodically. Four out of five schools participate in this program,

Water-Soluble Vitamins							Minerals					
Ascorbic Acid (mg)	Folacin[f] (μg)	Niacin[g] (mg)	Riboflavin (mg)	Thiamin (mg)	Vitamin B_6 (mg)	Vitamin B_{12} (μg)	Calcium (mg)	Phosphorus (mg)	Iodine (μg)	Iron (mg)	Magnesium (mg)	Zinc (mg)
35	50	5	0.4	0.3	0.3	0.3	360	240	35	10	60	3
35	50	8	0.6	0.5	0.4	0.3	540	400	45	15	70	5
40	100	9	0.8	0.7	0.6	1.0	800	800	60	15	150	10
40	200	12	1.1	0.9	0.9	1.5	800	800	80	10	200	10
40	300	16	1.2	1.2	1.2	2.0	800	800	110	10	250	10
45	400	18	1.5	1.4	1.6	3.0	1,200	1,200	130	18	350	15
45	400	20	1.8	1.5	2.0	3.0	1,200	1,200	150	18	400	15
45	400	20	1.8	1.5	2.0	3.0	800	800	140	10	350	15
45	400	18	1.6	1.4	2.0	3.0	800	800	130	10	350	15
45	400	16	1.5	1.2	2.0	3.0	800	800	110	10	350	15
45	400	16	1.3	1.2	1.6	3.0	1,200	1,200	115	18	300	15
45	400	14	1.4	1.1	2.0	3.0	1,200	1,200	115	18	300	15
45	400	14	1.4	1.1	2.0	3.0	800	800	100	18	300	15
45	400	13	1.2	1.0	2.0	3.0	800	800	100	18	300	15
45	400	12	1.1	1.0	2.0	3.0	800	800	80	10	300	15
60	800	+2	+0.3	+0.3	2.5	4.0	1,200	1,200	125	18+[h]	450	20
80	600	+4	+0.5	+0.3	2.5	4.0	1,200	1,200	150	18	450	25

[e] Total vitamin E activity, estimated to be 80 percent as α-tocopherol and 20 percent other tocopherols. See text for variation in allowances.

[f] The folacin allowances refer to dietary sources as determined by *Lactobacillus casei* assay. Pure forms of folacin may be effective in doses less than one fourth of the recommended dietary allowance.

[g] Although allowances are expressed as niacin, it is recognized that on the average 1 mg of niacin is derived from each 60 mg of dietary tryptophan.

[h] This increased requirement cannot be met by ordinary diets; therefore, the use of supplemental iron is recommended.

From: *Recommended Dietary Allowances*, 8th ed., Washington, D.C.: National Academy of Sciences, 1974. p. 129.

and in 1974, 57 percent of the enrolled students patronized it. (Status of Children.)

The school lunch program is designed to teach nutrition education, provide ⅓ of the child's daily nutritional needs and promote the use of U.S. agricultural products. The United States Department of Agriculture established prescribed meal patterns which designate portion sizes for children from birth through age 21 to serve as guidelines for food services in public institutions and in residential care centers.

Schools participating in the National School Lunch Program are required to furnish reduced prices or free meals to children whose families cannot afford to buy their food. In 1974, about a third of all school lunches were provided on this basis. Federal monies are also made available for schools to offer breakfast and dinner programs, provide additional milk, purchase food production equipment and transport and serve meals. Special provisions have been made to help ensure good nutrition for economically needy, migrant and ADC (Aid to Dependent Children) students. The federal government has required that schools keep records of the number of free and reduced-price meals served but has also said that children receiving these meals cannot be identified as such to their peers. In order to maintain the self-respect of these children some schools have lists of all children who have paid for their meals and who are eligible for free or reduced-priced meals at the cash register for checking. Others use a system of ID cards with symbolic codes concerning lunch status. Still others employ numerically coded lunch tickets. They have found that children will more readily participate when no one knows their nonpaying status, whereas they would formerly skip the meal rather than have others know they could not afford to buy it.

Teachers of elementary school children can contribute to their students' food habits and nutritive status in a number of ways. They can set a good example of food consumption and provide encouragement to children to eat balanced meals. They can help see that the facilities where school meals are eaten are clean, cheerful, uncrowded and conducive to visiting with one's friends. They can help children learn to accept new foods with curiosity rather than skepticism through classroom tasting parties, stories, experiments. Field trips to food processing plants, farms, markets can increase awareness and interest in food. Animal feeding experiments and personal improvement projects related to food habits are enjoyable to children at this age. Social studies units about foods in other parts of the world foster acceptance and understanding of others.

The need for a relaxing atmosphere during mealtime is not met in many schools where quiet in the cafeteria is expected. Some schools sponsor contests among classes to foster this expectation, awarding the quietest class with a movie or special outing. Mealtime is an appropriate time for socializing and recovering from the pressures of the classroom. Children need a degree of freedom at this period and can be helped to develop acceptable standards of behavior without imposition of rules which are not conducive to good development and growth. Mealtime should also be unhurried as far as possible. Manners and digestion are both better when adequate eating time is allowed. Strenuous exercise immediately following a meal is also not good since the body's primary task at that time is processing of the meal.

Evidence seems to support the fact that when teachers are educated in nutrition, they do a better job of effecting learning and its application in their children. In a recent California study (Lovett et al., 1970) involving 306 second grade classrooms, children whose teachers had received specific nutrition-related training and materials increased 151 percent in their ability to apply nutrition knowledge, while those whose teachers received only the materials improved only 39 percent. Those whose teachers worked only from general objectives increased in their ability only 22 percent.

The Parents' Role

The school cannot be charged with providing for the total nutritional needs and attitudes during the middle years of childhood. Parents will play a major role in shaping the attitudes of their children toward food and eating, and in the home the child should receive from one-half to two-thirds of his daily nutrients, depending on the amounts provided in school meals. Parents will need to assist children in checking the adequacy of their daily intake, by providing appetizing, nourishing meals on a schedule convenient for the family, by eating a wide variety of foods themselves, and by complimenting the children on their consumption.

Sometime during the elementary years almost every child decides he would like to take a packed lunch to school. If properly planned, these lunches can still fulfill his nutritional needs. But when children are left unsupervised to prepare their own lunch, protein and vitamin content of the menu may be low. The school lunch pattern is a good guide for both packed lunches and meals served to the family at home (McWilliams, 1967).

Vitamin supplements are often used by parents in an attempt to ensure proper nutrition for their children. Although there are times in one's life when these dietary supplements are advisable, as during pregnancy or following injury, there are some facts in this connection which should be considered prior to their prescription: Dietary supplements are unnecessary and in a sense a waste of money if a proper diet is being consumed. All vitamins in excess of those actually needed by the body are either stored (vitamins A and D) or excreted (vitamins C and B). If stored in excess in the body vitamins A and D can cause a disease called hyperavitaminosis, characterized by such symptoms as skin lesions, growth retardation, poor bone formation, abnormal reproduction, blood clotting, and hemorrhage. Through consumption of large amounts of vitamins it is possible to actually raise the body maintenance level, particularly in children; hence heightened amounts will be needed throughout life. And, those depending on vitamin supplements instead of natural foods for their vitamin requirements may miss the additional contributions the natural foods could have made, in terms of roughage, water, protein, and minerals (Fleck and Munves, 1966; Wilson et al., 1965). Physicians often routinely prescribe vitamin supplements for healthy children; parents who are providing a nutritionally adequate diet for their family can probably avoid this added expense.

Health and Fitness

Normally the period from age 6 or 8 to puberty is a healthy age. Health conditions in childhood are closely associated with the socioeconomic status of the family—with respect to diet, attitude toward health care, and availability of such care. A child's state of general health is revealed in his appearance and in his behavior patterns. One can make a fair assessment of his health status through observation. Hurlock (1972, p. 122) has characterized the healthy child as follows:

> In appearance, practically all healthy children have certain common characteristics. The mucous membranes (especially of the lips) are definitely pink; the facial expression is serene or happy, often radiant; the eyes are bright and responsive; the skin is smooth and elastic; the limbs are rounded because of a sufficient layer of subcutaneous fat; the muscles are well formed, and their tonus is good; the stance is well balanced and posture is erect; the limb muscles are almost straight; the spine is straight; the shoulder girdles do not droop; the arches of the feet are well formed; and the movements of the limbs and body in walking and running are characterized by elasticity, vigor, and poise. . . . The healthy child is alert, full of energy, and anxious to be on the go. When given a choice of play activities he will prefer those which require bodily activity.
>
> By contrast, the child whose health is poor is either underweight or soft and flabby; his posture is poor, his shoulders are rounded, his legs tend to be bowed, and his teeth are likely to be carious. He is usually shorter than one would expect from his family background, and his growth is at a slower rate than is normal for his age. . . . The child in poor health will select sedentary activities, such as watching television or going to the movies.

Sleep and Rest

Sleep and rest are protective functions of the body, allowing for repair and recovery of tissues after activity. By the end of the preschool period, the average child sleeps about 11 hours of the 24. But there is a wide variance in the number of hours, the distribution between night and day, the consistency of the pattern, and the soundness and the effects of the various influences on sleep. There is no set rule concerning the amount of sleep needed at various ages, but one can generally assess sleep adequacy by observing readiness to arise in the morning, emotional state, cheerfulness, activity in play, brightness of eyes, and enthusiasm. Since there is not rapid growth during the 6-12 years, the elementary school-age child may not require the amount of sleep that a preschooler and an adolescent do. He may benefit, however, from brief rest periods, particularly following active play. Parents are not usually willing to allow children to regulate their own sleeping patterns, and most children are able to learn to sleep approximately when the family does. It is not uncommon for schoolage children to arise particularly early on the weekends in order to have a longer day in which to play and yet to find it exceedingly difficult to awaken on school mornings.

During sleep each night persons experience four to six periods when dreaming occurs, accompanied by rapid movement of the eyes, observable through the lids. This type of sleep is called REM sleep, designating rapid-eye movement periods. REM sleep is likely to occur during the latter portion of the night, although each person has an individual sleep pattern as unique as his fingerprints. Each person requires a certain amount of REM sleep, and deprivation of this can cause personality changes. There is a decreasing need for REM sleep with increasing age. (See Figure 6-12.) Lost

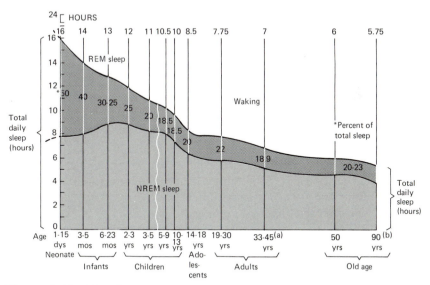

Figure 6-12. REM sleep/NREM sleep relationship throughout human life. (From "Ontogenetic Development of the Human Sleep-Dream Cycle," by H. P. Roffwarg et al., *Science*, 152:604–617, April 29, 1966, Fig. 1. Copyright 1966 by the American Association for the Advancement of Science. Revised since publication in *Science* by Dr. Roffwarg. Used by permission of Dr. Roffwarg and the publisher.)

REM sleep must be made up by the body before the sleeping pattern returns to normal. It is harder to awaken a person during REM sleep than during periods without dreaming . External factors influence the amount of REM sleep one can achieve: sedative drugs reduce it, and alcohol found in two cocktails reduces REM sleep by 15 percent. There is no way to induce increase of REM sleep. Some sleeping pills prevent it; all reduce it. If possible parents should avoid waking children while they are experiencing REM sleep (Levine, 1969).

Injury and Illness

In 1973 among the 5–14 years age group, the accident rate was 21.3 deaths per 100,000 population, a 16 percent increase since 1963. Accidents accounted for 48.7 percent of the deaths, cancer for 14.4 percent and congenital anomalies another 5.4 percent. Motor vehicles were the leading cause of accidents, followed by drowning, fire and burns (Status of Children).

Some children tend to be accident- or illness-prone, having more than their share of illness and being sicker when illness does strike. Among the factors contributing to this phenomenon are repeated frustration, hostility toward adult authority, broken homes, authoritarian discipline methods, poor social adjustment, and being a latter-born (Hurlock, 1964). Accident reoccurrence may be a sign of family problems, and medical treatment may not be enough. Research indicates that individual maladjustment is an important variable in accident liability, and familial pathology is related to personal pathology. Plionis (1977) studied the association between the adequacy of family functioning and the children's repetitive accident rate, finding a significant relationship in children ages 3–11. A higher accident rate was noted when their was a disturbance in the marital relationship which threatened family solidarity. A history of illness in the children was also related to high accident rates. Variables not found significant included parent-child relationship, father absence, and sibling relationships.

Respiratory and gastrointestinal upsets are the most frequent types of illness. Communicable diseases common around age 5 or 6 diminish during the 6–12 period. Immunization, good nutrition, adequate rest and exercise can help fortify the child's body to resist disease. Children by this age need to be taught self-care for such prevention.

With the near eradication of the once dreaded childhood diseases such as diptheria and whooping cough, the rate of unimmunized children has begun to increase in recent years. About 20 percent of American children under age 13 are not adequately immunized against diptheria, tetanus, and whooping cough. Thirty-five percent have not received measles and rubella vaccines. The number being immunized against polio is decreasing. More than 5 million children are inadequately protected against these diseases (Status of Children).

United Nations figures indicate that the mortality rate for U.S. children ages 1–14 years in 1969 was 42.2 per 100,000. The leading causes of death were cancer, diseases of the nervous and circulatory systems. More boys than girls succombed to death, and slightly more at ages 5–9 than between 10 and 14. The United Nations estimates that by 1980 approximately 16 percent of the North American population will be between ages 5 and 14 (Jeanneret and Raymond, 1975).

Tragic numbers of children are killed or injured annually due to poisoning or explosions resulting from experimenting with or mistaking as harmless common household products: furniture polish, iodine, bleach, cleaning compounds, aerosol sprays, medicine, kerosene, to name a few. Children should be taught early the symbols denoting poison, and their respect for chemicals should be fostered through learning and storage precautions.

Over 2 million children under age 14 are living with disabilities that are permanent or of indefinite duration, orthopedic defects being the most frequent, then speech, hearing, and visual defects. Among children 6 to 11, 8 percent have speech defects while 11 percent suffer from visual handicaps. Any of these has a potential adverse effect on growth (Legislative Reference Service, 1964). Other conditions that retard growth include hookworm, rheumatic fever, diabetes, and chronically infected tonsils and adenoids (Breckenridge and Vincent, 1965).

Sickle cell disease is an inherited disorder that affects black people almost exclusively. It is accompanied by severe anemia, and markedly reduces life expectancy, the victim not usually living beyond the third decade. Sickle cell anemia is not curable, and early recognition of the condition is vital to proper care of the affected child.

The child with sickle cell anemia has to visit the doctor and the hospital regularly. He takes special medications and needs protection from colds, pneumonia, intestinal upsets, and other infections that may cause weeklong crisis periods in his disease several times each year. He is thin and small for his age, and may have feelings of inferiority because of his inability to compete physically with his peers. The condition does not affect intelligence, but he is frequently absent from school because of illness and is sometimes behind his age group as a result. He may ask questions his parents are unprepared to answer: Am I going to get well? Am I going to die from this? (Duckett, 1971).

Why the disease is particularly prevalent among the black race is an interesting question. The sickle gene, producing elongated instead of round blood cells, is believed to have arisen by spontaneous mutation in equatorial Africa thousands of years ago. This trait seems to enhance one's resistance to malaria, resulting in natural selection for persons with the sickle

Table 6-3 Chronic Illnesses—Prevalence

| Chronic Health Problem | Age and Sex | | | | | | Total |
| | 0–4 | | 5–9 | | 10–14 | | |
	Male	Female	Male	Female	Male	Female	
Asthma	98	71	122	75	82	36	484
Social problems (economic, housing, parental conflict, etc.)	98	77	72	43	39	39	368
Congenital malformations (excluding heart and cleft palate and lip)	98	45	18	18	11	13	243
Epilepsy	20	19	14	24	15	11	103
Hyperkinesis	2	3	35	10	20	5	75
Congenital heart disease	15	13	5	3	3	1	40
Scoliosis	—	—	3	8	7	8	26
Diabetes mellitus	—	3	7	2	12	1	25
Nephritis and nephrosis	3	—	5	3	4	5	20
Psoriasis	2	—	1	6	4	3	16
Rheumatic heart disease and hypertension	1	1	—	7	3	2	14
All malignant neoplasms	1	4	2	2	2	1	12
Purpura and hemorrhagic conditions	1	2	2	2	2	2	11
Glaucoma	3	—	2	2	2	—	9
Schizophrenia and organic psychoses	—	—	3	1	2	2	8
Cataract	1	2	—	—	4	—	7
Gastric and duodenal ulcer and ulcerative colitis	—	1	—	1	3	1	6
Rheumatoid arthritis	—	—	—	3	2	1	6
Cleft palate	—	2	1	1	—	1	5
CNS vascular lesions	3	—	—	1	—	—	4
Total, all diseases	—	—	—	—	—	—	1,482

From Fromm, p. 78, based on 25,391 cases in Rochester, N.Y. 1971–1973.

cell trait. The slave trade during the sixteenth to eighteenth centuries is believed to have distributed the sickle gene to other parts of the world. A small number of persons of Italian, Greek, Near Eastern, and Indian descent have also been found to have the sickle cell trait. About 1 in 12 black Americans is a carrier. Approximately 1 in 500 has the disease. Prevention through genetic counseling is currently the only method of avoiding the spread of the disorder to later generations. When two carriers of the trait become parents, one child in four will inherit sickle cell anemia, two will become carriers, and one will be free of the disease (Pearson, 1971). (See Figure 6-13.)

Hyperkineticism or hyperactivity is a condition affecting from 3 to 5 percent of U.S. children. It is characterized by lack of self control and a preponderance of activity. The condition may be evident prenatally or in early infancy. Ten times as many boys than girls have been so diagnosed, according to Bettleheim (1976). During early elementary school most of these children perform at average or slow learner levels on tests, and some perform at very high levels. But their measurable intellect tends to decline from grades three or four as their disruptive behavior patterns interfere with their intellectual growth. The condition usually lessens with the approach of puberty, but the damage to self-concept may have permanent ramifications (Wunderlich, 1970).

The hyperactive children react to their environment far more than the average child, being stimulated by everything they see, hear and feel. They are likely to be out of their seats a lot, and some part of their body is always in motion. Their low attention span makes them poor listeners, and often incessant talkers. They are easily distracted and typically difficult to discipline. Hyperkinetic children may have many characteristics of the passive withdrawer: respond negatively to demands they feel unable to meet, refuse to perform, do not understand what is asked of them, make mistakes which seem stupid. They forget what they seemed to learn yesterday. They fight back through restlessness and defiance of adult authority (Wunderlich, 1970; Bettleheim, 1976).

The cause of this condition may be neurological damage, called Strauss Syndrome; the result of an hereditary temperament; or allergy-based. All lead to lack of inner control. Some children have developed an overactive behavior profile as a defense against further emotional damage, Bettleheim suggests. Typically one or both parents of hyperactive children is restless, short-tempered, insists on "nice" behavior through many "do's," "don'ts" and "behave-yourselfs." Parents who see their normally active toddlers as rambunctious and who set unrealistic demands for quiet or body cleanliness can pattern them into hyperkinetic patterns. Children with only mild undiagnosed neurological disorders may have mild tendencies toward overaction which shapes their care-givers into high attention patterns during infancy. As they mature, the lack of external control pattern intensifies, and by school age, the children are exhibiting problems similar to those with more severe neurological damage or emotionally-based problems.

The reaction of these hyperactive children to such school demands as sitting for long periods, and engaging in seemingly meaningless tasks is a desire for activity. The preponderance of negative responses of primary school teachers toward boys (90 percent) may be related to the 10 to 1 ratio of hyperkineticism in boys and girls. The severity of the condition may be related to the degree normal boyishness was tolerated prior to

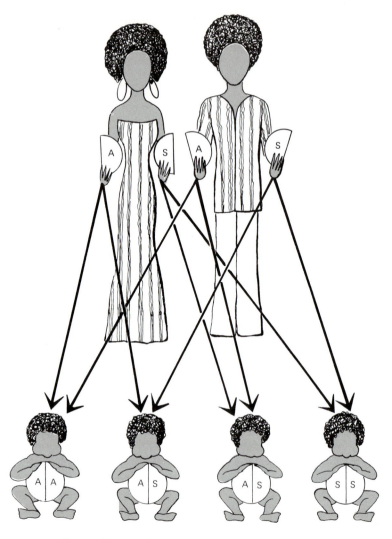

Parents who are carriers of the sickle cell trait do not show symptoms of the disease because hemoglobin A (the normal form of hemoglobin) in their red blood cells protects them from hemoglobin S (the sickling form). But when two carriers become parents, the possibilities are:

☐ One child in four will inherit all normal hemoglobin (AA) and thus be free of the disease.

☐ Two children in four will inherit both hemoglobin A and hemoglobin S (AS) and thus become carriers of the trait like their parents.

☐ One child in four will inherit all sickling hemoglobin (SS) and thus become a victim of sickle cell anemia.

Figure 6-13. How parents transmit sickle cell disease. (From *Children Today,* November–December 1971. Washington, D.C.: Office of Child Development, Department of Health, Education, and Welfare.)

school entrance (Bettleheim, 1976). Treatment for children whose high activity is due to their early environment involves rewarding them for good behavior, helping them to ask for attention in positive ways.

During the past decade stimulant drugs have been widely used in treatment of childen with this problem, with 50 to 67 percent success. In 1974 two hundred thousand children were receiving drugs for the disorder. The potential harm of this approach is not clear, but drugs do not cure; they merely help children respond to counseling and educational efforts better. Other children are responding to diet restrictions which eliminate artificial colorings and flavorings (Feingold, 1975), but it is postulated that the Hawthorne effect is in operation in these cases.

Options are confusing to the hyperkinetic child. He requires a calm, stable, resolute person to help him learn the feeling of inner control. This person should be kind, fair, and consistent.

Bettleheim recommends vigorous activity such as running prior to the need for concentration. Wunderlich proposes introduction of an external stabilizing influence which truly inhibits motor activity for short periods of time, increasing gradually, then decreased as the child's stable behavior rises.

Although corporal punishment is ill-advised, other physical contact such as touching, holding, caressing, patting seems to be effective as a means of external stability. It is advisable to interrupt a child's overactive manifestations immediately and to interject the element of stability in the environment. His attention span can be lengthened through such activities as playing records, playing with wheel toys, and stirring food—the circular motions involved tend to captivate and calm this type of child.

Allergies plague many children during middle childhood, often having begun in infancy. They tend to run in families and are related to such conditions as asthma, recurrent bronchitis, eczema, reaction to foods and drugs, recurrent nose-bleeds, and even bedwetting. Allergies are thought to be related to hyperkineticism, and brain injured children often are also allergic. It is not known if the allergy restricts nutrients to the brain, thus causing the damage, or if the destruction of brain tissue creates an antibody to the brain itself, the latter process having been demonstrated in animal studies (Wunderlich, 1970). An allergic tension-fatigue disorder has been identified which affects children, and one of the commonest allergic problems is congestion of the Eustachian tube. Allergies can be treated with antihistamine or cortisone drugs, desentizing vaccines, chiropractic, or by removal of the offensive substance. Feather pillows, pollens, stuffed animals, wool, such foods as chocolate, wheat, milk, eggs, oranges, hydrocarbon fumes and smoke are all common allergens.

There is increasing evidence on the harmful effects of sidestream smoke on the respiration of children as well as adults. Respiratory disorders are twice as common among children whose parents smoke. Some harmful compounds are far more prevalent in sidestream smoke than in the mainstream smoke inhaled by the smoker. Among the products of smoking which affect the respiratory organs are nitrogen dioxide, hydrogen cyanide, and cadmium. Once some of these substances reach the lungs, they remain permanently (Second-hand Smoke, 1975).

Children whose allergies are being properly managed are apt to feel better and have improved disposition, better food absorption, improved sleep and reduced fatigue, better family relationships. Such physical signs as sneezing, dark circles beneath the eyes, excessive sweating and chronic mouth breathing are likely to disappear.

The impact of disabilities on growth and personality varies from little to extensive among various children, depending on the type and severity of the physical condition as well as the way it is regarded by those around the child. The better the defect can be camouflaged, the less serious its effect will be. The time of the onset of the impairment will also be a consideration: he can usually adjust better if it occurs prior to the establishment of his own independence (Cruickshank and Johnson, 1958). Some children try to compensate for a physical defect by excelling in intellectual or creative endeavors. More develop neuroses or other manifestations of maladjustment.

The child's handicap is interpreted to him in terms of the values of those closest to him. In one study (Goodman et al., 1963) various groups of children were asked to rank five disabilities. The normative group judged obesity as most undesirable, facial disfigurement next, and confinement to a wheelchair least undesirable. Jewish children ranked confinement to a wheelchair worse than obesity and obesity worse than facial disfigurement. Italian children ranked the handicaps in still another order.

The child's attitudes toward any illness, accident, impairment, or hospitalization will be best if parental attitudes are wholesome, and family life continues in regular fashion. Of all the people whose attitudes toward impairments matter, parents are paramount. There is the tendency to be overprotective, making the child feel inferior and depriving him of the incentive to learn to adjust. There is the tendency for the mother to withdraw from social activities because of the "burden" of caring for her child. She may neglect other family members. The father may view the child as a financial and social liability (Boles, 1959). Siblings generally reflect parental attitudes toward an afflicted child. If the affliction is not readily noticeable, outsiders may view the child as spoiled, withdrawn, stupid.

Effects of Illness

Being ill may have varying effects on children. Heightened emotionality or reduced social status in the peer group could result. Schoolwork usually suffers when the child feels ill or is absent because of illness. Behavior difficulties may follow illness if the child has enjoyed being catered to, coaxed, or bribed. He may rebel at having to return to his regular daily routine and responsibilities, even though physically he is quite able to do so. Personality changes may be observed, from increased dependence and shyness to aggression. Illness can cause such physical manifestations as weight loss. Prolonged illness could diminish ultimate height if it coincided with a period of relatively rapid growth.

Canalization is the term given to the body's returning to normal growth pattern after being pushed off by disease, malnutrition, or trauma. A catch-up mechanism, a regulatory system within the body—perhaps the hypothalamus at the base of the brain—seeks to compensate for slowing of growth due to malnutrition or hormone lack. Although not fully understood, it is believed to go into operation as soon as conditions are again optimum and to help the body catch up with its natural growth pattern. Apparently it allows the organism to "know" when to stop the catch-up velocity. If the growth arrest has been prolonged, the catch-up may be incomplete, however. Girls are better canalized than boys, showing less growth retardation as a result of these factors. Although there is no direct evidence of the extent of canalization in brain growth or mental ability, it is believed that the principle also applies during the time the brain is undergoing rapid development. The earlier and more prolonged the stress, the more difficult is total restoration (Tanner, 1970).

Think Back

To some illness or medical treatment you received but did not understand:
How you felt about it.
Who helped you understand it.
If you thought it was worth the trouble afterward.
What you told your friends about it.

Any child who is injured or ill, for whatever periods of time, may suffer from feelings of guilt. In our culture parents teach children that bodily harm comes from doing bad things, like playing in the rain, staying up too late, not minding Mother, not eating rutabagas, and the like. Naturally, when the child becomes hurt or ill, he can think immediately of something he has done which might have caused the infirmity. Most often, it is not of his own doing, of course. Another feeling common among sick children is anger, particularly toward siblings. They are in a sense jealous, too, that the siblings remain well while they are infirmed and restricted in activity. Their anger is partially due to their knowledge that the siblings have also done things that were wrong—yet they have not been made to suffer for their misdoings. And fear is common among ill or hurt children. By school-age they are aware of death, and they may think death will come because of their state of ill health. They do not understand the cause, the treatment, the extent, or the duration of their infirmity unless someone carefully explains it to them. Even after such explanations they may not understand adequately enough to alleviate their fear. They also fear what separation from the peer group will do to their standing.

Treatment and Hospitalization

The fear of doctors is thought to be universal, primarily due to the doctor's role as a pain-inflicting figure. Children typically learn this fear from parents who themselves fear physicians, and use them as threats to achieve compliance to their demands. Another factor instilling distrust and alienation between children and medical personnel is the practice of assuring them given procedures will not be painful when indeed they are. Children often ascribe certain magical powers to physicians and assume they know all and see all, particularly shameful things.

The child entering middle childhood takes extraordinary pride in his body and experiences exquisite anxiety about its welfare. On the other hand, at this age the child has learned that being brave and unafraid is a sign of being grown-up, a role he strongly desires to portray. The conflict resulting from these two facets of his personality is revealed in the medical arena. For this reason, it may be well to limit the medical and surgical procedures to which children this age are subjected. Elective surgery should be scheduled prior to age four or after age seven whenever possible.

Because of their fear of doctors, children may not always be fully honest

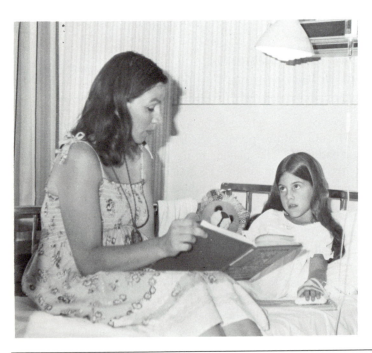

Hospitalized children are often handicapped by their fears and fantasies. Parents can often aid recovery by their presence. (Photo by Lin Mitchell.)

with respect to reporting pain or other symptoms of illness. At this age "to examine" may imply to tear down or disassemble, as in the case of a car or clock. Their concepts of injections or surgery may be greatly exaggerated and unrealistic.

The more freely children express such emotions as fear, anger and sadness, the less damage will occur through psychosomatic illness. For example, one boy who vehemently protested receiving a shot left the office to resume his full play repertoire; his companion who had accepted the procedure placidly went home to bed with a migraine because of his internalized anxiety.

Children fear anesthesia highly. They tend to associate accounts of pets who have been "put to sleep" or acquaintances who have "gone to sleep" with the anesthesia experience they may be facing. This causes them to falsely assume they will never wake up, as in the case of the dead pet or person. They also worry about doing something shameful while under the influence of the anesthesia, such as wetting themselves or telling carefully concealed personal secrets.

Parents separated from their child because of medical procedures often suffer guilt. This can impede their cooperation with the physician and cause them to make demands that the child be brought home earlier than is expedient or they may express a desire to change doctors. Parental emotions such as anxiety are transferable to children, compounding the situation (Bird, 1973).

If hospitalized, they are virtually cut off from their friends becuse most hospitals prohibit child visitors. Although there are good reasons for such restrictions, the sick or injured child does not know them or does not understand them. Mothers are very important during children's illnesses. Their presence can do wonders for the child's spirits. More and more hospitals are realizing the positive effect of mothers and are allowing parents to remain with their hospitalized child as much as they wish. Not only do the mother's hands help with routine chores, but her presence contributes to the child's feeling of security and his will to recover.

If at all possible it is highly desirable to prepare a child for hospitalization. The first step is preparation of the parents, including knowledge of the necessity of the hospitalization and of the procedures that will be conducted while the child is there. The child of school-age should be told one or two days in advance of his going to the hospital. He should be allowed to ask questions and should understand that the stay will be only temporary. To dwell on the unpleasant aspects is unwise, but to paint a completely rosy picture is also unfair. Brevity and honesty are important. Mention that he can expect to stay in bed, see other sick people, eat from a tray, follow certain hospital rules, and eventually feel much better and go home. For the young school-age child there are books about visiting the hospital. An older child may receive solace from discussing hospitalization with his friends or older persons who have been hospitalized. Regardless of the preparation, the child's emotional behavior may be different. He may cry for no good reason, or have a return of such old anxieties as fear of the dark. He may act in other ways younger than his age. Boys especially may show anger at having to wear regulation hospital gowns or sleeping in beds with side rails. Parents should explain the necessity of such procedures and assure them that all is being done to make them well.

In a recent 7-year period, the number of hospitals providing sleep in arrangements for parents in the pediatric section has increased 5-fold (Viorst, 1977). This is one step hospitals are taking as the sensitivity to the emotional aspect of hospitalization increases. Medical personnel are recognizing more and more that children, particularly, are handicapped by their fears, fantasies about pain, separation, and loss of body parts and functions during hospitalization. They ask themselves "Will I ever get to go home? Will I be the same afterwards? Am I being punished for being bad?" The Childrens Hospital National Medical Center in Washington, D.C. has taken definite steps to make the experience as pleasant and supportive as possible for its young patrons. A few innovations are playrooms, bright decor, colored nursing smocks, beds for parents, and assignment of "primary nurses" to a small group of children whom they are responsible for, rather than to certain medical procedures. A Child Life Director coordinates activities for the child's welfare. To allay fears, parents are given pamphlets to help them, take tours, and hold discussions with the hospital staff concerning their child's confinement. Human requirements supersede efficiency when taking more time to perform a task will reduce emotional stress without endangering health status. Parents hold their child's hand until an anesthetic has taken effect before surgery. Children's requests for a hamburger at 6 a.m. are honored when diet will permit. Parental visiting hours are virtually unlimited. Children are encouraged to share their misconceptions, and they are dealt with: one fearing that removal of his adenoids would necessitate removal of his nose had a picture drawn to show the relationship of the two. Another fearing his navel would be excised during surgery was comforted by the placing of a large sign taped to his navel: DO NOT TOUCH. As one physician observed, children will tolerate large doses of hurt if they know the persons doing it really like them!

Eighty-two fatally ill children and their parents were involved in a longitudinal study at the City of Hope Medical Center to assess the value of parent participation in the care of their dying children (Hamovitch, 1964). Parents were able to stay at the center up to full-time, and a supportive staff of social workers and medical personnel was an integral part of the arrangement. The major findings were that inclusion of parents in the hospitalization care of such children helps both the child and the family to deal with the catastrophe in a constructive manner. The marital status of the couple seemed to be the key to the family's coping ability and served as an index to their characteristic pattern of coping with problems. Parent participation was more positive in cases where the child's illness was operable as opposed to cases where surgery did not extend the hope for recovery. Parents whose children were beyond age ten were the most uncomfortable and experienced more guilt. Those children ages 5–9 experienced the most tranquil course in their illness: they were old enough to handle the separation from home but not old enough to sense the gravity of their condition. The nursing personnel found the presence of parents highly beneficial and reportedly felt less personal loss when a child patient died, because they did not have to assume the parental role during care.

Fewer problems were noted when the participation of parents was moderate as opposed to high or low: spending considerable time with the hospitalized child but also attending to home and personal affairs and spending time with at-home siblings. Parents reported that the first three months following the loss of the child is particularly difficult in terms of adjustment. During this period they reported that relatives and friends avoided them when they yearned for company and an opportunity to discuss their loss experience. Fathers seemed to suffer more than mothers, possibly because of the fact that mothers were able to experience more anticipatory grief because they were with the child more, prior to death. Siblings nearest the age of the deceased child reportedly suffered considerably during this period, partially from the loss and partially from the prolonged absences of mothers during the hospital care period. Parents were highly appreciative of the participation program which afforded them more time with their ill childen as well as a chance to realize that theirs was not the only fatally-stricken child. The program was deemed a success in terms of mitigating trauma associated with the illness and the hospitalization process. Both the presence and the participation in care by parents were cited as important facets of this conclusion.

Motor Development

Motor Skills

The achievement of the developmental task of perfection of skills necessary for sports and games is one index of a child's physical development. In our culture it is more impotant to have general motor ability than to perfect specific fine motor talents which are highly valued in other cultures. Perhaps this has led to the generalized physical education programs in the public schools and playgrounds, recreation centers, parks, and community programs such as the YMCA.

There are a number of reasons why it is important for the school-age child to develop motor abilities. They allow him to enter into the peer group projects, whether these are hide and seek, ice-skating, modeling with clay, hiking, digging a cave, or water-skiing. Practice of such skills contrib-

The adventure brought through motor skill development greatly increases in middle childhood. (Photo by Jonathan Burnette.)

utes to all aspects of his total development: social, emotional, physical, and mental. Lack of motor ability may cause him to be excluded, and possibly hinder all aspects of his development. He also derives many hours of self-entertainment through the practice and refinement of motor abilities, whether the activity is playing jacks, tree climbing, piano playing, jump rope, snow sculpture, or skating. With increased motor abilities, his independence grows. The preschooler who needed help dessing, brushing his teeth, bathing, and putting away his toys no longer requires this assistance as his motor skills develop during the ages 6–12. The child who has mastered the art of bike riding has expanded his navigable world immeasurably. And physical skills carry with them prestige value which contributes to a heightened self-image. As he continues to master various motor-related obstacles, he becomes more willing to try new ones, thus broadening his mental, social, and emotional world along with his physical one. The child who does not perfect motor skills, on the other hand, feels insecure, shy, rejected, depressed, and his personality adjustment suffers. Of course, the new independence and freedom brought about by motor skill perfection can be the source of conflict between children and parents, children and their siblings, or even with their peers. But for the most part, their acquisition carries more advantages than disadvantages (Hurlock, 1972).

Healthy children of school-age are typically bounding with energy and bursting with curiosity about their ever-expanding world. The traditional classroom, which requires an appreciable amount of quiet sitting, offers a sizable challenge to these youngsters. In open classrooms teachers are finding that freedom to move around and talk does not interfere with learning. Even when prolonged study and concentration are necessary, periodic breaks that involve physical activity rejuvenate the mind and body. Particularly at recess and lunchtime children need to be allowed to jump, run, talk, laugh, and relax in order to vent their inner urge for movement. Short periods in the out-of-doors lend themselves best to this exercise of muscle and lungs.

Although heredity practically determines one's motor ability potential, environment determines to what extent any individual will achieve his genetic possibilities. Maturation must precede learning. Before skilled movements can be learned, the muscular mechanism must be sufficiently matured to allow such learning. Voluntary muscles are controlled by nerves and nerve centers. Until these have sufficiently developed, coordinated action of a voluntary type will be impossible (Martin and Vincent, 1960). Such development occurs gradually throughout the years of childhood. Training a child prior to the time he is maturationally able to learn may produce temporary gains, but the long-term effects may be more damaging than enhancing.

An example might be found in bicycle riding. The child who is encouraged to attempt perfection of this skill prior to the time his muscles, coordination, and sense of balance have developed to a sufficient degree may experience such failure, develop such fear, and suffer enough physical injuries to hinder his normal progress even when he is maturationally ready for this feat.

Motivation plays an important part in achievement of motor skills. Living in a society that places such great value on coordination of the body, American children usually receive adequate stimulus to produce inner-motivation. The next step is opportunity to learn and practice. Many families do not accept any great personal responsibility for actual teaching in the motor realm; however, most children have opportunities at school and in the community to develop in this area.

The research relative to motor skills of children is summarized by Cratty (1970). It is not as extensive as study of other aspects of development, and the variables have not been as carefully controlled. The majority of emphasis has been given to differences between the sexes and changes with age, although some attempts have been made to relate motor ability to intellectual functioning and sociocultural change. Although early success at motor tasks may contribute in a general way to a child's aspirations in such related areas as writing or play, the idea that motor development forms the basis of the intellect does not seem clearly borne out by research. In fact, simple correlations between classroom learning, intelligence and physical fitness show little or no relationship between academic achievement and physical fitness. The size and strength of the present generation has been shown significantly different from that of previous generations. The impact of physique has often been ignored in data collection, yet it is thought to be an important variable in performance.

The major methods for assessing children's motor performance between ages 6 and 12 include the Denver Developmental Screening Test which contains subtests to evaluate the perceptual motor attributes of children, and the Lincoln-Oseretsky battery containing an even greater variety of items for evaluation of both fine and gross motor skills (see page 292). The Kraus-Weber Test is composed of six simple items which measure strength and flexibility of large muscle. It is the instrument that produced a comparison of American and European children. This resulted in the increased emphasis on U.S. physical fitness beginning in the 1960's.

The components of motor development include strength or power, flexibility, impulsion, speed, precision, coordination, balance, and rhythm.

The motor development between ages 6 and 12 shows regular improvement in a rough linear form, along with such structural changes as increased long-bone growth, higher muscle density and power, and greater force. Although boys may excel girls in such tasks as speed, running and throwing, girls often demonstrate superiority in agility, rhythm and hopping speed and accuracy.

Strength, being the amount of force one can exert, is most often measured in grip strength, and marked changes in this attribute are noted during middle childhood. Boys' average grip strength excels girls during this period, perhaps because of hand size, cultural expectations or muscle efficiency. Little difference is usually found between left and right hands. Low to moderate correlations have been reported among the strength measures in various parts of the body, because muscle strength in various body regions increases at uneven rates. Shoulder strength and flexion rise until age 8, and back strength improves throughout early childhood but is less pronounced at age 12. Ankle strength and flexion improves regularly at all ages in childhood.

Table 6-4 Percent Pure Versus Mixed Sensory Dominance by Age

		Age			
	Dominance	* 4 yrs	** 5–6 yrs	7–8 yrs	9–11 yrs
Handedness	Pure (right and left)	92%	81 %	81 %	94 %
	Mixed	8%	19 %	19 %	6 %
Eyedness	Pure	97%	73 %	68.7%	78.8%
	Mixed	3%	27 %	31.3%	21.2%
Footedness	Pure	No Data	94 %	94 %	98 %
	Mixed	No Data	6 %	6 %	2 %
Hand-eye Preference	Pure	No Data	37.5%	41.7%	63.5%
	Mixed	No Data	62.5%	49.3%	36.5%

* After Flick (1967); N = 453.
** After Belmont and Birch (1963); N = 148.
From Corbin, p. 143.

The National Bureau of Standards has recently been engaged in research to determine children's strength in relation to twisting, squeezing, pushing, pulling and pulling apart in order to provide scientific data for use by manufacturers of children's products in making the items tamper-proof and self-injury-proof. Earlier studies of this type have resulted in current refrigerator doors being magnetic to allow escape from the inside.

Flexibility, or the freedom to bend and otherwise move the body, in this age group has received little research attention, yet it is one of the greatest contributors to motor ability. Flexibility is contingent upon the ability of the muscles to stretch and relax. Girls have been found to lose flexibility in knees, thighs, and shoulders while increasing their flexibility in the trunk, wrists, and legs. This suggests children may grow more flexible in some body regions while the quality diminishes in other regions.

Impulsion is the rate of initiating movements from a stationary position. Reaction time research is also sparse in the literature. In simple reaction time problems, 5-year-olds take twice as long as adults. Ineptitude at initiating a task is thought to contribute to this fact, and differentiation between thinking time and acting time is difficult to ascertain. In adults, about ten times more time has been found necessary to make decisions concerning the positioning of the body for a motor task than is needed for the final decision to reach the muscles involved.

By age 6, normal children can run well, jump vertically and horizontally, and skip. Some can hop rhythmically from one foot to the other while in place. At age 7, both sexes can jump about 7 inches straight upward, and then there develops about a 1-inch mean difference between the performance of boys and girls, with boys excelling. Boys are slightly more successful than girls at the standing broad jump, and better jumpers of both sexes tend to use their arms more and evidence a more pronounced knee bend.

Speed is considered to be the rate of movements once initiation has occurred. Speed in running tasks is a common measurement of this component. Both boys and girls run about 1 foot per second faster each year from ages 6 to 12. Toward the end of this period, girls generally run about 1 foot per second slower than boys. Agility and running ability on specified courses, such as shuttle runs, increases substantially between ages 8 and 9 for boys and between ages 6 and 7 for girls. Boys are still slightly faster.

Precision involves tracing, threading, pursuit aiming, finger and hand dexterity. It is refined with age as hand-eye *coordination* increases. *Balance* is a type of precision and concerns control of the body against the forces of gravity. It can be studied in its static or dynamic states, the former involving maintaining a given posture, the latter requiring movement down a balance beam. This attribute matures slightly earlier in life than strength and improvement is manifest in two or more periods during childhood. Boys seem to improve their balance most between 7 and 9 and again at age 10, whereas girls show more marked improvement between 6 and 7 and again between 10 and 11. The average child of both sexes can maintain balance on one foot with arms folded across the chest for 4 to 6 seconds with eyes open but cannot accomplish this task with closed eyes. By age 7 they can usually maintain closed eyes balance on the floor while using their arms for equilibrium. Ability to balance increases markedly during middle childhood and reaches maturity prior to the teen years.

Girls excel boys in hopping on grids, such as hopscotch, until about age 9. Girls are generally superior in tasks involving precise movement of the feet. Not until age 8 can more than half of children of either sex be expected to hop *rhythmically* in a two-two pattern without breaking cadence. Children seem to have difficulty recognizing when their limbs have moved a given number of times, a problem also observable in attempts to reproduce tapping movements with the upper limbs.

Middle childhood people spend a large amount of time playing with balls of various sizes. A reasonable mature throwing pattern with a weight shift and a step with the foot opposite the throwing arm is evident by age 6 in boys. Girls often step with the foot on the throwing side. Boys throw farther than girls at each age, the difference being more marked by ages 10

Tee-ball allows children to develop precision without the factor of a moving object to contend with. (Photo by Lin Mitchell.)

and 11. Boys' superior strength and frequent exposure to the task are thought to explain this finding. They also throw more accurately. Children between ages 7 and 10 have been found to throw twice as far as they could at age 6, and the distance tripled by age 12. Intercepting balls, or catching, is more difficult than impelling, or throwing. Catching accuracy lags several years behind throwing accuracy. Failure to catch can be among the most socially traumatic of skill deficiencies, especially since it is a key to success in such little league sports as baseball, teeball and football. Kicking accuracy improves with age until the ninth year, when a plateau is reached. Boys excel girls in this task as well as in batting, perhaps due to experience and cultural expectations.

Motor learning progresses from simple to complex, gross to refined, large to small. Maturation must precede practice for the practice to be productive. And still, practice may not necessarily make perfect. Movement abilities improve when the learner intends them to and frequent short practice is more effective for young or beginning learners than massed practice. Motor learning is characterized by the gradual elimination of superfluous and tense movement and the acquisition of effective action and good coordination. The better perceived and learned, the better and longer a skill will be remembered. Simpson (1966) defined the sequence of psychomotor learning as: observation, imitation, practice and modification.

The motor abilities of children have been largely unestimated. During the elementary school years motor development is primarily the attainment of mature patterns of performance, since the basic motor skills are attained between birth and age 5. Definite sex differences emerge in this period, probably more a result of socialization than physiological determinants. Eighty-five to 90 percent of the recreational skills are learned before age 12, and work by Nash (1960) suggests that there is an essential skill learning decade when most people learn physical skills which influence recreational choices in adulthood. This decade has been proposed as 2–12, 4–14 or 6–16 years of age.

A child's motor development and abilities have a partial genetic basis which may or may not predispose him toward motor skill and susceptibility to proficiency in motor tasks. During middle childhood motor performance is largely unaffected by physique, except in extremes; is moderately related to skeletal age; and is negatively related to subcutaneous fat in certain tasks.

At puberty male and adrenal hormons are secreted to increase the muscle weight and enlarge muscle fibers. The female hormones inhibit excessive muscle growth in girls. Exercise promotes the protein-building power of the body in much the same way that the hormones work during puberty. For physical fitness to be achieved, muscles must be overloaded or required to perform at a level higher than normal activity demands. Since the average child does not encounter situations in every day living which provide physiological overloads, such activity has to be planned (Corbin, 1969).

Simpson (1966) formulated a taxonomy for learning in the psychomotor domain, enumerating five levels: perception, set, guided response, mechanism, and complex overt response. She delineated sublevels for the levels. Perception is composed of sensory stimulation, cue selection as a guide to action, and translation of the perception into action. Set encompasses mental readiness, focus of the physical body on the task, and possession of an emotional readiness for task performance. The guided response begins with imitation of a model and proceeds to a trial and error level. The mechanism level is represented by habit or patterning of action. The last level is characterized by a high degree of skill gained through practice and resolution of uncertainty in task performance. Simpson also suggested a higher level of competence termed *adapting* or *originating* in which the learner innovates with the acquired skill.

Perceptual-Motor Development

With refinement in the perceptual-motor aspect of development, the child gains greater control over motor responses during middle childhood. He becomes more adaptive to environmental circumstances as he is able to perceive more about the spatial components of his world. Three major changes are apparent during this stage: There is a shift from tactile-kinesthetic dominance to visual dominance as a basis for regulating or modifying motor acts. Therefore, the older child is more rapid and precise in his judgments, performing better coordinated acts. There is increasing ability to use multi-sensory systems rather than single sensory systems in deciding on a given motor movement. There is also increasing discrimination and differentiation by each sensory system yielding better coordination of the whole body during middle childhood. (Williams, 1973)

Specific perceptual motor abilities increase during this period: By age 8 or 9 children have considerable ability to judge the speed and direction of a moving target, but they are still relatively unable to judge time-space-force concepts. With age, the accuracy of responses to moving objects increases, and by age 11 they show smooth and skillful behavioral responses to objects moving in space.

Whole-part perception also increases as the child's ability to differentiate and use perceptual detail increases. The selection of relevant information and the simultaneous processing of many different bits of visual information seems the key to this ability. Children's drawings of the human body demonstrate this quality. Whereas 5-year-olds draw the figure with a distinct body, head and limbs, by age 9 drawings of the body are integrated and the parts more related to the whole. Viewing a drawing of a body composed of various fruits, the younger child would either report seeing a man or seeing a banana and a pear and an apple. The older child typically would report a man made of fruit.

Handedness is generally established by age 4, but between ages 5 and 8 some ambivalence may emerge which is a reflection of the increased hand-eye coordination of the child and the freedom his growing skills allow him in manipulating objects in the environment. By 9 or 10 there is a return to a decided and stable hand in most children. Footedness seems well determined by age 5 with no later ambivalence manifest. Eyedness is not clear cut up to age ten in 20 to 25 percent of children. Many children may never establish an eye preference. Right-left discrimination is spontaneously present by the majority of children by 6 years of age, but it is not until ages 8–9 that this concept is fully established by most children.

Laterality

One concern of parents and teachers in motor skill development of some children is related to laterality, particularly in relation to handwriting. Children may show hand preference as early as 6 months of age, others at 1 year, and still others are not sure of their laterality at nursery school age. Our society is essentially constructed for right-handed persons, although in the last generation concessions such as left-handed desks have been made

Table 6-5 Sample Score Sheet for the Lincoln–Oseretsky Motor Development Scale

	Description	R-L	Trials	Pts.	Notes
1	Walking backwards, 6 ft.		2		
2	Crouching on tiptoe		2		
3	Standing on one foot	R/L	2/2	/	
4	Touching nose		1		
5	Touching fingertips	R/L	2/2	/	
6	Tapping rhythmically with feet and fingers		1		
7	Jumping over a rope		1		
8	Finger movement		3		
9	Standing heel to toe		2		
10	Close and open hands alternately		3		
11	Making dots		2		
12	Catching a ball	R/L	5/5	/	
13	Making a ball	R/L	2/2	/	
14	Winding thread	R/L	1/1	/	
15	Balancing a rod crosswise	R/L	3/3	/	
16	Describing circles in the air		1		
17	Tapping (15″)	R/L	2/2	/	
18	Placing coins and matchsticks		1		
19	Jump and turn about		1		
20	Putting matchsticks in a box		1		
21	Winding thread while walking	R/L	1/1	/	
22	Throwing a ball	R/L	5/5	/	
23	Sorting matchsticks	R/L	1/1	/	
24	Drawing lines	R/L	2/2	/	
25	Cutting a circle	R/L	1/1	/	
26	Putting coins in box (15″)	R/L	1/1	/	
27	Tracing mazes	R/L	1/1	/	
28	Balancing on tiptoe		1		
29	Tapping with feet and fingers		1		
30	Jump, touch heels		1		
31	Tap feet and describe circles		1		
32	Stand on one foot	R/L	1/1	/	
33	Jumping and clapping		1		
34	Balancing on tiptoe	R/L	1/1	/	
35	Opening and closing hands		1		
36	Balancing a rod vertically	R/L	3/3	/	

Source: From William Sloan, "The Lincoln-Oseretsky Motor Development Scale," *Genetic Psychology Monographs,* **51,** Table 5, p. 247. Copyright © 1955, The Journal Press. Reprinted by permission of the author and the publisher.

to accommodate the 10 percent of the population who are left-handed. Recently in the U.S. entire conferences have been devoted to the topic of left-handedness, also called sinistrality. Among the questions discussed are: the possibility of natural superiority, advantage or preference for a particular cognitive mode as being related to this characteristic.

We are unsure why some people show a tendency to use the left side of their body. The cerebral dominance theory suggests that it depends on which side of the brain is more fully developed. Some contend it may be due to brain damage. Many feel right-handedness is environmentally taught by example and admonition and that if no such pressure were exerted, there would be a 50–50 incidence of the left-handed phenomenon. Still others hypothesize the position of the fetus in the uterus affects laterality. The incidence of left-handedness rises in times of crisis, as war or depression, suggesting environmental origins (*New York Times Report,* 1959). It also varies from one culture to another: In Italy, where it is regarded as a moral and personal defect, the incidence is almost zero (Young and Knapp, 1965). Wunderlich (1970) declares it is unquestionably genetic in origin but contends some children are more genetically-based than others. He says this explains why many children with this weak bias can change their handedness.

It is common belief that changing a person's handedness will cause serious emotional upsets, apparent most often in speech disorders. However, experience has shown that both children and older persons can acquire new skills with either hand without suffering any emotional problems. Still, parents are often reticent to interfere with hand dominance for fear of causing upsets in their children. Whatever their decision, it is advantageous for the child to establish his pattern as early as possible so that skills can begin developing. Those who are slow in acquiring handedness preference are somewhat deficient in the use of both hands, and usually have less strength, speed, and accuracy in movement than the child who is either left- or right-handed. A degree of bilaterality is also necessary to perform two-handed tasks with skill.

The child who does show left dominance may have difficulty in learning to write and doing such manipulative skills as hand-sewing, tying a bow, drawing, or throwing a ball, mainly because demonstrations are not usually given from his orientation. When trying to transfer the demonstration and imitate it, he can develop awkward and inefficient movements. Whether being different will affect the child's personality probably depends on the attention called to his difference by his family, peers, and others in his environment; the degree to which the dominance is established; the methods used; and the degree of natural dominance. Six prognostic indicators have been identified by Hildreth (1950) on which a parent may wish to decide the advisability of attempting to facilitate a change: if the child is under age 6, is of above-average intelligence, is agreeable to the change, shows no problems during a trial period, has a bilateral hand index, and uses both hands interchangeably. Many left-handed persons achieve well and even derive some distinction from their difference.

Teachers should probably not undertake a change in handedness without first discussing the proposal with the child and his parents. They should also refrain from calling undue attention to the incidence of left-handedness in their classes, thus minimizing any feelings on the part of students that this condition is undesirable or freakish.

Play

Traditionally viewed as a rather useless activity, play and its peculiar function has been largely disregarded in favor of its role in reducing tension, developing sociability, and fostering physical growth. In the literature of the past decade, a new attitude toward the significance of play and games has emerged, namely, that play's function be explored in its own right. (Sutton-Smith, 1972). It is currently being identified with exploratory behavior and as an intellectual response in fantasy because one cannot make

Play is a term that encompasses sedentary arts and crafts as well as active sports and games. (Photo by Lin Mitchell.)

the response in reality for fear of losing his autonomy. Play is believed to consolidate previous learnings and to help one in social understanding because one has to take into account the role of another in his own actions. For example, in hide and seek it is useless to hide unless there is also someone to look for you.

Play has been found to be related to creativity, although the question arises if intelligence is actually the intervening variable in the relationship. It has been impossible to determine if play expresses a pre-existing status of the child's cognition or if it contributes actively to the character of that status. Therefore, it is not now known if the player learns anything through play, per se. There is evidence that play, games and cognitive development are functionally related. Play does not appear to be adaptive in any strictly utilitarian sense, as are laughter, humor and art.

"Play is older than culture . . . human civilization has added no essential feature to the general idea of play. Animals play just like men." (Huizinga, 1970, p. 19). The concept of play is a universal one, but there is no agreement on its definition. Although its variety of benefits are widely recognized, it has received little attention in formal research. The fun of playing resists all logical analysis.

All play has meaning, and it is believed to prepare one for the serious work of life later on. It helps teach sex role and build self-concept. It helps teach restraint and is an outlet for impulses. Many attest that it serves some deeper purpose than mere diversion, and Huizinga contends "pure play is one of the main bases of civilization" (p. 23). Play is voluntary activity, not activity imposed by moral duty nor physical necessity. Play is freedom, a temporary sphere of pretend activity. Although it is defined by both space and time, it can be replayed by the memory. Play is order of some sort, yet involves the "chanciness" which tests the player's courage, tenacity, resources, and fairness. In play one is free to discover himself as well as learn much about the world. He learns about the rights and feelings of others. He develops skills and strengths, gradually becoming acclimated to the risks of life through such adventures as jumping from high places or wading in the surf.

Caplan (1973) has called the power of play all pervasive and extraordinary. He cites its contributions to development as: strengthening of personality, encouraging interpersonal relations, furthering creativity, and advancement of learning. He says play is a happy activity which begins in delight and ends in wisdom. Through play the child learns to imitate, explore, and test his ideas. He learns to gratify his basic needs for independence through planning, making judgments, creating and controlling the sequence of events. He begins to see himself as an active agent in his environment, free to experience trials and errors without fear of failing. Play provides that imaginary world where a child can manipulate and maneuver things to suit his whims. He can feel larger than life itself as he disregards the laws of reality.

Play allows for the experiencing of such concepts as low, rough, long, loud. It nourishes the vocabulary, associative memory, reflective thinking, and the labeling and naming necessary for eventual mastery of reading. Play provides opportunity for adjustment to various social groupings that help one find himself in the social world.

According to Caplan, the most intense period of play ends about age 8. From ages 4 to 8, dramatic play is at its height. Dramatic plays motifs typically include protection, power, attack and destruction. Innermost concerns, anti-social feelings and self concept are exposed through this type of play. Well adjusted children shift from one theme to another in their play, while disturbed ones become pre-occupied with only one theme. Children in this period of development create the make believe world because they lack the logical thought processes to cope with the real world and its demands. They escape the restraints of reality to fortify their inner feelings of power. They may retreat to this imaginary world when they feel unable to handle external circumstances. The healthy child knows quite well he is only pretending.

Children's interest in building materials begins in the early years and continues into middle childhood. This interest may be due to their desire to work with things they can tower over. Their fascination with wheel toys gives them a feeling of being in the driver's seat, in charge of things. Through doll play they may relive experiences in their own life that they can now be in control of. Water play also offers delight through control of a non-threatening substance. Water and sand play are common mediums for treatment of disturbed children during play therapy. Disturbed children tend to play as if they were younger than they actually are. Other signs of disturbance that are observable in play include arranging toys only in neat patterns, avoidance of messy or dirty play, playing silently or engaging in constant chatter or in aimless handling of a series of play items without actually playing with any of them.

Before entering school, the child's play group begins to expand. By age 5 he is able to follow simple rules in playing and to initiate group activity. The play group is the most informal of peer groupings and is essentially an alliance of equals to share common equipment and space. From ages 6 through 12 these groupings provide for much learning about property rights and taking turns. Play activities allow outlets for dominance, display of prowess, and destruction. Children who are unable to express these feelings singly often do so in play groups. Through games children learn to win and lose with grace. They also can learn to enjoy playing for the challenge and companionship of others. If a dichotomy between play and work is drawn at school entrance, an antipathy for school may result. The play interests of children 6 to 8 revolve around family, occupations, neighborhood activities, current events and transportation. Nondiscriminate collecting also is beginning at this age, although it becomes more organized as cognitive powers include classification and ordering. Rules become very important in play at this period. Making things, reading, guessing games and games involving chance are popular.

With increasing age, games demanding physical dexterity are fascinating to children. Games requiring decision-making with varying consequences are appropriate from age 8 onward as are competitive group games or teams. Academic games that allow children to learn through manipulation have been found successful. Caplan summarizes the result of this approach "I hear and I forget. I see and I remember. I do and I understand" (p. 127). Such teaching games contribute to the development of analytical, intuitive and problem-solving skills.

Children between ages 8 and 12 enjoy more elaborate collections, models, sports, and musical instruments as part of their play. They are able to use a sewing machine, a potter's wheel, and simple motor driven tools by the end of this period. Crafts and hobbies gain in popularity, as do club memberships. At this age they give up toys for ideas in their play. In later middle childhood interests expand to include gardening, photography, writing, woodworking, dancing, discussing. The peer group takes on increasing significance. Serious hobbies and occupational plans become more realistic.

Pet-owning is a popular recreational activity among children 5–12. The mere selection of pets encourages decision-making, and the daily care of them furthers the ability to make choices and take action. Younger children may not fully comprehend the continuity pet-care demands, but they

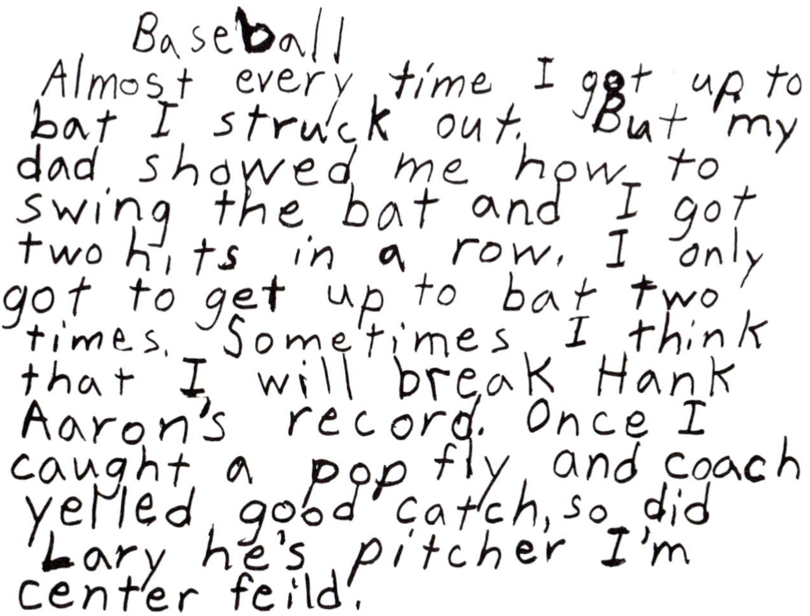

> **Baseball**
> Almost every time I get up to bat I struck out. But my dad showed me how to swing the bat and I got two hits in a row. I only got to get up to bat two times. Sometimes I think that I will break Hank Aaron's record. Once I caught a pop fly and coach yelled good catch, so did Lary he's pitcher I'm center feild.

Figure 6-14. Written by a nine-year-old.

can learn with skillful adult guidance. An animal companion helps satisfy a child's need for unrestrained loyalty and love and provides a rare opportunity to be in charge of something in their world which is largely controlled by adults and older children. Caring for pets encourages children to sharpen their observational abilities, and their verbal skills are perfected by discussing the animal. Pet-keeping also fosters a caring attitude toward all living things, including other people.

Sutton-Smith (1976) discussed the value of play using as examples four levels of play which help build the concepts of chasing, capturing, escaping and rescuing with increasing spacial and temporal parameters with which the children must contend. Magical IT figures were cast in: Hide and Seek, appropriate for ages 5 and 6; Release, suitable for ages 7 and 8; Red Rover, popular with ages 9 and 10; and Prisoner's Base, a game suited to 11- and 12-year-olds. He points out that flexibility, imaginative capacity, physical and strategic competence are demanded in the increasingly complex demands of the four games. In Hide-and-Seek, the IT has power over fugitive players and safe and dangerous areas designated may for children represent the sacred and profane in an adult's religious world. In Release, the idea is of one against many. IT must find all players, but any player can rescue another from the captive base. Red Rover demands that as IT catches players, they become his allies to catch the others. There are two safe bases from which to operate. In Prisoner's Base, two teams hunt one another over a large defined territory.

Caplan predicts more research on the value of play, safer toys of higher quality, an increase in the museums of play and fantasy, and more education for parenting through play.

Families should provide some requisites for developmental play: time, space, equipment and materials, companions, encouragement, and ideas. The old adage is true: "All work and no play makes Jack a dull boy"—also true for Jill! The child whose schedule is so filled with homework, household duties and routines, and formal commitments—such as Scouts, meetings, and music lessons—may have little time for perfecting his motor skills through play. In addition to time, this type of perfection through practice requires a fair amount of space, both indoors and outdoors.

Equipment need not be elaborate, but it must be safe, versatile, and durable. The price is not always indicative of these characteristics either. Children are quite ingenious at making meaningful use of the simplest equipment—consider the possibility offered by trees, wooden boxes, balls, broomsticks, tarpaper, sand and water!

Children who live in the slums learn to play in trash heaps, junkyards, cluttered streets, in attics, on the front steps, in traffic—anywhere. They must be more creative to have fun under these conditions than does the middle class child with a tree house, shiny toys, and a place on the Little League team.

In the United States those playgrounds that feature only the traditional ball diamond, tennis courts, slides, swings, seesaws, and jungle gyms have not been set up to stimulate creativity and ingenuity. In some areas, including the Scandinavian countries, play areas are purposely made to demand creativity. A play street featuring space but no elaborate equipment is one example. A collection of logs, old tires, a concrete pipe, a large beer barrel, a cargo net and cable spools, a shallow canal with rope swings are other items that are inexpensive, yet lend themselves to innovation by resourceful chilren. "Junk" playgrounds are also found in Europe. One in England allows children to build each spring a series of "shacks," using available materials. When winter comes, the area is leveled in preparation for rebuilding by a new group of children. Wendy Houses (taken from Peter Pan) in Stockholm, Sweden, simulate a little community in which children visitors can set up housekeeping and pretend they have their own tiny neighborhood. An artificial stream for boat-sailing, old airplanes and fire equipment for climbing and imagining, and a traffic playground for practicing safety are among other less traditional provisions in various parts of America.

Friendship and motor skill development combine to provide hours of fun in such activities as hopscotch. (Photo by Lin Mitchell.)

Equipment and materials when purchased should be selected in relation to the age and interests of the child, the facilities for storage and use, the other items the family already owns, and certain wishes of parents, and even neighbors.

Many children live in locations where play companions are readily available most hours in the day. Parents whose children lack companions because of the location of their dwelling may wish to "import" playmates fairly frequently in order to contribute to the normal social growth of their children.

Encouragement may be needed particularly in constructive and creative play activities, and ideas are usually needed most on rainy or cold days when play may be confined to the indoors. A special closet to house materials for such times is a good idea.

Think Back

To your favorite play activities at various ages:
Things you built yourself or with the gang.
Making presents for family members.
The programs you and your friends put on.
A team you played on.
Collections you had.

What's Next?

1. Publications for professionals working with school-age children are available at nominal fees from the American Dental Society, 211 E. Chicago Ave., Chicago, Illinoise 60611.

   Your Child's Teeth, S7B.
   You Can Prevent Tooth Decay, P6
   Healthy Teeth, A Happier School Child, G13.
   Dental Health Facts for Teachers, S13.

2. *Your Child from 6–12.* U.S. Government Printing Office, 1966.
3. *Accidents and Children.* U.S. Government Printing Office, 1963.
4. *Nutrition in Infancy and Childhood,* P.L. Pipes. St. Louis: Mosby, 1977.
5. *Nutrition: Concepts & Controversies,* E. Whitney and M. Hamilton. St. Paul: West Pub., 1979.
6. Children's Play and Playgrounds. J. L. Frost and B. L. Klein. Boston: Allyn & Bacon, 1979.

7. *Child Development Through Literature,* Landau et al. Englewood Cliffs, N.J.: Prentice-Hall, 1972: "Castle in the Sand," by I. Orgel,pp. 303–308.
8. *A Textbook of Motor Development,* C. B. Corbin. Dubuque, Ia.: Wm. C. Brown, 1973.
9. Film: *Looking at Children.* Metropolitan Life Insurance Company, 1 Madison Avenue, New York, N.Y. 10010. (24 min/color.)
10. Film: When a Child Enters the Hospital. Polymorph Films, 331 Newbury St., Boston, Mass., 02115. (16 min/color).
11. Film: We Won't Leave You (Hospitals) M.D. Films, 58 Fenwood Rd., Boston, Mass. 02115.
12. Film: *Children's Chants and Games.* BFA Educational Media, 2211 Michigan Ave., Santa Monica, CA. 90406. (15 min/color.)
13. Film: *Child's Play and the Real World.* Sterling Educational Films, 241 E 34th St., New York 10016. (16 min/color.)

Catalysts for Discussion

I. Playthings

Play equipment to aid development during the early school years:
   Bicycle, roller skates, ice skates, slide, trapeze, croquet set, jump rope, balls.
   Easy games of skill such as tiddlywinks, Chinese checkers, Parchesi, checkers, simple card games, anagrams, dominoes, games which teach words and numbers.
   Books and records.
   Construction sets, such as Erector, Tinker Toys, Lincoln Logs, puzzles.
   Doll house, paper dolls, hand puppets.
   Dress-up box.
   Paints, crayons, finger paints, clay.
Recreation aids for development during the intermediate school years:
   Tumbling mats and other stunt rigs.
   Throwing and catching games.
   Running games, such as tag, red light, cops and robbers, old mother witch.
   Kites, tops, marbles, skates, bicycle, jump rope.
   Card games such as rummy, hearts, Pit, authors, old maid.
   Board games, as Monopoly, Lotto, Aggravation, Yahtzee, Sorry, Scrabble.
   Sports games: baseball, glove and bat; football, basketball and basket hoops.
   Crafts: shrink art, plaster casting, string art, paint by number, chip carving.
Recreation plans for preadolescence:
   Team games and sports.
   Picnics, wiener roasts, hikes, movie parties, snack parties.
   Social dancing, folk dancing.
   Tennis, archery, ping-pong, swimming, riding, shuffleboard, skateboard, frisbee.
   Band and orchestra.
   Hobbies, collections.

Chemistry sets, airplane construction sets, miniature cars and trains, telescopes and star studies, electricity and radio construction sets, workbench.

Crafts: leatherwork, beadwork, wood carving, weaving, macrame, decoupage.

Cooking and sewing equipment and materials.

Advanced table games as chess, Camelot, Defense, Backgammon, Probe.

Books, records and tapes.

II. Test Your Skill

Based on your knowledge of age characteristics and recreational interests, suggest suitable gifts for the following children:

5-year-old boy who lives in an apartment complex in the North.
6-year-old girl with a leg brace.
7-year-old boy who lives on a farm in the South and is an only child.
8-year-old twins (boy and girl) with no near-by neighbors.
9-year-old boy with four brothers within 3 years of his age.
10-year-old girl who is visually handicapped.
11-year-old boy whose parents have already given him everything imaginable.
12-year-old girl who is socially mature for her age.

In each selection, identify the characteristic to which it is related and suggest what area(s) of development it will foster.

III. Children's Comments

An 8-year-old said:

"The hospital is lots of things—
like lots of windows—
and beds—
and temperatures—
and shots—
and nurses working—
and doctors looking—
and babies crying and crying
a pretty long time." (Smith, 1962)

Beyond the Classroom Experiences

1. Record the height and weight of a group of children of similar age. Note the range. Try to relate differences to heredity and environmental factors. For some children use the mid-parent stature chart to see how parent height relates to child height.

2. Talk to a child about his freckles or moles to see if he notices them and how he feels about them. Ask children how to get rid of styes and warts. Interview some children who wear glasses or hearing or dental appliances. Find out how they feel about this and see if they understand the purpose they serve.

3. Through a series of pictures, elicit from children their feelings toward persons wearing glasses, hearing, or dental appliances. Be sure to help them see the purpose served by these devices and encourage understanding toward those who wear them.

4. Watch children to see how changing dentition affects their life: status, eating, speaking, self-confidence. Talk to them to see how they feel about this phenomenon. Discuss with them their tooth care routine and see if they understand how brushing, diet, flossing, and regular checkups relate to a healthy mouth.

5. Ask children to keep a record of their food intake for a three-day period. Check these diets against the Basic Four Guide and the Recommended Dietary Allowances. Do the same thing for your own diet. Note where deficiencies occur.

6. Interview children concerning the advantages of buying and bringing their lunch. Ask what things they like about the lunchroom and what they would like to see changed.

7. Talk with parents of a child who has sickle cell disease or some other permanent disability. Note its effects on the child and the family. Find out how the family has helped the child to live with the impairment.

8. Use a series of pictures to ellicit from children their attitudes toward being ill, visiting the dentist, doctor, hospital, certain health practices, and treatments for injury.

9. Visit the children's ward of a hospital to see what special provisions have been made for young patients. Talk with the Child Life Director in the hospital about programs designed for children. Talk to a child who has been hospitalized to see what he thought of the experience. Ask him to write a letter to another child who will be going to the hospital, telling him what to expect. Discuss this letter with him.

10. Administer the Kraus-Weber Test and the Lincoln-Oseretsky Motor Development scale to children. Note how age affects their performance. Do not attempt to score. Test kit may be available at movement science laboratory or physical education department.

11. View some creations and collections of middle childhood people. Discuss their work with them. Attend a children's neighborhood talent show (or help them organize one). Note the variety and levels of talent. Inquire which talents are the result of lessons and which are self-taught.

12. Attend a birthday party and list the gifts. Then evaluate each gift relative to its appropriateness for the age of the child, its safety, versatility, and cost.

Chapter 7

Personality and Emotions

This chapter is designed to help you:

- understand the complexity of personality.
- realize the role of basic needs in behavior.
- become acquainted with the nature of self-concept and its implications.
- examine the role of traits in personality.
- think about the development and effects of emotions.
- appreciate the effects of skin color and sex role on self-concept.
- understand the role of achievement and motivation in behavior.
- see the importance of maintenance of mental health and treatment of mental illness during childhood.

General Theories of Personality Development

The personality is an illusive composite of behavioral tendencies and personal preference patterns which defies definition yet controls destiny. It is a dynamic, developmental and socially-oriented entity which encompasses values, roles, beliefs, traits and actions. Personality emerges over time, changes under pressure, responds to therapy, can be classified but not completely understood. Each personality is as unique as a voice print or a snowflake.

Current psychologists strongly believe that the basic personality is well established by age 5. This does not mean to say that persons will act at this age exactly as they will act for the remainder of their lives. But evidence seems to suggest strongly that unless psychotherapy or a major crisis intervenes, one's outlook on life, concept of self, and general methods of handling stress, success, and other variables of life will remain the same.

What causes personality? A child is not simply a piece of clay on which impressions are made; nor is he a sponge which merely soaks up every stimulus. Because of native endowments, assimilation of experience, growth and development, each child uses his resources in a particular way, straining out of life things which have meaning for him. Perceptions of reality and cognitive style affect personality. Other factors include ordinal position and family composition, cultural heritage and neighborhood friends and foes.

Is it possible to program a personality? Can its development be broken into stages or parts? Many theories have been postulated. But never has one been universally or even nationally accepted. Each theorist "slices" the personality loaf a bit differently.

Corsini (1977) in his review of current personality theories, delineated eight aspects of this psychological phenomenon. Temperament is cited as a biologically-based component; character as a moral aspect; mood refers to emotional set; and traits are classified as ways of behaving; attitude refers to value set; and in addition, disposition, trend, and habit are included.

One problem in personality theory is semantics or word use. Many words are used by different theorists to mean slightly different things. Theories also tend to vary with regard to their emphasis on time: the past, present, or future. Some theories consider the total person whereas others relate to specific parts of the whole. Theories differ with respect to how learning occurs in the human organism, and another dimension of variation is the relationship of the body to the mind.

Eysenck (1970) calls traits the building stones of higher order concepts in personality. He points out that although traits are readily cited and tested, it is highly difficult to separate their overlap and interaction on one another. He cautions "traits must not be postulated without adequate proof" (p. 98).

Mussen, Conger and Kagan (1969) explain motives as an integral part of personality or behavior (p. 32).

1. Motive for physical contact—as expressed in hugging, hand-holding.
2. Motive for positive evaluation from others—as shown in attempts to gain approval, recognition and praise.
3. Motive for instrumental aid or help from others—as seen in requests for assistance in homework.
4. Motive to reduce uncertainty—as evidenced by the desire for rules and signs which help prepare him for future happenings.
5. Motive for autonomy—as expressed in the child's striving for independence from parents and other adults.
6. Motive to dominate others—shown in power struggles among children and adults.
7. Motive to cause harm or anxiety to another—as seen in children's wishes that misfortune come to anyone who frustrates or threatens them.
8. Motive for genital stimulation—evidenced in the heterosexual phase as sex exploration, typical of adolescence.
9. Motive for competence—seen in the child's striving to perfect motor skills and master various tasks.
10. Motive to maximize congruence between one's behavior, motives or thoughts and previously acquired standards—shown in the child's attempts to conform in both action and thought to the norms of the important groups in his life.

A recent listing of major personality theorists by Corsini (1977) is shown in Table 7-1. We have chosen to cite herein some of the major theories which are developmental in nature, that is, those which include the concept of step-by-step progression through various stages.

Freud (1949) hypothesized that the topography of personality consisted of the id, ego, and superego and further suggested a series of psychosexual stages through which personality development proceeds: oral, anal, early genital, latency, pubescence, young adulthood, adulthood, and maturity.

Havighurst, as seen in Chapter 1, identified a series of developmental tasks, the successful achievement of which contributes to satisfactory personality growth during various times of life. Maslow (1970) has identified

Table 7-1 A Partial List of Current Personality Theories

Abelson, R. P.	Least effort	Jung, Carl	Analytical psychology
Adler, Alfred	Individual psychology	Kelly, Charles	Neo-Reichian theory
Allport, G. W.	Personalism	Kelly, George A.	Personal constructs
Angyll, Andreas	Organismic theory	Kohlberg, Lawrence	Moral developmental
Assiogoli, Roberto	Psychosynthesis		theory
Bandura, Albert	Social learning theory	Korsybski, Alfred	General semantics
Berne, Eric	Transactional	Lecky, P.	Self-consistency
	analysis	Lewin, Kurt	Topological psy-
Binswanger, Ludwig	Daseinsanalysis		chology
Blake, R. R.	Grid theory	Low, A. A.	Semantic theory
Branden, Nathaniel	Biocentrism	Lowen, Alexander	Bio-energetics
Burrow, Trigant	Phyloanalysis	Maltz, Albert	Psychocybernetics
Buhler, Charlotte	Humanistic psy-	Maslow, Abraham	Self-actualization
	chology	May, Rollo	Existentialism
Buhler, Karl	Funktionslust	Mead, G. H.	Social interaction
Boss, Medard	Daseinsanalysis	Meyer, Adolf	Psychobiological
Cattell, Raymond B.	Multivariate exper-		theory
	imental theory	Miller, Neal	Learning theory
Combs, Arthur	Phenomenology	Moreno, J. L.	Sociometry
Dollard, John	Learning theory	Mowrer, O. H.	Two-factor theory
Ellis, Albert	Rational-emotive	Murphy, Gardner	Biosocial theory
	theory	Murray, H. A.	Need-press theory
Erikson, Erik	Developmental theory	Osgood, Charles	Congruity theory
Eysenck, Hans	Factor theory	Perls, Frederick	Gestalt therapy theory
Feldenkreis, Moishe	Body awareness	Piaget, Jean	Developmental theory
Festinger, Leon	Cognitive dissonance	Rank, Otto	Will theory
Fisher, Seymour	Body image theory	Reich, Wilhelm	Character analysis
Frankl, Viktor	Logotherapy	Rogers, Carl	Person-centered
Freud, Sigmund	Psychoanalysis		theory
Fromm, Erich	Humanistic psycho-	Rolf, Ida	Structural integration
	analysis		theory
Gendlin, Eugene	Experiential theory	Rotter, Julian	Social learning
Glasser, William	Reality theory	Sarbin, Theodore	Role theory
Goldstein, Kurt	Organismic theory	Schutz, William	Open encounter
Greenwald, Harold	Direct decision theory	Sheldon, William H.	Morphological theory
Guilford, J. P.	Factor theory	Skinner, B. F.	Operant conditioning
Harvey, O. J.	Conceptual systems	Snygg, Donald	Phenomenology
Heider, F.	Balance theory	Sullivan, H. S.	Interpersonal theory
Horney, Karen	Sociopsychological	Thorne, Frederick	Eclecticism
	theory	Thurstone, L. L.	Experimental theory
Hubbard, H. Ron	Scientology	Van Kaam, Adrian	Transpersonal psy-
Jackins, Harvey	Reevaluation coun-		chology
	seling	Walters, Bernard	Observational learning
Jackson, Don	Systems theory	Werner, Heinz	Developmental psy-
Janov, Arthur	Primal theory		chology
Jourard, Sydney	Transparency theory	Wolpe, Joseph	Behavior theory

From Corsini, p. 9.

seven basic needs and arranged five of them into a hierarchy. (See Figure 7-1) The sixth need, knowing and understanding, and the seventh related to esthetics he did not include in the hierarchal arrangement. Maslow suggests that the lower needs are stronger and play the foremost role in motivation until "fairly well" gratified, allowing the next higher need to assume prepotency, thus becoming the dominant motivation source. The proportion of the need that must be met in order for another need to assume control decreases with ascendance of the pyramid. And the sequence is not immutable, sometimes occurring in reverse order. Physical needs of hunger, thirst, sex and breathing represent the foundation of the hierarchy. Safety-security needs for freedom from fear, protection, and order are seen at the next highest level. The needs for belonging, giving and receiving love and enjoying an intimate place in a couple or a group are placed in the third position. The need for esteem both from self and others, including achievement, status, independence and appreciation rests upon the three lower designations. And at the apex of Maslow's scheme is seen the need for self-actualization, to become all that one is capable of becoming, self-fulfillment and expression. Maslow believes a child cannot give attention to achievement if he is hungry or realize his potential if he feels unloved, or fearful. The theory has many applications in child-guidance.

Kohlberg (1970) and Piaget (1970) both expound theories which relate to personal functioning in terms of moral decisions and cognitive growth. These are dealt with in detail in Chapters 8 and 9, and are both developmental in nature. Erikson (1963) proposed a personality model involving eight stages which commence at birth or before and extend throughout the life span. He believes that the successful accomplishment of each stage is

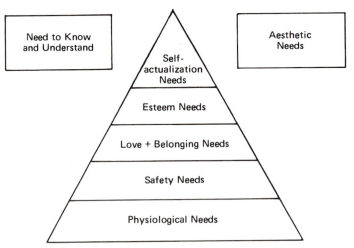

Figure 7-1. Maslow's hierarchy of needs. (Based on A. H. Maslow, *Motivation and Personality*, 2nd ed., New York: Harper & Row, Publishers, 1970.)

paramount for success in succeeding stages and that the final stage is a culmination of the other seven. Erikson divides personality into eight senses: trust, autonomy, initiative, industry (duty and accomplishment), identity, intimacy, generativity, and integrity.

By school age the child will normally be working on Erikson's fourth sense—that of industry and accomplishment. One of the dangers of this period is not having successfully completed former stages: namely, trust, autonomy, and initiative. Trust is ideally learned in infancy through others' satisfying the child's needs and through beginning to trust self in such ventures as walking. Much trust learning centers around food and its consumption. Trust is thought to be the most important element in personality, and most infants acquire it with ease and pleasure.

Autonomy is a sense usually fostered during the second and third year of life, as the child learns that he is a distinct being with a mind and will of his own. For him to develop autonomy he needs opportunities to make choices, yet learn to live within certain restrictions imposed by his environment. In the American culture autonomy is a highly prized quality. Adults who are secure in their own autonomy are better able to foster this characteristic in their children. A strong sense of personal worth and autonomy will fortify the child for attacks at all stages of development.

The sense of initiative is concerned with the period of doing, of imagination and enterprise, which is also greatly valued in our society. At this period, between ages 3 and 5, creativity and fantasy in play allow the child to "do" many things he cannot yet perform in reality. Helping adults perform routines, excursions in the community, and emerging abilities to care for one's own physical needs are other manifestations of this personality component.

By school age the child is ready for larger worlds of thought and action. He is capable of becoming less self-centered and more other-centered. His imagination must now deal with reality and his concepts with the laws of such impersonal things as the three R's. He begins to derive joy and satisfaction from producing, and demonstrating his abilities in ways that will "prove" he is growing up: riding his bike to the corner grocery, cooperating successfully in group projects, expressing his feelings in socially acceptable ways, spending the night with peers, and making decisions and living with the consequences.

During middle childhood the child learns the pleasure of work and its results and is able to focus his attention for extended periods of time while working diligently on the task at hand. During this period the culture begins to provide systematic instruction and many opportunities to help him develop his emerging abilities—through school, Scouts, community involvement, and service. Rewards for accomplishment are found in the form of badges, grades, and money. His skill in the use of manipulative tools, symbolic tools in math and reading, and management of available resources increases greatly. His citizenship talents are formed: leading, following, cooperating. The rudiments of fair play and the relationship of effort and accomplishment become real.

Among the dangers of this period are failure of the cultural institutions to build on past experience and allow innate motivation to operate, which may result in seeking recognition through delinquent acts. Constriction of horizons through stereotyping, labeling, or grouping children in detrimental arrangements can also stifle the sense of industry, leading to development of feelings of inferiority, inadequacy, hopelessness, and powerlessness because of repeated failure experiences.

The challenge to those guiding the child during the development of a sense of industry and accomplishment is to provide opportunities for success experiences for all and thus keep creativity and optimism alive. They should foster positive feelings about accomplishment and work and at the same time help him maintain a balance between personal autonomy and good cooperation.

In Erikson's scheme, the sense of identity is primary in early adolescence when the youth seeks to clarify his role in society in terms of who he is and what he will become. This sense is necessary for him to be able to see purpose and continuity in life and to prepare for his adult role. Failure to achieve a sense of identity can lead to emotional inadequacies.

In later adolescence the sense of intimacy, or ability to be intimate with those of the opposite sex, normally emerges. This ability is vital in establishing sound heterosexual relationships. Failure to grow in this sense

Self-concept is the perception one has of one's self, quite different from the image reflected in the mirror. (Photo by Rick Coleman.)

CHAPTER 7 / PERSONALITY AND EMOTIONS

results in a type of alienation from others and the inner conflict resulting from such a state.

Erikson has identified two senses that ordinarily develop in adulthood as generativity and integrity. The desire to care for others rather than being cared for characterizes one who has developed the sense of generativity. This is often found in parenting, the willingness of one to postpone his own need for gratification while ministering to the needs of those smaller or less able than he. This sense is exemplified by good parents and teachers. The person who has achieved the sense of integrity has accepted his own life cycle and realizes that one's life is one's own responsibility. He has developed a feeling of comradeship with those who, living before him, have evolved a philosophy of human dignity and love, duty, honor, grace, and enlightened self-discipline.

Each of Erikson's personality components extends beyond its point of beginning; for example, trust must be nourished throughout life. Each component develops on the foundation laid by previously developed ones.

Self Concept

Whereas personality is the composite picture others see of a person, the self-concept is an internal construct by which the person views himself—his abilities, identity, weaknesses—those perceptions, beliefs, feelings, attitudes and values which the person considers descriptive of himself. The self-concept or self-image is the result of a cyclic process in which others identify one's characteristics, communicate this perception to him, and he, in turn, projects these characteristics for still others to react to. Self-concept is a self-fulfilling prophecy—a commitment rather than a true description of self, according to Jourard (1974). Self-concept is so personal that it cannot be measured beyond mere positiveness and negativeness. It often does not correspond to objective appraisals, possibly because of one's inner desire to preserve the approval of others. Wylie (1968) proposes one may ignore certain self characteristics, thus forming an incomplete self-concept, in order to minimize anxiety over possible lack of approval.

The self-concept consciously and unconsciously guides behavior and influences attitudes and relationships. It has been termed the core of personality. It is revealed in posture, stance, gait, eye contact, a handshake, facial expressions—in social contacts and skills, treatment of others, care of one's body and clothing; in decisions, goal-setting, problem-solving, language and voice. People learn things more readily if they are consistent with their self-concept. Those with inaccurate notions of self are likely to receive unexpected reactions from others, thus compounding their own anxiety and mechanisms of defense. Evaluation of others is a function of self evaluation (Wylie, 1968).

The idea of self is encompassed in virtually all theories of personality, and a number of theorists include the terminology "self" in their explanations, among them Rogers, Adler, Horney, Jung, and Maslow. One's picture of himself begins the day of birth, and some have suggested even prenatally. Early care and attention help shape the infant's sense of security, of being wanted and accepted. Normally it is the mother who has the earliest opportunity to transmit good "self-feelings" to the child. Other family members add to her initial impact. The child whose surroundings permit him to do things on his own and to be successful because the tasks are suited to his level of development grows in self confidence and self respect. By school entrance friends and peers in the neighborhood, the mass media, and even strangers on the street have provided important clues to who he is and how important he is to the society. This may or may not be how he is in reality. But the way he perceives himself to be, he gradually becomes. It is important for a child to learn not only to accept himself but also to perceive himself as accurately as possible.

Jourard (1968, p. 158) sums up the process: "I have a certain concept of my being, of myself. This is my self-concept. It is my belief about my own being. My being discloses itself to me in the form of my intentional experience of myself. I experience the feel of my body's existence. I experience my own action from the inside. I form a concept of myself—what I am like, how I react, what I am capable of and what I cannot do—on the basis of this self experience. You may also tell me what and who you think I am, on the basis of your experience of the outside of my being; and I take your belief into account. We may agree that I am thus and such a kind of person . . . Once I have formed this concept of who and what I am, I proceed to behave in the world as if this is all and everything I am or can be. My behavior, my self-disclosure, endlessly confirms my self-concept. It is as if I have taken a pledge to present this and only this as my being."

Along with the self-concept, there exists for each person the construct of an ideal self, or a model of personality toward which to strive. The ideal self reflects ones socialization, values, taboos, and it serves as a yardstick for behavior. The ideal self is a sort of conscience phenomenon. It may be a composite of several other persons, or it may be a replica of one significant person in the figure's life. Parents may serve this function when a child is around age ten; but after entering adolescence ideals are usually chosen outside the family. Parental pressure may cause a child to form a self-ideal beyond his capabilities, thus causing conflict and frustration between what he is and what he feels he must become. The poorly adjusted child may grossly overestimate what he should become, leading to feelings of inadequacy and rebellion.

Whereas self-concept is one's picture of self and ideal self the possible goal toward which one is striving, self esteem is a measure of personal worth or value. It reflects how important one feels himself to be in the world. It ranges from self love to self deprecation. Ironically, the child who appears to love himself to the point of conceit may actually hate himself to the point of disdain and use boastfulness to cover his true feelings of low self esteem. Self esteem, like self-concept, is a reflection of others' opinions and treatment of the child. Feelings of personal usefulness and unworthiness can be learned through continual criticism, failure and punishment. Feelings of high esteem come from success, encouragement, praise. Self-concept and self esteem are sometimes used interchangeably in discussing one's feelings about himself.

As Rod MacLeish (1976) observed, when children put on Halloween masks their real self disappears, and they become a ghost, goblin or some other creature in full control of the situation. Becoming situation controllers is essential from time to time for children since childhood is largely spent on the receiving line of indignity.

In discussing the self-concept of the preadolescent, Gordon (1969) notes that parents and teachers are poor judges of this aspect of their development. He reports that children in middle childhood evaluate themselves consciously and that their evaluations are more related to activities than feelings, and regard specifics more than over-all worth. He sees a movement toward a more stable image of self at the end of preadolescence and perceives a generally positive, optimistic view of self by these children. Children seem to be reliable in self-reporting if the time period between reports is not too great. They tend to evaluate themselves on the positive side, probably due to cultural conditioning. Thus, their accuracy may not be as high as their reliability. Gordon (1969, p. 264) suggests children's ability to view themselves and report what they see is related to their degree of comfort with themselves. He postulates "What we may have (in middle childhood) is a pattern of movement from a global view ("I'm a good boy") through the preadolescent differentiated view ("I'm good at sports, but I'm not good in arithmetic, and I don't think much about how I am over-all") toward the mature position (I see myself as generally adequate, but I recognize differentiated abilities within myself")."

There are four major ways to assess self-concept in children: Observation and inference; projective techniques such as TAT, Rorschach and sentence-completion sets; such objective tests as vocational interest forms and personality scales; and self-reporting devices such as Q-sorts cards.

We cannot expect the child of the middle years to accurately evaluate himself outright since at this age there is a tendency to emphasize favorable traits and de-emphasize undesirable ones, because of cultural conditioning. Yet all measures of self-concept include the idea of desirability and undesirability. In most measures a number of terms, traits, values, or characteristics are presented to the subjects. The form in which they are presented provides the variety of assessment (McCandless, 1967).

One approach requires subjects to assign to each trait a rating, signifying the degree to which they identify with the given characteristic:

1 Very much like me.
2 A lot like me.
3 Somewhat like me.
4 Not very much like me.
5 Not at all like me.

Traits rated might include brave, beautiful, sensitive, ambitious. Each choice thus indicated is assigned a positive, neutral, or negative rating, resulting in a total score designated as an index to self-concept.

The semantic differential is another form in which traits may be presented. Subjects are asked to rate themselves somewhere along a line between two extremes, often on a 7-point scale. For example:

| Warm and outgoing | 1 2 3 4 5 6 7 | Cool and self-contained |
| Always on the go | 1 2 3 4 5 6 7 | Relaxed and a little lazy |

Again the ratings are assigned positive, neutral, or negative connotation to derive a total index score.

A less-structured but more challenging method in terms of scoring is found in the open-ended question Who Am I? Essay responses to this question are analyzed to locate both positive and negative statements concerning self. To ascertain the subject's relative value of such characteristics, investigators may ask that each person indicate the traits that they believe are socially desirable, unimportant socially, or socially undesirable.

Using the Q-sort technique, persons can reflect their self-concept. In this approach characteristics are written on cards, and the subject is asked to distribute the cards according to a predesigned system into categories ranging from "most applicable" to "least applicable." He is forced to place a specific number of cards in each of a number of piles. In determining his relative self-concept projection, each selected trait is then examined for its location in the distribution.

A projective technique, such as the Thematic Apperception Test or CAT, adapted for children, may be utilized by those having the background necessary to interpret results. This method involves presentation of a series of pictures. The subject is asked to interpret the action and relationships in the picture. Those trained in the use of the instrument are able to determine with whom the subject most closely identifies and thus rate the characteristics assigned to this character by the subject as though he were describing himself.

Variations of all these methods have been used with children in attempts to measure self-concept. Studies of this type with children under the age of 4 are rare because reading and writing deficiencies at younger ages require individualized testing, and such individualized attention is thought to influence the results. Tests of the reliability of self-concept measures indicate they are moderately stable over time. Younger children showed as high a level of stability in response as older children, and boys' responses were as stable as girls' (Engel, 1959).

Early-formed self-concepts stay with persons throughout life. This does not mean that self-concept cannot be changed, but usually it is not. What are the chances of altering a person's self-concept? Maturation is a natural shaper of self-concept, hence alterer, for better or worse. Psychotherapy can also produce marked changes in self-concept and thus changes in personality. Remedial teaching can change the self-concept, as a person begins to grasp knowledge and skills, whose lack have probably contributed to a low self-concept. Other successes, as well as failures, can affect one's view of himself, especially if the success or failure experience has affected his perception of how others see him. Basing his conclusion on a series of studies, McCandless (1967) has suggested other conditions which may contribute to such change: If through mild pressure or reward a person can be induced to do something contrary to his present self-concept, he may well alter his self-concept in the direction of his spoken opinion or overt action, as in the case of a child who did not consider himself a good speaker. He happened to, perhaps in unthinking excitement, address his class on a subject about which he felt strongly—and did it well. He was probably able to rethink his feeling about speaking and alter his self-concept accordingly. If behavior incongruous with one's self-concept becomes known by others important in his life, his self-concept might be altered, as others' perceptions of him are altered; for example, a child whose academic accomplishments improve so that he makes the Honor Roll. As important other people thus recognize him as a good student, his own idea of himself as a student could change, altering his self-concept.

Self-concept may be incongruent with level of development, thus causing problems. A child who is physically mature may still perceive himself as a child, perhaps because of parental treatment. He may act accordingly. To those outside his family, he appears mature but acts immaturely; therefore his behavior does not conform to the societal expectations. On the other hand, a child may be emotionally mature but physically immature in appearance, causing potentially similar problems.

Because of the varied roles he must fill, the child has need to develop flexibility. If his self-concept is "good," he is able to fulfill varied roles and expectations. He must be able to perceive himself a leader on the playground and act accordingly; however, a few minutes later he must perceive

Figure 7-2. First graders reveal aspects of their self-concepts in their self portraits and dictated statements.

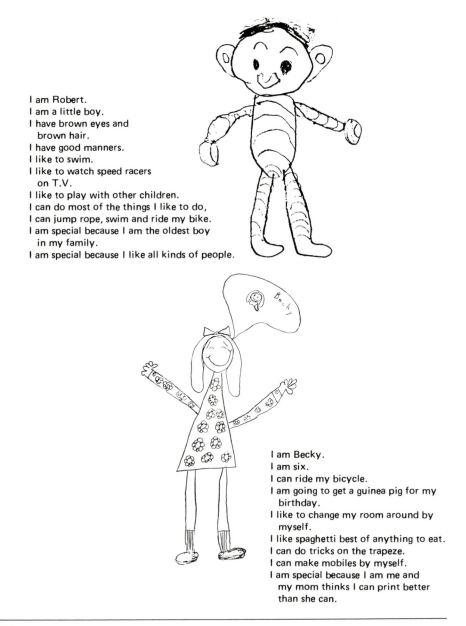

I am Robert.
I am a little boy.
I have brown eyes and
  brown hair.
I have good manners.
I like to swim.
I like to watch speed racers
  on T.V.
I like to play with other children.
I can do most of the things I like to do,
I can jump rope, swim and ride my bike.
I am special because I am the oldest boy
  in my family.
I am special because I like all kinds of people.

I am Becky.
I am six.
I can ride my bicycle.
I am going to get a guinea pig for my
  birthday.
I like to change my room around by
  myself.
I like spaghetti best of anything to eat.
I can do tricks on the trapeze.
I can make mobiles by myself.
I am special because I am me and
  my mom thinks I can print better
  than she can.

I am Feisal.
I cannot ride a bike but I want
  to learn.
I came from India with my family.
I like to play with Layon and
  Daron.
I like baseball, football, and
  basketball.
I want to have a walkie-talkie.
I like to watch cartoons on T.V.
I can do cartwheels.
I can make a fort.
I can change my clothes and
  tie my shoes.
I can do almost everything.
I am special because no one is
  like me.

I am James Robert
I like to ride my bike.
I like to read books.
I like spaghetti, chili dogs,
  my puppy and my fort.
I like Marie, Jack, Harry,
  and Mommy.
I like to play baseball.
I can do exercises, ride
  my bike, tie my shoes,
  dress my self, brush my
  teeth, pick up my
  things, shower and
  shampoo.
I am special because there
  is nobody else like me.
I love Snoopy, Mommy,
  Sister, Daddy and Jesus.

SELF CONCEPT

I am Michael.
I am a little boy.
I have a cat and two dogs.
I have a mamma, grandmamma,
  a twin brother, and a sister.
I like spaghetti and big wheels.
I like a nice home, ice-cream,
  and cookies.
I can leap, sleep, eat, run, walk
  and play football.
I am special because I am a boy;
I see; I can ride a big bicycle.

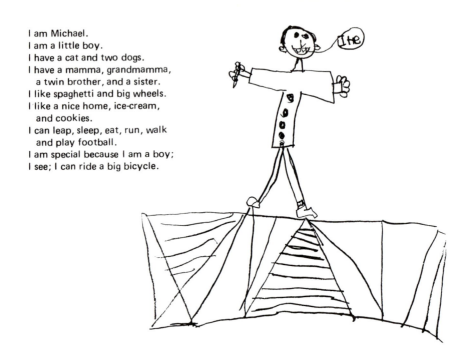

I am April.
I am six years old.
I help take out the trash and set
  the table.
I put up my clothes sometimes.
I like pretty clothes, dogs, food,
  coloring books, and things to
  ride.
I can play ball, tie my shoes, read,
  and button my clothes.
I am special because I am me and
  my Mother's baby girl.

CHAPTER 7 / PERSONALITY AND EMOTIONS

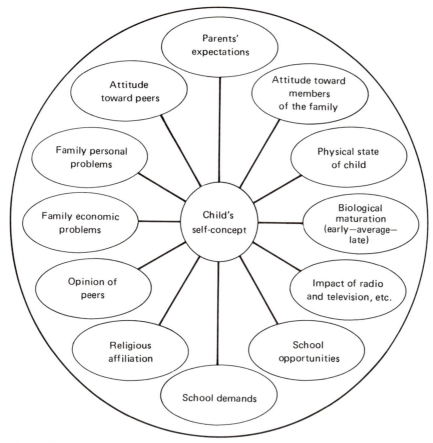

Figure 7-3.

himself a follower under the teacher's leadership. At home he may have to assume roles beyond his normal age, whereas at school he is expected to act like all the others his age. At school he is to be an independent learner, whereas at home he may be treated as if he knows little or nothing.

To preserve a good self-concept, persons select mainly those endeavors that will enhance them. If, for example, one feels inadequate in sports, he may avoid such involvement by choosing other activities or by making excuses, such as feigned illness or injury. The child who does not consider himself a good speller may actually become ill on the day of the six-weeks spelling test.

We behave in ways congruent with our concept of self. If we perceive people as liking us, we act differently than on occasions when we are with people who, we feel, do not like us. The child with a good self-concept will develop and demonstrate self-confidence, the ability to see himself realistically, and there will be little defensive behavior such as shyness or withdrawal. Thereby, he will make better social adjustment, have higher social acceptance, which in turn will reinforce his positive self-concept. The child with a negative self-concept will act accordingly, thereby opening himself to less social interaction and success, which reinforces his poor self-image. This can become a vicious circle. Self-concept seems to definitely affect school achievement and adjustment since, as a whole, those with poor self-esteem are more anxious, less popular, less effective in groups, and more defensive (McCandless, 1967). Fear of failure may prevent their even trying in some instances.

A child's successes and failures, then, have great effect on his self-concept. And since life is filled with both for most people, children must learn to weather them without crippling trauma. Those who have never known a failure have quite vulnerable self-concepts. Those who have never known a success—and there are children who fit into this category—have a negative self-concept to begin with. Helping children accept both failure and success is a prime responsibility of adults living and dealing with them. Letting them feel assured that they are worthy and normal under both circumstances is vital.

There are specific other factors that seem to contribute considerably to self-concept formation. Among these are family size and status, childrearing methods, age, sex, and ordinal position. During middle childhood the child's good feelings about himself decline, as he no longer can rely on his baby charm to gain support and acceptance from others. Adults who are important to him can help him assess himself in new ways so that he may continue to see himself as a worthwhile person.

The child who has been the center of attention in his home may well perceive himself as quite important. When in the classroom, where he must share the teacher's attention with thirty other children, his self-concept may change as he sees himself as not so important. If a child is unable to make such an alteration—still perceiving himself as the most important person in the situation, unable to realize that in school he must share the attention—he may well become a discipline problem. He may dislike school and report to his family that the teacher does not like him. He is exposed to an ever-widening circle of peers, many of whom are insensitive to his needs. He attends a school in which age is a symbol of maturity and status, and except in the highest grade in such an order, he is somewhat of an underling. Adults dominate his life to a considerable degree, often imposing their wills on his. He is in the process of establishing his identity, but it is not yet fully enough established to give him a feeling of security.

Likewise, if a drastic change occurs in the child's family, such as a divorce or the arrival of another child, the self-concept may suffer. The child in a divorce situation may perceive himself as being the cause of the divorce, thus heaping guilt and remorse upon himself, becoming withdrawn or irritable. Or, having to share the love of family with yet another sibling, he may perceive himself as being rejected and show increased aggression or hostility in an attempt to regain the lost love.

The size of the family may affect the children's self-concepts, smaller families generally fostering better ones due perhaps to more time for individual help and attention. Ordinal position within the family plays a part, first-borns and only children having more positive concepts of self. Once again this may be due to greater parental attention and the status of first-born in the family. Data indicate girls also have a higher correlation between self and ideal self than boys, and this correlation increases over time. Fourth- and sixth-grade girls in Bledsoe's (1972) research rated themselves significantly higher on a self-concept scale than boys in the same sample. This may be due to the greater availability of models in mothers, baby-sitters, teachers, and other females with whom they are almost constantly in contact. Another reason for this trend is that in our society more support and praise are given in upper- and middle-class situations to girls for being clean, dainty, polite, quiet. Boys are often thought of as dirty, aggressive, noisy, mischievous—behaviors that are more likely to command correction. Intelligence and academic achievement were positively correlated with self-concept in boys only, however. Manifest anxiety was negatively related with self-concept for both sexes.

Children from families with higher socioeconomic status likewise have better self-concepts, as their opportunities are greater for learning the socially acceptable behaviors of the broader culture. Parental self-concepts also impinge upon children's self-concepts; parents with good feelings about themselves more often produce children with good feelings about themselves.

Disadvantaged children have been thought to mirror others' negative attitudes of them, resulting in negative self-concepts. Their parents may give less attention to psychological aspects of life, yielding lower motivation for improvement. Disadvantaged children may have less models with whom to identify, and they are more apt to give up trying to achieve. However, Soares and Soares (1972) compared the self-concept of disadvantaged and advantaged children in grades 4–8 in an urban setting, collecting data from 514 children with respect to self-concept, ideal self and reflected self in the eyes of teachers, peers and parents. The five measures were obtained through use of a questionnaire containing 20 pairs of bi-polar traits to which students responded. Both groups indicated moderate positive self-perceptions, with the disadvantaged group demonstrating higher self-perceptions than the advantaged group. Since both samples attended neighborhood schools, they were only exposed to children in their same life conditions and did not perceive themselves as being better or worse than their peers.

Within the past decade, researchers have been taking a much closer look at the psychosocial functioning of the black child in an attempt to draw more conclusive determinations concerning such issues as self esteem. Such studies have characteristically sought to use more direct, sophisticated methods with fairly large samples stratified by age, sex, socioeconomic class and education level. Rosenberg and Simmons (1971) conducted an exceptional study with 1,988 subjects in grades 3 through 12 in Baltimore. They reported that when socioeconomic status and age are controlled, black children showed higher self esteem than white children, a fact contrary to the conclusions of long-accepted work. To explain their results, they investigated factors commonly assumed to cause the differences in blacks and whites. They found that the racial insulation created by the predominantly black social context in which black children are reared contributed to their high self-esteem and established certain barriers to assaults upon feelings of self worth such as direct expressions of prejudice. They reported black children use as their "mirror" for measuring self-worth the significant others in their lives more than they reflect society's relative low regard for their racial group. They discovered that black children use as a standard for assessing their personal attractiveness other black children rather than white children, so that even skin color was not a major debilatating factor. The authors stated that whereas school integration may create contextual dissonance for black children, the positive effects of the practice offset any negative effects on feelings of self-worth. They concluded that black children filter white world experiences through a black frame of reference and develop their self-concepts within a black context which protects and maintains their positive self esteem. They do not passively internalize negative definitions or assessments of themselves spawned by the white majority. Many black children and youths have high self esteem despite the family instability, relative social isolation and caste victimization which they may experience; calling upon the resources in their black communities and using personal ingenuity they can still find satisfaction with the kind of persons they are.

The potential impact of one's name on his self-image and success in friendship, school and work has been the focus of research. It has been found that persons who like their names like themselves better. Children bearing unpopular names have been found the most unpopular by their peers. Children with names their teachers liked are better adjusted, have higher expectations for academic success and score higher on achievement tests. Males with unusual names are more likely to be neurotic, while women prefer unusual names. A study of the attitudes of kindergarteners, third and sixth graders toward names revealed the youngest group did not hold the common adult conceptions of name stereotypes, but the two older groups did. Johns are considered kind and trustworthy, Jameses and Michaels as quite masculine. Tonys are thought to be sociable and Robins young. Wendys are stereotyped as quite feminine, Agneses as old, Anns as nonaggressive and Matildas as unattractive. (Marcus, 1975)

Democratic methods of child rearing are more likely to produce children with higher self-concepts than do authoritarian or laissez-faire approaches. This is doubtless due to the fact that in the democratic style, the parents show definite interest in the child's activities and his stage of development. The parents are warm and affectionate. They respect the child's point of view and have carefully outlined standards of behavior which assist the child in knowing how to act to please those around him. Discipline within this method is also consistent and fair rather than harsh, sporadic, or nonexistent.

Think Back

About your self-concept as a child:
What about yourself you liked, disliked.
What you thought you did best, least well.
Who you sought to emulate.

There is a vast amount concerning self-concept and achievement during childhood that is still unknown. Gordon (1969) suggests the relationships between the two follows a pattern of "experience→reinforcing experience→self-concept→seeking experience." (p. 267) As self-concept has become more recognized as an important commodity in personality development, its enhancement has become valuable as an education goal in its own right. Parent study groups and teachers are being helped to assess and foster its development in children of all ages. The use of token rewards has been a popular method in teaching children their own worth. But social reinforcement through positive comments and praise has proven even more beneficial. Helping children learn to praise themselves through suggestion of appropriate selfreinforcement comments has also been effective in increasing feelings of self-worth (Robeck, 1978).

Bloom (1977) proposes there is an academic self-concept clearly defined by the end of the primary grades and strongly related to school achievement for the top and bottom 20% of children. He contends that there is also the non-academic self-concept which encompasses success at athletics, appearance and peer relations. Up to half of the students with poor nonacademic self-concepts also have low academic ones, according to his estimates. (See Figure 7-4.) Through the arts, trades and athletics, the ones with low academic self-concepts can sometimes find sufficient success to avoid a total sense of failure related to the educational process. The average student has few hours during which he is not being judged, and often in comparison with others. There are also very few times when he is not judging himself. A good self-concept is a foundation for a happy, successful life. Bloom charges schools can systematically destroy the self-concept of many children as early as second grade!

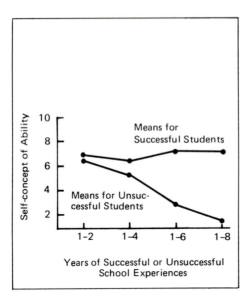

Figure 7-4. (From B. S. Bloom, "Affective Outcomes of School Learning," *Phi Delta Kappa*, **59**, Nov. 1977, p. 197.)

To measure the relative effect of classroom climate and teacher preparation on children's self-concepts, Perkins (1972) involved 251 fourth and sixth graders in suburban schools in a study using the Q-sort method. Congruency between perceived and ideal self was noted. Girls showed more congruency than boys, and sixth graders more than fourth graders. Children in child-centered classrooms whose teachers had completed a three-year child study program revealed higher congruency than those in teacher-centered classrooms where teachers had not received this educational opportunity. The factors of school achievement and peer acceptance did not prove important in this analysis.

Parents and teachers are seldom consciously aware of the self-concept being developed by their children, and few try to assist them toward formulation of realistic and favorable ones. The seriousness of such a situation is emphasized by Jersild (1951, p. 122):

> From an early age, without being deliberate about it, he [the child] acquires ideas and attitudes about himself and others. These are woven into the pattern of his life. They may be true or false, healthy or morbid. Their development is left largely to chance. . . . A large proportion of children will move into adulthood troubled and unhappy about many things. Many will be afflicted by irrational fears which do not represent dangers in the external environment but unresolved problems within themselves. Many, as adults, will suffer from attitudes of hostility, vindictiveness, and defensiveness which are not a response to hostile forces in the outside world but represent attitudes carried over from unresolved childhood struggles. Many persons similarly will acquire persisting feelings of inferiority or other unhealthy attitudes regarding their personal worth which represent either an irrational estimate of themselves or a failure to accept themselves realistically as they are. In numerous ways there is a vast

carry-over of unhealthy attitudes regarding self and others from childhood and adolescence into adult life.

Skin Color

Skin color is a factor that affects personality, as it elicits feelings and feedback from those who observe it. It is genetically endowed but culturally defined. To notice differences in skin color is normal, and as young as age 4, children make comments in reference to this trait. To ignore the obvious differences in skin tone by pretending it does not exist may signify a root of prejudice. McDonald (1970) reported a child who was trying to identify another child in her school group to her father who had visited, but she had forgotten the child's name. In describing this classmate she mentioned many features such as dress, size—but not skin color. Another youngster was trying to help his mother recall a friend of the family who was black. He provided all the clues he could think of and then said in exasperation, "She's not exactly the same color as we are," immediately disclosing her identity. This may be a defense reaction denoting a devaluation of other than white skin rather than a mask of real acceptance as some have believed. It may be more mature to recognize black without devaluing it. Perhaps some are afraid to recognize black, thinking that to admit it exists is to mark it bad.

Perhaps not since the Declaration of Independence has a public federal document had such an impact on personal feelings as did the Supreme Court's Brown decision on May 17, 1954, outlawing public school segregation. M. E. Goodman (1964) wrote: "It is all too clear that Negro children not yet five can sense that they are marked, and grow uneasy. They can like enormously what they see across the color line, and find it hard to like what they see on their side. In this there is scant comfort or security, and in it are the dynamics for rendering personality asunder."

Whereas the topic of skin color is usually taken for granted, and specific statements concerning it are rare, an excellent and lengthy report about the psychiatric aspects of school integration includes the following pertinent remarks on the topic (Committee on Social Issues, 1957, p. 207):

> Through lifelong association of specific meanings to certain colors, there is an automatic tendency to impute to those presenting a particular color psychological qualities which they may or may not possess. . . . Skin contacts form an essential part of the important relationships from infancy through childhood, and a variety of emotional attitudes come to be associated with particular colors, forms, and textures of the skin. . . . In this culture, yellow, brown, or black tend to be associated with ideas of dirtiness or destructiveness or unpleasant smell, while light colors, especially white and pink, tend to be associated with ideas of cleanliness, purity, innocence, and chastity. Since the skin and its

extensions—the hair and nails—cloak the entire body, it becomes that part of a person most quickly accessible to superficial perception and evaluation. Consequently, the association of particular meanings to certain colors and textures of skin often determines the manner in which one person relates to another. It would seem that negative associations to their skin color combine with the other reasons . . . in accounting for the disesteem of Negroes in this country. That it cannot be the sole factor is shown, for instance, by the high social value placed on sun tan by many white people.

In his extensive work, Coles (1964, p. 337) documented the anxiety of black children about their color, revealed by both children and adults. A child's grandmother in an interview shares the following insight: "It takes a lot of preparing before you can let a child loose in a white world. If you're black in Louisiana it's like cloudy weather; you just don't see the sun much."

In the same vein, a black child drew a picture of herself and then explained it: "That's me, and the Lord made me. When I grow up my momma says I may not like how He made me, but I must always remember that He did it, and it's His idea. So when I draw the Lord He'll be a real big man. He has to be to explain about the way things are" (Coles, 1964, p. 71). In the late sixties reports of improved self-esteem among black children were appearing. They emanated from the black's growing awareness of himself as a person and his increasing ability to channel his aggressive feelings outward. Coles (1964) reported that since beginning his work a sense of racial pride has become more evident among black children even as many continue to struggle with feelings of shame and worthlessness.

Black parents whose children are weathering the integration of schools and communities have been concerned about their identity. If they are helped to feel a spirit of community with other black people, they will understand they are not alone in the struggle. Encouraging them to know and be proud of their history and heritage is beneficial. Parental involvement in community programs and politics, coupled with opportunities for black children to develop the social and intellectual skills necessary for effective living, prevent the feelings of powerlessness that has haunted so many in the past. Black parents who can rid themselves of deep-rooted shame at being black and a secret desire to be white will add much to the identity of their children. Even parents who refer to long, straight hair as "good" hair are showing their distaste for "nappy" hair which their children may have. The black child will be more likely to develop a sound sense of self-worth when his family respects the dignity of all people and refrains from making derogatory remarks about other minorities.

In preparing a black child to face the prejudices of others, parents should generally not initiate racial discussions. They should instead answer a child's natural questions without degrading him or the people who may show prejudice toward him. Instilling pride in oneself is best done in everyday ways rather than through indoctrination, as drilling young children in such slogans as "Black is beautiful" or "I am an Afro-American." Nor can material gifts be relied upon to enhance self-worth. They may instead inject a false sense of power. They should not be taught to be subservient to any person but to develop the balance between control and display of all their emotions. Directing aggressive energies into games and active sports, projects, and programs will not only aid emotional health but help develop new skills and abilities in cooperation, organization, and problem solving (Poussaint and Comer, 1971).

Sex Role

A major portion of one's personality revolves around his sex-role development, and in most cultures, this process of sex-typing begins early in life. Currently the society is engaged in exploration and examination of sex roles which could lead to a new era in which an individuals' biologically endowed gender is no longer perceived as a limit to the realization of human potential. Or, as Rosenberg (1972) suggests, if a society without sex stereotypes is much less interesting and productive than one with definitions of sex role behavior, men and women may invent new techniques for polarization.

Lee and Gropper (1974) have identified nine distinctive features of sex-roles in North America. The sexes are socialized differently through child-rearing practices and expectations. There are recognized expressive styles, both verbal and non-verbal which differentiate between boys and girls, men and women. Physical gestures such as posture, stance, gait, and limb movement are typically different. Group affiliations are often sex delineated: Boy Scouts, Girl Scouts, sororities and fraternities, interest clubs such as sewing and flying. Dress customs vary both by style and place of purchase. Such cultural artifacts as toys and other possessions are traditionally sex-linked. Roles, expressive vs. occupational, nurturant vs. disciplining are usually sex related. Games and pastimes—low or high risk—vary between the two groups. Competencies—interpersonal vs. mechanical are typically sex-based.

A child decides what events, objects and actions are masculine or feminine by considering the ratio of males and females associated with that event or action in his repertoire of knowledge and experience. If the distribution is skewed in one direction, that activity is assigned to that sex-role in his mind. Any 5-year-old will assign fishing to boys and sewing to girls. School is usually assigned to girlness by 6-year-olds possibly because over 90 percent of the nation's primary teachers are women.

Lee and Gropper maintain sex role differences continue because of the

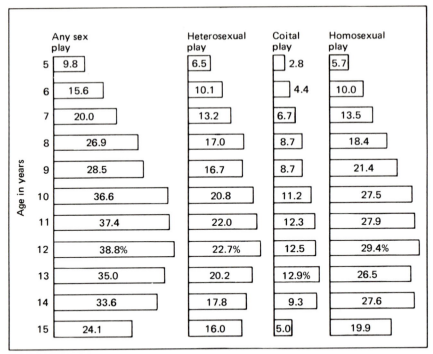

Figure 7-5. Sex play among boys. (Adapted from A. C. Kinsey, W. B. Pomeroy, and C. E. Martin, *Sexual Behavior in the Human Male.* Copyright © 1948, W. B. Saunders Company. Used by permission.)

comfort of habit and tradition, a resistance to change, and psychological survival and association of moralism with sex role conformity. They contend children should have equal access to educational and cultural resources so that their choices can be based on individual differences in interests and aptitudes.

Today's children are meanwhile continuing to be socialized generally as their parents have been socialized, and the following observations have been made by Yorburg (1974) with regard to differences between the sexes, be they genetic or learned: males are more physically aggressive and show less guilt or anxiety about expression of this aggression than females; females seem to have strong concern for popularity, seek help and approval from authority figures, are more conforming to rules, exhibit a more conservative approach to taking risks and are more susceptible to propaganda than males. More females than males develop sympathy, affection and helpfulness, confide readily in others, know intimate details about others; more females than males have better verbal skills, learn to speak sooner, use longer sentences and better grammar; females are more likely to receive better grades in elementary school and high school and do equally as well on all subjects as males; males tend to do well in courses which interest them, and poorly in subjects they dislike. In doll play projective tests more girls than boys make people responses; girls have better memory for faces than boys, although there seems to be no difference in rote memory; males are higher in achievement motivation, whereas females opt for sociability and popularity instead of career achievement. Women college students in contrast to male college students are less likely to cut classes and to participate in controversial classroom discussions, are more likely to have fewer reading problems, be more accurate in grammar and spelling, sit more quietly, take more notes, write longer papers and exams. Females are taught to be more conforming, more obedient than males.

"Generally, and despite many exceptions and much overlapping, more females than males are passive (less active, less overtly dominating and aggressive), dependent (helpless, conforming, obedient, suggestible), nurturing (helpful to others, sympathetic and empathetic), highly verbal, affiliative (sociable, popularity-oriented), and sexually restrained. More males are achievement-motivated (for power and fame in political and economic activities) and, in adulthood, are physically aggressive, emotionally inexpressive and assertive about displaying and utilizing their intelligence."

Sex-role tends to affect every area of living, from interest in school subjects to objects of irritation among children in middle childhood. Bledsoe and Brown (1972) surveyed fourth, sixth, and eighth graders to determine their interests in 8 important areas: art, music, social studies, active play, quiet play, manual arts, home arts, and science. No significant differences were noted for boys between grades 4 and 6, a trend which continued through eighth grade only in the area of active play. Girls in fourth grade indicated significantly higher interest than sixth grade girls in social studies, quiet play, manual and home arts, and science. Between the sixth and eighth grade, there was a decline in quiet play, manual arts and science for girls. Swimming was among the first two choices of both sexes at all ages. At least five of the ten most desired activities for each age and sex were from the active play category (See Table 7-2 and 7-3).

Sixth graders were asked to list all things which irritate, annoy or bother them to formulate an instrument administered to another group of sixth graders (Zeligs, 1972). The subjects responded on a five-point Likert scale from "hate much" to "like" in expressing their feelings. Girls reportedly are more often and more extremely annoyed than boys, but there are many situations in the daily lives of both sexes which annoy them. Boys reportedly hate most to take castor oil, to see dry plays, to eat something they don't like (cabbage family the most hated), to have no time for play, and accidents. Girls cited as their foremost hates: to have scarlet fever, to read dry books, to eat disliked food (Limburger cheese and beer most mentioned), to not go to the movies, and to have accidents. Six illness related hates were significantly more mentioned by girls than boys, whereas three fine art activities were significantly more cited by boys than girls.

Table 7-2 Percentages by Grade and Sex of "Yes" Responses to Scale of the "What I Like To Do" Interest Inventory

| | Grade Level | | | | | |
| | Fourth | | Sixth | | Eighth | |
Scales	Boys	Girls	Boys	Girls	Boys	Girls
Art	53	65	50	58	39	49
Music	40	60	37	50	27	44
Social Studies	72	70	68	60	53	52
Active Play	75	65	69	59	63	54
Quiet Play	66	70	55	55	48	44
Manual Arts	60	49	54	42	48	33
Home Arts	42	68	38	57	26	53
Science	79	70	69	58	53	43

Identification refers to the process of becoming like another individual, group of people or like those within a given category.

Role refers to a body of behaviors. Sex-role identification refers to the *internalization* of aspects of a role considered appropriate to a given sex and to unconscious reactions characteristic of that role. Sex role *adoption* refers to the *acting out* of behavior characteristic of one sex, and sex-role *preference* refers to the *desire* to adopt behavior associated with one sex.

Lynn (1969) provides a comprehensive review of literature relative to sexual identity, citing generalizations on the process and pointing out influencing factors from infancy to adulthood. He notes that both male and female infants usually establish their primary sex identification with the mother or mother surrogate, because they have more interaction with this figure. Therefore, it is generally claimed that the mother makes the biggest impact on this aspect of behavior.

When, at the relatively early age of two or three, the boy realizes somehow that he belongs not in her sex category but in his father's, or to some other familiar male figure in his environment, the shift begins from female to masculine identity, as the child adapts himself to physical-social reality. By age 5, children can make clear differentiation between the more obvious biological cues of maleness and femaleness and psychological cues of masculinity and femininity. They have been taught the need for this shift by subtle treatment such as handling and toy availability, guidance techniques and activities. Because American fathers are not present in their children's lives as frequently as mothers and since most fathers spend only a few minutes daily interacting with their children, the male child has a distinctly difficult time making the shift from mother—to father—identification. However, this does not mean to imply that fathers

Table 7-3 The Ten Activities of the "What I Like To Do" Interest Inventory Most Preferred by Boys and Girls in Decreasing Order of Preference at Fourth-, Sixth-, and Eighth-Grade Levels

Activity	Boys	Girls

Fourth Grade

Boys	Girls
1. Go camping	1. Make candy or ice cream
2. Go swimming	2. Go swimming
3. Go bike riding	3. Go to movies
4. Go hunting	4. Go bike riding
5. Go fishing	5. See the kinds of money used all over the world
6. Shoot at targets	6. Go sledding in the snow
7. Hear about life in the jungles	7. Take care of a pet animal
8. See a display of old weapons	8. Bake cakes, pies, or cookies
9. Find out about animals that lived thousands of years ago	9. Build things out of snow
10. Explore caves	10. Roller skate

Sixth Grade

Boys	Girls
1. Go swimming	1. Go swimming
2. Play baseball	2. Play table games like "Monopoly"
3. Shoot at targets	3. Ride horseback
4. Go hunting	4. Take care of a pet animal
5. Go camping	5. Go to movies
6. Go fishing	6. Build things out of snow
7. Go sledding in the snow	7. Go bike riding
8. Take care of a pet animal	8. Bake cakes, pies, or cookies
9. See a display of old weapons	9. Arrange the furniture in your room
10. Go to movies	10. Ice skate

Eighth Grade

Boys	Girls
1. Go swimming	1. Go to movies
2. Play football	2. Listen to popular music on the radio
3. Go hunting	3. Go bike riding
4. Go to movies	4. Go swimming
5. Go bike riding	5. Take pictures with a camera
6. See a display of old weapons	6. Play basketball
7. Play volleyball	7. Play table games like "Monopoly"
8. Ride horseback	8. Go sledding in the snow
9. Go camping	9. Build things out of snow
10. Go fishing	10. Play volleyball

Interests of Boys and Girls. From the *Changing Child: Readings in Child Development*, pp. 112–113.

are not contributing to the process. Fathers define standards of masculine behavior and exact a degree of adherence to these standards. They define the role more effectively than they model it.

Others in the boy's environment also contribute to the defining of the male role he is expected to assume—mothers, teachers, peers and even male characters in the mass media to which he is exposed. Lynn points out that whereas girls usually form parental identification with their mothers, boys form a sex-role identification with the generalized male role of the culture.

The ways in which sexual identification is transmitted seems to vary between the sexes. Girls are believed to learn their identification by imitating the mother or her surrogate, including covert practice of her behaviors. They receive positive reinforcement for mother-similar tendencies. They are generally developing a cognitive style which involves developing a personal relationship but calling for little or no experimentation and concluding about their sexual identity. On the other hand, boys must discover "maleness" more through trial and error, fostering a cognitive style which involves defining the goal, restructuring the field and abstracting principles. These differences in early cognitive style could lead to the divergence of characteristics in later life, such as obedience versus aggression. Whereas the mother-identification does not require girls to deviate but merely to copy, the masculine role identification calls for boys to learn things through such admonitions as "don't be a sissy," what being a boy and ultimately a man entails. In a nutshell, girls must learn not to be babies, whereas boys must learn not to be girls.

Lynn postulates that girls, then, have only a lesson to learn whereas boys have a problem to solve. Girls could, then, be conditioned to be relatively poor at problem-solving, or generally field dependent. Sons who are extremely close to their fathers might also develop field dependence, not having to seek an identity but merely imitating the male model. Likewise, mothers who are not in close proximity to their daughters may foster more field independence or ability to solve problems since their daughters are required to search more for sexual identity. If either parent is extremely brutal or detached, the same sexed child could be expected to experience a decline in cognitive functioning. Figure 7-6 and 7-7 attempt to demonstrate graphically the relationship of field independence and distance between the parent and child. In Figure 7-6 more fathers are hypothesized to be largely absent or distant from their sons than warm and close to them, resulting in more boys with high problem-solving skills and field independence. In Figure 7-7 more mothers are thought to be close than distant, and to have a close relationship with their daughters, contributing to more girls with lower problem-solving skills and field independence.

There is a paucity of reported research related to parental sex-typing practices, but it is generally thought that parents' attempts are more in terms of what the child should not do or be rather than what they should do or be: for boys, "not being girl-like." Boys are expected to learn to

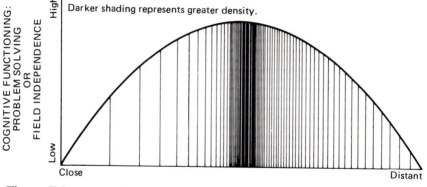

Figure 7-6.　　　DISTANCE OF PARENT FROM SAME SEX CHILD

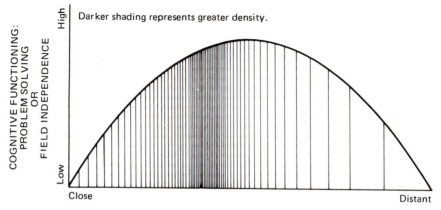

Figure 7-7.　　　DISTANCE OF PARENT FROM SAME SEX CHILD

From *Parental and Sex-Role Identification* ed. by D. B. Lynn. Berkeley: McCutchan Publishing Corporation, 1969. Reprinted by permission of the Publisher.

"deviate" from the early mother-identity, to solve a problem rather than merely learn a lesson. This requires that they restructure their field of reference and draw certain conclusions from observations and experiences, leading to a trial and error approach which often results in more negative than positive responses from those attempting to shape boys' sexual identity. Perhaps due to this complex approach, there seem to be more male casualities than female ones in sex-typing, manifest in such inversions as homosexuality and transsexualism or the desire for surgical transformation into the opposite sex. If boys fail to make the initial shift from mother to masculine identification or become fixated on early perceptions, they may fail to profit from the elaborate reinforcement systems aimed as acculturating them according to biological endowments. Whereas absence, emotional distance or abuse of the father might contribute to this failure to shift, emotional smothering, idolization or excessive attachment by the mother could also be factors. Girls who experience similar problems with sexual identification may have a serious disruption in the relationship with their mothers or an early abnormal attachment to their fathers. Also, if mothers deny or despise their own femininity and therefore exhibit distorted feminine models for daughters, sex-role inversion may occur. It is suggested that perhaps the incidence of the formerly-noted conditions is higher than those noted later, resulting in more males experiencing inversion. Also, since learning under negative feedback is known to be more difficult than under positive reinforcement, the technique used in socializing is thought to be a factor. Too, the socialization process in the culture seems to produce differences in the way males and females view one another. Most boys learn to prefer, adopt, and eventually identify with the role assigned to their sex. Girls learn to prefer the masculine role many times because they see it related to more privileges and prestige. Whereas boys' opinions of the female status decline, girls' opinions of the male status increase and their feelings toward their own sex status deteriorate. Girls are not given the same degree of negative feedback for dressing like males or playing with such toys as cars or guns that boys receive for dressing like females and playing with dolls and tea sets. Girls, therefore, have more freedom to experiment with their role and to indicate preference for the opposite one. Because the society has primarily perceived the central role of women to be in connection with marriage and motherhood, girls can take less action toward realization of this primary role until later in life than boys can move toward active identification with their assigned primary role of occupation.

Research relative to the impact of siblings, ordinal position, rivalry, child-rearing practices, age of parents is complex because of the interaction of these variables in the area of sexual identity. The place of peers in the process is recognized, but whether they impact on boys or girls in greater degree remains a moot question. That peers are not as important as adults in sex-typing seems supported by the fact that a power-envy basis takes precedence over status-envy.

The peer group does reinforce sex-role typing. Children learn about their sexuality through curiosity which leads to exploratory activities with the same and opposite sex. They even learn in this manner some of the feelings from such activity. As children in the 9–12 age range develop intense friendships with peers of the same sex, it is not uncommon for there to occur exchanges of genital manipulation and exploration. Parents or other adults, fearing this action as the sign of sexual maladjustment, can themselves contribute to exactly what they are trying to prevent: through horrified reactions they confirm for the children involved that sex *is* dirty. Although the opportunities are few, children this age also engage in heterosexual play during prepuberty, but without the emotional aspects of love that will later be attached to such activities. The high incidence of children in prepuberty who report having a sweetheart, liking love scenes in the movies, or expressing the wish to someday be married is an indication that the majority are not totally uninterested in the opposite sex. The boys' professing their hate of girls at this age is probably more an attempt to consolidate masculinity than an expression of homosexual tendencies (Kirkendall and Rubin, 1969).

Although it is generally agreed that improper sex-role development precedes the school-age period, some safeguards against such development can be built into the life of the school-age child (Brown, 1960):

- Never threaten or shame a child for his curiosity over sex differences.
- Avoid overstimulating a child through love play which may cause in him guilt feelings. Such feelings could cause him to withdraw from normal relations with the opposite sex.
- Try to establish a warm tie between the same-sexed parent, thus fostering emulation of this parent and facilitating proper sex-role development.
- Show love and respect for each sex child. Avoid making a child feel badly about the sex he or she is.

Some activities often interpreted by parents as being signs of improper development include exploratory sex play and masturbation. The overreaction of adults may actually serve as the catalyst for them to take an abnormal turn. Extreme compulsion in either might be a sign of deeper difficulties warranting professional help.

That children's involvement in sexual activity is not evil and rare but normal and common comes as a shock to some. (See page 330.) Normal heterosexual development is dependent on a child's relationships within the family and on social experiences. Broderick (1969) has suggested three primary conditions necessary in this connection:

- The same sex parent or parent substitute must not be so weak or so punishing as to make the child's identification with him impossible.
- The opposite sex parent must not be so seductive, punishing, or emotionally erratic as to cause the child to mistrust the opposite sex.
- The parents must not systematically reject the child's biological sex and attempt to teach him cross-sex behavior.

We do not become sexual all at once. Childhood experiences make their contribution to psychosexual experiences. About half of all adults report having engaged in some form of sex play as children, and the actual number may far exceed half. Many recall they were at the time concerned with being found out—but why? Was it that they inherently "knew it was wrong"? Was it because of the real content of the acts? Or was it because of the mystery and lure of the forbidden? A small number of children are involved in sociosexual activity during preadolescence, most of it initiated by adults. For the majority little apparently follows from it. Whether the reactions which follow come from the actual involvement or from the strong reactions of others is hard to tell. During the transition from childhood to adolescence many boys report arousal and orgasm while doing nonsexual things, such as climbing trees, sliding down banisters, riding bicycles, and other activities that involve genital contact. More important than all these happenings are the values or feelings that children pick up about sex. Childhood is a crucial time in the development of sexuality, not because of sexual occurrences, but because of nonsexual development which will lay the foundation for later judgments of encounters with sexuality (Simon and Gagnon, 1969).

Achievement Motivation

Atkinson and his colleagues (Atkinson and Raynor, 1974; Atkinson and Feather, 1966) have sought to explain one aspect of personality—that of motivation to achieve. They postulate that two factors which interact in this connection are one's tendency to achieve and one's tendency to avoid failure. Both factors are present in most persons, but which is dominant determines much of one's actions.

The tendency to achieve is expressed in the interest and performance level of a task and is a function of interplay among three variables: (1) a desire for success, that they believe to be a general, stable aspect of personality measurable by a projective thematic apperception technique; (2) the strength of expectancy of success in a task; and (3) the incentive value or relative attractiveness of that particular task. Persons with high achievement motivation find a task more attractive if it is more difficult. However, they are likely to choose tasks with intermediate probability of success rather than very difficult or very easy ones. They are able to do this because of their ability to judge their personal capacities better than low achievement persons. Those with high motivation to achieve are willing to risk failure in the intermediately difficult task rather than pursue sure success in easy ones because they will receive greater satisfaction and reward from the former.

The tendency to avoid failure is associated with anxiety and is a function of three other variables: (1) motive, postulated as a disposition of the personality related to the capacity to react with humiliation and shame when one fails, the anxiety measurable by test anxiety questionnaire; (2) expectation of failure following some task; and (3) negative incentive value of failure: failure is to be avoided at all costs. Persons with high achievement motivation may perceive the repulsiveness of failure to be greater as the task becomes easier. Their tendency to avoid failure may cause them to select tasks in the easy range, avoiding those they could surely do and those which neither they nor anyone else could expect them to do.

Achievement motivation theory is based on the assumption that all individuals have some interest or capacity for the achievement of success and some capacity for anxiety regarding failure. Both factors come into play in situations where performance is to be evaluated according to some standard: one produces the tendency to undertake the task, the other produces a tendency to avoid it. The result is an achievement-oriented tendency which is to approach or to avoid, depending on which factor is more dominant. If the avoidance tendency is dominant, such extrinsic motivators as authority figures may over-rule it. In this case, the person is likely to select a low-difficulty task where success is almost assured rather than risk failure in an intermediate or difficult task.

According to this theory, what happens when a child succeeds or fails? It would depend on whether he has a dominant tendency to achieve or a dominant tendency to avoid failure. A child with a tendency to achieve raises his aspirations when he succeeds, selects a more difficult task, considering it intermediate in difficulty. He is not content with mere repetition of a task he has mastered but is interested in the new, more challenging experience. To this child, failure causes him to think of an easier task as intermediate as he lowers his expectations to a more realistic level. This child is more likely to persist in a task he fails at, if he had considered it easy than if he had perceived it difficult from the beginning, because the failed task can be reconsidered as intermediate in difficulty with appropriate risk involved to hold his interest.

For the child with the tendency to avoid failure, success at a task may cause him to lower his aspirations and select easier tasks in order to be assured of continued certainty of success. When he fails, on the other hand, he is likely to raise his aspirations to unrealistic heights as a defensive mechanism. He is more likely to persist at difficult tasks and give up quite quickly on easy ones. He reasons that his continued failure at the difficult task makes them less risky whereas his failure at simple ones raises them to the intermediate level where he doesn't usually operate.

Atkinson and his associates suggest inadequate motivation in children may be a personality deficiency in which the motivation to achieve or the motivation to avoid failure is too strong. In these cases, the tendency to resist achievement may be overcome through extrinsic motivators, such as tokens or tangible rewards. Or perhaps there is lack of sufficient challenge to the child: all the tasks may be too hard or too easy.

In a study of the effect of ability grouping on school performance and interest (O'Connor and Atkinson, 1966), sixth graders with high achievement motivation in relation to test anxiety were found to have higher interest in school and greater learning than the ungrouped controls. This finding held for all levels of ability. Those with low achievement motivation and high test anxiety showed lower interest in school but not the expected lower performance in comparison with the ungrouped controls. All the children in the study did equally well with respect to their fifth grade performance, perhaps due to the extrinsic motivation provided.

Emotions

Another primary contributor to total personality patterns is the emotional nature of the child, which affects all behavior. Although investigators do not fully agree on the origin and pattern of development of this component of personality, we may be safe in saying that like other aspects of development, emotionality is contingent on both hereditary and environmental influences, since it seems to be a conglomerate of autonomic nervous system functioning, biochemical composition, nutrition, maturation, and patterning (Rogers, 1969).

Bridges' early investigations (1932) concerning the differentiation of emotions in the young child strongly indicates that by school entrance the major expressions have appeared and are fairly established into thought and behavior patterns. (See Figure 7-8.) Therefore, guidance toward healthy emotional development is necessary prior to the 5–12 age period. However, there are still considerations of emotionality which demand the attention of the adults involved with the middle childhood people.

Of paramount importance is knowledge concerning emotionally healthy behavior, in order to locate help for the child whose emotional behavior is atypical. In 1968 approximately 10 percent of America's million schoolage children had moderate to severe emotional problems. Boys are more frequently treated for these problems than girls. Contrary to the first thought of many, an emotionally healthy person is not void of such emotions as fear, anger, jealousy, disgust, or despair; nor totally given to emotions of joy, love, hope, elation, affection, and delight. His behavior instead exhibits a combination of both types of emotions but in a controlled manner, at appropriate times and in socially accepted ways. Rogers (1962, pp. 108–109) has characterized this person as follows:

> He accepts his right to be human; he laughs with gusto; he expresses normal anger or fear without feeling guilty about it. He does, however, discriminate between appropriate and inappropriate circumstances for showing emotion. He controls his emotions; they do not control him. He experiences an inner freedom derived from confidence in his ability to utilize emotions properly. Expression for him is no all-or-none affair; he can express feelings in whatever gradation required. If the door is stuck he does not smash it down. He also discriminates between positive and negative aspects of emotion. He recognizes that mild fear, worry, and anxiety may be stimulants to the right actions; his goal is not cowlike contentment. He does, however, avoid the excessive tension that paralyzes action.

So, then, we can expect children during middle childhood to get mad, to be afraid, to have feelings of jealousy, and to exhibit frustrations. And indeed they *will* do all these things. But we can likewise look forward to their giggling with delight, crying with excitement, and showing love and

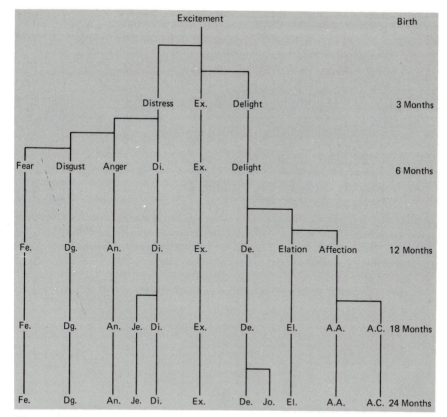

Figure 7-8. Bridges' schematic representation of the differentiation of emotion from general excitement in the newborn to 11 types of emotion at two years. (Reprinted by permission from K. M. B. Bridges, "Emotional Development in Early Infancy," *Child Development,* 3:324–341, 1932, Fig. 1. Copyright © 1932, The Society for Research in Child Development, Inc.)

affection for both adults and other children. What determines the degree of emotional control and constitutes appropriate times and ways of expressing feelings will be the level of maturation of the child and the emotional norms of the society in which he functions. Therefore, when children of similar ages but differing maturational levels congregate, and when these children represent a wide range of subcultures, each having slightly varying standards for expression of emotions, such as occurs in the elementary school classroom, one can expect heterogeneity in emotional behavior and control. This may make it wise and necessary for the adult leader or teacher to help the class group establish some emotional standards to which all can subscribe and toward which to strive.

Emotion is a three-part drama. First comes the subjective feeling known only to the individual, followed by such physiological changes as flushed face, dry mouth, sweating palms, pounding heart, rise in blood sugar.

Then there is the behavior that others label and interpret. When a feeling is aroused in a situation in which it is impossible to respond authentically, the feeling may be displaced to a person or other situation. An example of this is found in a play entitled *The Case of the Missing Handshake* (Stirling, 1952). A ten-year-old comes home and is rude to a guest of her mother's, who is the director of a camp she wants to attend. The parents are upset and shocked at the child's rudeness. After Miss Crosby, the guest, leaves, the following conversation occurs:

> VAL: . . . Grownups. I hate grownups. I hate that Miss Grierson worst of all.
> FRANK: Who?
> SARA: Your history teacher?
> FRANK: What did she do?
> VAL: She gave me a C minus, that's what she did. And that Patricia Connelly, the fat slob, just because she brings her presents . . . she gave her an A.
> FRANK: That's ridiculous, teachers don't do that. Anyway, what has that to do with Miss Crosby?
> VAL: I didn't say it had anything to do with her. I just don't like her. I don't like grownups. I'm going to run away from home and live in a cave all by myself.

Val's experiences with Miss Grierson and Patricia Connelly had caused her to feel frustrated and unhappy. She vented her feelings at home where she felt safe to let down her guard. A home atmosphere that allows this "venting" behavior enables children to manage their feelings in acceptable ways away from home.

When people do not know that feelings are legitimate, deep emotions are often frightening. Such feelings may be suppressed or masked because of guilt feelings, emerging as apathy or I-don't-care attitudes. Many people find it difficult to say "I love you" even to a child. Yet if adults are able to face and express their feelings, even intense ones, children learn that it is all right to feel. And they also learn they do not need to act out every feeling but that there are other ways of using emotional energy.

Adults put high premium on such feelings as joy, happiness, wonder, and affection and are less accepting of fear, anger, and jealousy. Some have called the former type *integrative* and the latter type *disintegrative*. However, it is not the emotion but, rather, the way in which it is expressed and how it affects those experiencing it that determines whether it builds or damages personality and adjustment. It is good to be happy, but it is more important to be authentic. To be untrue to one's feelings merely to maintain "peace in the family" is to teach children that to feel and work through these feelings is unacceptable behavior.

Parents play a central role in children's emotional development and control. They are the models for emotional management that children tend to emulate. They are the reinforcers of emotional expressions, often through negative comments such as "Don't cry," which may teach children to deny or ignore their true feelings. Parents often view such emotions as anger or fear as disruptive of family functioning. But such feelings serve a fuse function, alerting the person that something may need to be checked out in a relationship, experience, or decision. To deny or ignore a feeling is allowing the feeling to manage rather than be managed. Parents also constitute the major stimuli for children's emotions, both positive ones and negative ones. They can do more than any other to help children develop into emotionally healthy individuals.

Anger and Aggression

A child's anger is usually due to inability to cope with some situation within the environment. He experiences it when he is unable to do what he wants to do because of restraint, inhibition, or lack of skill. He may be angry with the circumstances (rain), the materials (stubborn rain boots, tough meat), peers, or even himself. Adults are common causes of anger, as they seek to set and enforce limits.

At young ages children express anger physically, but with increasing age, they tend to use more verbal means. Anger is more likely to appear during periods of hunger, fatigue, or when they are strangers in the group. Children's angry outbursts may increase if they "pay off" or if the children perceive that parents are overconcerned about their exhibiting good behavior, as when guests are present.

With increasing ability to control his body and to use words, as well as to internalize the culture's behavior norms, the child during the middle years should be able to bring anger under control. The transition from home to school—about age 5 or 6—as well as the age of criticism and teasing—about age 8 or 9—may prove challenges to this control. Covert anger in such forms as impertinence and sulkiness may replace such overt anger forms as fighting. Children express anger in such devious ways as sneering, belittling through gossip, plotting, or even imagining situations that would bring sorrow to their enemy. Anger may be evidenced in the way they do their jobs, psychologically withdrawing from the situation by doing poorly. Scapegoating is another means of expressing anger.

In many homes there is a definite lack of suggestions concerning ways children may express anger or vent their anger in sociably acceptable ways. The time-honored system of counting to ten seems to have disappeared from today's child culture. Psychologists emphasize the extreme desirability of children's being able to express their anger verbally toward parents and other adults, but the majority of adult authority figures are not emotionally able to accept a child's saying "I hate you," or something similar. Whereas parents would like angry children to think and speak rationally, in lowered tones, with controlled feeling, they themselves employ far angrier methods. It is a difficult situation for all. It is helpful to remember that the child's outburst is not motivated in the same way as an adult's.

The child has fewer means of control and regulation. His emotions are near the surface.

Activities that tend to help vent frustration or anger include physical exercise, such as bike-riding, wood-chopping, drawer-straightening, room-cleaning, or running; creative endeavors such as puppetry, role playing, painting or piano playing; mental exercises including writing poison pen letters (destroying them prior to delivery, of course), making lists, making a written account of the anger-provoking circumstances; social activities such as gossiping, arguing, name-calling. Crying, fighting, and tongue sticking-out are popular, too. Some of these are socially wise; others are not. A few may be done almost anywhere; most require certain facilities. The wise parent or other adult living with children will remember the limited alternatives available for their expressions of anger and help them accordingly. He will not tell a child not to get angry!

It is well to help children know that all people may be angry but that as people grow older they will become angry about different things. Children are angered by things that upset their routine or their plans; their anger is often self-centered. With healthy maturity, anger is more often triggered by injustices to others or social conditions that make growth difficult or impossible. Such individuals use anger as an energizing force to initiate action, to right wrongs, and to meet needs.

Think Back

About things which made you mad as a child:
What you argued about with friends.
What you got mad at your family about.
How people could tell when you were angry.
What you did to feel better.

A group of children listed the following items as anger-producing:

STIMULI	CHILDREN 6–8
Peers and siblings:	Sister won't do her part of the work.
	Friend will not walk home with me.
	Somebody hits me.
Adults:	Mother makes me take the trash out and clean up my room.
	Teacher is mad at me.
	Dad whips me.
Wants denied:	Someone butts in when I'm talking.
	Sister gets to go but I have to stay home.
	I don't get my allowance.

Possessions threatened:	Someone breaks something of mine.
	Mother lets my brother play with my toys.
	Sister comes in my room.
	Someone uses up my glue without my permission.
Abilities questioned:	I can't find something I want.
	I am the last one chosen for a team at school.
	Getting tackled in football.

STIMULI	**CHILDREN 9–11**
Peers and siblings:	Sister makes up lies about me.
	My friend is on the opposite team.
	My little brother hangs around when my friends are over.
	Boys make fun of me.
Adults:	Mother makes me do the dishes.
	I have to go with my parents instead of the kids.
Wants denied:	Being grounded.
	The Cub pack doesn't meet.
	Having to go to bed in the middle of a project.
	I can't touch things in a store.
Possessions threatened:	My brother breaks something precious of mine.
Abilities questioned:	Throwing a perfect pass and somebody misses it.
	My teacher won't call on me to answer a question.
	Mother standing over me while I'm practicing the piano.

Aggressive behavior is different from simply expressions of anger. It may be described as behavior that results in injury to or destruction of animal or human or inanimate objects and is intentional in nature. Such behavior can be seen in childrens' social interactions with peers, parents, and authority in general. Control of such behavior is a basic developmental problem for the child. He must learn to inhibit his rage responses, to differentiate between situations where aggressive behavior is appropriate and where it is not, and in any situation to respond in relation to the frustration encountered (Feshbach, 1970).

While aggression appears to be linked to biological states and structures, it is at the same time a social act that is strongly influenced by the family and other cultural factors. According to Feshbach (1970, p. 164), Nunberg (1965) and Saul (1956) represent the extremes of the continuum in this regard:

the former finding evidence of the death instinct (which he believes to be the expression of innate aggression) in the mouthing by an infant of his body extremities; the latter arguing that the roots of aggression are in the child's experiences during his early formative years. In Saul's view, hostility is basically a reflection of developmental disturbances arising from diverse sources such as overindulgence of the child, inadequate handling of sibling and other familial relationships, parental rejection, and identification with punitive parental images.

The frustration-aggression hypothesis (Dollard, Dobb, Miller, Mower, and Sears, 1939) suggests a reaction theory of aggression and assumes that aggression results from exposure to frustrating experiences, rather than stemming from a death instinct or an aggressive instinct. All aggressive behavior is to some degree acquired. Even if aggression were innate, as it is considered by some, and simply called forth by frustrating events, it must be noted that the conditions that produce such frustrations are defined by learning.

Behaviors that are labeled aggressive may be very unlike each other in regard to causes, concomitant behavior, and effects. A particular behavior may have a quite different meaning from one child to another, or even in the same child at various times. For example, children hit other children for numerous reasons: the hitter may like to hit; he may want a toy in the possession of the other child, which he may or may not have tried to obtain by other means; the hitter may be angry about something else and the other child may be the first available target. While the behavior is the same, the mediative processes are not the same. The child in each case must be dealt with in different ways, for each has distinct needs.

One point that must be considered in dealing with destructive-aggressive acts of children is to determine whether they are intentional or accidental. A clumsy or hyperactive child may be destructive, inflict injury, or cause pain to another without intending to. "Intentional" or "motivated" aggression, even though the child may not be consciously aware of this intention, is the behavior here under discussion. A further subdivision of intentional aggression (Sears, Maccoby, Levin, 1957) is instrumental aggression, directed toward the achievement of nonaggressive goals, and hostile aggression through which the child intends to deliver injury to some object. If a child wants an object which another child possesses he may resort to hitting in order to get the toy. This is an instrumental aggressive act rather than aggressive behavior emerging from hostility.

Certain patterns of aggression appear in the middle years of childhood. Although there is little research concerning changes that occur in expression of aggression during the childhood years, in contrast to preschool years, Kagan and Moss (1962) found physical aggression toward peers quite stable over the first ten years. During the 10-to-14-year period this behavior was not rated because of its low occurrence, which in itself is significant. These researchers also reported a fairly high level of stability of patterns of aggression established in childhood and adolescence into adulthood.

Sears, Maccoby, and Levin (1957) reported that the greatest childrearing distinction made by parents between boys and girls is in the area of aggression. Boys are expected to be aggressive; girls are not. This is particularly true in the case of physical aggressiveness. This could result not only from cultural determinants of aggressiveness but also from constitutional determinants which affect aggressive behavior: differences in physical strength, motoric impulses, and skin sensitivity.

Data concerning relationships between social class background and aggressive behavior are contradictory. One thing is clear. It cannot be generalized that aggression is suppressed in middle class families and permitted or encouraged in lower-class families.

In most cultures, the aggressive child is the deviant child whose behavior is disruptive. However, aggressive behavior is not a simple act that can or should be extinguished or overlooked. Butcher (1965) found that boys with low aggression scores, as well as boys with high aggression scores, were more disturbed than boys whose aggression scores fell in the middle range. The low aggression boys were more neurotic, withdrawn, socially inhibited. The high aggression boys were more rebellious, excitable, and schizoid. Licht (1967) suggested that although an individual with high self-esteem may typically behave in a nonaggressive manner, he may be freer to respond aggressively to provocation. There must be differentiation between persistent aggressive behavior and an aggressive response to a provocation.

According to Mallick and McCandless (1966), reasonable interpretation of the behavior of a frustrating person to a child during the middle childhood period is effective in reducing both behavior and verbal aggression toward that person. Feshbach (1970, p. 243) draws a provocative conclusion in relation to management of aggression or angry responses: "in reinforcing nonangry behaviors, one may also be modifying the responsiveness to other affective stimuli. The child who has difficulty in experiencing anger may have difficulty in experiencing pleasure."

In dealing with any part of the child's behavior, the totality of the child must be considered: his relationships with others in his environment, and the models with whom he identifies.

Fear and Worry

Fear and worry during the middle school years are largely due to the expanding world of children. Almost daily they encounter new people and circumstances for which they have no preconceived or practiced behavior pattern. Ignorance of the environment and curiosity concerning it combine to cause some fears and worries. Developmental inabilities compound the problem. Some typical worries of this age are parental illness and death, doing poorly in school, getting into trouble, not being liked, getting hurt. Interestingly enough, many of the feared objects or occurrences have never been encountered by the child reporting fear of them: the boy who is afraid of snakes, although he has never seen a snake; the girl afraid to sleep upstairs, even though she has never done it.

Fears and worries are learned. And it cannot be correctly assumed that they will disappear with age. In one study (Holmes, 1935) 40 percent of the childhood fears of personal failure, inadequacy, and ridicule persisted into adulthood. Imitation is a method of learning fear. The sex differences in feared objects is a form of this type of learning: girls learn it is appropriate because of their sex role for them to fear bugs and snakes; boys learn that to fear such creatures would brand them "sissies." Other fears are the result of unpleasant experiences, as in the case of medical treatments. Still other fears emanate from vicarious experiences through such mass media as books, television, and movies. Other fears seem to have no basis in reality. One Kansas youngster listed his two main fears as sabertoothed tigers and man-eating sharks. The peak ages for fear as determined by Mac-Farlane, Allen, and Honzik (1954) are ages 3 and 11. Whereas the early fear is in relation to people, objects, or animals in the environment, the preadolescent fears were more generalized, taking the form of anxiety or worry.

A great number of children's fears are unrelated to actual experiences they have had. In the following listing, note how often the three "most frightening things" have no connection with the "worst" thing that ever happened to the child:

Age of Child	Most Frightening Things	Worst Thing That Ever Happened
7, boy	Kids ganging up on me Doing something real bad	Chipping a tooth
7, girl	Riding on the rollo-rocket Dark nights	Falling off a table as a baby
8, boy	Scary movies Big boys Dark plases [sic]	A thorn in the leg
8, girl	The devil Thunder Going to the graveyard at night	Father's lether [sic] belt
9, boy	Dark places Pits Spankens [sic]	Bike chain broke going down a dead man's curve
9, girl	Untamed lion Poisonous snakes A mean mother	Having to stay inside four days because it was raining
10, girl	Floods Fires Sirens	Being in a air tent in the hospital
10, boy	College kids hitting me Dogs Bats	Having stitches in elbo [sic]

11, girl	Camping out	A broken arm
	A loose criminal	
	Someone in the family getting hurt	
11, girl	Strange men following me	A mean babysitter
	Teenage boys	
	Getting lost	

Children are likely to worry more about family and school than about personal and social inadequacy early in middle childhood. With age they become increasingly worried about self, more fearful of scolding, embarrassment, guilt, and failure. Through cognitive development, earlier fears of supernatural beings, deformities, and the dark become less threatening.

With maturity fear fastens more and more on realistic objects, depending more on experience than instructional learning. The intensity of the child's fears depends for the most part on family relationships. The increased exposure to mass media may be affecting their awareness, which results in their fearing such things as air pollution, cigarette smoke, cancer, and strikes (Thiesing, 1971).

Maurer's (1965) five-year study of children ranging in age from 5½ to 14½ years revealed interesting findings: Fear of animals is nearly universal, the snake being the most unpopular. Fear greatly diminishes with age. Fear of the dark largely disappears after age 7. Fears of such nonexistent entities as monsters, the boogie man, ghosts, witches, and animated skeletons are abandoned around age 10; horror films prior to age 9 or 10 may well be traumatic, but in later ages serve a therapeutic purpose. With age, fears become more realistic and more closely tied to learned or experienced objects and situations; fear of natural hazards, including fire, poison oak, deep water, and the desert increases after age 7. Fear of hazards that are man-made and a result of an industrial society also rose with age. Automobiles were mentioned by only 15 percent of the children ages 7–14. Trains were mentioned more than weapons. Other items listed included rusty nails, the electric chair, falling bricks, and a stairwell.

Incidence of the fear of people and their actions more than doubled from ages 5 to 12. Among the fearful people and actions were divorce, people with guns, and child enticers. Such things as traffic, germs, and kidnappers were rarely mentioned. Punishment, war, and the atomic bomb were also scarcely noted.

Croake (1969) studied fears in children from grades three and six to determine the relation of type and number of their past, present, and future fears. Girls were found to have more fears than boys, and those from the lower socioeconomic groups more fearful than upper socioeconomic children. They reported having had more fears in the past than at the present and saw themselves as having even fewer in the future. Political fears such as war and the Communists taking over were the most common both in present and future for sixth-graders. They were also the most common future fear of third-graders. The past fears of the younger group were most often natural phenomena, while sixth grade boys reported having previously feared supernatural phenomena, and sixth grade girls said natural phenomena and animals had been their most common past fears. Children were generally unable to cite the origin of their fears.

Fear as a warning of danger can be a valuable thing for a child if it does not become too intense. Excess fear or anxiety can be damaging to the self-concept. It can narrow one's field of experience. It can trigger various behaviors which may mask the child's real problem.

Think Back

About what you feared as a child:
What caused you to be afraid.
How you managed your fear.
How you overcame it.
What your friends feared.

Anxiety can manifest itself in a variety of ways, among them daydreaming, nightmares, bedwetting, insomnia, psychosomatic illness, withdrawal, overaggressiveness and rebelliousness. Often the clues to anxiety are not recognized for their true significance, and insensitive treatment of the anxious child may intensify the original condition. A variety of experiences can help children overcome or avoid fears and anxiety. A healthy self-concept will counteract overfearfulness. Good models help immeasurably, and a minimal amount of attention or flurry concerning fears will contribute to their disappearance. As a child develops skill and knowledge, he becomes less fearful because he is able to control the situation.

Boredom

Jersild (1968) has included boredom in his discussion of emotions. Calling it an absence of activity pleasure, he postulates that much of children's misbehavior and mischieveousness is due to the feeling there is nothing to do. Tiredness and even some pain can be caused by boredom rather than by fatigue or organic problems. Children fight boredom with inventiveness and daring. Much boredom centers in the school, primarily among children who are not challenged and kept meaningfully occupied in their learning. One fourth grade boy described by his teacher as bored received disapproval from her for doing his math problems in Roman rather than Arabic numerals. He told his mother he did it to make the work more interesting! Another form of boredom may be seen in a person who cannot abide solitude—is bored with himself. A person who is thus bored is not at ease with himself. He is probably anxious and unsure, not merely bored.

Jealousy

Since jealousy is another universal emotion and thought virtually unavoidable in children, its origin and handling bear mention. This emotion arises from insecurity in relationships and often accompanies feelings of anger and inferiority. It is expressed in many forms, from temper tantrums to allergies, bed-wetting, or cruelty to animals. Quite often it occurs at the arrival of a new sibling. The older child perceives the new family member as a threat to his kingdom of parental attention.

Sending the school-age child away from home on the arrival of the new sibling is not a recommended procedure. Instead the older child should be made to feel he is needed to welcome and enjoy the new arrival. Ways to alleviate new-baby jealousy include allowing the older children to help in selecting clothing, furnishings, and even names for the new sibling; planning special activites with the older children while the baby stays home; allowing them to help in the enjoyable aspects of baby care, as rocking, strolling, and feeding; not requiring them to assist with such duties as diapering, calming while crying, and clothes washing. Friends can also help prevent rivalry by remembering to acknowledge the presence of the older children before "making over" the new arrival and by bringing a small gift, such as an inexpensive toy or book, to the older siblings when they bring the traditional gift to the new arrival.

Younger children may experience feelings of jealousy because of privileges granted to older children in the family. Parents may seem to show favoritism among the siblings, thus fostering jealous feelings among the less-favored. Jealousy may stem from envy of others because of their physical abilities, material possessions, or popularity among peers. It may arise in connection with relationships with adults or children outside the family: the Scout leader, a favorite teacher, or popular peers.

Girls are more likely to be jealous than boys (MacFarlane, et al., 1954), and persons of higher intellect are more often jealous (Koch, 1960). The oldest child is more prone to jealous feelings, and this emotion is more common in families with two or three children than in large families or families with only one child (Vollmer, 1946). Children are more likely to be jealous if their mothers coddle them or are inconsistent in administering discipline (Bousfield and Orbison, 1952). Reducing jealousy may be accomplished through building a child's image of himself, diverting his attention from himself, and providing him satisfying experiences. Jealousy has been termed a "withering emotion," and since it is a difficulty that is almost inevitable at some points in a child's life, adults must be ready to help children deal with it. Perhaps it is well that jealousy often appears in young children so that they can be supported by family as they work through its difficult feelings and reactions.

In the area of emotional development, far more research and writing is done concerning the so-called disintegrative emotions than the integrative ones. Perhaps it is because the incidence of the latter brings general pleasure to the society, whereas expressions of the former more often cause concern. Another reason may be that whereas anger, fear and jealousy in many forms are readily distinguishable, delight, love, hope, and joy may be less discernible. But whatever the cause, no disucssion of emotional development would be complete without attention to the vital need for love and affection in childhood.

Love and Affection

Affection seems deeply and closely related to the basic need to belong and to be with others. Explanations of its origin are still not fully adequate. But we do know that love is related to the helpless dependency of the infant on those around him. And it is suggested that love grows through conditioning. If love and affection are provided for the child, these emotional manifestations are evident in his behavior during the early and middle years of childhood. The capacity to love is thought to be innate even though learning plays a role in terms of the objects toward which the child directs his affection or admiration.

Although the ratio of friendly and competitive feelings with others varies from child to child, on the average the greater proportion of behavior is freindly. All children need love, and during elementary school days the deep need for affection (approval) is shown in their great desire to be accepted by the peer group. Persons suffering from "diseases of nonattachment" or lack of love are typically characterized as having an impoverished emotional range. They experience no joy, grief, guilt, or remorse. An advertisement picturing two boys with their arms around each other was captioned "Everybody needs somebody." The text included these words: "If you're a kid, it's a friend who sticks up for you. If you're an adult, it's someone who understands you." So true. Everyone needs someone to love him in order that his growth and development proceed normally.

Prescott (1952) has formulated five hypotheses about the role of love in the lives of children and their families which have become classic:

- Being loved affords the human being much-needed basic security.
- Being loved makes it possible to learn to love oneself as well as others.
- Being loved and loving others makes it possible to belong in groups.
- Being loved and loving allows for identification with others and the appropriate internalization of adequate values and attitudes.
- Being loved and loving makes it easier to adjust to situations that involve strong and unpleasant emotions.

The ability to love (Jourard, 1974) is a result of having early love needs met. One who is able to give love does so out of his abundance of it rather than out of the needs of the persons whom he loves. He has plenty to share because he has received much in his earlier life. Self-loving provides practice in loving, making it possible to love others.

Socially, children deprived of love are less able to relate to others satisfactorily. They may be uncooperative or even hostile. Feeling inadequate, they can become overly aggressive, dependent, and disobedient. Mentally, the unloved child lacks the ability to concentrate and is easily distracted. His speech development may be delayed. If deprived of love in infancy, children can develop psychosomatic illness and establish apathetic, listless activity patterns, which in turn can impair proper physical development.

Deprivation of affection can have serious effects on a child's total emotional development, causing irritability, cantankerousness, and unreasonableness in children of school age. Hate, hostility, and vengefulness can be caused by rejection. Children who are seeking love and approval can become overachievers to gain parental and teacher approval—or underachievers because of having virtually given up. They may turn to delinquent behavior in an effort to meet their needs for affection, approval, and recognition.

The school-age child may consider overt expression of love childish and resort to other methods for demonstrating this integrative emotion to family and freinds. He will be more adept at displaying or hiding his affectional feelings by this age. And he may find it more difficult to accept than to give affection, particularly in public. Love for parents will be shown less through preschool kissing and hugging and more by wanting to be with them, doing things for and with them, and sharing his problems with them. He will perceive that they love him as they show genuine interest in him, his interests, and activities. But his affectional feelings will be broadening to include peers too.

Expressions of affection for peers will be evident in the insatiable desire to be in their presence, day and night; in the secret clubs and codes they share; and in the notes, letters, and telephone calls by which they keep in touch. Girls are generally more affectionate than boys, in keeping with the cultural norm. They will demonstrate their love for friends by giving small presents, doing things together, and selecting a best friend with whom to play and share. Boys demonstrate this same emotion in their friendly wrestling, punching, and hitting of one another.

Joy

Joy comes to children from many sources: activity, satisfaction of curiosity, surprises, and finishing a project. They find joy in learning to do something new. One youngster, age 7, described the happiest day of her life as the one when she learned to "take away" (subtract in mathematics). Children could well write their own Happiness Books. They have defined joy or happiness in many ways. Happiness is:

- feeling better after telling the truth.
- new neighbors my own age.
- to have happy dreams.
- finishing a puzzle.
- when somebody talks to me and listens.
- being in the kick ball circle longest.
- having somebody walk you home.

Think Back

To the happiest things that happened to you as a child:
What caused the happiness.
How long it lasted.
How you shared it.
How you showed it.

Every child enters the world capable of pleasant and unpleasant feelings. The type that becomes a habit is dependent on the kind of relationships he establishes with those he knows and the environment in which he grows. Childhood is a crucial time for development of emotional habit patterns. All emotions can be good if they are understood and wisely used. Fear and caution are closely related. Anger and disgust can lead to concern and reform. Distress may lead to sympathy, compassion, and sharing. Joy, delight, and affection can be experiences of love. Jealousy can aid empathy and identify or it can be damaging, without proper channeling. Fear can become phobia, crippling the spirit of adventure or causing total withdrawal. Anger can turn to rage, dulling judgment and perception, and preventing constructive action.

Traits

Another personality dimension in which there is wide individual variation is traits. The casual observer probably assesses personality most often in terms of the characteristics displayed by a person, such as friendliness, bravery, selfishness. Most traits are emotion-related. Traits are learned in the home and school and elsewhere by imitation of persons with whom a child identifies. Some are learned by trial and error through everyday experience. If a child happens on a behavior bit which brings him a desired outcome, he may try it in similar situations in the future. With extended successful use he may incorporate the trait into his personality pattern. On the other hand, if repeated use fails to bring about his desired results, he may eliminate it from his behavior or personality repertoire.

Although no one single trait distinguishes the popular child from the unpopular one, highly accepted children are expansive, dynamic, objective, and free from anxieties and fear. They are optimistic, happy, and good natured. They are group-centered rather than ego-centered and build others up instead of tearing them down to their own feelings of self-worth (Hurlock, 1964).

Children learn that certain traits appeal to some people while different traits please others in their environment. During the school-age period children will work on developing traits to please their peers, sometimes to the displeasure of their parents and other adults. Through sex-role typing, children come to learn traits that are culturally appropriate for their sex. Various subcultures within a given society quite often value differing traits. These, too, children are expected to learn. As in the case of emotional reactions, trait conglomerates and conflicts are quite often seen in elementary school classrooms. And the skillful teacher must seek to relate the variances without destroying the child's subcultural identity.

Work by Friedmen and Rosenman (1974) suggests that the traits of hostility, urgency and competitiveness raise serum cholesterol levels in the blood, contributing to a high incidence of coronary heart disease in persons whose lives are characterized by these traits. Since traits are acquired primarily in childhood, it is conceivable that children can be programmed for this type of physical weakness due to their early experiences and models.

Mental Health

Mental health is a term which is used to signify emotional-social well-being. Basically, good mental health is manifest in feeling comfortable and confident about oneself, feeling right and relating effectively with others, and being able to meet the demands of life in a positive way. Carl Rogers (1969) characterizes the mentally healthy person as one who is fully functioning, always discovering himself, always developing. He says mental health encompasses trusting oneself, living fully with ones feelings and reactions, being open to evidence from all sources. A mentally healthy person is experiencing optimum psychological growth, is self-enhancing, socialized and engages in appropriate behavior.

Todd (1973) expands on these ideas and states that mentally healthy persons can see the other person's point of view, see reasons for others' behavior, withhold premature judgment, learn from mistakes, see the need for others to help on occasion, appreciate their own abilities and limits, communicate their own needs and can listen to others, are committed to helping self and others, are concerned about others' rights, and show consistency between values, feelings and behavior.

Teachers and parents are the major sources for mental health, either helping or hurting this aspect of children's development. With increasing age, the peer group has increasing effect on this dimension, but the family remains crucial in its maintenance. Parents who are emotionally healthy themselves are best able to foster the quality in their children. When they allow them to develop as a unique persons, without imposition of their dreams, in a community which values and supports children, they foster mental healthiness. Respect, response to their needs, discipline which typifies approved behavior, all contribute to this condition. Even parents who have experienced mental illness can rear mentally healthy children if they have learned from their experience and found the kind of help which strengthened them.

A substantial but unkown number of children have mental health problems. Between 1969 and 1971, the number of reported cases of treatment of clients under 18 increased 32 percent. There was relatively high incidence of schizophrenia, depressive disorders, and disorders associated with drug abuse in this number. (Status of Children)

Estimates of the prevalence rates of severe mental illness among American children range from 2 to 4.5 per 10,000. In 1970, 402.6 children per 100,000 between ages 6 and 13 were admitted to outpatient psychiatric cinics in the U.S. A 1970 census conducted by the National Institute of Mental Health of state and county mental hospitals and outpatient psychiatric clinics indicated children's mental illness rates were higher when living with mother only than when living in intact homes. The rates were lowest when the children lived in families with six or more members.

There has been a considerable increase in services to this group in the last decade, through establishment of more agencies and more parent involvement in their treatment. Some signs of mental health breakdown in children are fear of the unfamiliar, stress in adapting to change, withdrawal, excessive fighting, school failure, rebellion, lack of stable relationships with other children, sleeping problems, refusal to eat almost all the time, inability to control elimination, temper tantrums and crying spells, difficulty working in groups, excessive name calling, inability to show or receive affection, or complete lack of emotional expression. No single symptom is abnormal, since even stable children manifest some of these characteristics at various times in normal development. The duration and severity of a symptom must be assessed before mental illness can be assumed.

A severely disturbed child is one who seems to suffer deeply and to be handicapped in every area of living: he may be fearful of everything at home and school, be unable to understand and react to the simple realities of life, and may appear not to understand anything parents or teachers say to him. Autism and schizophrenia are lables given to some forms of childhood psychoses. Although little is known about the cause of such disorders, one hypothesis is that there are predisposing inherited factors which are reinforced by environmental pressures.

Some children may not be emotionally disturbed but simply need firmer discipline. They may show some signs of anxiety or overexcitability but are at the same time able to develop warm relationships and accept and give love. They are generally able to use their abilities in constructive endeavors. This group is not large; most unhappy children receive discipline which is too firm, sometimes even cruel. (U.S. Facilities, 1974; Mental Health Is 1, 2, 3; Facts about the Mental Health of Children, 1972)

What's Next?

1. *A Child Called Noah,* J. Greenfield, N.Y.: Holt, Rinehart and Winston, 1972.
2. *Child Development Through Literature,* Landau et al. Englewood Cliffs, N.J.: Prentice-Hall, 1972: "The Dog," by C. Reilley, pp. 128–133; "The White Circle," by J. B. Clayton, pp. 156–162.
3. "Sex Role Stereotyping in the Schools," NEA, 1973.
4. "Changing Sexist Practices in the Classroom," M. Stern, ed. American Federation of Teachers.
5. Sexist Discussions: *Today's Education,* Dec., 1972
   Phi Delta Kappan, Oct., 1973
   Journal of Teacher Education, Winter 1975
   Social Education, March 1975
6. Film: *Shyness.* McGraw-Hill, 1221 Avenue of the Americas, New York, N.Y. 10019. (15 min/b/w.)
7. Film: *Angry Boy.* International Film Bureau, 332 S. Michigan Ave., Chicago, Ill. 60604. (33 min/b/w.)
8. Film: *The Quiet One.* Athena Films, 165 W. 46th Street, New York, N.Y. 10019. (67 min/b/w.)
9. Film: *Johnny Lingo.* Brigham Young University, Provo, Utah. 84602 (25 min/color.)
10. Film: Yellow Summer (self concept) Iowa PTA.
11. Film: *Cipher in the Snow.* Brigham Young University, Provo, Utah 84602 (24min/color).
12. Film:*Sex Role Development.* CRM Films, 1011 Camino Del Mar, Del Mar, CA 92104 (23 min/color).
13. Film: *Super and Spice* (non-sexist ed. environment). Odeon Films, 1619 Broadway, N.Y. 10019 (32 min) 1974.
14. Film: *Cross-cultural development of sex roles and social standards. Harper and Row Media. (25 min/color.)*

Catalysts for Discussion

I. "Cipher in the Snow" (Mizer, 1964).

It started with tragedy on a biting cold February morning. I was driving behind the Milford Corners bus as I did most snowy mornings on my way to school. It veered and stopped short at the hotel, which it had no business doing, and I was annoyed as I had to come to an unexpected stop. A boy lurched out of the bus, reeled, stumbled, and collapsed on the snowbank at the curb. The bus driver and I reached him at the same moment. His thin, hollow face was white even against the snow.

"He's dead," the driver whispered.

It didn't register for a minute. I glanced quickly at the scared young faces staring down at us from the school bus. "A doctor! Quick! I'll phone from the hotel. . . ."

"No use. I tell you he's dead." The driver looked down at the boy's still form. "He never even said he felt bad," he muttered, "just tapped me on the shoulder and said, real quiet, 'I'm sorry I have to get off at the hotel.' That's all. Polite and apologizing like."

At school, the giggling, shuffling morning noise quieted as the news went down the halls. I passed a huddle of girls. "Who was it? Who dropped dead on the way to school?" I heard one of them half-whisper.

"Don't know his name; some kid from Milford Corners," was the reply.

It was like that in the faculty room and the principal's office. "I'd appreciate your going out to tell the parents," the principal told me. "They haven't a phone and, anyway, somebody from school should go there in person. I'll cover your classes."

"Why me?" I asked. "Wouldn't it be better if you did it?"

"I don't know the boy," the principal admitted levelly. "And in last year's sophomore personalities column I note that you were listed as his favorite teacher."

I drove through the snow and cold down that bad canyon road to the Evans place and thought about the boy, Cliff Evans. His favorite teacher! I thought. He hasn't spoken two words to me in two years! I could see him in my mind's eye all right, sitting back there in the last seat in my afternoon literature class. He came in the room by himself and left by himself. "Cliff Evans," I muttered to myself, "a boy who never talked." I thought a minute. "A boy who never smiled. I never saw him smile once."

The big ranch kitchen was clean and warm. I blurted out my news somehow. Mrs. Evans reached blindly toward a chair. "He never said anything about being ailing."

His stepfather snorted. "He ain't said nothin' about anything since I moved in here."

Mrs. Evans pushed a pan to the back of the stove and began to untie her apron. "Now hold on," her husband snapped. "I got to have breakfast before I go to town. Nothin' we can do now anyway. If Cliff hadn't been so dumb, he'd have told us he didn't feel good."

After school I sat in the office and stared bleakly at the records spread out before me. I was to close the file and write the obituary for the school paper. The almost bare sheets mocked my effort. Cliff Evans, white, never legally adopted by stepfather, five young half-brothers and sisters. These meager strands of information and the list of D grades were all the records had to offer.

Cliff Evans had silently come in the school in the mornings and gone out the school door in the evenings, and that was all. He had never belonged to a club. He had never played on a team. He had never held an office. As far as I could tell, he had never done one happy, noisy kid thing. He had never been anybody at all.

How do you go about making a boy into a zero? The grade-school records showed me. The first and second grade teachers' annotations read "sweet, shy child"; "timid but eager." Then the third grade note had opened the attack. Some teacher had written in a good, firm hand, "Cliff won't talk. Uncooperative. Slow learner." The other academic sheet had followed with "dull"; "slow-witted"; "low IQ." They became correct. The boy's IQ score in the ninth grade was listed at 83. But his IQ in the third grade had been 106. The score didn't go under 100 until the seventh grade. Even shy, timid, sweet children have resilience. It takes time to break them.

I stomped to the typewriter and wrote a savage report pointing out what education had done to Cliff Evans. I slapped a copy on the principal's desk and another in the sad, dog-eared file. I banged the typewriter and slammed the file and crashed the doors shut, but I didn't feel much better. A little boy kept walking after me, a little boy with a peaked, pale face; a skinny body in faded jeans; and big eyes that had looked and searched for a long time and then had become veiled.

I could guess how many times he'd been chosen last to play sides in a game, how many whispered child conversations had excluded him, how many times he hadn't been asked. I could see and hear the faces and voices that said over and over, "You're a nothing, Cliff Evans."

A child is a believing creature. Cliff undoubtedly believed them. Suddenly it seemed clear to me: When finally there was nothing left at all for Cliff Evans, he collapsed on a snowback and went away. The doctor might list "heart failure" as the cause of death, but that wouldn't change my mind.

We couldn't find ten students in the school who had known Cliff well enough to attend the funeral as his friends. So the student body officers and a committee from the junior class went as a group to the church, being politely sad. I attended the services with them, and sat through it with a lump of cold lead in my chest and a big resolve growing through me.

I've never forgotten Cliff Evans nor that resolve. He has been my challenge year after year, class after class. I look up and down the rows carefully each September at the unfamiliar faces. I look for veiled eyes or bodies scrouged into a seat in an alien world. "Look, kids," I say silently, "I may not do anything else for you this year, but not one of you is going to come out of here a nobody. I'll work or fight to the bitter end doing battle with society and the school board, but I won't have one of you coming out of here thinking himself into a zero."

Most of the time—not always, but most of the time—I've succeeded.

ANGRY
by Angela Jones

Sometimes I feel so angry that I could
Rip up my dog's sweater
Throw him out the window
And toss him in the ocean.
I feel so angry
I could squeeze toothpaste
In my mother's turnip greens.

RIGHT NOW I FEEL VERY EXCITED
by Lloyd McKibbins

I am more excited than my whole class.
I am excited as a bunch of bees
That have some honey in a nest.
I am very excited today
Because we are having our annual carnival.
I feel so excited
That I can jump into the wall.
And I am so excited
That I can jump over the world.
And I can't wait to
Ride the bumper cars and
Taste the pickles.

JOY
by Lisa McFadden

My heart is pounding so hard with joy
That I can lay down and go to sleep.
My lungs are dancing inside of me.
My tonsils are singing.
My brains are going fast asleep.

LOVE
by Tempist Spikes

*Love is something that's real serious. Watch
out, for it can get you, right or wrong.*
*If I would get married I would not go with another man, because some men can be
jealous of the other man. And you can get hurt from your man.*
And sometimes your man can be going to another woman, and you can get jealous.

Beyond the Classroom Experiences

1. Describe incidents involving various emotions expressed by children over a period of time.

2. Through a picture series, ask children to respond to various emotions expressed by others. Ask them to suggest ways each emotion could be expressed without hurting others.

3. Ask children to tell what makes them angry or fearful. Compare their responses with those cited by research. Ask adults the same question. Note the differences and similarities between the two groups.

4. Ask children to complete the sentence: "Happiness is . . ." Talk with them about their responses.

5. Discuss with parents of Oriental, Black, Chicano, or Indian children ways they have prepared their children for possible reactions to their skin color and physical features. Discuss with Anglo-Saxon parents ways they have helped to encourage children's acceptance of persons who are physically different from themselves.

6. Explore children's sex-role identity through use of a series of pictures. Ask them to choose among occupations, play objects, other activities, and items that may be related to the traditional sex roles in our society. Discuss their decisions with them.

7. Examine textbooks and other mass media to see to what extent traditional sex roles are being portrayed to children. Interview parents to ascertain if they wish traditional or nontraditional sex-role identification in their children.

Chapter 8

How Children Think

This chapter is designed to help you:

- see varied factors which influence children's performance on measures of intelligence.
- see approaches that foster intelligence.
- explore theories of cognitive development and reasoning of school aged children.
- understand the problems in language and communication in middle childhood.
- see the role of memory in cognitive functioning.
- recognize the significance of children's humor.
- see the place of curiosity in children's development.

Intellectual Development

Most teachers probably perceive their major occupational task as fostering and evaluating the intellectual development of their pupils. And parents tend to express worry over this phase of growth in their children a great deal. Therefore, interest in mental growth and development holds a prominent place among those preparing for the vocations of teaching and parenting. Because of the value placed on mental development in the total society, its study is germane to any professional who will be working and living with children.

Just as the word *personality* carried for each of us a generalized meaning, so does the word *intelligence*. Specifically, intelligence refers to the capacity of an individual to learn, to link previous learnings with new ones, and mentally organize the accumulated knowledge into a usable store. In contrast, *intellect* is a term used to refer to the content of the mind, or the accumulated collection of learnings. Although the two go hand in hand in cognition and development, it is theoretically possible for an individual to possess one and not the other.

A prime goal of the child of the middle years is to organize and apply the multitude of facts he has been accumulating and will continue to accumulate. He becomes more refined in his ability to learn as his basic repertoire of knowledge grows, allowing him to relate new facts and concepts to his ever-broadening store. As he masters the basic skills of reading, writing, and numbering, he strengthens his skills of communication, thus opening new doors to even greater knowledge and understanding.

As he learns to deal with symbols, he will be able to expand his concept collection to include such abstractions as justice, zero, God. He shows flexibility in his thought as he recalls knowledge stored in the past to apply it to present situations and to plan for a future time. With age, his thought pattern becomes less self-centered and more concerned with the other person's point of view.

The problem is not that children are unable to cope with ideas, but rather that they deal with them in ways characteristic of their level of development. It is simply that they do not think in the same manner as adults. Children's words do not always have the same meaning for them as they do for their adult listeners, nor is their logic the same.

Almy (1961) believes the real danger in current attempts to change the notion that public schools are "easy" and that they encourage general mediocrity in thinking lies not so much in the attempt to inject more content into the curriculum but, rather, in a failure to recognize that "each level of development contributes its own special understandings of that content."

Perhaps he was wiser than we thought—the Prophet—when he wrote concerning children: "They have their own thoughts" (Gibran, 1945, p. 21). This might be amplified by adding "their own way of thinking." In this area of development, children are certainly not small replicas of adults, but are qualitatively and quantitatively different and change as they grow. Almy (1961) suggests we are often deceived by our own wishes with regard to how children think. For some persons, children's thinking processes are equated with IQ and its measurement.

Measurement and Testing

With mental development contingent on intelligence, or ability to learn, great effort has been expended to devise measures of this dimension of the being. These tests are measures of performance, although their results are often interpreted as being indications of potential.

Thurstone and Thurstone (1938) have enumerated eight abilities that may be identified through intelligence tests: (1) verbal ability, (2) number ability, (3) perceptual speed, (4) rote memory, (5) inductive reasoning, (6) deductive reasoning, (7) word fluency, and (8) ability to visualize objects in space. In assessing such abilities, tests include tasks representing situations scaled to the child's age level.

Among the more well-known tests of intelligence are the Stanford-Binet (Terman and Merrill, 1937) and the Wechsler Intelligence Scale for Children (Wechsler, 1949). Both are individually administered. The items in such instruments measure, among other things, object assembly (putting puzzles together), general information (From what animals do we get milk?), word comprehension, opposite analogies (snow is white, coal is ————), awareness of absurdities (What's silly about this?), and carrying out of simple commands.

In addition to these well-known individually administered measures, there are a number of intelligence tests that are administered to large groups of children. Whereas they conserve time and energy on the part of the testers, they are generally less accurate in depicting intelligence since they tend to rely more on the child's reading and writing ability and include items that are of necessity more shallow.

A child's score on this kind of test represents a comparison of his performance with that of the many children of his age on whom the instrument was standardized. The mental age thus determined may be compared to the child's chronological age and his relative IQ (intelligence quotient) determined: $IQ = MA/CA \times 100$. Therefore, the child with an IQ of 100 has a mental age equal to his chronological age. IQ's in the 90–110 range are usually considered normal. Below 90 is considered indicative of subnormal intelligence; those exceeding 110 may indicate above-average intelligence. (See Table 8-1.)

Since IQ tests are measures of performance, the effects of nonintellectual factors are apt to influence the child's score. Because of these factors it is probably rare that a child is able to perform in terms of his full abilities. The social and ethnic membership of the tester and testee may influence test performance because of language differences, anxiety level, and the group on which the measure was standardized.

Table 8-1 Distribution of IQ's in Children Tested in the Standardization of the Stanford–Binet Test in 1937

IQ	Percent	Classification
160–169	0.03	
150–159	0.2	Very superior
140–149	1.1	
130–139	3.1	Superior
120–129	8.2	
110–119	18.1	High average
100–109	23.5	Normal or average
90–99	23.0	
80–89	14.5	Low average
70–79	5.6	Borderline defective
60–69	2.0	
50–59	0.4	Mentally defective
40–49	0.2	
30–39	0.03	

Source: Reprinted by permission from L. M. Terman and M. A. Merrill, *Stanford-Binet Intelligence Scale* (Boston: Houghton Mifflin Company, 1960). Copyright © 1960, Houghton Mifflin Company. Used by permission.

Familiarity with test materials and procedures can also be a factor. The child who has had previous experience with testing or even with reading the "brainteasers" that are so common in children's magazines would have an advantage over the child to whom this is foreign material.

A teacher told of a child being given a test who was asked "What is a faucet?" The child made no attempt to answer this question. Because of her dealings with the child, she felt he understood this concept and so after the examiner had completed her task, she asked the child where he got water at his house. From a "spigot" was his answer. It was located outside the house and they had to wrap the pipes with rags in the winter time so the water would not freeze. They also have a special key, the operation of which the child could explain, for opening the spigot so their water would not be stolen. The child could reproduce on paper the pattern of pipes that led from the ground, under the house, to the "spigot." The youngster, however, was recorded as having no concept of "faucet," because the word was foreign to him.

The interest level of the testee and the degree of cooperation he lends to the testing situation can affect his score. This could be contingent on his activities immediately preceding the testing session, his general state of health, or the buildup he has received relative to the testing exercise. Even such superficial circumstances as the temperature or lighting level of the testing room, the comfortableness of his clothing, and whether or not he is hungry could conceivably affect his performance, hence his score.

How consistent is IQ? Realizing the many variables which may affect it, one wonders. Terman (Terman and Merrill, 1937), one of the authors of the Stanford-Binet Scale, indicated that chances are one in two that the IQ will increase as much as 6 points or decrease as much as 4 points over a period of time. The chances of larger shifts are not so great; and the older the child, the less the chance of fluctuation.

Repeated testings of a large group of children between the ages of 6 and 18 revealed that the IQ of over half the children "showed a variation of 15 or more points . . . at some time during the school years, and a third of the group varied as much as 20 points" (Honzik et al., 1948). Such variation in IQ scores may be attributed to the high dependence of such scores on external factors already discussed, the increasing "test wiseness" of many children, and the "catch-up" characteristic of enrichment education in the light of the culture-tied IQ tests.

What of the predictive value of intelligence tests? Consider the composite test scores of the children mentioned in the just-cited study. It can readily be seen that prediction of later test scores based on early ones is not high over a span of several years. But there is a fairly high relationship between children's test scores and their school performance, partly due to the similarity in the kinds of behavior assessed in both cases. The predictive value of IQ tests in relation to such fields of endeavor as music and manual arts and trades is much less accurate than for such academic areas as literature or mathematics (Mussen et al., 1969).

Think Back

To some standardized tests you took as a child:
How you felt.
What you thought about the test and results.
If they were easy or hard.
If they were fun or not.
If you were scared or not.

What does this say, then, about the great dependence placed on measures of intelligence? What are the implications in the classroom where a teacher treats children in terms of the IQ's recorded in their cumulative folders? What may be the outcomes of sharing with a child's parents his IQ score? How about telling the child himself? To carry the situation even further, how fair is it to group children on the basis of IQ; to grant or deny college entrance on the basis of test scores; to determine fitness for a job solely on such a basis? Such questions must be dealt with by those who work with children.

The IQ score is a psychological measure originally intended for use by the psychologist but which has been the subject of flagrant misuse by both parents and teachers in what Flescher (1972) has called the "illegitimate numbers racket." He charges IQ identification aggravates the process of dehumanization in schools, determining under- and over-achievement, forming the basis for ability grouping, and contributing to the pressurized character of the learning environment.

IQ tests intended for individual administration by psychologists quite often become group administered by teachers. Group-administered tests considerably diminish the confidence that can be placed in a given score, which is at best an indirect measure based on brief observations and not actually a full measure of intelligence. Performance in a testing group may be influenced by the child's mistakes in blacking in the blanks on the machine-scored answer sheet; illness or test anxiety; reading disabilities which decrease comprehension and increase reaction time; cultural deprivation factors; undetected auditory or visual problems; misinterpretation of verbal instructions; negative attitude toward test; emotional difficulties; suppressed self-esteem which may lower effort or encourage guessing; and teacher error in instructions or timing.

Flescher maintains that teachers who are less interested in "getting a child's number" may find themselves able to teach the "unteachable" when they rely on good professional judgment rather than overdepending on preexisting information in the pupil's personal folder.

There seems to be a natural tendency to treat persons in terms of our perception of them. In one study (Rosenthal and Jacobson, 1968), elementary school teachers were told that according to test results, five children in each of their classes were expected to show unusual intellectual gains during the school year. The children had actually been selected at random and therefore presumably differed from their classmates only in the minds of their teachers. Group IQ tests administered by the teachers during the school year revealed a gain by the first and second grade high expectancy children significantly higher than that of their classmates. While results of this study do not allow us to dismiss individual differences and innate capacity, they do point up the importance of expectations in the student-teacher relationship.

Range in IQ is wide, becoming apparent during the school years because of the great emphasis on learning. It is during the middle childhood years that most parents first gain some insight into their child's learning abilities, as he is compared with other children his age. Parents who place undue pressure for achievement on their children who scored high or those who degrade the child who has not scored average or above may actually create new problems with learning. The knowledge of one's measured IQ may affect the self-concept, perhaps causing depression because of a low score or on the other hand unrealistic feelings of self-worth over a high quotient. Teachers who hold that IQ is a completely valued and reliable measure, highly indicative of one's potential for success in academics or the world, have failed to consider the role of other factors in the learning process.

The whole area of testing has received closer scrutiny in the past few years, as we have realized the many nonintellectual factors that influence one's test performance. If mere scores computed mechanically are the prime determiners of a child's destiny, something is basically and drastically wrong with our concern for the future of our race. If, on the other hand, test scores are used not mainly as predictors of behavior but as tools to reveal differences in perceptual functioning, mental operations, level of mental development, and conceptual style and in turn as the basis for developing educational strategies suited to the needs of individual children, they are vital in our quest for a better society. The limitations of present-day intelligence tests, largely developed and standardized on middle-class white children, impose limitations on any comparison among socioeconomic, ethnic, or racial groups in the population.

There is no direct evidence that supports the view that there is an innate difference between members of different racial groups (Council of the Society for Psychological Study of Social Issues, 1969). When cultural and educational backgrounds are comparable, differences in inteligence scores diminish markedly. Since social inequalities prevent members of all races from leading comparable lives, a more accurate assessment of the contribution of heredity to intelligence will be possible only when more equitable social conditions for all races have existed for several generations. We know that environmental factors begin to impinge on development from the moment of conception, resulting in a lifelong interaction between heredity and environment.

Because of the importance of environmental as well as heredity factors in the total picture of intellectual development, it is well to look at these as we explore improved functioning. (See Chapter 2.) First hand experiences in which children can be physically involved and about which they are encouraged to talk both to other children and to adults allow them to be active participants in learning which seems to be important. Improved physical health allows children to take advantage of experiences around them: e.g. freedom from disease, nutritious food, rest, appropriate shelter and clothing to assure protection and security. Provision for mental health of children allows them to expend energy in learning: e.g., good feelings about themselves, ability to delay gratification and think in terms of long-range goals rather than short-term goals, adults who believe in the importance and worth of the child. Finally, if the environment offers work and play materials which the child can use to increase curiosity, discovery, creativity, and enjoyment, he will be in a better position to reach his intellectual potential.

The Development of Reasoning

In any discussion of intelligence or cognitive development, it is necessary to examine the work of Jean Piaget, a Swiss psychologist who has worked with children since 1920 and has published over 30 books. Accepting a position in the Binet Laboratory in Paris in 1920 to develop a standardized French version of certain English reasoning tests, he became interested in how children thought. As he tested them he found their incorrect answers far more interesting that their correct ones. Noting that among children of like age the same wrong answers occurred, he concluded that older children were not just smarter than younger ones but that "the thought of younger children was qualitatively different from that of older ones" (Ginsberg and Opper, 1969, p. 3).

He also came to feel that the standardized test was not the best way to study intelligence, and adapted the psychiatric method to examine children's thinking processes. In this approach the course of questioning was determined by the way a child answered rather than by some preconceived plan. Instead of directing him to choose from among given answers, Piaget

Children have their own ways of thinking things through.

followed the child's own line of thought, pursuing interesting answers given. Because of the deficient verbal abilities of abnormal children, he incorporated the manipulation of certain materials into the questioning sessions. This procedure was later applied to work done with normal children. Since his clinical method required a great deal of time with each subject, much of Piaget's early work is based on the observation of small numbers of children. His more recent work has involved large numbers of children.

Because of his interest in logic Piaget formulated a system of viewing children's thinking in terms of certain elementary logical operations. He coined the term "genetic epistemology" to express his idea that intellectual development is firmly rooted in biological foundations (Pulaski, 1971). He saw psychology as the link between his two great interests: biology, the study of life; and epistemology, the study of knowledge.

Ginsberg and Opper (1969) have presented the basic ideas or points of view that guided Piaget's experimentation on the nature of intelligence—its content, structure, and function. More recent contributions underscore the application of Piaget's theory to educational methods (Elkind, 1976; Flavell, 1977; Wadsworth, 1978). We shall draw heavily from their writing in the next section.

Defining of Terms

Piaget, with a broad flexible definition of intelligence, believes cognition to be a "mode of adaptation to the world" beginning with man's biological nature, innate reflexes, and proceeding by invariant stages to abstract logical reasoning (Sigel, 1977, p. 15). Piaget's theory (Sigel, 1977) includes the following major facets: (1) developmental point of view, which focuses on orderly stages of intellectual growth, with learning capabilities defined at each stage; (2) description of how children acquire information about the physical world (number, quantity, time, space), the social world (morality, social conventions), and logical-mathematical understandings (classification, seriation, hypothetical-deductive reasoning); and (3) methodology that deals with how children think rather than with what they know.

Mental activity is a vital component of intelligence, according to Piaget. Knowledge does not come to the passive observer but is discovered and constructed through the activity of the child. Piaget is concerned with what the individual does in his interaction with his world. "The Piagetian man actively selects and interprets environmental information in the construction of his own knowledge rather than passively copying the information just as it is presented to his senses," and in addition, "reconstructs and reinterprets that environment to make it fit with his own existing mental framework." (Flavell, 1977, p. 6). This process is carried out through two "invariant functions."

The *function* factor in intelligence is of biological origin. All species of life have two basic tendencies or "invariant functions" which define the very essence of intelligent behavior: organization and adaptation. Organization refers to the "tendency for all species to systematize or organize their processes into coherent systems which may be either physical or psychological" (Ginsberg and Opper, 1969, p. 17). On the physical level, the fish has many structures that must interact and be coordinated to allow the fish to function in water. The infant has the physical ability to look at objects and to grasp objects. Through development, he organizes his looking and grasping structures into a higher-order system which enables him to grasp something at the same time he looks at it, thus illustrating a higher psychological level of organization.

Adaptation is the tendency of all organisms to adjust to their environment and is composed of the twin processes *assimilation* and *accommodation*. Adaptation methods vary from organism to organism and within a given individual from one stage in development to the next. *Assimilation* is seen as one deals with the environment in terms of his structures: a child picking up a toy assimilates it into the framework of his grasping structure. *Accommodation* involves the transformation of his structures in response to the environment: the child's fingers accommodate to the shape of the toy. Using his knowledge about sand and heat, a child may construct his own concept of desert.

A child might "assimilate a seashell as a cup, that is the child is pretending that a shell is a cup or is interpreting an external object in terms of his way of thinking about things." Most play is assimilation. Accommodation means taking into account the real properties of an object or event and behaving mentally accordingly. The child who imitates the gestures or actions of a parent or teacher is "accommodating" his mental apparatus to this new behavior.

Flavel (1977) further illustrates the interrelationship of these processes by suggesting that if you see a symmetrical ink blot, you might suppose it looked like a bat. This would mean you had "accommodated to certain physical features of the blot and used these as the basis for assimilating the blot to your internal concept of a bat." Of course, you did not just discover a bat in the blot, he continued, but rather you had to already have a conception of a bat in your cognitive repertoire or you would not have interpreted the blot as you did. The blot had to have some bat-like qualities to which you could accommodate and you had to have a bat conception into which you could assimilate the blot. There is continuous interaction between the internal cognitive system and the external environment in the construction and use of knowledge. This accommodation-assimilation model accounts in part for development and movement to higher stages of cognitive levels. Each transaction causes a stretch, which allows the child to change a bit and thus be ready for slightly different or more stretch adaptation, another time. After each such interaction, the child is different or new in some way in his approach to himself and his world. This development, of course, is slow and gradual.

The *content* aspect of intelligence refers to what a person thinks about, "the terms in which he contemplates a given problem." When a mechanic is asked what makes a car go, he talks about explosion of gas, movement of pistons, and transfer of power. But a child might talk about the horses inside the car or how the car feels about the matter of going: it goes because it wants to or has somewhere to go. The content with which a child works is quite different from that of the mechanic, because he has had different experiences and he uses his memory in a different way: he does not consciously "rehearse" things in order to remember them.

Structure, like content and unlike function, changes with age, and it is this development with which Piaget is chiefly concerned. Structures are the "organizational properties of intelligence, organizations created through functioning and inferable from the behavioral contents whose nature they determine . . . mediations imposed between the invariant functions on the one hand and the variegated behavior contents on the other hand" (Flavell, 1963, p. 7).

Structure in intelligence refers to both physical mechanisms and automatic behavioral reactions such as reflexes. For example, humans inherit a nervous system and sensory organs that are unlike those of the fish. The fact that our vision is binocular and our perception three-dimensional affects our intelligence. The role of reflexes or automatic patterns of nervous behavior is minor in human intelligence since during the first few days of life reflexes are modified by experience into a new type of mechanism, psychological structure, which is not hereditary. These psychological structures are formed through a complex interaction between biological and experiential factors.

In an attempt to explain a particular phenomenon, a child may say that one object sinks because it is heavy, while another sinks because it is light. Certain structural properties are responsible for this faulty content.

> First the child is *phenomenistic* in the sense that his cognitive structure is so organized that the surface appearance of things are unattended to; his thought is dominated by the environmental qualities which strike him first and move vividly—in this case the lightness or heaviness of the object. Second, he fails to relate in a logical way successive, cognitive impressions, thus, heaviness and lightness are successively involved as explanatory principles with no thought to the contradiction involved, as though the need to reconcile opposing impressions were not a characteristic of his cognitive structure. (Flavell, 1963, pp. 17–18.)

Cognitive change is inevitable, as the organism adapts repeatedly, with each adaptation setting the stage for the next one. Not everything, however, can be assimilated by an organism at a given point in his development. He can take in only that reality which his current structure can assimilate without drastic change.

The term *schema* plays an important role in the account of cognitive development: "an established pattern of a meaningful, repeatable psychological unit of intellectual behavior or its prerequisites" (Maier, 1969, p. 106). Schemas form a structural system, not tied to any one developmental level, through which incoming data may be assimilated. They are labeled by the behavior sequences to which they refer: sucking, prehension, sight in infancy, and in middle childhood there is a "schema of intuitive qualitative correspondence" (Flavell, 1963).

But schemas are more than simply action sequences: the grasping schema is more than grasping behavior. It implies a specific cognitive structure—an "organized disposition to grasp objects on repeated occasions." The idea of schema means that a change had been made in the child's overall cognitive organization so that the new "behavioral totality" has become a part of the child's intellectual skills.

Even though he grants that individual differences in intelligence exist, Piaget does not stress them. He is interested in describing the general form of thought, not in setting norms or determining IQ. He places little emphasis on such emotions as anxiety, although he recognizes that emotions influence thought and represent the "energizing or motivational aspect of intellectual activity" (Ginsberg and Opper, 1969, p. 15). He began his work with concern for verbal communication and moral judgment. More recently he has stressed understanding of various scientific and mathematical concepts: movement, speed, one-to-one correspondence, time, causality.

Piaget's Periods of Cognitive Development

Piaget conceptualized stages, or phases, of cognitive development. The sequence of the stages is invariant, all children passing through each in the same order. However, the speed with which a child moves from one phase to another varies among children. The age norms assigned each stage are only approximate, depending on such factors as the growth-speed of the child, the nature of his social environment, and his physical condition. Development is a continuous process. There are no sudden shifts from one stage to another; each stage grows out of the one before and serves as a foundation for the one following. Cognitive development is gradual and continuous, as is physical development. The stages are not all "pure"; that is, children may exhibit a number of cognitive behaviors simultaneously—some characteristic of one stage, others representative of a higher level of function. In each phase there is a repetition of processes of the previous level in a different form of organization (schema) (Maier, 1969). Each child is unique and progresses at his own rate in this realm of development.

In various presentations of Piaget's work, and in his own writings, there is inconsistency in the labels applied to periods and stages of development. This in no way detracts from the constancy of the cognitive behavior changes which occur as the child grows; rather this informality may reflect the idea that the stages, as such, are simply abstracted to aid developmental analysis rather than "concrete immutables actually engraved in ontogenesis" (Flavell, 1963, p. 86). The following outline is from Flavell, who presents three main periods. Periods may be divided into subperiods and these into stages and substages.

I. *Period of sensory-motor intelligence* (0 to 2 years)
   During this period the infant moves from a "neonatal, reflex level of complete self-world undifferentiation to a relatively coherent organization of sensory-motor actions vis-à-vis his immediate surroundings" (p. 86). This organization does not involve symbolic manipulation, but only perceptual and motor adjustments. Six major stages are described for this period.

II. *Period of preparation for and organization of concrete operations* (2–11 years)

A. Preoperational representations (2 to 7 years)

Characterized by egocentric thinking expressed through transductive reasoning, juxtaposition, syncretism, realism, artificialism, animism.

1. Beginnings of representational thought (2–4 years)
2. Simple representations or intuitions (4–5½ years)
3. Articulated representations or intuitions (5½–7 years)

B. Concrete operations (7–11 years)

Characterized by logical thought in relation to concrete things; use of operations of classification, seriation, hierarchal arrangement; emergence of the schema of reversibility; assumption that mental activities depend largely on perception, yet child is not tied to phenomenalistic appearance.

III. *Period of formal operations* (11–15 years)

During this period the adolescent learns to deal with pure possibility, abstractions, propositional statements. Where the concrete operational child can deal effectively only with the reality before him, the formal operational individual is not bound in this way.

The first stage, sensory-motor (birth to about two years) is characterized by a significant achievement: object permanence, an understanding that objects continue to exist even though they cannot be seen. The child becomes more exploratory and curious and works at solving problems through organized, purposeful behavior. Increasing physical control (sitting, standing, walking) gives the child a new perspective of the world. Near the end of the period, the child shows capacity for primitive symbolic representations which ushers in the semiotic function: ability to use language, signs and symbols to express thought. No longer will the child have to depend on motoric exploration alone.

The child moves into the second stage: preoperational level, from two to seven years, approximately. Flavell (1963) defines this period as "preoperational representation." The first representational activities, *deferred imitation,* are seen in the sensory-motor child. For example, Piaget described one of his children imitating the actions of a temper tantrum she had witnessed in another child on the preceding day. Symbolic functioning, however, is the real breakthrough during the first part of this period. This symbolic function is manifested in a variety of ways: symbolic play, drawings, verbal evocation (ability to talk about events not occurring at the time). Developmentally, the use of graphic symbols is the most advanced: cues, identification of an object based on seeing only a part of it, e.g., recognizing a tree from its leaf or its silhouette; symbol, a stylized cue, e.g., a map or a road sign; sign, arbitrary abstractions that represent something else, e.g., letters, numbers, words.

Sigel (1977) labels the two-to-seven-year stage the Preoperational Phase and distinguishes between the early Preoperational Period (two to four years) and the Intuitive Phase (four to seven years). During this time two cognitive invariants are acquired: qualitative (as different from quantitative) identities and functions. That is, the child knows that even when you roll a ball of clay into a different shape it is the same clay. He may also think it is more or less than the other ball of clay not so transformed. He cannot yet logically deal with the quantity of the clay, but he has an understanding of its "same thingness." This was also true of a wire bent into various shapes. Typically, a five-year-old readily accepted the fact that it was the same wire, but did not accept that it was always the same length.

These children are also able to understand that change in one thing tends to be associated with change in another, but cannot quantify that change. In one experiment, using strings and springs and weights, the children understood that when weights were shifted, the spring would lengthen. They could not understand that the string was shortened to the same extent that the spring was lengthened, only that change occurred. In another test, the children were asked to give different amounts of "meat balls" to fish of varied sizes: the middle sized one was to get twice as much as the little one, the big one was to get three times as much as the little one. Five-year-olds could give the bigger fish more food, but could not make quantitative decisions about how much more. The important thing that happens to the child centers around the use of language and symbolic functioning. The child does not have to "think" through direct motor action as he did during the preceding stage. However, preoperational thought is not mature thought, rather it is perceptual-dominant.

Movement from Level to Level

Maturation. According to Piaget's theory, development from one stage or level to the next involves four processes: maturation, experience, social transmission and equilibration, which means finding a link between things already understood and new ideas. With the maturation of the central nervous system, cognitive abilities increase. Both motor coordination and the ability to speak are dependent on maturation of physical structures. Pulaski (1971) points out that just as the child makes use of developing muscles to walk, run, and climb, he also uses and exercises changing cognitive structures. She maintains that "a child is not capable of thinking like an adult because he simply does not have the logical structures, the organization of thought, and the methods of reasoning which would enable him to deal with adult problems" (Pulaski, 1971, p. 9). Maturation is vital in the development of such cognitive structures.

Experience. Experience, both *physical* and *logico-mathematical,* is another important factor. *Physical experiences* such as using magnets, rolling tires, playing baseball, and lifting weights are examples of direct sensory-motor activities often lacking among many urban children.

> The child who has never seen or smelled a fresh orange . . . who has never learned to climb a tree or balance himself on a railing, has missed some of the tremendously complex sensory and motor experiences that go to make up the

background of school learning. For such a child, pictures of trees and oranges in a book do not have much meaning. He must go back and explore the rich world of childhood—touching, smelling, climbing, digging—before he is ready to settle down to books full of squiggly, meaningless symbols called "letters." (Pulaski, 1971, p. 10).

Children who have missed smelling the orange or climbing a tree have often had other experiences of which the middle-class child or teacher is ignorant. If these experiences are known and built on, cognitive development might not be as hampered as it is when we are uncertain about or fearful of dealing with a past so different from our own. The principal of an elementary school in Arizona told of a first-grader who had never spoken a word since beginning school. His teacher referred to him as "that dumb Indian boy." During the spring the whole school planned and staged a world's fair for which each class was to study a country or culture and prepare exhibits and programs related to their study. The little boy's class was to learn about the Navajo culture, and one member pointed out that "the dumb Indian boy" was very adept at the difficult hoop dance. This was his main contribution to the program his class gave for every other class in the school. And following the first performance, he began talking. He hasn't stopped yet; and nobody since refers to him as dumb! All experiences or knowledge of disadvantaged children are not as acceptable as the hoop dance! However, we must be ready to accept and use to the fullest whatever experiences or knowledge a child brings.

Logico-mathematical experiences foster knowledge that is a result of mental actions performed on objects rather than as a direct result of perceiving objects. Piaget (1964, p. 12) cites the experience of a friend about age 5 which illustrates this concept:

> He was seated on the ground in his garden and he was counting pebbles. Now to count these pebbles he put them in a row and he counted them one, two, three up to ten. Then he finished counting them and started to count them in the other direction. He began by the end and once again found he had ten. He found this marvelous. . . . So he put them in a circle and counted them that way and found ten once again.

Ginsberg and Opper (1969, pp. 170–171) interpret the experience:

> Through repetitions of counting and recounting, or arranging and rearranging, the child learned an important property of number: it stays the same despite different order of counting and despite physical arrangements. In this case, Piaget maintains, the child did not discover a physical property of pebbles; rather he learned something about his own actions (logico-mathematical experience) and only secondarily from the world of things (physical experience).

Social Transmission. Social transmission is a third component of cognitive development. This includes instruction or explanation given by parents or teachers, information learned reading a book, discussions with peers, or imitation of a model. The worth of social transmission is, however, contingent on the possession of certain cognitive structures.

Although language is one of the important social factors, Piaget believes that logical thinking is really born out of action rather than out of language: images are part of the figurative aspect of cognition gained through imitation of actions of persons and things, symbolic play. Deaf children who may speak very little and hear not at all are capable of mental operations—logical thinking—when they have reached a certain age. Furthermore, even children who verbally identify "blue triangle" or "red circle" are still unable to classify or use "operations." All this points to the importance of action in cognitive growth.

Equilibration. The fourth factor to be considered is equilibration. Pulaski (1971) pointed out that just as there must be a physiological state of equilibrium between exercise and rest, or hunger and overeating, so there must be a mental state of equilibrium between what the child understands and what he experiences in his environment. Piaget (1962, p. 120) defines equilibration as a "compensation for an external disturbance" (Piaget, 1970, p. 725) accomplished through activity. Equilibration, then, is not a state of rest, not an exact automatic balance, but alludes to movement, change. "Compensation is the annulling of a transformation" (Piaget, 1962, p. 120) which implies the idea of reversibility, characteristic of all operations of intelligence. It is not the same as reversibility (final state) but is, rather, a self-regulating process that leads to the final state. It is the means by which progress from less mature to more mature ways of perceiving and thinking is brought about.

For example, the cognitive structures guaranteeing conservation are achieved in a four-step equilibration process (Flavell, 1963). When a child watches a clay ball change by several successive transformations into a sausage shape, he makes different responses, depending on available structures. In Steps One and Two, the subject concentrates on only one property of the object, length or width; he cannot take both into consideration. At first he centers on one or the other, later he substitutes centration on one property for centration on the other as continuing changes force him to account for differences. Step Three is an intermediate stage between clearcut nonconservation and clear-cut conservation, Step Four, when the subject understands that the change in length is compensated for by a change in width. This is what happens. But how does it happen? Piaget suggests that continuous performance at Step One makes transition to Step Two more probable; performance at Step Two makes transition to Step Three more probable and so on, until a behavior is reached (conservation of mass in this case) which is a permanent and best solution to the problem. Berlyn (1970, p. 69) suggested this definition of equilibration: "a form of learning, limited by maturational factors, that is motivated by conflict and reinforced by conflict resolution."

While Piaget believes that environment exerts influence on the child and his intellectual development, he does not see behavior as simply molded by the environment. The energetic growing child is not passive, but active, and seeks contact with people and things around him. His curiosity leads him to search out increased levels of stimulation. He does not simply register a stimulus; he interprets it. It is this interpretation that affects his behavior. Thus the same situation may elicit quite different behavior or reactions in one child than in another.

Middle Childhood Thinking

We will now focus specifically on cognitive development and thinking during middle childhood years. At the beginning of this time, the child is in the intuitive stage of the preoperational period. At the close he will be ready for the period of formal operations which will characterize his thinking during the rest of his growth.

Preoperational Thinking (4 to 7 years)

The thought of the preoperational child is characterized by his *egocentrism,* meaning he cannot take the point of view of another person but extends his own immediate view to all others. Egocentrism is not to be confused with being egotistical, which means selfish or self-centered. The young child feels he has captured *the* view of the world and that everyone shares a like view.

The egocentric child believes, for instance, that the moon moves along with him, that mountains change as he walks around them. He makes no real effort to adapt his speech to the needs of his listeners. He may speak in words or phrases that have no meaning for the listener and be surprised when he is not understood, or when his stand is challenged. He feels no necessity to justify his reasonings to others, nor to look for contradictions in his logic. He believes that other persons know what he knows and see what he sees.

He cannot imagine that a thing looks different to a person who is seeing it from another perspective. The "three mountains experiment" (Figure 8-1) illustrates this. The child sits at one side of a table where there are three cardboard mountains of different heights and sizes mounted on a square in the center of the table. A doll is moved around the table and the child is asked to tell or show from pictures or drawings what the doll sees from various vantage points. The preoperational child cannot do this. He believes the doll sees what he sees, no matter the angle. The concrete oper-

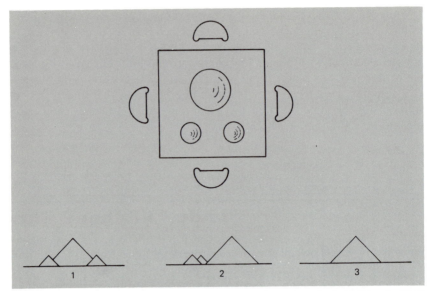

Figure 8-1. From *The Origins of Intellect: Piaget's Theory* by John L. Phillips, Jr. W. H. Freeman and Company. Copyright © 1969.

ational child can perform this task with confidence and accuracy only toward the end of the period.

The ability to see things from the other person's point of view while at the same time retaining one's own point of view, and the corresponding ability to be logically consistent, are acquired gradually. This is made possible through repeated interactions in which children are compelled to take account of the viewpoint of others—in play and in work.

The preoperational child is trapped by *centration*, or the inability to decentrate. That is, he can deal only with one characteristic of an object at a time, so neglects other aspects, and therefore makes judgments intuitively rather than logically. For example, when a child at this stage is presented with two balls of clay which he perceives to be the same, and one ball is rolled into a sausage shape, he no longer perceives them to be the same. His reasoning: one is longer (or higher), therefore it is more than before. A child in this period of development matches two lines of pennies in a one-to-one fashion. But when he sees one line elongated, or one line bunched together, he no longer believes there are the same number of pennies in both lines—simply because one line is longer than the other. He changes his opinion because of his new perception. He cannot evaluate both line length and object density simultaneously.

In the water and beaker problem, where water is transferred from a short, fat beaker to a tall, thin one, the child centers on either the new taller height or the new narrower width and makes his decision that there is more or less water in the new container than in the old one. This is true even when the transfer has been made in his presence as he watched.

Not only is centering a problem when dealing with objects, but also in dealing with actions. The child at this stage reacts to states, rather than transformations from one state to another, which makes preoperational thought static and immobile. If a child is shown an illustration of a bar in an upright position, then one in which the bar has fallen to a horizontal position, he finds it difficult to draw the bar in various positions of the fall—as a series of still pictures. He sometimes depicts the intervening state by drawing the bar bent into a right angle.

He thinks only in terms of the end stage or end product of an experience, rather than in terms of changing states. A car toy that gets to the finish line first is fastest, with no regard for distance covered; work finished first is easiest. The child has little notion of variation or relativity; for him there is always a "best" and a "worst."

The preoperational child does not yet use certain mental operations but, instead, depends on his perception of things. Thinking at this stage of development is marked by *transduction*—a process by which the child reasons from particular to particular, rather than by induction—a process by which one moves from particular to universal—or by deduction—a process by which one moves from a generalization to a particular. The concept of transductive thinking is a logical explanation for many illogical or unrelated reasons that children may give for the same effect: "a large boat floats because it is heavy, a small one because it is light, a raft because it is flat, a needle because it is thin" (Beard, 1969, p. 47).

Phillips (1969) chose two illustrations to point this up. Jacqueline Piaget saw her father getting hot water, so concluded he was going to shave. To the child, it is not different to think "Daddy's shave requires hot water" and to think "hot water requires Daddy's shave." The child moves from particular to particular. On another occasion, Jacqueline wanted a doll dress from a cold room upstairs. Both her mother and father refused to get it for her because it was too cold. After a silence she said: "Not too cold . . . in room." When asked why it was not too cold in the room, she replied: "Get dress." Phillips pointed out that here again the child is reasoning from particular to particular: "a warm room makes it possible to get the dress" seems to her no different than "getting the dress makes the room warm." This helps explain childish insistence in getting what he wants. If he is told that he can go outside when it is "not raining" he might reason that "going out to play" will make it "not raining." His insistence is based on reasoning that is qualitatively different from that of the adult.

Juxtaposition, another characteristic of children's thought, deals with the child's tendency to concentrate on the parts, rather than to see the parts in relation to the whole. A group of children asked to complete "because" sentences did not give reasons for behavior but, instead, seemed to reverse cause and effect: "I've lost my pen because . . . I'm not writing." "The man fell off his bicycle because . . . he broke his arm." Rather than giving a cause for the effect stated, they more often stated another effect which in some cases might have caused the original situation (Beard, 1969, p. 59). Young children asked to draw a bicycle drew separate parts scattered all over the page—next to each other but not related. In the preoperational period, children do not consider the connections but simply place events side by side.

In contrast, children's thinking is also characterized by *syncretism,* causing them to link together unrelated things because of the tendency to see the whole with no regard for the parts that make it up. Syncretism accounts for the child's inability to understand the underlying meanings of proverbs. Instead they seem to catch on to one word or phrase that is familiar and assign that meaning to the whole proverb. For example, a child might explain the meaning of "make hay while the sun shines" by saying "The sun makes the hay dry." He knows the sun is hot and drying and so applies this concept to the whole saying.

Early childhood thinking is marked by *nominal realism:* these children cannot distinguish clearly between the symbol and the thing symbolized. The symbol becomes real: dreams "come in the window"; the name of the moon is in the moon. Dreams and names, thoughts and imaginary friends are marked with this same realness. Play has all the elements of reality.

Childhood thinking is marked by *artificialism,* which causes children to think of natural events in the world as caused or made by people. For instance, a child saw the dawn beginning and said, "Now, they've put on the light outside." Another characteristic is *animism,* by which they attribute characteristics of life and will to all objects. One boy remarked after having missed the train: "Doesn't the train know we're not on it?" Another child, hearing the wind in the trees, remarked: "The trees must have something to say to us today."

Reversibility is lacking in the thought of the preoperational child. A preoperational child cannot move from one point in thought to another and then move back through the operations to the beginning point. Prior to age 6 or 7, the child who has lost something searches for it in every room where he has been. The older child is able to sit still and think reflectively about where he has been and logically conclude where he may have left the lost item. He is able to reverse his actions in his thought.

During the preoperational period, a child has difficulty seeing whole-part relationships or the relation of a class and its subclasses. For example, he can answer correctly that there are ten flowers in a vase and that six of them are buttercups. But he also believes there are more buttercups than flowers, because there are only four flowers. In a box of wooden beads, some of which are white and some are brown, he knows there are four white ones and six brown ones, but he does not know there are more wooden beads than brown beads.

Because of their inability to consider a number of factors at the same time, preoperational children cannot make comparisons, so thinking is dominated by immediate impressions. These children find it difficult to stick to an opinion on a subject or a classification task. Opinions change as they get new perspectives. An example by Beard (1969) illustrates their need to act out their thinking in the absence of mental structures needed for such comparisons. A small square was drawn in the middle of a larger square of paper, and subjects were asked to draw the smallest and largest squares possible on this paper. Children in the preoperational period drew a square slightly smaller than the original one and another square a bit larger than the original one. In successive trials they drew smaller and larger squares but never arrived at the "largest square possible" concept. Children in the Period of Concrete Operations, over age 7 or 8, drew a very tiny square, then another following the outline of the paper. The younger children seemed to need to find out through experimentation how much space would be required for their succession of squares. Each time they tried it, they saw more space and so drew larger squares. They were depending solely on "how it looked" to guide their actions.

It must be remembered that children can use language quite well. They can use appropriate sounding words without understanding the meaning and may understand and use words in ways quite different from adults. These children are literal and concrete in interpretation of verbal directions. One can never be sure a child understands what is being said simply because he can repeat the words he hears!

Period of Concrete Operations (7 to 11 years)

Thought of children during the Period of Concrete Operations is marked by mental actions or operations. An "operation" is defined as: "an action which takes place within the imagination" (Beard, 1969); "an action that can return to the starting point, and that can be integrated with other actions also possessing this feature of reversibility . . . [and] is internalized" (Phillips, 1969, p. 53); "activities of the mind, as opposed to the bodily activities of the sensory-motor period" (Pulaski, 1971, p. 53). Children at this stage of development seem to have in their command a coherent and integrated cognitive *system* with which they organize and manipulate the world around them (Flavell, 1963).

Throughout development, cognition is characterized by real action of the subject, external and observable in the case of the infant, but becoming more internalized, schematic, mobile, and abstract as the child develops. These internal representational cognitive actions form integrated systems of action which Piaget calls cognitive operations. There are many such operations: classification, seriation, hierarchal arrangement, numerical operations. Flavell (1963, p. 166) suggests as a "rule of thumb" that all actions implied by common mathematical symbols (+, −, ×, ÷, <, >) belong to the domain of intellectual operation. A "class" is not meaningful unless there is an understanding of the classification system: add classes to form supraordinate classes; subtract classes from one another; these are examples of such mathematical actions.

Reversibility is an operation that allows the child to return to the starting point in his thought. The concrete operational child is able to conserve, in part, because of this ability. At first he can simply know that in the clay problems, the sausage shape can be rolled back into a ball, which Piaget (1972) labels the "identity" reason. Nothing has been added or taken away; it is the same. With increasing experience, the child is able to use two other reasons for his stand: reciprocity and negation. He understands that the change in height is compensated for (reciprocity) by the change in the width of the beaker in the water problem. He also understands that there are actions which negate other actions, that it is possible to undo certain kinds of things. He can subtract; go back to the beginning. Water can be poured back into the original container.

A second operation is *classification*. Children in this stage of development no longer center on only one aspect, but can attend to more than one attribute simultaneously and so can solve the brown bead-white bead problem. They can also classify in an hierarchal order; that is, they are reaching the understanding that a class, animals for example, is made up of other sub classes, horses and dogs, and each of these may also be made up of other subclasses. Their ability to *decenter* fosters a flexible approach to thinking and allows solutions to class-inclusion problems, e.g., horses can be in the class of animals that are pets, or in the class of animals that work, or in a combination class of animals that are pets and work.

These children are able to classify objects, taking into account multiple characteristics. They are not confused by centering. They know a person can be a member of two classes (e.g., a person can be one who lives in Chicago and at the same time be one who lives in Illinois). Their ability to deal with multiple classification comes into play when they must solve such problems as: Choose an *even* number *between 11 and 19;* Name a *yellow* flower that *begins with* D. In order to answer they take into consideration two aspects or variables.

At first, children classify on the basis of structural similarities, "all have doors," and similarity of use, "you wear them all" (Sigel, 1976). As children grow older, they use "conceptual or categorical labels": buildings, clothing. Class-inclusion becomes more extensive as children grow older and gain more experience. When familiar items are dealt with, children earlier classify at a more mature level than when classifying unfamiliar items.

Seriation, another operation, is the ability to order elements of increasing or decreasing size. Concrete operational children seem to form a strategy for this, picking out the shortest stick, placing it, then picking the shortest stick from among those remaining and so on. Their ability to use mental operations can be seen in their ability to order a series of sticks after looking at them a bit and without physically comparing each stick with all the others. They can finish the task much more quickly than a younger child. During this period their skill increases so that they can order a set of numbers such as 1897, 1518, 2732, 2042. By the close of the period they can understand ordering that demands attention to two directions. For example, they can match age and birth dates and understand that *increasing* ages correspond to decreasing birth year numbers: a child who is a year *older* was born a year *earlier*.

Children at this stage can add new members to the seriation. They understand ordinal (first, second) and cardinal (one, two, three) numbers. They know that when they have placed the fifth one, there are exactly five sticks in place.

The concrete operational child can measure with reference to two or more axes: so he can locate a place on a map by using "A" and "37" as markers on the two edges. He understands symmetrical relationships: he has a brother and is a brother so that his brother also has a brother. He can also understand friends, enemies, participation in games.

Transivity is the ability to deduce that when A is greater than B and B is greater than C, then A is greater than C, without comparing A and C directly. Mary is taller than her sister Jane; Jane is taller than her cousin Joan. Who is tallest? The child must "discriminate the relevant variable," must focus on height, not relationship (Sigel, 1976, p. 75). He can skip one unit or one relationship and reach a logical conclusion.

By about age 7 the child conserves quantity (amount of space taken up by the object) but does not conserve weight until about age 9, and cannot conserve volume (how much water will be displaced; the ball and sausage) until much later Piaget (1972) places the ages much later: 8, 10, and 12 years respectively. Beard (1969, p. 84) reports an experiment in which 240 children from 40 schools were given two large glasses containing equal amounts of water. One glass was emptied into two smaller glasses and then into five still smaller glasses. Only 10 percent of the 6-year-olds were able to give correct responses as to the unchanged amount of water; 63 percent of the 9-year-olds did so. Even children who were able to state that two pints make one quart were not able to manage the above transformation. Less than 10 percent of the oldest children in this study knew that when two same-sized cans were immersed in water, they would displace the same amount of liquid even when one of the cans was filled with a heavier substance than the other.

This "gap" phenomena is referred to as *decalage*. Horizontal decalage connotes inability to deal logically with all phases of conservation in the early operational stage; vertical decalage refers to evidence of thinking at different levels of development in the same child (Wadsworth, 1978). With concepts with which they have had more experience, children are able to think more logically at an earlier age.

Flavell (1976) points to the quantitative attitude of the elementary school child as a distinguishing characteristic. This child seems to understand that certain problems have "precise, specific, potentially quantifiable solutions" (p. 85) and that these solutions can be reached with measurement units and actions. Such operations make conservation possible since the child can infer reality; he is no longer tied to perceived appearances. The child has the tools to discover when something *looks* larger and when it is really, really bigger.

Egocentricity decreases and the child can imagine views other than his own. Cooperation with others, therefore, increases and with it there is a decrease in isolated play or play simply in the company of others. He can now appreciate relationships, including those of his peers. Too, he has more opportunities for and support for competitive tasks and for discussions that will enable him to correct misconceptions. The concrete operational child can shift back and forth from his own viewpoint to that of other persons. Cooperation is possible, so he becomes interested in group games with rules and teams.

Even at the beginning of this period, the child has superior ability to communicate, as compared with the preoperational child. He is more accomplished in sending messages and in receiving them. He can follow directions and influence the behavior of others. He becomes increasingly skilled at eliciting desired behavior from others. This communication ability shows a developmental trend: first he is able to receive messages from others, then send messages to others, and finally send messages to himself. During this period, he becomes more able to exert control over his own behavior and speech. He learns during this period to initiate a behavior plan and follow it, to inhibit certain actions, to postpone or delay gratification and other self control strategies. Luria (1961) suggested that this regulation or control stems from speech development: its origin (other-internal, self-external, self-internal) and its nature: impulsive (does not carry symbolic meaning, e.g., a sudden loud noise inhibits behavior) or semantic which places emphasis on what is said, reasoning. Flavell's (1976) point is that while there is strong evidence for "some sort of general ability to guide or regulate ones own behavior by internal means," it is likely not verbal in its origin. An interesting test of this sort of control is the appearance of the children's game called "Simon Says."

It seems wise to point out again that development is all-of-a-part, continuous, ongoing. There are no sudden shifts; children gradually progress, acquire new structures, and exhibit different behavior. They are in constant transition—assimilating new information and making new accommodations. Experience and maturation play a part. The integrating principle is Piaget's concept of equilibration. There is a functional continuity uniting the highest forms of intellectual thought with certain primitive beginnings.

Limitations During Concrete Operations Period

We must also look at the limitations of thinking during this period. These are summarized by Beard (1969, pp. 85–88).

1. Limitations in verbal reasoning are still characteristic. *Question:* Edith is fairer than Susan; Edith is darker than Lily. Who is the darkest of the three? This is rarely solved before the age of twelve. The reasoning before that time seems to be: Edith and Susan are fair; Edith and Lily are dark. Therefore, Lily is darkest and Susan is fairest and Edith is in between. When concrete operational children deal with verbal propositions they consider one statement at a time, just as children in the intuitive stage (preoperational period) consider one characteristic at a time in dealing with objects.
2. When asked to explain absurdities the child cannot accept the premises and reason from them. The response of children to this problem is illustrative: "If ever I kill myself from despair, I won't choose a Friday, because Friday is a bad day and would bring me ill luck." Children's comments vary, but fail to account for the absurdity in the statement: "People can kill themselves any day, they don't need to kill themselves on Friday"; "he doesn't know if it will bring him ill-luck"; "perhaps Friday will bring him good luck." They do not see the contradiction in the statement because they do not see the situation from the speaker's point of view. Another illustration (*Developmental Psychology Today*, 1971, p. 266) supports this: "If a three-headed fish flew four miles the first day and five miles the second day, how many miles did it fly altogether?" Children find it impossible to deal with the basic question, but answer: "no fish can have three heads" or "fish can't fly."
3. Piaget could not persuade children to accept a suggested assumption unless he forced them to believe it as an affirmative. For example, he presented this problem to children: "If there were no air in this room would this (an object suspended by a string which was swung around rapidly) make a draft?" Most of the children answered yes. Why? "Because there is always air in the room." Even when Piaget insisted that all the air had been taken away, the children were sure there would still be some air left!
4. Failure to see general law. In explaining a thing they related only to that particular instance rather than having in mind a general rule. Another problem will illustrate this: "Paul says he saw a little cat eating a big dog. His friend says that is impossible because . . ." The child may answer: "because the cat is little and the dog is big." He cannot yet generalize: little cats do not eat big dogs.
5. Giving meaningful definitions is difficult. During the intuitive stage, the child defines in terms of the use to which an article is put: a mother cooks or takes care of you. In the concrete operations period, definitions first have to do with genus or class: a mother is a lady; later, definitions involve multiple classifications: a mother is a lady who has children. The following excerpt from a newspaper column (Battelle, 1967) illustrates this definition difficulty: One child asserted that she wouldn't be a doctor for anything. "I'm

going to be a plain ordinary mother." When it was pointed out to her that a mother often had to take care of sick children, she snapped: "I'm not going to have any children. I'm going to be a plain mother, I said." Later on, children are able to give more absolute definitions.

Period of Formal Operations
(11 years to Adulthood)

The period of formal operations is marked by changes. Instead of proceeding by trial and error, as a younger child would, the child at this stage of development makes plans based on hypotheses which he tests. He is able to foresee end results; "If this happens, then that is also likely to happen" or "If Jim had passed the ball instead of shooting, then . . ." In addition, according to Beard (1969, p. 13), he "sees all-embracing causes or explanations and general laws where the (younger) child merely describes or is content with partial explanations."

Cooperation with others seems to be the initiator of the period of formal operations. During adolescence, social life enters a new phase with increasing interchange involving examination of various points of view and discussion of their merits before joint control of the group is possible. This leads to greater mutual understanding and gives adolescents the habit of constantly placing themselves at points of view which they did not previously hold. They are able to make assumptions, to reflect, and to meditate. They are no longer tied to the here and now, but mentally survey many possibilities, form theories, and conceive new worlds! Their new interests make them critical of their own standards, so they begin to be more objective about themselves and of the practices and attitudes of various groups of which they are members.

Implications for Education

Those concerned with the education of children should be aware of certain pitfalls that exist because of the reasoning patterns, abilities, and inabilities of those at various developmental levels. The first is that if teaching or training is conducted only verbally and is not accompanied by meaningful activity, it will not be maximally effective. Children may repeat weight tables but be unable to use this knowledge in manipulating a scale or balance. They may memorize multiplication tables but fail to see the relationships they express. They may know equivalent capacities but not see that volume or capacity is conserved when sand or liquids are transferred from one size container to another. For greatest learning to occur, children should be motorically involved in the process.

The second is that a child's use of a word does not necessarily indicate he knows its normal meaning—nor that other children interpret a given word in the same context as does the speaker. Scott and Myers (1923) found that children in grades 5–8 could use words without really being able to define them: 41 percent could name two explorers but could not tell what an explorer was; 31 percent could name two nations but could not state with reasonable correctness what a nation was. They conclude a correct answer is not proof a child really knows what he seems to know and that children often have vague and incorrect notions of the terms they frequently use and hear.

Also, the child's speech is not always communicative. In Beard's (1969) study of school-age children, she found only about ⅔ of their speech could be called socialized or communicative. The rest was classified as repetition or monologue. Even in communicative speech there are serious deficiencies: children do not always attempt to explain events to one another; they often do not speak in terms of causes of events; they do not give proof or logical justification for what they have proposed; it does not usually occur to them that listeners will have contrary opinions.

The communicative problem is not totally the fault of the speaker. The listener contributes to his own misunderstanding: He always thinks he understands, even when the meaning is obscure. As the speaker's remarks bring forth a kind of free-association pattern in him, the listener assimilates the information he hears into his own scheme of things, which may have little relation to what is being communicated. He then mentally elaborates on what he has "heard."

In an experiment (Beard, 1969) pairs of subjects ages 6–8 were asked to tell stories to each other which had previously been told to one of each pair by the investigator. The following characteristics of these stories demonstrates that even communicative language has egocentric tendencies:

1. Faulty use of pronouns and demonstrative pronouns; missing antecedents.
2. Incorrect ordering of events.
3. Failure to point out how one event caused or was related to another.
4. Tendency to omit important features.
5. Little logical movement from one event to another in relating a series of events.

A study (Krauss and Glucksberg, 1972) which also illustrates this phenomenon utilized novel designs characterized by their low codeability (see Figure 8-2). The focus was the communication ability of children, taking into account the age and grade level of both speaker and listener. The speaker described a design (which was printed on a block) while the listener built a tower utilizing the blocks he thought were being described by the speaker. In an earlier study of nursery school children, the same researchers (Krauss and Glucksberg, 1969) attributed the poor communication to the idiosyncratic and egocentric nature of the transmitted

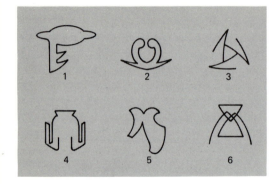

Figure 8-2. Designs children attempted to explain. (From "Some Characteristics of Children's Messages," R. M. Krauss and S. Glucksberg. Paper delivered at the meetings of the Society for Research in Child Development at Santa Monica, California, April 1969. Reprinted by permission of the authors.)

messages. While the block descriptions could not be interpreted correctly by adults nor other children, they resulted in extremely accurate behavior when quoted back to the subjects who had originally given the description. The message, then, was "meaningful," but private rather than social.

The children's abilities to communicate effectively with peers increased with age, either age of the speaker or of the listener. The eighth-graders had higher communication scores than first- or fifth-graders. Even kindergarteners' scores were higher when the listener was an eighth-grader than when he was a first-grader or another kindergartener, which points out the vital role of the listener in communication.

For effective communication to occur, the speaker must have a repertoire of concepts from which to draw, as in describing the novel designs. He must have word labels that can express such concepts (e.g., a saucer and snake in referring to Design 1; a spaceship in referring to Design 2; a triangle used to describe Design 3). He needs to know which of the concepts or encodings will be meaningful to the person to whom he is talking. For instance, describing a design as being similar to "Mommy's hat" would not prove meaningful since the other child's mother might not have a similar hat. With increasing age, children use more general concepts. Among eighth-graders about 35 percent of the concepts used in descriptions were employed by more than one person. The level of commonality was lower for fifth-graders and still lower for kindergarteners.

A look at what children talk about will also indicate educational implications. The following summary by Baker (1942) shows changes from grades 2 to 6.

1. Personal activities account for 61 percent of the conversations of second graders but for only 18 percent of that of sixth graders.
2. Current happenings in the world at large make up 60 percent of the discussion topics for sixth graders, but only 18 percent in the second grade.
3. Older children are more ready to deal with activities and people other than themselves or those they have witnessed. Personal experiences, things that had actually happened to them or things they had witnessed, accounted for

the topics of discussion of 83 percent of the second graders, but only 25 percent of the sixth graders.
4. Media such as books, magazines, radio, and personal conversations were the sources of discussion topics for 56 percent of the sixth graders but for only 16 percent of the second graders.
5. A change in the manner in which children carry on discussions showed 5 percent of the second graders continued the topic under discussion with their contributions, while 40 percent of the contributions from fourth graders and sixth graders could be so classified. There was little meeting of the mind among second graders, while about half of the discussion of the fourth and sixth graders was of this type.

As they grow, children become less egocentric in their conversation and more interested in people outside their families, outside their own realm of experience. They become involved with their peers and in the world they live in. This happens as they become able to take the other person's point of view and understand there are differences of opinion among people.

We must understand that experience plays a vital part in the development of the cognitive structures, which Piaget defines as underpinning the appearance of logical reasoning within the child. For example, it is easier for children to understand inclusion of one class within another if one talks about "children" including "boys" and "girls" instead of "flowers" including "yellow primroses" and "red poppies," or "wooden beads" including "brown ones" and "yellow ones." In a 1953 report (Beard, 1969) only 7 out of 60 six- and seven-year-olds understood the concept of "pilot's view" and could reproduce it in a drawing. By way of contrast, in her 1964 study (Beard, 1969) almost all eight-year-olds understood this. Perhaps this was due to: familiarity with aerial photographs on television, use of simple construction toys which are made into models on the floor, and study of diagrams of plans.

Experience is a tricky commodity—it varies with age and across social classes. It is likely that varied experiences are assimilated in different ways and therefore contribute to development and learning differently from child to child. One child was asked what he would do if he saw a train wreck occur. He said he would go for help. Another child said he would run away before anyone could blame him for the accident. In the light of their experiences, each child probably arrived at a logical and wise decision.

Zimiles (1968) reported the performance of advantaged and disadvantaged children on four classification tasks. In the two simpler tasks there were differences in performance, but these were not great. On the complex classification tasks, however, there was a gap between performance of the two groups, with advantaged children performing at higher levels. It was noted, however, that even when the children responded incorrectly, as did about three-fourths of the disadvantaged sample on the two-way classification test at kindergarten through third grade level, their incorrect responses seemed to be based on a strategy. The social-cultural backgrounds and therefore the experiences of the two groups were widely different.

Farnham-Diggory (1972) suggested that the child responds to training or education in the light of not only cognitive structures, but also in the light of previous experience which allows him to profit from or fail to profit from such training. In this experiment the child learned to construct string patterns and then learned their meaning: two strings laid vertically represented a river; a single string or two strings crossed over each other represented roads; a three-string design represented a bridge. Then the child was asked to "Make a bridge, going across a river, with a road on each side." One of the difficulties encountered by between 25 and 40 percent of both black and white children in lower-class or ghetto districts was failure to discriminate between short strings (used for underpinnings on the bridge) and long strings (used for all other parts of the puzzles). If the child failed to make even this distinction, the author predicted a much lower probability of their connecting with such concepts as "across" or "on each side of." White children's performance was better on this task than black children's, but all children improved with increased age.

The second part of the study dealt with the validity of verbal pretraining or sensory-motor, nonverbal training for accelerating this kind of synthesis. In two other tasks, a combination of verbal and action training increased performance. This was not true on the map problem. In the case of lower-class districts other than the ghetto, girls performed better than black boys, but white boys performed far better than everyone else, including white girls.

Farnham-Diggory hypothesized that perhaps the white boys had experience with fathers and with certain play equipment such as tinker toys and erector sets which had provided enrichment or training for this task. But this did not account for the superiority of black girls in "edgetown or milltown" communities. Perhaps housekeeping chores give opportunity to practice symbolic operations of this sort, table setting for example. Housekeeping chores seem to increase as class decreases. And indeed, lower-class girls performed the map task better than middle-class girls.

However, ghetto second grade boys from a rioting inner-city section were better at the task than suburban fourth grade black boys. Many of these boys had no father model, so the researcher hypothesized that in father-absent or father-weak homes, boys had to develop perceptual abilities in order to survive, particularly in dangerous periods. She found that indeed boys from fatherless or father-weak homes performed significantly better than did boys who came from father-present homes.

On this particular task it was found that verbal training was beneficial to girls, but not to boys. Therefore, it was suggested that there is interaction between where you live and what sex you are, which dictates in part your experiences, which in turn determine the kinds or types of enrichment or pretraining that can be effectively used.

For the boys, the kind of pretraining that helps the girls may be disruptive. For the girls, the kind of pretraining that helps the boys may be disruptive. Presumably in both cases the disruption results from the intrusion of intersensory associative systems which the respective sexes do not normally use in performing mental operations of this type. The boys are negatively affected by verbal pretraining, and the girls are negatively affected by the ghetto life. (Farnham-Diggory, 1972, p. 304)

It is necessary to take into consideration the kinds of experiences children have had, as further educational activities are planned.

Another thing to bear in mind is that there may be situations in which children must be taught to act in certain ways that they may not be able to understand, given the limitations of their intellectual development. For example, children very early must begin to deal with "rights of others." According to Piaget, the very young child is not able to approach the concept from a logical standpoint. He can, however, be conditioned to be aware of and interpret certain stimuli and so "act out" certain acceptable responses *as if* he were able to "take the viewpoint" of the other person. This sort of behavior helps the child to be involved with his peers and so to learn from them. Of course, there is always the risk that words or superficial actions will continue to be a substitute for real growth and understanding.

A paragraph from *Developmental Psychology Today* (1971, p. 73) serves as a final summary note of caution:

There is little doubt that Piaget's statements about the developmental changes in conservation of mass, class inclusion or serialization are generally true for Western children. But the concepts with which Piaget has worked—mass, quantity, weight, volume, space, number and time—and the operations he defines—reversibility, class inclusion, and serial ordering—are most relevant to math and physics. Their relevance to biological and social phenomena, which seldom show reversibility or obey class inclusion rules, is less clear. The relation between a whole and its parts in mathematics is not necessarily applicable to living things or to the behavior of people. The concept of a crowd is more than the sum of the people in the crowd. The child discovers that life itself, unlike the quantity of water, is not conserved: there is no reversible operation that restores life when a child kills a butterfly.

Language and Communication

Language development is basic to concept formation and use of the intellect, a major component of language being vocabulary. Active, or derived, vocabulary is that used in speaking: while passive, or basic, vocabulary refers to words that are understood but not employed by one in his speech, the latter being larger.

As the child's language activities become more complex with the introduction of reading, writing, spelling, and grammar, his conceptualization must of necessity expand. He must learn to communicate with and relate to persons with varying conceptions of words. Subtle differences become increasingly important. Consider the dilemma of the first-grader who when told by the teacher to go to the bathroom replied, "I don't have to." The teacher interpreted this as a sign of rebellion against authority, when in reality the child meant to tell her his bladder did not need emptying! Words are the mediators for concepts. Children use words to represent the ideas or things to which adults have assigned them. They often use words they really do not understand, sometimes in amazingly correct context. But such usage does not assure their grasp of the appropriate concept. On the other hand, they may have a clear understanding of a concept, but lack the language necessary to express it fully.

How they learn words through verbal context was studied by Werner and Kaplan (1950). Each of twelve nonsense words was presented in six different contexts. Children were asked to determine the word from the context in which it appeared. Under 10 or 11 years of age, children were

"Who's playin' house? We're playin' CASA!" (Used by permission.)

not able to differentiate between the word and its context. The younger children did not use the cues furnished by the sentences to determine the word represented by the nonsense term. Try your skill in such a task:

1. All the children will lidber at Mary's party.
2. The police did not allow the people to lidber on the street.
3. The people lidbered about the speaker when he finished his talk.
4. People lidber quickly when there is an accident.
5. The more flowers you lidber, the more you will have.
6. Jimmy lidbered stamps from all countries.

There are some 5 million children in American schools with limited or no command of English. The toll in discouragement and eventual dropout is high. And the federal government is spending $35 million a year to develop bilingual programs mainly at the elementary level to help overcome the language handicap and keep children in school. Over 200 bilingual programs in over half the states are serving 100,000 children who speak 19 languages other than English. The Spanish-speaking and American Indian children compose the largest groups with language barriers to learning. In some programs there is complete instruction in the child's native tongue; others feature initial teaching in native tongue and gradual introduction of English.

A large group who experience language difficulties are, however, not accorded such consideration, for few really are aware of the language gap that exists for black children, particularly when they enter school. There are distinct differences in Black English and standard English: how words sound, what they mean, and how they are used grammatically. Although the grammar and pronunciation of blacks have traditionally been considered inferior by scholars, currently emphasis is being placed on realizing language forms are a part of one's culture. Differences in sound in Black English result partly from anatomical differences in the vocal mechanisms, according to Marshal Howard (Askins, 1972), a black linguist. Another cause of sound variations comes from the African heritage of musical, fluid language. "Th" is pronounced "D" at the beginning of a word (dem instead of them), "V" in the middle of a word (muvver for mother), and "F" at the end (mouf for mouth), for example.

The meanings of words differ also. "The cat split the hammer" carries quite a different connotation for some, but a black child would know it meant some man left the presence of a rather unattractive woman. Among the grammatical hallmarks of Black English are double subjects (that man, he ain't here); double negatives (nobody can't run as fast as me); the elimination of some possessive pronouns (they got in they car); the use of "done" to show completion (done walked too far); and the substitution of of "mona" and "mon" for *gone;* and "gonna" for *shall, will,* and *going to* (I'mona get married; you gonna get hurt).

To assess the effects of black dialect on the learning of black children, third- and fifth-graders from inner-city and suburban schools in Washington, D.C., were asked to repeat thirty sentences (Caratz, 1969). Half the subjects were white, half black. Half the sentences were in standard English: "I asked Tom if he wanted to go to the picture that was playing at the Howard." Half were in nonstandard English: "I asks Tom do he wanna go ta the picture that be playin' at the Howard." Data indicated white subjects were better in repeating standard English sentences, while black children were better in repeating nonstandard ones. The black children "translated" standard sentences into nonstandard construction; white children "translated" nonstandard sentences into standard construction. The results suggested that whereas two dialects are involved in the education of black children, black children are usually not bidialectal. There is evidence that their dialect interferes with their attempts to use standard English. Black children who speak Black English have trouble learning if they cannot understand nor be understood by their teachers. Their quietness in class may be due to this problem rather than emotional problems or retardation.

Black children suffer from mutual misunderstanding because of their language, and many prevailing curricula and techniques do not help them. A child who read the sentence "The girl ran through the meadow" defined "meadow" by pointing to the handle of the closet door. Confused about the similarity in sound of *metal, meadow, medal,* a child does not understand the meaning of some words. Because much of their lives is chaos, they scarcely expect even sequences in stories to fit together into wholes: looking at comic books, they do not try to read or even view the pictures in logical order but instead skip around, seeing each frame separately but not in relation to the frames on either side of it. Being taught various facets of language separately—phonics skills, auditory perception, silent reading for meaning, and structural skills—does not help them see or learn the total message. Ways to give coherence and continuity might include hearing the story prior to reading it, listening to tapes of their reading material. But when very little in school seems logical, the child no longer expects learning to make sense, and he is likely to become the passive pupil who doesn't question, nor try to reason nor to learn (*Teaching Language in a Harlem School,* 1969).

Communication is important to children, and necessary steps must be taken in the school system to understand children and put them in real touch with each other and with their community. In the Ontario Crippled Children's Center in Toronto a system to help severely handicapped children in this area is being explored. Currently in use are about 200 symbols, developed by Charles Bliss, an Austrian-born chemical engineer, with the hope they would be used to promote international understanding. The symbols are arranged on wooden trays attached to wheelchairs. Six brain-damaged children are learning to use their fingers or a special clock hand fastened to the tray to point to the symbols that express what they want to say.

The ability to communicate, even on this quite simple level, has had remarkable effects. The children seem to be less frustrated since they can express themselves and so are more relaxed. This makes possible better use of whatever slight physical and verbal abilities they may have. Their previous apathy and withdrawal have been replaced by a new capacity to share in family life.

Memory

Memory, storage of experiences after they have occurred, is a cognitive process that has received new emphasis recently because of controversy over the distinction between short- and long-term memory (Adams, 1967). Older concepts dealt with memory in terms of registration and retrieval, with the idea that all encoded events were registered initially with equal strength. The distinction now being made is that short-term memory means information is available only for about 30 seconds, and without special control processes the information is not transferred to long-term memory and so cannot be retrieved at a later time.

Short-term memory seems to increase each year from ages 5 to 10. Whereas the typical 5-year-old can recall four or five numbers read to him, the 10-year-old may recall up to six or seven. With age, children seem to develop schemes or tricks to aid their memory (Flavell, Beach, and Chinsky, 1966). About 5 to 10 percent of American school-age children have eidetic imagery, the ability to maintain a complete mental picture of what they have seen (Haber and Haber, 1964). The vast majority rely on words and concepts to store and recall.

Memory varies from individual to individual. Kagan and Kogan (1970) suggest four dimensions to account for this: availability and use of vocabulary units to encode the event; attention; cognitive control of leveling-sharpening; and motivation.

Language is an important tool in mental operations, so when a child lacks ability to formulate his experience by way of "inner speech" or by way of language that is used to communicate with others, encoding processes are inhibited. It is likely that encoding, rather than forgetting, is the process that influences utilization of short-term versus long-term memory. Children from language-poor environments do not perform as well on memory tasks, nor do they assimilate new information with the accuracy or the extensiveness of children with richer language resources (Kagan and Kogan, 1970).

Children differ in their ability to attend selectively to an event, which is likely the result of interfering responses—preoccupation with other thoughts—and distracting stimuli. Poor attention to an event leads to imperfect registration or encoding. Anxiety is one factor that creates distracting stimuli that deflect attention from relevant incoming information; anxious children show poorer recall than children who store material under anxiety-free conditions. Messer's data (1968) illustrated this. A story was read to a group of third grade boys about a horse called "Man of War" who was "brown with a red mane." In the story a group of children visited the horse, watched him run, and afterward were served "hot chocolate, biscuits and fudge." The group of boys who had been subjected to a failure experience before the story, and were therefore judged to be anxious in the new testing situation, performed quite differently in recall than the nonanxious subjects. The anxiety boys distorted details, failing to remember the name of the horse ("war horse" or "a horse that fought in the war") and substituting other colors and other foods for those given in the story.

Leveling-sharpening refers to the manner in which a child remembers gradually changing sequential stimuli: the sharpener keeps a separation between the memory of previous stimuli and the new information; the leveler does not maintain this separation, but merges the new information with memory of preceding stimuli, altering both the perception of the new and the memory of the old in the direction of greater similarity. The memory of the various events remains discrete for the sharpeners, but tends to lose this characteristic for levelers (Kagan and Kogan, 1970). Differences were found in two groups of children labeled "levelers" and "sharpeners" in the number of elements accurately recalled and the number of contaminated elements produced when a story was passed from one person to another in each group in the manner of the game called "Gossip." The levelers produced a story with more mistakes, both fewer accuracies and greater numbers of inaccuracies than the sharpeners (Gardner and Moriarty, 1968). The leveling-sharpening scores of younger and older children, 10.5 to 12.1 years, indicated development toward greater accuracy during this short period of time. Gardner and Moriarty (1968) suggest greater concentration on the part of the older child and thus more vivid perception, or maturational changes in the perceptual and memoric apparatuses as reasons for greater occurrence of sharpening with increased age. Santostefano (1964) tested children from three age groups, 6, 9, and 12 years, using a simpler device than the Schematizing Test (a series of squares of graduated sizes) used by Gardner. Again, the younger children tended toward leveling; older children, toward sharpening.

M. E. Smith's work (1952) illustrates this concept from another point of view. When adults recall childhood memories, experiences that have occurred repeatedly do not stand out, but tend to merge together. They are often inaccurately recalled. More likely to be remembered are out-of-the-ordinary events: an unexpected gift, for example, is more often recalled than an expected one, even though the latter may have been greatly treasured.

The child's motivation also plays a part in memory. Retrieval of information requires effort, and the child who works harder and longer is likely to recall more information.

Kagan and Kogan (1970, p. 1304) summarized the variations in the quality of recall among children as due to "differences in available mediational units or their use, anxiety, focused attention, susceptibility to distraction and motivation. One of the perplexing problems is the fact that it is still not clear whether, or to what degree, recall failure is the result of imperfect registration, deficient rehearsal, or the effect of interference on the recall process."

Memories are constructions rather than reproductions. Jersild (1968, p. 472) points out that they have a strong subjective cast; they are not like a sound video tape of what has happened. "They represent events of the past as perceived at that time and edited in light of later experiences." Some investigators have suggested that errors in recall may be due to an attempt to lessen guilt (Smith, M. E., 1952); difficulty in perceiving self-behavior as other people perceive it (Jayaswal, 1955); the mood of the person, one with a cheerful view of life being more likely to remember happy experiences (Kadis, 1957).

Think Back

About some memory crutches you used to use:

Where they came from.

How helpful they were.

When you stopped using them.

Why you stopped using them.

Humor

Humor is one sign of the ability to communicate and reason. Not only is laughter essential in good mental health, Wolfenstein (1954) has called the construction of a joke one of the most complex products of the human mind. Some children laugh quite easily; others appear almost never to even smile. This is related to the kinds of experiences a child has had and how these experiences are interpreted by him. Such experience can lead him to see the world as kindly and enjoyable or unpleasant and not very promising. Our culture also dictates in part where and when we laugh: not at church; not at handicapped people. Children must learn these rules.

Parents and teachers need to be aware of humor and its meaning to children from ages 6 to 12. Most humor during these years is off-color, dealing with things that are slightly if not entirely taboo, such as sex and body functions. Young children use humor to express hostility and to make people, particularly authority figures, look foolish. There is also an increasing involvement with word play. Sometimes through jokes a child tries to make light of his own difficulties. If one laughs at one's own problems or differentness, he cannot be hurt; or he can more easily hide his hurt when others laugh.

Many times the clown in the group is in this position. He may feel insecure and inferior to other children; but if he "makes a joke" or acts "silly," he can cover up some of his loneliness and fear. The role of the clown is sometimes a protective device. This child needs help in establishing techniques for being part of the group in more acceptable ways.

With maturation and experience there is a shift in the type of things perceived as "funny" by children. Children delight in incongruities, probably because of a twist or turn given to something they have learned to understand in a different way. For example, punning jokes are funny to children: A man was locked up in a house with a calendar and a bed. How did he stay alive? He ate dates from the calendar and drank water from the springs on the bed. Another version adds a piano and asks how he got out. The answer: He played the piano till he found the right key (along with other variations). With increased age the degree of sophistication and the subleties increase, but the basic themes continue.

School-age children like concise jokes with a punch line or surprise ending. They repeat jokes they overhear from adult conversation, sometimes not fully understanding the source of the humor. They use humor to release tension and relieve anxiety. The little moron stories were popular a generation ago, followed by knock-knock jokes, cruelty jokes, dumb Polack jokes. Riddles are ageless in their popularity with children.

Giggling reaches a peak during the middle childhood years. Girls giggle together; so do boys. They themselves do not know what is funny— perhaps nothing. At times giggling may be a means of covering embarrassment in an unfamiliar situation. It may be simply a way to use excessive energy in a situation where there is nothing else to do. If children do not know the "answer" or understand what is expected of them, giggling may be their out. Of course, giggling may also spring from sheer joy of living! It is easier for adults to live with this if they can remember it is a pretty normal phenomenon.

Some attempts at humor are designed to make the listener look stupid, or to express hostility.

Laughter is essential to good mental health and also is one sign of ability to reason and communicate.

Row, Row, Row your boat,
Gently down the stream,
Throw your teacher overboard,
And listen to her scream.

What's eight and eight?
Sixteen.
Stick your head in kerosene
Wipe it off with ice cream
Show it to the king and queen.

CHILD: Do you know my name?
ADULT: Of course I know your name.
CHILD: Will you know me a month from now?
ADULT: Yes.
CHILD: Will you know me a year from now?
ADULT: Yes.
CHILD: Knock, knock.
ADULT: Who's there?
CHILD: Boo hoo—you've already forgotten me!

Others demonstrate the child's expanding vocabulary and understanding of word play:

CHILD: Daddy, have you ever shaken a tower?
DADDY: No.
CHILD: Well, have you ever taken a shower?

At times there is quite elaborate word play leading the victim into a carefully laid trap. One such trick will illustrate this:

What's one and one?
Two.
What's a word that means also?
Too.
What was the last name of the man who wrote Tom Sawyer?
Twain.
Now, can you remember all the answers and say them over again?
Two; too; Twain.
When you get a little older, I'll teach you to say locomotive!

And another:

Do you want to take an intelligence test?
    What color is the sky?
    What is two and two?
    What color is grass?
    How many stars in the flag?
    What was the first question I asked you?

Sometimes jokes simply reflect word play:

Once there was a man and woman who lived in Russia. The man's name was Rudolph and his wife's name was Helga. One day, Helga looked out the window and said to her husband: "Look! it's snowing." Rudolph looked out the window and said, "No, it's raining." She insisted it was snowing and he insisted it was raining. Finally, to end the argument he said: "Rudolph, the Red, knows rain, dear!"

They may employ humor to show their understanding of natural phenomena:

CHILD: Granny, did you hear about the two cross-eyed men who bumped into each other in the post office?
GRANNY: No, I didn't. What happened?
CHILD: One said, "I wish you'd look where you're going." The other one said, "I wish you'd go where you're looking."

Fun based on incongruities:

Where is that man going with that sack of fertilizer?
He's going to put it on his strawberries.
Oh! I always put sugar and cream on my strawberries.

They may use a joke to explain some action they have taken: choosing the largest piece of cake. That's like the story of the two Scotchmen having supper. Both ordered fish, and when they were brought on the platter, one was big and the other little. One man took the big fish, and the other said, "If I'd chosen first, I'd have taken the smaller fish." And the first man replied, "Well, what are you fussing about, then?"

A sign of creativity may be seen in the child who constructs his own jokes or adapts others to his circumstances. Children do not always understand the jokes they tell or laugh at. One youngster shared a joke riddle: What's black and white and red all over? He acknowledged the "right" answer as "newspaper." He and the other children present chuckled over this. The next day he was asked to explain why the joke was funny. His answer was that the newspaper was white with black printing and the red came on Sunday in the stripes on Charlie Brown's shirt.

Another child asked: Why did the man take a ladder to the restaurant? The answer was: Because the meal was on the house. Pressed for an explanation, the boy and his brother explained that "on the house" meant that it was "high—you know like the roof of a house." A "high meal" was one consisting of "steak and wine and all that kind of stuff." Both boys thought the joke very funny!

This is particularly true for "off-color" stories they overhear or report. Following are a few of the very mild examples in this category:

Yankee Doodle went to town, riding on a turtle.
He turned the corner just in time to see a lady's girdle.

What did one strawberry say to the other?
If you hadn't been so fresh, we wouldn't be in this jam.

What is black and white with a red bottom?
A skunk with diaper rash.

An off-color joke is not reason for undue concern. In fact, too great a reaction or apparent shock might have only the effect of causing the children to find out the reason for so much concern. At times, children do not see the "under-the-counter" implications of simple-sounding stories. It is better to hear the stories children tell, which is one way to be aware of their interests and the information they have. If one knows what they are thinking, he can more easily determine the direction or action that will be meaningful to the children. At any rate, an admonition of "Don't you ever let me hear you tell a story like that again," or "Say a word like that again and I'll . . . ," will have little effect, other than to send the storyteller underground. "Aren't you ashamed?" and the soap-in-the-mouth routine are not very helpful either. Children won't let you hear them tell such stories again, but will likely go right on telling them. Children are trying to deal with the world—rather frightening in some aspects. Parents and teachers need to help them learn to manage their feelings: curiosity, anger, fear. Children must be led to become skillful in techniques for relating to other people and feeling good about themselves.

How can we handle the dirty joke or the unacceptable language? It will depend a great deal on who the child is and one's relationship with him. In general, a good policy is to ignore the behavior in question. Do not let it pay off; the child may be waiting for your shocked reaction and his elevation to "hero status." Giving the child an interesting assignment may serve to change the manner of his expression. A simple statement may be in order: "That's not the kind of joke I like to hear. It makes fun of some pretty important ideas"; or, "I know you are pretty excited (or angry, or in a hurry), but I think you can find a better word than that one."

Here, again, it is dangerous to talk about techniques or formulas for dealing with behavior. One must consider the child, the group, and the situation and then make a decision about what can or cannot be permitted.

Wolfenstein (1972) reported an investigation of children's ability to distinguish between joking and nonjoking talk. She told jokes and asked the children if they were funny. Then she supplied "logical" answers and asked for their evaluation of these answers. She used the man-locked-in-a-house joke including both predicaments: how did he stay alive and how did he get out? Children of all ages fell into four groups: (1) no apparent acknowledgement of joke conventions; no differentiation between joking and nonjoking answers; (2) rejection of nonjoking answers as not funny, but then becoming involved in the problem situation, discussing solutions from the standpoint of practicality, dropping consideration of joke conventions; (3) attempting to exclude nonjoking solutions by limiting the situation so this was not possible (no chimney, walls ten feet thick); (4) rejection of nonjoking alternatives as inappropriate to the joke or riddle.

> While joke comprehension tends to increase with age, there are other important factors to which it is related. Intelligence and interest in jokes are both relevant. The rules of correct joke construction are something the child has to learn.

Other things being equal, the child of good intelligence who generally learns easily will also master with greater facility the modes of joke formation. Dull children or those retarded in learning are slower to grasp the rules implicit in jokes. But motivation is also a major determinant. A child who has found in joking a particularly valuable device for solving emotional difficulties, or for expressing otherwise unacceptable impulses, is apt to gain a quicker mastery of the joke technique. (Wolfenstein, 1972, p. 223).

Think Back

About things you thought were funny:
Where you heard them.
Who you shared them with.
What you thought of them.
How you remembered riddles and jokes.

Curiosity

The job of the teacher is to help children sidestep or move above rote learning. A teacher must nourish the children's urge to inquire, invent, and perform. John Holt (1967), a fifth grade teacher, in answer to his own question concerning what happens to the capacity for learning, for intellectual growth (present during early years in all children except the grossly retarded), said:

> What happens is that it is destroyed . . . by the process we misname education—a process that goes on in most homes and schools. We adults destroy most of the intellectual and creative capacity of children by the things we do to them and make them do. We destroy this capacity by making them afraid, afraid of not doing what other people want. We make them afraid to gamble, afraid to experiment, afraid to try the difficult and unknown.

One task of the teacher is to whet the curiosity of a child. Curiosity is certainly one of the avenues leading to creative "finding out," but it is not a natural phenomenon. It has been suggested that sustained involvement of any child in an activity is dependent on that child's having acquired a set of hypotheses appropriate to the object. This concept is illustrated in the two following examples (Kagan, 1968).

A teacher brought to her class a dozen packs of Cape Cod seaweed stuffed with attractive samples of shells of many kinds. She gave a package to each pair of 6-year-olds, expecting them to display natural curiosity. Each child devoted less than ten seconds to the material before returning to his previous game. The teacher had not prepared the children for the experience; they did not know how to ask questions, nor what questions to ask.

The second incident concerned an infant rhesus monkey raised from birth by a student of Kagan's. His sixth grade daughter asked to see the monkey, so arrangements were made to have the student come to dinner and bring the animal. The girl excitedly informed the neighborhood; and in a few minutes after the student and the monkey had arrived, six children, ages 7 to 11, came trooping in. They ran to the monkey, looked and poked for about two minutes, then casually walked off one by one, for more interesting activities. The children had not been prepared to ask questions about the monkey: What makes him afraid? What makes him run? What makes him smack his lips?

In addition to helping children find ways of exploring new experiences, adults must provide models of curiosity and learning. Children identify with important adults and, early in their lives, attach importance to things that seem important to these adults. Arbuthnot (1957) has suggested if we would encourage children to read, then reading must be given the prestige of adult enjoyment. This same philosophy might well be applied to other activities.

Sylvia Ashton-Warner, in her book *Teacher* (1963), writes warmly and with understanding about children's ability to learn and emulate the role of the teacher. In relating her experiences as a teacher in the "infant rooms" in New Zealand, she states: "What a dangerous activity reading is; teaching is. All this plastering on of foreign stuff. Why plaster on at all when there's so much inside already? So much locked in? If only I could get it out and use it as working material. And not draw it out either. If I had a light enough touch, it would just come out under its own volcanic power" (p. 14).

This seems to sum up the "duties" of the teacher. He must know the children he teaches, be aware of the level of their development, then provide the environmental equipment and opportunities in which they can find out for themselves. This is the light touch of the creative, caring teacher.

According to Ack (1970), certain principles must be considered if learning is to take place:

1. Material must be relevant.
2. Learner must be active.
3. Activity must be pleasurable.
4. Affect as well as cognition must be involved.
5. A significant human relationship must be involved.
6. The learner must feel respected.

To ensure relevance of material, the learner must be consulted. What do children want to learn? What makes reading so much more important than mechanics, or calculus more worthwhile than carpentry? To help children know what they want to learn might mean a demonstration by the instructor of the importance of certain materials and experiences to current life needs and goals. For example, some things are relevant simply because they are beautiful.

Activity is important: building a Nigerian village; having a party for the elderly folk who live in a nursing home; packing a box of everyday things for far-away friends; writing a story; making a play; putting together a community collage; printing a newspaper; making a gift; looking up important information; drawing a map. Activity also involves asking questions, bringing up different points of view or new ways of approaching problems, and solving problems.

At times, by the terminology used, adults set children's teeth on edge in relation to learning. "When you learn this (whatever it is) you can play." This almost sounds like punishment. "Learning" is the price one must pay for playing. Learning in such a context is something to be suffered through in order to get to the fun part. To say that learning must be pleasurable does not mean that all learning is conflict-free. This is impossible, and perhaps not to be desired. However, successful work, finding a solution to a problem, is pleasurable and fulfilling.

There must be attention to feelings as well as to cognitive activities. Behavior is the result, not simply of what is known, but the attitudes one has about this knowledge. Logical and mature behavior does not result just from knowing.

Most important is the teacher. Techniques of teaching run a poor second to the quality of the relationship between the teacher and the child. Emphasis must be placed not on what to "do" with a child but on how to develop a relationship with a child—a relationship in which he feels respected and fulfilled. A person who values the child and is valued by the child will indeed help him grow.

Catalysts for Discussion

I. Try your hand on this "IQ Test" developed for ghetto children:

1. Which word is out of place here?
   a. splib   d. spook
   b. blood   e. black
   c. grey
2. A "handkerchief head" is:
   a. a cool cat   d. a hoddi
   b. a porter   e. a "preacher"
   c. an "Uncle Tom"

3. Cheap chitlings will taste rubbery until they are cooked long enough. How soon can you quit cooking them to eat and enjoy them?
   a. 15 minutes
   b. 2 hours
   c. 24 hours
   d. 1 week on a low flame
   e. 1 hour
4. Hattie Mae Johnson is on the county. She has four children and her husband is now in jail for nonsupport, as he was unemployed and was not able to give her any money. Her welfare check is now $286 per month. Last night she went out with the biggest player in town. If she got pregnant, then nine months from now, how much more will her welfare check be?
   a. $80
   b. $2 less
   c. $35
   d. $150
   e. $100
5. "Hully Gully" came from:
   a. East Oakland
   b. Fillmore
   c. Watts
   d. Harlem
   e. Motor City

Now think how you felt taking this test. Try to imagine what children from nonwhite, nonmiddle-class, non-English-speaking cultures think and feel taking the Stanford-Binet or other similar measures of intelligence. What implications would these feelings and thoughts have for their performance? (In each question answer c is correct.) "Chitling Test," *Newsweek* (November 15, 1968)

Beyond the Classroom Experiences

1. With children conduct some of the experiments of Piaget with regard to conservation of number, weight, and volume—related to classifying. See where each child is in his cognitive development according to Piaget's theory.
2. Present some brainteasers, proverbs, and absurdities to children. Note the processes they use to try to solve or explain them.
3. Listen to the conversations of children in early and late elementary grades. Code the topics they discuss, and compare with the findings of Baker in 1942. Try to account for any differences noted.
4. Ask children to tell you some of their favorite jokes. Try to get them to explain what is funny about each. Try to determine in which of Wolfenstein's stages they are.
5. Set up some memory tasks for children to see how they approach the problem and how well they remember. Check their eidetic imagery and memory crutches they employ.
6. Ask children of different ages to explain or describe the Krauss designs.

Chapter 9

Moral
and
Religious
Development

This chapter is designed to help you:

- see the role of cognition, socialization, and religion in moral development.
- become acquainted with the stages of moral development and relate them to children's moral behavior
- explore the motives behind children's moral judgments.
- realize how guidance techniques affect moral behavior.
- identify some ways to foster the child's development of religious concepts.

An Age-Old Challenge

Down through the centuries each succeeding generation has been concerned with the moral fiber of their children. The following item appeared in the "Trade Winds" section of the *Saturday Review* (Beatty, 1968):

"An angry father asked his teen-age son, 'Where did you go?' The boy, trying to sneak home late at night, answered, 'Nowhere.'

" 'Grow up,' the father chided him. 'Stop hanging around the public square, wandering up and down the street. Go to school. Night and day you torture me. Night and day you waste your time having fun.' "

"That familiar dialogue is four thousand years old. It was translated from Sumerian clay tablets." Moral development and internalization of a system of values have been long-standing concerns.

How do children learn right from wrong? How is conscience developed? What about a moral code? Morality concerns conduct, but also judgment about or reasons for particular behavior. A child's actions may change little, but his reasons for his actions likely change greatly as he grows. A moral code consists of what a child thinks is good and bad, what he thinks he should do or not do, and the standards by which he judges the rightness of thoughts and actions.

The family group is the first teacher of such ideas or values, not just through spoken words, but also through activity choices, treatment of one another, financial expenditures, discipline styles, housing type and location, and countless other life choices. The young child accepts the values and standards his family sees as important, and as he incorporates these values into his personality pattern, he receives reinforcement through their love, affection, and praise for doing so.

With increased age the child senses that other children and families have different value systems from his own. And by school entrance, this diversity is compounded appreciably. Parents are concerned that their children retain the basic values that reflect the goals and practices of their families.

McCandless (1967) states that one must hold honest evaluation of his own value system in order to realistically evaluate and appreciate those of another person or group. Only when one has thought through the advantages and disadvantages of his value system can he work and live successfully and harmoniously with persons who hold differing or even opposing values.

Although it is important to help children understand why their families make certain decisions based on their values, it is equally important that they realize that other families operate differently for various reasons and that they learn an accepting attitude toward all people, regardless of their values. If children are able to see the why behind family actions and values, they are more likely to continue to practice them in their lives, even as they are exposed to alternate ones. But if they follow family values only out of fear or blind respect, they may be more likely to change when the opportunity arises.

One method of helping children bear in mind the basic values of their heritage is through conscience development, or moral development. The middle childhood years is a time when the conscience develops at a rapid rate. It begins to move beyond rules about specific behavior and becomes more generally oriented to abstract standards. It becomes less exclusively regulated by rewards and punishments, and more by internal sanctions. It begins to consider not only what one should not do but what one should do.

Unless a reasonable amount of conscience development occurs during the elementary school years, the child as an adult is more apt to yield to social temptations or to his own urges for uncontrolled behavior. On the other hand, if the conscience is overly developed, crippling of the personality because of guilt and attendant defense mechanisms may lead to serious psychological problems (Mussen, Conger, and Kagan, 1969).

Investigators are virtually unanimous in their conclusion that moral character cannot be adequately measured by mere assessment of moral knowledge or attitudes, as revealed in questionnaires. Moral character is not simply a set of good habits which can be inculcated by moral education. It does not seem likely that increase in long-term, internalized, moral behavior is related to the use of physical punishment for misdeeds.

Kohlberg (1964, p. 389) points out that moral conduct may more profitably be viewed as stemming from "ego abilities rather than moral habits or feelings." He discussed the following variables which researchers have regarded as correlating with moral character:

- General intelligence.
- Tendency to anticipate future events and to choose the greater remote outcome over the lesser immediate outcome.
- Capacity to maintain stable, focused attention.
- Capacity to control unsocialized fantasies.
- Self-esteem or satisfaction with the self and the environment.

Kohlberg (1964, p. 391) suggests that such findings support the idea that moral conduct represents "decision-making capacities rather than fixed behavior traits." He concludes that it is "safe to tell parents that rejecting their children, being harsh and unreasoning, and using strong physical punishment are unlikely to produce effective learning of parental expectations in moral or other domains of socialization" (p. 423).

Studies reveal that parental attempts at specific training in such good habits as responsibility and obedience fail to have appreciable impact on consistent moral behavior. Chilman (1966) suggests the following actions that parents may find helpful in assisting the child toward conscience or moral strengthening: parental example of desired behaviors; discussion and clarification of moral values in keeping with the child's slowly developing ability for moral judgment; and democratic methods, including mild, reasonable, and consistent discipline.

Moral Development Is More Than Adjustment

Moral development is more than adjustment to the group, or more than mental health. It is different from the internalization of exterior cultural norms, although it may involve this. This is highlighted by the work done in the 1920s by Hartshorne and May (1930), who found very little evidence of unified character traits: honesty, service (altruism or generosity), self-control, persistence. In regard to honesty, a summary of the findings follows (Hartshorne and May, 1963).*

1. There is not an "honesty trait" which one has or does not have. In 23 tests presented to a large group of children, there were few who cheated 23 times and few who were honest in all 23 situations.
2. Whether or not a person cheats depends on the situation rather than on a trait of honesty.
3. What a child knows about the rightness or wrongness of a situation has little effect on whether or not he cheats. Honest children and cheaters give about the same kinds of answers to a list of what-would-you-do kinds of questions.
4. While there is practically no correlation between age and honesty, older children were slightly more inclined to be deceptive than younger ones.
5. There was no difference between boys and girls in honesty and cheating.
6. More intelligent children are more inclined to be honest.

* Hugh Hartshorne and Mark A. May, "Studies in the Organization of Character" (adapted and abridged). In Raymond T. Kuhlen and George C. Thompson, eds., *Psychological Studies of Human Development*, 2nd ed. (New York: Appleton-Century-Crofts, 1963), pp. 432–441.

7. Dishonest children more often came from homes where there are poor parental example, parental discord, bad discipline, and unsocial attitudes toward children.
8. Dishonest children, more often than honest children, come from impoverished communities.
9. Honest children were more often enrolled in Sunday school than were other children. There was no relationship, however, between Sunday school attendance and honesty; sporadic attenders were as honest as regular attenders.
10. Some classroom situations seemed to generate more honest responses than others. Children were more likely to be honest when the teacher's attitude was cooperative and sympathetic.

These findings indicate that honesty is determined by external factors such as punishment, reward, group pressures, and group values rather than an internal character or conscience (*Developmental Psychology Today,* 1971). However, commonsense concepts of moral development suggest that an individual's morality does not change when the expectations of the social order vary, as they did, for example, in pre-Nazi and post-Nazi Germany. In a later analysis of the original Hartshorn and May data, Burton (1963) confirmed the rejection of the extreme trait model but suggested individual differences along a broad dimension of resistance to temptation. Burton's (1976) social learning model focuses on learning experiences which might lead individuals to be relatively consistent in honesty, others to be relatively dishonest.

Krebs (1970) asked teachers to rate children on three scales of morality: trustworthiness, obedience, and respect for others' rights. Girls were rated as more moral on all three scales. When the children were tested, through a "Moral Judgment Inventory" and two "cheating task opportunities," girls did not make more moral decisions than boys; indeed, middle class boys made more moral choices. There was no difference between the groups in their overt action in the laboratory situation.

Where do teachers come by the idea that girls are more moral than boys? Possible explanations are that girls conform more than boys, which is confused with morality; girls may be more eager to please, which teachers define as morality; since the boys Krebs tested had a less positive self-image than the girls, teachers may react to the way boys feel about themselves rather than to their actual behavior.

Cognitive-Developmental Approach

Rather than looking at morality as a bag of virtues that children internalize, it will be profitable to examine two basic approaches to the developmental process. The first, Piaget's cognitive-developmental approach, stresses the cognitive changes that come with increasing age as a major influence in moral development. The second, social learning theory, stresses the importance of the social environment, particularly parental socialization techniques.

Piaget's early work was concerned with how children perceive rules which he explored as he played marbles with children, observed them play, and talked with them about it. He suggested a developmental sequence through which children move in their interpretations or understanding of rules which seems to be duplicated in approaches to the problems they face in the moral realm: lying, stealing, interpreting punishment.

Egocentric Stage—4 to 7 years of age

Children do not follow the rules but insist they do. They "imitate" the rules. Two children, even though playing together, are not using the same set of rules nor are they competing with each other. "Winning" means having a good time.

Incipient Cooperation—7 to 10 or 11 years of age

Games acquire a genuinely social character. There is fascination with rules. There is cooperation (agreement on rules) and competition (each tries to win).

Genuine Cooperation—11 and above

Children come to an understanding about rules, even invent their own. They use rules, rather than being used by them.

Piaget conceived two broad stages of moral development which deal with respect for rules and sense of justice. The first stage is labeled in various ways: moral realism, absolutistic morality, morality of constraint, heteronomous morality. The more advanced stage is referred to in various ways: moral relativism, morality of cooperation, autonomous morality.

When the child operates at the first stage, he believes that some authority originated the rules and that they are unchangeable, sacred. While he may be willing to accept changes, he does so because he believes the new ones are alternatives rather than alterations in the old ones. Rules are simply placed upon him; they do not alter his behavior. A little later he refuses to accept any changes in rules. He asserts there is "one way." Any change is "not fair." By later childhood he understands rules can be changed; that they were originated through human invention and are maintained by mutual consent among equals. He participates in making rules and is willing to follow them.

This is illustrated in an incident during a checker game. One boy cheated; nothing was said about this. A few minutes later, the second boy cheated. Again, nothing was said. The observer, however, asked about this behavior. "Oh," responded one, "we made up a rule that we could each cheat once."

Piaget implied that young children operate from the base of moral realism which grows out of adult constraint—adults tell them what to do. At this level of understanding, an untruth is labeled a lie and therefore bad, with no reference to whether there was intention to deceive or simply that a mistake was made. If a child repeated as true something that had no basis in fact (seeing a dog as big as a horse), it is perceived as a bigger lie, and a greater wrong than something that could conceivably happen (re-

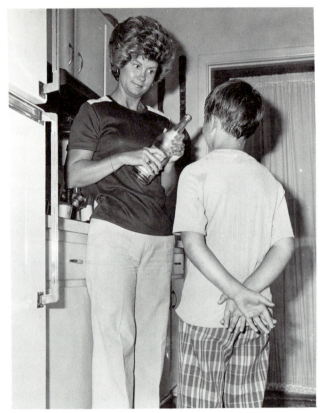

There are rituals among middle childhood people that "cover" lying, such as finger-crossing (Photo by Lin Mitchell.)

porting a good grade on a test when the reality was a poor grade). It is *possible* to get a good grade, whereas a dog-as-big-as-a-horse is clearly beyond the limits of imagination!

Very few children think it is all right to tell a lie. However, when they give reasons for this opinion, real differences emerge. According to Medinnus (1963), almost twice as many younger children as older ones (six- and eight-year-olds versus ten- and twelve-year-olds) think that a lie is wrong because it is forbidden and will be punished (external). On the other hand, four times as many older as younger children give answers that demonstrate a concern from the consequences of a lie (internal): you hurt others; you don't get any place; it just leads to more lies.

The young child judges an act only by its results—destruction of property or punishment to himself—rather than in the light of the reason for the behavior. A child who makes a very small inkblot on the tablecoth playing with his father's forbidden pen is a lesser culprit than the child who makes a large inkblot on the tablecloth while attempting to help his mother put things away. The size of the inkblot is the determining factor; circumstances or motivation behind the acts play no part in the young child's judgment.

A boy who steals a candy bar is worse than the girl who steals a piece of ribbon, because the candy costs more. A child who whispers in class and gets spanked for it has done a greater wrong than another child who tosses a ball through a window and breaks it but is only reprimanded for his act.

According to Medinnus (1963), these attitudes may be related to at least three factors: (1) Adults, by their manner as well as by their verbalization, many times communicate greater concern for objective responsibility than for subjective intentions. (2) Unilateral respect—children do not feel mutual respect; parents make the rules, so they are obeyed for that reason. (3) Egocentric patterns of thought—the child cannot see the need others have for truth, so is not aware of the fact that his lies (which he himself often believes) are deceiving to listeners.

According to Piaget (1965) this same sort of evolution takes place in the child's understanding of justice and its corollary—punishment. He has set forth the following stages:

Immanent Justice

Punishment for wrongdoing is believed to be automatic without the necessity of a punishing person. If a boy plays on the edge of a stack of barrels where he has been told not to play, and falls and breaks his leg, young children tend to feel this serves him right. He shouldn't have played here. Punishment is necessary and sure and grows out of the wrong itself.

Retributive Justice

When a rule is violated, which is a type of breach in the social bond, something must be done about it in order for reinstatement to take place. There are two levels of retributive justice:

1. *Expiation:* the one who does a wrong must suffer for it; the more pain the better. Such pain is a moral requirement, which makes punishment necessary in and of itself.
2. *Reciprocity:* the one who has done a wrong must take the consequences or make some restitution—put things right. Children see punishment as having value as a preventive measure for further deviant acts. Punishments children choose may be grouped in the following categories:

- Isolation from social groups; if a child cheats, the others exclude him from the group.
- Punishment which deals with the immediate and material consequences of the act; if a child fails to come in on time, he misses the planned trip to the circus.
- Deprive the child of the thing he misuses; he cannot play with the cards he mutilates.
- Doing to the child exactly what he had done to another; hitting a child who has hit someone.
- Restitution, which means replacing what was destroyed or misused; out of allowance, pay to replace a broken window, or clean the mud off the garagae door used as a battle target.
- Censure only, which makes the violator know he has broken the unity of the group.

Distributive Justice or Equalitarian Justice

The child has moved beyond the idea that "just" is what is commanded by the adult and reached the point of recognizing equal rights among children. This is closely linked to the development of autonomy and mutual dependence. Equalitarianism develops to the level of equity, which allows the child to take into consideration particular situations as he deals with the equal rights of the individual. In deciding on the right of an individual, he takes into account the personal circumstances of the individual.

Moral development is dependent on mutual respect and cooperation. The first cooperation is between children, and then between child and adult as the child comes to consider himself an equal of the adult. How do children reason morally? Two illustrations (Brearley and Hitchfield, 1970) depict changes over time in children's approaches to fairness in particular situations.

A story was told of two boys each of whom took paper from his father's desk for his own drawing. The father of one boy was angry and whipped him. The father of the other boy did not punish him, but explained to him this wasn't right or good action. The father pointed out that he did not take the boy's toys without permission, nor should the boy use his father's possessions without asking. It so happened that after a few days the boy in each story found his father's pencil in the garden—a pencil each father thought had been lost somewhere else and so could not be found. The subjects in the study were told that one boy returned the pencil to his father, the other kept it, and then they were asked to guess which was which. Younger children, 6 to 8, voted that the boy who had been punished would give the pencil back; the one who had only been talked to would keep it. They agreed that the explaining father was the "best sport," but the punishing father was the "fairer" one. These children believed punishment was morally necessary and educationally useful to prevent the wrong being done again.

A different type of moral attitude was exhibited by children slightly older—8 and 9 years of age. They chose the boy who was not punished as the one who gave the pencil back to the father. The children gave as their reasons for this that the boy knew the father would be pleased. These children were the ones who thought it was fairer and wiser to explain rather than to punish.

The second illustration deals with another decision that schoolchildren must make: to tell tales or not to tell them. "Tattletales" seem annoying to children and teachers alike:

Tattletale, tattletale
Your tongue shall be split
And every dog in town
Shall get a little bit.

In one situation, children responded to a story that concerned a man who had two sons and went away on a trip. One son was asked to watch the other child carefully and report to the father when he returned. Now it happened that indeed the brother who was to be watched did something silly. The question for the child was, when the father came home, what should the first son do? Should he tell about his brother's silliness or not?

Here again there were two levels. Nearly nine-tenths of those who were 6 or 7 years of age believed the father should be told everything. A majority of the children over 8 years of age thought that nothing should be told. In fact, some opted for telling a lie rather than to betray the brother.

This was a hard decision because "on the one hand is law and authority; since you are asked to tell tales, it is fair to tell tales; on the other there is the solidarity between children: it is wrong to be betray an equal for the benefit of an adult, or at any rate it is illegitimate to interfere in your neighbor's business" (Brearley and Hitchfield, 1970, p. 137). This again illustrates the two levels of morality: adult constraint and mutual cooperation.

Think Back

About some dilemmas you had concerning right and wrong:
When you told a lie.
Something you did which you knew to be wrong.
How you felt about others who didn't obey the rules.
When your conscience hurt.
How it felt to be generous.

Related to the work of Piaget, Kohlberg (1970) labeled the child a "moral philosopher" and hypothesized a series of invariant levels and stages of moral development through which children move. He points out that children have many ways of making judgments that are not "internalized" from the outside and do not really come in any direct way from parents or teachers or peers. Each of the levels or stages he describes are presented as "separate moral philosphies, distinct views of the socio-moral world." We have paraphrased Kohlberg's (1970) presentation of his model as follows:

Preconventional Level—4 to 10 years of age
Child is usually "well behaved," responsive to cultural labels of good and bad which he interprets in terms of physical consequences and the physical power of those who set forth the rules and labels. He may engage in quite cruel behavior when there are holes in the power structure.

Stage 1: Concern with punishment; unquestioning deference to superior power.

Stage 2: Right action is that which instrumentally satisfies one's own needs and occasionally those of others. They are willing to do good turns for others if they see a profit for themselves.

Conventional Level—10 years of age and above

Child conforms to and maintains the expectations and rules of his family, group, nation—which is seen as valuable in its own right.

Stage 3: Good behavior is behavior that pleases or helps others and is approved by them.

Stage 4: Good behavior consists of doing one's duty, showing respect, performing dutifully.

Postconventional Level (Principled)

Behavior is guided by autonomous moral principles that have validity apart from authority or persons who also hold such values.

Stage 5: Right action is that which is defined in terms of general rights and standards that have been critically examined and agreed upon by the whole society.

Stage 6: Right action is based on conscience and self-chosen ethical principles.

In his research Kohlberg has defined 25 basic moral concepts or aspects which he has operationally illustrated at each of the six stages of development. In this way, moral development can be examined more objectively. One such concept is "the value of human life." The six stages of development of this concept are (Kohlberg, 1964, p. 402):

Stage 1. The value of a human life is confused with the value of physical objects and is based on the social status or physical attributes of the possessor.

Stage 2. The value of a human life is seen as instrumental to the satisfaction of the needs of its possessor or of other persons.

Stage 3. The value of a human life is based on the empathy and affection of family members and others toward its possessor.

Stage 4. Life is conceived as sacred in terms of its place in a categorical moral or religious order of rights and duties.

Stage 5. Life is valued both in terms of its relation to community welfare and in terms of life's being a universal human right.

Stage 6. Belief in the sacredness of human life is seen as representing a universal human value of respect for the individual.

To pinpoint the level of moral development, a person may be given a number of situations and asked for solutions. For example: Is it better to save the life of one important person or a lot of unimportant people? Kohlberg (1967, pp. 111–112) presented the following answers to illustrate the varied stages of development:

Stage 1. "All the people that aren't important because one man just has one house, maybe a lot of furniture, but a whole bunch of people have an awful lot of furniture and some of these poor people might have a lot of money and it doesn't look it."

"Should a doctor 'mercy kill' a fatally ill woman requesting death because of her pain?"

Stage 2. "Maybe it would be good to put her out of her pain, she'd be better off that way. But the husband wouldn't want it, it's not like an animal. If a pet dies you can get along without it—it isn't something you really need. Well, you can get a new wife, but it's not really the same."

Stage 3. "It might be best for her, but her husband—it's a human life—not like an animal; it just doesn't have the same relationship that a human being does to a family. You can become attached to a dog, but nothing like a human you know."

Stage 4. "In one way, it's murder, it's not a right or privilege of man to decide who shall live and who should die. Got put life into everybody on earth and you're taking away something from that person that came directly fom God, and you're destroying something that is very sacred, it's in a way part of God and it's almost destroying a part of God when you kill a person. There's something of God in everyone."

Stage 5. "There are more and more people in the medical profession who think it is a hardship on everyone, the person, the family, when you know they are going to die. When a person is kept alive by an artificial lung or kidney it's more like being a vegetable than a human being. If it's her own choice, I think there are certain rights and privileges that go along with being a human being. I am a human being and have certain desires for life and I think everybody else does too. You have a world of which you are the center, and everybody else does too and in that sense we're all equal."

Stage 6. "A human life takes precedence over any other moral or legal value, whoever it is. A human life has inherent value whether or not it is valued by a particular individual. The worth of the individual human being is central where the principles of justice and love are normative for all human relationships.

Kohlberg (1967, p. 112) says that this latter young man has "moved step by step through a sequence culminating in a definition of human life as centrally valuable rather than derived from or dependent on social or divine authority."

Kohlberg's stages 1 to 4 have elements of Piaget's heteronomous stage, and his stages 5 to 6 have elements of Piaget's autonomous stage. There are differences; in the explanation of obedience in young children; in designating the age of autonomous action; in acceptance of the view that moral development follows an invariant and universal sequence.

According to Piaget, the young child has a strong respect for authority; he relies on the adult for a definition of right and wrong. The child therefore conforms out of respect, and not because he is afraid of punishment or because he is constrained. Kohlberg sees greater conflict between child and parent. He suggests that the young child obeys rules, not because of reverence for adult values, but simply to avoid punishment. He is not cognitively able to be moral at this level of development.

Kohlberg believes that children who are 10 or 11 are far removed from a fully autonomous and mature morality, and are still externally motivated. Piaget places them well into his autonomous stage by this age. Kohlberg's last three stages go into late adolescence and early adulthood. Kohlberg places more stress on cognitive development, while Piaget takes more account of social determinants in this area.

The following chart summarizes, generally, characteristics of the cognitive developmental approach to moral development. There are not fixed ages at which a child changes, nor are such changes automatic. Each child moves at his own pace which is determined by his inherited growth pattern and neurological framework, his environment, his experiences.

Before Seven—Characterized By:	After Seven—Characterized By:
Moral realism	Moral relativism
Moral behavior based on specific rules	Moral behavior based on more general concepts of what is right and wrong
Belief that rules are arbitrary, fixed, eternal	Belief that rules grow out of mutual consent
Dependence on adults	Peer group solidarity
Morality of adult constraint	Morality of mutual cooperation
Moral conduct in response to external demands: heteronomous	Moral conduct in response to internal standards which are adopted as their own: autonomous
Attention to objective responsibility only	Understanding of importance of subjective intentions
Immanent justice; justice of expiation	Justice of reciprocity and equality
Judgment of acts in terms of physical consequences	Judgment of acts in terms of intent to deceive or do harm
Judgment of seriousness of act in terms of seriousness of punishment	Judgment of acts according to harm done or whether or not a rule was violated
Necessity of judging acts of others according to inflexible standards	Ability to judge acts of others according to circumstances in which action occurred and underlying motivation
Belief that an act is totally right or totally wrong; adult view is always right	Awareness of steps of rightness and wrongness; of differences in points of view; adult may be mistaken

Kohlberg's (1976) position is that to understand moral stage, one must place it alongside other sequential factors in personality development: logical reasoning or intelligence as defined by Piaget (1967) in which a child moves through three major stages: intuitive, concrete operations, formal operations; social perception or role taking as defined by Selman (1976) in which the child moves through five stages of the differentiation of himself and others, and of ways in which he relates these perspectives to each other. Although moral development requires certain cognitive development, that development will not assure equal moral development. Putting oneself in the place of various people involved, or attainment of a given role-taking stage, is a necessary but insufficient condition for moral development. As an example, Tomlinson-Keasey and Keasey (1974) compared the performance of sixth grade girls and college coeds when presented with six Kohlberg dilemmas. There was a high correlation between cognition levels (concrete, transitional and formal) and moral judgment stages (preconventional, conventional and principled). Ten of the sixth graders were still at the concrete stage of reasoning; four were classified at the formal stage and twelve as transitional; but none was placed at the principled level of moral judgment. Four coeds were classified at the principled level of moral judgment and only one was not also classified at the formal stage of reasoning. However, thirteen of the coeds were classified at the formal reasoning stage, but only at the conventional level of moral development.

In addition the provision for role-taking activities in the family, peer group and school will afford the child opportunities for moral development. The more distant, impersonal, and influential in society these roles are, the greater the breadth to the child's development, which means the middle class child is in a more favorable position than the lower class child because of the greater variety of role-taking opportunities open to him. According to Keasey (1971), children who were more frequently involved in social organizations and who were perceived by teachers and peers as popular and as leaders had more role-taking opportunities and, therefore, were likely to be more advanced in moral reasoning than less involved and less popular children. Mutual role-taking is necessary along with participation. That is, we must take into account the moral atmosphere of the group: is the child's point of view considered and respected? Kohlberg refers to the "justice structure" of the institution—home, school, community—as being important in helping the child know how to resolve conflicting points of view from the standpoint of applying principles of justice.

The third condition necessary in movement from one stage of moral development to the next is cognitive-moral conflict (Kohlberg, 1976): exposure to discrepant moral reasoning by a significant other or exposure to a situation (discussion or live) which points up contradictions and in which decisions must be made. This conflict causing disequilibrium between where the child is in his approach to the problem and new information, pushes the child to restructure his thinking and so to move to a higher stage of judgment which allows use of the new point of view or the new information.

This concept has been the basis of the moral discussion programs, based on the presentation of moral dilemmas, which have been implemented in the public schools by Kohlberg. Moral stage changes have occurred when children were exposed to next-stage higher reasoning. The research of Rothman (1976) presents conflicting evidence in regard to this concept as it relates to behavior choices. One-hundred-forty-four seventh-, eighth-, and ninth-grade boys, through use of Kohlberg's conflict stories, were classified at Stage 3 or 4 in moral development and were placed in one of four experimental conditions: (1) presentation of two choices with reasoning; half presented reasoning one step above where they were $(+1)$, half presented reasoning one step below where they were (-1); (2) two choices, no reasoning; (3) one choice with and without reasoning, half of the subjects in each situation; and (4) condition one presented as a hypothetical dilemma.

With no reasons for starting or stopping the game (which were the choices offered), all subjects were more likely to continue than to stop. Presentation of $+1$ reasoning was more effective in changing behavior of Stage 4 subjects than Stage 3 subjects. At both stages, more subjects chose to stop when reasons were presented, regardless of the level of presentation. However, when subjects were asked which of the adults made the better choice (based on the reasoning they had shared) a majority of the subjects chose the $+1$ advice, no matter if it were stopping or continuing the game, and no matter what choice the subject had actually made in the situation.

Rest (1976) rejects both Piaget's and Kohlberg's methods of evaluating the material they gathered through interviews with children and other subjects (in terms of either moral development stages or a Moral Judgment Quotient). In Piaget's paired stories, the subject may choose one child as naughtier without understanding the contrast in the stories (high damage—good intentions versus low damage—poor intentions or severe punishment versus light or lack of punishment). It is assumed that one choice or the other marks the difference between attention to external punishment and rules or to intentionality. In most of Piaget's stories, however, the high damage-good intentions characters have a service motivation for the action which caused the damage, whereas this is not true of the low damage-poor intentions subjects. This, Keasey (1977) says, further confounds Piaget's scoring or assigning moral development levels on this basis.

Kohlberg's dilemmas have a multitude of aspects that make responses hard to code or compare. A classic one concerns Heinz, whose wife is dying of cancer. A druggist in the town has a supply of a drug he invented, which will save the wife's life, but he refuses to sell it except for an exorbitant price. Heinz raises half the money, but the druggist will not lower the price nor allow a partial payment. The question is: Should Heinz steal the drug? Answers must be justified. Judges classify these answers according to their orientation toward one of the six stages outlined by Kohlberg; for example, "toward avoidance of punishment and deference to authority (Stage 1), toward prudent and purely self-centered concerns (Stage 2), toward a husband's natural love and affection for his wife (Stage 3), toward the necessity of unwavering adherence to society's system or rules in order to prevent social chaos (Stage 4), and so on" (Rest, p. 199). It is the reasoning rather than the choice that is important. Kohlberg's system of scoring is difficult, involving six stages and 25 aspects in each (125 scoring possibilities).

In addition to the complicated, subjective scoring, Rest (1976) questions Kohlberg's method of assessing moral judgment in terms of simply predominate use of a stage.

Other difficulties Rest points out in assessing moral judgment include: stories that are more explicit or familiar produce more advanced reasoning; the amount of information with which the child must deal affects the response; subjects are more inconsistent from one judgment to the next when they are in transition stages or moving from one stage to the next.

In relation to the inappropriateness of the subject matter, Biskin and Hoskisson (1977) suggest that rather than using Kohlberg's dilemmas in the discussion groups in school for training in moral judgment or encouraging moral development, that stories from children's literature be used. This position is that such materials enhance role-taking, can be used by most teachers in the classroom because of the reflective questioning method proposed by the authors (to replace the dependence on extensive knowledge of developmental psychology and group processes needed to conduct the Kohlberg program), and provide a greater variety.

Seven stories were selected (see list at end of chapter); the dilemmas were identified; the moral issues at conflict were identified. A basic question along with follow-up questions were written which dealt with facts, interpretation (what did the author mean) and evaluation (how do you feel about what the author meant). Fourth and fifth grade students were assigned to an experimental group which for seven weeks read and discussed one story each week. Control group subjects simply read the stories. In both groups the experimenters worked with the children individually to be certain they had the facts of the story correct. Before and after the discussions, children were tested with Kohlberg's Moral Judgment Interview (1973). The moral maturity score increased significantly for the experimental group. A second test period ran for 18 weeks using 17 stories and again moral maturity scores increased for the experimental group. The authors believed that the longer training period was associated with greater increases than occurred during the shorter training period.

In order to deal with the other difficulties which he raised, Rest (1976) proposed another method for assessing moral judgment, the Defining Issues Test (DIT) which presents subjects with the major issues involved in the dilemmas. In each of the six Kohlberg dilemmas the subject is asked to rate a set of 12 issues, each representing a stage of moral reasoning, as to how important each issue is in deciding what ought to be done: most important, much, some, little, no. Subjects are also asked to rank the four most important issues. In drafting these issue statements there has been an attempt to word them in such a manner that choices really represent agree-

---

ment with the reasoning presented rather than simply with the conclusion. Among the 12 statements there are a few added items that use "high sounding phrases" in order to check whether the subject is responding to the meaning or just to the verbiage, a sort of "lie scale." This is an attempt to assess moral judgment by an objective format: standardized stimuli and test conditions and asking subjects to respond with rating and ranking instead of in free-response mode.

Kurtines and Grief (1974) reviewed the work of Kohlberg and research using the cognitive model of moral development which he proposed. They found this research "beset with a multitude of problems" which they approached from four standpoints.

The Formation of the Moral Judgment Scale. The general meaningfulness of the intuitively derived six stages of moral reasoning is not clear. The scale is not standardized, either in administration or in scoring. There are nine moral dilemmas, some of which grow out of others and therefore are not independent, from which researchers may choose some or all and there is no proof that all of them tap the same cognitive dimension. Main characters in the stories are male which may account for the finding of higher moral reasoning among males than females. There are five different ways of scoring, all of which are complicated, subjective, and require special training.

The Reliability of the Scale Has Not Been Demonstrated. Scores vary greatly over short periods of time. There are no estimates of internal consistency nor reports of standard deviations of scores. There have been no complete reports of inter-rater reliability in scoring interview protocols.

Predictive Validity Has Not Been Established. Although Kohlberg's framework does not require it, when scores on the Moral Judgment Scale are related to nontest criteria, there is no clear-cut connection between moral judgment and moral action. "There is no evidence to indicate that the six distinct stages, particularly the final three stages, add predictive power to the scale or much beyond that which would be obtained with a simple dichotomy classification of high-low or mature-immature" (p. 468).

There Is Little Construct Validity for the Scale or the Model. Four types of evidence offered to support the invariant sequence, cross cultural, statistical, longitudinal, and experimental, were examined and found not to support the major assumptions of the model. There was failure to show that people move through the stages in a pre-set order or that people move through each distinct stage. No evidence was found to support the idea that each new stage was qualitatively different from the previous one, and grew out of it.

There was evidence to suggest that certain of these assumptions may be incorrect. For example, Hogan (1970) maintained that what Kohlberg defines as progressive stages (5 and 6) may be equally defensible moral postures. His work also pointed to personality differences as important determinants of a person's moral reasoning. Kurtines and Grief (1974) concluded their review with the idea that Kohlberg's stages model may indeed reflect moral development, and that the evidence may point to the inadequacy of the measuring devices used to assess the stages of moral reasoning.

Biskin and Hoskisson (1977) suggest questions that may well be asked in further research concerning concomitant changes which accompany moral development:

1. Were the children better able to communicate with one another after the discussion sessions?
2. Were the children more aware of moral conflicts?
3. Were the children able to justify their attitudes and their behavior to others in artificial and in real-life situations? (p. 414)

Indications of changes in these characteristics may be easier to evaluate than changes in moral reasoning, particularly in hard-to-administer tests such as Kohlberg's.

Social-Learning Approach

Social learning theorists have been concerned with the emotional and motivational aspects of moral development rather than the cognitive aspects. Mere knowledge of moral standards, which may be learned quite easily—and quite passively—does not guarantee moral behavior nor the development of conscience. Then how does it happen?

Certain moral characteristics in children seem to be related to particular child-rearing practices, especially disciplinary or guidance techniques. Bandura (1971b) reminds us that the mother does not remain the primary socializing agent. Siblings, peers, nonfamilial adults, and models from television and literature as well as selected individuals from the whole community influence the child's development. Although the parent is certainly a powerful socializing agent in the child's life, the effects of parental guidance seem to vary and require explanation from the standpoint of how such moral development is effected by parent-child interaction.

Several hypotheses have been offered to explain the underlying processes by which parent-practices are effective, so that "the child who is pleasure dominated and amoral develops moral standards to which he is internally committed" (Hoffman, 1970, p. 282).

> The model presented by parents during a disciplinary encounter is a factor: openly expressed anger versus controlled anger. If child is discouraged from expressing anger through the controlled model, he turns it inward, and guilt capacity is developed (Allinsmith and Greening, 1955).

Duration of punishment must be considered. Physical punishment is over quickly, reducing child's motivation to change behavior. Other types of discipline last longer so the child may be forced to try to begin a parent-approved action, which then is reinforced.

The child wants his mother near. Punishment by withdrawal of love makes him feel and remember her loss at the time of subsequent misdeeds (Sears, Maccoby, and Levin, 1957). In order to keep from losing his parent he takes on the characteristics of the parent in the situation: criticizing, evaluating, punishing his own behavior and taking on the moral values and behaviors which he knows are more acceptable to his parent. Actually, in this sort of identification, he becomes the parent.

Timing of punishment is important (Hill, 1960). Physical punishment often occurs at the time of the deviant act, while love-withdrawal as punishment usually terminates at the time of some corrective act: confession, restitution. The punishment iself then may reinforce the poor behavior or the acceptable behavior.

Explanation offered by the parent may help a child to examine his actions and accept responsibility for them.

In order to examine these hypotheses, Hoffman (1970) classified pertinent child-rearing practices; defined internalization concepts, a basic aspect of morality; and then examined the relationship between each of the practices and each of the indices.

The following child-rearing practices in the area of guidance (discipline) have been carefully defined and used by a great many researchers in an attempt to assess their effect on the child's moral development.

1. *Power-Assertive Discipline:* the parent attempts to control the child by using his physical power or control over the child's material resources. The parent does not try to use or develop the child's inner resources, but uses punishment or fear of punishment for control.

> Physical punishment
> Deprivation of material objects or privileges
> Direct application of force
> Threat of any of these

2. *Nonpower-Assertive Discipline:* there are two main types of nonpower techniques, the first quite punitive.

> A. *Love-Withdrawal Techniques:* These have a highly punitive quality and may be more emotionally devastating to the child than the power-assertive techniques listed above. This kind of control is prolonged, makes an ultimate threat of abandonment or separation, and the child has no idea when the punishment will be over. This is direct but non-physical expression of anger or disappointment in the child because of his undesirable behavior.
>
> > Ignoring the child
> > Turning one's back
> > Refusing to speak to or listen to the child

Isolating the child

Threatening to leave the child

B. *Induction:* These techniques are less punitive than power-assertive or love-withdrawal techniques; the parent gives reasons or explanations for requiring child to change behavior. The effectiveness of induction as discipline seems to be that the child comprehends the situation and controls his own behavior accordingly.

Pointing out physical requirement of situation

Stating harmful consequences of behavior for himself or others

Appeal to conformity-inducing agents which exist in the child:

Appeal to the child's pride

Appeal to strivings for mastery and to be "grown up"

Concern for others

Other-oriented induction techniques are references to the implications of the child's behavior for other people:

Explaining nature of consequences

Pointing out need or desires of others

Explaining motives underlying peer behavior

3. *Parental Affection:* Although this is not a form of discipline in the same sense as those listed above, it does have effect on moral development. Being loved provides the emotional security necessary for considering the needs of others. The child may attempt to control behavior to please affectionate parents; this become a generalized reaction so the child controls behavior out of consideration for other people.

The social learning approach to moral development is more concerned with conduct and with forces shaping moral responses than with reasoning or judgment. There are, however, important forces operating within the individual which give direction to action. To move from the knowledge and understanding of, or the capability to perform prosocial behavior, to actual moral conduct in specific situations requires attention to the person's expectancies and subjective values regarding those expectancies (Mischel and Mischel, 1976). The choices of particular behaviors in a specific situation is guided by the subject's own behavior-outcome expectancies, which may grow out of previous direct experience or out of observations of the consequences of such action when performed by other people. After observing other people (models) receiving positive consequences for a particular action, there is a tendency to behave in a similar manner. Negative consequences following behavior also alter behavior by inhibiting the tendency to engage in such behavior.

The effectiveness of the model depends on the attributes of the model and of the observer. If the model has prestige, stature, power, is similar to the observer, and if the model-observer relationship is marked by nurturance and warmth there is greater likelihood that the modeled behavior will influence the observer's actions (Bandura and Walters, 1963; Mischel and Mischel, 1976). This is certainly supportive of research reporting correlations between affection and nurturance of parents and the prosocial behavior of children (Hoffman and Saltzstein, 1967).

For modeling to be most effective, provision must be made for the following components (Bandura, 1973): responses repeatedly performed in a variety of ways and by a number of people; opportunity for practice of the modeled behavior with guidance and support until it can be performed skillfully and spontaneously; successful consequences following behavior. Although symbolic modeling, demonstration of desired response, may be adequate for modifying behavior in some cases, it is better to provide demonstration, practice and feedback concerning performance until a high level of skill is acquired.

Direct training for prosocial behavior may include a number of activities such as role-taking opportunities and reasoning with children to help them understand and engage in activities which show responsibility, empathy, and consideration for others (Mischel and Mischel, 1976). Consideration for others is learned more quickly when exhortation is accompanied by greater interpersonal obligations and responsibilities. Mischel and Mischel (1976) indicate this occurs because successful execution of such responsibilities generate long-lasting expectations of their positive consequences, and so serve to increase their likelihood.

It must be kept in mind, however, that people subjectively value particular consequences in different ways and this affects the choice of behavior patterns. For example, parental approval may be less important for a particular child in a particular situation than peer approval, which will influence behavior choices the child makes. These value systems have the effect of furnishing incentive or reinforcement for the child's behavior. Such values may be modified and certainly change with age. Bandura (1973) suggests that if the model, in addition to demonstrating prosocial behavior, also verbally supports this behavior, there is greater possibility of bringing about a change in this basis of self-satisfaction. In some instances, subjective values may be relatively the same for quite different groups, but the individuals within the group may tolerate, to different degrees, deviance from these prosocial values which they have endorsed "in principle" (Gordon, et al, 1963).

Self-regulatory systems, the ability to control behavior in the face of strong temptation and situational pressures for long periods of time in the absence of obvious rewards or supports, are critical in moral conduct. An important component is the adoption of a set of rules to guide behavior that specifies what is appropriate, sets standards of performance, and determines consequences of achievement or failure (Mischel and Mischel, 1976). These rules are derived from models and socialization experiences. The child is affected by both the model's actions and words. When there is discrepancy in the standards followed and the standards taught, the child is more likely to adopt the less stringent set of standards.

Another important consideration in self-regulation is performance of

To cheat or to fail—that is sometimes the choice. (Photo by Lin Mitchell.)

"cognitive transformations" on stimuli, (Mischel, 1974) focusing on selected aspects of the stimulus that may change the influence of that stimulus on behavior. How well a person attends to a task or how well the person resists distraction are related to some indices of moral behavior
(Hartshorne and May, 1928; Grim, Kohlberg, and White, 1968). On the
other hand, *not* attending to a goal (potential reward) was what contributed to self-control most dramatically in a study of delay of gratification
(Mischel, Ebbesen, and Zeiss, 1972). How one focuses in the situation
seems to be more important than whether one focuses. The objects can be
cognitively transformed in such a way as to permit or prevent effective
delay of gratification, e.g., pretzels can be little brown sticks, or crunchy,
salty, appetizing tidbits; marshmallows can be cotton balls, or can be
thought of as chewy, soft, sweet confections (Mischel, 1974). One can
focus on arousing or non-arousing aspects of the stimulus and thus regulate on control one's behavior. One child willed herself to go to sleep!

Finally, the self-regulating system includes attention to how the individual sets priorities for sequencing and stopping behavior, which have to do
with the planning process which is adopted. The plan includes behavior intentions and a series of contracts in regard to these intentions or goals.

Moral development, by whatever means, involves internalization of certain standards, inhibitions, mandates, and taboos. Although society's norms are at the beginning foreign to the child, he adopts them largely through early control by others (parent is the chief "other"). This outside control is replaced by self-control. When the standard is internalized, the child's actions are based not on concern over external sanctions but rather on his own sanctions or those of a valued reference group or person.

Hoffman (1970) reviewed four aspects of internalization which appear in parent-child research literature. He used this to define a child morality index. These four indices represent affective, cognitive, and overt levels of behavior. They are presented, not as an underlying continuum of moral growth but as different aspects which indeed may increase with age, which may appear and reach maturity at various ages and result from quite different processes mediated by varied parent practices.

Internalization Concepts

1. *Resistance to pressures to deviate*

    This is an important index of conscience. It represents the degree to which an individual can resist pressures to deviate from standards even when probability of detection is slight.

2. *Guilt*

    One view is that this is a conscious experience following violation of an internalized standard. Guilt is not really a goal of society, since overt behavior is more important than internal responses; however, guilt is an emotional response to a completed act and therefore important. Some "guilt" reactions are probably not triggered by increased internalization, but by such external factors as fear of punishment.

3. *Internal versus external orientation*

    This dimension examines whether or not child accepts responsibility for deviation and tries to correct situation without blaming external forces; making reparation or modifying his behavior in the direction of being socially acceptable. With internal orientation the child is concerned with future events rather than punishment; he understands the differences in "crime," e.g., stealing versus breach of trust.

4. *Confession*

    This involves openly accepting responsibility for one's deeds even when detection is unlikely. Some children have learned that "confession" is approved by parents and therefore simply go through the form of confession based on this external force.

These moral indices were examined by the use of story-situations in which the child was asked to tell how the hero felt and what he did. His answers were coded in various manners placing the child along a continuum in one or more of the particular aspects of internalization. Some researchers also used laboratory settings in which children were placed in possible cheating situations, for example, and their overt behavior was observed and scored. At the same time, parents, through interviews and questionnaires, outlined as fully as possible their child-rearing practices in relation to guidance and discipline.

The overall pattern of findings is as follows:

- Frequent use of power assertion by mothers associated with weak moral development.
- Induction and affection are associated with advanced moral development, although positive relationship is not as strong as previous negative relationship.
- Love withdrawal overall is not significantly related to any of the moral indices; in the instances where a relationship was found, no pattern was established.
- The above relationships were most direct for the two internal indices, internal orientation and guilt, and less clear-cut for the two overt indices, resistance to temptation and confession.

While there are not a great many relationships between the father's practices and the child's moral development, there is evidence that the father's presence is important for growth in this area. Father seems to play an important role in the boy's moral development, although his method of discipline does not seem to be the key. It may be that the father furnishes "cognitive content of the child's moral standards by direct instruction in nondiscipline situations rather than by his discipline techniques" (Hoffman, 1970, p. 294).

Hoffman (1970, p. 294) suggests another hypothesis to explain the role of the father:

> the father's role is ordinarily latent in its effects and only becomes manifest under exceptional circumstances such as those often associated with delinquency. That is, under normal conditions with the father away working most of the time and the mother handling most of the discipline, the father's importance may lie mainly in providing an adequate role model that operates in the background as a necessary supporting factor. Under these conditions the specific lines along which the child's moral dvelopment proceeds may be determined primarily by the mother's discipline, that is, individual differences in children's moral orientations may be due mainly to the mother's discipline. An adequate role model is lacking, however, in extreme cases, as when there is no father, when the father is a criminal, or when the father is at home but unemployed.

The reported findings apply to middle-class families only. In one study (Hoffman and Saltzstein, 1967), when middle-class and lower-class parents were contrasted according to the same schema, there were few significant relationships between child performance and parent practices. Hoffman explored varied explanations for this outcome. Internalization makes little sense, he felt, in the lower class and therefore should not be expected to be related to parental discipline. Members of the lower class have less stake in the social order; occupations followed by many lower-class persons require standardization and direct supervision, the following of specific rules, in contrast to middle-class occupations which allow more self-direction and make success dependent on one's own action thus fostering internalization. Kohn (1959a; 1959b) reported that expressed child-rearing goals of lower-class parents were focused more on immediate compliance and less on long-range character development, in contrast to middle-class parents.

Lower-class parents use predominately power-assertive discipline techniques, rather than induction and affection. It may be that all interactions between parent and child have a power-assertive cast, so few differences among various practices can be measured. Another point for consideration is the possibility of the mother's being less effective in the use of discipline, in part because of her own makeup and in part because discipline is more widely shared with father, siblings, extended family, and peers.

Any disciplinary technique, to be successful in underscoring moral development, must use existing emotional and motivational resources in the child. A strong one is the need for approval, which requires a high level of affection from the parent. Any disciplinary action arouses in the child some need to show he is worthy of his parents' approval. The parent-child interaction, to be successful, should be of such nature that it gets his attention, helps him to stop what he is doing, and helps him to attend to the information concerning why his action is unacceptable. If the interaction is too harsh, too much anxiety may be generated in the child so that he cannot attend or act constructively.

Two other internal motives are useful in helping the child change undesirable behavior and develop moral standards: the child's mastery strivings and his capacity for empathy. A child wants to do the mature or grown-up thing. He may also respond to the successfully communicated idea that he is able to reason through situations and make wise behavior choices.

A child often experiences vicarious pain from having harmed another; then he has greater motivation to learn moral rules and control his impulses. Other-oriented induction relates most directly and positively to tapping and using children's feelings of empathy. Induction, or reasoning, directs the child's attention to the other person's distress and communicates to the child his responsibility for the distress. This capacity for empathy forms a motive or basis for positive morality—in contrast to simple repression of impulses.

In an effort to define specific socializing techniques, Hoffman (1969) identified childen who showed signs of internalized, humanistic, flexible conscience, then looked for the antecedents of such a conscience in the parental practices to which the children had been exposed. He contrasted this group of children with a group whose conscience was more rigid and conventional, although also internalized. A third group of children were characterized as having externally oriented moral standards.

The first group of children were described as follows: In making moral judgments they emphasized consequences of behavior for others, or stressed certain interpersonal moral values such as trust (humanistic); they took into account extenuating circumstances in applying standards (flexible). The second group of children were different: In making moral judgments they emphasized violation of the institutional mores, legal or religious (conventional); and failed to give weight to the circumstances in which an act was committed (rigid).

The external group was lower in IQ and did not score as high on the internalization concepts as the other two groups: guilt intensity; teacher rating on the extent to which the child accepted responsibility for misbehavior; parental report of child's confession after wrongdoing. It turned out that in the humanistic-flexible subjects, in contrast to the conventional-rigid subjects, guilt was in reference to actual harm done to others rather than in reference to their own feelings in the situation.

The parents of both internal groups received higher scores on induction and affection and lower scores on power assertion than those in the external group. However, there were differences between the humanistic-flexible and conventional-rigid group. We have paraphrased selected findings that Hoffman reported concerning these differences, as follows:

> Conventional-rigid parents more often used love withdrawal as a disciplinary technique, especially in regard to the child's anger, which is in contrast to other research which pointed to the importance of low power assertion and high induction and affection as leading to internalization of standards. This greater use of love withdrawal may color all other disciplinary techniques which foster development of flexibility and humanistic tendencies, so that while the children develop internal standards they become quite rigid and conventional so that they run no risk of losing the parent's love.
>
> Humanistic-flexible parents showed different reactions to the child's anger; anger was handled firmly but with little threat; the focus was on the issue that caused the anger. Such action tones down anxiety since it communicates that anger is inappropriate because it makes it difficult to deal with the issue rather than because it is intrinsically objectionable.
>
> Both groups of parents disapproved of hurting another child or destroying his property; both placed emphasis on how the other child felt about this. The humanistic-flexible parents also placed emphasis on restitution and repair of damage where possible.
>
> The humanistic-flexible group more often used power assertion than the conventional-rigid group. The child saw this, however, as giving reasons for required behavior. Power assertion evidently was not used indiscriminately, but only in instances where the importance of the situation demanded immediate action on the part of the child. It was used as a follow-through technique when the child was defiant, which helped the child attend to the reasoning of the parent. Conventional-rigid parents, on the other hand, refused any open confrontation with the child along this line.
>
> In accident situations, the conventional-rigid parents responded with love withdrawal which produced anxiety in the child. The humanistic-flexible parents, on the other hand, responded in a highly permissive manner. They realized that this behavior was outside the child's point of view.

In summary, the conventional-rigid parents seemed to use love withdrawal, no matter what the situation, whereas the flexible-humanistic parents used more varied techniques ranging from power assertiveness to permissiveness. This group focused on the precipitating issue, suggested reparation where possible. They were able to look at behavior in the larger context, from the doer's point of view and to consider his intentions, abilities, and limitations. On the other hand, the conventional-rigid parents were more likely to ignore the situation and judge specific acts by rigid standards of good or bad behavior and act accordingly. In a double way, then, parents seem to affect the moral development of their children: by the methods of control they use and by the model they present to their children as they use these techniques.

There is little understanding of how parents really transmit values to their children, but that such transmission occurs there is little doubt. Stinnett and Kreps (1972) developed the Positive Value Character List, composed of 16 value items gleaned from the literature and validated by a panel of eight family life experts. The items were rated by college students in the light of their own learning experiences.

Positive Value Character List

- Determination and perseverance
- Self-reliance
- Seeing each person as having dignity and worth
- Moral courage (courage to stand by one's inner convictions)
- Spiritual development
- Cooperation
- Honesty and integrity
- Loyalty
- Self-discipline
- Feeling genuine concern and responsibility toward others
- Initiative
- Intellectual inquisitiveness
- Responsibility in performing tasks
- Self-respect
- Friendliness
- Appreciation

The students chose five as most important for parents to teach their children; three values they believed parents were most successful in teaching their children, and the three they believed parents most often failed to help their children learn. The most important values were:

- Honesty and integrity
- Spiritual development
- Seeing each person as having dignity and worth
- Self respect
- Moral courage

The students felt that those which parents were most successful in teaching were honesty and integrity, friendliness and self-reliance. One of these values appeared in the top five. The three values most difficult to teach, in which parents were least successful, were spiritual development, genuine concern and responsibility toward others, and moral courage. Two of these were in the most important five.

The students felt that the greatest influence in character development was the family, with particular emphasis on the mother. The peer group was also frequently selected as having influence on the development of these values. The influence of the church was considered to be the least influential of the community groups.

The researchers concluded:

> The finding that feeling genuine concern and responsibility for others was so frequently selected as a value parents most often fail to help children learn and so infrequently selected as a value which parents are successful in helping children learn, may reflect the revolution toward more humanistic values which is taking place among the younger generations.

The Role of Religion

Research releative to the role of religion in the moral development of children is sparse. Many of the things dealt with in religious education are in the subjective realm of faith, hope, and love. It is difficult to measure attitudes of compassion and humility, and of religious conviction and commitment. It is difficult to score such attributes as peace of mind, absence of guilt, patience, forgiveness, and generosity. Suffice it to say that throughout the ages one of the major objectives of spiritual fellowship has been to guide moral behavior.

Even though religion and idealism do not play as great a part in the thinking of middle childhood people as it does in that of adolescents, it is nevertheless a real part of their life, and the church is a viable agency in their ecological unit. Because there is a vast discrepancy between what church members profess and the way they act, children face confusion. In addition, there is confusion in regard to theological concepts which teachers and parents attempt to teach children and the manner in which they are assimilated. Children, because of their cognitive development, interpret what is said concerning God and other spiritual truths in a concrete manner. What one teaches and what children learn may be two quite different things.

Elkind (1971) makes several generalizations about the growth of religious concepts. Personal religion, in contrast to institutional religion, develops along two fronts: spontaneous and acquired. The first involves the child's own interpretations of religious ideas or practices; the second is a function of religious education. Both of these responses are regulated by cognitive development, experiences, and parent-child interaction. As a child's ability to understand abstract concepts increases, his interpretation of religious ideas changes. These principles can be illustrated through examination of two concepts: understanding of personal religious identity and meaning of prayer.

Through questioning several hundred children of varied religious orientation, Elkind (1961, 1962, 1963) tested Piaget's contention that concepts develop in discernible stages which follow a regular sequence related to age. Children were asked the following questions (which were changed appropriately for Catholic and Protestant children): Is your family Jewish? Are you Jewish? Are all boys and girls Jewish? Can a dog or a cat be Jewish? How do you become a Jew? What is a Jew? How can you tell if a person is Jewish? Can you be Jewish and American at the same time? In addition to answering the questions, the children were asked to give their reasons.

There were three distinct stages or levels in the evolution of the child's understanding of his religious identity. When the children were asked "What is a Jew?" They responded at varied levels of development.

STAGE ONE: *Global undifferentiated concept—5 to 6 years*
Jew: Cause some people have black hair and some people have blonde.
Catholic: A person.
Protestant: Maybe it's something that makes you happy.
All boys and girls are not Jews because some are colored, they speak another language.
A dog cannot be Jewish because it goes bow-wow.
The child seems to have some general notion of the meaning of these words but he confuses them with national and racial designations.
STAGE TWO: *Differentiated but concrete concept—7 to 9 years*
Jew: A person who goes to temple and Hebrew School.
Catholic: He goes to Mass every Sunday and goes to Catholic School.
Protestant: He belongs to a Protestant family; he gets bap-a-tized.
All boys and girls are not Jews because some are Catholic and some are Protestant . . . there is somp'in like Buddhist, but I don't know what the others are.
Dogs and cats cannot be Jewish . . . they cannot go to Synagogue or say prayers . . . but I guess if they belonged to a Jewish family they could be Jewish.
They do not confuse religious denominations with other designations, realize one can be Protestant and American, and think of their denomination in terms of practical, appropriate actions.
STAGE THREE: *Differentiated and abstract concept—10 to 12 years*
Jew: A person of a different faith. He believes in one God.
Catholic: A person who believes in the truths of the Roman Catholic Church.
Protestant: A person who believes in God and Christ and is loving to other men.

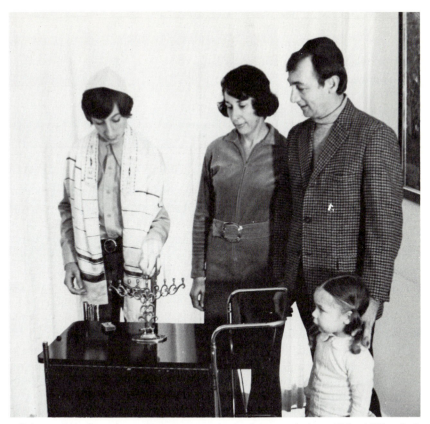

Religion and idealism play an important part in development during middle childhood; the church is a viable agency in the ecological unit. (Photo by Rick Coleman.)

All boys and girls are not Jewish because God made all different religions.
Dogs and cats cannot be Jewish because they are not human and would not
   understand religion.
   His understanding now is an acquired one. He thinks in more abstract
terms rather than in relation to particular actions.

Understanding of prayer (Elkind, 1971) moves through the same developmental stages. For young children, prayer is simply asking God for things. They "get mad" or "yell and scream" or "get angry at God" if prayers are not answered. Later prayer is thought of as talking to God. Children in this stage pray for their families and their pets as well as for themselves. They are disappointed, but look for reasons why, if their prayers are not answered. In the third stage, prayer is understood as a private communication. The child's prayers are more altruistic and general. They argue that prayer can be answered only as they share some responsibility for its fulfillment.

THE ROLE OF RELIGION

To the religious training you received as a child:
Who provided it.
What you thought of it.
What about it you did not understand.
What you prayed about.

_____

This same developmental sequence was highlighted when a group of children enrolled in Sunday school classes were interviewed and asked to "tell me something" about God, prayer, Jesus, heaven, sin, and the Bible. God was identified by younger children as Creator of everything—churches, houses, as well as seeds and trees and "a baby next June." Sixth-graders gave broader answers, but still with a concrete ring: "He is father of all people on earth"; "He created earth; we're made out of his image"; "he's sort of our leader"; "he thought up the Bible." One second-grader stated: "He loves people. He stays with you all the time. Sometimes He helps you."

Younger children, more than older children, dwelt on the posture of prayer: folded hands and bowed head. One-third of the children made reference to when prayers were said: at the table and before bed. A second-grader gave this thought-provoking answer: "It makes you think what Jesus did." Of course, this gives no clue as to what the second-grader thought Jesus did. A fifth-grader "felt" his way through this answer: "It's our connection with God. It's the communication God provided if you needed things he could give you."

In commenting about Jesus, a second-grader said simply: "He's a nice man"; while another questioned: "Is he the one that got killed and came alive again?" A third-grader stated: "He made the world. He's nice. He's old." The answer of one sixth-grader was indicative of those given by other children of this age: "It's one man God chose to tell people about him. He died for us. If you followed his ways, you'd become better people. He cured bunches of people of sickness."

A second-grader explained heaven as "God lives there. When people die, that is where they go. God's king and Mary's queen. Mary has to be queen if Jesus is to be God's Son. Mary has to have a prince." And another second-grader offered this testimony: "You can't see it. The space astronauts can. It's behind the clouds. God lives in it." With a faraway look in his eyes, a third-grader remarked: "I hear it's a very beautiful place. It's the farthest thing up in the sky." A sixth-grader volunteered: "Sort of a kingdom of God. When you die, you live on, and your spirit goes to heaven. It's God's kingdom, and He watches over us."

Half of the children made no responses at all to the idea of sin. Only 13 percent of the children below the third grade attempted an explanation, and one of these equated sin with her mother's blindness. Third- and fourth-graders defined sin as bad things people do. Answers from two sixth-grade boys are worth noting: "Every person does, almost everyone. It's usually real bad. Pray for forgiveness. If you do too much, you go to hell. But I don't believe that. It's the things you shouldn't do, like stealing and murder." And from the other: "When you do wrong to God and bad to mankind; do what God doesn't want you to do."

In reference to the Bible, younger children were more apt to talk about its physical properties: "it's a big book; it has a lot of words in it"; "the guy who invented the press decided to print the most famous book in the world, so he printed the Bible"; "it's thick and large"; "in red, Jesus said it"; "a long book." Sixth-graders gave these answers: "New Testament is like the biography of Jesus, and the Old Testament is when He created the earth." "It's the book of God. It tells all about Him. It was what the prophets and disciples wrote down so it would not get lost."

Older and younger children approach these teachings at different levels of mental functioning and so must assimilate the teachings in different ways. It is well to talk with children about things they are not ready to fully understand, but the adult in the situation should understand that simply repetition of phrases or memorization of Scripture does not guarantee that the child has incorporated the concepts as they are understood by older children and adults.

A second important point is the need to listen to what children have to say; they need encouragement to talk about their ideas of God, the church or Temple, the Scriptures, and prayer. They need help to clarify their ideas and may show far more insight and readiness to learn than is indicated by pat assertions that simply mimic adult teachings.

It is important to be honest with children as they question. Perhaps all questions children ask are religious questions: concerning life, death, the world, ways of dealing with sorrow, disappointment, disaster, the whys of personal hurt, crisis periods, social ills.

Children can experience the awe and wonder of life and love, an apple tree in bloom, a tiny baby, or a deep tragedy. Children can experience joy and sadness. Adults must be willing to think with children about these experiences as they sort and classify them.

What's Next?

1. Stories from children's literature chosen for moral development discussions: *The Samaritan. Galaxies.* Harper, Richard. Glenview, Illinois: Scott, Foresman, 1969.

Old Ben Bailey Meets His Match. Bridges. Justus, M. Scott, Foresman Reading Systems. Glenview, Illinois: Scott, Foresman, 1970. pp. 73–79.

The Lost Gold Piece. Pollack, C. Reader's Digest Advanced Skill Builders I. Pleasantville, New York: Reader's Digest Services, 1973.

Be Nice to Josephine. Windows. Howath, B. Scott, Foresman Reading Systems. Glenview, Illinois: Scott, Foresman, 1970, pp. 1–14.

The Old Man and His Grandson. With Skies and Wings. Grim, Jacob. (Ginn 360 Level 9). Boston: Ginn and Co., 1970, pp. 250–252.

The Bullock. The Sun That Warms. McCullough, Constance. (Ginn 360 Level 12). Boston: Ginn and Co., 1970, pp. 354–366.

George Washington Boy. Unknown.

2. *Exploring the Child's World,* H. Parkhurst. New York: Appleton-Century-Crofts, 1951.

3. *God Is a Good Friend to Have,* E. Marshall and S. Hample. New York: Simon and Schuster, 1969.

4. *The Sound of Summer Voices,* H. Tucker. New York: Stein and Day, 1969, pp. 42–43, 47.

5. "The Language of Prejudice," S. Steinberg. *Today's Education,* February 14, 1971, pp. 14, 16–17.

6. *Child Development Through Literature,* Landau et al. Englewood Cliffs, N.J.: Prentice-Hall, 1972: "The Dawn of Hate," by P. Horgan, pp. 396–405; "A Glory of the Moon," by J. Cary, pp. 293–295; "Death in the Fifth Grade," by M. Marks, pp. 418–423; "A Day's Wait," by E. Hemingway, pp. 137–139.

7. Film: *Angry Boy.* International Film Bureau, 332 S. Michigan Ave., Chicago, Illinois 60604. (33 min/b/w.)

Catalysts for Discussion

I. Kohlberg (1976) points out that "the most obvious characteristic of cognitive-developmental theories is their use of some type of stage concept, of some notion of age-linked sequential reorganizations in the development of moral attitudes." He continues by suggesting other assumptions underlying this approach and the social-learning approach.

A. Assumptions underlying cognitive developmental theories:

1. Moral development has a basic cognitive-structural or moral judgmental component.

2. The basic motivation for morality is a generalized motivation for acceptance, competence, self-esteem, or self-realization, rather than for meeting biological needs and reducing anxiety or fear.

3. Major aspects of moral development are culturally universal, because all cultures have common sources of social interaction, role taking, and social conflict, which require moral integration.

4. Basic moral norms and principles are structures arising through experiences of social interaction, rather than through internalization of rules that exist as external structures; moral stages are not defined by internalized rules, but by structures of interaction between the self and others.

5. Environmental influences in moral development are defined by the general quality and extent of cognitive and social stimulation throughout the child's development, rather than by specific experiences with parents or experiences of discipline, punishment, reward.

B. Assumptions underlying social-learning theories:

1. Moral development is growth of behavioral and affective conformity to moral rules rather than cognitive-structural change.

2. The basic motivation for morality at every point of moral development is rooted in biological needs or the pursuit of social reward and avoidance of social punishment.

3. Moral development or morality is culturally relative.

4. Basic moral norms are the internalization of external cultural rules.

5. Environmental influences on normal moral development are defined by quantitative variations in strength of reward, punishment, prohibitions, and modeling of conforming behavior by parents and other socializing agents.

II. "It's O.K., Son, Everybody Does It" (Griffin, 1965)

When Johnny was six years old, he was with his father when they were caught speeding. His father handed the officer a five-dollar bill with his driver's license. "It's O.K., Son," his father said as they drove off. "Everybody does it."

When he was eight, he was permitted at a family council, presided over by Uncle George, to hear the surest means to shave points off the income tax return. "It's O.K., Kid," his uncle said. "Everybody does it."

When he was nine, his mother took him to his first theater production. The box office man couldn't find any seats until his mother discovered an extra two dollars in her purse. "It's O.K., Son," she said. "Everybody does it."

When he was 12, he broke his glasses on the way to school. His Aunt Francine persuaded the insurance company that they had been stolen and they collected $27. "It's O.K., Kid," she said. "Everybody does it."

When he was 15, he made right guard on the high school football team. His coach showed him how to block and at the same time grab the opposing end by the shirt so that the official couldn't see it. "It's O.K., Kid," the coach said. "Everybody does it."

When he was 16, he took his first summer job at the big market. His assignment was to put the over-ripe tomatoes in the bottom of the boxes and the good ones on top where they would show. "It's O.K., Kid," the manager said. "Everybody does it."

When he was 18, Johnny and a neighbor applied for a college scholarship. Johnny was a marginal student. His neighbor was in the upper three per cent of his class, but he couldn't play right guard. Johnny got the assignment. "It's O.K.," they told him. "Everybody does it."

When he was 19, he was approached by an upper classman who offered the test answers for three dollars. "It's O.K.," he said. "Everybody does it."

Johnny was caught and sent home in disgrace. "How could you do this to your mother and me?" his father said. "You never learned anything like this at home." His aunt and uncle were also shocked.

If there's one thing the adult world can't stand, it's a kid who cheats. . . ."

Beyond the Classroom Experiences

1. Interview children individually concerning lying: if it is all right; why or why not. Compare with the findings of Medinnus.

2. Present some hypothetical stealing behaviors to children and ask them to tell which is worse. See if you can establish any trends. Discuss their decisions with them, and try to see at what stage of moral development they are.

3. Through projective techniques, perhaps pictures or stories, ask children to tell what is "right" to do in certain situations. Evaluate their responses in the light of ideas presented in the chapter.

4. Ask parents to rate the items in the Positive Value Character List in ways reported by Stinnett and Kreps. Compare your findings with theirs.

5. Try some of Elkind's questions about religion with children. See if their concepts are similar or different from his findings.

Chapter 10

The Child in the Marketplace

This chapter is designed to help you:

- see how children influence the economy.
- realize the economic impact of children on the family.
- understand how clothing and housing can affect development.
- become aware of toy hazards and laws designed to eliminate them.
- consider the role of work opportunities in children's development
- become familiar with the techniques employed by advertisers seeking child patronage.
- examine the involvement of children in advertisements

The Cost of a Child

The cost and value of children has only received scholarly attention in the past decade, and the past five years have witnessed tremendous growth in understanding these concepts and their potential impact on parent-child relationships and future facility and family planning. Children have both non-economic and economic values. Among the non-economic ones are feelings of prestige, creativity, accomplishment and "immortality" on the part of parents. Their economic value as productive agents in the home, on the farm, or in the family business has declined with modernization and industrialization of the United States. Although they still perform some economic functions in care of the home, disposal of garbage, babysitting and yard and car maintenance, their over-all economic benefits have been termed negligible by population economists. Their potential as sources of economic security for parents in case of emergency or in old age has been diminished by Social Security and insurance programs (Espanshade, 1977).

As living standards have continued to rise, parental conceptions of what they should provide for children have also risen, contributing to the spiraling cost of rearing a family. The direct maintenance costs for children today do not seem to vary consistently between farm, rural non-farm, and urban families; but the geographic region, level of living, race of head of household, parental educational level, and tastes and preferences for life style do cause the expense level to vary. It is more expensive to rear children in the West, according to data from the USDA. Families living on $10,500 to $13,500 annual incomes after taxes correspond roughly to USDA low-cost food plan designation. Those in the $16,500 to $20,000 disposable income range constitute the USDA moderate-cost level category. The latter group spends about 50 percent more on food than the former. The variation caused by level of living and region is reflected in the fact that a rural non-farm family on low-cost plan in the North Central region will spend an estimated $31,675 to rear a child to age 18 whereas a rural non-farm family in the Western region on a moderate-cost plan will expend $58,255. Of course, in averaging, a great many differences from one family to another are hidden. Medical care is an example: dental care, braces, regular health checkups would all make great variations from one age level to the next. After school care, music and dancing lessons, tutoring and club memberships account for some of the differences. Families with more money to spend are the families who buy such services. The leading item in child rearing costs is housing, claiming 32.3 percent of the total. Food is estimated to claim 24.3 percent, followed by 16.1 percent transportation, 9.5 percent clothing, 5.3 percent medical care, 1.5 percent education and 11 percent for all other expenses. Projections are that by 1990 today's one-year-old will need $47,330 to attend a state university or $82,830 for a private one for four years.

Aside from direct maintenance costs of rearing children, economists are estimating the opportunity costs involved. These include the loss of earnings if mothers are unemployed while performing child-care functions, the reduced opportunities to invest and save, and the relinquishment of certain consumptive expenditures which lower the family's standard of living. They compute the opportunity costs for the first child to be $75,000 for the least-educated mothers and $155,000 for those with post graduate educations, with an average of $100,000. They conclude that direct maintenance and opportunity costs of rearing children are about equal.

While the real income tends to increase over the family life cycle, the level of living generally declines for families with children; it generally rises for childless couples. Therefore, the family standard of living typically declines as children grow older and rises when the first child becomes financially independent.

The Child as a Consumer

To talk about the child as a consumer is a two-pronged topic: there must be concern for the child as a user of many items, but there must also be concern for his actual role in the marketplace. He is a consumer of food, housing, clothing, toys, medical skills and drugs, educational supplies, entertainment, and out-of-home care. All these must be examined, planned, provided for. In addition, as the child exercises a more active role as a selector and buyer, he becomes a more profitable target of advertising and special merchandising. He is given more room for choice: he may have an allowance to spend, and many times a part-time job. In addition, he is more able to know what he wants, influenced by his own likes and the need to conform to his peers.

Legislation has been enacted to protect the child in his passive role as consumer, and to help him be better informed in his active consumer role.

Of course, legislation cannot do the whole job of protection; adults in contact with the child must take responsibility: (1) reading labels or otherwise discovering the quality of the product or service intended for the child's use; (2) helping the child make wise use of food, clothing, and toys; (3) planning for educational experiences for the child so that he becomes a wise consumer, in just the same way experiences are planned so that he becomes an effective reader or skilled in physical performance or social relations.

McNeal (1965) conducted personal interviews with middle class children ages 5, 7, and 9 to determine whether or not adult consumer behavior has its roots in childhood. He posed questions about their consumer experiences, desires and economic knowledge. The younger children typically received their money as gifts or allowances, but it was not very meaningful to them. Seven-year-olds more often reported regular allowances and saw the funds as a necessity to acquire goods. They reported shopping independently in a couple of stores to purchase items for their own use or staples for the family. The oldest subjects received allowances and did odd jobs. They viewed money to spend as less exciting and reported shopping in more stores and for larger items. Shopping independence was granted earlier to boys; but by age 9 girls reported patronizing more stores, and having more interest and experience in shopping. Between age 5 and 9 there is a rapid growth in independent consumer behavior. Children are considered potential consumers from age 7, when they begin to understand what money can do. All children in the study said they accompany their mothers shopping, and almost all make suggestions about the purchases made. With age, their suggestions about family goods increases. Three fourths said their parents explain why they do not follow their suggestions. About half of the 7-and-9 year olds said they influence their friends purchases.

The children had definite preferences for shopping places: five-year-olds like grocery stores the most and department stores least. Seven-year-olds like supermarkets and discount houses. These younger subjects dislike crowdedness and having to wait in lines, as well as lack of cleanliness and certain desired items for purchase. By age nine, there was less expressed antipathy toward stores, probably because this age only go to the ones they like. All ages said they hold conversations with the store personnel.

The marketing knowledge of the children increased greatly between ages 5 and 9, and was about equal for boys and girls. Whereas the youngest knew about farms, 7-year-olds were aware of manufacturing and nines about processors. Knowledge about wholesalers and transportation of goods was low for all ages. Over 60 percent of all age groups were brand conscious, and all ages considered shopping exciting. The majority saw it as a feminine function in adults.

Consumer education as a separate entity in the elementary curriculum is a reality in many school systems. It involves much more than merely preparation for buying things. It can include value clarification, need satisfaction, goal conflicts, concern for quality housing in the community, clear air and water, the general welfare of others. Some important units typically include occupation and income; resource management, including time and energy as well as money; economic choicemaking; information sources, advertising and motivators; buymanship; consumer credit; insurance; savings and investments; taxation; laws and agencies for protection; consumers rights and responsibilities; the economy; the consumer and the environment.

Children engaged in consumer education enjoy: games in which they can practice their consumer skills, field trips to see production and marketing functions, record-keeping of their resource use; ad analysis; projects and experiments related to pricing, packaging, sales, and product testing. Relating their activities to their own consumer role makes learning more fun: studying school insurance, budgeting their own allowance.

Consumer education helps children develop skills, knowledge and attitudes which assist them in being more successful in their marketplace roles. This education supplements the abilities they acquire in the home through observing and imitating parents' consumerism (Rader, 1972).

Advertising

It does not come as a surprise that teen-agers have money to spend—more than $10 billion a year, not counting what is spent on them by parents. They have become a major market in our economy, and many products are designed for them especially. The middle childhood people also are targets of advertising for their own spending and because they have a choice in what products are bought, not only for their own use, but also for family consumption.

A committee of the Federal Trade Commission in February, 1978 termed TV advertising aimed at children under age 8 unscrupulous, and proposed a ban on it. Additionally, the committee proposed that ads for high sugar foods intended for viewers under age 11 were ill-advised due to the poor eating habits and tooth decay they foster. They estimated children see 20,000 ads annually.

Children are often involved in advertising products for adults as well as for children. Their cherubic faces appeal to the consumer's affinity for youth, and their cute dialogue is apt to ring in one's ears as an effective reminder to buy one product or service over another. To associate children's charm or testimonies with products to enhance sales is as ethically questionable as to employ a well-known adult to endorse a child's product in attempting to influence their purchases.

Many children's products such as toys and games are direct outgrowths of characters they have met in first-run movies or on weekly TV shows designed to appeal to youth. Among the currently marketed are a number of dolls and accessories: Cher with clothes, Charlie's Angels with make-up center and clothes; Donnie and Marie Osmond with van, mike, phonograph; The Waltons' mom and pop; Star Wars creatures, toothbrush and linens; Evel Knievel with bike; Fonzie Doll; Bionic Woman with beauty salon and dome house; Six Million Dollar Man with repair station, porta communicator, critical assignment arms and legs; and Sesame Street puppets and neighborhood storefronts. Board games are available related to *Welcome Back, Kotter; Happy Days; Star Wars; Laverne and Shirley; Kojak; the Waltons; Six Million Dollar Man;* and *Bionic Woman.* Viewing a show featuring a character that is associated with a toy, game or other product constitutes a virtual advertisement which lures the child purchaser into the marketplace.

An analysis of advertising on cereals in one outlet of a large supermarket chain yielded astounding emphasis on items which would appeal to children in the 5–12 age range. The top shelf held 33 cereals representing 9 brands. Three manufacturers featured no ads, but 63 percent of the boxes carried high-color illustrations of items ranging from a free 30″ x 36″ kite, "easy to put together and fly"; to a free chance for a $10,000 Hawaiian vacation, boat, car or van. Items offered for sale went from a 3-piece pocket tool set or an 11″ x 14″ cross stitch with floss, needle, and instructions, each for $1.50; to a $13.50 jogging outfit, in conjunction with a Bruce Jenner endorsement of physical fitness. One item was especially designed for sale to children: a brass door plaque, "personalized" to "make your room look distinctive, really yours. Be the first to have this." The cost for this item was $2.25, with a promised refund if not completely satisfied.

The center shelf was stocked with boxes even more appealing to youngsters. There were 11 brands, with 3 companies not featuring advertising on their products. Of the 30 cereals, 90 percent featured giveaways or items for sale. Thirteen had free items inside the cereal box or printed on the package itself. A 5-inch fishing rod and reel, sugarless bubble gum, a glow-in-the-dark plastic dinosaur skeleton, and Star Wars character stick-on were representative of these prizes.

One cereal offered five possible give-aways inside with no indication which was included in any particular box. Two described a 50¢ to $1 refund on any of four toys by a specified manufacturer with a proof of purchase seal from the cereal and the toy. Another featured a free Amtrak trip for a child under 12, "anywhere in the U.S.", for 3 box tops and an adult paid fare. Several cereals by one processor gave details for a poster contest offering a free coloring book and set of liquid crayons for all entrants and 2,000 cartridge tele-games systems to the winners. Two box tops and original artwork meeting contest specifications were required for participation in the contest. For sale were a pocket calculator for $6.95 and two tops; a basketball, soccer ball or football for $6.99 and two tops; a poncho-blanket, 50″ x 60″, "virgin acrylic" in blue, or red for $8.95 and two tops.

The bottom shelf held 23 cereals from 6 companies. Two manufacturers featured no ads on their products, but 78 percent of the cereals had advertising, mainly appealing to children. Again items inside the boxes were common, including iron-on designs and posters. One cereal is pushing a collection of 50 metallic coins (1-1/2″) one for each state, embossed with the state flag, date admitted to the union, number of sq. miles, the state flower, capital, shape and nickname. One comes inside each box with no designation of the state on the outside. A pro-curve practice baseball, free film processing, and flower seeds were offered for proof-of-purchase seals only. An instamatic camera was offered for $17.95 and two box tops. The art contest and Amtrak free trip were also featured on the bottom shelf.

Advertising on cereal boxes can affect children in a number of ways. It may help determine what kind they eat, often depending on the offers on the outside more than the nutrition inside. It may help determine the amount they consume, particularly if they need to accumulate a number of tops or seals to get the items offered. It may help teach them the "something for nothing" concept, as in the case of the sweepstakes with prizes worth thousands of dollars or the "free" toys in the package. It tempts them to purchase items sight-unseen, and without adequate comparison shopping through vivid descriptions and sometimes deceiving pictures or endorsements. There is the powerful pull of conformity to have what peers have in order to trade, barter and play with them. Advertising capitalizes on their other interests by offering items related to popular movies, sports stars, or cartoon characters. It may instill some consumer attitudes and practices, including brand loyalties, that will last the child's entire life.

Children hear advertisements of many of these items on television along with their favorite cartoon fare. They are lured by the "free items." In addition, there seems to be an appeal to "sending off," to receiving mail, which children enjoy responding to. Cereal makers are important buyers of time on children's programs.

Children are subjected to a great deal of selling pressure as they watch television. More families in America have television sets than have telephones or bath tubs. By the time a child enters school he has watched about 4,000 hours of television, which is more hours than he will spend in school during the following six years. By the time children finish high school they have spent 22,000 hours in front of the TV, compared to 11,000 hours in classrooms. Much of the TV fare for children is cartoons and advertisements (McDaniel, 1972).

In 1½ hours one Saturday morning (from 7:00 A.M. until 8:30) children saw 3 cartoon series, 31 ad segments and 2 "In the News" presentations of 2½ minutes each. (The latter is the CBS attempt to add something worthwhile to children's programming.) The cartoons were broken in the first half-hour segment into three separate stories of 6 to 7 minutes each. The other two series were each divided into four segments of approximately 5 minutes each. Even when the content is completely ignored—which is another topic in itself—this sort of programming may well teach children not to really attend. Certainly it does not enhance staying power, or developmnent of attention span.

In each half hour approximately 8 minutes was devoted to ads, which is within the guidelines of the National Association of Broadcasters' Code which permits 16 minutes of commercials per program hour on children's shows, but only 8 minutes during prime time adult shows. An advertising minute on a morning children's cartoon show costs about $8,000; on a nighttime show, the price goes to $80,000 per commercial minute.

On the average, children see about 20 ads per hour, but what they see and how it is presented constitutes the real problem. During the Saturday morning period, 12 advertisements dealt with what the child should eat or drink. Other surveys place this higher—up to 50 percent of all ads. The children were admonished to eat a particular cereal so they could get Bobby Sherman records; to ask for a particular kind of vitamin "shaped for grown up kids"; to eat pancakes, powdered juice, milk shakes from a particular chain, a candy bar which was said to have a "chocolaty taste," and many cereals.

Other commercials dealt with things children were to buy or ask for, for themselves: Ding-alings, Zoomer-Boomers, Spin Buggies (that are "wild—too wild to stay on a track" and which are sold alone or in sets), Feed the Monkey game (featured on "Romper Room").

The commercials were fast moving; children were shown having a wonderful, laughing time with the product. Many items were in a set series, so that first purchases would make subsequent purchases necessary, or certainly desirable. Several of the commercials were repeated verbatim during the hour-and-a-half. There seemed not to be a desire to impart information, but to create a feeling or attitude about the product as a "must" thing—and an "in" thing.

During another hour on Saturday, 8:55 to 9:55AM, *The Popeye Hour* was the feature. Its continuity was broken by the showing of 16 ads, two "In the News" features, one dope education spot, and 1 NASA spot explaining the work of IUE, the International Ultraviolet Explorer. Of the 16 ads, 13 were for products, two plugged other TV shows featuring soul music and high adventure, and one was related to bus transportation to a college football game. The products advertised included two dolls; one chocolate drink mix; peanut butter cookies made by elves; one type of candy that makes you blast off; two hamburger chains with attendant clown and magician; three games; a construction set; and a toy rocket set. Each ad included catchy music and strong admonitions concerning the potential role of the product in the lives of young viewers.

Bob McKenzie of the *Oakland* (California) *Tribune* summed the ad situation as follows: "The rocking, socking hard sell of children's ads make adult commercials sound like apologetic murmurs. The makers of $15 toys know that the juvenile must be worked up to a fever pitch if he is to have sufficient fanatical gleam in his eye to wrest that much cash from Dad, so they pour on the juice."

Some protection has been given children. Particular manufacturers have been called to task for false advertisement. It is no longer possible to have a professional race driver, for instance, endorse a toy race car, because he really has no special competence to judge toys that are desirable for children. The practice of having the master of ceremonies—Captain Kangaroo, for example—do the advertising of products on the show is not allowed. There must be an effort to show the real size of the product, in relation to children.

Examples of charges against advertisements that were removed from the air because of unfair exploitation of children: special filming that exaggerated the performance or appearance of a racing car toy; a dancing doll that appeared to dance by itself, but really needed the assistance of an operator.

Another source of protection is the child himself. Perhaps in their frenzy to sell their products, the ad men are going too far. A recent study (McGregor, 1971), directed by a Harvard Business School professor, underscored the need to tone down or eliminate "pitches" to children. The ads are losing their credibility. By the second grade children have begun to develop a cynicism and slight negative association toward commercials. By the sixth grade they respond with "global mistrust" and "general contemptuous rejection." This attitude, while it may protect them from overzealous manufacturers of many things, may also generalize to all sorts of forms of public information so that children may be unable to avail themselves of any public information source. This points up the need for early and regular consumer education.

Clothing

Clothing helps contribute to the identity of the person who wears it, and children in the middle years use clothes as a clue to sex role, occupation, relative financial status, and to identify such groups as Cub Scouts. By adolescence obsession with the style and condition of apparel and other physical endowments becomes paramount, particularly for girls. While clothes can be more a source of positive feelings toward self than of negative ones, for some children their clothing is a definite source of embarrassment, discomfort, or deprecation.

Read (1950) has summarized the role of clothing in the lives of children:

> Children do like clothes and find real satisfaction in them. Bright colors and gay materials, the feel of different textures in clothing, the comfortable, familiar garment as well as the new one—these are all things that bring pleasure to the child. Clothes make a contribution to the process of growing up when they are right from his standpoint. They can help to make the man.

School-age children's clothing is important to them for many reasons. What their friends think about it, whether or not it enables them to be active, how it feels, and whether or not they can manipulate the fasteners are all important considerations. They are not very concerned about durability, safety, price, becomingness, variety or cleanliness in clothing—considerations left up to parents.

By age 8 or 9, when it becomes important to the child to be like his friends or associates, he may become slavishly conventional about his clothing. Whereas earlier he might have enjoyed dressing like a sibling, by this age he chooses to conform to his peers rather than to his family. Hand-me-downs need to be remade or individualized by some ornamentation to make them acceptable to him and in keeping with current fashion. With the rise in sex-role identification, children have a distinct desire to wear what is appropriate for their sex, although today this may constitute only such subtle differences as the side of the garment on which the buttons are sewn.

An obsession over clothes, cleanliness, or neatness may signal a personality disorder in children. The child who deliberately appears unkempt may be indicating his hostility or defiance of authority through his dress rather than ignorance or lack of proper clothing and grooming aids with which to work. If clothing and appearance are very important to his parents, the unloved child can find a very effective means of punishing them through his dress.

Children do not have the same feeling as adults about what goes together or what is appropriate. It is important that children feel good about what they wear. They may need help in learning how to choose clothing and how to care for it. Preferences for various elements of design in clothing seem to change with age. Older children show a decreasing interest in bright colors, and red as the favorite hue of 5- and 6-year-olds bows to blue and green by grades 5 and 6. Checks and stripes gain in popularity with older children as use of solid colors declines (Hunt, 1959). The age at which the overall design of the garment becomes important is not clear, but with age there is a definite rise in clothing interest and awareness of clothing fads, such as jeans, patches, embroidery, nailheads, and printed tee shirts.

With the greater general affluence clothing manufacturers have used television to help sell children's clothing, capitalizing on the popularity of particular shows through merchandise tie-ins with them. Manufacturers of children's clothing items capitalize when possible on their attraction to TV and comic book characters, such as the Disney animals. There are Happy Birthday Mickey and Tom and Jerry sleepwear items; Billy the Kid swim trunks, jackets and shirts; Raggedy Ann and Andy overalls; Winnie the Pooh prints in various clothing items. Pre-teens are being encouraged to sew their clothes using patterns endorsed by Marie Osmond, and a whole line called Olive's (Osmond) Kids capitalizes on the famous family's name and image. Jumpsuits with career badges, such as crew chief, railroad engineer, trucker or military appeal to the children's interest in occupations, and major league sports. Symbolism appears on a host of items from belts to jackets and p.j.'s.

All this tells us that children are important as consumers and that they are the target of ad agencies. To be aware of this is to be more able to protect them and to plan a more meaningful system of consumer education, beginning with very young children.

By preadolescence there is concern over fit of clothing. Poor fit has been a prime complaint of the child of the middle years and a frequent reason for this age group's not liking their clothing. Sources of discomfort have included garments that were too tight, too small, too large, too short, or too long; and those that were too hot, scratchy, or hard to get on. (Cassidy, 1958; Tate et al., 1960; Miller, 1957).

Since dress constitutes a potential conflict-area for children and adults, there is need for children to be advised concerning fashion that is suitable, but it is also important that they be allowed a choice within the limits of propriety. The influence of the teacher on dress among children in the middle years has received almost no attention from research.

The general pattern is for mothers to purchase the clothing for the school-age child, often accompanied by the child. Girls more often go shopping for clothes than boys; however, boys have indicated an interest in doing so. With age, confidence in self-selection of clothing seems to rise, 8- and 9-year-olds showing little independence in their selections, 10-year-olds being more independent, and 11- and 12-year-olds having even more confidence.

The Haley-Hendrickson Person Preference Test (1974) features a series of ink drawn female stimulus-figures approximately eight years of age presented in sets of four with controlled variation in hair and clothing styles and posture, body type and face held constant. Second-grade students asked to select their preferred figure in each set indicated a difference in choice when hair and clothing were manipulated. Both boys and girls expressed stronger feelings relative to hair style than to clothing. They expressed choices indicating a preference for a feminine stereotype in girls their approximate age. Girls were more opinionated in their selections than boys. The children did not seem to match hair and clothing according to the personality types they were drawn to represent.

Clothing for children between ages 6 and 12 should allow for vigorous use of the arms and legs, and the fabric must be able to withstand hard wear and soiling. Poor fit is a common complaint of children with respect to their clothing. Clothes are sized by body build rather than age. The five measurements involved are chest, waist, hips, height and weight. The correct size is the one that best corresponds to these five measurements of the child. Children sometimes skip sizes due to their growth spurts. Buying clothes that are too large is not economical for this reason. Deep hems or tucks, deep cuffs, generous seams, raglan sleeves, elastic waist insets are features of clothing which hedge against growth.

Children distinctly dislike heavy, stiff and rough fabrics. The fabric should be machine washable and soil resistant, pre-shrunk, and colorfast. Stretch and knit fabrics allow for more growth than woven ones. Firm weaves and knits withstand strain better, and prints show soil and wrinkles less than solid colors. Reinforced seams and knees, shank buttons, and interfaced buttonholes contribute to longer-wearing clothing. Children enjoy having pockets in their clothing to carry their treasures. Girls enjoy pants or shorts coordinated with their dresses in the interest of modesty. Both boys and girls enjoy wearing pants, and sweaters and knit shirts (Roberts and McKee, 1976).

Shoes are one article of apparel that should not be handed-down. Each new shoe takes on the shape of its original wearer's feet, and subsequent wearers' feet will never be exactly the same. Shoes cannot be altered to fit, and they should be carefully fitted when purchased. Both feet should be measured and the shoes purchased to fit the larger foot. The child should stand on both feet to assess the fit. Shoes need to be ½ to ¾ inches longer than the longest toe, and if they are the correct width, it should be possible to pinch a small crease in the upper part of the shoe when the child is standing. The sides should not gape out when the foot is bent, and there should be room to move the toes when walking. There should be room in the heel to insert a finger between the back of the shoe and the foot (Roberts and Baker, 1977).

The care of clothing seems to be of little concern at this age. Leaving garments where they are removed is the most common practice. By ages 11 or 12 the very best dress or suit might be treated with better care. Girls in the lower-middle socioeconomic group reportedly participate more in the care of their clothing than those in the upper-middle or upper-lower groups.

Each year one million people are burned in their homes when clothing catches fire, causing 175,000 burn injuries and at least 4,000 deaths (Flaming Clothes, 1971). Most of the victims are children, the poor, the elderly, and the infirm. In 1953 the Federal Flammable Fabrics Act was passed, which helped rid the country of explosively flammable clothing. Amendments to the Act in 1967 broadened the categories covered to include hats, gloves, and footwear. The Act makes it unlawful to manufacture, import, or sell fabrics that are dangerously flammable.

Action by the Consumer Products Safety Commission in 1977 banned the use of the flame-retardant chemical Tris in children's sleepwear through size 14 after it was found to cause changes in cells and cancer. Even though the danger to children from sleepwear has been lessened, Tris is also used in a number of other products to which they are routinely exposed: doll's clothing, toy sewing kits, draperies, furniture upholstery and tent fabric, polyurethane foam mattresses, auto seat cushions, automobile headliners, Christmas decorations, plastic products, fiberboard back panels for TV sets. (Molloy, 1977). Although most difficult, parents need to remain informed on developments in industry and legislation by government impinging on their children's clothing and other products. Theirs is the last line of protection for the well-being of America's youth.

Housing

There is increasing concern for dealing with the human aspects of housing, perhaps most visible in planning housing for the elderly, the handicapped and the disadvantaged. There is need for greater attention to the child as a housing consumer. Write (1951, p. 21) has stated this well:

> Home should be a place in which parents, children, friends and pets all find equal enjoyment—a place to which adults could invite their friends without apology, youngsters play without endless taboos, and the family cats and dogs nap peacefully without having to keep a weather eye out for approaching punishment.

The house serves functions for children as well as for adults. The house should contribute toward their fulfillment of security, affection, intimacy, and loyalty, but often housing thwarts and obstructs the achievement of these goals. Housing exerts a powerful influence on mental stability, emotional maturity, and total personality. The very nature of a house may help develop in children judgment, taste, courtesy, comradeship, fairness, and lasting memories. Furnishings in the home either help or inhibit growth in self-reliance, and if they are not sized and arranged with children's needs in mind, they may be inhibitory. Modern houses are perhaps better designed for children than older ones. They tend to feature more light, more space and storage space, less fragile furnishings; but in the inner-city the physical facilities for rearing children are probably poorer than they were a century ago (Mumford, 1940).

Figure 10-1.

Whereas we commonly think a family needs in its housing hot and cold water, air-conditioning and heating systems, glassed-in showers, electronic ranges, and king-size beds, the family's basic need is for space—to romp, to sulk, to study, and to socialize. Reimer (1945) studied maladjustment of 300 families and found this problem was most strikingly related to crowding.

Perhaps children's values in housing were represented in recent experimental workshops for 7- to 12-year-olds based on the assumption that children are natural architects. Supported by a grant from the National Endowment for the Arts, the project resulted in a show entitled "Kids As Architects," in the Renwick Gallery. Participants were given no technical instructions but only suggested topics to design: Energy House, using sun, water and air for power; Snug-A-Bug House, taking its inspiration from the shell homes of snails and turtles; Hideaway for Two in some remote spot as underwater, or on an iceberg; and Kids-Only-Town. The industrial and architectural designer in charge was well pleased with their creations. (See Figure 10-1.)

Children in 40 families (Riebel, 1950) listed some of their gripes and dissatisfactions with their homes. Among them were: no modern conveniences; insufficient space for storage, play, and study; condition and location of house; and household chores. With the current emphasis on low-income housing, there should be corresponding concern for providing features that will enhance the development of children. High-rise apartment living makes it difficult for parents to supervise the play of the very young unless they are outside with them. Even 5- to 7-year-olds need some supervision at times. In housing developments provision should be made for adequate outside space for the probable number of children in the various age groups who will live in the area. Separation of very young from school-age children is highly desirable with respect to play space.

Ground floor bathroom facilities and water fountains are necessities if children must use elevators to reach their own home areas. A better solution is to plan family housing units other than high-rise dwellings. Whether in suburbia or the inner city, every family needs a bit of outside "private" space, such as a small plot of green earth or a patio. Outside storage space is vital for upkeep and protection of property and belongings. An out-of-sight area for garbage cans is also desirable.

Johnson (1952) suggested that toy storage may be centralized in the child's room or decentralized according to type in various areas of the home: quiet play materials (books, puzzles) in the living room; creative (water colors, scissors, glue) and experimental items in the kitchen; active play materials (skooters, wagons, skates) in the garage or carport; floating toys in the bathroom. Areas designated for play in various parts of the home and specific storage areas give children a feeling of security.

Storage is a prime concern if children are expected to keep their belongings neat. Even a spot to keep a box of their very own will help! A private place is quite important. Closet space designed at the proper height for younger children also encourages orderliness. Children will appreciate some locked storage space for safe-keeping of such special items as bird nests, diaries, or jewelry.

The growth and development of children bring many changes in family patterns of living and in the demands made on the family dwelling. Children need space, not only to eat, sleep, dress, and bathe, but to play, paint, conduct projects and experiments, keep collections, and study. Children's parties, planned or spontaneous, make certain demands on the home. Children's increase in age is likely to call for more interior space and more outdoor play area. A bedroom for two children of the same sex or separate bedrooms for children of opposite sexes is a worthy goal during middle childhood, as the desire for privacy grows.

The way the family plays together may dictate housing needs. If divergence of interests is great several areas for pursuit of interests may be needed; whereas, if the family does many things together, size rather than number of rooms may be more important. Kitchen arrangements that do not encourage children's running through reduce kitchen accidents such as burns or falls (Agan and Luchsinger, 1965).

Changes in the house and its furnishings are needed as the children grow, not only to reduce the chance of accidents but to allow children to feel "at home" in their own house. Among the features that can contribute to this feeling are outdoor play space, indoor play area, a place to keep private possessions, low shelves and hooks, simple and sturdy furniture, upholstery that is washable or Scotchgarded, a place where children's ongoing projects can be left standing from day to day, and allowing children to help in the selection, arrangement, and care of home furnishings. When housing is not planned with children in mind, health and emotional problems likely include fatigue, disagreement among children, nagging by parents, and leaving home for fun (Gries and Ford, 1932).

Furnishings that children use should be suited to their size and proportion, with allowances made for growth. Furniture should be able to withstand hard usage, not prone to tipping over, and yet light enough for children to move. Sharp corners and rough edges along with chances for pinched fingers should be avoided. Every living room should have at least one chair to fit each child.

The lack of design progress in children's furniture is due to a controversy over whether it should be designed for the child's convenience or of adult dimensions because children quickly outgrow small-scaled pieces. The ideal would be pieces that would allow for growth by accommodating to the user's satisfaction, without forcing poor and unnatural postures and uncomfortable positions. One piece of furniture that is both necessary and versatile for the child is a table. Among the many uses of this item are not only writing, drawing, and eating but also climbing, sewing, sitting, table games, tea partying, displaying art, studying, and imaginary play as a tent, boat, chimney for Santa, and garage for small cars. A large proportion of desks and tables used by children at home are not the correct height. Day (1960) designed a three-height table adjustable to serve the needs of children from early childhood to adulthood. Testing it with a sample ranging in age from 18 months to 18 years she found that the frequency of its use was similar for all age groups. Even the parents of the subjects used the experimental table as a stepstool, footstool, a place to write, stack clothes, and eat. Parents noted certain changes in children's habits while using the table: less study on the bed and floor, greater enjoyment of homework and table games, and play and study materials centered rather than scattered.

Wallace (1978) designed a unique children's furnishing especially for 3- to 6-year-olds in group settings. Tested in children's centers, its multifunctional nature was found to stimulate motor development, foster small muscle coordination, and lead children to cooperative and imaginative play. The design features three major parts—a seating panel, a rear leg panel, and a front leg panel—and giant nuts and bolts effecting easy assembly for 5- and 6-year-olds without adult assistance. Younger children typically needed some assistance to execute their creations. Children were found to make from these basic components not only regular chairs but also loungers and rockers, benches, thrones, stools, houses, tunnels, forts, fences, sliding boards, and climbing structures. The components can also be used to make giant building blocks and open storage shelves. Disassembled, the parts can be nested in relatively little space. The molded plywood construction can support up to 150 pounds when bolts are securely fastened, and the sizing of components is anthropometrically correct for children in this age group.

Toy Safety

There are approximately 1,200 toy manufacturers in the United States producing between 2½ billion and 3 billion dollars worth of toys each year. In addition, there are about 83,000 entries of imported toys annually. Children are the recipients of most of these items, tokens of love. It is most unfortunate when one of these articles causes hurt instead of happiness to a child.

Toy injuries accounted for less than 5 percent of the around-home injuries as they are compiled by the Food and Drug Administration. Bicycles were involved in the majority of toy-connected injuries. Most of the others were accounted for by other vehicle type toys: roller skates, sleds, and tricycles. Protecting children from unsafe toys and substances is the job of the parent as well as lawmaking bodies. Each year 170,000 persons are treated in hospital emergency rooms for toy-associated injuries. Hosts of others are treated at home and in the offices of physicians. The primary hazards in toys are sharp edges, small parts, loud noises, sharp points, propelled objects, electrical toys, and the wrong toy for the wrong age child. The U.S. Consumer Product Safety Commission does not have the authority to inspect toys for safety prior to marketing. However, it can ban products which are called to the attention of the Commission and are found to be hazardous. To report such items, write TOYS, U.S. Consumer Product Safety Commission, Washington, D.C. 20207. Under Federal Hazardous Substances Act, electrical toys must have age recommendation labels. Toys with heating elements, for example, must be labeled for use by children ages 8 and over.

Safety depends on the product, but also on the child. One child may be able to handle a toy that would be dangerous for another. A child should be taught general safety rules for using toys: bicycle riders must learn traffic regulations and refrain from "horseplay" while riding. The buyer should reject obvious pitfalls: sharp parts, brittle plastic or glass that can be easily broken, open flames, poorly constructed toys that expose sharp points when pulled apart, toys with moving parts (gears or springs) that may pinch fingers or catch hair, whistle mouthpieces that could be swallowed.

In order to protect children from household hazards more effectively, the Child Protection Act of 1966 was passed, which amended the Federal Hazardous Substances Labeling Act of 1960. The original Act required labeling that would alert buyers to potential dangers of articles commonly stored around the home. It also required that the label give directions for what to do in the event a person was injured by the substance. There were loopholes in this law. If an article was not used primarily "in and around the household," it did not come under the law. If an article was indeed labeled as hazardous, it could not be removed from the market, no matter how dangerous it seemed to be. If the item were not sold in a package, it did not come under the provisions of the labeling act.

Two examples can be cited of such loopholes. At one Easter time stores throughout the country sold imported toy ducklings, potentially dangerous, but not packaged, and therefore not required to be labeled. The novelties were made from stuffed skins of slaughtered ducklings and were found to contain high concentrations of benzene hexachloride, a poisonous insecticide that had been added as a preservative. Other such toys contained arsenic compounds or were contaminated with a microorganism, Salmonella. Other unpackaged items that escaped the regulation were jewelry made of jequirity beans, bright red and black and deadly poisonous. One bean chewed and swallowed could cause death within hours.

The Child Protection Act of 1966 amended the original act in three ways:

- All hazardous substances, regardless of wrapping or lack of it, were brought under the safeguards of the Federal Hazardous Substances Labeling Act. The word "labeling" was removed.
- Household substances so hazardous that warning labels were not adequate safeguards were banned from interstate commerce.
- Any toy or other children's article containing hazardous substances, regardless of packaging, was banned.

Because of these regulations, the Food and Drug Administration, charged with enforcing them, has been able to prohibit the importing of a type of fireworks known as "cracker balls," a small ball that explodes on impact. It is inevitable that children mistake the small round objects for candies. About 30 cases of injuries occurred in which children bit into a ball causing loosened teeth, burns, and cuts on the gums, tongue, and cheeks. FDA has also prevented the importing of certain dolls made in England and Poland which had a face made of nitrocellulose, "gun cotton," which burned at the rate of 1 inch per three seconds. The hair was made of a cellulose type material and burned even faster, two inches per second.

Some children's items that have hazardous substances are not banned because they are meant for children old enough to read labels and be governed accordingly: chemistry sets, preserved biological specimens, and chemicals to be used in school.

The law deals specifically with fireworks. Fireworks may be exempted from the banned toy classification "to the extent that they can be adequately labeled to protect purchasers and users thereof." Banned are cherry bombs, salutes, and firecrackers more than 1½ inches in length and ¼ inch in diameter and containing more than 2 grams of powder. Also banned from interstate commerce are kits intended for making explosive fireworks. Any state is free to ban the sale of whatever other fireworks it chooses.

Some fireworks were exempted from the regulations: those used for protecting crops from damage by birds and other wildlife and large items intended for public fireworks displays. These are not intended for general use. However, since accidents involving banned fireworks continue to occur (41 injuries and 8 fatalities were investigated by FDA after the regulations went into effect), new interpretations were made. Each manufacturer, wholesaler, and retailer of fireworks for agricultural purposes is to keep a record of production and receipt of distribution of such materials, being sure each container is labeled properly, and prohibiting distribution of such fireworks in any state that does not specifically provide for their use. Now 18 states ban fireworks altogether, and 8 others allow only the sparkler. In other states, the sale of some or all of the fireworks not banned by federal law is permitted.

In 1969 the Child Protection and Toy Safety Act was passed which amended the Federal Hazardous Substance Act by authorizing the Food and Drug Administration to remove from or keep off the market any toy or "other article intended for use by children" that presents an electrical, mechanical, or thermal hazard.

- *Electrical hazard:* In normal use or when subjected to reasonably foreseeable damage or abuse, its design or manufacture may cause personal injury or illness by electric shock.
- *Mechanical hazard:* In normal use or when subjected to reasonably foreseeable damage or abuse, its design or manufacture presents an unreasonable risk of personal injury or illness.
- *Thermal:* In normal use or when subjected to reasonably foreseeable damage or abuse, its design or manufacture presents an unreasonable risk of personal injury or illness because of heat or from heated parts, substances or surfaces.

In line with these regulations several toys have been removed from the market or redesigned to remove specific hazards: a coiled metal strip used for landing toy automobiles with a knifelike edge that could inflict a cut; an electrical pencil kit for making etchings on wood that was found to be capable of exploding when it was heated; a storage battery-powered riding toy which could short-circuit and cause electrical shock and also contained batteries that sometimes leaked sulphuric acid.

Regulations were set by FDA to define each of the injuries. Banned were toys that could produce a puncture wound and toys that produced sound levels over 100 decibels. A toy stove was discovered, and removed from the market, that heated up to 300 degrees on the outside and to over 600 degrees on the inside.

In November and December of 1971 at least 75 toys were removed from the market because of violation of these regulations. In many cases the toy was redesigned to eliminate the hazard, then redistributed. Some of the causes for removal from the market were:

- Sharp edges and small objects exposed.
- Sharp wires in various parts of the toy.
- Pinching hazard.
- Eyes could be pulled out.
- Metal rod used in construction was a puncture hazard.
- T-pins or straight pins used to hold on bows or caps.

Among toys that have appeared on the banned products listing in the recent past are: a spray adhesive for model-making—exposure to which may cause chromosome damage and birth defects; a toy umbrella which was flammable; a doll whose clothing or hair contained straight pins; a stuffed animal with sharp wires or removable squeaker; a ranch rifle with impulse type sound above 138 decibels; a mini car with a sulfuric acid battery susceptible to access by children. Manufacturers can review banned products and remarket them within safety requirements (Banned products, 1973).

Two manufacturers of bubble bath for children had to change the formula of their products because of complaints of irritation and urinary tract infection. The lotion and cream in a play kit for little shavers were found to contain bacteria that could cause infection in eyes, skin, nose, and throat. These products were banned from the market. The hazard of projectile toys is currently being investigated.

Even more recently another protective act for children was passed: The Poison Prevention Packaging Act of 1970. This provides that any hazardous household substance must be packaged in a way that it is "significantly difficult for children under five years of age to open or obtain a toxic or harmful amount of the substance contained therein within a reasonable time and not difficult for normal adults to use properly."

Along the same line, new school bus safety standards have been issued by the Transportation Department in order to reduce the number of school bus accidents which cause injury and death: identification, operation and maintenance of bus, and training of drivers.

Children and Work

Children entering middle childhood seem to have an innate desire to help. They like to help make decisions about the work to be done, as well as to perform the labor. They enjoy being an assistant to older persons. This is the age at which to foster a good attitude toward work through establishing a partnership program rather than a master and slave concept (Durrant, 1976).

Children work slowly and often messily. Their workmanship quality is likely to be lower than adults might wish. They may need help to complete the task and helping at their invitation develops them more than impatient prompting. They may need frequent re-assignment to prevent discouragement or boredom. Children's interest in a task is lost when they perceive it to be torturous, lonely or unappreciated.

Often work is assigned to children that adults disdain: taking out the garbage, cleaning the toilet, raking the yard, washing the car. Children quickly realize they have the dregs and gain little learning or satisfaction from the tasks. Such jobs carry less stigma when assigned randomly and rotated frequently. Children may volunteer for jobs of which they are not fully capable: shopping for groceries, paying the bills, painting the house. They can be made part of a team to accomplish these larger tasks and therein develop the skills to fit them for later assuming the job independently.

Working with persons whom they admire makes any job more enjoyable for children. They are great handers of tools, chef's assistants, "lieutenant" house cleaners. The side effects of such working arrangements are meaningful conversation, a cooperative spirit, and a good feeling when the job is done. Children learn to work better when they are not overwhelmed by the magnitude of the task. Raking one segment of the yard or vacuuming one bedroom may leave them anxious to take on another. Being assigned the whole yard or the whole house may tempt them to slop through, abandon the task or rebel at work altogether. One 7-year-old is always happy when his father has to be out-of-town on Saturday so he won't have to work. His 12-year-old brother likes to spend Friday night with a friend and thus accomplish the same goal.

It is vital that children receive praise for the work they do. Recognition in front of others may be far more meaningful than payment in cash or other tangible rewards. They learn to take pride in their portion of the work load when others know they have done it well.

Children early in middle childhood tend to wish to earn money. Their first desires may be to be paid for home chores. Later they offer to help neighbors or friends by shoveling snow, walking dogs, or cleaning in the home or yard. More creative children may invent ways to earn money either sporadically or regularly. One youngster set up a rent-a-plant business in which he rooted and potted cuttings and delivered them to the offices or homes of his clients. Another middle childhood boy made a craft item that his father sold regularly in a little shop. Two children in one family set up a stand and sold frozen sweets made in Mom's freezer to passersby.

Nine youngsters age 10 to 14 spawned a million dollar extortion scheme designed to gain funds and equipment from a large retailer to purchase and equip a large farm in a neighboring state. In a note they threatened to blow up the store unless their demands of a million dollars in cash plus merchandise marked in the enclosed company catalogue were delivered in three trucks of a specified type. Investigators were able to trace the origin of the package through postal officials who distinctly remembered it because despite its 100 page contents, the children had affixed only a 10¢ stamp. The leader in the plot was age 12, and he had chosen the other boys according to their particular skill or knowledge: one was selected because of his first aid knowledge in case a shootout with police was necessary to carry out their plans!

While most adults are happy to cooperate to help children earn spending money, because of unscrupulous employment of children for long hours in undesirable working conditions around the beginning of the century, the national child labor laws were established. Their purpose is not to prevent children from working but rather to see that the jobs in which they do work do not adversely affect their physical development, do not expose them to physical injury, and do not interfere with their opportunity to obtain an education. Some of their provisions (Working Children, 1971) are as follows:

- Minors under 16 may not be employed during the hours schools are in session.
- They may work outside school hours 3 hours on a school day and 8 hours in the summer and in vacation times from school.
- Work is not permitted before 7 A.M. or after 7 P.M. (9 P.M. from June 1 through Labor Day).
- No work is permitted in manufacturing and/or processing occupations or in nonagricultural hazardous jobs.
- Unless otherwise exempt, covered minor employees must be paid in accordance with the minimum wage, overtime, and equal pay provisions of the Fair Labor Standards Act.

In spite of such provisions many minors are illegally employed. The school has in the past decade aided the work-education of youngsters, beginning with kindergarteners. These efforts are commonly called career education. The premise of career education is that the traditional approach to preparing children for entering the job market has been ineffective. It features the conscious integration of work related skills into the curricula.

Elementary school children are exposed to varying kinds of work through the characters in their reading, the problems in mathematics, the projects in social studies and science. There is emphasis on the career

Career planning in middle childhood.

implications of all phases of the curriculum and introduction of practical problems in each unit of study. Simulation of work experiences through production activities is intended to teach the social significance of work, the interdependence of workers and the principle of completion of one's duty. Appreciation of work in general is a desired outcome as well as stimulation of children's thought concerning how they will contribute to the world of work when they complete their formal education.

What's Next?

1. "How TV Threatens Your Child," E. Sarson. *Parents Magazine*, August 1972, pp. 39, 88, 92–93.
2. *Child Development Through Literature*, Landau et al. Englewood Cliffs, N.J.: Prentice-Hall, 1972: "My Little Boy," by C. Ewald, pp. 249–255.
3. *Career Education and the Elementary School Teacher*. K. B. Hoyt, N. M. Pinson, D. Laramore & G. L. Mangum. Salt Lake City: Olympus, 1973.
4. *Children and Money: A Guide for Parents*, G. Weinstein, NY: Charterhouse Books, 1975.

5. *Good Cents: Every Kid's Guide to Money Making.* Boston: Houghton-Mifflin, 1974.

6. *Environments for Children,* M. & N. McGrath, Morrow, Inc, 1978.

Catalysts for Discussion

I. Some ways youngsters earn money at this age:

Collecting scrap metal for re-cycling
Dog walking agency in large apartment building area
Plant watering service for vacationers
Car-washing raffle (will wash only car of winning ticket)
Homemade sandwiches sold at supermarket or delicatessen
Selling polished apples at sports events in the community
Record and comic book exchange
Delivering handbills with supermarket ads
Back-rubbing service for tired executives and homemakers
Selling whittled items (letter openers) door-to-door
Selling lightbulbs, candy-bars and greeting cards in the mall
Making Christmas candles, woven pot holders and sugar Easter Eggs on special order
Sweeping the beauty shop on Saturday (a 9-year-old told a shop manager who had
    refused her a job: "You haven't given me a fair chance yet—" And she got the job.)
Lending clean socks to sister for a price.
Walking a mile in a community fund-raising.
Conducting a drive (giving the money to charity).

II. One family has a rather unique way of getting the housework done. The house becomes
a hospital. The mother is Nurse Melony. The daughter is Nurse Nancy; the son is Dr.
Davy. Each child makes out a roster of work. Even the boy, who cannot read, insists that
his sister make one for him. He will not let the mother do this. As each chore is completed, it is crossed off the list. When the chores are completed in the lobby (living room)
they move to the cafeteria (kitchen), unless it is time to discharge a patient. This is when
the bedrooms are cleaned. They have been playing the game for about two years.

Beyond the Classroom Experiences

1. Talk with middle childhood people about their clothing preferences with respect to
   color, style, and care. Compare findings with those noted in this chapter. Or take a
   child "window" shopping, noting his likes and dislikes in clothes. This could also be
   done by use of a catalog.

2. Hold a group interview with children relative to their likes and dislikes about their

housing. Note mention of privacy, quiet, space, and storage space. Use magazine pictures to elicit feelings about others' housing.

3. Read the *Toy Review,* a quarterly publication related to safety. Share findings with parents of middle childhood people. Visit local stores to see toys mentioned. Or examine a child's toy possessions, and tabulate dangerous features. Note which might be illegal under the various laws currently in effect.

4. Discuss home duties with children and/or parents. Note which are related to sex role and which are suitable to the child's developmental level.

5. Spend a morning watching children's TV programs. Note the frequency and "pitch" of ads they watch. Discuss some of the ads with the children and try to assess their impact on the children.

6. Write to your local TV station or national network to protest any programs or ads that are not in children's best interest. Be sure to give developmental or legal reasons for your complaints.

7. Write a sponsor, local or network station to praise a program or product which fosters the development of children. Give developmental reason for your praise.

8. Interview parents, asking them to designate which of their children's possessions were purchased because of the child's prompting after advertising exposure. Note percentages.

9. Give a child a hypothetical $100 to spend, using a mail order catalogue or during a chaperoned visit to a mall or shopping area with a variety of store types. Analyze his imaginary purchases in terms of comparison shopping, ability to judge quality, intended use (for self or others), and so on.

10. Ask children to draw some housing using such categories as those discussed in conjunction with Kids As Architects. Discuss the feasibility of their ideas afterwards, looking for their logic, and motivations.

Chapter 11

Guidance

This chapter is designed to help you:

- realize there are no magic formulas for rearing "good" children.
- distinguish between discipline and punishment.
- see how development and other factors contribute to the need for guidance.
- understand the role of parental personality in guidance styles.
- explore the styles and techniques of guidance and see their advantages and disadvantages.
- examine parenting education concepts, their implications, and ways they may be fostered.
- formulate a workable philosophy for guiding middle childhood people.

Introduction

Noted anthropologist Margaret Mead (1972), asked what future generations would deem the greatest accomplishment of twentieth-century man, replied that among them would be the discovery of the nature of childhood and the attempt to apply the knowledge in rearing children. Our time has seen the realization that there are a great many "right" ways to perform this important task. Around the world, basic beliefs and attitudes about children differ greatly: The Russians believe the newborn is so strong that they swaddle it firmly to protect it from itself; the French, believing the child to be quite fragile, wrap it gently and softly. The Balinese refer to a baby as a caterpillar or a mouse until the age of three months, when it is given a human name and is recognized as a participating member of the family.

The Chinese provide many opportunities for babies to look without touching; whereas in America we encourage them to move around, explore the world, and be aggressively involved with objects and persons. To the English, a child is a plant, and parents are gardeners tending it; but to Germans the child is more like a flowerpot in which the seeds of flowers and weeds are sprouting, and parents are meant not only to care for the flowers but uproot the weeds. During this century we have acknowledged that there are both regularities in growth and development patterns and numerous routes from childhood to adulthood. We have begun to see a connection between what happens in the child's experiences and what he can become. In our beginning attempts to apply the new knowledge and attitudes to child rearing we have had inconsistencies, reversals, misconceptions, and mistakes. But at least we have broadened our conceptions and laid a foundation on which future generations may build.

Guidance—Discipline—Punishment

Since a major concern of modern parents and teachers is the area of guiding children toward acceptable and satisfying behavior, many times persons involved in educational projects expect to receive specific formulas for use in making children behave well. However, one who becomes familiar with normal social, emotional, physical, and mental growth of children realizes that no such magic answers exist. Such knowledge should shed sufficient light and understanding on various situations to be encountered with children that one so informed is able to make intelligent deductions concerning guiding childhood behavior patterns, realizing that each child, each situation, and each relationship is unique.

There is a great deal of controversy today over "discipline." In the face of disorder and riots, there is a cry that children need discipline. Many adults feel that college students would not be acting out their feelings in the present manner if they had been disciplined when they were young. It is not quite clear what people mean when the word "discipline" is used; but many seem to equate the word with punishment, restriction, or overriding or breaking the will of the child, "showing him who's boss." Sometimes, by the expression "That child needs discipline" what the speaker really means to say is "That child needs punishment," or more specifically, "a good spanking." It is too bad if all our discussion of discipline is understood in the general framework of bad behavior or changing bad behavior, by whatever means may be chosen. It is more fruitful to consider discipline in the framework of guidance or teaching, for certainly this is the basic meaning of the word.

A disciplinarian is one who teaches. For one to grow into a productive, adjusted adult, discipline is certainly necessary. If a child is to live happily as he grows up and is to learn the ways of his society in order to be acceptable to himself and others, he must certainly be disciplined! This does not mean he must be punished, but instead that he must be taught; he must be guided. Discipline is guidance, not necessarily correction. It is certainly not limited to punishment.

Discipline carries the idea of control: at first, control by others; later, self-control or self-discipline. Some adult control is necessary throughout a child's growing years: certain behavior must be insisted on, other behavior cannot be allowed; limits must be set; a child cannot be allowed to injure himself; rights of others must not be violated. Questions revolve around when and how these kinds of control shall be exerted. Ideas of "right" and "wrong" vary from group to group, depending on child-rearing practices employed and value systems espoused. In addition, children are different from each other and respond to controls in various ways.

The goal of discipline or guidance is to help the child progress toward

Discipline should be considered in the framework of guidance or teaching, for this is the basic meaning of the word. (Photo by Rick Coleman.)

self-discipline so that indeed he need not be dependent on external forces to govern his behavior. He needs to learn to channel his behavior, to control and use his impulses in a manner that is not only acceptable in society but that will also help him move constructively toward his own personal goals and a sense of fulfillment or self-actualization.

Need for Guidance

What about children ages 5–12 causes them to need guidance? Their *developmental level* is a major factor. Consider the implications of misconceptions and concepts that are not fully developed. Think of the possible results of being emotionally immature. Imagine what could occur when typical curiosity, creativity, desire for independence, and high energy level combine. Recall the role of forgetting because of preoccupation. Remember the perils inherent in judgment not yet fully developed. The wonder of it is that children during middle childhood are not constantly in trouble. We might deduct that much of the time they err unintentionally.

The National Survey of Children (1976) conducted in the Fall of 1976 consisted of interviews with 2,200 children between 7 and 11 years of age along with 1,700 of their parents. The interviews were designed to explore the children's perceptions, feelings, attitudes, and values in relation to their families, friends, school, health and neighborhood activities. Although a majority of children felt good about themselves and things going on in their lives, a substantial minority reported negative feelings: often got angry, worried about things a lot, often got scared, felt lonely a lot and felt bored because there was nothing to do on most afternoons.

Sometimes children exhibit planned misbehavior. This type is often their attempt to strike back at what they perceive to be injustices dealt them by peers or adults. They *are* capable of planning and plotting mischief or destruction. Some misbehavior may be either consciously or unconsciously inspired to gain attention or exert their power over others. Some psychologists attribute much misbehavior to these goals; fighting is a prime example. Common home misdemeanors associated with the period of middle childhood include defiance of adult authority, aggressive verbal attacks on siblings, dawdling over routine activities, temper outbursts, shirking responsibilities, lying, sneakiness, breaking and spilling things, and rudeness to relatives or family friends (Gesell, et al., 1956). Those reportedly related to school are inattentiveness, "cutting up," vandalism, lying, carelessness in work. By age 12 such misbehaviors as the following may make their appearance in some children: smoking, swearing, stealing, drinking, illicit sex acts, and unexcused absences (Eaton, D'Amico, and Phillips, 1956).

Excluding traffic offenses, almost a million children were involved in more than a million (1.1 million) juvenile delinquency cases in 1973, which was a 3 percent increase over the year before (Snapper, 1975). Of all arrests made in 1973, 9 percent involved children under 15 years of age and 25 percent involved persons below 18.

By 1974, the number of juvenile delinquency incidents among children from 10 to 17 years of age reached 1,250,000 (Statistical Abstracts, 1977—98th Ed. p. 187. T. #314). Children between 10 and 12 years of age who participated in the General Mills study (1978), reported they

Percentage Distribution of Arrests of Persons under 15 Years of Age: 1973

Larceny-Theft	24%
Violation of Curfew; Loitering Ordinance; Runaways	17%
Breaking or Entering	12%
Vandalism	8%
Drunkenness and Disorderly Conduct	7%
Robbery; Auto Theft	5%
Drug and Liquor Laws	4%
Assaults	4%
Other	19%

From: Snapper, Status of Children, 1975.

knew children who had been in trouble with the police (43 percent); children who had taken something that didn't belong to them (61 percent); and children who had run away from home (28 percent).

The use of drugs is a growing problem at this age. Sniffing inhalants are commonly the "drugs" of youngsters in middle childhood. Children as young as 6 or 7 are motivated by curiosity and peer pressure to try "getting high," and the substances they employ to experience that pleasant sensation and giggly, cheerful excited behavior are often common household products: glue, hair spray, paint thinner, nail polish remover, and furniture

"I leave the beer cans around to reassure my folks—They'd freak out if they suspected I was doin' dope!" Marlette; in the *Charlotte Observer*. Used by permission.

polish. Many are unaware of the potential damage to their liver and kidneys or of the fact that the gas in spray cans can freeze the larynx and respiratory system, resulting in almost instant death. They fail to realize that even these milder drugs can cause the body to build up a tolerance, requiring larger and larger amounts to produce the same effect. As with all drug education, the best approach to sniffing is a calm, matter-of-fact one. Exaggeration and scare tactics should be avoided. For most children, a warning about sniffing can be given just as a warning about crossing streets. When children disregard the facts, they may be wishing to harm themselves and may need psychological treatment (Child Study Association, 1971).

A large number of children have mental health problems; in 1971, about 772,000 children under age 18 were involved in psychiatric patient care episodes. This was about one-fifth of all patient care episodes; about 82 percent were handled on an out-patient basis. Males have a higher admission rate than females. There was a 32 percent increase in patient episodes involving children (140,000) over a two-year period. Based on parent reports (National Survey of Children, 1976) just under 5 percent of 7 to 11 year olds received professional help during the preceding year for an "emotional, behavior, mental or learning problem." About 26 of every 1,000 had been to a psychologist or psychiatrist within the previous year. According to parent reports, only one-third of the children who needed professional help for some problem actually got it.

Children are also frequent victims of crime, with the highest rate between the ages of 12 and 19. The most common crime is personal larceny followed by simple and aggravated assaults. In the National Survey of Children (1976), two-thirds of the children said they were afraid "somebody bad might get into the house" and one quarter were afraid someone might hurt them when they went outside. According to the parents who participated in the survey, about 20 percent of the children lived in neighborhoods where there are "undesirable people in the street, parks or playgrounds, such as drunks, drug addicts, or tough older kids" and 15 percent live in areas where "neighborhood crime" is a problem. The majority of the children who report being afraid to go outside also report they have been bothered when they were outside at some time or other. More than 40 percent said they had been bothered by older children and in 1 in 8 cases had been bothered by a grown-up. They had been beaten, hit with something, and had possessions or money taken from them.

By seventh grade, 63 percent of all males and 54 percent of all females have tried alcoholic beverages. Other drugs are used and abused. Children below 15 years of age compose 22 percent of the population in America and make up 7 percent of the drug-abusing population. The most widely used drug for children from 10 to 19 is marijuana with hallucinogens (notably LSD) next in line (Snapper, 1975).

The wise adult dealing with a child's apparent misbehavior will take time to analyze the underlying cause. He might even ask the child to help think through this puzzle, and then act accordingly. Much of what we consider misbehavior may be left untreated; other types may call for action on the part of the guiding adult.

Variations in the need for and response to discipline are influenced by *health* and *energy level, emotional status, time* of day and week, and *age* and *sex* of the child. (See Figure 11-1.) Feeling ill or tired decreases a child's self-control and heightens the possibility that he may offend others by his actions or reactions. Heightened emotions, such as excitement, may have a similar effect. Times related to eating, dressing and going to bed tend to increase the need for guidance, since children naturally would prefer to play than to submit to routine. Parents may also be more tense at these times, causing changes in their emotional control. So it is with the days of the week, Mondays and weekends being the times of highest incidence of problems. Normally, older children need correction less often than younger ones; as age increases so does maturity and communication

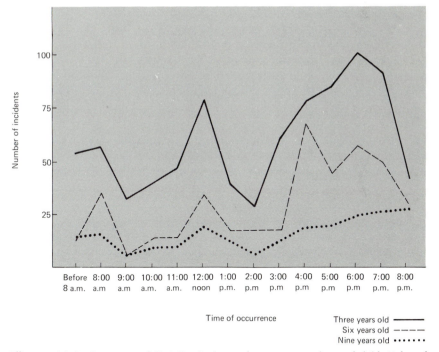

Figure 11-1. Frequency of discipline by hour of occurrence and age of child. (Adapted from E. Clifford, "Discipline in the Home: A Controlled Observational Study of Parental Practices," *Journal of Genetic Psychology, 95, 1959.* Used by permission of the author and the publisher.)

To things you did as a child which were considered "bad":
What they were.
Why you did them.
Who found out about them.
What happened then.
How you tried to prevent repeat performances.
How you felt about your act and its consequences.

that facilitate living up to desired standards (Clifford, 1959). Because of cultural expectations of aggression and daring, boys may need discipline more often than girls.

Children are subjected to *pressures* of all kinds, some so great that suicide is attempted. Their little time is filled with this and that very important activity: school, Scouts, choir, glee club, dancing lessons, music lessons, acrobatics, baton twirling, football and baseball practice. There is very little time to "tinker," "stare into space," or just "mess around." Mothers complain of chauffeuring their children to various activities, but it is the child who must take part in all these activities!

Increasingly, the child is pressured at home and at school about academic achievement. Homework assignments increase. Anxiety over doing an assignment well tends to make a child fearful and uncertain. For many children, knowing the right answer becomes a great deal more important than how one finds out or how a task is accomplished. Asking questions seems not as important as "getting it right." And this is because his important adults are confused. Perhaps adults would do well to take time out to ask: "What is it all for? In what ways are children being pressured? And why?"

A child is also placed under pressure by conflicting values in society: war, riots, civil disobedience, cigarette consumption in relation to the health hazards involved, drugs, and alcohol. He needs adults who can listen to him, talk with him, and help him to understand "this I believe" convictions. Other conditions that may be anxiety producing in children are sickness, hospitalization, death of someone dear or even someone whom they only know slightly, father absence—either temporarily, sporadically, or permanently—and employment of mother. Poverty or anxiety over finances on the part of parents also leave their mark upon children.

Two other pressures are the athletic field and the social front. At increasingly younger ages, children are expected to compete in leagues: biscuit, cracker, pony. The important thing becomes winning the game rather than learning it. Parents and coaches seem to expect children to defend or expand their own ego through their championship play in various parks and playgrounds. Dances, dating, beauty pageants, and other teen-age and adult activities are being cut down to middle childhood size.

On this subject Graves (1969, p. 28) stated:

> Too much of any one of these pressures—to excel academically, athletically, or socially—is enough to make childhood painful. Combined they often make life almost intolerable for a child. When he reacts in despair or anger, parents become alarmed. And parents have every reason to feel apprehensive, for either deliberately or inadvertently, it is they who have distorted their child's sense of values.

Correction of such distortion requires common sense and time. The child's hurts must be attended, and in addition there must be exploration with him of various alternatives, standards, and values.

Special Tasks

Thoughtful guidance during middle childhood is vital in developing independence, fostering moral judgment, transmitting sex roles, and reducing adjustment conflicts (adapted from A. W. Blair and W. H. Burton, *Growth and Development of the Preadolescent,* 1951, ch. 7). An attempt to understand the rationale, challenges, and varied approaches in connection with guidance of middle childhood people is important.

Developing Independence

Whereas security as a basic need was of primary importance during earlier years, in middle childhood the need for self-expression and self-development comes to the fore. Freedom with security is necessary if these needs are to be fulfilled. Adults often find it difficult or even painful to accept behavior tht exemplifies the inner urges to become self-directive. Yet failure to recognize the developmental nature of growing independence may give the child feelings of rejection which can lead to extreme behavior problems or even delinquent conduct. For the growing child to fulfill the expectations of both parents and peers without offending either is not an easy task. His feelings about each will fluctuate; and the continuing security of the home and school is of highest importance.

During middle childhood, independence seems to be one of the chief requirements for membership in the "gang." Physically these children are capable of carrying on many activities that afford them increasing independence status. Intellectually they are also ready for increasing independent activities. Both at school and at home there must be provision of opportunities for children to grow in independence from adult domination: for responsible action, for real choice-making. It helps if adults take interest in aspects of life they have long since outgrown, and accept without great alarm types of behavior that seem to them silly or unreasonable.

To allow children to host friends in their home as well as be guests in the homes of their peers contributes to their development of independent feelings. Trips alone to the homes of relatives, camping, as well as harmless adventures with the gang are also helpful. Opportunities to make decisions about the expenditure of allowance, clothing selection, and such out-of-family experiences as club membership allow the child to "try his wings" and live with the consequences.

Whereas there may be instances of irresponsibility, instability, disobedience, and restlessness, children grow as they are able to make their own kind of arrangements with respect to family and home routines. Including children in planning and decision-making in the home and classroom, allowing them to set their own standards on certain occasions, and basing some family, club, and class activities on small spontaneous groups of age-sex mates—all allow the pigtail set to practice and feel independence. Extreme adult concern over reading or achievement in general may lead to emotional conflict that further retards performance.

Opportunities to apply emerging physical and mental skills in hobbies are appropriate. Provisions for experimentation and problem solving involving causal relationships are valuable. Encouragement to find answers to why? how? what? and why not? by applying his reading skill contributes to the child's need for self-direction and self-development.

Fostering Moral Judgment

As the child progresses from dependence toward independence in his decision-making, he will develop increasing capacity to "judge" situations for himself. He will make mistakes as he explores cause and effect in human relationships, but will be learning to do things because there is satisfaction in doing them—not just because of what people will think or because they will contribute to his development of responsibility. His mistakes should not be allowed to evoke overreaction from adults. Often standards regarding honesty, tidiness, and cleanliness are too high, resulting in tension and conflict.

To help teach moral judgment it is more meaningful at this age to foster consideration of immediate effects of actions than to discuss morals and values of specific behavior. Providing experiences that permit dealing with reality is an effective way to foster desirable personal evaluation. Habits and social conformity learned through imitation and admonition of adults in earlier years are tried and tested. By this age most children can be allowed to face the consequences of their mistakes, if these consequences are not too serious.

As their world continues to expand, middle childhood people realize that there are many standards of right and wrong. The gang may force consideration for others through lessons that may even be harsh. Faults are openly discussed, and discipline is prompt and relentless. Whereas the adult role in this process is not one of restraint or too direct control, failure to provide any supervision of the gang, or rejection of the child because of his gang activities, may result in delinquent behavior.

Transmitting Sex Roles

This is the prime time for patterning according to the appropriate sex role. With traditional sex roles becoming less clearly defined in our society, the task is becoming a bit more difficult for youngsters. The group or gang life provides almost the sole opportunity children have for play activities in which they can express masculinity or femininity. Grouping them for formal instruction should be done with the realization that girls are at this age likely to be more mature both socially and intellectually because of their rapid physical maturation. Boys of this age need opportunities to associate closely with men to a greater extent than is common in the home and school, since some of their undesirable behavior appears to be overcompensation for the lack of a realistic conception of the male role.

The youngster whose growth pattern places him at the extremes either in size or maturity in his peer group may suffer in his adjustment. The ability to compete physically is of prime importance in achieving confidence and security in one's sex role. Help in developing the peer-expected skills such as those required in games and manual manipulation will contribute to self-esteem. Some children will need assistance in assuming a more subordinating or more dominating role in the group. Still others may need to be encouraged to eliminate habits or traits that are characteristic of the opposite sex. The home, school, and community can help by making possible large amounts of physical activity.

As each sex perceives that there are activities and attitudes that differentiate it from the other, there is growing antagonism between the boys and girls. This feeling is reduced when boys and girls are not placed together in highly competitive situations. Imposition of the same standards on all the children of the same age, sex, or class group probably intensifies antagonism. The more advanced language skills of girls makes comparison in schoolwork undesirable, and the selection of subject matter material and instructional activities should reflect some differences because of varying interests and skills of the two groups. This is particularly important in the physical education curriculum. During middle childhood, a measure of a child's social maturity is his imitation of others in the same age and sex group and his disregard for the opposite sex.

Reducing Adjustment Conflicts

Sound personal and social integration during middle childhood can lessen the strains and conflicts of adolescent adjustment. If a child receives satisfaction from his relationships with adults as he tries out the new social contacts during elementary school years, he is more likely to have confidence in the adults who strive to help him achieve social adjustment during the teen years. His feeling of growing independence and self-assurance, his success in gaining the approval of his peers, the degree to which he has been able to identify with his sex role, and the opportunities to make decisions in terms of his emerging value system and to live with the consequences will all contribute toward successful adjustment as an adolescent.

Guidance in Relation to Dimensions of Parental Personality

Child-rearing practices, or patterns of guidance, are really dimensions of the personalities of parents, and all interactions between parent and child affect the child in some way. However, in light of the relativism of child development, Kagan (1974) pointed out that after food, physical comfort, and protection from excessive disease are guaranteed, it is reasonable to ask "What do children need?" His answer to this question was that children do not require any specific actions from adults to develop optimally. "There is no good evidence to indicate that children must have a certain amount or schedule of cuddling, kissing, spanking, holding or deprivation of privileges in order to become gratified and productive adults" (p. 88). There is no fixed list of parental behaviors that can guarantee the meeting of the critical psychological needs of children. To meet these needs, we must know the demands which the society will make upon the adult.

This is not to say that child-rearing practices are the only factors that affect the child's growth; account must be taken of the child's constitutional endowment, his experiences, other people in his life, his ecological unit—the community in which he lives. Nevertheless, guidance techniques used by his parents make a lasting impression. Not all interactions, of course, are intended by the parents as training for the child, whatever his age. Some are simply for care-taking; others are expressions of love or concern—reactions with no real purpose for present control of the child or to improve his future actions. All interactions, however, do have an effect on him—elicit reactions from him. All such actions, Sears (1957) pointed out, whether by intention or not, change the child's potentialities for future behavior. Such parental behaviors—child-rearing practices, or discipline—grow out of parents' personalities. Who they are determines what they do with children.

In this section we will be concerned with child behaviors emanating from personality characteristics of parents. Even as we give our attention to this, it is necessary to remember that children differ in their genetically based temperamental characteristics and therefore in their interpretation of particular parental behaviors and attitudes. It is also true that different social and economic circumstances and varying role structures in the family give rise to variations in the effect of particular parental behaviors. For example, middle-class parents, in contrast to lower-class parents, seem to provide more warmth, use more love-oriented discipline, and act more permissively in regard to demands for attention by the child, sex behavior, routines (bedtime, eating, chores), aggression toward parents, and general obedience.

The interplay of sex of parents and sex of children also plays an important role. The mother seems to be more loving and nurturant than the father. She uses more psychological control, especially with girls. Fathers are stricter and use more physical punishment, especially with boys. They are also more fear arousing. The opposite-sex parent grants more autonomy while the same-sex parent is less benevolent and more frustrating, especially to older children.

A number of studies dealing with discipline have focused on parental type. Figure 11-2 (Schaefer, 1959) illustrates how a number of these types may be classified in terms of two dimensions of maternal behavior growing out of personality structure: love-hostility and control-autonomy.

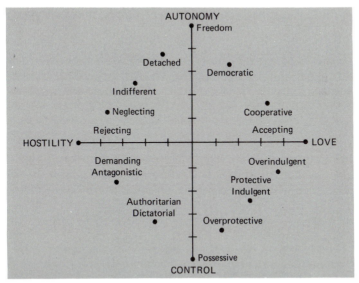

Figure 11-2. From E. S. Schaefer, "A Circumplex Model for Maternal Behavior." *Journal of Abnormal Social Psychology,* 59:232 (1959). Copyright 1959 by the American Psychological Association. Used by permission.

The love-hostility axis is in reference to the warmth and acceptance of the child or lack of these on the part of his parents. It includes expression of affection and realistic expectations in regard to the child's behavior or performance. Control-autonomy has to do with the amount of choice-making activity the child is allowed, and the kind of involvement planned for the child in the total interaction and decision-making process in the family. It grows out of the parents' need to control and lack of ability to allow the child to be separate and grow. In this framework, for example, a democratic mother is high on the love continuum and on the autonomy dimension; a protective mother is high on the love dimension but also highly controlling.

Becker (1964) added to this model (Figure 11-3) a third dimension that brings into play important affective considerations. He redefined and divided Schaefer's control-autonomy axis into restrictiveness-permissiveness and anxious emotional involvement-calm detachment. The love-hostility dimension he relabeled warmth-hostility, defining the warmth end of the continuum with such phrases as accepting, affectionate, approving, understanding, child-centered, frequent use of explanations and reasons, high use of praise and low use of physical punishment. The restrictive end of the restrictiveness-permissiveness continuum is marked by strict enforcement of demands in such areas as sex play, modesty, toilet training, orderliness, noise, obedience and aggression to sibs, peers, and parents. The anxious involvement-calm detachment continuum is defined at the anxious end by high emotionality in relation to the child, babying, and protectiveness.

Using this scheme the democratic parent and the indulgent parent, both high in warmth and permissiveness, are differentiated by their placement on the emotional involvement axis: the democratic parent tends to be calm and detached, whereas the indulgent parent is high in anxious emotional involvement. Both the organized-effective parent and the overprotective parent are warm and restrictive. The overprotective parent is more anxious and emotionally involved, whereas the organized-effective parent is more calm and detached.

This model points up the importance of consideration of affectional relationships between parent and child as well as behavior sequences in assessing the meaning of various interactions. In addition, parents who seem to be permissive may be at any point on the warmth-hostility continuum, which is also true of restrictive parents. Interplay among these various traits or positions make a particular technique come through quite differently from one parent-child group to another.

Hostility vs. Warmth Dimension

The use of praise and reasons (love-oriented techniques) has been found repeatedly associated with the warmth variables and the use of physical

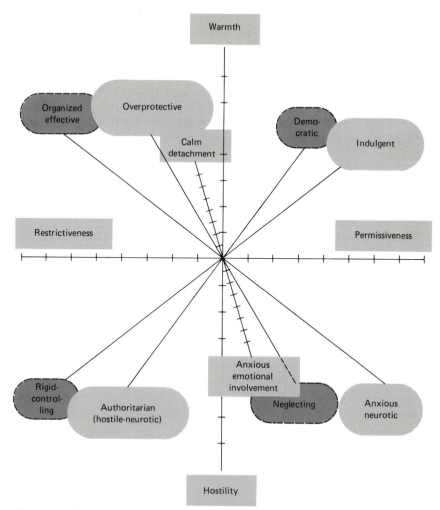

Figure 11-3. From *Review of Child Development Research*, Vol. I., figure 2, p. 175, by M. L. Hoffman and L. W. Hoffman, © 1964 by Russell Sage Foundation, Publishers, New York. Used by permission.

punishment has been associated with hostility. It is well to remember that permissiveness is not the same as warmth. Permissive parents (or restrictive) are neither predominantly hostile nor warm, but may be placed anywhere along this continuum. For a discussion of love-oriented versus power-assertive discipline techniques, refer to Chapter 9. Becker's summary (1964, p. 189) of the results of use of these techniques follows:

• *Power-Assertive Techniques,* more often used by hostile parents, tend to promote in children
—aggressiveness
—resistance to authority

—power assertion to other children

—externalized reactions to transgressions

- The aggression so generated probably results from

    —increased frustration in the child which leads to an aggressive anger reaction

    —model of aggressive behavior set by parent sanctions aggression

    —hostile punitive parents probably directly reinforce aggression: e.g. they admonish child to fight for his rights.

- *Love-Oriented Techniques,* more often used by warm parents, tend to promote in children

    —acceptance of self-responsibility

    —internalized reaction to transgressions

- These reactions probably result from

    —the parent, because of his warmth, is important to the child, so more severe forms of discipline are not necessary to insure compliance

    —parent provides a model of controlled behavior

    —verbal cues are provided for the child so he understands what is expected and anticipates consequences

    —the timing of the termination of punishment reinforces acceptable behavior, rather than being linked to the unacceptable behavior.

Restrictiveness vs. Permissiveness Dimension

This dimension can be defined in relation to the way the parent makes demands on the child and insists on compliance. There is a strong tendency for parents who are strict or demanding in one area to be strict and demanding in all areas. It can be thought of as a parent characteristic, rather than as simply a guidance technique. Generally, the commonsense supposition is supported by research, that children who have been subjected to restrictive discipline exhibit inhibited behavior, while those who have been involved with more permissive discipline are much less inhibited, more outgoing, daring, and expansive.

Permissiveness combined with hostility produces aggressive, poorly controlled behavior. Parents of delinquents have been found to have poor affective relations with their children and to exert little control over them. This is a prime example of permissive-hostile interaction. When restrictiveness is combined with hostility the result may be self-aggression, social withdrawal, and signs of internal conflict on the part of the child. This situation probably fosters a great deal of resentment; some of it is turned inward, against the child himself. Parents of neurotics have been found to have this sort of interaction with their children: restrictive-hostile.

Watson's study (1957) indicated that in a warm, permissive home some children were more independent; more cooperative with adults; not compulsively persistent on an impossible task, yet persisted for a time; more creative; less hostile. For children reared in a warm-restrictive home, there was a tendency to be dependent, unfriendly, less creative, more hostile, and more extreme in persistence.

Becker (1964, p. 197) summed up his review of the research in this area:

> Both restrictiveness and permissiveness entail certain risks. Restrictiveness, while fostering well-controlled, socialized behavior, tends also to lead to fearful, dependent, and submissive behaviors, a dulling of intellectual striving and inhibited hostility. Permissiveness on the other hand, while fostering outgoing, sociable, assertive behaviors and intellectual striving, tends also to lead to less persistence and increased aggressiveness.

Emotional-Involvement vs. Calm-Detachment Dimension

While this seems to be a part of the total interaction pattern, no direct research can be reported concerning the resulting child behaviors. This is another commonsense proposition. The emotional reaction pattern of the adult has a great influence on his ability to be effective in interactions with the child. The father who confessed he would have to take tranquilizers when he was told that some behavior of his child ought to be ignored was saying more about himself than he probably realized. The paradox is that adults wish children to act in ways in which they themselves have trouble acting. The parent who flies into a rage when a child screams "I hate you" has never learned much emotional control himself. When children's acts become mere occasions for the venting of parental aggression, the effect of the "guidance" is questionable in terms of the child's learning inner-control.

Parent-Child Relationships—Summary

Walters and Stinnett (1971) made a survey of a decade of research in parent-child relationships. The conclusions, which we have paraphrased, follow:

1. There is a distrust of simplistic explanations concerning direction of causality in exploring the nature of parent-child relationships. Children are not only a product of their parents' influence, they themselves exert powerful influence on parent-child relationships.
2. While the majority of the literature on parent-child relationships is concerned with mother-child interaction, there is indication of a significant impact of fathers, particularly on development of sons.
3. Children learn patterns of interaction primarily from their parents. Authority patterns established in the family have far-reaching effects.
4. There is an increase in parental authoritarianism and a decrease in parent-child communication as family size increases.
5. There is a differential impact of parents upon children, according to sex of child. Boys are probably more susceptible than girls to parental influence.
6. Parental warmth influences occupational choices among children as well as their academic achievement, leadership, and creative thinking. Aggres-

siveness and antisocial behavior are related to poor parent-child relationships. "Extreme parental restrictiveness, authoritarianism, and punitiveness, without acceptance, warmth and love tend to be negatively related to a child's positive self-concept, emotional and social development" (p. 101).

7. "Middle class parents tend to be more controlling and supportive of their children than lower class parents and they are more likely to discipline their children by utilizing reasons and appeals to guilt and are less likely to use physical punishment" (p. 101).

8. Parents have a differential impact among various ethnic groups and this impact is different at various stages of the family life cycle.

9. The peer group is of greater importance in role learning as children approach adolescence. In reality they are being guided by other children. Although some decisions of youth are a reflection of the values of their parents, other decisions are a reflection of values of their age mates.

10. In Western Society the responsibility of rearing children rests with the parents. A disadvantage of so completely localizing this responsibility is that it places extensive responsibility on parents who may be inadequate. There is little encouragement given to the establishment of relationships with adults outside the family except for such association provided in the school system.

Philosophies or Styles of Guidance

There are three general styles of guidance with many variations open to those involved in human relationships: *authoritarian, laissez-faire,* and *democratic.* These styles can be employed by the foreman on a construction job, by the teacher in the classroom, and by the parent in the home. Each has specific characteristics, and although exclusive use of one style is rare, it is usually possible to determine on inspection which style prevails in one's dealing with others, whether they are children or adults.

The Authoritarian Style

The *authoritarian* style of guidance enjoys the distinction of having been around longer than the others. It is a vestige of the paternalistic family pattern in which the father was undisputed head of his household and his word was law. This type of guidance was brought to America by its European founders and still remains in many homes. It is characterized by rigid restraints, control through external force in the form of punishment, and severe punishments for failure to live up to the established standards of behavior. Whereas it can be warm, this style often fails to incorporate praise for achievement of the goals and does not typically involve the child in decisions regarding the consequences of his misbehavior. It diminishes his opportunities to learn to control his own behavior, since it is controlled for him by the parent or other authority figure. As children begin to perceive their rights as individuals, this type of guidance seems to them incongruent with the democratic ideals to which our society seems committed. In such instances, they may lose respect and even rebel under this guidance.

The Laissez-faire Style

At the other end of the guidance spectrum is the *laissez-faire* philosophy by which children receive little or no direction or help in establishing or evaluating their behavior patterns. No punishment is employed, and it is often held that such a form of guidance will avoid the possible damage that may be caused by authoritarian methods, thus precluding indoctrination and inferiority complexes and allowing self-expression. Some parents espousing this philosophy leave children alone to grope through problems that may be well beyond their capabilities, unaided by adult wisdom. Laissez-faire discipline is for many parents a protest against the authoritarian style by which they were reared. Mothers tend to be more permissive than fathers, yielding to children's accusations that they are "mean." This also may result from rejection of the child or abdication from the parental role.

The Democratic Style

Near the middle in child guidance philosophy and orientation there lies the *democratic, or developmental,* method. It is based on the idea that children need to be involved in decisions that affect them and that children will naturally err, often not meaning to do so. It incorporates certain standards for behavior and includes reinforcement for attaining these standards. It involves penalties for willfully failing to live up to the established and agreed-upon goals of behavior which seek to foster inner-control in the child. The educational rather than the punitive aspect of guidance is emphasized in this method. It is the style most child developmentalists espouse.

Research in Patterns of Leadership

One of the best-known experiments (Lippitt and White, 1966) in the area of guidance concerns itself with various group atmospheres, or management, and corresponding effects on the activity of children within the groups. Groups of carefully matched 11-year-old boys were placed in situations with one of three patterns of leadership: authoritarian, democratic, and laissez-faire.

The autocratic leader determined all the policies of the group. Techniques were communicated one unit at a time, and future steps were concealed. The boys had no idea of the goal toward which they were working. They were not given choices as to whom they would work with or what they would make; indeed, they made no choices at all—the leader made them. The leader did not clarify his standards for good work; the boys were not sure which activity would bring praise or criticism. The leader did not become a part of the group, but demonstrated procedures and gave orders.

In the laissez-faire group, the leader played a passive role, giving the boys complete freedom in relation to activity and group procedures. The leader simply made materials available and gave information or help when asked. The leader made no attempt to evaluate negatively or positively the work going on. Although he was friendly, he was certainly not a part of the group.

The democratic leader provided a situation in which policy-making was a matter of group discussion and decision. There was active encouragement and assistance on the part of the leader, who helped in clarifying the goal desired and the steps for reaching that goal. When a problem arose, the leader suggested alternate procedures from which the group could make a choice. The members decided their projects, and everyone was free to work with whomever he chose. The leader tried to be a regular group member in spirit; the boys knew "where they stood" with him and the standards he held for good work.

The actions of the leaders in each of the groups were observed and recorded, then coded or labeled. Three classifications of behavior—"giving orders," "disrupting commands" (an order that interrupted ongoing activity and started things in a new direction), and "nonconstructive criticism"—were seen as limiting the spontaneity of the child's behavior. These categories accounted for about 60 percent of the behavior of the autocratic leaders and only about 5 percent of the behavior of the democratic and laissez-faire leaders.

Three other classifications—"guiding suggestions," "extending knowledge," and "stimulating self-guidance"—were thought of as extending the freedom of the child and the group. These behaviors were found to a far greater extent among democratic leaders than among autocratic leaders.

While laissez-faire leaders engaged in a great deal of behavior coded "extending knowledge," much of this behavior contributed very little to "stimulating self-guidance" on the part of the child. More often than any of the others, the democratic leaders requested the child's opinions about group plans, used the child's judgment as criteria for action, and took consensus of opinion. Democratic leaders stimulated independence in the child about eight times more often than authoritarian leaders and about twice as much as the laissez-faire leaders.

A classification labeled "genial and confident" indicated how often the leader talked about personal matters unrelated to the activities going on in the club and how often he joked on a friendly basis with the children. The democratic leader had a great many more interactions of this type than either the autocratic or laissez-faire leaders.

Now, what happened to the children in these situations?

Relationship with the club leader was different in each situation. There was greater dependence on the authoritarian leader and a greater feeling of discontent in this group. The children engaged in more friendly, personal contact with leaders in the democratic and laissez-faire clubs than in the autocratic club. The children in the democratic club felt free to make suggestsions concerning group policy.

Relationships among club members developed along different lines in the clubs. Aggressiveness and irritability toward other boys occurred more often in both autocratic and laissez-faire clubs than in the democratic one. The children in the democratic group depended more on each other for special recognition and were more willing to give approval and recognition to each other than did members of autocratic or laissez-faire groups. There was friendliness among the boys in the autocratic group, but the cohesion was often due to a feeling of rebellion against the leaders. The youngsters seemed to be bound together by a desire to "get the leader." There was greater cohesion among the democratic group members when a "stranger" (part of the experiment) came into the room and criticized the work of one of the children.

Activity when the leader was not present was different in these groups. In the autocratic group, work dropped to a minimum when the leader was out of the room; while in the democratic group, there was little difference in work involvement whether the leader was in or out. On two or three occasions when the laissez-faire leader left the group, one of the boys took over the leadership role, and an increase in group activity was noted.

A leader must recognize the impact of the group atmosphere on the child which in turn affects the child's activities, attitudes, and learning. It would be well for any adult who works with children to take a look at his own mode of operation and the manner in which children respond.

Guidance Techniques

Now, how does one discipline a child? How does one help him to be "at home" with himself, his peers, and his family? How does one help him to internalize the values and attitudes that are considered important? In today's world parents find themselves at the mercy of a society that imposes pressures and priorities which allow neither the time nor place for meaningful activities and relations between children and adults, which downgrades the role of parents and the functions of parenthood and which prevents the parent from doing things he wants to do as a guide, friend and companion to his child (White House Conference on Children, Report to the President, 1970).

Hymes (1966) suggests that adults should exploit two great silent forces that are at work within the child: the push of maturation and the pull of identification. As the child matures physically, he leaves behind many habits that are annoying to adults. Take the matter of cleanliness and neatness. In this area, the 9-year-old seems a catastrophe: his hair is never combed; his shoes are impossible; his hands are always dirty; there is always a rip or a button missing. But inside him the growth push is at work. The time comes when he spends hours in the bathroom: showering, shaving, and giving careful attention to hair and clothing. Just any shirt will not do; he needs a particular one. Nine-year-old boys who refuse to stand next to a girl not only will grow out of this antipathy, but later will seek out girls and try to please them. This is maturation. Much behavior is a result of the level of maturation. If parents will wait for a while, behavior will change. Be patient. Capitalize on growth.

The second phenomenon is the pull of identification. Children have a deep-seated desire to please important adults in their lives. They please adults by trying to be like them. In the realm of values and attitudes, adults influence children perhaps more than it is possible to realize. Later they are interested in pleasing peers. As the influence of peers increases, overt influence of parents seems to wane, but already strong foundations for action and attitudes have been laid. Perhaps parents teach children how to be men and women; peers teach children how to be boys and girls.

This does not mean we can simply follow the line of least resistance and wait for children to grow up and catch on. Discipline (guidance or teaching) also involves active direction of the child. There are numerous ways in which this active direction can be achieved:

- Reasoning with the child.
- Helping him to understand why or why not.
- Setting down limits; holding up standards.
- Using physical restraint or encouragement.
- Praising successful endeavors.
- Providing an atmosphere in which he can grow.

The total environment and relationship is important for growth—we cannot settle for a list of do's and don't's. Bee (1967) carried out a study that supports the importance of the total parent-child relationship. A sample of 136 nine-year-olds was divided into two groups in terms of their ability to withstand distractions. Each child was given problems to solve in a situation in which parents were allowed to interact with them. The children were scored on the number of times they asked for help.

There was no difference in the amount of interaction in the two groups, but there was a difference in the pattern of interaction. Parents of nondistractible children more often than other parents made remarks that were related to previous comments. There seemed to be more continuity in conversation with their children. Parents of distractible children made greater use of suggestions with sons than with daughters. The opposite was true for parents of nondistractible children. Parents of nondistractible children gave greater encouragement for persistence, and their children more often rejected offered help than did distractible children. Parents of nondistractible children gave general kinds of help or suggestions which encouraged independent thought, for example: "What kind of letter does every word have to have?"

People seem to assume there are only two alternatives to disciplining (guiding) children: punish them or let them alone. This, of course, is not true. Discipline includes everything that regulates behavior in such a way that children grow up to be healthy, well-organized, and reasonably happy young men and women. Punishment is certainly included in this repertoire, but is not the most important tool available for shaping behavior, guiding, or teaching. In fact, when punishment is administered in anger, the child may receive a completely wrong message. He may fail to learn anything about the misbehavior under attack for which he was punished; he may learn only that he must be more careful next time so as not to get caught. Spanking may stop a particular behavior, at least temporarily, and it may relieve a parent's frustration; but it teaches the child very little about correct or acceptable behavior. Spanking may keep a boy out of a dangerous swimming hole (may, mind you!), but it will never help him learn the long, slow lessons of generosity, kindness, and concern for other people.

The most effective punishment is that which follows as a natural consequence of behavior. If a child is late coming home and misses a special treat that had been planned, he learns that decisions he makes have consequences. He learns that while he can make choices, he cannot always choose the results of his choices. If he makes or helps to make reparations for a destructive act, he learns something about cause and effect in regard to his own behavior. What type of actions are open to the adult who wishes to help a child deal with his behavior? There are a number that may be used both from the standpoint of inhibiting certain behaviors and encouraging others.

If punishment seems to be indicated, it should be directly related to the misbehavior, when possible. If a child becomes undependable about coming home, for instance, some of his freedom in choosing where and when he will go may be curtailed. In the long run, however, we will do better to work with a child about limits and standards, and try to help him remember by reasoning with him or setting up checks and balances regarding his behavior. *Corporal punishment* (spanking and slapping) is probably used by parents more than any other because they have never learned more creative ways to teach children proper behavior. It is not generally effective after age 2, at which time children are quite able to understand language other than that of the hand or the hickory stick. Corporal punishment is usually administered when the adult is highly emotional, and there is always danger of actually injuring a child. The child is likely to associate the pain with the administrator of it more often than with the deed for which he is receiving the lashing. Even though hitting, slapping, or spanking seems the most expedient and natural way to let a child know he has done wrong, it is certainly not the best for his total peronality development.

Within the past decade child battering has become a major societal concern of those involved in child health and welfare, as thousands of children are victims of parental mistreatment each year. (See Figure 11-4.) In New York City in 1970 there were 7,000 reported cases of child beating ("Help for Child Beaters," 1972). Doctors estimate that one child was killed each week by drug-addicted parents. This, of course, does not present the whole picture, since many cases undoubtedly go unreported.

Child abuse and neglect must be examined from many angles: legal and social implications, physical and mental health implications. There is no certain knowledge about the number of cases (see Chapter 3), but child abuse and neglect is the largest cause of death among children, resulting in

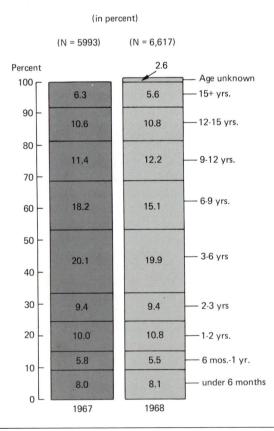

Figure 11-4.

6,000 deaths annually (Snapper, 1975). A number of programs have been established to assist parents who may be prone to child abuse which to some extent is a self-perpetuating problem: children who are abused are likely to have parents who were themselves abused as children.

The incidence of this practice spans all races and economic groups. There are numbers of causes underlying child battering. Unrealistic parental expectations of their offspring with subsequent failure by children to achieve to the expected level precipitate some of this mistreatment. Parents who were physically or emotionally abused and those who see in their children some of their own traits that they hate number high among the offenders. These parents are deeply suspicious of authority and carefully seek out different doctors and hospitals after each episode of child beating. They want, at all costs, to protect themselves from being attacked as "bad" parents. Two new factors are probably contributing to the present rapid increase in this crime: drug addiction, and marriage and childbirth at an age when the parents are scarcely beyond childhood themselves.

The attitude of child-battering parents often is that children exist to satisfy parental needs and that children's needs are unimportant. Each instance of less-than-perfect behavior by a child is seen in the battering parent's eyes as a sign of his own failure. To be cruel is not their usual intent; to have well-behaved children through punishment is the goal. Unable to cope with the pressures and tensions of modern living, they take out their frustrations on the relatively defenseless child. Abusing parents tend to be withdrawn, with few satisfying relationships, generally feeling let down by those around them. Most battering mothers are emotionally disturbed, and battering fathers tend to have just lost their tempers while disciplining a child.

After age 2 the chances of abuse are halved, but children who suffer from it into later years often come to depend on the rough treatment as the only demonstration of concern they receive. Most agencies do not seek to punish offending parents but, rather, to locate the needed help that can rehabilitate the family. All fifty states have laws that require reporting of child abuse.

A self-help group called "Mothers Anonymous" has now been established. One of the major purposes is to assure the parents of their personal worth. The members call on one another when they feel tempted to abuse their children and either talk out their frustrations or arrange for their child to stay with a fellow member until they can pull themselves back together. Professionals with skills to aid these parents in solving their personality problems are also available through the program.

Isolating the child and depriving him of familiar or desired persons, objects, or activities is another common way of telling him he has not done the right thing. The relative worth of such actions will depend upon their relation to the act for which they are being assigned. The most effective discipline is directly related to the misdemeanor.

The use of *natural results of conduct* as a guidance method is one that has become embodied in the teleoanalytic theory of child rearing, based on Adlerian psychology, and currently spreading across the nation in both homes and classrooms: Systematic Training for Effective Parenting—STEP (Dinkmeyer & McKay, 1976). When the child is allowed to experience the natural or logical consequences of his misbehavior, he is readily able to see how he can avoid such suffering by altering his behavior in the future. He cannot blame others for his suffering, and he is learning how in the larger life discipline often occurs. The *teleoanalytic* technique embodies certain guidelines that are applicable in other guidance methods also: learn when not to talk; avoid promoting competition between children; use the family council to air and settle problems; concentrate on one area of behavior at a time; avoid overprotection, physical punishment, feeling sorry for the child, and use of threats, rewards and punishment (Dreikurs and Grey, 1970).

The *family council* is a plan for involving the whole family in decisions which regulate their interaction with each other: rules are set, chores are distributed. Everyone has an equal vote, is free to express feelings and ideas, and takes a turn in presiding over the meeting. The success of this plan lies in the parents' ability to help the children understand the results or consequences of decisions which are made and to arrange "logical consequences" that will bring poor decisions into bold relief! (Allred, 1968)

Verbal appeals or scoldings may have little impact on children's behavior because the listening child is likely to be highly excited, afraid, or otherwise too emotional to hear what is being said to him. Many children report that they prefer a spanking to a talking to; it's quicker and they don't have to look at the angry parent while it's being administered. Quiet discussions, on the other hand, may have more important impact on the child's thinking. These may be scheduled after tempers have quieted down and the situation can be considered matter-of-factly. In such discussions attention can be given to the reasons behind the misdemeanor and the possible consequences on the welfare of the family or the neighborhood or the whole society if everyone acted in such a fashion. The school-age child will be able to apply his knowledge and begin to understand why he must avoid repeat performances of the undesirable act.

Gordon's (1975) P.E.T., *Parent Effectiveness Training,* system of guidance places emphasis on learning communication skills in order to help the child be aware of his behavior: passive and active listening in which the parent listens helps the child verbalize the problem and then reflects the child's feelings so that the child can get to the solution of his problem; I-messages, through which the child is told how the parent feels and what actions are desired in light of certain behaviors of the child; and recognition of problem ownership, whether the behavior is the child's problem (okay with parent) or the parent's problem (okay with child). He also makes use of the "no-lose" problem solving technique, replacing the "parent-wins" (use of arbitrary parental authority) and the "child-wins" (total parental resignation to the child's wishes) alternatives. In a situation where the parent cannot allow certain behavior and the child cannot or does not wish to come into line with the parent's wishes in the matter, Gordon suggests that all alternatives be written down, that unacceptable ones (either from the point of view of the child or the parent) be eliminated, and then a solution be agreed upon from the alternatives that remain.

Three of the most psychologically devastating guidance techniques employed by parents include *withdrawing love, frightening,* and *shaming* children. All that has been said concerning the need for children to develop feelings of security and self-worth is voided if one subscribes to these methods to bring about desired behavior.

When a child misbehaves he feels badly enough, without adding to his feelings the fear of the loss of respect and love of those on whom he depends, namely his parents or other significant adults. The skilled adult will carefully point out that although he cannot condone the act, he continues to love the actor. And it is out of this love that he takes steps to help the child avoid repeat performances. Degrading a child for his behavior may have exactly the opposite of the desired effect—he may decide "I'm no good anyway. I'll really show her how I feel." On the other hand, if his good qualities are cited and he is made to feel that with a little more effort he can enhance himself even more, he is likely to feel encouraged and as a result try even harder to attain the behavior standards that the family or class holds as important. To base good behavior on fear is not a good practice, although, admittedly, many phases of life are so based. To predicate good behavior on love and respect for one's fellow man and on self-respect has a much better effect on self-concept and mental health.

Ignoring as a guidance method may carry two connotations. One is a form of love withdrawal in which the child is ignored following his misbehavior; the other is a way of ignoring the misbehavior action rather than the child. To ignore the action is to acknowledge that much of what children do is unintentional and accidental. Therefore, such treatment is beneficial. The parent and teacher who call attention to every little error may not only be turned off by the child but may be perceived as overcritical. And if taken seriously, such parents and teachers may damage self-concept through their continued derogatory comments. On the other hand, to show selective displeasure brings emphasis when it can be meaningful.

Rewards, usually referring to material objects, and praise or social reinforcement, are common methods for modification of behavior. Positive reinforcement for approved behaviors and consistent ignoring of undesirable behaviors are powerful shaping tools. The RAID program, based on this sort of behavior modification, combines rules, approval, ignoring and disapproval, and was formulated by Charles and Clifford Madsen (Madsen and Madsen, 1976). One criticism of the use of approval in shaping behavior is that children may begin to behave in certain ways for the wrong reasons. In situations where they are not then rewarded for good behavior, they may lose their desire to act properly. The extent to which this would hold true would be dependent, of course, on many factors.

In discussing parent-child interaction, Elkind (1971) distinguished three types of arrangements: the bargain, the agreement and the contract. The most temporary and simplest is the *bargain,* by which a parent offers some reward or withholds some punishment in return for a particular behavior on the part of the child: the parent offers the child a trip to the variety store if he will feed the baby. Children become adept at such bargaining: "I'll pick up the bottles in the garage if I can stay up for the late show."

In an *agreement* the parent and child arrange to abide by certain rules over a period of time. Agreements change in content and may become more positive as the child grows older. For the young child a possible arrangement might be: "If you argue over that game you'll have to put it away." The agreement is the children can play together with the game cooperatively, but will have to forfeit use of it if they argue over it. For the older child: "If you keep the tomatoes weeded, I'll see that your Scout uniform is clean."

The *contract* is the most complex and least explicit, consisting of unspoken demands that determine expectations of each other. Usually it is only a breach of the contract that brings it into the open. Contracts vary in content according to age and sex of the child and the family life-style. All contain three elements: responsibility-freedom clause; achievement-support clause; and loyalty-commitment clause. During the middle childhood period, the parents demand that children take many responsibilities: care of clothing, room, and younger siblings. Children in response to this want greater freedom in staying away from home for longer periods and going farther away.

Think Back

About the punishments you were given as a child:
Who gave them.
How you felt toward that person afterward.
What you thought would be a better punishment.
How you thought you would discipline your own children.
The kinds of discipline your friends received for similar misdemeanors.

When the child enters school, parental demands for achievement center on academic performance, athletic skill, and social popularity. In return children want financial and psychological support for these activities. In addition parents expect family loyalty to continue and supersede loyalties to outside-the-family adults and peers. The child wants to be sure of the parents' commitments to him and asks for this assurance in terms of time and interest of parents devoted to activities in which he takes part. Such a scheme for parent-child interaction holds for the middle class intact family, not for others.

Nearly three fourths of the survey children (National Survey of Children, 1975) reported they get verbal praise as a reward for being good; more than two thirds get hugged or kissed and almost two thirds report that they receive a gift such as a toy or ice cream. More than half reported something special to eat as a reward and four of ten get money or extra allowance. As to punishment, eight of ten get yelled at; two thirds report getting a spanking; six of ten are sent to their rooms or isolated in some other way; about half are not allowed to play with friends and the same number lose television privileges. Only six children of one hundred report that their mothers make fun of them and three of one hundred report she says "she doesn't love you."

The National Survey of Children also had some data about rules: more than half reported they could watch television whenever they wished; 25 percent were allowed snacks and ate whenever they wanted to. Whereas 95 percent of the parents classified discipline as "very important," about 17 percent of the children indicated their parents made them follow the rules "just some of the time" or "hardly ever."

The choice of guidance techniques must be considered carefully for this certainly has impact on the child's personality development. Kagan and Ender (1975) made a study of rural Mexican, Anglo-American and Mexican-American mothers and their children in a success-failure situation in which the mothers could choose to reward, punish, or make no response to a performance by their child. The data suggested that non-contingent reinforcement and punishment (the categories most regularly chosen by the rural Mexican mothers and the low income mothers regardless of culture) are important in the development of compliance, low achievement motivation and a sense of external control. Anglo children, whose mothers were more likely to base reinforcement or reward on performance and did not ignore or punish, were more assertive, competitive, less submissive, more field independent and nonconforming, than the other groups of children. There was no attempt to judge which of these two approaches was the best, only to point out the relationships.

Guidance Concepts

In the American Family Report (General Mills, 1977) a total of 1,230 families were interviewed, including parents and children. Parents listed the following influences in society that made it hard to rear children:

- Drugs
- Broken marriages
- Inflation
- Permissiveness in child rearing
- Crime and violence in the streets
- Both parents having to work to get along financially
- Breakdown of traditional values
- Decline of religion
- Parents being more selfish and less willing to sacrifice for their children
- Insecurity about jobs and unemployment
- Television
- Quality of education

From a list of 48 concerns, parents were to list their personal concerns. The ten most frequently named concerns centered on parental shortcomings, impact of television on children, and intake of non-nutritive food. Their own shortcomings were being too permissive, feeling insecure and guilty, and expecting too much from the children. In addition, there were the nagging problems created by children—the kinds of things that irritate parents, create tensions, and generate arguments. These included:

- Eating habits: both the prevalence of between-meal snacking (34%) and the children's refusal to eat what they should (27%)
- Bad tempered behavior: children crying and whining (24% among parents of older children, but 42% among parents of young children; having temper tantrums (18%)
- The "gimmies": children asking for things they see advertised (28%)
- Disrespect and irresponsibility: children talking back (29%); not doing their chores (36%); and not coming home when supposed to (10%)
- Television: children spending too much time in front of the set (30%)
- Bedtime: children not going to bed on time (24%)
- Falsehood: children not telling the truth (10%)

Except for yelling and scolding, spanking is still the most frequently used form of punishment for children under 13 years of age. Strict parents use this form of punishment (59%) more often than the more permissive parents (39%). Parents who were more likely to have lost control recently, and punished their children more than they deserved, were the strict disciplinarians who were also the most inconsistent in their punishment. A third of all parents reported their loss of control, and almost three-fifths of the parents reported their inconsistency.

After a hug or kiss, the most often used rewards for good behavior were:

- Taking the children some place special   48%
- Buying them something special   40%
- Giving them something special to eat   26%
- Giving them money   20%
- Letting them watch extra television   20%

Children's views of their parents' expectations of them included:

- Do well in school   75%
- Go to college   56%
- Go to church; synagogue   50%
- Set an example for other children   38%
- Save money   38%
- Be the best in the class   30%
- Be popular   25%
- Be good at sports   24%
- Win at games   12%

Whereas no theory or set of rules will appeal to all parents or other adults working and living with children, acquaintance with many can allow them to develop specific techniques that work best in their situation. However, there are some underlying principles of guidance which may well be incorporated, whatever the approach. Waring (1952) has enumerated four principles (Figure 11-5) on which effective guidance is built: *affection, respect, help, and approval.* When the child knows he is loved, he derives a sense of security in his relationships. As he is respected as a growing, capable individual, he builds his self-respect. As he is given the help he needs for independent action, he improves his abilities to deal with life's problems. As he receives approval for good work, he learns to value that behavior as satisfying both to others and to himself.

Consistency is a requisite for effective guidance. Lack of it retards any learning in which the child may be engaged. Inconsistency may be more damaging than the degree of severity of discipline, for the child is unsure of limits and of the consequences that exceeding set limits will bring. Mothers tend to be less consistent in guidance than fathers, partly because they are with the child more, perhaps because of their increased understanding of the causes of misbehavior; and the good mother stereotype of our culture does not typically include strictness in discipline (Jackson, 1956). Studies of vacillating mothers (Clifford, 1959) revealed that they tend to fluctuate between hostility and concern for the welfare of their children; they threaten but do not impose penalties for misdoings; they impose restrictions but later apologize for their action; they complain that their children do not obey them. Children typically try to outwit their mothers and purposefully engage in antisocial behavior to tantalize them.

Parents are not only inconsistent in the things for which a penalty is assigned; they are inconsistent in the type of penalty they select. Because of orientation and belief concerning guidance techniques, parents subject chil-

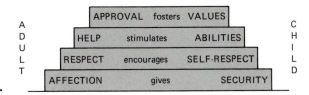

Figure 11-5.

dren to inconsistency from parent to parent. Whereas parents may never agree totally on specific discipline measures for all occasions, it is important that they stick together once one has made a decision and that they work out their differences of opinion apart from the children's hearing. Both these admonitions are difficult to follow; but energies so directed are well spent. Otherwise, the child may play the parents against each other purposefully and lose respect for them as authority figures. Such loss of respect for authority may then spread to other authority figures, including teachers and officers of the law.

Good models are another aspect of effective guidance. The child who is told "Do as I say and not as I do" is receiving little help toward the achievement of acceptable behavior goals. He learns instead that at certain later ages proper behavior becomes less important as power increases. This would be an unfortunate learning to impart.

Children are due one more "courtesy" with respect to guidance related to their misbehavior; *the incident should be treated and then forgotten.* Whereas adults have acquired the ability to harbor a grudge, children in the 5–12 age span have not yet solidified this characteristic in their personality pattern. After age 6, children's initial reaction to disciplinary measures is typically anger; the average time for such a feeling has been set at about five minutes (Clifford, 1959). Thereafter, they desire to forget the consequences of errant action. Parents who continue to dwell on the misdemeanor and its attendant results only prolong the feelings of guilt and shame that the child may have experienced.

To help children learn *to accept and cope with the less-than-good aspects of their personalities* is a primary ingredient in emotional health. Although adults know that no one, including children, is perfect all the time, they tend to set this goal for the children under their guidance. Many times adults are unable to admit their own wrongdoings, projecting the perfection model to children. This is not good. Children need to know that everyone makes mistakes. One first-grader, having erred, was being comforted by his teacher. When she assured him "Everyone makes mistakes," he responded, "My mother doesn't." Children who learn they must always be good try to split away the unwanted part of themselves, but instead of shedding the thought or feeling, they really lock it away inside. And when enough of these "bad" feelings accumulate, there may be an uncontrollable explosion: mental or physical illness or extreme antisocial acts may result.

Children are continually struggling with good and bad. While they cannot always be allowed to express hostility openly nor indiscriminately impose the results of their feelings on others, they can be reassured that it is nomal to have "bad" thoughts and urges and that everyone has to learn to deal with them. When children can accept all parts of their minds and bodies as normal and controllable, not viewing some as too terrible to be tolerated, they are free to feel comfortable with themselves and enjoy life more fully.

The concept of *freedom to fail* was presented at the American Home Economics Family Life Education Workshop (Kennedy, 1971). If a child is to know himself as a person able to accept responsibility, he must have trustworthy feedback from his environment. There is danger that parents and teachers may block such growth by overprotection, growing out of their own lack of ability and discomfort in dealing with failure.

If a child is to be free to succeed he must experience genuine situations that carry possibility of failure. As long as a child is protected from failure, he will not experientially know what capabilities he possesses. He will not know the moral quality that arises from the existential moment of risking himself in action for which he bears decision-making responsibility. Moreover, as long as he is protected from failure, he will exaggerate its trauma and be unaware of the growth-promoting qualities of its feedback.

Protectiveness encourages a child to fear failure as a *bad* thing, rather than to see its usefulness in a problem-solving approach to life. Protectiveness suggests that life is a fixed pattern demanding specific behaviors, probably beyond the potential of the individual. In contrast, growth-producing situations encourage the child to see life as a continuous unfolding. Change is valued, and the child is valued for his uniqueness and his potential. Growth situations accept the child where he is and encourage him to thus accept himself, accept responsibility for his behavior, and build new understandings and competencies on the feedback from each new experience. The child who is free to fail is the child who also is free to succeed.

In the meantime, of course, children are exposed to other *pressures to conform*—from peers, the school, the community, and the mass media. A recent cartoon pictured a small, disheveled boy with a black eye and torn trousers. Cap in hand, he squarely faced his quite evidently irate mother. The caption read: "Guess who was forced, on his way home, to disobey, against his own will, his mother's instructions not to fight?"

In the midst of such pressures, adult guidance can support the child in his development as he learns to know and value himself. Out of a child's general good adustment, one can expect responsible, helpful, and productive behavior.

In discussing the strengths and weaknesses of the ghetto child, the following suggestions were made for using positive resources within the child (Obsatz, 1967). These suggestions need not be limited only to dealings with disadvantaged children. All children profit from such attention and treatment.

- Give him credit.
- Don't force him to be dependent on the teacher.

- Make school work relevant to life.
- Encourage social interaction in class.
- Respect him and his possessions.
- Be genuine to the child.
- Be consistent.
- Don't be too rigid.
- Let the child know you are on his side.
- Admit when you are wrong.
- Give him alternatives in his school work (or in anything).
- Be aware of physical conditions.

Education for Parenting

One of the great needs in our society is an emphasis on parent education or education for parenting. Perhaps nothing we do is of such vital importance nor demands so much time, money, and commitment, and is prepared for so haphazardly. Bronfenbrenner (1974) pointed out the decreasing amount of interaction between parents and children, the vacuum being filled by age-segregated peer groups. His thesis is that this condition has resulted in a growing alienation of children and youth from society. This has not come about because parents do not care about their children, but rather because parents have come to feel powerless as forces in the lives of their children. Rapid change in technology, living styles, and value systems has left a void in knowledge and coping abilities.

This idea is expanded through excerpts from the report of Forum 15 at the White House Conference on Children (1971):

In our modern way of life, children are deprived not only of parents but of people in general. A host of factors conspire to isolate children from the rest of society. The fragmentation of the extended family, the separation of residential and business areas, the disappearance of neighborhoods, zoning ordinances, occupational mobility, child labor laws, the abolishment of the apprentice system, consolidated schools, television, separate patterns of social life for different age groups, the working mother, the delegation of child care to specialists—all these manifestations of progress operate to decrease opportunity and incentive for meaningful contact between children and persons older, or younger, than themselves.

And here we confront a fundamental and disturbing fact: Children need people in order to become human. The fact is fundamental because it is firmly grounded both in scientific research and in human experience. It is disturbing because the isolation of children from adults simultaneously threatens the growth of the individual and the survival of the society. The young cannot pull themselves up by their own bootstraps. It is primarily through observing, play-

Bringing adults back into the lives of children is a way to socialize youngsters more effectively. (Photo by Rick Coleman.)

ing, and working with others older and younger than himself that a child discovers both what he can do and who he can become—that he develops both his ability and his identity. It is primarily through exposure and interaction with adults and children of different ages that a child acquires new interests and skills and learns the meaning of tolerance, cooperation, and compassion. Hence to relegate children to a world of their own is to deprive them of their humanity, and ourselves as well.

Yet, this is what is happening in America today. We are experiencing a breakdown in the process of making human beings human. By isolating our children from the rest of society, we abandon them to a world devoid of adults and ruled by the destructive impulses and compelling pressures both of the age-segregated peer group and the aggressive and exploitive television screen. By setting our priorities elsewhere and putting children and families last, by claiming one set of values while pursuing another, we leave our children bereft of standards and support and our own lives impoverished and corrupted. . . . What is needed is a change in our patterns of living which will once again bring people back into the lives of children and children back into the lives of people.

In order to enhance the parenthood role, change the alienation trend, and reorder priorities, Bronfenbrenner (1971(b)) made several suggestions:

1. Making available developmental day care services, reinvolving and strengthening the family through such programs. This means real parent participation.
2. Provision of increased opportunities (number) and reward (status) for part-time employment for both men and women.
3. Modification of work schedules and obligations to allow employees more time at home, fewer moves, maternal and child care leaves, fewer job-related social obligations.
4. Reacquainting children with adults as participants in the world of work: e.g.: a shop or business adopt a group of children (a particular classroom) and arrange visits back and forth between the children and workmen in the classroom and on the job.
5. Assign to children genuine responsibilities, for children learn to cope with different situations as they take on responsibility and are held accountable for their performance.
6. Involvement of the school in community and of school children with each other: learning from the activities going on in the community; utilizing skills of community people; having older children being reponsible for and sharing with younger children. Functional courses in human development should be begun in which children participate in day care programs, Head Start classrooms, with the aged, with those living alone. Through such contacts the children would have opportunities not only to work with other people, but to know the families and understand and appreciate the life styles of families different from their own.
7. Development of family support systems in the neighborhood and throughout the community which would strengthen the role of the family in meeting the needs of the child and involving him with people:
   a. Commission for children and families
   b. Neighborhood Family Centers
   c. Community and Neighborhood projects
   d. Participation of youth in local policy boards
   e. Community and Neighborhood Planning

Concepts of Parenting Education

Some adults experience feelings of guilt themselves because they do not feel astute in child guidance. People vary in their abilities to relate to and work successfully with various ages and stages in the cycle of growth. Some feel more at ease with young children or infants. Others may find they relate best to adolescents or aging persons. Hopefully, there are many who find their strength lies in guidance of the child of the middle years. But few will be good with all ages, and some may not be particularly outstanding with any group.

To when you were growing up:
How you celebrated holidays and birthdays.
About family rituals.
What special privileges you were given.
Things you were denied.

Much of the guilt of modern parents may lie in their feeling that they should be all things to all children at all stages in their growth. In former days the extended family pattern provided a variety of adults in the home and thus many talents suitable for dealing with child guidance. In the current nuclear pattern, two parents cannot possibly become experts in all the necessary roles. But adults working with children can gain some basic understanding about guiding them which will facilitate the awesome task.

To set down a few basic principles about child development and parent-child interaction is important. This compilation is by no means exhaustive. As you read and think you may want to add other concepts to this list:

1. There are patterns of development or stages of growth. Some behaviors that are "normal" may be difficult to accept unless seen as a developmental step in growing up, e.g., terrible two's; school teacher crush; sass and pulling away from home in middle childhood; peer group attachment.
2. Each child *reacts* as well as is acted upon. His reaction in turn affects the parents' actions and feelings.
3. Children learn within a relationship—this relationship is more important than particular techniques. The child's perception of this relationship is a crucial factor.
4. Some people are more important to children than others. These are the significant others. Those near him. They internalize values of these people, their ways of acting, their roles.
5. Children become increasingly influenced by adults outside their home after they go to school—and then by their peers. To understand and accept this allows the child to use these resources and still to retain his contact with the family. They learn other ways of doing things and other value systems as they range away from home.
6. Children need to be allowed to make decisions. This must be learned; they need support in this activity. Start early; give increasing opportunity and responsibility.
7. Children must know they are seen as responsible worthwhile family members—persons. Interaction in the family is important. They need feedback on how they "come on." They should know what is expected of them.
8. Children learn in subtle ways. Many things are "caught" rather than "taught." They pick up feelings; indeed they seem to be equipped with

radar. They learn things never intended which are inferred from our actions. We think we teach one thing and in reality may teach something quite different. We must examine what children learn from our actions, as well as from our words.

9. Children must be dependent on adults before they can be truly independent. They must trust grown-ups and the world so they can learn to assert themselves (show autonomy) and show initiative (try things out for themselves).

10. Children need to see themselves as succeeders—as good people. They learn this (or the opposite) from people who are important to them. They need success experiences rather than only failure experiences.

11. Children have feelings that must be accepted. They learn to understand, to use, and to control feelings as they see other people do this and talk about it.

12. Children must be allowed to grow at their own rate and in their own style rather than be called on to fulfill the ambitions of parents and other adults.

13. In order to allow a child to grow, not to burden him with tasks too big for him, parents must be growing mature people, finding ways to meet their own needs; e.g., good adult-adult relationships.

14. Parents must realize children attempt to manipulate them. Set limits. Limits give security. Enforce limits. Be consistent.

15. At the same time—listen to children. Be ready to listen and evaluate new materials or information they bring to the situation. Consistency means being willing to listen to new evidence as well as never changing a stand or "giving in."

16. Keep lines of communication open. Don't embarrass children or make fun of them. Let them set the stage for the manner in which their problems should be received and reviewed and worked out. "Little" problems may be quite big—important—to children. Treat them so.

17. Talk with children—not just with words. Parents must be available to children. Answer questions honestly, as fully as they desire at the time of the question.

18. Be honest with children about personal feelings. Share awe and wonder with them. Do not overburden or overwhelm them with adult problems and concerns. But share with them sadness and anger and grief on occasion—as well as joy and delight and laughter.

19. Include children in family activities—allow them to help plan as well as to participate in the action.

20. Know about community opportunities and resources for children. However, as you broaden their horizons, try not to clutter their lives. Give them time to think; to "mess around." They must have time and freedom to appropriate what they can and will do.

What's Next?

1. *Between Parent and Child,* H. Ginott. New York: Macmillan, 1965.
2. *Between Teacher and Child,* H. Ginott. New York: Macmillan, 1972.
3. *The Prophet,* K. Gibran. New York: Knopf, 1955, pp. 15–18.
4. *Child Development Through Literature,* Landau et al. Englewood Cliffs, N.J.: Prentice-Hall, 1972: "The Stone Boy," G. Berriault, pp. 261–270.
5. "For My Son." In R. McKuen, *Lonesome Cities.* New York: Random House, 1968.
6. Drug Information. National Clearinghouse on Drug Information, Box 1706, Rockville, Maryland 20850.
7. Play: *The Case of the Missing Handshake,* N. Stirling. American Theatre Wing Community Plays, Human Relations Aids, 225 Park Avenue, S., New York, N.Y. 10003.
8. Play: *The Daily Special,* N. Stirling. American Theatre Wing Community Plays, Human Relations Aids, 225 Park Avenue, S., New York, N.Y. 10003.
9. Play: *There Was a Little Boy,* B. Davidson. Mental Health Materials Center, 419 Park Avenue, S., New York, N.Y. 10016.
10. Film: *Who Cares About Jamie?* Smart Family Foundation, 65 E. South Water, Chicago, Illinois 60601.
11. *P.E.T. Parent Effectiveness Training,* Thomas Gordon. New York: New American Library, 1975.
12. *P.E.T. in Action,* Thomas Gordon. New York: Bantam Books, 1976.
13. *Children: The Challenge,* Dreikurs, Rudolph and Vicki Stoltz. New York: Hawthorn Books, 1964.
14. *Teaching/Discipline,* Charles H. and Clifford K. Madsen. Boston: Allyn and Bacon, 1976.
15. *Parent and Child Relations: An Introduction to Parenting,* Bigner, J. J. New York: Macmillan, 1979.
16. Filmstrip: *The Forgotten Years: Understanding Children from 6 to 12.* Parents Magazine Films, Inc., Department A., 52 Vanderbilt Ave., New York, New York. 10017.

Catalysts for Discussion

I. A recollection (Bruner, 1970)

When I was in the fourth grade—no it was the third grade
The boy he stole my glove.
He took my glove and said that his father found it downtown on the ground (And you fight him?)
I told him that it was impossible for him to find it downtown 'cause all those people was walking by and just his father was the only one that found it?
So he got all (mad).
So then I fought him.

I knocked him all out in the street.
So he say he give and I kept on hitting him.
Then he started crying and ran home to his father.
And the father told him that he didn't find no glove.

II. Dear Dad (source unknown):

"When I tried to explain to you how I got that green paint on the Kitchen floor, the hall carpet, all over the basement, upstairs in the bathroom, and all over me, you were too mad to listen. If you've cooled off a little now, maybe you could try to understand that I was only trying to help. Honest.

"You know that Mom's been bugging you to paint the porch chairs all summer. You kept saying you were too busy. So I thought it would make both of you happy if I painted them. I didn't know you'd go yelling that it took longer to clean up the mess I made than to paint the chairs yourself. Honest.

"Dad, I tried not to make a mess. I couldn't paint outside because it was raining. I did spread papers down all over the basement. How was I to know you hadn't read them yet?

"I did put on old clothes. You saw that. I didn't know that shirt was Mom's favorite because it matched my eyes. Jeeps, women are buggy about what a guy wears! The reason paint got all over my legs was because I was wearing those old jeans I cut off to make a pirate costume for day camp. I thought it was a good idea to go barefoot, so I wouldn't ruin any good socks, if something dripped. I didn't know I was making green footprints all over the basement. Honest.

"Dad, I did wipe the paint brush on the edge of the can every time I dipped it in, like you said. Honest, I did. I think. I don't know how come the paint got all over the papers. And I did not know I was stepping in it until I saw all those green tracks. That's when I went to the laundry room and got an old pair of your socks. Well, I thought they were your old socks. I can't explain how paint got all over them, too.

"After I finished the first chair, I had to go back upstairs to the porch to get another one. That must have been when the paint got on the basement stairs. I didn't mean to break the glass on the kitchen counter. I just couldn't see it when I was carrying the chair. I thought I did clean up all the broken glass. How was I to know you'd step on that piece way over by the refrigerator?

"Dad, I did try to clean up the mess myself. Honest. It took me a while to find the paint remover. That must have been when I got the green paint on your tools. How could I get the paint off my hands until I found the paint remover?

"I couldn't get the lid off the can and I couldn't find anything in the basement to pry it off, and I didn't want to bother you or Mom, so I went up to the kitchen to get a knife. How was I to know the lid would come off right then and would spill all over the kitchen floor. The color isn't off the floor forever, is it?

"Even with the paint remover, I couldn't get all the gunk off my feet. I couldn't put the socks back on because they were all painty. That's when I got this great idea of making myself shoes out of aluminum foil. They were pretty neat shoes! How was I to know one of them would come off when I was halfway up the front stairs to the bathroom? I'll try some paint remover on the stair carpet if you want me to.

"I know I made an awful green ring in the bathtub. But I was just trying to get the rest of the paint off me. Honest, I did try to scrub away the ring. That's when Mom yelled at me for getting green paint on the guest towels. The reason I cut off part of my hair was because the paint wouldn't come out. I didn't know Mom was going to cry when she saw it. It'll grow out in a week or so, won't it?

"Dad, I don't blame you for being mad about the mess. It sure makes me feel stupid. I must be an awful dumb nut. But, honest, Dad, I was just trying to help.

Your loving son,
Chris"

III. Some techniques for minimizing aggressive behavior in children. (Adapted from F. Redl and D. Wineman, *Controls from Within*. New York: Macmillan, 1952):

Ignore the behavior if it is likely to stop.

Use a warning signal, as a glance or some other symbol, denoting the behavior is out of bounds.

Come close to the youngster to calm and reassure him—without hostile intent.

Show interest in something the child is doing, while suggesting new acceptable ways to behave.

Give sympathetic support by expressing understanding of the problem causing the child's behavior.

Kid the child out of his misbehavior.

Provide "hurdle help" just prior to an emotional explosion, thus circumventing it.

Interfere with the behavior by verbal interpretation, suggesting something which could have caused his bad feelings.

Regroup children who do not seem to get along together well.

Drop an activity in which tension is mounting and begin a different one.

Limit space and tools to separate child from objects which may be contributing to misbehavior.

Remove the child from a conflict situation without showing emotional involvement—as in emergencies when physical harm is likely.

Hold the child in a calm, friendly, non-aggressive restraining way during a temper outburst.

IV. Where to go for information, counseling and help: Family Service Centers; Family Counseling Centers; Mental Health Associations for Retarded Children; Jewish Family Services; United Charities Associations; Catholic Charities Associations; Counseling Services on University and College Campuses; Synanon; Alateen; Child Guidance Associates; Association for Care of Children in Hospitals; Parents Anonymous.

Beyond the Classroom Experiences

1. Note the actions of middle childhood people over a period of time, and make anecdotal records of things that call for guidance. Later determine the probable cause of the behavior: developmental, circumstantial, or otherwise.

2. Clip from current periodicals articles related to child abuse. Look for factors in the offenders' lives which might account for this behavior. If possible, attend the court proceedings for a child abuse offense. Attend the meeting of a Mothers Anonymous group, or a similar group.

3. Set up a family council in your family, or visit the home of children who have a family council. Note the process, its strengths and weaknesses.

4. Record incidents where an adult was actively engaged in providing guidance for a child. Discuss this with respect to the information in this chapter.

5. Attend several groups related to parenting education—such as Parents Without Partners, church groups, Family Services groups. Note the emphases and compare the principles taught with those in this chapter. Observe the reactions of the parents, and note specific problems they relate.

6. Recall from your middle childhood one or more incidents involving guidance. Write a brief account expressing how you felt and what happened. If possible, ask the adult involved to recall the same incident and write an account from his or her viewpoint. Compare them.

7. In your community, contact the various agencies offering services for families. Collect information concerning their services, costs, clientele, professional staff and so on.

Chapter 12

Children's Concepts

This chapter is designed to help you:

- recognize the role of concept development in children's thought and actions and component parts of the process
- discover how prejudice develops and how it can be minimized
- plan and evaluate sex education in the home and community
- understand how children may view divorce and ways to deal with its effects on them
- explore children's concepts of aging and the aged and plan ways to help them relate to both
- understand the grief process and ways to deal with children experiencing it
- see how children may be helped to develop money concepts
- understand how children's political concepts change with age

Concept Development

It is their concepts that makes the middle childhood people so fascinating to study: only at this time can you lose your teeth and be happy about it; that you will walk your friend home, and she will walk you home, and you will walk her home again, sometimes until dark. Only in these years do you hate the opposite sex so much you won't even hold hands in a circle game and do you invent such marvelous memory crutches as "A rat in Tom's house may eat Tom's ice cream" to remember how to spell arithmetic. Now is when you learn to put a ball and bat at the end of a sentence to show that it is an excited statement and when you buy cereals according to what's pictured on the outside instead of what's packaged inside. Middle childhood is when you idolize Fat Albert, Fonzie, and Wonder Woman, when you stuff your pockets with Star Wars cards, bullet casings, and cellophane strips off cigarette packs because a friend told you that if you could save a pound of them you can get a free leader dog for a blind person.

It's a common idea during middle childhood that your dad can beat any other kid's dad blindfolded and that when you grow up you can become an Indian or work in the daytime as a doctor and at night as a fireman. You are convinced the peanut butter sandwiches your mom packs in your lunch are better than the fried chicken lunch they serve in the school cafeteria. And without a doubt, you know that cutting your arm and placing it on the cut arm of your best friend will make you blood brothers for life. It's only middle childhood people who write cryptic messages in lemon juice and bring them to visibility over a warm light bulb and who meet secretly where knowledge and pacts are formed, forever banned from the ears of adults. This is when you learn not to slide on first base but to run like fury if the catcher misses the ball on your third strike; when you perfect the skill of giving Indian wrist burns; and when such mystic acts as tying knots in string, stepping on sidewalk cracks and kissing your elbow can accomplish feats far beyond the mind of a mature adult!

The world is made up of innumerable sights, sounds, smells, and tastes. Color, texture, firmness, and temperature are a few of the stimuli that must be interpreted through the sensory organs by the central nervous system. At first a child is only vaguely aware of these things. He must learn to understand, label, and invest them with meaning. In addition, a child must be able to perceive new clues about objects he is already familiar with. Even when he knows about a cow, it takes time to attend to the shadows and other hints that will make him know that a cow at a distance is not really as small as it looks, nor is the animal flat. He must learn to "see" these properties of the "cow at a distance."

To bring order out of this great amount of information input, a system of concepts must be developed. Concepts are regarded as the fabric of mental life; they serve to carve up the person's world into functional units. To define "concept," however, is difficult indeed; it is easier to describe and discuss various concepts than to formulate a definition. A dictionary meaning of concept is "an idea of something formed by mentally combining all of its characteristics and particulars." In an effort to obtain a clearer definition, Flavell (1970) suggested certain similarities among concepts and certain variations which go a long way toward solving the definition problem.

The first common attribute he presented was the notion of *equivalence responses:* all concepts imply similar or same reactions to dissimilar environmental inputs. This means that we must locate concepts in the organism—the person—not in their external milieus. In this vein, Harvey, Hunt, and Schroder (1961, p. 1) stated "a concept is a system of ordering that serves as a mediating linkage between the input side (stimuli) and the output side (response)." The concept, when it is formed, serves as a filter through which all events are screened, a process which determines for the most part what the responses will be.

This leads to two *functional* similarities. The first function, an absolutely essential one, is that of "reducing the complexity of sensory input to manageable proportions" (Flavell, 1970, p. 985). This simplification function, the classification and categorization of objects and events, allows one to anticipate future events from present ones. For example, to know that a particular thing is part of a certain class or group is to know a great deal about the thing which may not be immediately perceptible.

A second function, building on the first, is that a concept may be regarded as a network of sign-significant information which "makes it possible for the organism to 'go beyond the information given' in all manner of adaptive ways" (Flavell, 1970, p. 986).

A third common property characterizing concepts is the interdependence among concepts forming conceptual systems. Concepts are defined in terms of other concepts. This interlocking gives "the temporal flow of most thinking its smooth, continuous and effortless quality" (Flavell, 1970, p. 986).

When we talk of diversity among concepts we must distinguish between variation "associated with concepts taken in their public, consensually valid aspect . . . [and variation] in their relation to the individual who uses them" (Flavell, 1970, p. 986). There is public and private content of a concept; one may understand "a" concept, but not "your" concept, in a particular instance.

Flavell (1970) presents seven ways in which concepts may vary:

1. *Attributes*—characteristics which an instance of the concept will invariably possess. These may be intrinsic, measurable, physical properties such as red, round, 4 pounds; they may refer to function or activity such as washable, fire resistant, bio-degradable; they may refer to role or status such as class assignment, friend, best alternative.

2. *Structure*—the manner in which the attributes must be combined or related in the definition of the concept. For some concepts two particular attributes must be present (conjunction): a mother must be both female and have a child. In others any one of two or more attributes may define the concept (dysjunction): either a sister or brother can be labeled sibling. In still other concepts, certain attributes must be present in particular relationships to each other (relational); equilateral triangles include only those triangles whose sides are equal.

3. *Abstractness*—there is a wide range from concrete, tangible objects and events (ball, apartment, rainy day, school prom) to abstract, intangible ones (justice, happiness, communism, between).

4. *Inclusiveness*—variation in number of instances included; from only one, Paige's baby sister, to a very large number, stars.

5. *Generality*—variation in the position in the classification hierarchy they occupy: Jiggs, the new puppy next door, is a very specific concept; Boston Bull dog, a more general one; canines, a still more general one.

6. *Precision*—there is a variation in the extent to which or manner in which a concept may be explicitly defined so that instances may be clearly distinguished from non-instances by a group. Some concepts are quite precise: mumps, postage stamps; others are quite imprecise: beautiful woman, good weather, adequate performance.

7. *Power*—power is determined by whether most people agree the concept is an important one and whether the understanding of the concept makes possible the understanding of other important concepts. Flavell (1970, p. 988) points out that while the understanding of "cat may be of significance in the child's intellectual growth, it certainly does not have the formative, development-impelling power of 'permanent object' or 'measurement unit.' "

Another set of variations concern the *subject-concept relationship*. The private meaning of a concept may vary from the public or standard meaning (validity). The subject's definition of the concept may be narrower or broader, less definite or fixed, than standard. Therefore, the private concept may be different from and more unstable than the accepted or standard concept. In the child the concept of quantity illustrates this. "More" may mean only "taller" or "wider," not both; and may refer to one dimension (height) in one situation and to another (width) in a different situation.

The second varying relationship is the degree to which the person is a *concept-user* and a *concept understander*. One can use a concept without being able to articulate it, or even being aware of it; the opposite is not true. One can think with a concept before one can think about it, but not vice versa. People vary in the extent to which a concept is for them an intellectual object as well as an intellectual instrument. Flavell (1970) used the "grammatical English sentence" as an illustration of this. Children operate in terms of this concept before they can name it, let alone define and discuss it.

There is also variation in *accessibility*. An individual may have a concept given yet for a number of reasons be unable to use it on a give appropriate occasion. For example, one may have acquired the concept of "consideration" and yet on a particular occasion is not able to call forth ways of being considerate of other people.

With any child some concepts may be fully and accurately developed, others only partially developed, and still others quite inaccurate. Differences in particular areas appear from one child to the next depending on developmental level and experiences.

There are two major types of concepts to be learned, according to Gagne (1977). Such concrete concepts as red, house, and round can be readily observed and even experienced. However, other concepts are abstract and their learning involves rules which show relationships or classifications typically given in verbal definitions: mass, aunt, temperature. By entrance into kindergarten many children have workable concepts of such common objects as chair, flower, book, and those of placements as, under, behind, around. But the less tangible ideas of early and late, more than, the next one, and double may prove a challenge for several years. Primary youngsters can often count to 10 but cannot yet envision one-ness nor ten-ness. Their concept of these terms is still limited.

Through experience and instruction, the concept collection expands with age. The repertoire of printed symbols gradually encompasses mathematical notations, letters which form words which convey meaning, punctuation marks, and even comic strip symbolism. One second-grader wanted to attend the parent orientation at his school. His mother pointed out the notice specifically said "No children tonight." He queried, "Were they excited when they wrote that"? He merely wanted to know if the sentence had ended with an exclamation point! Gagne cautions against verbal superficiality. Children often use words of which their concept is foggy: they can name three inventors but don't know what makes a person an inventor. They listen to stories containing unfamiliar words often without inquiring concerning their meaning. Even adults skip over words as they read, unaware of their meaning, and deduce the message due to general context.

Gagne defines three steps which lead to concept building. *Discrimination* or learning to locate similarities and differences in objects or ideas is a prerequisite to this process. How can a child tell a dog from a cat? He has learned to look for the distinguishing features of each. This leads to the next step, that of *generalization* or application of the concept in another context, as dog and wolf or cat and tiger. *Practice* making decisions based on one's ability to discriminate and generalize helps develop a full range of the given concept including specific breeds of dogs or cats. Two conditions facilitate this progress: *reinforcement* or feedback concerning accuracy of judgments, and *contiguity* or the quality of being closely related to an already-acquired concept. It is the absence of contiguity which causes trial and error learning to be slow. The condition of repetition is not now thought to be necessary for good concept learning, if the other conditions are met. Perhaps the idea of repetition could be represented in the practice step noted above.

Concept learning is not necessarily a verbal process, but verbal cues make it easier if meaningful concrete situations have occurred in which discrimination has been well established. Diagrams and pictures also assist in children's grasping of concepts because they provide concrete images to aid encoding and cue sources for later retrieval of the concept. Such abstract concepts as justice, courtesy and loyalty may be better fostered through drama or literature. Learning by doing aids concept building far more than rote memorizing.

Concepts provide concrete references for thinking and communicating. They free thought and facilitate further learning. Linked together they form principles which guide decision-making and behavior. In an effort to build concepts through definitions, it is helpful to include four types of cues:

1. A thing-concept which is the superordinate of the concept
   (TOY: doll; ANIMAL: pig)
2. A set of characteristics or features of this superordinate class
   (inanimate; alive)
3. A relational concept showing function
   (to play with; to eat)
4. Another thing-concept related to the function
   (doll clothes; bacon)

With these types of cues and a rich vocabulary and experience, learners can readily acquire new concepts. If there is a lack in referential meanings and relational concepts, acquisition of new concepts is impeded.

To acquire a new concept the learner must have in his working memory the component concepts that are represented in the definition of the to-be-learned concept. Evidence the concept has been learned may be seen as the learner's ability to demonstrate it in art, action or decision-making improves.

The development of children's concepts have been characterized by Russell (1956) as changing in several ways:

- From simple to complex, e.g., structures of society move from an understanding of the family to the neighborhood, community, school, church, state;
- From concrete to abstract, e.g., the child becomes increasingly free from the immediately perceived characteristics of an object and able to deal with them in terms of their general properties; the younger child may draw pictures of particular persons such as himself or his parents, while an older child is able to produce pictures of persons older or younger than himself—a composite sort of person;
- From undifferentiated (or diffuse) to differentiated, e.g., concept of self changes from a simple awareness of body and relationships to others to well defined understandings of roles, attitudes, values, traits;
- Discrete to organized, e.g., organization proceeds along vertical lines, Tabby, cat, animal, living thing;
- Egocentric to more social (or objective), e.g., the young child may think the teacher knows what he is thinking or all about his family, while older children are able to separate objects and people from themselves and see them as distinct and apart from themselves.

Vinacke (1954) adds two other changes that take place with age:

- Movement from variable to more stable concepts, e.g., words which at first had no stable meaning, increasingly come to signify specific objects and characteristics of objects; certain procedures come to be recognized as fixed;
- Movement from inconsistent to more consistent and accurate concepts, e.g., a first grader may classify all red vehicles as fire trucks or may classify any building with red clap boards as a barn; older children classify more accurately.

Concept formation involves processes different from those involved in increase in mental age or growth of vocabulary. Concepts are individualized in that no two children will have exactly the same concept of any thing or idea. They are cumulative in that new concepts are welded to old ones, modifying and enlarging them. They are emotionally weighted, as the new learning is often accompanied with certain feelings about the learning. For example, the child's concept of school is altered or reinforced upon school entrance. If this is a pleasant experience, the school concept carries a positive value. If it is a bad one, he may associate bad feelings with the word school. Such a weighting can impede changing of concepts. Concepts are usually maintained until they are replaced by alternative ones which are more convincing or more satisfying. Social pressures and intellectual maturity play a part in such change.

The ability to conceptualize grows steadily and continuously during middle childhood. Guided experience seems to play a part in fostering conceptualization growth, according to Gordon (1969). Research seems to support the notion that what children are does not necessarily determine what they may become. The effect of specific training techniques in concept development needs considerable investigation. Even though we recog-

Concept building is a continuous process, not fully understood.

nize that such things as age, socioeconomic status, sex, and emotional factors influence this type of growth, we still know relatively little about how children develop concepts, how they integrate their experiences, and how self-concept influences development of other concepts.

What besides intelligence contributes to concept development? Sensory exploration offers the first clues to understanding the world, followed by motor manipulation. Asking questions becomes a major source as language develops. Pictorial mass media play an important role; and reading, when this skill is developed, supplements other methods greatly. Variation in the state of concept development among children can be accounted for by their exposure to opportunities to build concepts in these ways.

Obviously, the child with incomplete sensory facilities will have more trouble building concepts than the one who has the full use of all senses. Imagine a blind child trying to gain the concept of "pretty" or "cloud" or "bright." Or a deaf child who is striving to learn the concept of "music" or "shrill" or "whisper." Likewise, the child who has impaired motor manipulation may suffer from less developed concepts since he is not as free to learn by exploring his world. He may find difficulty with such concepts as "stretch" or "tiptoe" or "tumble."

The extent to which questioning can contribute to concept development will depend largely on the availability of persons to whom questions may be addressed and the correctness of the answers they provide. Persons in the environment who encourage questioning and guide the child in observing, manipulating, questioning, and relating environmental objects and actions help concept development immeasurably. Likewise, if toys, recreational activities, and mass media are carefully planned with concept development in mind, the child benefits.

Older children display more fully developed concepts because they have had more learning opportunities and more experiences. Children from different cultures or groups develop different concepts because of the variety of experiences they have had. A lower-class child attaches a quite different meaning and feeling to the word "maid" than does the middle class child. The same is true for such words as "school" or "job."

The sex and personality of the child play a part. Being a boy or a girl influences the feelings one develops. A "fight" is different for a boy and a girl; so are concepts relating to parties and clothing.

Generally, children who are happy and well adjusted have more accurate concepts than less well-adjusted children. The well-adjusted child feels good about himself and does not need to withdraw to a fantasy world. The well-adjusted child can give his attention to objects and people within his environment.

The amount of guidance a child receives and the type of mass media to which he is exposed must also be considered in concept development. This, of course, is closely associated with the quality of learning opportunities and experiences and with what a child understands is important. One study (Lawson, 1963) comparing the patriotic attitudes of children in 1961 with those of children in 1936 indicated these social concepts are appearing earlier in today's children than those of yesteryear, suggesting the influence of the culture on concept development. Learning opportunities and types of experiences are important in concept development.

Since concepts are built through experience and incidental learning as much as through formal instruction, they often are in part or totally erroneous. These have been the subject of many stories and jokes about both children and adults. Language is often the culprit, as in the case of the boy who drew a picture of the Holy Family on the journey to escape the wrath of King Herod: they were in an airplane, and he explained that the fourth person in the picture was Pontius, the pilot. Another child, in illustrating "America the Beautiful," drew an airplane covered with oranges, apples, bananas and grapes thereon, interpreting it as "the fruited plane."

Incorrect information due to poor information sources or misunderstood explanations contribute to misconceptions. Superstitions are a lucid example of this. Vivid imaginations of children may build on truth but so embellish it that faulty concepts emerge. Faulty reasoning due to lack of information or inexperience or lack of guidance also contribute. A school-age child when asked to tell why a bandage is placed on a wound explained that the whiteness of the bandage drew out the darkness of the scab, making the skin beneath white again.

Think Back

About some misconceptions you had as a child:
Who knew about them.
Where you acquired them.
How you found out they were wrong.
What you did about them.

Misconceptions are serious if they are uncorrected, both in the intellectual and social realms. Children's misconceptions seem to abound in relation to such areas as death, bodily functions, God, and illness. But is this not also true of many adults, because of sheer lack of information?

According to Blair and Burton (1951), intellectual activity is marked by certain changes during middle childhood years: a seeking for reality; increasing use of causal relationships in physical and mechanical fields; and increased reading skills. These changes contribute to rapid growth in concepts.

As children grow older, they become more prone to ask such questions as "Could it really happen?" Because of this seeking to know, they are eager for information. Accurate information makes children more courageous in their exploration of cause and effect in the physical world and in group relationships.

Children's readings and questions show growing interest in the physical environment. Young children are interested in talking animal stories; 8-year-olds like fairy tales; magazines on mechanics are popular among many boys by the fourth grade. Interest in real stories begins to develop at about the age of 9. Interest in current events increases with age.

With increasing use of causal relationships, the generalizations that children reach are more accurate. Children move during the period from giving animistic explanations about reasons for things that happen toward logical explanations. Remember that first-graders may think things move of their own accord or as the first-grader himself moves. Perhaps you can remember from your childhood the trips you took at night, and the wonder of the moon's moving right along with the car, keeping up with you no matter how fast you moved and changing from one side of the road to the other! Young children think clouds are alive because they move, that the sun shines because it wants to, or a car runs over a dog because the car is angry with the dog. Later, the child uses more logical deductions.

CONCEPT DEVELOPMENT

Children's understanding of cause and effect in the area of social relationships is not as clear-cut nor advanced as their understanding of cause and effect in the mechanical world. The child finds it difficult to understand the reasons for some of the requests made by his parents. The values and rewards for most desirable social habits are dependent on the ability to see long-range consequences of immediate actions. This applies to keeping clean, being courteous, careful use of language, study habits, and neatness.

This objectivity or desire for reality is seen in personal relations. Children tend to be factual, accurate, cool, and insensitive. They can be cruel in their criticisms. Children increasingly want their friends to be loyal and courageous, but are not so interested during these years in friends being kind or generous.

Some Concepts Demanding Struggle

Even though the majority of concepts middle childhood people encounter are readily grasped by them, there are some which baffle even the significant others who serve as their models. Some concepts tend to cause many misconceptions for children because of their intangible nature, their involvement with emotions and the varying societal approaches to their management.

> A 9-year-old girl, asked about God, replied: "We don't know why God does what he does. It's kind of like a cat that doesn't know why his owner leaves in the morning. We just can't comprehend His actions."
>
> Tiffany, age 6, reported that a Jew was a person born in December, while a Catholic was a person born in January and a Protestant was someone born in September.
>
> A youthful remedy for fainting: "Rub the person's chest, or if it is a lady, rub her arm above the hand."
>
> Some thoughts about Easter from a 6-year-old: "Easter comes around summer—all the eggs are hatching. Easter is celebrating all the new babies. Put eggs in basket because all animals are born in eggs!!"
>
> Happiness is . . . a bull frog that doesn't give warts and you get a hold of him!

Prejudice

In order to test adult behavior toward children of two different races, Coates (1972) enlisted 2 black and 2 white nine-year olds as confederates in his study. He asked 24 male and 24 female white college student volunteers to teach a discrimination task to one child of each race. Each adult was asked to complete a rating scale about each child he or she taught, and to read one statement to each child at the end of each teaching trial. The statements ranged from positive to negative, and no other talking was allowed. The college students were provided bogus feedback about the learning curve of the children they were teaching, and it was all reportedly low. The student volunteers rated black children more unfavorably than white ones, using such terms as dull, passive and unfriendly. They read more negative statements than positive ones in the teaching situation. The male volunteers used significantly more negative statements to black children than to white children. These performances indicate some degree of internal predispositions with respect to race on the part of the college students.

One of the most pressing problems today deals with relationships among people, particularly those who are different from one another—so we are confronted with prejudice. What is prejudice? Where and how does it begin? How can it be handled?

Based on a study of the "authoritarian personality" (Adorno et al., 1950) which included interviews with 1500 boys and girls between 11 and 16 years of age, Clark (1963) listed the following statements as characteristic of the prejudiced person:

- He worships the strong and despises the weak.
- He has strong impulses toward cruelty toward others and sometimes toward himself.
- He is incapable of genuine feelings of love.
- He is rigid, compulsive, and punitive in his ideas and behavior.
- He is constantly striving for superficial social status; he is willing to grovel before those whom he believes to be his superiors while he is contemptuous of those whom he considers his inferiors.
- Even his feelings toward his parents and others in authority are not without deep conflicts; on the one hand he subjugates his own desires to their demands while on the other hand he hates them.
- Because he cannot face his negative feelings toward parents and other authorities, he takes out his frustration by aggressions against those whom he considers weak and acceptable as victims.

Prejudice is not inborn; rather, it is learned early in life and taught in subtle ways by people with whom the child identifies and wants to please in some way. Children as young as 4 years of age show prejudiced attitudes and behavior. No one sets out to teach a child to hate; the child simply incorporates the attitudes of his family and, later, those of his community. Such simple things as the use of the word "boy" in reference to black males of all ages is a degrading and dehumanizing action. The careful avoidance of titles such as Mister and Doctor; the back-door policy; restriction of playmates; stereotyping of people of other races as "rough," "lazy," "dirty"; ignorance of the contributions of other races to the American way of life; lack of knowledge of the work and community acivities of educated, productive, minority-group men and women in one's own community—these all say to children: "We don't like them; they are not very worthwhile." At least, this is the message children receive, whether or not this is what we mean to convey.

Prejudice really means prejudging people without knowledge, thought, or reason, or judging all people of a group on the basis of what has been noticed about or connected with only a few members of that group. While such a preconceived feeling may be either favorable or unfavorable, it is usually unfavorable, unreasonable, and hostile. Prejudice can be directed toward a racial group, religious group, political group, national group, or even against the very old, the very young, or people who live in a particular community, or are engaged in a particular occupation. It is really intolerance of differences and the assignment of that group believed to be different to an inferior position.

Frenkel-Brunswik (1966) examined the development of the intensely prejudiced person in the light of certain child-rearing practices. The parents of ethnocentric (prejudiced) children possessed an exaggerated concern with social status: anxiety about status, rigid social conformity, and compulsive quest for acceptability. They held a rigid and externalized set of values and insisted that children conform to these inflexible rules, suppressing all impulses unacceptable to the parents. They discouraged spontaneous, genuine expressions of feelings. They used harsh and rigid forms of punishment to which the children submitted, but which they did not seem to understand or accept. On the surface the children seemed to idealize the parents, but there was an underlying lack of genuine affection for them.

Liberal children (nonprejudiced) were treated as equals by their parents and were given opportunity to express their feelings of rebellion and disagreement. They learned at home an individualized approach to people, to avoid stereotyping. Their parents were less strict and encouraged exploration, questioning, decision-making.

While such interaction does not guarantee an "ideal" personality, these latter children will more likely be able to handle the conflicts they face. For example, they will be more able to express rebellion or aggression openly and appropriately, rather than finding it necessary to scapegoat their hostility on weak and convenient individuals or groups within the society.

Clark (1963, p. 70) contends that

the more prejudiced the individual the less he will be able to modify his behavior when objective conditions require it; that prejudiced individuals have a more constricted range of general interests; that they show less interest and originality in their thinking; that they demonstrate a lower capacity to understand the problems of others; that they have a smaller range of emotional responses; that they show less insight into themselves; and that they are generally more inhibited.

A study (Gough, et al., 1950) of the relationship between personality and ethnic attitudes among fourth-, fifth-, and sixth-graders, revealed that children who were more intolerant tended to be generally more fearful, less confident and secure, and more suspicious than were tolerant children. They feared and distrusted other people, lacked confidence in themselves, and reacted with hostility toward persons different from themselves.

Prejudice, then, is not a single attitude that can be "corrected." It is either a pervading influence in the personality of the child affecting his attitudes toward himself, his relationship to authority figures, his ability to trust others, and his ability to function with confidence and ease; or it is one of a cluster of traits or attitudes that develop out of a personality structure that fosters such traits. At any rate, prejudice affects the child who is prejudiced as well as the victim of his prejudice.

What can be done about this? Preliminary findings of a survey concerning anti-Semitism in the United States revealed that over one-third of the population of the United States is anti-Semitic, although most of this prejudice is in passive form. The other two-thirds includes a majority who is apathetic toward discrimination against the Jews. According to the survey, simplistic beliefs, ignorance, and low tolerance for social and political diversity go hand in hand. A rather frightening implication was that in time of crisis, the power of the anti-Semites (or the anti-anything group) is vastly increased by those who are tolerant of anti-Semitism. To put it another way, the whole problem of overcoming prejudice is not a simple one of "live and let live," but rather "live and help live." Each person must take an active part, not only in shunning poor attitudes, but in espousing and building positive, action-oriented attitudes, especially in children.

A rural third grade teacher gave her pupils a real lesson in discrimination ("Inferior Kids Reacted With Anger," 1968). To help the youngsters in a northeast Iowa community become aware of color discrimination, the teacher divided the class into two groups: those with blue eyes and those with brown eyes. On one day the brown-eyed group was given special privileges denied the blue-eyed group; and the next day the roles were reversed. Then the children wrote about their feelings. The children's reactions can best be seen through their own words:

"The people with blue eyes could not do the things the people with brown eyes did. . . . I felt left out because I have blue eyes. I felt like giving them all black eyes."

"I felt like slapping a brown-eyed person. It made me mad. Then I felt like kicking a brown-eyed person. I felt like quitting school. The brown-eyed people got five extra minutes of recess. I would not like to be angry all my life."

"I didn't want to work. I didn't feel like I was very big."

"Discrimination is not fun at all. I am glad I am not a Negro and being judged by my skin."

The next step in leading an individual child out of prejudice must be helping him understand that no one need be judged good or bad on the basis of his skin color or his eye color or any other external characteristic.

It is better to enjoy and appreciate other people from whatever group they come, and to attempt to understand and to accept all persons in spite of differences.

The real problem in prejudice is the child's attitude toward authority. Forced submission to authority, at home or in the society, produces only surface conformity and generates underlying destructiveness, dangerous to the very society in which there seems to be conformity.

> Only a frightened and frustrated child will tend to gain safety and security by oversimplified black-white schematizations and categorizations on the basis of crude, external characteristics. Deliberately planned democratic participation in school and family, individualized approach to the child, and the right proportion of permissiveness and guidance may be instrumental in bringing about the attitude necessary for genuine identification with society and thus for internalized understanding (Frenkel-Brunswik, 1948, p. 306).

What can parents do to help their children develop more positive racial attitudes and therefore adjust more effectively to the rapid changes in race relations? Clark (1963) makes the following suggestions:

- Exercise control over their own racial feelings.
- Face their own prejudice and recognize its manifestations.
- Encourage and reinforce favorable expressions of racial democracy on the part of their child.
- Set up no special requirements nor allowances for friends of minority groups.
- Set an example for children by nature and quality of personal relationships with members of other races and groups, recognizing the wide range of differences that exist among minority groups as well as among majority groups.
- Help children deal with the pressures they face by providing warmth, love, understanding and guidance which have been found necessary for the healthy growth of all children.
- Do not evade, minimize or exaggerate a child's questions about race, religion or nationality. If a child is old enough to ask questions, he is ready to receive honest and appropriate answers.
- Discuss achievements of people of minority groups; do not allow child to use minority status as an excuse for inferior achievement or lack of personal integrity.

Adults must talk with children about prejudice and explore with them their feelings and actions. In the final analysis, children take on the attitudes—good or bad—of their parents and other significant adults, which are modified by peers, community influences, and school experiences. Children do not learn as easily what adults say as they learn what adults are. In discovering who he is, what a child feels is more important than what he knows. It is easier to teach math or geography than to help a child learn to like himself and to relate in a caring constructive fashion to other people.

Sex

Some views of children on where babies come from:

> A 5-year-old boy says: "I'll tell you if you keep it secret. Babies come from baby-sitters and the mothers and fathers have to go and pick them up."
>
> A 4-year-old explains: "Babies come from a seed. A little baby angel with white wings flies into the house and puts a seed into the mommy's tummy."
>
> A 7-year old girl says: "All I can tell you is how we got here. I have nine brothers and sisters and here's what happened. My dad bought a ticket in a store and won us."
>
> A 9-year-old boy explains "Babies fly on planes from somewhere in the sky—but not heaven. Pilots have to fly the planes because the mothers have to hold the baby."
>
> A 6-year-old explains: "Babies hop out of their mother's stomach. They don't like to sit in that dark tummy so they say: "Let me out!"

Freud advanced the idea that during the years of middle childhood the natural interest in sex enters a period of latency, being submerged as the child turns his interests to intellectual pursuits, game skills, and other endeavors. This view is being increasingly challenged. Current writers are suggesting that interest in sex-related matters is not lost; it takes its place beside the many other interests of childhood but can still be the basis for

Children often turn to peers for sex information during middle childhood. (Photo by Lin Mitchell.)

learning, decisions, and feelings. They caution that if opportunities to explore the other interests are not found, sexual curiosity and behavior may become exaggerated. Another facet of reality may also be that children by this age sense that the adults in their lives do not approve of such interests; therefore, they pretend to suppress them, turning to peers instead of parents and other adults for information. Correct knowledge of sex and its normal development helps prevent anxiety and equips the growing child to develop a healthy and positive attitude toward his own body and his adult sex role.

Preschoolers are aware of the anatomical differences in boys and girls and such sex-related functions as mothers having babies and fathers paying bills. During middle childhood interest in sex continues and may even heighten because of the children's own physical development, peer association, exposure to mass media, and listening to adult conversations. Yet many American parents do little about this aspect of normal growth. A great many adults today have inherited their inadequate knowledge and hesitant attitudes from past generations whose attempts at sex education were what could be considered quite crude. Because of this heritage they feel ill at ease in helping their children in this phase of development. Whereas some other cultures far surpass us in transmission of sex-related knowledge and attitudes, others equal us in their backward beliefs and approaches to the problem.

Parents feel unsure not only about the facts but about when instruction should begin. They commonly ask what form it should take and which parent should be responsible. They wonder what is important to tell and how much they can expect the child to pick up from others.

The wise parent has begun sex education long before school age. He has demonstrated genuine love in his relationship with the other parent and in his dealings with all members of the family. He has dealt with such questions as Where do babies come from? What is the difference between boys and girls? and Why do people get married? He has treated them as matter-of-factly as those concerning road-building, making lemonade, or buying toys. He has answered inquiries briefly and honestly, without undue elaboration and encouraged the child to ask such questions anytime they arise in his mind. He has always demonstrated and taught the use of proper terminology for body parts and processes and corrected misconceptions which became apparent to him through the child's conversations or actions. He has avoided inculcating fear, guilt, or shame in children because of their interest in sex. In all these matters he has been calm, unemotional, objective, and correct in the information imparted. He has not told the questioning child to ask the other parent later, to ask some of his playmates, or to wait until he is older to ask about the subject. Now that the child is of school age, he can supplement these early learnings and attitudes with proper literature written especially for such a time and purpose.

With varying degrees of knowledge and motivation, teachers are including sex education in the classrooms—more in secondary than in elementary schools, however. Many feel as inadequate as parents in this new role. Few have had any formal preparation in college but are finding help through extension and graduate work in health, science, and family relations as well as from workshops and other in-service education. A study (Benell, 1969) revealed that teachers are more prone to have misconceptions in the sociophysiological area than in the biological area of sex-related topics. Elementary teachers demonstrated a greater need than secondary ones for instruction to remove misconceptions about sex. And those with the greatest number of misconceptions were least willing to teach the subject in their classes.

For sex education in public schools to be successful, it is necessary to have the support of the parents and the community. This has not come in the majority of America's cities and towns. Sex education has been a controversial subject for over half a century. The issue in years past was, "Should youth be told about sex?" Today the controversy rages over "What, when, and by whom should they be told?" The mass media have done a lot of sex education, not in a formal sense, but through highly glamourized or vulgarized episodes more often depicting illicit or perverted than well-adjusted sexuality. An estimated 80 percent of youth receive their "sex knowledge" from their friends, the basis of such exchange often being misinformation, old wives' tales, and jet-age fantasies, mixed with the salaciousness attached to a forbidden subject (Gendel, 1969).

Churchmen plead for the job so that morality can accompany sexuality and training can be spiritual as well as factual. Parents claim sex education is a parental privilege and that they know best when their particular child is "ready" for such information. Some parents see it as a way to develop confidence and communication from the day the child asks, "Mommie, where do babies come from?" School systems point out their contact with all children as a rationale for sex education, supported by prepared personnel, materials, and continuing curricula.

Think Back

To your early sex education:
Who provided it.
What you thought about it.
Who you told about it.
Things you tried related to it.
Questions you were afraid to ask.
Misconceptions you later remedied.

Groups across the nation have been organized to fight public school sex education. Some oppose it on the grounds that it is a Communist plot to demoralize American youth. Some approach the subject from a religious viewpoint, saying that sex is sacred and should be learned in the sanctity of the church or home. Others cite belief in Freud's latency period. Still others claim it is a diabolical plot by pornographers to break down modesty, lead to promiscuity, and teach raw sex.

A prime target of such groups has been the Sex Information and Education Council of the U.S., Inc., commonly known as SIECUS. This is a voluntary health organization chartered in 1964 to "establish man's sexuality as a health entity." It does not produce curricula, classroom materials, or sex education programs for schools. It does publish the SIECUS Newsletter in which sex education materials are reviewed but not endorsed. It sponsors a national consultant program which furnishes resource persons on request to community, educational, religious, and other professional groups. It is supported by individual contributions, foundation grants, and memorial gifts and bequests. SIECUS is staffed by professionals in the field of medicine, public health, education, and community organization and has a board of directors composed of representatives from many disciplines, including law, counseling, religion, psychiatry, sociology, and education.

Some goals of sex education as delineated by SIECUS follow:

- To provide for the individual an adequate knowledge of his own physical, mental and emotional maturation processes as related to sex.
- To eliminate fears and anxieties in relation to individual sexual development and adjustments.
- To develop objective and understanding attitudes toward sex in all of its various manifestations—in the individual and in others.
- To give the individual insight concerning his relationships to members of both sexes and to help him understand his obligations and responsibilities to others.
- To provide an appreciation of the positive satisfaction that wholesome human relations can bring in both individual and family living.
- To build an understanding of the need for the moral values that are essential to provide rational bases for making decisions.
- To provide enough knowledge about the misuses of sex to enable the individual to protect himself against exploitation and against injury to his physical and mental health.
- To provide an incentive to work for a society in which such evils as prostitution and illegitimacy, archaic sex laws, irrational fears of sex, and sexual exploitation are nonexistent.
- To provide the understanding and conditioning that will enable each individual to utilize his sexuality effectively and creatively in his several roles, e.g. as spouse, parent, community worker, and citizen (Kirkendall, 1965).

Values that should underlie a science, according to the National Education Association and the American Association of School Administrators (*Education and the Spirit of Science*, 1966), are:

1. Longing to know and understand.
2. Questioning of all things.
3. Search for data and their meaning.
4. Demand for verification.
5. Respect for logic.
6. Consideration of premises.
7. Consideration of consequences.

Those involved in sex education as a science could well apply these values in assessing the approaches and information provided through educational programs. In some instances sex educators employ methods in which logic, verification, and meaningful data may be overlooked. Even the use of such terms as "normal," "immature," "unhealthy," and "perverse" are not scientific but disguised value judgments. Since parental moral values and those of teachers or other sex educators may not coincide, to eliminate moral value judgments seems desirable. The role, then, is to provide information on which the learners may make decisions by applying their own moral values. To imply that any child's values are inferior or inappropriate is not the task of the sex educator; this may merely serve as a deterrent to future learning, contributing to lowered self-concept or even triggering overt rebellion.

Among the weaknesses common to most sex education programs designed for children and adolescents are the *strong emphases on reproduction* or *moral judgments*. Whereas the biological aspects are important to children and are appropriate to the developmental level of those in middle childhood, by adolescence there emerges the need to relate sex to interpersonal relations and standards. This vital application of knowledge is left largely to chance in most instances, and the peer group exerts more influence than do parents or educators.

Whereas one way to begin to relate the application of attitudes toward life is through example, sex education is more often thought of in terms of a telling process. Some of the most potent sex education is transmitted nonverbally in the normal living within the home and the larger community. That it might serve to enrich the lives of children and their families is often overlooked because the prevention of moral disaster is cited as the real need for children to be exposed to this information.

Divorce

Over 1,200,000 children under age 18 in the U.S. experienced divorce in their families during 1975. There are now over 13 million such children in the nation, constituting 20 percent of the elementary school population. The concepts they hold of this social practice are many and varied, but a few are typical during middle childhood. The younger ones may wish bad things on their parents to punish them, and experience both grief and guilt if the projected happenings actually occur. Children in this age group may develop the mean-Mother, good-guy Father concepts if they live with the mother who must handle the weekly routine, and spend time with their father only on weekends when they can have fun. Some children interpret Mother's entering the labor force as a sign that she no longer loves them, if the divorce has caused her to seek employment for the first time. Many worry that the persons their parents now date will sap the parents' love from them. Children may idealize the absent parent, hoping he or she will improve and cause a reconciliation for the family. They may over-idealize a new step-parent and thereby suffer serious disappointment. They may even form negative feelings about marrying themselves.

In his book written for children of divorcing families, Gardner (1970) offers help for both the parent and the child. He points out that children are more capable of accepting the painful realities of a dissolving marriage than many might think and calls for sharing as much information with them as will be psychologically helpful to the children. He cautions that although truth engenders trust, half-truths lead to confusion. For example, he points out that children should not be told repeatedly how much the absent parent loves them if that parent demonstrates no signs of such love. Neither should parents paint glowing, untrue pictures of one another merely for the child's solace.

Gardner enumerates the following behaviors that are often associated with children whose families are experiencing or have undergone a divorce:

1. Pretending nothing is wrong, acting disinterested or unconcerned about the situation, actually an attempt to mask true sadness and fear
2. Loss of interest in school and play
3. Poor eating and sleeping patterns
4. Moping, crying, feeling ashamed of parents
5. Lying to peers about family situation, not inviting them to the home
6. Blaming self for the divorce, thinking their misbehavior was the cause
7. Feeling sorry for themselves and refusing to do home chores
8. Living in the past, wishing parents would remarry
9. Feeling parents no longer love them, reasoning if they did, they would become re-united
10. Jealousy and anger when parents begin to date other people
11. Worrying that something will happen to remaining parent leaving them with no one to care for them

Gardner provides for his child reader definite suggestions for handling such difficult situations as a parent who invites him to become his bed mate, to serve as a spy on the absent parent, and poor step-parent relationships. He tries to help the child feel he can be in control and make his situation better through certain behaviors and problem-solving techniques.

Children's feelings, fears and concepts about divorces that have occurred in their families have been dealt with successfully in group sessions held by elementary guidance counselors (Wilkinson and Bleck, 1977). In eight 45-

minute sessions involving 7 children and a counselor, children are helped through art, role-playing, puppetry, visual aids, and informal discussion to clarify their feelings, gain realistic concepts, learn ways to cope with their divorce-related feelings, and realize that others have similar ones. Every child involved in the project reported liking the experience, and 75 percent said it helped them act differently outside the group. Eighty-percent learned their feelings were common to others. Typical comments were: "It helped me and was fun." "It was terrific." "I liked it better than anything else in school."

Aging

By the year 2000 it is expected that 12 percent of the U.S. population will be over 64. One hundred eighty children, 20 at each age 3 to 11, were asked how they felt about growing old, what they know about the elderly and how they interacted with older people. Children at all ages had limited knowledge, and only 39 were able to name an older person outside their family. They said being old is terrible, ugly, wrinkled and short, having gray hair, not going out much, having heart attacks and dying, watching TV in rocking chairs. They saw aging as a passive, unattractive, and unproductive time of life, with no diversity of interests, activities, or life styles. They knew death was closer in old age and felt that life holds few pleasures for the elderly. The group did not want to grow old themselves, but some knew it was inevitable. Only 11 percent mentioned a positive aspect of aging, like owning a home (Serock, et al, 1977). These children had definite concepts of old age. They expressed deep affection for older persons, calling them "rich, wonderful and good." They said they loved their grandparents—just didn't want to be like them. They thought of themselves as helping their elders, and of the elders helping them with homework, reading to them and teaching them.

Shown sketches of 20-year-old and 80-year-old men, the majority expressed preference for the younger one. Some older children selected the octegenarian. Rural children perceived older people as being more active than those from urban or suburban areas. The older children had less negative concepts than the younger ones.

When told "Your grandmother grows older every day," younger children did not agree, indicating lack of concept of continuousness of aging. This same deficiency was noted in their expressed beliefs that they could eventually catch up in age with someone five years older than they.

Children 4–5, 8–9, and 11–12 were studied to see what perceptions they held of grandparents (Kahana, 1968). The younger group focused on physical characteristics, the middle group on behaviors, and the oldest group on interpersonal orientation aspects. The younger children preferred older grandparents whereas the older children preferred young ones. These choices are perhaps related to the more affectional need of the younger

Experiences with older persons can affect children's perceptions of aging. (Photo by Lin Mitchell.)

group and the action need of older children. The conclusion is that the grandparent role is related to the needs of the developing child.

In an exploratory study third graders wrote paragraphs on feelings and thoughts they had about old people. They characterized them as either very nice to children or quite mean and wicked, and as very lonely, bored and inactive with much leisure time. Expanding the study to include 8, 12, 15, and 19 year olds, the researchers noted distinctly different perceptions of persons 25, 45, 65, and 85 years of age. The older the adults, the less pleasant the image of aging held by the child (Hickey and Kalish, 1968).

Attitudes toward aging and the aged during middle childhood are a result of individual experience and exposure to media stereotypes of this process and group. One child's view: "That's awful—being old is being sick, helpless, and ugly. I just don't want to get old." Another said, "They're good, wonderful; they love you. You can sit on their lap and they'll talk to you." (Seefeldt, 1977) Another exclaimed, "This makes me not dread getting old. In fact, I think I will like it" (Whitley, 1976).

"This", in the latter statement was a regular involvement with adopted grandparents in nursing homes that second and third grade children experienced through their teacher's efforts, in Gainesville, Florida. Positive attitude changes were revealed in post-testing of the children who were involved in the project. They visited, wrote, read to, gave parties for and performed drama for the elderly. They planted a cooperative flower garden and did arts and crafts together. The activities helped to reduce the typical grim concepts of aging American children have, and made them feel happy by making others happy. The aged participants provided a link with the values and traditions of the past. They taught games, songs, crafts to the children. They discussed their former careers. They taught the children, even in their deaths, that life continues and grief can be overcome.

Schools have begun regular classroom participation with elders as aids and resource persons. There are over twenty million Americans over age 65. American children generally have limited contact with them. They characterize them into strong physical and behavioral stereotypes. They think of older persons in terms of wrinkles, sadness, sitting in wheel chairs all day, chewing funny, and walking with canes. Their attitudes toward the care of the elderly is related to their general feeling about aging. In order to accept their own aging, they need positive feelings about the process. They need contact with older persons in many roles and settings. With increased grouping of the elderly in "homes" and communities apart from the rest of the population, children's exposure is limited. As nuclear families in a mobile society more often move away from grandparents, the children are denied even regular association with aging kin.

Death

Death is universally frightening, has always been and probably always will be. Perhaps all that changes over time is the way we cope with the dying person. The society used to allow death to occur in familiar home settings, with children present. The current gruesome, lonely and mechanical death among busy strangers in the hospital is unkind to all involved. While every man tries to postpone the death issue in his life until forced to face it, the only way to "grow" in this attitude is to start to conceive of one's own death.

The goal in death education is to help persons accept death without guilt. Listening to the dying or their loved-ones performs a great service. Allowing them to ventilate their rational and irrational feelings is important. Support and involvement are keys.

As death moved to hospitals, children were sent away or told stories such as "Mother has taken a long trip . . . Aunt Suzie has gone to sleep . . . God loves little children and has taken your brother to be with Him . . ." Adults began to avoid their questions altogether and to give diversionary gifts. These actions cause unresolved grief, anger at God, fear of dying yourself.

Children are often the forgotten ones at a time of death, and adults find it difficult to discuss the subject with them. Before age 5, they view death as temporary, much like burying a bulb in the ground and later seeing it burst forth again. TV characters who die in one episode but are later seen in another role reinforce this notion for them. After 5, they envision death as a bogey-man, coming to take people away. Not until about age 9 or 10 do children sense the permanence of dying. Because youngsters cannot separate a death wish from the death occurrence, they may experience guilt when someone they know dies. Perhaps they have at sometime thought badly about the person or even wished the individual were dead or would die. They may fear some awful punishment for their thoughts. By adolescence these fears typically disappear.

Death, though younger children may not comprehend it, is a concept the school-age child can deal with. Kubler-Ross (1976) reminds us that there are hardly any children who by maturity have not experienced the illness, death, and funeral of at least one person meaningful in their lives. In the event of the death of a parent, there may have been a long illness during which they was an attempt to shield the child from the truth of the situation. At this age, to know that the ill parent may not live may cause considerable worry; but for him to be completely unaware of the possibility can result in great shock at the time of death. In some ways, of course, it is impossible to shield a child from any knowledge of impending sorrow or tragedy. He will likely feel it in the air, and needs help in dealing with his own fears and anxieties. He may not know the exact nature of the trouble, but he will surely be aware of the tension of other people in the family. It may be difficult to share with him, but it will likely be best from a long-term point of view.

Children should not be sent away at such a time. There is value in their being with the family, feeling needed, loved, important, and included. They need to be assured that life will continue for them. Children need time to talk about death, particularly the death of a parent, a sibling, or a friend near their own age.

Little research has been done concerning the feelings of children in regard to death. Bowlby (1961) examined the long-term effects of the death of a father or mother during the child's growing years. The incidence of such loss is greater among adult depressives than in the general adult population. (See Figure 12-1.) Loss of father during later childhood seemed to be more damaging than such loss at earlier periods.

Jackson (1965) suggests that children try to deal with grief in ways which mask their real feelings and make it difficult for adults to understand, and even harder for them to deal with the resulting behavior. Children play at being dead, having funerals, about which adults have ambivalent feelings, at least. A child may show grief through anger because he

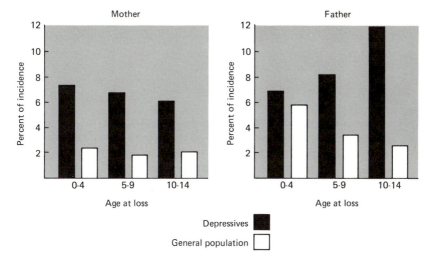

Figure 12-1. Long-term effects of parental death during childhood. (Adapted from J. Bowlby, "Childhood Mourning and Its Implications for Psychiatry," *The American Journal of Psychiatry,* 118: 481–498, 1961. Copyright 1961, the American Psychiatric Association. Used by permission of the author and the publisher.)

feels deprived; he may have an overwhelming fear of being abandoned causing him to cling tenaciously to the remaining parent; he may become noisy and boisterous as if to reassure himself by his own noise, or may laugh hilariously at things that are not really funny in an attempt to use humor to bring down to size this thing which is too big for him to handle alone. At other times, parents are amazed at a child's apparent unconcern at the time of death of a person close to him; other children become truant, delinquent, defiant and provocative at a time when the family is occupied with other things and unable to pay attention (Kubler-Ross, 1976).

Adults find this subject a difficult one to deal with because of the mystery that surrounds it, because of our lack of certainty about what death means and what comes after death. For this generation, death seems to bear the kind of taboo that sex bore for the previous one. Whatever our religious convictions, we must be willing to share with children our own wonderings, our own questions, and our own faith and hope.

When a death has occurred, children must be given a realistic view of what this means in terms of changes in life-style. This does not mean that children must be burdened with adult problems, but it does mean that they need to know there may be less income; Mother may need to work; Father may need to employ someone to help in the home; a move to another neighborhood may be necessary.

If possible, steps should be taken to spare the child's being sent away to live with another family. To lose not only a parent but also a neighborhood, friends, teachers, and, for all practical purposes, the other parent, is almost too much for a child to bear. While there are not simple rules about how to handle this situation, some suggestions may be helpful.

Prepare a child for this event in a gentle way, if possible. Include him in the family's "circle of grief," helping him to talk about how he feels about the loss. There is a tendency to try to change the subject when a child is discussing his sadness, but this emotion needs to be recognized and dealt with, just as other emotions need to be dealt with. Spend time talking with the child about the absent parent—happy things and not-so-happy times as well. It is a mistake to try to idealize the parent who has died. Sometimes it is well to say, for example, "You remember how mad your dad got when you left your bicycle in the driveway?" Try not to be shocked if a child asks rather earthy questions about death—what happens to a person when he's put in the ground. This is part of his curiosity, his education, and his understanding. It is better to talk about such things than for him to simply wonder, with no help to think it through.

Death is a concept school-age children can deal with, and they often ask questions about it which are difficult to answer. (Photo by Lin Mitchell.)

A different problem arises when the child is terminally ill. Bluebond-Langner (1978) deals with this subject from the standpoints of children, parents, and health professionals. Her point of view is that children come to know they are dying even though no one tells them, and that many of them decide not to reveal this awareness because of their knowledge of the order they have been socialized where death seems to have little place. Children possess a self, can interpret the behavior of others, and act on the basis of these interpretations. Children's experiences with death and dying described by Bluebond-Langner will be helpful to those who wish to understand more of children's feelings and adult actions during terminal illness.

Think Back

To your first contact with death:
The circumstances.
Your feelings.
What people told you about death.

Money

An examination of the child's concept of money has a direct application to the student of child development, for there are steps that may be taken to contribute to understanding of money and its related terms and activities. Even during the middle years of childhood, misconceptions or gross lack of knowledge in this phase of living is not uncommon. Yet adults are expected to show considerable expertise in this area.

Parents greatly influence the child's concepts of money by the attitudes they display in their actions and conversations about property and money. But it is as a child handles money—uses it himself—that he develops his concept of money. School entrance provides for many children the first such opportunity. Here again, however, there are differences from one child to the next, which grow out of his experiences and his developing interests.

Simple knowledge of money is one example. The 5-year-old typically identifies only pennies. A year later he can name pennies, nickels, and dimes. However, a 5-year-old in a Head Start program was able not only to identify various coins in his pocket, but could tell that with "this" one you could buy an ice cream cone, with this one a package of chewing gum, and with this one two candy bars.

The 7-year-old knows what a quarter is and may be able to ask for correct change in a store. Between ages 8 and 9 the child becomes able to match equivalent amounts with different coins (Marshall, 1964; Terman and Merrill, 1960). With increasing age the buying power of various coins becomes known, as the young child perceives that money is needed to purchase goods or services.

Much of the following is adapted from Gruenberg's (1958) *The Parents' Guide to Everyday Problems of Boys and Girls,* ch. 15. Certain conditions or experiences seem to contribute to more accurate money concepts: earning money; freedom in spending allowance money; being male; having a working mother; few siblings (Gesell et al., 1956; Marshall and Magruder, 1960). The child who receives all his money as a gift or an allowance may not equate work with money; whereas he who rakes lawns, washes dishes, or delivers papers gains some idea of the amount of energy that must be expended to gain a given sum of money. The child whose parents closely guard his expenditures may deprive him of the experience provided through poor purchases or impulse buying, thereby giving him a faulty sense of confidence and less than realistic concepts of the money he spends. Boys typically are given greater freedom in earning and spending money; hence through such experience they gain better money concepts than do girls. Too, our culture expects money management to be primarily an ability related to the male sex role.

The children of the working mother are probably given more home duties involving money, such as the payment of some bills and the purchase of some goods. Also, they may receive more money through allowance because of their mother's employment. And they may place greater value on money since they are deprived of their mother's presence in the home while she earns funds for the family's use. Fewer children in the family contributes to better money concepts since there is, at least theoretically, more money for each child to spend. There may also be more money-related opportunities for children with fewer siblings.

Children receive money with which to learn in four main ways: gifts, the dole, the allowance, and working. The relative value of each method is worth mentioning.

Gifts at any age are an unexpected pleasure. For this very reason they cannot contribute as much as other sources to the child's money concepts. Receiving money in this way may impart to the child the idea that money is a reward for good behavior or that love can be bought. Since money gifts cannot be counted on but are given at the whim of the giver, they do not encourage planned spending but may lead to hoarding, which is not a desired practice by children or by adults. Gifts of money are nice as supplements to other sources of income but probably should not constitute a child's major source of funding.

The dole is a term given to the practice of giving a child money whenever he needs or wants it. It is a common method of providing funds for the school-age child, since his needs may be relatively small and his wants less extensive than those of the adolescent. Probably most families that

As children use money—handle it themselves—they develop their own concepts of money. (Photo by Rick Coleman.)

employ this method are not consciously aware of the money concepts thus imparted. The dole does little or nothing to encourage planning in money matters. Instead it teaches the child that there is always more money available. Instead of helping him learn to manage money, he learns to manage the source of the money, namely his parents. He may become quite expert at asking the right parent at the most opportune time. He sees little need for saving or thinking ahead since under the dole plan neither is vital. There is always the possibility when employing this method that the child begins to perceive money the reward for good behavior or cunning ways and that he considers the parents unkind, unfair, or poor managers when they cannot meet his continuing demands for funds. Parents usually find this method the most expensive of all, and many eventually change to the allowance or insist the child must earn his own money.

The child who earns the money he needs for living will develop better money concepts than he who receives it under one of the other methods. However, until he is old enough to so finance his needs, the allowance may serve well. The allowance has been modified by some parents so that the child actually "earns" money through home duties or through good behavior. When this is done, the allowance becomes a disciplinary technique and not a vehicle for learning to manage money or understanding economic principles. Besides sabotaging a good learning opportunity, this sort of "correction" or "punishment" doesn't work very well at the outset!

An allowance is a sum of money given regularly to a child just because he is a member of the family. It should not be contingent on any behavior level or performance of assigned responsibilities. Through an allowance parents can say to the child: "We believe that by providing a certain sum of money for you regularly we are contributing to your growth and development just as we do by providing your clothes, food, and recreation materials." If given in this manner, the child does not begin to think of money as a reward but as a necessity to life, which indeed it is. His money is not withdrawn for bad behavior any more than his clothes would be taken away in such a circumstance. In addition, there are certain chores the child should be responsible for because he is a family member. It is most unfortunate if the idea grows within him that everything one does has a price!

The amount of the allowance should be commensurate with his age and that received by his peers; relative to the items for which it is responsible; and must include an amount to be used solely at the discretion of the child. If given in a businesslike manner, regularly and without undue admonition, the child perceives it seriously and will be more likely to use it seriously. His requests for a raise in the sum should be considered in terms of the total family budget, and if unable to meet his demands, the parents should explain the reasons matter-of-factly and help him understand them.

Think Back

About your early experiences with money:
How you got it.
Where you kept it.
How you felt when it was lost, spent wisely, spent foolishly, all gone.
How you spent it: corner store, mail-order, for self, for others.

It is entirely possible that a child's allowance may be too small to serve its teaching purpose. A weekly sum of ten or fifteen cents may appear adequate for a first-grader. But when one considers that the only items available for such paltry sums are either junk, as candy or gum, which are quite nondurable, the need for larger amounts is evident. The child who must try to learn management on such small amounts is likely to hoard, give up, or never learn to make a purchase that will bring him lasting satisfaction. As the child gains more experience his allowance may expand to take care of many regular expenditures: school lunches, Scout dues, church contributions, and small school supplies. This gives him the chance to deal with fixed expenditures as well as with discretionary spending. He has reason as well as opportunity to plan ahead.

One mother set her son's allowance at $5.00 per week. To her friends this seemed unduly high for a five-year-old. But when she explained that out of this amount he had to pay $4.75 each Monday to his kindergarten teacher, it seemed a wise plan. This child was learning the very important fact that much of one's income is committed before it is received.

Young children receiving allowances may lose their money or spend the total amount in one purchase. In such cases, parental expression of understanding is in order, along with an offer to help them think of ways to better manage their money. Provision of a small change purse can help prevent loss, as can the suggestion that only the money to be used on a given day be taken along. Simple discussion of where the money went seems more advisable than requiring detailed records of each expenditure, a method whereby children may infer it's easier to hoard than to spend and learn.

The allowance should not be replaced if it is lost or spent unwisely. It is probably not wise to advance money on the next week's allowance. There might be some help in finding a job around the house for which the child can be paid. This should be beyond his regular chores and it should be a real and necessary task, not simply busy work in order to allow him extra money! Or savings, if any exist, might be used.

Children reportedly prefer to save out of their own decision rather than out of parental requirement. Parents should certainly acquaint them with this aspect of money management but probably should not insist on it. For the child, saving for something as far away as next summer's vacation or a college education is quite unrealistic and difficult. They do better if they decide to save for a new baseball or a gift for someone on a soon-to-occur occasion.

The hoarding child may be helped to overcome this habit by encouraging him to make a purchase that will bring him pleasure, or by giving him a gift requiring that he make additional purchases in order to enjoy it (such as a record player). Making supportive comments about the purchases he makes will help provide encouragement for him to make other expenditures.

The child whose major source of income is a job will be gaining many experiences preparatory for adult roles. The role of the parent of such a child includes supervision in the selection of a job. There are five standards identified by Gruenberg (1958) in this connection:

1. Safe.
2. Within the child's ability.
3. Not overly demanding in terms of time.
4. Involves no undesirable conditions nor companions.
5. Fairly paid.

Children, in their eagerness to earn money, may wish to do work that would endanger their physical or moral safety. Their first impulse is often to work every available minute, shunning play and study. They easily overestimate their strength and ability in performing tasks over an extended period of time, and they may either overestimate or underestimate their monetary worth. Fair pay should be determined on the basis of what others are receiving for the same job, the amount of responsibility or skill required by the job, and the level of quality the child is able to maintain.

Opportunities to use their concepts of money may be provided for children in relation to family finances. If the family is suffering from financial reverses, children of school age should be encouraged to share the parental courage over the crisis, and not the fears. They need reassurance that the situation is being dealt with, and the parents are confident it will be remedied. The children can help economize by limiting expensive recreational activities, wearing their clothing longer, even perhaps getting a job to replace their allowance.

Another involvement with family financial matters is afforded when decisions related to family money are made, including vacation activities, home redecoration, and the purchase of a new car. Whereas children cannot make the final decision in some cases, they can assist in gathering pertinent information and in helping to weigh the pros and cons.

Think Back

About some jobs you had to earn money:
If they were hard or easy.
If they were regular or sporadic.
If they were fairly paid or not.
If they met the criteria for jobs.
If they taught you the value of money or not.

Politics

Out of cognitive development and the internalization of moral standards grow attitudes and actions that govern the child's increasing participation in his community. Hess (1969) collected data on political knowledge, attitudes, and behavior of 12,000 children and teachers in grades 2 through 8 from eight cities. Subjects came from both large and small cities, both middleclass and working-class areas.

The child's early conception of the government and the nation, although vague, was favorable. There was a strong emotional attachment to the President; the children ranked him in helpfulness close to policemen and fathers. He was considered personally responsive to children's wishes. Laws were viewed as powerful and benevolent, helpful and protective, just and unchanging.

This allegiance was transferred by older children from officials to offices and institutions. In a democracy the idealized acceptance of the authority, omniscience, and benevolence of the political system does not fit well with the need for a critical examination of public policy. The citizen must see the need to influence governmental actions, as well as to be a loyal supporter.

With increasing age, perception of how things really were became more realistic. The belief that punishment inevitably follows crime dropped from 57 percent in the second grade, to 16 percent in the eighth, to 2 percent among teachers. As children grew older there was less inclination to argue that "all laws are fair," even though there was still consensus that "laws are to keep us safe." The discrepancy between ideal and actual could be the basis for disillusionment or an incentive to action.

There was an eagerness on the part of children to minimize political conflict of all sorts, among candidates and between parties. One of the largest differences between teachers and eighth-graders was in the ability to tolerate political disagreement. Children seemed to be committed to the need for consensus and majority rule without appreciation of the role of debate, disagreement, and conflict.

Think Back

Regarding the political happenings when you were 5-12:
Who the President, governor and mayor were.
What the national political issues were.
Whether you considered yourself a Democrat or Republican.
How you compared America's form of government with other governments.

Children did not recognize that government and lawmaking are influenced by interest groups. Children believed the average citizen's influence in lawmaking was equal or superior to big companies, rich people, newspapers and churches. Teachers were not in agreement with children on this dimension.

One of the most striking differences between middle class and working-class children was the feeling of personal effectiveness in government operation. Lower-status children rated themselves less influential than higher-status students. The difference increased with age. This may point up the more realistic orientation of the working-class children.

Hess (1969, p. 28) concluded:

---

it makes very little sense to instill in children a superficial faith in institutions under attack, to gloss over social realities, and to obscure many of the routes effective action can take. More useful would be a candid acknowledgement of political and social facts and, especially, a clear explanation of the ways that institutions can be influenced and changed.

Between ages nine and thirteen, children move from near ignorance of politics to awareness of most of the conspicuous features of the adult political arena. With their cognitive progress away from self and toward the larger world, they are readily impressed and interested in the political discussions of their parents, as well as the media coverage of major political events and personalities. Some knowledge is gained through school-sponsored activities related to patriotic holidays and elections. This age rarely closely attends to political newscasting, and the majority of their learning is informal and casually acquired. (Greenstein, 1965).

Children are relatively unaware they are forming basic attitudes about the politics of their world, yet it is hypothesized that the stability of the American system of government is rooted in the early positiveness instilled in children with regard to the Presidency. This respect for the highest office in the system extends to other parts of the political structure, providing life-long allegiance for most Americans. Favorable conceptions of political authority emerge well before the child gains much political information or knowledge. It is not until early adolescence that negative attitudes arrive in his repertoire of political feelings.

Children typically have much more favorable attitudes toward political figures than do their elders. They do not share the distrust of the system of adult citizens nor criticize the leaders in it.

Some preschoolers show respectful awareness of the President and are far more likely to know the name of the President than of their local mayor. Presidential work was conceptualized by a 7-year-old as telling important people goodbye, being on programs and studying important things like what's happening and the weather. This age is likely to consider the President more important than a doctor or a school teacher. A fourth grader saw the President's role as providing safety, and a fifth grader as making peace. Fifth graders saw the work of a mayor as making or repairing parks and swings, removing snow from roads, and providing for the needs of schools and stores (Greenstein, 1965).

Between grades 4 and 8, there is slightly less idealization of political leaders and much more information about political issues, parties and personalities is gained. The more important a political orientation is to adults, the earlier it will be learned by children, according to Greenstein. Children typically learn about federal and local politics before state ones, and about the executive leaders prior to the legislative ones. Fourth graders in a New Haven study generally understood the President's role, whereas it is not until the fifth grade that a majority comprehend the role of the mayor.

Sixth graders could explain the governor's functions, but not until seventh grade could a majority discuss the work of Congress to any degree.

Children are quite willing to rate public officials, but they find it difficult to distinguish between the Democratic and Republican parties except in such broad strokes as "The Democrats spend too much money," or "Republicans are richer." It is believed that party identification development proceeds similarly to ethnic and religious ones: with little explicit teaching but inherent pride in identification with parents.

In the New Haven study of fourth to eighth graders, Greenstein found the majority of sixth graders mentioned political issues in responding to a "Wish to change the world" item. The common response was related to peace.

Boys are generally more politically informed than girls and tend to identify more with public figures, perhaps due to the patterns of male socialization in the culture. Children from lower socioeconomic classes tend to perceive themselves as less able to judge political events than those from middle class families. They have less political information and less skills for political action and communication, probably because of the authority-compliance child-rearing patterns under which they are socialized.

What's Next?

A Death in the Family. J. Agee, Grossett and Dunlap, 1967.

Discussing Death: A Guide to Death Education, Mills, et al. ETC Pub., 1975.

Death, Society and Human Experience. R. Kastenbaum. Mosby, 1977.

Not by the Color of Their Skin, M. McDonald. New York: International Universities Press, 1970.

Prejudice and Your Child, 2nd ed., K. B. Clark. Boston: Beacon, 1963.

Children of Crisis, R. Coles, Boston: Little, Brown, 1964.

"The Language of Prejudice," S. Steinberg. *Today's Education,* February 14, 1971, pp. 14, 16–17.

"What White Parents Should Know About Children and Prejudice," A. F. Poussaint and J. P. Comer. *Redbook,* May 1972, pp. 62–63, 122–123.

God Is a Good Friend to Have, E. Marshall and S. Hample, New York: Simon and Schuster, 1969.

Film: *Day Grandpa Died,* BFA Ed. Media, 2211 Michigan Ave., Santa Monica, CA 90406 (12 min/color).

Film: *Old Enough to Know* (sex education), Planned Parenthood, 810 7th Ave.,N.Y. 10019 (20 min/color).

Hello Up There (concepts of life in the family), Learning Corp of America, 1350 Avenue of the Americas, N.Y. 10019 (9 min/color).

Catalysts for Discussion

1. The Dream of Martin Luther King:

"I have a dream that my four little children will one day live in a nation where they will not be judged by the color of their skin, but by the content of their character."

II. "Children and War" (Skard, 1972, pp. 33–34)

We hesitate to talk to children about war, atom bombs, destruction, loss of human lives. We do not want to disturb their peaceful existence, their confidence in life, their feeling of safety. But can we protect them against the hard realities of our time? And, for how long a time? Let us hear what the children say themselves. I refer to a conversation in a family with five children. For clarification purposes let us call them Eleven, Ten, Eight, Seven, and Three according to their ages.

ELEVEN starts out: Mummy, why do you look so serious? Are you sick? Does it hurt somewhere?

MOTHER: No, no, it is nothing present here, it is just something happening somewhere in the world.

TEN: What is it? What is happening?

FATHER: It is so far away, it does not happen here.

EIGHT: But when you look so serious, it must be here anyway.

MOTHER: It is way, way off,—far away in Asia.

ELEVEN: You must tell us about it, tell us all that is wrong, so that we do not think you are mad at us when you look so serious.

EIGHT: But it is useless to tell to Three, for she is so little, she understands nothing at all.

TEN: No, you must try to be gay and friendly to Three anyway, even if you are very sorry inside yourself, so that little Three may be happy even so.

SEVEN: I do not understand all you say, Daddy,—but when you talk about America and England and Russia and such matters, I think of it inside myself, I think and think, and sometimes I understand more of it after a while.

EIGHT: You had better talk about it all, so that we are informed.

ELEVEN: But we do not manage to understand all you talk about when you grown-ups talk. And you must talk about many other things than just the sad and serious problems. And you must be a bit happy also, so that we may have fun. We cannot think of all that is serious and sad all the time.

TEN: But you should rather talk about all that is difficult a little every day, so that we are prepared for it all when we grow up, and so that things do not happen too suddenly without our knowing anything about it ahead of time.

EIGHT: I know what is worst of all: it is when you look terribly sad, and then you say: "It is something you do not understand."

SEVEN: Yes, that is true. It is much better when you talk a lot that we do not understand or that we only understand a bit.

TEN: But that is not the case of Three. She is so little it is no use to talk to her. She only needs to have us happy.

ELEVEN: I cannot stand being serious all the time,—even if it is terribly dangerous and awfully miserable some places in the world.

This conversation gives us some clues as to the desires of the children for insight into the actual and difficult questions that pose themselves in connection with the news from TV, radio, and newspapers, and their wish to understand the feelings that arise in the grown-ups in the struggle with the problems of the modern world. Should we extract some important points from what the children said, it might be the following:

Whatever we say or do must be related to the age of the child. It is useless to talk to the very small ones, they "only need to have us happy." With them we must try to push aside our worries and give ourselves fully to the play and care, feeling strongly how happy we are with our small toddlers and how much joy that is to be found in the budding and growing little child. When the children grow a little older, even at the age of five-six, they notice all by themselves that we turn serious and look sad, and they need to be assured that it is not they themselves who are the source of our quandary. Gradually we can explain more and more, rather too much than too little: The worst of all is to be told that "it is something you do not understand." But when we have explained and when we have answered questions as far as we are able to and perhaps even further than children can grasp, we should try to turn to the situation here and now, because children "cannot think of all that is serious and sad all the time."

III. Children's Concepts in Fantasy (From Rubin, 1976, p. 66)

On election day, students presented their platforms and held a small mock election on the basis of the platforms.

by Angela Jones

If I were govenor of Georgia I would make sure that food prices go down. I will be the nicest govenor Georgia ever had. I will make sure people use the peace sign wisely. I will throw every bottle of liquor away, and burn bad drugs.

This fantasy was started by the phrase: If I had a million dollars. . . .

by Angel Williams

If I had a million dollars I would buy me a Eldorado. I would like to take a trip to New York, California, New Jersey. I would have servants to bring my food and to go get my children. I would have a car for my daughter and a car for me and my husband. I would have a police to stand out and guard. I would have two of them to be in the house because I do not want to be threatened. That is what I am going to do with my money.

IV. Lane's (1964) adaptation of Tuckman-Lorge "Old People Questionnaire," p. 231

WHAT ARE YOUR ATTITUDES TOWARD THE AGED?

Answer "Yes" or "No."

Do you feel that persons over 65

1. think young parents do not know how to bring up children properly?
2. are careless about their table manners?
3. make bad patients when ill?
4. feel that young parents rear their children wisely?
5. feel secure?
6. are bossy?
7. dislike any change or interference with established ways of doing things?
8. usually look on the bright side of things?
9. hoard their money?
10. get easily upset?
11. are easy to care for when ill?
12. respect a person's need for privacy?

13. are grouchy?
14. like to gossip?
15. think the future is hopeless?
16. like to be waited on?
17. feel miserable most of the time?
18. are good company?
19. accept suggestions readily?
20. remember names well?
21. keep up with current ideas and events?
22. are critical of the younger generation?
23. rarely get upset?
24. feel other people must manage their business for them?
25. like to learn new ways of doing things?
26. feel that their children neglect them?
27. are fussy about food?
28. are very stubborn?
29. are self-reliant?

30. meddle in other people's affairs?
31. are very helpful around the house?
32. have good table manners?
33. are insecure?
34. approve of the younger generation?
35. prefer to support themselves?
36. are in the way?
37. are easy to get along with?
38. find ways to take care of themselves?
39. are out of step with the times?
40. are tidy and careful about their appearance?

To indicate a favorable attitude toward the aged, questions 1, 2, 3, 6, 7, 9, 10, 13, 14, 15, 16, 17, 22, 24, 26, 27, 28, 30, 33, 36, and 39 should be answered *No;* the remainder should be answered *Yes.*

V. Misconceptions of children with respect to money-related terms (Williams, 1970):

Poverty is people going around cheering.
A gift and a prize are the same thing except you don't wrap a gift.
To labor is to sleep.
Paying interest is liking something a lot.
If you employ someone you don't like them so well.
Thrift is to do something in a hurry.
Currency is how fast the wind is blowing.
Free enterprise is giving something away free.
Inflation is like pollution; it kills something in the air.
A luxury is a man who carries old ladies' luggage.

VI. "Nurses in Colored Uniforms" (Howe, 1969)

School-age children seem leery of nurses who are not dressed in the traditional white uniform by which they can be readily identified as persons who help doctors care for sick people. There is a tendency for them to view nurses dressed otherwise as "just ladies," not nurses, regardless of the nursing functions they perform. Consider the statement of a nine-year-old: "I've been here (in the hospital) six days, and I haven't seen a nurse yet." Another school-age patient reflected a similar idea, declaring, "You're a nurse? You don't look like no nurse I ever seen. You ain't no nurse."

Beyond the Classroom Experiences

1. Survey children as to their source of money and the weekly amounts they have to spend and how they manage it. Discuss their feelings about the allowance concept as compared to the gift, dole, and salary.

2. Talk with parents of a child who has recently had a death in his family. Note ways he was or was not included in the "circle of grief," how he was prepared for the loss, and how he is being helped to adjust to it.

3. Talk with children about politics and political matters. Ask them to interpret a news item in this connection. See if they realize some of the strengths and weaknesses of a democratic form of government and other forms.

4. Analyze yourself with respect to Clark's characteristics of prejudice. See if you can account for any prejudiced feelings you have. Make definite plans to overcome them, if possible, drawing help from the list by Frenkel-Brunswik.

5. Administer Lane's questionnaire about aging to children. Discuss their concepts and their possible sources.

6. Ask some college-age friends and some parents of school-age children to write about their earliest sex education. Note feelings and misconceptions.

7. Visit some formal sex education classes for children or adults in the community. Note relative emphasis on physiology, sex role, relationships, emotions, morality. Note strengths and possible ways to improve. Compare with SIECUS goals.

8. Talk with parents about their feelings on sex education for children. Ask what they do and what challenges they see in home and school-based sex education.

9. Interview a single parent and children about their divorce experience and what advice they would give to others facing divorce.

10. Plan some activities involving children and older persons to foster communication and respect between the age groups. Refer to Whitley's project for ideas.

Epilogue

My world, as a kid, was full of things that grownups didn't care about. My fear now is that all of us grownups have become so childish that we don't leave the kids much room to move around in, that we foolishly believe that we understand them so well because we share things with them.

This is not only folly, it is not fair. At somebody's house one night, a harassed father who was trying to talk to grownups with his brood around, finally spoke a simple sentence of despair, "For Gossakes, go up upstairs or downstairs!"

He was, I believe, asking for privacy. He was, I believe, entitled to it.

I think kids are, too.

Let them moon, let them babble, let them be scared.

I guess what I am saying is that people who don't have nightmares don't have dreams.

If you will excuse me, I have an appointment with myself to sit on the front steps and watch some grass growing. (Smith, 1957, pp. 123–124.)

Bibliography

Abel, John D. The family and child television viewing. *Journal of Marriage and the Family* **38**:2 (1976), 331–335.

Abraham, W. *The Slow Learner.* New York: Center for Applied Research in Education, Inc., 1964.

Accidents and Children. Washington, D.C.: U.S. Government Printing Office, 1963.

Ack, M. Is education relevant? *Journal of Home Economics,* **62**:9 (1970), 647–651.

Adams, R. L., and Phillips, B. N. Motivational and achievement differences among children of various ordinal birth positions. *Child Development* **43**:1 (1972), 155–164.

Adorno, T. W., Frenkel-Brunswik, E., Levinson, D. J., and Sanford, R. N. *The Authoritarian Personality.* New York: Harper & Row, 1950.

Agan, T., and Luchsinger, E. *The House.* Philadelphia: Lippincott, 1965.

Agee, J. *Death in the Family.* New York: Avon, 1959.

Aginsky, B. W. An Indian's soliloquy. *The American Journal of Sociology,* **46** (1940), 43–44.

Allinsmith, W., and Greening, T. C. Guilt over anger as predicted from parental discipline: A study of superego development. *American Psychologist,* **10** (1955), 10, 32. (Abstract.)

Allred, G. H. *Mission for Mother: Guiding the Child.* Salt Lake City: Bookcraft, 1968, pp. 71–72.

Almy, M. Wishful thinking about children's thinking? *Teachers College Record,* **62** (1961), 396–406.

American Association of School Administrators. *Education and the Spirit of Science.* Arlington, Va.: Education Policies Commission, 1971.

American Library Association. *Basic Book Collection for Elementary Grades.* Chicago, 1960.

American Library Association. *I Read, We Read, You Read.* Chicago, 1971.

Angove, R. He's the housewife, she pays the rent. *Tallahassee Democrat,* **67**:1 (May 26, 1972).

Ansbacher, H. L., and Ansbacher, R. R., eds. *The Individual Psychology of Alfred Adler.* New York: Harper & Row, 1956.

Arbuthnot, M. H. *Children and Books.* Chicago: Scott, Foresman, 1957.

Arbuthnot, M. H. *Children's Reading in the Home.* Glenview, Ill.: Scott, Foresman, 1969.

Arbuthnot, M. H. *Children's Books Too Good to Miss.* Cleveland: The Press of Case Western Reserve University, 1971.

Arbuthnot, May H., and Broderick, Dorothy M. (Compilers). *The Arbuthnot's Anthology of Children's Literature* (4th ed.). Glenview, Ill.: Scott, Foresman, 1976.

Armor, D. J. The evidence on busing. *Public Interest,* **28** (1972), 90–126.

Arnold, L. Eugene (ed.). *Helping Parents Help their Children.* New York: Brunner/Mazel, 1978.

Ashton-Warner, S. *Teacher.* New York: Simon and Schuster, 1963.

Askins, J. Black English "Different strokes for different folks." *Tallahassee Democrat* (July 30, 1972), A8.

Atkinson, J. W., and Feather, N. T. (eds.). *A Theory of Achievement Motivation.* New York: Wiley, 1966.

Atkinson, J. W., and Raynor, J. O. *Motivation and Achievement.* New York: John Wiley, 1974.

Axline. V. *Dibs: In Search of Self.* Boston: Houghton Mifflin, 1964.

Bachrach, Riva, Huesmann, L. Rowell, and Peterson, Rolf A. The relation between locus of control and the development of moral judgment. *Child Development,* **48** (1977), 1340–1352.

Baker, H. V. Children's contributions in elementary school general discussions. *Child Development Monographs,* No. 29 (1942), 32–33.

Ban, P., and Lewis, M. *Mothers and Fathers, Girls and Boys: Attachment Behavior in the One-year-old.* Paper presented at the Eastern Psychological Association Meeting, New York, April 1971.

Bandura, A. *Aggression: A Social Learning Analysis.* Englewood Cliffs, N.J.: Prentice-Hall, 1973.

Bandura, A. *A Social Learning Theory.* New York: General Learning, 1971.

Bandura, A. *Principles of Behavior Modification.* New York: Holt, 1969.

Bandura, A., Ross, D., and Ross, S. A. Imitation of film mediated aggression models. *Journal of Abnormal and Social Psychology,* **66** (1963), 3–11.(a)

Bandura, A., Ross, D., and Ross, S. A. Vicarious reinforcement and imitation learning. *Journal of Abnormal and Social Psychology,* **67** (1963), 601–617.(b)

Bandura, A., and Walters, R. H. *Social Learning and Personality Development.* New York: Holt, Rinehart and Winston, 1963.

Banned Products (Consumer Products Safety Commission, Vol. II, Part 1). October 1973.

Barth, R. S. When children enjoy school—Some lessons from Britain. *Childhood Education* (January 1970), 195–204.

Barrett, Curtis, and Noble, Helen. Mothers' anxieties versus the effects of long distance move on children. *Journal of Marriage and Family,* **35**:2 (1973), 181–188.

Battelle, P. *Chicago Daily News,* November 6, 1967.

Baumrind, D. Current patterns of parental authority. *Developmental Psychology Monographs,* 1971, **4** (1).

Bayley, N. Individual patterns of development. *Child Development,* **27** (1956), 45–74.

Bayley, N. Growth curves of height and weight by age for boys and girls scaled according to physical maturity. *Journal of Pediatrics,* **48** (1956), 187–194.

Bayley, N., and Bayer, L. M. The assessment of somatic androgyny. *American Journal of Physical Anthropology,* 4 N.S. (1946), 433–461.

Beard, R. M. *An Outline of Piaget's Developmental Psychology.* New York: Basic Books, 1969; London: Routledge & Kegan Paul, 1969.

Beatty, J. Trade winds. *Saturday Review* (March 16, 1968), 10.

Beck, Dorothy F. *Marriage and the Family Under Challenge* (2nd ed.). New York: Family Service Association of America, 1976.

Becker, W. C. Consequences of different kinds of parental discipline. In M. L. Hoffman and L. W. Hoffman, eds., *Review of Child Development Research.* Vol. I. New York: Russell Sage Foundation, 1964, pp. 169–208.

Bee, H. Parent-child interaction and distractibility in nine-year-old children. *Merrill-Palmer Quarterly,* **13**:3 (July 1967), 175–190.

Behrens, H. D., and Maynard, G. Historical perspective. In H. D. Behrens, and G. Maynard (eds.), *The Changing Child: Readings in Child Development.* Glenview, Ill.: Scott, Foresman, 1972, 2–3.

Behrens, H. D. and Maynard, G. The child: development of the self concept. In H. D. Behrens and G. Maynard (eds.), *The Changing Child: Readings in Child Development.* Glenview, Ill.: Scott, Foresman, 1972, 44–45.

Bell, R. R. *Marriage and Family Interaction.* Homewood, Ill.: Dorsey, 1963.

Bell, R. R. The one-parent mother in the Negro lower class. Paper read at the meeting of the Eastern Sociological Society, New York, 1965.

Bellak, L. *The Thematic Apperception Test and The Children's Apperception Test in Clinical Use.* New York: Grune and Stratton, 1954.

Benell, F. B. Frequency of misconceptions and reluctance to teach controversial topics related to sex among teachers. *The Research Quarterly,* **40**:1 (1969), 11–16.

Bennett, William J. Let's bring back heroes. *Newsweek* (August 15, 1977), p. 3.

Berenda, R. W. *The Influence of the Group on the Judgments of Children.* New York: King's Crown Press, 1950. Cited in M. L. and N. R. Haimowitz, eds., *Human Development: Selected Readings.* 2nd ed. New York: Crowell, 1966, pp. 366–376.

Berlyne, D. E. Children's reasoning and thinking. In P. H. Mussen, ed., *Carmichael's Manual of Child Psychology.* Vol. 1, 3rd ed. New York: Wiley, 1970, pp. 939–981.

Bernard, H. W. *Human Development in Western Culture* (2nd. ed.). Boston: Allyn and Bacon, 1966.

Bernstein, Joanne. *Books to Help Children Cope With Separation and Loss.* New York: R. R. Bowker, 1977.

Bettleheim, B. Bringing up children. In S. White (ed.), *Human Development in Today's World,* Boston: Educational Associates, 1976, 284–286.

Bigelow, Brian J. Children's friendship expectations: A cognitive-developmental study. *Child Development,* **48** (1977), 246–253.

Bigner, Jerry J. Attitudes toward fathering and father-child activity. *Home Economics Research Journal,* **6**:2 (1977), 98–106.

Bigner, Jerry J. A Wernerian development analysis of children's descriptions of siblings. *Child Development,* **45** (1974), 317–323.

Bigner, J. J. *Parent and Child Relations: An Introduction to Parenting.* New York: Macmillian, 1979.

Bijou, S. W., and Baer, D. M. The laboratory-experimental study of child behavior. In P. H. Mussen, ed., *Handbook of Research in Child Development.* New York: Wiley, 1960, pp. 140–197.

Biller, H. B. A multiaspect investigation of masculine development in kindergarten age boys. *Genetic Psychological Monograph,* 1968a, **76,** 89.

Biller, H. B. Father absence and the personality development of the male child. *Developmental Psychology,* **2** (1970), 181–201.

Biller, H. B. *Father, Child and Sex Role.* Lexington, Mass.: Lexington Books, D.C. Heath, 1971.

Biller, H. B. *Paternal Deprivation.* Lexington, Mass.: Lexington Books, D. C. Heath, 1974.

Bird, B. *Talking With Patients.* Philadelphia: Lippincott, 1973.

Biskin, Donald S., and Hoskisson, Kenneth. An experimental test of the effects of structured discussion of moral dilemmas found in children's literature on moral reasoning. *The Elementary School Journal,* 1977, 407–415.

Blaine, Graham B. The effect of divorce upon the personality development of children and youth. In E. A. Grollman (ed.), *Explaining Divorce to Children.* Boston: Beacon Press, 1969.

Blair, A. W., and Burton, W. H. *Growth and Development of the Preadolescent.* New York: Appleton-Century-Crofts, 1951.

Bledsoe, J. C. Self-concepts of children and their intelligence, achievement, interests and anxiety. In H. D. Behrens and G. Maynard (eds.), *The Changing Child: Readings in Child Development.* Glenview, Ill.: Scott, Foresman, 1972, 69–72.

Bledsoe, J. C. and Brown, I. D. The interests of preadolescents: a longitudinal study. In H. D. Behrens and G. Maynard (eds.), *The Changing Child: Readings in Child Development.* Glenview, Ill.: Scott, Foresman, 1972, 107–116.

Blood, R. O. and Wolfe, D. M. *Husbands and Wives.* New York: Free Press, 1960.

Bloom, B. S. Affective outcomes of school learning. *Phi Delta Kappan,* **59** (November, 1977), 193–198.

Bloom, Benjamin. *Human Characteristics and School Learning.* New York: McGraw-Hill, 1976.

Bluebond-Langner, Myra. *The Private Worlds of Dying Children.* Princeton: Princeton University Press, 1978.

Bluefarb, S. M. The skin and its disorders. In D. G. Cooley, ed., *Family Medical Guide.* New York: Meredith Press, 1964, pp. 167–196.

Bocks, W. M. Non-promotion: a year to grow? *Education Leader,* **34** (February 1977), 379–383.

Boehm, L. The development of independence: A comparative study. *Child Development,* **28** (1957), 85–92.

Bohannon, John Neil, III. The relationship between syntax discrimination and sentence imitation in children. *Child Development,* **46** (1975), 444–451.

Bolstad, O. D., and Johnson, S. M. The relationship between teachers' assessment of students and the students' actual behavior in the classroom. *Child Development,* **48** (1977), 570–578.

Boroson, W. First-born—A head start on life. *St. Petersburg Times* (January 7, 1971), 1.

Bossard, J. H. S., and Boll, E. S. *The Large Family System*. Philadelphia: University of Pennsylvania Press, 1956.

Bossard, J. H. S., and Boll, E. S. *The Sociology of Child Development*. New York: Harper & Row, 1960.

Bossard, J. H. S., and Sanger, W. P. The large family system—A research report. *American Sociological Review*, **17** (1952), 3–9.

Bousfield, W. A., and Orbison, W. D. Ontogenesis of emotional behavior. *Psychological Review*, **59** (1952), 1–7.

Bowlby, J. Childhood mourning and its implications for psychiatry. *American Journal of Psychiatry*, **117** (1961), 481–498.

Braddock, C. Teach it that way. *Florida Schools* (May–June 1969), 11–13.

Brazelton, T. B. What makes a good father. *Redbook*, **74** (June 1970), 121, 123.

Brazelton, T. B. How to tame the TV monster: A pediatrician's advice. *Redbook*, **138** (April 1972), 47, 49, 51.

Brearley, M., and Hitchfield, E. *A Teacher's Guide to Reading Piaget*. New York: Schocken Books, 1970; London: Routledge & Kegan Paul, 1966.

Breckenridge, M. E., and Vincent, E. L. *Child Development*. 5th ed. Philadelphia: Saunders, 1965.

Breland, H. M. Birth order, family configuration, and verbal achievement. *Child Development*, **45**:4 (1974), 1011–1019.

Brewer, A. On Indian education. *Integrateducation*, **15** (May–June 1977), 21–23.

Bridges, K. M. Emotional development in early infancy. *Child Development*, **3** (1932), 324–341.

Broderick, C. B. Normal socio-sexual development. In C. B. Broderick and J. Bernard, eds., *The Individual, Sex and Society: A SIECUS Handbook for Teachers and Counselors*. Baltimore: Johns-Hopkins Press, 1969.

Brodinsky, B. Back to the basics: the movement and its meaning. *Phi Delta Kappan*, **58** (March, 1977), 522–526.

Brodzinsky, David M. Children's comprehension and appreciation of verbal jokes in relation to conceptual tempo. *Child Development*, **48** (1977), 960–967.

Bronfenbrenner, U. *Two Worlds of Childhood*. New York: Russell Sage Foundation, 1970.

Bronfenbrenner, U. *On Making Human Beings Human*. Detroit: Merrill-Palmer Institute, June 8, 1971. (a)

Bronfenbrenner, U. We must increase our own influence on kids. *Today's Child*, **19**:2 (February 1971), 1, 4. (b)

Bronfenbrenner, Urie. Reported by Pam Moore. A look at the disintegrating world of childhood. *Psychology Today*, **9**:1 (1975), 32–36.

Bronfenbrenner, Urie. Nobody home. *Psychology Today*, **10**:12 (1977), 41–47.

Bronfenbrenner, Urie. The roots of alienation. In Nathan B. Talbot (ed.), *Raising Children in Modern America*. Boston: Little, Brown, 1974, 157–172.

Bronfenbrenner, Urie, Devereux, E. C., Jr., Suci, G. J., and Rodgers, R. R. *Adults and Peers as Sources of Conformity and Autonomy*. Paper presented at the conference on Socialization for Competence, sponsored by the Social Research Council, Puerto Rico, 1965.

Brown, C. *Manchild in the Promised Land*. New York: Signet, 1965.

Brown, D. G. Psychosexual development in childhood in relation to adult sexual maladjustment. Paper read at the 1960 meeting of the National Council on Family Relations, New York City. Cited in Hawkes and Pease, 1962.

Brown J. L. Differential hand usage in 3-year-old children. *Journal of Genetic Psychology,* **100** (1962), 67–75.

Brownfain, J. J. Stability of the self-concept as a dimension of personality. *Journal of Abnormal Psychology,* **47** (1952), 597–606.

Bruner, J. S. *Poverty and Childhood.* Detroit: Merrill-Palmer Institute, 1970.

Burton, R. Honesty and dishonesty. In Thomas Lickona (ed.), *Moral Development and Behavior: Theory, Research, and Social Issues.* New York: Holt, Rinehart and Winston, 1976, 173–197.

Burton, R. V. The generality of honesty reconsidered. *Psychological Review,* **70** (1963), 481–499.

Butcher, J. Manifest aggression: MMPI correlates in normal boys. *Journal of Consulting Psychology,* **29** (1965), 446–454.

Caldwell, B. M. Early childhood in art. In J. D. Andrews (ed.), *Early Childhood Education: It's an Art? It's a Science?* Washington, D. C.: National Association for the Education of Young Children, 1976, 183–206.

The Canadian School Library Association. *Basic Book List for Canadian Schools, Elementary Division Grades 1–6.* Ottawa, 1968.

Caratz, J. C. A bi-dialectal task for determining economically disadvantaged Negro children. *Child Development,* **40**:3 (September 1969), 889–901.

Caspari, E. Gene action as applied to behavior. In J. Hirsh (ed.), *Behavior-Genetic Analysis.* New York: McGraw-Hill, 1967, 112–134.

Cassidy, M. L. Clothing preferences of 150 pre-adolescent girls and 50 of their mothers. Master's thesis, Iowa State University, 1958.

Chaffee, S. H., and McLeod, J. M. Adolescent television use in the family context. In G. A. Comstock and E. A. Reubenstein (eds.), *Television and Social Behavior. Vol. 3 Television and Adolescent Aggressiveness.* Washington, D.C.: U.S. Government Printing Office, 1972.

Challenge for the Third Century: Education in a Safe Environment (Final report of the Nature and Prevention of School Violence and Vandalism). Washington, D.C.: U.S. Government Printing Office, February 1977.

Child Study Association of America. *You, Your Child and Drugs.* New York: Child Study Press, 1971.

Chilman, C. D. *Growing Up Poor,* #13. Washington, D.C.: U.S. Government Printing Office, 1966.

Clark, K. B. *Prejudice and Your Child.* 2nd ed. Boston: Beacon Press, 1963.

Clifford, E. Discipline in the home. A controlled observational study of parental practices. *Journal of Genetic Psychology,* **95** (1959), 45–82.

Clorox. Rejoice. In S. M. Joseph, ed., *The Me Nobody Knows.* New York: Avon, 1969.

Coates, B. White adult behavior toward black and white children. *Child Development,* **43**:1 (March, 1972), 143–154.

Coburn, J. A community-based Indian curriculum development program. *Ed. Leader,* **34** (1977), 284–287.

Cole, L. *Teaching in the Elementary School.* New York: Rinehart, 1939.

Coleman, J. S. *Equality of Educational Opportunity.* Washington, D.C.: Office of Education, 1966.

Coles, R. *Children of Crisis.* Boston: Little, Brown, 1964.

Coles, R. Like it is in the alley. *Daedalus,* **97** (Fall 1968), 1315–1320.

Coles, R. *Children of Crisis, Vol. IV: Chicanos, Eskimos, Indians.* Boston: Little, Brown, 1976.

Coles, R. *Children of Crisis, Vol. V: Privileged Ones.* Boston: Little, Brown, 1977.

Coles, R., and Erickson, J. *Middle Americans: Proud and Uncertain.* Boston: Little, Brown, 1971.

Committee on Social Issues. *Psychiatric Aspects of School Desegregation,* Report No. 37. Group for the Advancement of Psychiatry, 1957. Cited in McDonald, 1970.

Condry, John, and Siman, Michael L. Characteristics of peer- and adult-oriented children. *Journal of Marriage and the Family,* **36** (1974), 543–554.

Coopersmith, S. Studies in self-esteem. *Scientific American,* **218** (1968), 96–106.

Corbin, C. B. *A Textbook of Motor Development.* Dubuque: Brown Co., 1973.

Corbin, C. B. *Becoming Physically Educated in the Elementary School.* Philadelphia: Lea and Febiger, 1969.

Corey, S. M. Poor scholar's soliloquy. *Childhood Education,* **20**:5 (January 1944), 219ff.

Corsini, R. J. *Current Personality Theories.* Itasca, Ill.: Peacock, 1977.

Cottle, T. J., and Edelman, M. W. Our country's neglected children. *Parents Magazine,* (December 1975), pp. 36–37; 56–57.

Council of the Society for the Psychological Study of Social Issues. Racial factors in intelligence—A rebuttal. *Trans-Action,* **6**:7 (June 1969), 6, and 75.

Cowen, E. L., Pederson, A., Babigian, H., Izzo, L. D., and Trost, M. A. Long-term follow-up of early detected vulnerable children. *Journal of Consulting and Clinical Psychology,* **41** (1973), 438–446.

Cowen, E. Mothers in the classroom. *Psychology Today* (December 1969), 36–39.

Croake, J. W. Fears of children. *Human Development,* **12** (1969), 239–247.

Cruickshank, W. M., and Johnson, G. O. *Education of Exceptional Children and Youth,* Englewood Cliffs, N. J.: Prentice-Hall, 1958.

Cratty, B. J. *Perceptual and Motor Development in Infants and Children.* New York: Macmillan, 1970.

Crockett, W. H. Cognitive complexity and impression formation. In B. A. Maher (Ed.), *Exploration in Experimental Personality Research* (Vol. 2). New York: Academic, 1965.

Cullen, C. "Incident: Baltimore." In *On These I Stand* by Countee Cullen. New York: Harper & Row, 1925.

Daly, E., ed. *Profile of Youth.* Philadelphia: Lippincott, 1951. Cited in Rogers, 1969.

Davis, A., and Havighurst, R. Social class and color differences in child rearing. *American Sociological Review,* **II** (1946), 698–710.

Davis, C. M. Self selection of diet by newly weaned infants. *American Journal of the Diseases of Children,* **36**:4 (October 1928), 651–679.

Day, S. S. *Design, Use and Space Needs of a Three-Height Table for Children.* Research report #1. Women's College and Agricultural Experiment Station of the University of North Carolina at Greensboro, 1960.

De Bono, E. *Children Solve Problems.* London: Penguin, 1972.

Decker, S. *The Empty Spoon.* New York: Harper & Row, 1969.

DeFee, J. F., and Himelstein, P. Children's fears in a dental situation as a function of birth order. *Journal of Genetic Psychology,* **115**:2 (December 1969), 253–255.

Developmental Psychology Today. Del Mar, Calif.: Communications Research Machines, Inc., 1971.

Dennis, W., and Sayegh, Yvonne. The effect of supplementary experiences upon the behavioral development of infants in institutions. *Child Development,* **36** (1965), 81–90.

Dennison, G. *The Lives of Children.* New York: Vintage, 1969.

Dinkmeyer, D. C. *Child Development: The Emerging Self,* Englewood Cliffs, N.J.: Prentice-Hall, 1965.

Dinkmeyer, D. C., and Dreikurs, R. *Encouraging Children to Learn: The Encouragement Process.* Englewood Cliffs, N.J.: Prentice-Hall, 1963.

Dinkmeyer, Don C., and McKay, Gary D. *Systematic Training for Effective Parenting.* Circle Times, Minn.: The American Guidance Service, 1976.

Dobbs, V. and Neville, D. The effects of non-promotion on the achievement of groups matched from retained first-graders and promoted second graders. *Journal of Education Review,* (July-August 1967), 472–75.

Dodge, L. *Creative Approaches to Tutoring.* Washington, D.C.: National Student Association, Tutorial Assistance Center, 1966.

Dollard, J., Dobb, L. W., Miller, N. E., Mowrer, O. H., and Sears, R. R. *Frustration and Aggression.* New Haven, Conn.: Yale University Press, 1939.

Drawing a hand. Editorial in the *Baltimore Sun,* November 24, 1960; November 23, 1961.

Dreikurs, R., and Grey, L. *A Parents' Guide to Child Discipline.* New York: Hawthorn, 1970.

Dreikurs, Rudolph, and Stoltz, Vicki. *Children: the Challenge.* New York: Hawthorn Books, 1964.

Drillien, G. M. The social and economic factors affecting the incidence of premature birth. I. Premature births without complications of pregnancy. *Journal of Obstetrics and Gynecology, British Empire,* **64** (1957), 161–184.

Duckett, C. L. Caring for children with sickle cell anemia. *Children,* **18**:6 (November–December 1971), 227–231.

Duberman, Lucille. *The Reconstituted Family.* Chicago: Nelson-Hall, 1975.

Durrant, G. D. Teaching your children to work. *Love at Home Starring Father,* Salt Lake City: Bookcraft, 1976, pp. 51–58.

Duvall, E. *Family Development.* Philadelphia: Lippincott, 1957.

Eaton, M. T., D'Amico, L. A., and Phillips, B. N. Problem behaviors in school. *Journal of Educational Psychology,* **470** (1956), 350–357.

Education and the Spirit of Science. Education Policies Commission of the National Education Association and the American Association of School Administrators, 1966.

Eichorn, D. H. Variations in growth rate. In H. D. Behrens and G. Maynard, (Eds.), *The Changing child: Readings in Child Development.* Glenview, Ill.: Scott, Foresman, 1972, 214–219.

Elkind, D. The child's conception of his religious denomination. I: The Jewish child. *Journal of Genetic Psychology,* **99** (1961), 209–225.

Elkind, D. The child's conception of his religious denomination. II: The Catholic child. *Journal of Genetic Psychology,* **101** (1962), 185–194.

Elkind, D. The child's conception of his religious denomination. III: The Protestant child. *Journal of Genetic Psychology,* **103** (1963), 291–304.

Elkind, D. *A Sympathetic Understanding of the Child Six to Sixteen.* Boston: Allyn and Bacon, 1971.

Elkind, David. *Child Development and Education.* New York: Oxford University Press, 1976.

Elkind, D. Humanizing the curriculum. *Childhood Education,* **53** (1977), 178–182.

Engel, M. The development and applications of the children's insight test. *Journal of Projective Techniques,* **22**:1 (1958).

Engel, M. The stability of the self-concept in adolescence. *Journal of Abnormal Psychology,* **58** (1959), 211–215.

Erikson, E. H. *Childhood and Society.* New York: Norton, 1963.

Espanshade, T. J. The value and cost of children (Population Bulletin, Vol. 32, No. 1). Washington, D.C.: Population Reference Bureau, Inc., April 1977.

Eysenck, H. J. *The Structure of Human Personality.* London: Methuen and Co., 1970.

Facts about the Mental Health of Children. Rockville, Md.: NIMH, 1972.

Fancher, E. C., and Weinstein, M. A. A Szondi study of the developmental and cultural factors in personality: The 7-year-old. *Journal of Genetic Psychology,* **88** (1958), 81–88.

Farber, B. and Jenne, W. C. Family organization: parents and siblings of a retarded child. *Monographs of the Society for Research in Child Development,* **28** (1963), 1–78.

Faris, R. E. L. Sociological causes of genius. *American Sociological Review,* **5** (1940), 689–699.

Farnham-Diggory, S. The growth of symbolic abilities in black and white children. A report to the Society for Research in Child Development, Santa Monica, Calif., 1969. In R. C. Smart and M. S. Smart, eds., *Readings in Child Development and Relationships,* New York: Macmillan, Inc., 1972, pp. 297–304.

Farr, R. Is Johnny's reading getting worse? *Ed. Leader,* **34** (April, 1977), 521–527.

Fedder, R. *Guidance Through Club Activities.* New York: Teachers College Press, Teachers College, Columbia University, 1965.

Feingold, B. F. Hyperkinesis and learning disabilities linked to artificial food flavors and colors. *American Journal of Nursing* (1975), 797.

Feinman, S., and Entwisle, D. R. Children's ability to recognize other children's faces. *Child Development,* **47** (1976), 506–510.

Feinman, S., and Entwisle, D. R. *Person Perception According to Race.* Paper presented at the Annual Research Institute of the District of Columbia Sociological Association, March 1976.

Fellows, M. Student classification and legal implications for administrators. *Clearing House,* **51**:2 (1977), 80–85.

Fenwick, J. J. Insights into the middle school years. *Ed. Leader,* **34** (April 1977), 528–535.

Ferguson, C. P. *Preadolescent Children's Attitudes Toward Television Commercials.* Austin: University of Texas, 1975.

Feshbach, S. Aggression. In P. H. Mussen, ed., *Carmichael's Manual of Child Psychology,* Vol. 2. 3rd ed. New York: Wiley, 1970, pp. 159–369.

Finkelstein, I. E. *The Marking System in Theory and Practice,* Educational Psychology Monographs #10. G. M. Whipple, ed. Baltimore: Warwick and York, 1913.

Finlayson, H. J. Non-promotion and self concept development. *Phi Delta Kappan,* **59** (November 1977), 205–206.

Flaming clothes. *Everybody's Money,* **11**:3 (1971), 21–22.

Flatt, A. E. Bones and muscles and their disorders. In D. G. Cooley, ed., *Family Medical Guide.* New York: Meredith Press, 1964, pp. 591–626.

Flavell, J. H. *The Developmental Psychology of Jean Piaget.* Princeton, N.J.: Van Nostrand, 1963.

Flavell, J. H. Concept development. In P. H. Mussen, ed., *Carmichael's Manual of Child Psychology,* Vol. 1, 3rd ed. New York: Wiley, 1970, pp. 983–1059.

Flavell, John H. *Cognitive Development.* Englewood Cliffs. N.J.: Prentice-Hall, 1977.

Flavell, J. H., Beach, D. R., and Chinsky, J. M. Spontaneous verbal rehearsal in a memory task as a function of age. *Child Development,* **57** (1966), 284–299.

Fleck, H., and Munves, E. *Introduction to Nutrition.* New York: Macmillan, Inc., 1966.

Flescher, I. *Children in the Learning Factory.* New York: Chilton, 1972.

Forssman, H., and Thuwe, I. One hundred and twenty children born after application for therapeutic abortion refused. *ACTA Psychiat. Scand.,* **42** (1966), 71–88.

Freidman, M., and Rosenman, R. H. *Type A Behavior and Your Heart.* New York: Knopf, 1974.

Friedrich, L. K., and Stein, A. H. Aggressive and pro-social television programs and the natural behavior of preschool children. *Monograph of the Society for Research in Child Development,* **38**:4 (1973), Serial No. 151.

Frenkel-Brunswik, E. A study of prejudice in children. *Human Relations,* **1**:3 (1948), 295–306.

Freud, S. *An Outline of Psychoanalysis. New York: Norton, 1949.*

Fromm, J. Prevalence and natural history of chronic diseases in childhood. (In *Chronic Childhood Illness, Assessment of Outcome.* National Institute of Health). Washington, D.C.: U.S. Government Printing Office, 1973, 77–81.

Fry, E. A readability formula that saves time. *Journal of Reading,* **11** (April 1968), 514–516, 575–578.

Gallup, G. H. 8th annual Gallup Poll of the public's attitudes toward the public schools. *Phi Delta Kappan,* October 1976, pp. 187–200.

Gagne, Robert M. *The Conditions of Learning* (3rd ed.). New York: Holt, Rinehart and Winston, 1977.

Garbarino, James. The human ecology of child maltreatment: a conceptual model for research. *Journal of Marriage and the Family,* **39** (1977), 721–735.

Gardner, R. A. *The Boys and Girls Book About Divorce.* New York: Science House, 1970.

Gardner, R. W., and Moriarty, A. *Personality Development at Preadolescence.* Seattle: University of Washington Press, 1968.

Garn, S. M., Clark, D. C., and Guire, K. E. Growth, body composition, and development of obese and lean children. In M. Winick (ed.), *Childhood Obesity.* New York: Wiley and Sons, 1975, 23–46.

Garn, S. M., and Rohmann, C. G. Interaction of nutrition and genetics in the timing of growth and development. *Pediatric Clinics of North America,* **13** (1966), 353–379.

Garn, S. M., Clark, A., Landkof, L., and Newell, L. Parental body build and developmental progress in the off-spring. *Science,* **132** (1960), 1555–1556.

Gendel, E. S. Sex education program and controversy. *Health Education in Kansas* 27:5 (May 1969), 3.

General Mills Study. *The American Family Report,* 1977.

Gerald, H. B., and Rabbie, J. M., Fear and social comparison. *Journal of Abnormal and Social Psychology,* **62** (1961), 586–592.

Gerbner, G. Violence in television drama: trend in symbolic functions. In G. A. Comstock and E. A. Rubenstein (eds.), *Television and Social Behavior (Vol. I) Media Content and Control.* Washington, D.C.: U.S. Government Printing Office, 1972.

Gerbner, G., and Gross, L. P. *The Violence People, V: Trends in Network Television Drama and Viewers Conceptions of Reality.* Unpublished manuscript, University of Pennsylvania, 1973.

Gesell, A., and Amatruda, C. *Developmental Diagnosis,* New York: Hoeber, 1951.

Gesell, A., Ilg. F. L., and Ames. L. B. *Youth: The Years from 10 to 16.* New York: Harper & Row, 1956.

Gibran, K. *The Prophet.* New York: Knopf, 1945.

Gildea, M. C., Glidewell, J. C., and Kantor, M. B. Maternal attitudes on general adjustment in school children. In J. C. Glidewell, ed., *Parental Attitudes and Child Behavior.* Springfield, Ill.: C. C. Thomas, 1961.

Gil, D. G. *Violence Against Children: Physical Child Abuse in the United States.* Cambridge, Mass.: Harvard University Press, 1970.

Ginott, H. *Between Parent and Child.* New York: Macmillan, Inc., 1965.

Ginott, H. *Between Teacher and Child.* New York: Macmillan, Inc., 1972.

Ginsberg, H., and Opper, S. *Piaget's Theory of Intellectual Development: An Introduction.* Englewood Cliffs, N.J.: Prentice-Hall, 1969.

Glassow, R. B., and Kruse, R. Motor performance of girls 6 to 13 years. *Research Quarterly,* **31** (1960), 426–433.

Glick, Paul C. Updating the life cycle in the family. *Journal of Marriage and the Family,* **39**:1 (1977), 5–13.

Godfrey, E. The Tragedy of Failure. *North Carolina Education,* October 1971, 10–11.

Gold, D., and Andres, D. Relations between maternal employment and development of nursery school children. *Canadian Journal of Behavioral Science,* In press.

Goldberg, M. L. Adapting teacher style to pupil differences: teachers for disadvantaged children. In J. F. Rosenblith and W. Allinsmith (eds.), *The Causes of Behavior II.* Boston: Allyn and Bacon, 1966.

Goodman, M. E. *Race Awareness in Young Children.* Cambridge, Mass.: Addison-Wesley, 1952. New, rev. ed., New York: Collier Books, 1964.

Goodman, Mary Ellen, and Beman, Alma. Child's-eye view of life in an urban barrio. In Nathaniel N. Wagner and Marsh J. Haley (eds.), *Chicanos: Social and Psychological Perspectives.* St. Louis: C. V. Mosby, 1971, 109–122.

Goodman, N., Richardson, S. A., Dornbusch, S. M., and Hastorf, A. H. Variant reactions to physical disabilities. *American Sociological Review,* **28** (1963), 429–435.

Gordon, I. J. *Human Development from Birth Through Adolescence.* New York: Harper & Row, 1969.

Gordon, R., Short, J., Cartwright, D., and Strodtbeck, F. Values and gang delinquency. *American Journal of Sociology,* **69** (1963), 109–128.

Gordon, Thomas. *P.E.T. in Action.* New York: Bantam Books, 1976.

Gordon, Thomas. *P.E.T. Parent Effectiveness Training.* New York: New American Library, 1975.

Gottman, John. M. Toward a definition of social isolation in children. *Child Development,* **48**:2 (1977), 513–517.

Gough, H. B., Harris, D. B., Martin, W. E., and Edwards, M. Children's ethnic attitudes: I. Relationship to certain personality factors. *Child Development,* **21** (1950), 83–91.

Graves, D. The many pressured pupil. *The PTA Magazine,* **63**:6 (1969), 27–29.

Green, G. *To Brooklyn with Love.* New York: Trident Press, 1967.

Greenfield, J. *A Child Called Noah.* New York: Holt, Rinehart and Winston, 1972.

Greenstein, F. I. *Children and Politics.* New Haven, Conn.: Yale University Press, 1965.

Greulich, W. W. A Comparison of the physical growth and development of American born and native Japanese children. *American Journal of Physical Anthropology,* **15** (1957), 489–515.

Gries, J. M., and Ford, J. *Homemaking, Home Furnishings and Information Services,* reports of the Committees on Homemaking—Housing and Family Life, Home Furnishings and Decoration and Home Information Services of the President's Conference on Home Building and Home Ownership. Washington, D.C.: Nation's Capitol Press, 1932.

Griffin, J. "It's O.K., Son, Everybody Does it." *Ann Landers Column,* 1965.

Grim, P. F., Kohlberg, L., and White, S. H. Some relationships between conscience and attentional processes. *Journal of Personality and Social Psychology,* **8** (1968), 239–252.

Grinspoon, L., and Singer, S. Amphetamines in the treatment of hyperkinetic children. *Harvard Ed. Review,* **43**:4 (1973), 515–555.

Grollman, Earl A. (ed.). *Explaining Death to Children.* Boston: Beacon, 1967.

Grollman, Earl A. *Explaining Divorce to Children.* Boston: Beacon, 1969.

Gronlund, N. E. *Sociometry in the Classroom.* New York: Harper & Row, 1959.

Gross, D. W. Improving the quality of family life. *Childhood Education,* November-December 1977, 50–54.

Grotberg, Edith H. (ed.). *200 Years of Children.* Washington, D.C.: U.S. Government Printing Office, 1976.

Grotberg, E. H. *Child Development* (In *200 Years of Children,* Department of Health, Education, and Welfare). Washington, D.C.: 1976, 391–420.

Grottman, John M. Toward a definition of social isolation in children. *Child Development,* **48** (1977), 513–517.

Gruenberg, S. *The Parents' Guide to Everyday Problems of Boys and Girls.* New York: Random House, 1958.

Guilford, J. P. A system of psychomotor abilities. *American Journal of Psychology,* **71** (1957), 164–174.

Haber, R. N., and Haber, R. B. Eidetic imagery. *Perceptual Motor Skills,* **19** (1964), 131–138.

Haley, E. G., and Hendrickson, N. J. Children's preferences for clothing and hair styles. *Research Journal of Home Economics,* **2**:3 (March, 1974), 176–193.

Hamovitch, M. B. *The Parent and the Fatally Ill Child.* Duarte, Calif.: City of Hope Medical Center, 1964.

Hartshorne, H., and May, M. A. Studies in the Organization of Character. In Raymond T. Kuhlen and George C. Thompson, eds., *Psychological Studies of Human Development,* 2nd ed. New York: Appleton-Century-Crofts, 1963.

Harvey, O. J., Hunt, D. E., and Schroder, H. M. *Conceptual Systems and Personality Organization.* New York: Wiley, 1961.

Hathaway, M. I. *Heights and Weights of Children and Youths in the U.S.* Home economics research report #2. Washington, D.C.: U.S. Department of Agriculture, 1957.

Havighurst, R. J. *Developmental Tasks and Education.* New York: McKay, 1952.

Havighurst, R. J., Bowman, P. H., Liddle, G. P., Matthews, C. V., and Pierce, J. V. *Growing Up in River City.* New York: Wiley, 1962.

Havighurst, R. J., and Morehead, T. E. The disadvantaged in industrial cities. In P. A. Witty (ed.), *The Educationally Retarded and Disadvantaged, 66th Yearbook, Part I.* Chicago: National Society for the Study of Education, 1967, 8–20.

Harvey, K., and Horton, L. Bloom's human characteristics and school learning. *Phi Delta Kappen,* **59** (November 1977).

Hawkes, G. R., and Pease, D. *Behavior and Development from 5 to 12.* New York: Harper & Row, 1962.

Healthy Teeth—A Happier School Child. Chicago: American Dental Association, G13.

Heil, L. M., and Washburne, C. Characteristics of teachers related to children's progress. *Journal of Teacher Education,* **12** (1961), 401–406.

Help for child beaters. *Newsweek* (July 24, 1972), 66–69.

Henry, W. E. Projective techniques. In P. H. Mussen, ed., *Handbook of Research in Child Development.* New York: Wiley, 1960, pp. 603–644.

Herndon, J. *The Way It Spozed to Be.* New York: Bantam, 1968.

Herron, R. E. A biomedical perspective on stereographic anthropometry. In F. D. Thomas and E. Sellers, eds., *Biomedical Instrumentation.* Vol. 6: *Imagery in Medicine.* Pittsburgh: Instrument Society of America, 1969.

Herron, R. E. Stereophotogrammerty in biology and medicine. *Photographic Applications in Science, Technology and Medicine,* **5** (1970), 26–35.

Herzog, E. Some assumptions about the poor. *Social Service Review,* **37** (December 1963), 4.

Herzog, E., and Sudia, C. D. Fatherless homes. *Children,* **15** (September-October 1968), 177–182.

Hess, R. D. Political attitudes of children. *Psychology Today,* **2**:8 (January 1969), 24–28.

Hess, R. D. Social class and ethnic influences upon socialization. In P. H. Mussen, ed., *Carmichael's Manual of Child Psychology,* Vol. 2. 3rd ed. New York: Wiley, 1970, pp. 457–557.

Hickey, T., and Kalish, R. A. Young people's perceptions of adults. *Journal of Gerontology,* **23** (1968), 215–219.

Hicks, L. H., and Buhler, J. H. Schools children like: what do they say about them? *Ed. Leader,* **34** (February 1977), 388–392.

Hildreth, G. The development and training of hand dominance: V. Training of handedness. *Journal of Genetic Psychology,* **76** (1950), 101–144.

Hill, Susan J., and Waggoner, Dorothy. Children from non-English speaking background. *Children Today,* **6**:3 (1977), 24–25.

Hill, W. F. *Learning: A Survey of Psychological Interpretations.* San Francisco: Chandler, 1960.

Hilton, I. Differences in the behavior of mothers toward first and later born children. *Journal of Personality and Social Psychology,* **7** (1967), 282–290.

Himmelweit, H. T., Oppenheim, A. N., Vince, P., et al. *Television and the Child.* London: Oxford University Press, 1958.

Hirsch, J. Behavior-genetic analysis. In J. Hirsch (ed.), *Behavior-Genetic Analysis.* New York: McGraw-Hill, 1967, 416–435.

Hirsch, J. and Han, P. W. Cellularity of rat adipose tissue. *Journal of Lipid Research,* **10** (1969), 77.

Hoffman, M. L. *Conscience, Personality Structure, and Socialization Techniques.* Ann Arbor: University of Michigan: Mimeographed, 1969.

Hoffman, M. L. Moral development. In P. H. Mussen, ed., *Carmichael's Manual of Child Psychology,* Vol. 2. 3rd ed. New York: Wiley, 1970, pp. 261–359.

Hoffman, M. L., and Saltzstein, H. D. Parent discipline and the child's moral development. *Journal of Personality and Social Psychology,* **5** (1967), 45–57.

Hogan, R. A. A dimension of moral judgment. *Journal of Consulting and Clinical Psychology,* **35** (1970), 205–212.

Holmes, F. B. *Children's Fears.* New York: Bureau of Publications, Teachers College, Columbia University, 1935.

Holt, J. *How Children Fail.* New York: Pitman, 1964.

Holt, J. *How Children Learn.* New York: Pitman, 1967.

Holt, J. *Freedom to Learn.* Columbus, Ohio: Merrill, 1969.

Holt, J. *Instead of Education: Ways to Help People Do Things Better.* New York: Dutton, 1976.

Honzik, M. P., Macfarlane, J. W., and Allen, L. The stability of mental test performance between 2 and 18 years. *Journal of Experimental Education,* **17** (1948), 309–324.

Howe, J. What's all this about colored uniforms? *American Journal of Nursing,* **69**:8 (August 1969), 1665–1667.

Hunt, J. McV. Black genes—white environment. *Trans-Action,* **6** (1969), 12–22.

Hunt, L. A. A developmental study of factors related to children's clothing preferences. *Society for Research in Child Development Monographs,* **24** (1959), 3–47.

Hurlock, E. *Child Development.* 4th ed. New York: McGraw-Hill, 1964.

Hurlock, E. *Child Development.* 5th ed. New York: McGraw-Hill, 1972.

Hurlock, E. B. Encouraging laughter. *Today's Health* (February 1957), 58–59.

Hymes, J. *The Child Under Six.* Englewood Cliffs, N. J.: Prentice-Hall, 1966.

Inferior kids reacted with anger. *Charlotte Observer,* Saturday, July 13, 1968.

Irelan, L. M. *Low-Income Life Styles,* #14. Washington, D.C.: U.S. Government Printing Office, 1967.

Iscoe. I., Williams, M., and Harvey, J. Modification of children's judgments by a simulated group technique: A normative developmental study. *Child Development,* **34** (1953), 963–968.

Jackson, Edgar N. *Telling a Child About Death.* New York: Hawthorn, 1965.

Jackson, P. W. Verbal solution to parent-child problems. *Child Development,* **27** (1956), 339–349.

Jayaswal, S. R. Adult recall of early memories. *Uttara Bharati* (July 1955), 69–74.

Jeanneret, O., and Raymond, L. *Children of School Age and Their Mortality and Hospital Mortality Throughout the World* (World Health Statistics Report V, **28,** #4). Geneva, Switzerland: World Health Organization, 1975, 140–194.

Jencks, C. *Inequality.* New York: Basic Books, 1972.

Jennings, M. K., and Niemi, R. G. The transmission of political values from parent to child. *American Political Science Review,* **62** (1968), 169–184.

Jensen, Arthur R. How much can we boost IQ and scholastic achievement? *Harvard Educational Review,* **39**:1 (1969), 1–123.

Jersild, A. T. Self-understanding in childhood and adolescence. *American Psychologist,* **6** (1951), 122–126.

Jersild, A. T. *Child Psychology.* 6th ed. Englewood Cliffs, N. J.: Prentice-Hall, 1968.

Johnson, B. E. *Indoor Play Areas for the Pre-school Child,* #126. Tucson: University of Arizona College of Agriculture, 1952.

Johnson, G. O. *Education for the Slow Learner.* Englewood-Cliffs, N.J.: Prentice-Hall, 1963.

Johnson, R. C., and Medinnus, G. R. *Child Psychology Behavior and Development.* New York: Wiley, 1969.

Jones, E. E., and Gerard, H. B. *The Foundations of Social Psychology.* New York: Wiley, 1967.

Jordan, F., and Massey, J. *School Readiness Survey.* Palo Alto: Consulting Psychologists Press, 1967.

Jourard, S. M. *Disclosing Man to Himself.* Princeton, N.J.: Van-Nostrand, 1968.

Jourard, S. M. *Healthy Personality.* New York: Macmillan, 1974.

Kadis, A. Early childhood recollections as aids in group psychotherapy. *Journal of Individual Psychology,* **13** (1957), 182–187.

Kagan, J. The child: His struggle for identity. *Saturday Review* (December 7, 1968), 80–82, 87–90.

Kagan, J. The child: His struggle for identity. In H. D. Behrens and G. Maynard (Eds.), *The Changing Child: Readings in Child Development.* Glenview, Ill.: Scott, Foresman, 1972, 63–68.

Kagan, Jerome. The psychological requirement for human development. In Nathan B. Talbot (ed.), *Raising Children in Modern America.* Boston: Little, Brown, 1974, 86–97.

Kagan, J., and Kogan N. Individual variation in cognitive processes. In P. H. Mussen, ed., *Carmichael's Manual of Child Psychology,* Vol. 1, 3rd ed. New York: Wiley, 1970, pp. 1273–1365.

Kagan, J., and Moss, H. A. *Birth to Maturity.* New York: Wiley, 1962.

Kagan, Spencer, and Ender, Philip B. Maternal response to success and failure of Anglo-American, Mexican-American and Mexican children. *Child Development,* **46** (1975), 452–458.

Kahana, B. Grandparenthood from the perspective of the developing grandchild. *The Gerontologist, Part II,* **8** (Autumn, 1968) 31. (Abstract)

Kaplan, F., and Kaplan, T. *The Power of Play*. Garden City, N.J.: Anchor Press, 1973.

Keasey, C. B. Social participation as a factor in the moral development of preadolescents. *Developmental Psychology,* **5**:2 (1971), 216–220.

Keasey, Charles. Young children's attribution of intentionality to themselves and others. *Child Development,* **48** (1977), 261–264.

Keeney, A. H., and Keeney, V. T. *Dyslexia: Diagnosis and Treatment of Reading Disorders*. St. Louis: Mosby, 1968.

Kelley, J., and Wallerstein, J. Brief interventions with children in divorcing families. *American Journal of Orthopsychiatry,* **46**:1 (1976), 23–39.

Keniston, K. *All Our Children: The American Family Under Pressure*. New York: Harcourt, Brace and Jovanovich, 1977.

Kennedy, C. D. The individual's right to fail. In J. Baird and D. Keenan, eds., *Family Life Education Re-examined: Applications for Teachers*. Washington, D.C.: American Home Economics Association, 1971.

Kifer, E. The relationship between home and school in influencing the learning of children. *Research Teach. Eng.,* **11** (1971), 5–16.

Kimmel, C. Parent power: a plus for education. *Ed. Leadership,* **34** (October, 1976), 24–25.

Kinsey, A. C., Pomeroy, W. B., and Martin, C. E. *Sexual Behavior in the Human Male*. Philadelphia: Saunders, 1948.

Kirkendall, L. A. *Sex Education, SIECUS Study Guide #1*. New York: Sex Information and Education Council of the U.S., 1965.

Kirkendall, L. A., and Rubin, I. *Sexuality and the Life Cycle, SIECUS Study Guide #8*. New York: Sex Information and Education Council of the U.S., 1969.

Kirsten, G. G. *The Rich: Are They Different?* Boston: Houghton Mifflin, 1968.

Klapper, J. T. *The Effects of Mass Communication*. New York: Free Press, 1960.

Klausmeier, H. J., and Goodwin, W. *Learning and Human Abilities*. New York: Harper & Row, 1966.

Kleck, Robert E., Richardson, S. A., and Ronald, Linda. Physical appearance cues and interpersonal attractiveness of children. *Child Development,* **45** (1974), 305–310.

Knepp, T. H. *Human Reproduction: Health and Hygiene*. Carbondale, Ill: Southern Illinois University Press, 1967.

Koch, H. L. The relations of primary mental abilities in five- and six-year-olds to sex of child and characteristics of his sibling. *Child Development,* **25** (1954), 209–223.

Koch, H. L. The relation of certain formal attitudes of siblings to attitudes held toward each other and toward their parents. *Monograph of the Society for Research in Child Development,* **25**:4 (1960).

Kohlberg, L. Development of moral character and moral ideology. In M. L. and L. W. Hoffman, eds., *Review of Child Development Research,* Vol. 1. New York: Russell Sage Foundation, 1964.

Kohlberg, L. The child as a moral philosopher. In P. Cramer, ed., *Readings in Developmental Psychology Today*. Del Mar, Calif.: CRM Books, 1970, 109–115.

Kohlberg, L. *Scoring Manual for Assessing Moral Development*. Unpublished manuscript, Cambridge, Mass.: Harvard University, 1973.

Kohlberg, Lawrence. Moral stages and moralization: the cognitive-developmental approach. In Thomas Lickona (Ed.), *Moral Development and Behavior: Theory, Research and Social Issues*. New York: Holt, Rinehart, and Winston, 1976, 32–53.

Kohn, M. L. Social class and the exercise of parental authority. *American Sociological Review,* **24** (1959), 352–366. (a)

Kohn, M. L. Social class and parental values. *American Journal of Sociology,* **64** (1959), 337–351. (b)

Kozol, J. *Free Schools.* Boston: Houghton Mifflin, 1972.

Kraus, H., and Hirschland, R. P. Minimum muscular fitness tests in school children. *Research Quarterly,* **25** (1954), 178–185.

Krauss, R. M., and Glucksberg, S. The development of communication: Competence as a function of age. *Child Development,* **40** (1969), 255–266.

Krauss, R. M., and Glucksberg, S. Some characteristics of children's messages. In R. C. Smart and M. S. Smart, eds., *Readings in Child Development and Relationships.* New York: Macmillan, Inc., 1972, pp. 370–381.

Krebs, A. M. The determinants of conformity: age of independence training and achievement. *Journal of Abnormal and Social Psychology,* **56** (1958), 130–131.

Krebs, R. L. What are little girls made of? *Trans-Action,* **7:5** (1970), 8.

Kronus, S. *The Black Middle Class.* Columbus, Ohio: Merrill, 1971.

Kubler-Ross, Elisabeth. Helping parents teach their children about death and life. In L. Eugene Arnold (ed.), *Helping Parents Help Their Children.* New York: Brunner/Mazel, 1978, 270–278.

Kurtines, William, and Grief, Ester B. The development of moral thought: review and evaluation of Kohlberg's approach. *Psychological Bulletin,* **8** (1974), 453–470.

Kurtz, R. M. Body image—Male or female. *Trans-Action* (*December 1968*), 25–27.

Lamb, Michael. Father-infant and mother-infant interactions in the first year of life. *Child Development,* **48:1** (1977), 167–181.

Landau, E. D., Epstein, S. L., and Stone, A. P. *Child Development Through Literature.* Englewood Cliffs, N.J.: Prentice-Hall, 1972.

Landers, Ann. Tell principal to speak English. *Tallahassee Democrat,* (July 26, 1977), p. 11.

Lane, B. Attitudes of youth toward the aged. *Journal of Marriage and the Family,* **26** (May, 1964), 229–231.

Landis, J. T. The trauma of children when parents divorce. *Marriage and Family Living,* **22** (1960), 7–13.

Landis, P. H. Marriage preparation in two generations. *Marriage and Family Living,* **13** (1951), 155–156.

Landreth, C. *Early Childhood: Behavior and Learning.* New York: Knopf, 1967.

Larrick, N. *A Parent's Guide to Children's Reading.* 4th ed. Garden City, N.Y.: Doubleday, 1975.

Lasko, J. K. Parent behavior towards first and second children. *Genetic Psychological Monographs.* **49** (1954), 96–137.

Lawson, E. Development of patriotism in children—A second look. *Journal of Psychology,* **66** (1963), 279–286.

Lee, H. *To Kill a Mockingbird.* Philadelphia: Lippincott, 1960.

Lee, P. C., and Gropper, N. B. Sex-role culture and education practice. *Harvard Education Review,* **44:3** (August 1974), 369–410.

Lehane, S. The developmental curriculum: an articulation model for grades K-12. *Clearing House,* **51** (October 1977), 86–88.

Lehr, C. J., and Hendrickson, N. Children's attitudes toward a family move. *Mental Hygiene,* **52**:3 (July 1968), 381–385.

LeMasters, E. E. *Parents in Modern America* (3rd ed.). Homewood, Ill.: Dorsey Press, 1977.

Lerner, R. M., and Korn, S. J. The development of body-build stereotypes in males. *Child Development,* **43**:3 (1972), 908–920.

LeShan, E. J. *The Consipiracy Against Childhood.* New York: Atheneum, 1973.

Lesser, Gerald. Education and the mass media. In Nathan B. Talbot (ed.), *Raising Children in Modern America.* Boston: Little, Brown, 1974, 319–331.

Levine, D. U. The integration-compensatory education controversy. *Ed. Forum,* **32** (1968), 323–332.

Levine, M. E. *Introduction to Clinical Nursing.* Philadelphia: Davis, 1969.

Lewis, Oscar. The culture of poverty. In Saul Feldman and G. W. Thielbar (eds.), *Life Styles/Diversity in America.* Boston: Little, Brown, 1972, 175–184.

Licht, L. A. Direct and displaced physical aggression as a funciton of self-esteem and method of anger arousal. Unpublished Doctoral dissertation, University of California, Los Angeles, 1967.

Lickona, Thomas (ed.). *Moral Development and Behavior: Theory, Research, and Social Issues.* New York: Holt, Rinehart and Winston, 1976.

Liebert, R. M., and Neale, J. M. TV violence and child aggression. *Psychology Today,* **5**:11 (April 1972), 38–40.

Lindzey, G. *Projective Techniques and Their Application in Cross-Cultural Research.* New York: Appleton-Century-Crofts, 1960.

Lippitt, R., and White, R. K. An experimental study of leadership and group life. In M. L. Haimowitz and N. R. Haimowitz, eds., *Human Development: Selected Readings.* New York: Crowell, 1966, pp. 356–366.

Lobsenz, N. M. The plot to abolish childhood. *Redbook,* **31** (June 1962), 106–108, 112.

Lovett, R., Barker, E., and Marcus, B. The effect of a nutrition education program at the 2nd grade level. *Journal of Nutrition Education,* **2**:2 (1970), 81–95.

Luria, A. R. *The Role of Speech and the Regulation of Normal and Abnormal Behavior.* New York: Pergammon Press, 1961.

Lynn, D. B. *Parental and Sex-role Identification: A Theoretical Formulation.* Berkeley, Calif.: McCutchan Pub. Co., 1969.

Maccoby, E. E. Why do children watch television? *Public Opinion Quarterly,* **18** (1954), 239–244.

Maccoby, E. E., Gibbs, R. K., et al. Methods of child-rearing in two social classes. In W. E. Martin and C. B. Stendler, eds., *Readings in Child Development.* New York: Harcourt, Brace, 1954, pp. 380–396.

MacFarlane, J., Allen, L., and Honzik, M. P. *A Developmental Study of Behavior Problems of Normal Children Between Twenty-One Months and Fourteen Years.* Berkeley, Calif.: The University of California Press, 1954.

Machover, K. Drawing the human face: A method of personality investigation. In H. H. and G. L. Anderson, eds., *An Introduction to Projective Techniques.* Englewood Cliffs, N.J.: Prentice-Hall, 1951, pp. 341–369.

MacLeish, R. Points to ponder. *Reader's Digest* (October 1976), p. 208.

Madsen, Charles, and Madsen, Clifford. *Teaching/Discipline*. Boston: Allyn and Bacon, 1976.

Maier, H. W. *Three Theories of Child Development*. Rev. ed. New York: Harper & Row, 1969.

Mallick, S. K., and McCandless, B. R. A study of catharsis of aggression. *Journal of Personality and Social Psychology*, 4 (1966), 591–596.

Marcus, M. G. The power of a name. *Psychology Today* (October 1975), pp. 75–76, 108.

Marshall, E., and Hample, S. *God Is a Good Friend to Have*. New York: Simon and Schuster, 1969.

Marshall, H. R. The relation of giving children an allowance to children's money knowledge and responsibility and to other practices of parents. *Journal of Genetic Psychology*, 104 (1964), 35–37.

Marshall, H. R., and Magruder, L. Relations between parent and money education practices and children's knowledge and use of money. *Child Development*, 31 (1960), 253–284.

Martin, Barclay. Parent child relations. In Frances D. Horowitz (ed.), *Review of Child Development Research* (Vol. 4). Chicago: University of Chicago Press, 1975, 463–529.

Martin, E. A. *Roberts' Nutrition Work with Children*. Chicago: University of Chicago Press, 1954.

Martin, P. C., and Vincent, E. L. *Human Development*. New York: Ronald, 1960.

Maslow, A. *Motivation and Personality*. New York: Harper, 1954.

Maslow, A. H. *Motivation and Personality* (2nd Ed.). New York: Harper and Row, 1970.

Maurer, A. What children fear. *Journal of Genetic Psychology*, 106 (1965), 265–277.

Mayer, J. Obesity during childhood. In M. Winick (ed.), *Childhood Obesity*. New York: Wiley and Sons, 1975, 73–80.

McClendon, P. E. A criterion-referenced marking system. *Educational Technology*, 16 (August 1976), 23–25.

McCandless, B. R. *Children: Behavior and Development*. New York: Holt, Rinehart and Winston, 1967.

McCarthy, D. Language development. In L. Carmichael, ed., *Manual of Child Psychology*. 2nd ed. New York: Wiley, 1954, pp. 492–630.

McDaniel, C. G. TV: A wasteland for tots. *The Christian Century* (April 26, 1972), 492–494.

McDonald, A. P., Jr. Manifestations of differential levels of socialization by birth order. *Developmental Psychology*, 1 (1969), 485–492.

McDonald, M. *Not by the Color of Their Skin*. New York: International Universities Press, 1970.

McGhee, Paul E. Children's appreciation of humor: a test of the cognitive congruency principle. *Child Development*, 47 (1976), 420–426.

McGrath, L., and Scobey, J. *What Is a Mother?* New York: Simon and Schuster, 1968.

McGrath, M., and McGrath, N. *Environments for Children*. N.Y.: Morrow, 1978.

McGregor, J. Stung by criticism, TV moves to upgrade youngsters program. *Wall Street Journal*, 51:231 (September 10, 1971), 1, 13.

Mc Innis, J. H. *Family Perception as Expressed by Youth Ages 11–18.* Unpublished Doctoral dissertation, Florida State University, Tallahassee, Fla., 1972.

McKuen, R. For my son. *Lonesome Cities.* New York: Random House, 1968.

McLeod, J. M., Chaffee, S. H., and Eswara, H. S. *Family Communication Patterns and Communication Research.* A paper presented at the Association for Education in Journalism Conference, Iowa City, Iowa.

McNeal, J. U. An exploratory study of the consumer behavior of children. In J. U. McNeal (ed.), *Dimensions of Consumer Behavior.* New York: Appleton-Century-Crofts, 1965, 190–209.

McWilliams, M. *Nutrition for the Growing Years.* New York: Wiley, 1967.

Mead, M. A new understanding of childhood. *Redbook,* **138**:3 (January 1972), 49, 54.

Mead, Margaret. Anomalies in American post-divorce relationships. In Paul Bohanan (ed.), *Divorce and After.* Gardern City, N.Y.: Doubleday, 1970.

Mead, M., and Heyman, K. *Family.* New York: Macmillan, Inc., 1965.

Medinnus, G. R. Moral development in childhood. In R. G. Kuhlen and G. G. Thompson, eds., *Psychological Studies of Human Development.* New York: Appleton-Century-Crofts, 1963.

Mendelson, G., and Young, M. *Network Children's Programming: a Content Analysis of Black and Minority Treatment on Children's Television.* Boston: Action for Children's Television, 1972. (ERIC Document No. ED 067 889)

Mental Health is 1, 2, 3. Arlington, Virginia: National Association for Mental Health.

Merriam, E. *The Inner City Mother Goose.* New York: Simon and Schuster, 1969.

Messer, S. B. The effect of anxiety over intellectual performance on reflective and impulsive children. Unpublished Doctoral dissertation, Harvard University, 1968.

Miller, N. M. The attitudes toward their clothing of a selected group of eight- to twelve-year-old girls. Master's thesis, Oregon State College, 1957.

Mirandi, Alfredo. The Chicano family: a reanalysis of conflicting views. *Journal of Marriage and the Family,* **39**:4 (1977), 747–755.

Mischel, W. Processes in delay of gratification. In L. Berkowitz (ed.), *Advances in Social Psychology* (Vol. 7). New York: Academic, 1974.

Mischel, W., Ebbesen, E., and Zeiss, A. R. Cognitive and attentional mechanisms in delay of gratification. *Journal of Personality and Social Psychology,* **21** (1972), 204–218.

Mischel, W., Ebbesen, E., and Zeiss, A. R. Selective attention to the self: situational and dispositional determinants. *Journal of Personality and Social Psychology,* **22** (1973), 129–142.

Mischel, Walter, and Mischel, Harriet N. A cognitive social learning approach to morality and self-regulation. In Thomas Likona (ed.), *Moral Development and Behavior: Theory, Research, and Social Issues.* New York: Holt, Rinehart, and Winston, 1976, 84–107.

Mizer, J. E. Cipher in the snow. *NEA Journal* (November 1964), 8–10.

Molloy, John T. Tris: a health, business and governmental problem. *Tampa Tribune* (July 1976) p. 1 of feature section.

Moody, A. *Coming of Age in Mississippi.* New York: Dell, 1970.

More executives refusing to locate. *New York Times,* November 7, 1975, 1, 15.

Moreno, J. L. *Who Shall Survive?* Washington, D.C.: Nervous and Mental Disease Publishing Co., 1934.

Morgan, C. D., and Murray, H. A. A method for investigating phantasies: The thematic apperception test. *Arch. Neurol. Psychiat.,* **34** (1935), 289–306.

Moustakas, C. *The Authentic Teacher.* Cambridge, Mass.: Doyle, 1966.

Murphy, L. B. Child development now and then. In H. D. Behrens, and G. Maynard (eds.), *The Changing Child: Readings in Child Development.* Glenview, Ill.: Scott, Foresman, 1972, 3–7.

Murphy, L. B., and Morgan, C. J. A preliminary report—An individual action research method for intensive exploration of adaptive difficulties in the pre-puberty stage. *Progress Report,* USPHS Grant MH 04093-04, December 1963.

Mussen, P. H. Early socialization: learning and identification. In T. M. Newcomb (ed.), *New Directions in Psychology, III.* New York: Holt, Rinehart and Winston, 1967.

Mussen, P. H., Conger, J. J., and Kagan, J. *Child Development and Personality.* 3rd ed. New York: Harper & Row, 1969.

Napoli, P. J. Finger painting. In H. H. and G. L. Anderson, eds., *An Introduction to Projective Techniques.* Englewood Cliffs, N.J.: Prentice-Hall, 1951.

Nash, J. B. *Philosophy of Recreation and Leisure.* Dubuque: Brown Co., 1960.

National Research Council. *Toward a National Policy for Children and Families.* Washington, D.C.: National Academy of Sciences, 1976.

National Survey of Children. Foundation for Child Development, 345 East 46 Street, New York, New York 10017. Prelearning Department, 1976.

NEA Teacher Rights. Desegregation and equality. *Today's Education,* **66**:1 (January–February 1977), 22–25.

New York Times. Report: Left-handed find handicap grows. *The New York Times,* August 2, 1959.

Nunberg, H. *Principles of Psychoanalysis.* New York: International Universities Press, 1955.

Obsatz, M. Reaching and teaching the ghetto child. *Main Currents in Modern Thought,* **24**:4 (1967), 102–104.

O'Connor, P. Atkinson, J. W., and Horner, M. Motivational implications of ability groupings in schools. In J. W. Atkinson and N. T. Feather (eds.), *A Theory of Achievement Motivation.* New York: Wiley, 1966.

Oden, Sherri, and Asher, S. R. Coaching children in social skills for friendship making. *Child Development,* **48** (1977), 495–506.

Orfield, G. White flight research. *Education Forum* **40**:1 (1976), 525–536.

Orlich, D. C., and Ratcliff, J. L. Coping with the myth of accountability. *Ed. Leader,* **34** (January, 1977), 246–251.

Park, H. M. *A Study of a House of Average Rental Level in Terms of Family Living.* Unpublished Master's thesis, Cornell University, Ithaca, N.Y., 1939.

Parkhurst, H. *Exploring the Child's World.* New York: Appleton-Century-Crofts, 1951.

Parks, G. *The Learning Tree.* Greenwich, Conn.: Fawcett, 1963.

Pearson, H. A. Progress in early diagnosis of sickle cell disease. *Children,* **18**:6 (November-December 1971), 222–226.

Peckos, P. S. Nutrition during growth and development. *Child Development,* **28** (1957), 273–285.

Pedersen, Frank A. Does research on children reared in father absent families yield information on father influence? *The Family Coordinator,* **25**:4 (1976), 459–464.

Pendry, E. R., and Hartshorne, H. *Organizations for Youth.* New York: McGraw-Hill, 1935.

Pepper, F. C. Birth order. In A. G. Nikelly, ed., *Techniques for Behavior Change.* Springfield, Ill.: C. C. Thomas, 1971.

Perkins, H. V. Factors influencing changes in children's concepts. In H. D. Behrens and G. Maynard (eds.), *The Changing child: Readings in Child Development.* Glenview, Ill.: Scott, Foresman, 1972, 46–54.

Peterson, C. C. *A Child Grows Up.* New York: Alfred, 1974.

Phillips, J. L., Jr. *The Origins of Intellect: Piaget's Theory.* San Francisco: Freeman, 1969.

Piaget, J. The stages of intellectual development of the child. *Bulletin of the Menninger Clinic,* **26**:3 (1962), 120–145.

Piaget, J. Development and learning. In R. E. Ripple and V. N. Rockcastle, eds., *Piaget Rediscovered.* Ithaca, N.Y.: Cornell University Press, 1964.

Piaget, J. *The Moral Judgment of the Child.* New York: Free Press, 1965.

Piaget, Jean. *The Child and Reality.* New York: Grossman, 1973.

Piaget, Jean. *Six Psychological Studies.* New York: Random House, 1967.

Piaget, J. Piaget's theory. In P. H. Mussen, ed. *Carmichael's Manual of Child Psychology,* Vol. 1. 3rd ed. New York: Wiley, 1970, pp. 703–732.

Pien, Deana, and Rothbart, Mary K. Incongruity and resolution in children's humor: a re-examination. *Child Development,* **47** (1976), 966–971.

Pikunas, J. *Human Development: A Science of Growth.* New York: McGraw-Hill, 1961.

Pipes, P. L. *Nutrition in Infancy and Childhood.* St. Louis: Mosby, 1977.

Plionis, E. M. Family functioning and childhood accident occurrence. *American Journal Orthopsy,* **47** (April 1977), 250–263.

Plumb, J. H. The great change in children. In A. Skolnick (ed.), *Rethinking Childhood.* Boston: Little, Brown, and Co., 1976, 205–213.

Pollack, E. S. Mental health indices of family health. In *World Health Statistics Report* (Vol. 28, #7). Geneva, Switzerland: World Health Organization, 1975, 278–294.

Porter, D. G. The case against separate schools. *Clearing House,* **51** (November 1977) 125–130.

Poussaint, A. F., and Comer, J. P. The question every black parents asks: What shall I tell my child? *Redbook,* (January 1971), 64, 110–113.

Poussaint, A. F., and Comer, J. P. What white parents should know about children and prejudice. *Redbook* (May 1972), 62–63, 122–123.

Prescott, D. Role of love in human development. *Journal of Home Economics,* **44** (1952), 173–176.

Profiles of Children. Washington, D.C.: U.S. Government Printing Office, 1970.

Pulaski, M. A. S. *Understanding Piaget: An Introduction to Children's Cognitive Development.* New York: Harper & Row, 1971.

Rader, E. D. Working with your consumers in the classrooms. *Instructor,* (October 1972), 55–59.

Radloff, B. The tot in the gray flannel suit. In S. White (Ed.), *Human Development in Today's World.* Boston: Educational Associates, 1976, 274–275.

Rapaport, D., Gill, M., and Schafer, R. *Diagnostic Psychological Testing: The Theory, Statistical Evaluation, and Diagnostic Application of a Battery of Tests.* Chicago: Year Book Publ. Vol. 2, 1946.

Read, K. H. Clothes help build personality. *Journal of Home Economics,* **42** (1950), 348–350.

Redl, F. and Wineman, D. *Controls from Within.* NY: Macmillan, 1952.

Rebelsky, F., and Hands, C. Fathers' verbal interaction with infants in the first three months of life. *Child Development,* **42** (1971), 63.

Reese, H. W. Relations between self-acceptance and sociometric choices. *Journal of Abnormal and Social Psychology,* **62** (1961), 472–474.

Rest, James R. New approaches in the assessment of moral judgment. In Thomas Lickona (ed.), *Moral Development and Behavior: Theory, Research, and Social Issues.* New York: Holt, Rinehart, and Winston, 1976, 198–218.

Reuter, M. W., and Biller, H. B. Perceived paternal nurturance availability and personality adjustment among college males. *Journal of Consulting Clinical Psychology,* **40** (1973), 339.

Richardson, S. A., and Royce, J. Race and physical handicap in children's preference for other children. *Child Development,* 39:2 (June 1968), 467–480.

Riebel, L. J. A study of some ways children's activities and attitudes affect housing requirements on 188 owner-operated farms in Pennsylvania. Unpublished Master's thesis, Pennsylvania State University at University Park, 1950.

Riemer, S. Maladjustment to the family home. *American Sociological Review,* **10** (August 1945), 642–648.

Riessman, F. *The Culturally Deprived Child.* New York: Harper & Row, 1962.

Riessman, F. *Milwaukee Journal,* June 30, 1965.

Rivers, W. L., and Schramm, W. *Responsibility in Mass Communication.* Rev. ed. N.Y.: Harper & Row, 1969.

Robeck, M. C. *Infants and Children.* New York: McGraw-Hill, 1978.

Roberts, W. J., and Baker, W. M. *Footnotes on Children's Shoes.* University of Arkansas: Cooperative Extension Service Leaflet 483, 1977.

Roberts, W. J., and McKee, W. *Clothing for the Grade School Child.* University of Arkansas: Cooperative Extension Service Leaflet 493, 1976.

Rodham, H. Children under the law. In A. Skolnick (Ed.), *Rethinking Childhood.* Boston: Little, Brown and Co., 1976, 391–413.

Roff, M. B., Sells, S. B., and Golden, M. M. *Social Adjustment and Personality Development in Children,* Minneapolis: Univ. of Minn. Press, 1972.

Rogers, C. *Freedom to Learn.* Columbus, Ohio: Merrill, 1969.

Rogers, C. R. A Tentative scale for the measurement of process in psychotherapy. In I. E. Rubenstein and M. Parloff (eds.), *Research in Psychotherapy.* Washington, D.C.: American Psychological Association, 1962.

Rogers, D. *Child Psychology.* Belmont, Calif.: Brooks/Cole, 1969.

Rorschach, H. *Psychodiagnosis: A Diagnostic Test Based on Perception* 4th ed. New York: Grune and Stratton, 1942.

Rosen, B. C. Family structure and achievement motivation. *American Sociological Review,* **26** (1961), 575–585.

Rosenblatt, Paul C., and Cunningham, M. R. Television watching and family tensions. *Journal of Marriage and the Family,* 38:1 (1976), 105–111.

Rosenberg, B. G., and Sutton-Smith, B. *Sex and Identity.* New York: Holt, Rinehart and Winston, 1972.

Rosenburg, M. and Simmons, R. *Black and White Self-esteem: The Urban School Child.* Boston: American Sociological Association, 1971.

Rosenthal, R., and Jacobson, L. *Pygmalion in the Classroom,* New York: Holt, Rinehart and Winston, 1968.

Rosenheim, M. K. The child and the law. In E. H. Grotberg (ed.), *200 Years of Children.* Washington, D.C.: U.S. Department of Health, Education and Welfare (Office of Child Development), 423–486.

Ross, H. L., and Sawhill, Isabell V. *Time of Transition.* Washington, D.C.: The Urban Institute, 1976.

Rothman, Gold R. The influence of moral reasoning on behavioral choices. *Child Development,* **47** (1976), 397–406.

Rubin, M. When is Gladys Knight and the Pips art-in-education? Or Children teach the teacher how to teach. In *Demythologizing the Inner-city Child,* R. C. Granger and J. C. Young (eds.), Washington, D.C.: National Association for the Education of Young Children, 1976, pp. 59–69.

Rubin, K. H., and Scneider, F. W. The relationship between moral judgment, egocentrism, and altruistic behavior. *Child Development,* **44**:3 (1973), 661–665.

Rubinstein, E. A., Comstock, G. A., and Murray, J. P. *Television and Social Behavior.* Vol. 4: *Television and Day-to-Day Life: Patterns of Use.* Rockville, Md.: National Institute of Mental Health, 1972.

Russel, D. H. *Children's Thinking.* Boston: Ginn, 1956.

Rybash, John M., and Roodin, Paul A. A reinterpretation of the effects of videotape and verbal presentation modes on children's moral judgments. *Child Development,* **49** (1978), 228–230.

Rytina, W. H., Form, W. H., and Pease J. Income stratification ideology: beliefs about the American opportunity structure. *American Journal of Sociology,* **75** (1970), 703–716.

Sacks, J. M., and Levy, S. The sentence completion test. In L. E. Abt and L. Bellak, eds., *Projective Psychology.* New York: Knopf, 1950, pp. 358–402.

Sampson, E. E. Birth order, need achievement and conformity. *Journal of Abnormal Psychology,* **64** (1962), 155–159.

Santostefano, S. G. A developmental study of cognitive control "leveling-sharpening." *Merrill-Palmer Quarterly,* **10** (1964), 343–360.

Sarson, E. How TV threatens your child. *Parents' Magazine,* (August 1972), 39, 88, 92–93.

Saul, L. J. *The Hostile Mind.* New York: Random House, 1956.

Sax, G. *Empirical Foundations of Educational Research.* Englewood Cliffs, N.J.: Prentice-Hall, 1968.

Scarlett, Helaine H., Press, Allan N., and Crockett, Walter. Children's descriptions of peers: a Wernerian developmental analysis. *Child Development,* **42** (1971), 439–453.

Schachter, S. *The Psychology of Affiliation.* Stanford, Calif.: Stanford University Press, 1959.

Schaefer, E. S. Hypothetical circumplex model for maternal behavior. *Journal of Abnormal Social Psychology,* **59** (1959), 226–235.

Scheflin, A. A. Living space in Urban ghetto. *Family Process,* **10** (1971), 429–450.

Schlesinger, Benjamin, and Todrea, Ruben. Motherless families: an increasing societal pattern. *Child Welfare,* **55** (1976), 553–558.

Scott, F., and Myers, G. Children's empty and erroneous concepts of the commonplace. *Journal of Educational Research,* **8** (1923), 327–334.

Sears, R., Maccoby, E., and Levin, H. *Patterns of Child Rearing,* Evanston, Ill.: Row, Peterson, 1957.

Sears, R. R., Whiting, J. W. M., Nowlis, V., and Sears, P. S. Some child-rearing antecedents of aggression and dependency in young children. *Genetic Psychological Monograph,* **47** (1953), 135–236.

Second hand Smoke. American Lung Association, 1975.

Seefeldt, Carol. Young and old together. *Children Today,* (January–February 1977), 21–25.

Selman, Robert. Social-cognitive understanding: a guide to educational and clinical practice. In Thomas Lickona (ed.), *Moral Development and Behavior: Theory, Research, and Social Issues.* New York: Holt, Rinehart, and Winston, 1976, 299–316.

Serock, K., Seefeldt, C., Jantz, R. K., and Galper, A. As children see old folks. *Today's Education.* (May 1977), 6670–73.

Sewell, W. H. Social class and childhood personality. *Sociometry,* **24** (1961), 340–356.

Sheldon, W. H. *The Varieties of Human Physique.* New York: Harper & Row, 1940.

Shelton, B. O. Our stigmatized youth. *Education,* **87**:6 (February 1952), 341–342.

Shibler, H. D. Fable for school people. In E. C. Moore, Education as a social change agent, *Phi Kappa Phi Journal* (Summer 1972), 68–75.

Shneidman, E. S. *They Make a Picture Story Test.* New York: The Psychological Corporation, 1949.

Sigel, Irving E. and Cocking, Rodney R. *Cognitive Development from Childhood to Adolescence: A Constructivist Perspective.* New York: Holt, Rinehart, Winston, 1977.

Silberman, C. *Crisis in the Classroom.* New York: Random House, 1970.

Simon, S. B. Down with grades. *Today's Education,* **58**:4 (April 1969), 24.

Simon, W., and Gagnon, J. Psychosexual development. *Trans-Action* (March 1969), 9–17. Condensed from D. A. Goslin, ed., *Handbook of Socialization Theory and Research.* New York: Russel Sage Foundation, Rand McNally, 1969.

Simpson, B. J. The classification of education objectives, psychomotor domain. *Illinois Teacher of Home Economics,* **X**:4 (Winter 1966–67), pp. 110–144.

Singleton, L. C., and Asher, S. R. *Peer Preference and Social Interaction Among Third Grade Children in an Integrated School District.* Unpublished Manuscript, University of Illinois at Urbana-Champaign, 1976.

Skard, A. G. Children and war. *Delta Kappa Gamma Bulletin,* **38**:3 (Spring 1972), 33–38.

Skeels, H., and Dye, H. A study of the effect of differential stimulation on mentally retarded children. *Process of American Association on Mental Deficiency,* **44** (1939), 114–136.

Skinner, B. F. *Beyond Freedom and Dignity.* N.Y.: Knopf, 1972.

Skolnick, A. Introduction: rethinking childhood. In A. Skolnick (ed.), *Rethinking Childhood.* Boston: Little, Brown and Co., 1976, 1–15.

Sloan, W. The Lincoln-Oseretsky motor development scale. *Genetic Psychology Monographs,* **51** (1955), 183–251.

Smith, B. K. *Your Non-Learning Child*. Boston: Beacon Press, 1968.

Smith, B. K. *The Worth of a Boy*, Rev. ed. Austin, Texas: The Hogg Foundation for Mental Health, University of Texas, 1970.

Smith, Charles P. (ed.). *Achievement Related Motives in Children*. New York: Russell Sage Foundation, 1969.

Smith, G. H. Sociometric study of best liked and least liked children. *Elementary School Journal,* **51** (1950), 71–85.

Smith, G. J. The hospital is where they take care of you. *Parents Magazine,* (October 1962), p. 56.

Smith, M. E. Childhood memories compared with those of adult life. *Journal of Genetic Psychology,* **80** (1952), 151–182.

Smith, R. P. *Where Did You Go? Out. What Did You Do? Nothing.* New York: Norton, 1957.

Smith, M. E., Peck, R., and Weber, F. A consumer's guide to educational innovation. *Council for Basic Education,* Washington, D.C., 1972.

Snapper, Kurt J., Barriga, Harriet H., Baumgarner, Faye H., and Wagner, Charles S. (Eds.) *The Status of Children*. Washington, D.C.: George Washington University, Social Research Group, 1975.

Snipes, W. T. Promotion and moving. *Elementary School Journal,* **65** (May 1965), 429–433.

Soares, A. T., and Soares, L. M. Self-perceptions of culturally disadvantaged children. In H. D. Behrens and G. Maynard (eds.), *The Changing child: Readings in Child Development*. Glenview, Ill.: Scott, Foresman, 1972, 36–54.

Sontag, L. W., and Reynolds, E. L. The Fels composite sheet. I. A practical method for analyzing growth progress. *Journal of Pediatrics,* **26** (1945), 327–335.

Squeeze on the middle class. *U.S. News and World Report,* (May 2, 1977), pp. 50–57.

Statistical Abstracts (98th Edition). Washington, D.C.: U.S. Government Printing Office, 1977.

Stein, A. H., and Friedrich, L. K. Impact of television on children and youth. In E. M. Heatherington (ed.), *Review of Child Development Research* (Vol. 5). Chicago: The University of Chicago Press, 1975, 183–256.

Steinberg, S. The language of prejudice. *Today's Education* (February 14, 1971), 16–17.

Steiner, Gilbert. *The Children's Cause*. Washington, D.C.: The Brookings Institute, 1976.

Stern, W. Cloud pictures: A new method for testing imagination. *Character and Personality,* **6** (1938), 132–146.

Stirling, N. The case of the missing handshake. An American Theatre Wing Community Play. Rosslyn, Va.: National Association for Mental Health, 1952.

Stirling, N. The daily special. An American Theatre Wing Community Play. New York: Human Relations Aids, 1955.

Stinnett, N., and Kreps, C. A. Values relating to the development of character. *Journal of Home Economics,* **64**:3 (1972), 53–57.

Stith, M. *Inner City Report, Resource Supplement #24*. Manhattan, Kans.: Department of Family and Child Development, Kansas State University, HEW Contract #HSM 110–71–186, 1969.

Stone, L. J., and Church, J. *Psychology of Childhood and Adolescence.* New York: Random House, 1968.

Struve, K. Typische ablaufsformen des deutens bei 14–15 jährigen schulkindern. *Z Angrew Psycho.,* **37** (1932), 204–234.

Student attitudes toward busing in Louisville and Jefferson County. *Integrated Education,* **15** (May-June 1977), 40–43.

Sudea, Cecelia E. Historical trends in American family behavior. In Edith H. Grotberg (ed.), *200 Years of Children.* Washington, D.C.: U.S. Government Printing Office, 1976.

A summary of alternatives. NEA Task Force on Testing. *Today's Education,* **66** (March, 1977), 54–55.

Supnick, E. *Source of Information as a Factor Affecting the Impression of Others.* Unpublished doctoral dissertation, Clark University, 1967.

Sutton-Smith, B. Children at play. In Sheldon White (ed.), *Human Development in Today's World.* Boston: Educational Associates, 1976, 160–165.

Sutton-Smith, B. The role of play in cognitive development. In H. D. Behrens and G. Maynard (eds.), *The Changing child: Readings in Child Development.* Glenview, Ill.: Scott, Foresman, 1972, 305–313.

Sutton-Smith, B., Robert, J. M., and Rosenberg, B. G. Sibling association and role involvement. *Merrill Palmer Quarterly,* **10** (1964), 25–38.

Sutton-Smith, B., Rosenberg, B. G., and Morgan, E. The development of sex differences in play choices during preadolescence. *Child Development,* **34** (1963), 119–126.

Sutton-Smith, Brian, and Rosenberg, B. G. *The Sibling.* New York: Holt, Rinehart, and Winston, 1970.

Talbot, Nathan B. (ed.). *Raising children in Modern America.* Boston: Little, Brown, 1976.

Tanner, J. M. Physical growth, In P. H. Mussen, ed., *Carmichael's Manual of Child Psychology,* Vol. 1. 3rd ed. New York: Wiley, 1970, pp. 77–155.

Tanner, J. M., and Taylor, G. R. *Growth.* New York: Time-Life Books, 1969.

Tate, M. T., Glission, O., McClasky, B., and Groseclose, M. The Virginia elementary school-age child's clothing. Virginia Polytechnic Institute, 1960.

Teaching language in a Harlem school. *Trans-Action,* **7** (March 1969).

Tenezakis, Maria D. Linguistic subsystems and concrete operations. *Child Development,* **46** (1975), 430–436.

Terman, L. M. *Genetic Studies of Genius* (Vol. I-V). Stanford University Press, 1925–1959.

Terman, L. M., and Merrill, M. A. *Measuring Intelligence.* Boston: Houghton Mifflin, 1937.

Terman, L. M., and Merrill, M. A. *Stanford-Binet Intelligence Scale.* Boston: Houghton Mifflin, 1960.

Thiesing, C. B. Worries and fears of fourth-grade students in the public schools in Manhattan, Kansas. Unpublished Master's thesis, Kansas State University, 1971.

The exception. *The New Yorker Magazine* (September 18, 1954), 31.

Thompson, Vaida. Family size: implicit policies and assessed psychological outcomes. *Journal of Social Sciences,* **30**:4 (1974), 93–124.

Thoreau, H. D. *Walden.* Cleveland: World, 1942.

Thurston, L. L., and Thurstone, T. G. *Tests of Primary Mental Abilities*. Chicago: University of Chicago Press, 1938.

Todd, K. R. *Promoting Mental Health in the Classroom*. Rockville, Md.: National Institute of Mental Health, 1973.

Todhunter, E. N. Approaches to nutrition education. *Journal of Nutrition Education,* **1**:1 (September 1969), 8–9.

Toman, W. Birth order rules all. *Psychology Today* (December 1970), 45–49, 68–69.

Tomkins, S. S., and Miner, J. B. *Horn Picture Arrangement Test*. New York: Springer, 1957.

Tomlinson-Keasey, C., and Keasey C. B. The mediating role of cognitive development in moral judgment. *Child Development,* **45** (1974), 291–298.

Tooley, Kay. Antisocial behavior and social alienation post divorce: the "man of the house" and his mother. *American Journal of Orthopsychiatry,* **46**:1 (1976), 33–42.

Trubowitz, J. *Changing the Racial Attitudes of Children*. New York: Praeger, 1969.

Tryon, C. M. Evaluation of adolescent personality by adolescents. *Monographs of the Society for Research in Child Development,* **4**:4 (1939).

Tucker, H. *The Sound of Summer Voices*. New York: Stein and Day, 1969.

Ullman, C. A. Teachers, peers, and tests as predictors of adjustment. *Journal of Educational Psychology.* **48** (1957), 257–267.

Ulman, N. A. A delicate subject: Sex education courses are suddenly assailed by many parents' groups. *Wall Street Journal,* **49**:127 (April 11, 1969), 1 and 16.

United Nations Demographic Yearbook, 1973. New York: United Nations, 1974, pp. 371–372.

U.S. Bureau of the Census. *Mobility of the Population of the United States March 1970 to March 1971*. Series P-20, April 1972, #235. Washington, D.C.: U.S. Government Printing Office.

U.S. Department of Agriculture, *Food for Fitness: A Daily Food Guide*. Leaflet 424. Washington, D.C., 1967.

U.S. Department of Agriculture. *Cost of Raising a Child*, CFE-318, September 1971, Hyattsville, Md.

U.S. Department of Labor. *Working Children, A Report on Child Labor*, Bulletin #1323, April 1971.

U.S. Facilities and Programs for Children With Severe Mental Illness. Rockville, Md.: National Institute on Mental Health, 1974.

The use of stimulant drugs in treating hyperactive children. *Children,* **18**:3 (1971), 111.

Viorst, J. The hospital that has patience for its patients: a look at Children's Hospital in Washington, D.C. *Redbook,* (February 1977), pp. 48–54.

Vinacke, W. E. Concept formation in children of school age. *Education,* **74** (1954), 527–534.

Vollmer, H. Jealousy in children. *American Journal of Orthopsychiatry,* **16** (1946), 660–671.

Wadsworth, Barry J. *Piaget for the Classroom Teacher*. New York: Longman, 1978.

Wagner, R. F. *Dyslexia and Your Child: A Guide for Parents and Teachers*. New York: Harper & Row, 1971.

Wald, Michael S. Legal policies affecting children: a lawyer's request for aid. *Child Development,* **47** (1976), 1–5.

Waldrop, Mary F., and Halverson, Charles F. Jr., Intensive and extensive peer behavior: longitudinal and cross-sectional analysis. *Child Development,* **46** (1975), 19–26.

Wallace, J. Evolution of a child's chair. *Journal of Home Economics,* **70**:4 (Fall 1978), 29–30.

Wallerstein, Judith, and Kelly, Joan B. Divorce counseling: a community service for families in the midst of divorce. *American Journal of Orthopsychiatry,* **47** (1977), 4–22.

Wallerstein, J. S., and Kelly, J. The effects of parental divorce: Experiences of the preschool child. *Journal of American Academic Child Psychiatry,* **14**:4 (1975), 600–616.

Wallerstein, J., and Kelly, J. The effects of parental divorce: Experiences of the child in late latency. *American Journal of Orthopsychiatry,* **46**:2 (1976), 256–269.

Walters, J., and Stinnett, N. Parent-child relationships: A decade of research. *Journal of Marriage and the Family,* **33**:1 (1971), 70–118.

Ward, S., Reale, G., and Levinson, D. Children's perceptions, explanations and judgment of television advertising: A further explanation. In *Television and Social Behavior.* Vol IV: *Television in Day-to-Day Life.* National Institute on Mental Health, 1972.

Waring, E. B. *Principles for Child Guidance,* Extension Bulletin # 420. Ithaca, N.Y.: Cornell University, 1952.

Watson, G. Some personality differences in children related to strict or permissive parental discipline. *Journal of Psychology,* **44** (1957), 227–249.

Wechsler, D. *Wechsler Intelligence Scale for Children.* New York: Psychological Corporation, 1949.

Weinberg, G. H., and Schumaker, J. A. *Statistics, An Intuitive Approach.* Belmont, Calif.: Wadsworth, 1962.

Wellington, J. K. American education: Its failure and its future. *Phi Delta Kappan* **58** (March 1977), 527–530.

Werner, H., and Kaplan, E. Development of word meaning through verbal context: An experimental study. *Journal of Psychology,* **29** (1950), 251–257.

Westoff, L. A., and Westoff, C. F. *From Now to Zero.* Boston: Little, Brown, 1971.

Wetzel, N. C. Assessing physical condition of children: Components of the physical status and physical progress and their evaluation. *Journal of Pediatrics,* **22** (1943), 329–361.

White, B. L. *First Three Years of Life.* Englewood Cliffs, N.J.: Prentice-Hall, 1975.

White, B. L., Watts, J. C., et al. *Experience and Environment.* Englewood Cliffs, N.J.: Prentice-Hall, 1973.

White House Conference. *The Children's Charter.* New York: Century, 1933.

White House Conference on Children. *Profiles of Children.* Washington, D.C.: U.S. Government Printing Office, 1970.

White House Conference on Children, 1970. *Report to the President.* Washington, D.C.: U.S. Government Printing Office, 1970, 241–243.

Whitley, Esstoya. From time to time: a record of young children's relationships with the aged. *Research Monograph,* **17** (March 1976) (ED 128 088).

Whitney, E. and Hamilton, M. *Nutrition: Concepts and Controversies.* St. Paul: West Publishers, 1979.

Wichita City Teachers' Association. The teacher and I. *Potential,* **23,** Wichita, Kansas (1967–1968).

Wilkinson, G. S., and Bleck, R. T. Children's divorce groups. *Elementary School Guidance Counseling,* **11** (February 1977), 205–213.

Williams, H. G. Perceptual-motor development in children. In C. B. Corbin (ed.), *A Textbook of Motor Development.* Dubuque: Brown Co., 1973, 109–148.

Williams, John E., Best, Deborah, L., and Biswell, Donna A. Measurement of children's racial attitudes in the early school years. *Child Development,* **46** (1975), 494–500.

Williams, J. W. A gradient of the economic concepts of elementary school children and factors associated with cognition. *Journal of Consumer Affairs,* **4:**2 (Winter 1970), 113–123.

Wilson, E. D., Fisher, K. H., and Fuqua, M. E. *Principles of Nutrition.* New York: Wiley, 1965.

Winick, M. Introduction. In M. Winick (ed.), *Childhood Obesity.* New York: Wiley and Sons, 1975, 1–12.

Witty, P. A. Reading the comics—A comparative study. *Journal of Experimental Education,* **10** (1941), 105–109.

Winterbottom, M. R. The relation of need for achievement to learning experiences in independence and mastery. In J. W. Atkinson (ed.), *Motives in Fantasy, Action, and Society.* Princeton, N.J.: VanNostrand, 1958.

Wixan, B. N. *Children of the Rich.* New York: Crown, 1973.

Wolfenstein, M. *Children's Humor.* New York: Free Press, 1954.

Wolfenstein, M. Children's understanding of jokes. In A. R. Binter and S. H. Frey, eds., *The Psychology of the Elementary School Child.* Chicago: Rand McNally, 1972, pp. 215–226.

Wolynski, M. Confessions of a misspent youth. *Newsweek* (August 30, 1976), p. 11.

Wright, H. F. Observations on child study. In P. H. Mussen, ed., *Handbook of Research Methods in Child Development.* New York: Wiley, 1960, pp. 71–139.

Wright, R. The child proof house. *Glamour* (November 1951), 121+.

Wunderlich, R. C. *Kids, Brains and Learning.* St. Petersburg, Fla.: Reads, Inc., 1970.

Wylie, R. C. The present status of self theory. In E. F. Borgatta and W. W. Lambert (Eds), *Handbook of Personality Theory and Research.* Chicago: Rand McNally, 1968, 728–787.

Yando, R. M., and Kagan, J. The effect of teacher tempo on the child. *Child Development,* **39:**1 (March 1968), 27–34.

Yarrow, L. J. Interviewing children. In P. H. Mussen, ed., *Handbook of Research Methods in Child Development.* New York: Wiley, 1960, pp. 561–602.

Yarrow, M. R. The measurement of children's attitudes and values. In P. H. Mussen, ed., *Handbook of Research Methods in Child Development.* New York: Wiley, 1960, pp. 645–687.

Young, H. B., and Knapp, R. Personality characteristics of converted left-handers. *Perceptual and Motor Skills,* **23** (1965), 35–40.

Your Child's Teeth, Rev. Chicago: American Dental Society, S7B, 1962.

Yorburg, B. Sexual identity; sex roles and social change. New York: Wiley, 1974.

Zeligs, R. Children's attitudes toward annoyances. In H. D. Behrens and G. Maynard (eds.), *The Changing child: Readings in Child Development.* Glenview, Ill.: Scott, Foresman, 1972, 117–129.

Zimiles, H. Classification and inferential thinking in children of varying ages and social class. Paper presented at the Symposium on Comparative Studies of Conceptual Functioning in Young Children, American Psychological Meeting, San Francisco, 1968. Cited in Smart and Smart, 1967.

Zukerman, Paul, Ziegler, Mark, and Stevenson, Harold W. Children's viewing of television and recognition memory of commercials. *Child Development,* **49** (1978), 96–104.

Name Index

A

Abel, J. D., 82
Abraham, W., 172
Ack, M., 408
Adams, R. L., 128
Adorno, T. W., 529
Agan, T., 462
Agee, J., 41, 553
Aginsky, B. W., 133
Allen, L. (MacFarlane), 348, 351
Allinsmith, W., 429
Allred, G. H., 500
Almy, M., 366
Amatruda, C. (Gesell), 22
Ames, L. B. (Gesell), 478, 546
Andres, D. (Gold), 97
Angove, R., 93
Ansbacher, H. L., 126
Ansbacher, R. R. (Ansbacher, H.), 126
Arbuthnot, M. H., 74, 75, 408
Ariès, P., 39
Armor, D. J., 168
Asher, S. R. (Oden), 204
Ashton-Warner, S., 185, 408
Askins, J., 397
Atkinson, J. W., 338, 339
Axline, V., 41

B

Baer, D. M. (Bijou), 21
Baker, E. (Lovett), 268
Baker, H. V., 392, 410
Baker, W. M. (Roberts), 459
Bandura, A., 81, 429, 431, 432
Barrett, C., 70
Barth, R. S., 187
Battelle, P., 380
Baumrind, D., 112
Bayer, L. M. (Bayley), 256
Bayley, N., 22, 29, 256
Beach, D. R. (Flavell), 399
Beard, R. M., 384, 385, 387, 389, 390, 391, 393
Beatty, J., 413
Becker, W. C., 488, 489, 491
Bee, H., 496
Behrens, H. D., 11
Bell, R. R., 52
Bellak, L., 16
Beman, A. (Goodman), 69
Benell, F. B., 535
Bennett, W. J., 85
Berenda, R. W., 21, 202
Berlyn, D. E., 380
Best, D. L. (Williams), 66
Bettleheim, B., 275, 276
Bigelow, B. J., 208
Bigner, J. J., 116, 206, 207, 513
Bijou, S. W., 21
Biller, H. B., 115, 116
Bird, B., 281
Biskin, D. S., 429
Biswell, D. A. (Williams), 66
Blaine, G. B., 121
Blair, A. W., 110, 483, 527

Bleck, R. T. (Wilkinson), 38
Bledsoe, J. C., 323
Blood, R. O., 122
Bloom, B. S., 175, 185, 325
Bluebond-Langner, M., 545
Bluefarb, S. M., 247
Bocks, W. M., 165
Boehm, L., 218
Bolstad, O. D., 164
Boroson, W., 126
Bousfield, W. A., 351
Bowlby, J., 542, 543
Bowman, P. H. (Havighurst), 22
Brazelton, T. B., 85, 117
Brearley, M., 420, 421
Breckenridge, M. E., 245, 248, 273
Breland, H. M., 128
Brewer, A., 166
Bridges, K. M., 340, 341
Broderick, C. B., 337
Brodzinsky, D. M., 162
Bronfenbrenner, U., 96, 102, 125, 196, 508, 510
Brown, C., 41
Brown, D. G., 337
Brown, I. D. (Bledsoe), 331
Bruner, J. S., 86, 513
Buhler, J. H. (Hicks), 154
Burton, R. V., 416
Burton, W. H. (Blair), 110, 483, 527
Butcher, J., 347

C

Caldwell, B. M., 9
Caratz, J. C., 398
Cartwright, D. (Gordon), 432
Caspari, E., 32
Cassidy, M. L., 458
Chaffee, S. H., 82
Chinsky, J. M. (Flavell), 299
Chilman, C. D., 50, 58, 63, 414
Church, J. (Stone), 196
Clark, A. (Garn), 238
Clark, D. C. (Garn), 262
Clark, K. B., 529, 530, 532, 553
Clifford, E., 481, 482, 505, 506

Coates, B., 528
Coburn, J., 166
Cole, L., 188
Coleman, J. S., 51, 168
Coles, R., 53, 54, 85, 328, 553
Comer, J. P. (Poussaint), 329, 553
Conger, J. J. (Mussen), 85, 152, 308, 369, 414
Condry, J., 197
Coopersmith, S., 198
Corbin, C. B., 287, 290, 301
Corey, S. M., 188
Corsini, R. J., 307, 308, 309
Cottle, T. J., 39
Cowen, E., 182
Cratty, B. J., 286
Croake, J. W., 349
Crockett, W. (Scarlett), 205, 206
Cruickshank, W. M., 278
Cullen, C., 66
Cunningham, M. R. (Rosenblatt), 84

D

D'Amico, L. A. (Eaton), 478
Davidson, B., 513
Davis, A., 22
Davis, C. M., 263
Day, S. S., 463
Decker, S., 185
DeFee, J. F., 126, 127
Dennis, W., 46
Dennison, G., 185
Devereux, E. C. (Bronfenbrenner), 196
Dinkmeyer, D. C., 126, 500
Dobb, L. W. (Dollard), 346
Dobbs, V., 165
Dodge, L., 183
Dollard, J., 346
Dornbusch, S. M. (Goodman), 278
Dreikurs, R., 126, 500, 513
Drillien, G. M., 259
Duberman, L., 121, 122
Duckett, C. L., 273
Durrant, G. D., 468
Duvall, E., 132
Dye, H. (Skeels), 46

E

Eaton, M. T., 478
Ebbesen, E. (Mischel), 433
Edelman, M. W. (Cottle), 39
Edwards, M. (Gough), 530
Elkind, D., 160, 372, 439, 440, 441, 502
Ender, P. B. (Kagan), 503
Engel, M., 16, 317
Entwisle, D. R. (Feinman), 211
Epstein, S. L. (Landau), 85, 133, 185, 228, 301, 357, 444, 470, 513
Erikson, E. H., 310
Erickson, J. (Coles), 54
Espanshade, T. J., 449
Eysenck, H. J., 308

F

Francher, E. C., 16
Farber, B., 128
Farnham-Diggory, S., 394, 395
Farr, R., 161
Feather, N. T. (Atkinson), 338
Fedder, R., 218
Feingold, B. F., 277
Feinman, S., 211
Fellows, M., 158
Fenwick, J. J., 147
Ferguson, C. P., 80
Feshbach, S., 345, 347
Finkelstein, I. E., 188
Finlayson, H. J., 165
Fisher, K. H. (Wilson), 260, 269
Flatt, A. E., 246
Flavell, J. H., 372, 373, 374, 375, 376, 377, 380, 385, 386, 388, 399, 520, 521, 522
Fleck, H., 260, 269
Flescher, I., 369
Ford, J. (Gries), 463
Form, W. H. (Ratina), 64
Freidman, M., 355
Frenkel-Brunswik, E., 530, 532
Frenkel-Brunswik, E. (Adorno), 529
Freud, S., 308, 533
Friedrich, L. K., 81, 82, 83

Fromm, J., 274
Frost, J. L., 300
Fry, E., 74, 75
Fuqua, M. E. (Wilson), 260, 269

G

Gagne, R. M., 552
Gagnon, J. (Simon), 338
Gallup, G. H., 157
Galper, A. (Serock), 531
Garbarino, J., 124, 125
Gardner, R. A., 538
Gardner, R. W., 400
Garn, S. M., 238, 257, 258, 262
Gendel, E. S., 535
Gerald, H. B., 128
Gerard, H. B. (Jones), 198
Gerbner, G., 72, 80
Gesell, A., 22, 478, 546
Gibbs, R. K. (Maccoby), 22
Gibran, K., 366, 513
Gil, D. G., 51, 124
Gildea, M. C., 104
Gill, M. (Rapaport), 15
Ginott, H., 513
Ginsberg, H., 371, 372, 373, 375, 379
Glasser, W., 38
Glick, P. C., 95, 97, 101, 102
Glidewell, J. C. (Gildea), 104
Glisson, O. (Tate), 458
Glucksberg, S. (Krauss), 391, 392
Godfrey, E., 165
Gold, D., 97
Goldberg, M. L., 152
Goldstein, J., 39
Goodman, M. E., 69, 327
Goodman, N., 278
Goodwin, W. (Klausmeier), 178
Gordon, I. J., 315, 325, 524
Gordon, R., 432
Gordon, T., 500, 513
Gough, H. B., 530
Graves, D., 483
Green, G., 41
Greening, T. C. (Allinsmith), 429
Greenfield, J., 357

Greenstein, F. I., 552
Greulich, W. W., 257
Grey, L. (Dreikurs), 500
Grief, E. B. (Kurtines), 428, 429
Gries, J. M., 463
Griffin, J., 445
Grim, P. F., 433
Grimm, J., 444
Grollman, E. A., 133
Gronlund, N. E., 202, 203, 215
Gropper, N. B. (Lee), 329
Groseclose, M. (Tate), 458
Gross, D. W., 160
Gross, L. P. (Gerbner), 80
Grotberg, E. H., 9
Grottman, J. M., 203
Gruenberg, S., 546, 549
Guire, K. E. (Garn), 262

H

Haber, R. N., 399
Haber, R. B. (Haber), 399
Haley, E. G., 458
Halverson, C. F. (Waldrop), 209
Hamilton, M. (Whitney), 300
Hamovitch, M. B., 282
Hample, S. (Marshall), 444, 553
Han, P. W. (Hirsch), 262
Harper, R., 443
Harris, J. A., 236
Harris, D. B. (Gough), 530
Hartshorne, H., 415
Harvey, J. (Iscoe), 202
Harvey, K., 143
Harvey, O. J., 520
Hastorf, A. H. (Goodman), 278
Hathaway, M. I., 257
Havighurst, R. J., 22, 34, 35, 133, 168, 308
Hawkes, G. R., 173, 227
Heil, L. M., 153
Hendrickson, N. J. (Haley), 458
Hendrickson, N. (Lehr), 72
Henry, W. E., 15
Herron, R. E., 253, 255
Herzog, E., 14, 115
Hess, R. D., 46, 65, 104, 550, 551

Heyman, K. (Mead), 203
Hickey, T., 540
Hicks, L. H., 153
Hildreth, G., 293
Hill, S. J., 67
Hilton, I., 128
Himelstein, P. (De Fee), 126, 127
Himmelweit, H. T., 78, 83
Hirsch, J., 32, 262
Hitchfield, E. (Brearly), 420, 421
Hoffman, L. W. (Hoffman), 489
Hoffman, M. L., 429, 430, 432, 434, 435, 436, 489
Hogan, R. A., 429
Holmes, F. B., 348
Holt, J., 39, 158, 185, 407
Honzig, M. P., 368
Honzig, M. P. (MacFarlane), 348, 351
Horner, M. (O'Conner), 339
Hoskisson, K. (Biskin), 427, 429
Horton, L. (Harvey), 143
Howath, B., 444
Howe, J., 556
Hoyt, K. B., 470
Hunt, D. E. (Harvey), 520
Hunt, L. A., 457
Hunt, J. McV., 46
Hurlock, E., 31, 79, 84, 270, 272, 285, 355
Hymes, J., 496

I

Ilg, F. L. (Gesell), 478, 546
Irelan, L. M., 62, 63, 64, 113
Iscoe, I., 202

J

Jackson, E. N., 542
Jackson, P. W., 505
Jacobson, L. (Rosenthal), 370
Jantz, R. K. (Serock), 539
Jayaswal, S. R., 401
Jeanneret, O., 273
Jenks, C., 51

Jennings, M. K., 104
Jensen, A. R., 47
Jersild, A. T., 326, 350, 401
Johnson, B. E., 462
Johnson, G. O., 173, 278
Johnson, R. C., 17, 223
Johnson, S. M. (Bolstad), 164
Jones, E. E., 198
Jordan, F., 186
Joseph, S. M., 85
Jourard, S. M., 313, 314, 353
Justus, M., 444

K

Kadis, A., 401
Kagan, J., 7, 8, 47, 48, 85, 152, 308, 346,
    369, 399, 400, 401, 407, 408, 486, 414
Kagan, S., 503
Kalish, R. R. (Hickey), 540
Kantor, M. B. (Gildea), 104
Kaplan, E. (Werner), 396
Kaplan, F. T., 295, 296, 297
Kastenbaum, R., 553
Keasey, C. B., 425, 426
Keeney, A. H., 173
Keeney, V. T. (Keeney), 173
Kelly, J., 119, 120
Keniston, K., 55, 58, 59, 65
Kennedy, C. D., 507
Kifer, E., 443
Kimmel, C., 156
Kinsey, A. C., 330
Kirkendall, L. A., 337, 536
Kirsten, G. G., 52
Klapper, J. T., 77
Klausmeier, H. J., 178
Kleck, R. E., 210
Klein, B. L. (Frost), 300
Knapp, R. (Young), 293
Knepp, T. H., 249
Koch, H. L., 128, 351
Kogan, N. (Kagan), 399, 400, 401
Kohlberg, L., 310, 414, 415, 421, 422, 423,
    424, 425, 426, 427, 433, 444
Kohn, M. L., 435
Korn, S. J. (Lerner), 256

Kozol, J., 185
Krauss, R. M., 391, 392
Krebs, R. L., 416
Kreps, C. A. (Stinnett), 438
Kronus, S., 55
Kubler-Ross, E., 542, 543
Kurtines, W., 428, 429
Kurtz, R. M., 256

L

Lamb, M., 116
Landau, E. D., 85, 133, 185, 228, 301, 357,
    444, 470, 513
Landers, A., 152, 153
Landis, J. T., 117
Landkof, L. (Garn), 238
Landreth, C., 63, 259
Lane, B., 555
Larramore, D. (Hoyt), 470
Larrick, N., 76
Lasko, J. K., 128
Lee, H., 160
Lee, P. C., 329
Lehane, S., 161
Lehr, C. J., 72
LeMasters, E. E., 52, 108
Lerner, R. M., 256
LeShan, E. J., 8
Lesser, G., 80, 83
Levin, H. (Sears), 111, 430, 486, 346
Levine, D. U., 168
Levine, M. E., 272
Levinson, D. J. (Adorno), 529
Levinson, D. (Ward), 76, 77, 79
Levy, S. (Sacks), 16
Lewis, O., 61, 63, 64
Licht, L. A., 347
Liddle, G. P. (Havighurst), 22
Liebert, R. M., 85
Lindzey, G., 15
Lippitt, R., 493
Lobenz, N. M., 179
Lovett, R., 268
Luchsinger, E. (Agan), 462
Luria, A. R., 388
Lynn, D. B., 332, 334

M

Maccoby, E. (Sears), 22, 111, 346, 430, 486
MacDonald, A. P., 128
MacFarlane, J., 348, 351
Machover, K., 16
Madsen, Charles, 501, 513
Madsen, Clifford (Madsen), 501, 513
Magruder, L. (Marshall), 546
Maier, H. W., 375, 376
Mallick, S. K., 347
Mangum, G. L. (Hoyt), 470
Marcus, B. (Lovett), 268
Marcus, M. G., 324
Marshall, E., 444, 553
Marshall, H. R., 546
Martin, B., 113, 114, 128
Martin, C. E. (Kinsey), 330
Martin, E. A., 243, 260
Martin, P. C., 247, 285
Martin, W. E. (Gough), 530
Maslow, A., 205, 308, 310, 314
Massey, J. (Jordan), 186
Matthews, G. V. (Havighurst), 22
Maurer, A., 349
May, M. A. (Hartshorne), 415
Mayer, J., 263
Maynard, G. (Behrens), 11
McCandless, B. R., 54, 62, 315, 317, 322, 347, 414
McClasky, B. (Tate), 458
McClendon, P. E., 164
McCullough, C., 444
McDaniel, C. G., 454
McDonald, M., 327, 553
McGrath, L., 133
McGrath, M., 471
McGrath, N. (McGrath), 471
McGregor, J., 456
McInnis, J. H., 105
McKay, G. D. (Dinkmeyer), 500
McKee, W. (Roberts), 459
McKuen, R., 513
McLeod, J. M. (Chaffee), 82
McNeal, J. U., 451
McWilliams, M., 269
Mead, M., 203, 275
Medinnus, G. R., 17, 222, 418, 419

Mendelson, G., 83
Merriam, E., 85
Merrill, M. A. (Terman), 366, 367, 368, 546
Messer, S. B., 400
Miller, N. E. (Dollard), 346
Miller, N. M., 458
Miner, J. B. (Tomkins), 16
Mirandi, A., 68
Mischel, H. N. (Mischel), 431, 432
Mischel, W., 431, 432, 433
Mizer, J. E., 358
Molloy, J. T., 460
Moody, A., 41
Moorefield, T. E. (Havighurst), 168
Moreno, J. L., 212
Morgan, C. J. (Murphy), 181
Morgan, E. (Sutton-Smith), 210
Morgan, C. D., 16
Moriarty, A. (Gardner), 400
Moss, H. A. (Kagan), 346
Moustakas, C., 185
Mower, O. H. (Dollard), 346
Munves, E. (Fleck), 260, 269
Murphy, L. B., 11, 181
Murray, H. A. (Morgan), 16
Mussen, P. H., 85, 152, 308, 369, 414
Myers, G., 391

N

Napoli, P. J., 16
Nash, J. B., 291
Neale, J. M. (Liebert), 85
Neville, D. (Dobbs), 165
Newell, L. (Garn), 238
Niemi, R. G. (Jennings), 104
Noble, H. (Barrett), 70
Numberg, H., 345

O

Obsatz, M., 507
O'Connor, P., 339
Oden, S., 204
Oppenheimer, A. N. (Himmelweit), 78, 83

Opper, S. (Ginsberg), 371, 372, 373, 375, 379
Orbison, W. D. (Bousfield), 351
Orfield, G., 168
Orlich, D. C., 155

P

Parkhurst, H., 19, 89, 111, 444
Parks, G., 41
Pearson, H. A., 275
Pease, D. (Hawkes), 173, 227
Pease, J. (Rytina), 64
Peck, R. (Smith), 145
Peckos, P. S., 252
Pederson, F., 116
Pepper, F. C., 126
Perkins, H. V., 326
Peterson, C. C., 42
Phillips, B. N. (Eaton), 478
Phillips, B. N. (Adams), 128
Phillips, J. L., 381, 383, 385
Piagét, J., 206, 310, 371, 372, 373, 376, 377, 378, 379, 380, 381, 386, 387, 416, 417, 419, 421, 423, 424
Pierce, J. W. (Havighurst), 22
Pikunas, J., 33
Pinson, N. M. (Hoyt), 470
Pipes, P. L., 300
Plionis, E. M., 272
Plumb, J. H., 6, 7
Pollack, C., 444
Pomeroy, W. B. (Kinsey), 330
Porter, D. G., 166
Poussaint, A. F., 329, 553
Prescott, D., 352
Press, A. N. (Scarlett), 205, 206
Pulaski, M. A. S., 372, 378, 379

R

Rabbie, J. M. (Gerald), 128
Rader, E. D., 452
Radloff, B., 179
Rapaport, D., 15
Ratcliff, J. L. (Orlich), 155

Raymond, L. (Jeanneret), 273
Raynor, J. O. (Atkinson), 338
Read, K. H., 457
Reale, G. (Ward), 76, 77, 79
Redl, F., 515
Reese, H. W., 202
Reimer, S., 461
Rest, J. R., 426, 427
Reuter, M. W., 116
Reynolds, E. L. (Sontag), 253
Richardson, S. A. (Goodman), 278
Richardson, S. A., 201
Richardson, S. A. (Kleck), 210
Riebel, L. J., 461
Riessman, F., 61, 87
Rivers, W. L., 72, 73, 84
Robeck, M. C., 325
Roberts, W. J., 459
Rodgers, G. J. (Bronfenbrenner), 196
Rodham, H., 38, 39
Roffwarg, H. P., 271
Rogers, C., 148, 185, 195, 208, 314, 340, 355
Rogers, D., 202, 203
Rohmann, C. G. (Garn), 257, 258
Ronald, L. (Kleck), 210
Rorschach, H., 15
Rosenberg, M., 324
Rosenberg, B. G. (Sutton-Smith), 128, 130, 210, 329
Rosenblatt, P. C., 84
Rosenheim, M. K., 38
Rosenman, R. H. (Freidman), 355
Rosenthal, R., 370
Ross, D. (Bandura), 81
Ross, S. A. (Bandura), 81
Rothman, G. R., 425
Royce, J. (Richardson), 201
Rubin, M., 360, 555
Rubin, I. (Kirkendall), 337
Russell, D. H., 524
Rytina, W. H., 64

S

Sacks, J. M., 16
Saltzstein, H. D. (Hoffman), 432, 435

Sanford, R. N. (Adorno), 529
Santostefano, S. G., 400
Sarson, E., 470
Saul, L. J., 345
Sax, G., 30
Sayegh, Y. (Dennis), 46
Scarlett, H., 205, 206, 207
Schachter, S., 128
Schaefer, E. S., 487, 488
Schafer, R. (Rapaport), 15
Schramm, W. (Rivers), 72, 73, 83
Schroder, H. M. (Harvey), 520
Schumaker, J. A. (Weinberg), 30
Scobey, J. (McGrath), 133
Scott, F., 391
Sears, R., 111, 346, 430, 486
Seefeldt, C., 540, 539
Selman, R., 424
Serock, K., 539
Sewell, W. H., 104
Sheldon, W. H., 254
Shibler, H. D., 187
Shneidman, E. S., 16
Short, J. (Gordon), 432
Sigel, I. E., 373, 377, 386, 387
Silberman, C., 158, 159, 185
Siman, M. L. (Condry), 197
Simmons, B. (Rosenberg), 324
Simon, M. D., 237
Simon, S. B., 188
Simon, W., 338
Simpson, B. J., 290
Skard, A. G., 554
Skeels, H., 46
Skinner, B. F., 85
Skolnick, A., 7, 8
Sloan, W., 292
Smith, B. K., 174, 182, 183
Smith, G. H., 202
Smith, M. E., 145, 400, 401
Smith, R. P., 228
Snapper, K. J., 70, 98, 164, 478, 480, 499
Snipes, W. T., 180
Soares, A. T., 323
Soares, L. M. (Soares), 323
Sontag, L. W., 253
Stein, A. H., 81, 82, 83
Steinberg, S., 444, 553
Stern, W., 15, 357

Stinnett, N., 438
Stinnett, N. (Walters), 491
Stirling, N., 132, 342, 513
Stith, M., 58
Stoltz, V. (Dreikurs), 513
Stone, A. P. (Landau), 85, 133, 185, 228, 301, 357, 444, 470, 513
Stone, L. J., 196
Strodtbeck, F. (Gordon), 432
Struve, K., 15
Suci, G. J. (Bronfenbrenner), 196
Sudea, C. E., 91
Sudia, C. D. (Herzog), 115
Supnick, E., 206
Sutton-Smith, B., 128, 130, 210, 294, 298, 329

T

Talbot, N. B., 92, 101, 108
Tanner, J. M., 235, 238, 244, 248, 259, 279
Tate, M. T., 458
Taylor, G. R. (Tanner), 235
Terman, L. M., 175, 366, 367, 368, 546
Thiesing, C. B., 349
Thoreau, H. D., 181
Thurstone, L. L., 366
Thurstone, T. G. (Thurstone), 366
Thuwe, I. (Forssman), 123
Todd, K. R., 355
Toman, W., 126
Tomkins, S. S., 16
Tomlinson-Keasey, C., 425
Tryon, C. M., 215
Tucker, H., 444

U

Ullman, C. A., 204

V

Vinacke, W. E., 524
Vince, P. (Himmelweit), 78, 83

Vincent, E. L. (Breckenridge), 245, 248, 273
Vincent, E. L. (Martin), 247, 285
Viorst, J., 282
Vollmer, H., 351

W

Wadsworth, B. J., 373, 388
Waggoner, D. (Hill), 67
Wagner, R. F., 173, 174
Wald, M., 85
Waldrop, M. F., 209
Wallace, J., 463
Wallerstein, J. S., 119, 120
Walters, J., 491
Walters, R. H. (Bandura), 431
Ward, S., 76, 77, 79
Waring, E. B., 505
Washburne, C. (Heil), 153
Watson, G., 490
Watts, J. C. (White), 144
Weber, F. A. (Smith), 145
Wechsler, D., 366
Weinberg, G. H., 30
Weinstein, G., 470
Weinstein, M. A. (Fancher), 16
Wellington, J. K., 162
Werner, H., 396
Westoff, C. G. (Westoff), 124
Westoff, L. A., 124
Wetzel, N. C., 253
White, B. L., 143, 144
White, S. H. (Grim), 433
White, R. K. (Lippette), 493

Whitley, E., 540
Whitney, E., 300
Wilkinson, G. S., 538
Williams, H. G., 291
Williams, J. E., 66
Williams, J. W., 556
Wilson, E. D., 260, 269
Wineman, D. (Redl), 515
Winick, M., 262
Witty, P. A., 77
Wixen, B. N., 52, 53
Wolfe, D. N. (Blood), 122
Wolfenstein, M., 401, 406, 407
Wolynski, M., 158
Wright, H. F., 22
Wunderlich, R. C., 170, 171, 275, 277, 293
Wylie, R. C., 313, 314

Y

Yando, R. M., 152
Yarrow, L. J., 19
Yarrow, M. R., 17
Yorburg, B., 96, 330
Young, H. B., 293
Young, M. (Mendelson), 83

Z

Zeiss, A. R. (Mischel), 433
Zeligs, R., 331
Zimiles, H., 393

Subject Index

A

Accidents, 272
Accident proneness, 272
Acculturation, 84-85, 195-199
Achievement motivation, 338-339
Adaptation: accommodation and assimilation, 373-374
Advertising, *see* Television; Money
Aggression, 345-347
Aging, 539-541, 555-556
Allergy, 277-278
Allowance, 547-549
Androgyny, 256-257
Anger, 281, 343-345, 361, 542
Animism, 384, 527
Anxiety, 338, 350
Artificialism, 384
Autonomy, 311

B

Basic Four Food Groups, 264-266
Behavior modification, 501-502
Black English, 397-398
Body changes, 233-252
Body configuration, 237

C

Camping, 219-221
Canalization, 279

Career education, 470, 519
Centering, 382-383
Child abuse, 124-125, 498-499
Child development, field of study, 9-13
Child-rearing, 7-9, 324-325, 336, 415, 430-438, 508-512; costs of, 449-450; *see also* Guidance and Discipline
Children's rights, 37-39, 42, 111-112
Clothing, 456-459
Clubs, 195, 210-211; *see also* Youth organizations
Cognitive development, *see* Mental development
Comics, 76-78
Communication, *see* Language and communication
Competition, 178-179
Concept development, 36-37, 520-528
Concrete operations, 377-378, 385-390
Conformity, 202-203
Conscience, 37, 414
Consumer education, *see* Money
Corporal punishment, 277, 497-498, 504
Cost of a child, 449-450
Cultural deprivation, 59-60
Cultural influences, 48-69, 397-398, 503
Curiosity, 407-409

D

Death, 282-283, 541-545, 553
Development, 73, 103, 224-227; *see also* Growth; Emotional development; Men-

Development (*continued*)
tal development; Moral development; Physical development; Social development; Developmental principles and tasks
Developmental principles, 30-34, 40
Developmental tasks, 34-37, 48
Digestive system, 247
Discipline, 414, 429-437, 476, 497; corporal punishment, 497-498, 504; ignoring, 500; isolation, 499; love withdrawal, 430-431, 437; parental affection, 431, 488-490; power assertion, 430-436, 489-490; *see also* Guidance
Diseases, 273-278
Divorce, 117-123, 349, 537-539
Drugs, 479-480
Dyslexia, 173-174
Dysgradia, 52

E

Ears, 247
Education, 141-190, 390-395, 408-409, 504-505, 508; ability grouping, 339; alternative education, 158-160, 181-185; approaches, 145-147; back-to-basics, 161-162; busing, 166-168; competition, 178-179; failure, 164-165, 180, 358-359; financing, 154-155; gifted, 175-176; handicapped, 168-170; home-school cooperation, 143-144, 149-152, 177, 184; issues, 154-176; learning disabilities, 170-175; minority education, 165-167; parent involvement, 155-156; privacy, 157-158; readiness, 143-144, 186; retention, 164-165, 180; sex education, 534-535; student evaluation, 162-164, 179-180, 188-190; teacher roles, 147-154, 177; vandalism, 155; violence, 155
Egocentrism, 381-382
Emotional development, 80-81, 112, 340-360; affection, 352-353; aggression, 345-347; anger, 343-345, 360, 542; boredom, 350-351; excitement, 360; fear, 347-350; grief, 542-544; love, 352-353, 360; jealousy, 351-352; joy, 353-354, 360; pressure, 482, 483; worry, 338, 347-349
Endocrine system, 233-235
Entitlement, 53
Experimental laboratory, 21
Equilibration, 380
Eyes, 80, 247-248

F

Failure, 164-165, 180, 338-339, 358-359, 507
Family, 91-136, 503; child's view of, 104-107, 133, 477-478, 504, 519, 539-541; council, 500; composition, 97-104, 491; divorce, 117-123; father absence, 115-117; housing, 460-462; one-parent, 114-117; ordinal position, 126-130, 133-134; planning, 123-124; siblings, 105, 130-132; tension, 84
Family council, 500
Family planning, 123-124
Fathering-father absence, 115-117, 119, 332, 435
Fatty tissue, 246, 262
Fear, 280, 281, 347-350, 507, 543
Fels Composite Sheet, 253-254
Food and nutrition, 259-270; food selection, 263-266, 504; nutrients, 260-261; nutrition education, 268-269; obesity, 261-263; school food service, 265-268
Friends, 205-212, 299; *see also* Peers
Formal operations, 377, 390

G

Generativity, 312
Geographic locale, 69-72
Gifted children, 175-176
Group interview, 19-20
Growth, 32, 33, 224-227, 258; assessment, 252-259; physical, 233-252, rates, 33; *see also* Development
Growth hormone, *see* Somatotrophin
Guidance, 52-53, 62, 73, 104, 106, 108, 110, 112, 134-135, 269, 278, 324-325,

468, 475-515, 534; natural consequences, 500; parental personality, 486-492; special tasks, 483-486; styles, 492-495; techniques, 495-503; verbal appeals, 500; *see also* Discipline and Parenting

H

Handicaps, 168-170, 278
Hand preference, *see* Laterality
Happiness, 353-354
Health, 270-272
Height, 238-243
Heredity and environment, 7, 32, 45-46, 257, 285, 290, 371, 381, 496
History of childhood, 6-9, 235
Hoarding, 549
Hospitalization, 280-283, 302
Housing, 460-464
Humor, 401-407
Hyperactivity, Hyperkineticism, 275, 277

I

Identity, 312
Illness and injury, 272-283, 459-460, 464-467
IQ, 46-47, 366-370; computation, 367; distribution, 367; moral conduct, 414; tests, 366-369
Independence, 37, 200, 221, 284, 483-484
Industry, 311-312
Initiative, 311
Integrity, 312
Intellect, *see* IQ and Mental development
Interview, 18-20
Intimacy, 312

J

Jealousy, 130-132, 351, 352
Jobs, *see* Work

Jokes, *see* Humor
Joy, 353-354
Justice, 419-420
Juxtaposition, 383-384

L

Language and communication, 66-67, 385, 391-393, 395-399, 406
Laterality, 291-294
Learning disabilities, 170-175; dyslexia, 173-174; hyperkineticism, 275, 277
Lessons, 221-223
Leveling-sharpening, 400
Listening, 78-79
Little League, 219
Little League elbow, 244
Love, 352-353, 360, 430-431, 490

M

Magazines, 76
Mass media, 72-84, 88, 104, 527, 535
Masturbation, 337
Maternal employment, *see* Working mothers
Memory, 399-401, 523
Mental development, 365-410, 527; adaptation: accommodation and assimilation, 373-374; animism, 384, 527; artificialism, 384; centration, 382-383; classification, 385-386, 393-394; concepts, 365, 442-443, 517-556; concrete operations, 377-378, 385-390; curiosity, 407-409; decalage, 387-388; egocentrism, 381-382, 388, 417; equilibration, 380; experience, 378-379, 393-395, 408, 523, 526, 540, 545; formal operations, 377, 390; humor, 401-407; IQ, 366-370, 409-410; intelligence, 365-372, 525; juxtaposition, 383-384; language, 393-399, 406; leveling-sharpening, 400; maturation, 378; measurement, 366-371; memory, 399-401; nominal realism, 384;

Mental development (*continued*)
Piaget's theory, 371-390; preoperational thought, 377-378, 381-385; reasoning, 371-381, 389; reversibility, 384, 386; seriation, 386-387; social transmission, 379-380; syncretism, 384; terms in Piaget's theory, 373-376; transduction, 383; transivity, 387; verbal reasoning, 389

Mental health, 340, 355-357, 480

Mental retardation, *see* Learning disabilities

Minority groups, 51, 59, 166-169; *see also* Social class, Skin color, Prejudice

Mobility, 54-55, 70-72

Money, 449-472, 504-505, 545-550, 555; advertising, 452-456, 519; allowance, 547-549; children as consumers, 450-452; child labor laws, 469; work, 467-471, 547, 549-550

Moral development, 37, 413-444, 484-485, 506-507; cognitive, developmental approach, 416-429; honesty, 415-418, 433, 438, 445, 504; justice, 419-420; Kohlberg's theory, 421-427; parental affection, 431; Piaget's theory, 417-420, 423; role of religion, 439-443; rules, 417; social learning approach, 429-439, 445

Motivation, 285; achievement motivation, 338-339

Motor development, 35, 283-290, 292; flexibility, 287; impulsion, 287; precision, 288; speed, 288; strength, 286-287; tests of, 286, 292

Movies, 79

Muscle growth, 244, 290, 286-287

Myths of education, 176-180, 185-186; of parenthood, 108

N

Natural consequences, 500

Needs (basic needs by Maslow), 308, 310

Nervous system, 246

Newspapers, 76

Nutrition, *see* Food and Nutrition

O

Obesity, 261-263

Observation, 21, 26, 42

One-parent family, 114-117

Ordinal position, 126-130, 133-134, 336; first-born, 126-129; last born, 127-128; latter-borns, 128-129; middle child, 127; only child, 127

Orthodontic treatment, 252

P

Parenting, 107-114, 139-140, 475-515; concepts of parenting education, 510-512; myths of parenthood, 108; role of parental personality in guidance, 486-492

Peers, 36, 195-230, 283, 336, 483-484, 508, 513-514, 519; friendship, 205-212; functions, 198-205; group acceptance, 200-205; sociometry, 204, 212-216, 229

Perceptual, motor development, 290-294

Personality, 307-357; clothing as a factor, 458-459; emotions, 343-360; Erikson's stages, 310-312; mental health, 355-357; self-concept, 312-327, 358-359; sex role, 329-338; theories, 307-311; traits, 354-355, 506

PET (Parent Effectiveness Training), 500

Physical development, 233-300; assessing growth, 252-259; body changes, 233-252; dentition, 250-252; digestive system, 247; ears and eyes, 247-248; fatty tissue, 246, 262; food and nutrition, 259-270; health and fitness, 270-272; height, 238-244; hospitalization, 280-283; injury and illness, 272-283; laterality, 291-294; motor development, 283-300; muscles, 244, 286-287, 290; nervous system, 246; nutrition, 259-270, 300; perceptual-motor development, 290-294; play, 294-302; reproductive system, 248-249, 290; skeleton, 238-243, 245-246, 290; skin, 246; sleep, 270-272; teeth, 250-252, 300; weight, 238-242, 261-263

Play, 294-300, 301-302; equipment, 298-300
Political attitudes, Politics, 550-553, 555
Popularity, 200-205, 207-210
Prayer, 441-442
Prejudice, 37, 327-329, 528-532, 553
Preoperational thinking, 377-378, 381-385, 527
Pressure, 482-483, 505, 507
Principles of development, 30-34, 40
Projective technique, 15-17, 318-320
Puberty, 248-249

Q

Questionnaire, 17-18

R

Race, 47, 59, 257, 323-324, 327-329, 370-371, 393-394, 397-398, 527-532
RAID, 501-502
Reading, 73-78, books, 74-76; comics, 76-78; magazines, 76; newspapers, 76; readability graph, 75
Reasoning, 371-381, 389
Recommended Dietary Allowances, 263, 265-267
Religion, 439-443, 504-505; concepts, 442-443, 553; Elkind's stages, 440-441; prayer, 441-442
REM sleep, 271-272
Reproductive system, 248-249, 290
Research, 13-30; language, 26-30; methods, 15-23; problems, 13-14
Reversibility, 384, 386
Rights of children, *see* Children's Rights

S

Schema, 375-376
School, *see* Education
School food service, 265-268
Self-concept, 36, 312-327, 358-359; academic self-concept, 325; black

children's, 323-324; changing, 317; ideal self, 314; measurement, 315-317; moral conduct, 414; name, effect of, 324
Sensory-motor intelligence, 376-377
Sex education, 533-537, 553
Sex play, 330, 336, 337
Sex role, 36, 96-97, 329-338, 485; adoption of, 332; deviation, 335-337; identification, 332, 334; preference, 332; typing, 334-337
Sexuality, 48, 110, 329-338, 533-537
Siblings, 105, 130-132
Sickle cell anemia, 273-276
SIECUS, 536
Single parents, 114-117
Skeletal development, 238-243, 245-246, 290
Skin color, 327-329, 528-532, 553, 554
Sleep and rest, 259, 270-272
Smoke, 277-278
Social attitudes, 35-37, 83, 91; *see also* Prejudice
Social class, 48-65, 88, 323; lower class, 55-65, 85-87, 97, 113, 436, 507-508, 551; middle class, 51, 52, 54-55, 64, 97, 435, 551; upper class, 51-53, 64
Social development, 130-132, 195-230, 330-331; characteristics, 223-227; *see also* Family, Cultural influences, Social attitudes, Social Class
Sociogram, 213-215
Sociometry, 204, 212-216, 229
Somatotrophin, the growth hormone, 234-235
Somatotyping, 254-255
Statistics, *see* Research
STEP (Systematic Training for Effective Parenting), 500
Stereophotogrammetry anthropometry, 253-254
Syncretism, 384

T

Teachers, 54, 110, 147-154, 177, 178, 186-187, 416, 534-535; *see also* Education

Teeth, 243-244, 250-252, 300
Television, 79-83, 88, 503; advertising, 80, 200, 452-456, 504; violence, 81, 82, 85, 470
Toys, 298-299, 301-302, 464-467
Traits, 354-355
Transduction, 383

V

Values, 37, 104, 278, 414, 438-439, 461, 504, 536-537
Vitamin supplements, 261, 269

W

War, concept of, 554-555
Weight, 238-242, 261-263

Wetzel Grid, 253
Work, 468-471, 510; *see also* Money
Working mothers, 94-97, 136, 546
Worry, *see* Anxiety

X

X-ray, 238, 243, 245

Y

Youth organizations, 54, 216-222